DATE			

SECRECY
AND
FOREIGN POLICY

New York University
CENTER FOR INTERNATIONAL STUDIES
Studies in Peaceful Change

Why Federations Fail: An Inquiry into the Requisites for Successful Federalism, by Thomas M. Franck, Gisbert H. Flanz, Herbert J. Spiro, and Frank N. Trager, 1968.

A Free Trade Association, ed. Thomas M. Franck and Edward Weisband, 1968.

Comparative Constitutional Process, by Thomas M. Franck, 1968.

The Structure of Impartiality, by Thomas M. Franck, 1968.

Agents of Change: A Close Look at the Peace Corps, by David Hapgood and Meridan Bennett, 1968.

Law, Reason and Justice: Essays in Legal Philosophy, by Graham B. Hughes, 1969.

Czechoslovakia: Intervention and Impact, ed. I. William Zartman, 1970.

Sierra Leone: An Experiment in Democracy in an African Nation, by Gershon Collier, 1970.

Microstates and Micronesia: Problems of America's Pacific Islands and Other Minute Territories, by Stanley A. de Smith, 1970.

International Business Negotiations: A Study in India, by Ashok Kapoor, 1970.

Foreign Capital for Economic Development: A Korean Case Study, by Seung Hee Kim, 1970.

The Politics of Trade Negotiations Between Africa and the European Economic Community: The Weak Confront the Strong, by I. William Zartman, 1971.

Word Politics: Verbal Strategy Among the Superpowers, by Thomas M. Franck and Edward Weisband, 1971.

The United States and International Markets: Commercial Policy Options in an Age of Controls, by Robert G. Hawkins and Ingo Walter, 1972.

Developing Democracy, by William A. Douglas, 1972.

Turkish Foreign Policy 1943-1945: Small State Diplomacy and Great Power Politics, by Edward Weisband, 1973.

U.S. East-West Trade Policy: Economic Warfare Versus Economic Welfare, by Thomas A. Wolf, 1973.

The Ideology of American Foreign Policy: A Paradigm of Lockian Liberalism, by Edward Weisband, 1973.

International Law in the Western Hemisphere, ed. Nigel S. Rodley, 1973.

SECRECY
AND
FOREIGN POLICY

Edited by
Thomas M. Franck and Edward Weisband

New York
OXFORD UNIVERSITY PRESS
London   1974   Toronto

Second printing, 1974

Copyright © 1974 by Oxford University Press, Inc.
Library of Congress Catalogue Card Number: 73–87619
Printed in the United States of America

For the Friedlaender Family

Editor's Note

The Editors are grateful above all to the contributors to this book, who by their promptness in meeting deadlines and invariably amenable dispositions made the editing of this volume as pleasant as it was stimulating. The two-day Conference at which the next-to-final drafts were reviewed was sponsored by the Center for International Studies and the Law School of New York University, and we express deep gratitude to them; in particular, to Dean Robert McKay, who was not only a good host but also a most helpful participant in these meetings with the authors.

The gift of time and peace of mind was bestowed on us by the extraordinary administrative support we received from Phyllis Goldberg in organizing the conference of the authors and the coordination of their efforts; Rochelle Fenchel, Judith Chazen, Carol Yevcak, and Sandra Booth each played an important part in making the task possible and enjoyable.

The Consul General for Canada in New York, Bruce Rankin, exemplifies that rare balance, the diplomat-statesman-scholar-wit. His helpful participation in the organization of the manuscript conference and his excellent critiques have made this a better book than it would otherwise be. The Assistant Director of the Center for International Studies, Bert Lockwood, chaired several of the authors' meetings and contributed immeasurably to the organization and to the content of this project.

Although this book is intended to be read by non-lawyers as well as lawyers, legal citations are usually given in some variation of standard legal form—depending upon the chapter author's preference—and this may sometimes be unintelligible to the layman. When the reference involves an often-used source, a more fully descriptive equivalent is supplied on first appearance, thus: 29 Supreme Court Reports (hereinafter: S.C.R.) 326. In references to sources rarely cited, the equivalent is not usually given, as such entries involve chiefly the official or authoritative reports of statutes, regulations, or court cases of Canada or Great Britain. In any event, the reader can hie himself to the precincts of a law library, where he can as well consult the librarian.

The orthography current in England and Canada has been preserved in the chapters originating in those countries.

T. M. F.
E. W.

Contents

Foreword

Maxwell Cohen

Among the operational tensions within the democratic process are those between the privileged position, in the hands of those governing, of varieties of confidential information necessary for their decision-making, and the contrasting concept of a "right to know" by the governed. Indeed, that right is seen as part of the very act of decision-making in which the governed are promised their rightful role in the name of the democratic process.

It is a particular dilemma for the self-governing traditions of so-called free societies, therefore, that so much thought and imagination should be expended on the responsibility and responsiveness of governing bodies, while at the same time there is always a core of remoteness and secrecy within power, no matter how carefully circumscribed that power system may be so as to protect the rights of the many from the authority of the few. Indeed, probably what unites all power systems, from tribe to nation-state, from family to a people, from tyrant to town hall, is that somewhere in the process of action, decisions must be made and carried out and that such decisions cannot always be reconciled with an absolute concept of openness in decision-making or execution of policy itself. Hence, whether it is the body of Athenian citizens or a town meeting in Vermont, the Legislative process may have the appearance of public participation, but the Executive process in preparing for that public debate on the one hand and its responsibility to execute its commands on the other, may require, on the part of those pre-

Professor Cohen was Dean of the Faculty of Law of McGill University, 1964–69; Director of the Institute of Air and Space Law 1962–66; and a member of the Canadian Delegation to the 14th General Assembly of the United Nations 1959–60.

paring and those executing, data and administrative arrangements that cannot always be in the public domain if there is to be fairness and efficiency in governmental procedures.[1]

What is true of open societies and their need for secrecy or privacy of information in aid of Executive activities, is even more relevant to the special character of closed societies. For probably the common link between all coercive orders, whether popular or authoritarian, and however primitive the arena, is the need for a locus of power and the equivalent need for a degree of secrecy in preparing policy or in executing it. Secrecy is itself a prime factor in any power system; and the more authoritarian the system the greater the need for and use of secrecy. Conversely, the greater the use of secrecy, the greater the likelihood of approaching authoritarian models. Indeed, the fact that secrecy may be viewed as both symptom and source of authority demonstrates its uniqueness within a power system—as a measure and a tool. Only relatively open societies may have the institutional resiliency, and the political culture, to demand from those governing that secrecy be minimized in the process of exercising power whether for the making of policy or for its application.

In short, in its characterization as both means and end, secrecy fits into varieties of governmental models and becomes a significant determinant of the nature of the power system. Yet obviously such statements are rather simplistic generalizations reaching toward a kind of sub-theory of the nature of government and its means, of power systems and their mechanisms. In the literature on secrecy and disclosure that has been expanding in volume because of the growth of secret state activities in general, in particular during the Cold War and more recently the Vietnam War, it is surprising that no general theory of secrecy has evolved that would account for the role of secrecy within democratic orders and replace the anecdotal study of the problem with systematic analysis.

There is another difficulty in the way of studying secrecy systematically at this time. The matter is very much in flux, for in self-governing systems there are two contemporary challenges to the nature and use of power, and thus challenges to secrecy itself. On the one hand there is a decline in the credibility of power, a questioning of its legitimacy, that is part of the restiveness of the time, a *Zeitgeist* of this generation and, ironically, serving as a bridge across the celebrated "generation gap" itself. Evidence of this distrust of au-

---

1. For recent discussions of this general problem, see Great Britain, Home Office, Report of the Departmental Committee on Section 2 of the Official Secrets Act 1911, Lord Franks (1972), vol. 1, Cmnd. 5104, pp. 9–131 (hereinafter called Franks Report); Report of the Royal Commission on Security (abridged; Ottawa: Queens Printers, 1969), pp. 1–12 (hereinafter called Canadian Report); "The National Security Interest and Civil Liberties, Developments in the Law," 85 *Harv. L. Rev.* 1113 *et seq.* (1972) (hereinafter called Harvard Developments).

thority, and certainly disbelief in its infallibility, is to be found almost everywhere from the campus to the capital, and—perhaps more significant as a
barometer—at the walls of the Kremlin and even at the gates of the Vatican.
Under these conditions, of skeptical minds rejecting many old gods before
new ones have been fashioned, it is unlikely that even the most representative
of governmental systems, exercising an abundance of caution in its use of
power and of secrecy, can escape a demand for exposure of the means by
which power is exercised; a demand not only for a greater share in decision-
making but also for greater access to the actual data, which, through the instrument of secrecy, remain the natural ally and stuff of authority.

Hence the present volume is further witness to this new—or is it old?—
reservation about government, about power and its instruments. Even though
our study's more immediate stimulus may have been the particular crisis in
the debate over secrecy versus the right to know brought forward so sharply
by the Pentagon Papers and, to a lesser extent, the Watergate matter and its
by-products, the issues are transcendent. While the most important questions
may have their primary and present focus in the United States, with dramatic
scenarios that are uniquely American, the issues raised and the challenges
posed touch all self-governing societies and their operations.[2]

Another development that now complicates this debate is that the challenge to secrecy can be seen as a parallel to some extent, psychologically and
politically, to the new demand for "right to privacy." Among the strange,
contrapuntal arrangements of our time, special stress is now laid on these
new claims of right by the individual not to be exposed, or to have disclosed,
the many profiles of his personal life from family to foibles. This, in one
sense, is a rejection of the state's "right to know"—or, indeed, that of any
power system, public or private. The right is asserted equally vis-à-vis government statistics and files as against credit-rating data banks serving the
private sector for its own purposes.

Thus, in a curious way, claims by government for secrecy involve two conflicting sub-claims: the right of government to know more about everybody,
and the refusal by government to allow anyone to know much about it.[3]
Correspondingly, the citizen's heightened interest in personal privacy and
surveillance generally—from wire-tapping to State-operated or commercial
computers—reflects a claim of right to personal secrecy.[4] Indeed (put in its
simplest form), the civil libertarian should be able to argue a maximum of
personal secrecy as against a minimum of governmental secrecy. For their
part, the managers of government, whether democratic or otherwise, will
assert that there is, in the interests of effective social policy and administra-

2. For extensive bibliography on espionage and secrecy, see Selected Bibliography in
the Canadian Report, pp. 121–31.
3. For the range of intrusions see Canadian Report, pp. 27–38 and 91–98.
4. Harvard Developments, pp. 1244 ff.

tion, a need for a maximum application of the State's right to know as much as it believes it needs to know to carry out intricate and difficult social policies. Equally, they argue, the very making and execution of these policies require a degree of privacy, and so secrecy is justified as an instrument of an efficient and responsible government.

Any general theory of the democratic process, therefore, would have to take into account the particular function of secrecy and to accommodate within such a conceptual framework the peculiarly analogous demand for a personal secrecy in the name of "privacy" as a counterweight to Leviathan and its growing intrusions into the life of all—particularly if that social order is both popular and representative in the Western tradition. But whether such a general theory exists, some of the chapters of this book doubtless reflect implicit assumptions of a balance in the Western political tradition between secrecy and disclosure, even if few pretensions can be made to applying a developed, systematic framework to the problem.

The comparison of State conduct in the area of secrecy and the law, with particular attention to the impact of secrecy on international relations, will demonstrate that there is a community of shared values among the three countries represented in this study—the United States, the United Kingdom, and Canada. No doubt the differences to be found will be less those of general political theory than of specific divergencies in administrative technique, in political institutions, in the intensity of public attitudes—all reflected partly in law and machinery, and partly in social and political behavior patterns within or beyond the legal norms themselves. Indeed, it is not without significance that the Royal Commission on Security in Canada in 1969 discussed the problem of access to records in the field of international relations in comparative United Kingdom and United States terms, and made the observation that "it is important that our regulations should remain in step with those of Britain since our files (and especially the early ones) contain so much British material; it is also important that we remain in step with the United States."[5]

Clearly a Royal Commission with a mandate to examine Canada's security systems and structures understood that, for technical reasons at least, in the field of international relations documentation, there had to be certain basic similarities in Canadian practice when dealing with the two principal nations affecting Canada's social and political history. Moreover, while not so expressed, the Report was in truth articulating a general political philosophy concerning security or confidentiality, one that assumed a kind of unity in Anglo-Canadian-American experience and thus provided a triangular setting within which to express its findings and recommendations. Nor is it without significance that its findings match those of the Franks Report of the United Kingdom Departmental Committee on section 2 of the Officials Se-

5. Canadian Report. p. 81.

crets Act 1911, released as recently as September 1972.[6] At the same time a special study of U.S. documentation in the field of foreign policy, and the problems of its classification and declassification, was at the time of writing under way in a task force headed by John D. Eisenhower.[7]

The time is thus propitious for a comparison of the efforts of three great democracies, all sharing the tradition of the common law, to put in balance their competing needs for maximum informed public participation in the foreign policy process and the minimum secrecy needs of national security, effective decision-making, and responsible exercise of power. This book sets out the pragmatic struggle for balance waged by activists in three nations—politicians, civil libertarians, lawyers, journalists, and broadcasters. And, in its final chapter, it takes a large first step toward the evolution of an analytical theory of the role of secrecy in foreign policy.

6. *Ibid.*
7. *The New York Times,* December 31, 1972, sec. E, p. 9. Major Eisenhower has since resigned.

Part 1

The Executive Examines Its Secrecy Policies

. . . secrets are edged tools
That must be kept from children and from fools.

John Dryden

But Governments that want results
Must oft-times share their secrets with adults.

Anon.

1

Introduction:
Executive Secrecy
in Three Democracies:
The Parameters of Reform

THOMAS M. FRANCK AND EDWARD WEISBAND

On July 4, 1967, President Johnson signed the Freedom of Information Act (FOIA). Although he had not been a conspicuously enthusiastic supporter of the bill—at least as originally proposed, the President did rise to a certain rhetorical grandeur on the occasion of the signing. "I have always believed," he said, "that freedom of information is so vital that only the national security, not the desire of public officials or private citizens, should determine when it must be restricted." At this point in the ceremony (according to John Rothchild, writing in *The Washington Monthly*) some literal-minded reporter asked Mr. Johnson if he might see the original draft of the remarks just made. Mr. Johnson turned down this first post-FOIA request.

MR. FRANCK, former Director of the Center for International Studies, New York University, is presently Professor of Law, New York University, and Osgoode Hall Law School, York University, Toronto. He is a Senior Fellow at the NYU Center for International Studies; has received a Guggenheim Memorial Foundation Fellowship for the academic year 1973-74; and is Acting Director of the International Law Program of the Carnegie Endowment for International Peace in New York. His previously published studies include *Race and Nationalism, East African Unity Through Law, The Structure of Impartiality,* and *Comparative Constitutional Process.* He is currently completing with Professor Weisband a study of styles and ethics of resignation from high government offices in both England and the United States.

MR. WEISBAND is Director of International Studies and Associate Professor of Political Science, State University of New York at Binghamton. He is the co-author with Professor Thomas M. Franck of *Word Politics: Verbal Strategy among the Superpowers.* He has published several studies in foreign policy and international politics, including *Turkish Foreign Policy 1943-1945: Small State Diplomacy and Great Power Politics* and *The Ideology of American Foreign Policy: A Paradigm of Lockian Liberalism.* He is a member of the Governing Council of the International Studies Association and has served as consultant to a number of U.S. Government Departments that have required the handling and evaluation of confidential materials.

His refusal foreshadowed the ensuing attitude of most officials to the new legislation.[1]

Symptomatic of the problem is the *Assembly Manual for a Gyro Float,* issued in February of 1971 by the Air Force Space and Missile System Office. At the front of the book is this mind-bending notation: "Each section of this volume is in itself unclassified. To protect the compilation of information contained in the complete volume, the complete volume is confidential."

Public resistance to government secrecy and overclassification is scarcely a trendy development. Almost a quarter-century ago, an august committee consisting of Marion B. Folsom, Beardsley Ruml, and Will Clayton, asserted in its report that

> There is no more essential job to be done in America than to keep the
> sources of public information as free as possible from blocks and obstacles.
> . . . public opinion is not as self-evident as it should be so long as it de-
> pends largely on random exposure to news and comment.

The authors went on to warn against the "garrison-police state" in which,

> cut off from significant information . . . the process of public discussion
> atrophies. Political parties decline. The power of Congress dwindles. Admin-
> istration by civilians shrinks, relative to administration in uniform. The
> courts weaken. Cut off from information, the power of the citizen fades.
> Local plans are subordinated to central purposes. The free market is con-
> stricted. Labor is hedged in by special regulations. Consumers find their
> range of choice reduced. Decisions come to be made by an all-powerful gov-
> ernment. All freedoms suffer.

The report concluded that "Recently the line has been drawn heavily on the side of secrecy" and that "resistance to disclosure can be overcome only if there is positive pressure to release information."[2]

This report was published in 1949. While the direst of these eventualities have not yet come true, neither have we solved the problem to which it alludes. But if the past quarter-century has not produced definitive solutions, it has undoubtedly produced clearer definitions of the problem. The most recent, and one of the best, is that by President Nixon, quoted in Congressman Moorhead's Chapter 6:

> The many abuses of the security system can no longer be tolerated. Funda-
> mental to our way of life is the belief that when information which properly

---

1. John Rothchild, "Finding the Facts Bureaucrats Hide," *The Washington Monthly,* 3 (January 1972), p. 15.
2. *The New York Times,* December 15, 1949, p. 1.

belongs to the public is systematically withheld by those in power, the people soon become ignorant of their own affairs, distrustful of those who manage them, and—eventually—incapable of determining their own destinies.

There is, as one might guess, an "on the other hand." It was President Kennedy who cried aloud for a one-armed adviser who would not be able to say "on the other hand." But the President's caveat is as important as is his major premise.

> . . . since the early days of the Republic, Americans have also recognized that the Federal Government is obliged to protect certain information which might otherwise jeopardize the security of the country. That need has become particularly acute in recent years as the United States has assumed a powerful position in world affairs, and as world peace has come to depend in large part on how that position is safeguarded. We are also moving into an era of delicate negotiations in which it will be especially important that govern-- ments be able to communicate in confidence.
>
> Clearly, the two principles of an informed public and of confidentiality within the Government are irreconcilable in their purest forms, and a balance must be struck between them.

In the present book several leaders from three great democracies have been brought together to reflect on their experience in fighting secrecy and protecting the national security. They have attempted to advance the search for functional, country-specific solutions. Before the U.S. Congress are amendments that would restrict Executive privilege and secrecy classification, and a draft law that would make the leaking or theft of government information a serious criminal offense. In Canada the Government has just announced new guidelines for making government studies and reports available to Parliament, and a task force is studying the problem of secrecy with special emphasis on foreign relations. In Britain the Official Secrets Act and the question of substituting an Official Information Act for its section 2 have been under scrutiny by way of a government-authorized study directed by Lord Franks. This has produced insights on the balance between democracy and administrative efficiency relevant for all three countries.

The three countries studied in this book have in common the traditions of democratic decision-making. By examining the problem of secrecy in the contexts of a small, a middle, and a large power (Canada, England, and the United States) we can see the issues in relation to the facts of world power and responsibility.

Deliberately, but with regret, we have excluded from our consideration several subjects that are important and related to secrecy, yet do not come within the foreign policy framework of this symposium. Thus we have not included that obverse of the public's right to know, which is the *govern-*

ment's right to know and the collision of that right with another—namely, the privacy of the individual. Neither have we dealt with secrecy in semi-public institutions such as foundations that also affect our foreign relations. *The New York Times,* for example, refuses scholars access to its obituary files on grounds surprisingly like those used by the U.S. Government to deny Representative Patsy T. Mink access to information on the Cannikin tests: that the files contain a mixture of matters some of which it is not in the public interest to make known, and that manpower is not available to separate these matters from others in which the public has a legitimate interest.

BENEFITS OF GOVERNMENT SECRECY

It is clear from the reflections of our authors that government secrecy involves both real costs and real benefits for government and the public. Significantly, there is a large measure of agreement among our authors as to what these costs and these benefits are.

Chief among the *benefits* of secrecy is the maintenance of the minimal defense security that is still essential in a world of national rivalry. A second and almost equally important benefit is that secrecy preserves a certain flexibility among advisers and members of the Government negotiating with each other prior to reaching an official policy decision. As George Ignatieff stresses in Chapter 4, secrecy preserves flexibility among negotiators at international conferences. Positions that do not have to be taken publicly can be compromised without loss of prestige.

A third, related benefit is that secrecy makes it easier for opponents of a policy to oppose it from inside the government without having their loyalty questioned. The fourth benefit is that secrecy makes possible a higher level of candor in the routine exchange of confidences among governments. Not only does secrecy allow governments to negotiate certain issues; it also prevents them from being compromised by the private candor that makes diplomacy work.

Among authors of the chapters to follow there is little disagreement on the belief that governmental secrecy does have its beneficial uses. But there is much less agreement as to what categories of data are worthy of secrecy classification. In Britain, for example, the recent Franks Report (alluded to above and treated later on) recommended that protection be extended to Cabinet memos; to classified information on foreign relations, defense, internal security, and currency; to documents entrusted to Government by private persons or individuals; and to information likely to assist criminal activities or impede law enforcement.

In the United States the Freedom of Information Act (FOIA) makes provision for protecting matters pertaining to foreign policy and national defense, to trade secrets, investigatory files compiled for law enforcement, and intra-agency memoranda. The most recent Executive Order on classification embraced still other categories, and these have been questioned by Members of Congress—Senator Mathias and Congressman Moorhead among others—as excessively broad, broader, even, than the scope of FOIA.

Important, too, are differences as to whether these exemptive categories should be further narrowed by adding to them a "probable injury" rider. Both the Franks Report and the U.S. Espionage Statutes point in the direction of such refinement, suggesting as they do that information, to be entitled to secrecy, must not only fall within the described categories but must also, under the specific circumstances, be capable of causing harm if disclosed. At this writing there are in the Congressional hopper several proposals to remove from the Espionage Statutes the requirement for a positive showing, by the prosecution, of intent to injure and actual injury.

There is, further, the crucial question of how to apply exemptive categories. Who is to separate what is properly kept secret from what is wrongfully suppressed? This issue is raised by the *Mink* case (see Chapter 7 below). Who decides what is "harmful to the national interest" or pertains to "foreign policy"—the government classifiers themselves? the courts using principles of due process or natural justice, as in Britain's most recent cases on Executive privilege cited by Professor Street? or, as various authors from each of our three countries have suggested, a mixed tribunal of members of Executive, the Legislature, and the public?

There is, finally, the problem of finding a remedy for wrongful withholding of information. One approach is to permit self-help—that is, simply to repeal laws that make it a crime to possess and release official information that ought not to have been secret in the first place. This may be the approach indicated by the lacunae deliberately provided in the U.S. Espionage Statutes, at least as Leonard Boudin and Benno Schmidt read them (see Chapters 17 and 11). It is not the approach taken by the Franks Committee.

Another approach is to provide, as in the Freedom of Information Act, for a positive legal remedy to secure the release of classified materials improperly embargoed under the law. This is the activity in which Richard Frank and his public-interest lawyers are engaged, as he describes in Chapter 16. It is also, however, the remedy Congresswoman Mink failed to obtain in the action she describes in her chapter. The Supreme Court's denial of her request for information reinforces the search described in Congressman Moorhead's chapter for a way to amend FOIA, and perhaps also the Administrative Procedure Act, to facilitate public access to Executive information and decision-making—at least in respect of non-sensitive foreign relations.

COSTS OF GOVERNMENT SECRECY

In considering the *costs,* there is first the threat to the internal balance of power. As several of our authors have stated, information is power. The twentieth century has seen a tremendous growth in our respective governments' capability as the super-data generators and gatherers. Insofar as the data are withheld from those not in the government's inner circle, traditional balances of power within the community are upset. These imbalances, as Thomas Hughes suggests in Chapter 2, might arise even within the Executive Branch itself: vertically, as between, for example, the canaries of the State Department and the cats of the Department of Defense; or horizontally, as between the foxes in the intelligence community and *les petits princes* of policy-planning.

The balance might be upset even more fundamentally as between the Executive and the Legislature or between the government and the people. Historically, in each of our societies, the various forces in the community have never been in equilibrium, nor is it equilibrium that is being sought. Rather, there has been in the past a seesawing pattern, with various centers of power in the ascendant at different times. What concerns us now is that one factor —information, data—is becoming the crucial indicator of power, and that one power center, located within the Executive, seems to be obtaining an unbreakable near-monopoly on it, in which event the system will be permanently tilted in one direction. In his chapter Thomas Hughes makes a radical but practicable proposal for keeping the seesaw in motion.

A second cost of secrecy is the loss of public support for government policy, such as occurs when there is a real or imagined "credibility gap" based on evidence of frequent non-disclosure by a government. Closely related is a phenomenon more frequently alluded to by the British and Canadian authors: the loss of public interest in foreign affairs which sets in when a government refuses to let legislators and the public in on their deliberations. If foreign affairs is too sensitive for candid dialogue between Executive and Legislature, or the government and the people, there is not likely to be much public enthusiasm in those quarters for the government's pet foreign ventures. Public interest is closely related to public participation. Anthony Westell, from the journalist's perspective, George Ignatieff from the Executive side, and Gordon Fairweather from Parliament describe a recent Canadian experiment—not wholly successful but undeniably novel—for bringing the public into middle-range policy-making before decisions are made.

Still another disadvantage of secrecy—the obverse of one of its benefits—is that it obscures from the public the divisions and dissensions comprising the administrative history of most important Executive decisions. This means that when things go wrong there can be no heroes, only villains. And when things go seriously wrong, the surfeit of villains and paucity of heroes place a profound strain on the entire system.

Finally, to be counted among the costs of secrecy is the procedure known as "leaking." The cost of excessive secrecy is excessive leaking of confidential information—with its possible threat to national security. Both the Canadian and the American authors have noted the sharp increase in such leaks during the past few years.

THE ADVERSARY ROLE

Although, as we have seen, our authors agree in general as to both the benefits of secrecy and its costs, there are inevitable differences in the way each weighs the one against the other. Here our national ethos and experience become crucial. It is part of the Lockean tradition of the United States to see the government as an evil, albeit a necessary evil. As Senator Mathias has emphasized, the Constitution's description of the foreign relations power is "an invitation to struggle" among the three branches of government and as between government and the people. To Americans, suspicion of government, regardless of party, is a natural inclination. War between press and government is normal and, as Haynes Johnson suggests, perhaps desirable. Between these two adversaries (to quote one of Maxwell Cohen's famous aphorisms from another context), "truce is stranger than friction." The adversary role is normal to the American press: co-operation sometimes, but co-option never.

Authors Anthony Westell and Anthony Sampson have a quite different attitude toward government from that of Haynes Johnson. In Canada and Britain, between elections, governments tend to get the benefit of a presumption of trust. And if good government requires an element of secrecy, privacy—or call it discretion—so be it. Thus, when Quebec terrorists kidnapped two officials in October 1970, Americans were either dismayed or made envious by the secrecy, speed, and efficiency with which the Canadian Government was able to invoke the War Measures Act and detain the suspected villains with relatively little hindrance from public opinion, the courts, or Parliament. For their part the Canadians and the British find rather distasteful the adversary relation between press and government in America. As our contributor Kenneth Lamb emphasizes, the media are in a better position to fight the dangers of secrecy and suppression if they have developed a public reputation for strict impartiality, both because the public will then stand behind them and because a high level of credibility, even among opponents, becomes a powerful asset in a conflict. Yet the media in America have fought or been forced to fight government so hard as to be, themselves, perceived as advocates. The result may be a loss of credibility and public support comparable even to that imputed to the White House by the adversary press.

Characteristically, it is an English author, William Clark, who raises a question not asked by any of the Americans: What if the people, the press, the legislators, are wrong? Might it not have been better for Stanley Baldwin actually to have manufactured a crisis with Germany in 1936—a Gulf of Tonkin incident—which would have mobilized the somnolent "peace-at-any-price"-loving British public and press to deal preventively with Hitler? Is it not in the nature of leadership that it sometimes be allowed to be wiser than the people, and sometimes be expected to deceive the public into doing the right thing? William Clark's chapter seems to recommend the Macbeth test of what the public should let the Government put over on it: "If it were done when 'tis done, then 'twere well it were done quickly."

Readers should not expect this volume to reveal a three-nation consensus on anything so subjective as secrecy. The British experienced Munich, in which weak government, excessively influenced by public anti-war feelings, brought near-disaster through inaction. The United States experienced Vietnam, in which a strong government, too little restrained by public anti-war sentiment, led the nation into a divisive, costly, and inconclusive war. It is natural that in public attitudes there will be differences in regard to formal restraints on government, such as requirements for disclosure and public participation in the policy-making process. In this respect the Canadian perception is much closer to the British.

AREAS OF AGREEMENT

The Vietnam agony has separated the United States from these two Parliamentary democracies. Nevertheless, the comparative approach can be useful, and our three nations have much to learn from one another. There is much that we can explore jointly. Similarities mark our analyses of the central problem of power balance. We have already referred to the common inventory of costs and benefits. It is also apparent from these chapters that we employ a similar analytical vocabulary in dealing with the challenge of secrecy. For example, we all understand the difference, and the importance of the difference, between *secrets* and *information*. We understand the distinction between *the right to know* and the *right to participate*, the distinction between access to *official data* and access to *written opinions or advice of officials*. In each of our countries we speak of an *intelligence community* that is distinct from the *community of policy-makers*. We all understand the legal difference between *the right to know* and the *right to divulge*.

More, for each of our three countries we understand that Executive secrecy can mean (1) *the exercise of Executive privilege* or (2) *Executive classification of documents* or (3) *selective/distortive disclosure and leaking of information by the Executive*. We agree to the difference between *true* and *false* secrets—false referring to information so classified to protect not the *national* interest but the government's *political* interest. Our countries are quite different from those in which the *national* and *political* interests are, and are intended to remain, identical.

This similarity of national experiential vocabulary makes it possible for our authors to speak to publics in all three countries, and they have offered several highly imaginative proposals for the reader's consideration. Thus,

—that intelligence estimates be made available to a key group of legislators on a par with Cabinet members, these legislators to be given top security clearance;

—that committees of the Legislature dealing with foreign affairs should have the power to summon and examine Executive officers and to secure the release of information and documents;

—that Legislative committees dealing with foreign affairs should have extensive data-gathering and analyzing capability rivaling that of the Executive Branch;

—that the question of the Legislative Branch's information-getting prerogatives vis-à-vis the Executive could, at least in the United States, be resolved by litigation;

—that overclassification by civil servants should, like underclassification, be a punishable offense;

—that classification of documents or refusal to produce documents and data should in every case be subject to review either by a special tribunal composed of persons other than the classifiers, or by the courts, or by an ombudsman;

—that all documents should be automatically declassified in a relatively few years (2 to 10) except in rare circumstances determined by an independent review board;

—that the press should unilaterally terminate the vestiges of their "buddy" relation with government by refusing to participate in non-attributable briefings, not-for-quote "backgrounders," and other co-optive arrangements;

—that legislation punishing disclosure of government information be amended, clarified, and narrowed;

—that public-interest groups and affected individuals should have the right to
be heard, and to meet the arguments on the other side, in key decisions affecting trade, the environment, and other matters which, though pertaining
to foreign relations, are also of direct domestic concern;

—that more members of the Executive establishment should be encouraged,
or should seize the necessary courage, to resign over matters of conscience
and take their case to the public.

The time is right for public examination of these proposals. In Britain the
Franks Report has been published and action is pending. It has been criticized (by Professor Harry Street in this volume) for being too modest in its
aspirations and too restrictive in effect. In Canada, there are important departures from the British Parliamentary and Cabinet tradition, and these
may go far toward opening the windows on the foreign relations process. In
the United States the Freedom of Information Act has been seen to fail to
open U.S. foreign relations to public scrutiny; and the search is on for new
and better methods of implementing disclosure. The chapters that follow
should help to equip the citizen to participate in an informed way in that
search.

2

The Power To Speak and the Power To Listen:
Reflections on Bureaucratic Politics
and a Recommendation on Information Flows

THOMAS L. HUGHES

> In this vast external realm, with its important, complicated, delicate, and
> manifold problems, the President alone has the power to speak or listen. . . .

So wrote Justice Sutherland for the Supreme Court in his *obiter dicta* in the
landmark *Curtiss-Wright* case of 1936, proclaiming the "plenary and exclusive power of the President as the sole organ of the federal government in
the field of international relations."[1]

In the intervening decades much has happened to complicate Justice
Sutherland's fulsome allocation of power to the Executive in foreign affairs—much to confound both the power to speak and the power to listen. In
recent years the Executive Branch has spoken with many tongues—often
with forked tongues—to itself and to others, a complexity exceeded only by
the even more complicated conundrum: To whom and for what does the
Executive Branch listen? Competitive answers to that question can carry
major Constitutional consequences, and can increasingly set in motion
cross-currents and counter-claims on central issues influencing information
flow. The outcome could affect the control and circulation of information
not only outwardly from the Executive Branch but bureaucratically within
it as well. The scope of the debate itself clearly indicates how simplistic
was the solution, unresolved in many of its propositions, that the Supreme
Court thought it had found in 1936.

Sutherland, of course, was writing before World War II, before wartime
secrecy and the Office of Strategic Services, before the Cold War and the
Central Intelligence Agency, before the National Security Council and the
United States Intelligence Board, and well before the manifold Executive

Mr. Hughes is President of the Carnegie Endowment for International Peace. He was
formerly Director of Intelligence and Research, U.S. Department of State, and Minister, U.S. Embassy, London.
1. *United States* v. *Curtiss-Wright Export Corp. et al.,* 229 U.S. 304 (1936).

Branch proliferations that would later bedevil the issues of who speaks to whom and who listens to whom. Unaware of these subsequent issues of Who/Whom, the Justice had it in mind, of course, that the President should speak for the country to the world, and credited him with the means of assuring that the Executive Branch, when speaking, would present a united front. He noted that the Executive had agents and reporters who needed the protection of secrecy, indispensable alike to effective listening abroad and to responsible evaluation and presentation at home. Secrecy would thus enable the policy spokesman to speak with authority in the right manner at the right time. Contemplating the power to listen, the Court assumed that the component elements of the Executive Branch had an identity, not a conflict of interests.

Not contemplated was the unfolding prospect that as Big Government became bigger, the pluralization of the Executive Branch, operating in a context of ever larger pluralism, would sooner or later render it faintly odd to use the institutionalized terms Sutherland used imputing exclusivity, consistency, and singlemindedness to a whole branch of government. And most unforeseen of all at the time of *Curtiss-Wright* was the growth of a full-fledged, formally constituted intelligence community. In time the collective roles and missions of its component elements would come to control many of the instrumentalities and reach all of the substantive reporting on world affairs. Their purview would come close to constituting the full official power to listen on behalf of the President—to collect, assemble, analyze, package, and present the truth about world events and trends, the truth that was supposed to make Presidents free to act, or not to act, as objective evidence indicated.

Objectivity would require independence *within* the Executive Branch from policy command and control, and this independence, at least among the civilian elements of the intelligence community, would become explicit in theory and, until recently, honored in practice. For the power to listen for the truth would come to have an indispensable corollary: the power to speak truth to power.

INTELLIGENCE AND THE FOREIGN POLICY FREE-FOR-ALL

As the key (or deputy) State Department official in the intelligence community over a nine-year period under three Presidents, I propose to reflect upon that experience in the setting of the contemporary Presidential-Congressional confrontation over information sharing. The current swirling debate over secrecy and democracy covers many other familiar issues. Excessive classification, Executive privilege, non-accountability of important

Executive Branch personnel, and the overuse of Executive agreements—all of these testify that the field of foreign affairs poses the most vexing and unresolved problems in the deteriorating Executive-Legislative relation. The arguments are compounded in the present situation, in which a private President prides himself on exclusivity and surprise, the foreign policies he has successfully conducted have been full of pyrotechnic brilliance, the country remains deeply divided over major foreign policy issues, deference and respect for government in general are at low ebb, and the Congress itself is in the hands of the opposition party and therefore doubly frustrated over Executive ascendency, mitigated only by Watergate.

In a day when bureaucratic politics is a fashionable explanation of how governments function, I should like to reflect (within reason) on the flavor of those struggles as well. For the Washington-based men and organizations that were—and are—responsible for interpreting, presenting, and (in part) protecting the incoming information on trends and developments abroad were not immune from bureaucratic politics either, a fact which should be predictable from the very character of the organizations represented on the United States Intelligence Board (USIB) and among the even more variegated institutions constituting its interagency sub-system. Throughout the 1960's this self-styled intelligence community consisted of the State Department's Bureau of Intelligence and Research (INR), the Central Intelligence Agency (CIA), the Defense Intelligence Agency (DIA), plus the separately represented Army, Navy, and Air Force intelligence components, the National Security Agency (NSA), the Atomic Energy Commission (AEC), and the Federal Bureau of Investigation (FBI). The Treasury Department has since been added.

The variety of budgetary, organizational, and substantive struggles enveloping and investing this community could by no means be reduced to simple bureaucratic gamesmanship models of specific organizational interests let loose to pursue predictable organizational aggrandizements. Instead, the cross-cutting complexities were striking: position disputes within agencies, alliances shifting with issues, personal strayings from organizational loyalties, hierarchical differences between superiors and subordinates, horizontal rather than vertical affinities, and much *ad hoc* reaching for sustenance somewhere outside. Thus, while the struggles within the intelligence community sometimes mirrored simultaneous struggles in the larger policy community, they did so by no means invariably and never symmetrically.

Among the three major constituent elements, Defense, CIA, and State, certain inequalities of influence are evident without elaboration. They derive from obvious functional differences in size, weight, budgets, and numbers. The relative strength and persuasiveness of their leaders varied personally and politically in the White House and on Capitol Hill. From those

over-all departmental differences, certain intelligence agencies or units enjoyed derivative assets or liabilities that could be used at many points in
the information handling process—from initial fact gathering through several stages of production to final presentation.

Beyond that there were important bureaucratic-psychological differences.
More often than not, what David Halberstam has written about the climate
of Defense intelligence behavior, for example, has an authentic ring:

> It is the job of the military intelligence people to get along with their supe-
> riors. . . . The light colonels and bird colonels, bright men on their way up,
> are soldiers; they are in uniform, they know what the JCS wants, they are
> servants, and they have careers ahead. An Air Force intelligence officer will
> not, for instance, say that the bombing will not work.[2]

Collectors in the field, popular briefers in Washington, role players in the
Pentagon's civilian-military struggle, strategic planners, tacticians in battle
—there were overlapping ingredients on the soldier's side of intelligence
which no one else shared.

The CIA's situation was also many-sided. Its covert operational interests
abroad could conflict with the objectivity of its reporters in the field as well
as of its analysts in Washington. Its current intelligence carriers purveying
instant news were not necessarily on the same wavelength as its longer term,
big-picture estimators. Its director inevitably experienced several divergent
pulls as he tried equally to preside over these disparate activities. The Director of Central Intelligence (DCI) also wore other hats. Thus, for example, he distinguished his role as head of CIA from his role as coordinating
chairman of the USIB. By statute he was charged with protecting sources
and methods of intelligence collection, and hence was in a curtailing as well
as liberating role on information flow. In some incarnations he fancied himself as a policy adviser to the President. At times he certainly played a personal political role. Depending on the strength of his private convictions
about matters of high policy, he might expound his personal estimate orally
at Presidential meetings instead of in the official written estimate he had
signed on behalf of the intelligence community. A many-hatted director
headed a many-sided agency. The many role players pushed many contra-
dictory themes, as any comprehensive analysis of the CIA record on Vietnam throughout the 1960's is eventually bound to disclose.

The role of the State Department's Bureau of Intelligence and Research
(INR) was less encumbered and thus more coherent by far, but nevertheless

---

2. David Halberstam, *The Best and the Brightest* (New York: Random House, 1972),
p. 358.

anomalous for other reasons. Conflicts of interest were minimal by definition. INR had no agents abroad, conducted no covert operations, and had
no bureaucratic stake in or direct responsibility for Foreign Service reporting. Moreover, the bureau was given an explicit charter of independence
from State Department policy control. Except for a celebrated flurry in
1963 over INR's use of Joint Chiefs of Staff statistics against the JCS view,
the Secretary of State was meticulous in insisting on INR's complete freedom of choice of what to write about, how to write about it, and what conclusions to draw from it. This freedom extended specifically to the INR
drafts, which constituted the State Department's sole regular weekly contributions to the coordinated National Intelligence Estimates (NIE's). It
also extended specifically to the INR director's role in personally approving,
footnoting, or dissenting from a NIE as finally acted upon by him and his
USIB colleagues. The Secretary of State had repeated reason to know that
INR analysis was unhelpful to the pursuit of policies on which the Administration had embarked, and that INR papers were often being used against
arguments he was espousing. Never did this potentially embarrassing situation affect INR's daily access to the Secretary personally, or INR's independent role. Throughout the period 1961–69, INR operated in as free an
atmosphere of inquiry as is possible inside government—in terms of priorities and liberty of expression, utterly free.

The INR was therefore the least culture-bound, bureaucratically staked,
umbilically connected, or career-limited of the participants. It was, in addition, determined to organize its personnel in a manner contrived to sustain
and maximize its privileged, pressure-free situation. Thus it deliberately selected a judicious mix of officers with highly differentiated career patterns:
Foreign Service Officers chosen especially for their analytical expertise in
certain areas; civil servants guaranteed tenure and protected from the in-
roads of the Foreign Service promotion system; and academic experts
drawn from outside government and strategically placed in charge of research and analysis for Latin America, East Asia, Africa, the Near East,
and South Asia. Only for Europe did INR use careerist office directors, deliberately selecting two unusually gifted entrepreneurs, one for Eastern and
one for Western Europe; and their diverse products were better than they
would have been had there been a single research office for Europe.

Despite its intrinsic advantages, however, INR had to conduct business
in an uncertain milieu. The policy-makers at the State Department were,
after all, potentially the chief users of political estimates, and they were responsible for the public presentation of much of the policy. Yet in actuality
the enthusiasm for intelligence estimates among State Department's policy-
makers left something to be desired. Their attitudes normally were a compound of several ingredients:

1. A preference for "facts" over "opinions." Policy-makers did not relish having intelligence crowd them with estimates with which they themselves might differ.

2. Skepticism about the incremental value of more information for policy-making as such. Without overstating it—a common view was that on the whole much more information was already available than could be properly used. Policy-makers rarely thirsted for a greater over-all flow. They lacked eagerness for the specific piece of information that complicated or contradicted a policy the recipient was already championing.

3. Eager appreciation, by contrast, for the kind of information that would help convince the public or the Congress to support policies already decided upon, whether the purpose was to prove Chinese aggressiveness, the Soviet threat, Hanoi's control of the Viet Cong, or the infiltration rate into South Vietnam.

4. Dissatisfaction with the inadequacy of the existing armory of facts supportive of existing policy, especially when augmented by suspicions that fact gatherers were skeptical of the policy and therefore not wholeheartedly responsive to requests for more supporting facts.

5. Nervousness simultaneously about the methods, techniques, and provocations incident to the collecting of information by CIA, DIA, or NSA. The policy-makers most concerned about information gaps often turned out to be those most worried about the illegalities, costs, and potential political repercussions that filling those gaps might mean. A decade that began with a U-2 torpedoing the Eisenhower-Khrushchev Summit Conference certainly understood that the collection of information was not necessarily cost-free politically.

6. Heightened frustrations at the end of the process when, after fresh information was obtained, it often turned out to be politically impossible to use it publicly without credibility problems, jeopardy to sources and methods, or disclosing unpalatable techniques. In 1964–65, the closer the policy-makers came to escalation in Vietnam, the higher were the potential military costs involved in information collection. Techniques for collecting future tactical battle data would arguably be jeopardized in the process of proving infiltration rates; demonstrating Hanoi's involvement and capabilities would require publicly unacceptable or provocative measures. In order to assuage their credibility problem, the policy-makers discovered that they would have to engage in information collection practices that inevitably would increase their credibility problem.

This was one of the underlying and pervasively schizoid elements in a persistent Vietnam policy-information predicament. While additional information was thought to be marginal for Executive Branch policy decisions and costly to obtain, it was regarded as necessary for public consumption, yet ultimately unusable for it: the brokers who found themselves between the fact gatherers in the intelligence community and the fact consumers in the policy community never fully fought themselves out of that bag. Oscillating between the value and the cost of potential information, arguing over the quality, usability, and reliability of certain kinds of information over time, the policy-makers became accustomed to living with a self-fulfilling credibility gap. Their frustrations grew as their information grew, along with their inability to use it convincingly.

Especially on Vietnam, INR's role as objective analyst and interpreter had to find its place in an environment where others were seeking and supplying intelligence to please. It took its place, as it had to, at the interface of the intelligence and policy communities, both of them peopled by men in motion. The policy people ranged widely across the spectrum from procurement and production to presentation and protection; insistent requestors to quality controllers; can-do operators to nervous authorizers; insensitive technocrats to sometimes sensitive bureaucrats; high-risk collectors to low-risk decision-makers; eager analysts to reluctant ventilators; loose-lipped consultants to carefree classifiers; interested producers to half-interested consumers.

Viewed from above by the ranking policy-makers, the intelligence community often seemed cumbersome, expensive, loquacious, probing, querulous, and at times, axe-grinding. Viewed from below by the intelligence experts, the policy community often seemed determined to ignore evidence plainly before it—or (even worse) mistake the intelligence managers for the experts. Viewed from in between at the intelligence-policy interface, it looked like controlled chaos—and not surprisingly—for here .was where means and ends were brokered—jurisdictional rivalries compromised, contentious controversies delineated.

In the vast field of Executive Branch information handling, this was where the pressure tended to converge, where connections were made, where controversies were joined. In a formally structured interagency setting the ranking men of intelligence, armed with both the power to speak and the power to listen, played out their bureaucratic roles. Within the formal structure their own interactive lifestyles provided a free-form contrast to their formal written product. Their behavior testified to the fact that they were in touch with real cases, real controversies. It also proved that they were not by any means immune to the temptations of gamesmanship. It was normal bureaucratic politics, bound to be productive of a rich variety of vignettes.

Had an outsider had the power to listen to that cacophony, he would have heard the voices of men in many roles, demonstrating at times their power to listen to the experts below and to speak to the policy-makers above. At other times the demonstration was strictly vice versa. At still other times they were listening and speaking only to themselves. Better than most others, they had regular opportunities to learn that the power to speak can impede the power to listen. Some days the best Q's and A's were: *Who is speaking? Everybody. Who is listening? No one.* On other days it was just the usual bureaucratic jujitsu.

The cacophony nevertheless underlined a serious proposition: the institutions were weighty enough, the men were strong-willed enough, the issues were vital enough, so that the raw material for rivalries of significance was present. As we shall see later, the system worked: in terms of the quality of the formal product sought from it, the intelligence community's estimative system in the 1960's was probably the best that the U.S. Government could hope to have. One reason for this was the very fact that it proceeded from a base of men and institutions wide enough, deep enough, and mixed enough to assure both the connection with reality and the ability to reflect upon it. In the 1970's that base needs reinforcement.

To emphasize both points as vividly as possible, I propose to juxtapose discussions of the informal and the formal aspects of the process. Section 3 is subsequently devoted to an elaboration of what the public is now in a position to know about the record of National Intelligence Estimating on Vietnam. Section 4 draws some conclusions therefrom, and proposes a basic step in Executive-Legislative institutional reform.

First, however, I turn to a stream-of-consciousness anecdotal rendition of the life and times of the intelligence bureaucracy, in the hope of illustrating recurring categories of problems as the Executive Branch tries to come to grips with the production of useful information. The omission of names and dates is by no means intended to suggest that the vignettes are all apocryphal. The flavor is accurate, and the prototypes real. They once were in motion in the great 1960's foreign policy free-for-all. Things are apparently less exciting in the 1970's, but it is too much to believe that somewhere subsurface their counterparts are not comparably in motion today.[3]

BUREAUCRATIC HIGH LIFE: INTELLIGENCE IN MOTION

"I lived in the Government of the United States for many years," Woodrow Wilson once wrote, "and I never saw the Government of the United States." I never saw it either.

---

3. The United States experience should be distinguished sharply from that of the United Kingdom or Canada. While similarities inevitably occur in human and institutional behavior, the problems in London or Ottawa are not to be compared with those in Washington in terms of scale, scope, or Constitutional complexity. Moreover, in a manner of speaking, their national security bureaucracies have maintained a culture of secrecy up to now which we, to a significant degree, have lacked. Whether we are focusing on the President, the Congress, or the intelligence community, we are dealing with levels of independent activity which have no legal or philosophical counterparts elsewhere, including Parliamentary democracies. The checks and balances operating between our Executive and Legislative, and the quasi-independent status of our intelligence community within the Executive, are significantly unique.

In order to think about the Congress, one must pluralize it. In order to think about the Executive Branch, one must pluralize that as well. I have in mind more than the familiar tension between the Presidential government and the permanent government, between temporary Presidents and the careerists of the Civil Service and Foreign Service. I have in mind the splintering of those lesser governments into a more vigorous pluralism of levels, sectors, and personalities, all caught up in such intricate patterns of interaction as to render highly suspect any confident assumptions about consistency in their bureaucratic behavior. In the long run, as applied to the intelligence community, this is just as well—an extra safeguard against intelligence's becoming doctrinaire or predictable.

The intelligence bureaucracies were constantly in motion in the 1960's, which is another way of saying that few models of interagency relations stayed put. Trade-offs and compensations, repeatedly flavored with dashes of Hegelian dialectic, tended to enthrone relativities, not the conspiracies operating along regularized circuits which analysts of bureaucratic politics are fond of finding. Operating under formal methodologies, and regularly producing formal products, the intelligence community had to be considered a system—surely the largest and most comprehensive system working on an interagency basis within the Executive Branch in Washington. But looked at in its personalized and pluralistic dimensions, it was a system full of accidental cross-currents, strange bedfellows, and unexpected connections. A feeling for the whole will perhaps take on a more convincing real-life aspect if these samples are grouped under successive headings, and introduced without pausing to dwell on any one of them in particular.

1. *The politics of information-handling was often enlivened by hierarchical anomalies.* For example:

> —a ranking, politically appointed agency head fervently disagreeing with his own analysts on whether the Sino-Soviet rift was deep enough for any United States policies to be based upon it . . .
>
> —the Cabinet official seeking help in his awkward relation with a powerful subordinate, asking for a Special National Intelligence Estimate on the plausibility of an attack on the United States through the clandestine introduction of nuclear weapons, and mentioning in passing that a great many things were riding on the outcome . . .
>
> —the Secretary of a major department complaining that interagency task forces were forever expanding collection requirements, heedless of cost, and the chairman of USIB promptly dressing down the Secretary's nearest subordinate for exemplifying the Secretary's proposition in the task force he had just chaired . . .
>
> —the civilian Secretary emerging suddenly with a long-time personal connection with an Army general then serving in a subordinate position at CIA, a connection based on their mutual prior service with George C. Marshall . . .

—the Director of CIA, wearing one of his other hats at an interagency meeting, habitually turning to one of his deputies and inquiring: "Does CIA wish to speak?" . . .

—the Deputy Executive Secretary of State calling on Presidential instructions to order an Assistant Secretary of State as part of his intelligence responsibilities to prepare a political dossier on Senator Fulbright's Vietnam record, only to be countermanded by the Under Secretary when the Assistant Secretary, claiming that the order was improper (*ultra vires*), refused to comply . . .

—the ranking foreign visitor telling his American counterpart after a day of briefings on Mediterranean problems: "Oh, I agree with you, but your people don't" . . .

—the admiral freely confessing that one reason the Navy classified information was to keep it from civilians in the Defense Department . . .

—the CIA regional covert operator—alarmed at how the Soviet KGB (secret police) were taking over Africa—admitting to a "growing gap" on the issue between the covert and overt sides of the CIA and an "even greater gap" with the policy-makers . . .

—the colleague of the Secretary of State attempting to embarrass him at a meeting with the President by asking him to withdraw State (INR) footnotes to an estimate on Chinese militancy, since the Secretary personally disagreed with the footnotes . . .

—several prominent officials trying to contrive the consideration and approval at staff level of a significant interagency paper on atomic energy matters and its release at that level without higher interagency discussion and adoption—a device to by-pass the Arms Control and Disarmament Administration in a matter of vital interest to it . . .

—the Commander of the Korean theater whose idiosyncratic personal estimates (was Che Guevera in P'yŏngyang?) were perhaps of greater moment than they might otherwise have been had not he and a member of the Cabinet matriculated together at Oxford years ago.

Sometimes pursuing their conflicting bureaucratic mandates, sometimes simply off on frolics of their own, policy-makers and intelligence executives alike not only managed now and then to undermine one another, but their own or the other man's subordinates as well, all in the interests of more intelligent information handling. Not surprisingly, interagency conversations on the same subject at different bureaucratic levels often produced different results. But not even the units of the subsystem were predictably coherent; by no means did they necessarily project organizational views.

2. *Coordinators of information often attempted to prevent its misuse within the Executive Branch itself by restricting distribution.* There were regular interagency flaps over the predictable misuse by the armed services

of hypothetical worst-case assumptions ground into the multi-year projections on Soviet military force capabilities. Civilian agency representatives would express profound concern that such papers—likely to be styled "Intelligence Assumptions for Planning"—not be used by anyone as a forecast, i.e., as a plausible estimate for actual tables of organization and equipment for Soviet forces, since no one thought the Soviets could or would in fact do everything covered by the assumptions.

The ranking Pentagon representative present would be asked for a suggestion on how to restrict the paper's distribution and control its use. Something like the following conversation would ensue. *An Army general:* "I see no reason why CINCPAC (the Pacific Commander) needs it, for instance." *A Navy admiral:* "I am sure our senior planners do intend to manipulate this paper in just the dangerous way you suggest." *An Air Force general:* "Why else was the paper requested?" *A CIA admiral:* "Within the Navy, the Navy footnotes will be used." *An NSA general:* "I'm dubious about the whole document. It simply transfers the problem over to the interested users." *A DIA general:* "On the other hand, if we don't act on a community document, DIA will get asked—and that is worse."

Organized self-criticism could lead to embroiled discussions of the distribution of interagency committee papers. The subject might be a postmortem analysis of the deficiencies in information flow, the gaps in intelligence that had come to light in the process of writing an important estimate. The issues might be three: (1) whether the CIA board responsible for writing the final draft estimate was the best qualified to describe the gaps; (2) how to relate the gaps as seen by the estimators with the gaps as seen by interagency groups responsible for setting intelligence collection priorities; and (3) who would win the interagency jurisdictional struggle over which instrumentalities would be given the implementing assignments. Rather than air these issues widely—and some of them could have million-dollar budgetary consequences—there might be quick agreement that uncoordinated postmortems should not be distributed outside the intelligence community. The "hateful boo-boos" of unauthorized distributions would be corrected at once, with offending copies instantly recalled.

3. *Scoring jurisdictional points was commonplace at interagency sessions, and the subject matter could range from low comedy to consequential infighting on major issues of information management.* To wit:

From *CIA:* I will not sit here with responsibility for these expensive technological failures and have this go on. Maybe the Pentagon's got the wrong team operating this again. I'm dissatisfied, and so is the President—when I get through talking to him.

From State (after a mixed record of regular weekly briefings of the inter-agency Watch Report): How about an interagency review of the Watch Report's recent false alarms? *From CIA:* Our job is not tactical; we are usually wrong when we pinpoint; so let's stop doing it.

From NSA: God knows we have other problems, but lack of office space is no excuse for failure anywhere in the world.

From CIA: The Secretary of Defense and I developed this plan. I charged my station chief to prepare an analysis pursuant thereto. If the generals can't use our product, screw them.

From an ambassador in a Communist capital: The President tells me I am in charge of all U.S. activities here. My military attachés don't know it. Can the Secretary of State or the Director of Central Intelligence restrain excessive information collection by my attachés? *Tentative answer:* No.

From CIA: Why do we have to send the China estimate to U.S. military commands overseas just because that's where the action is? That's where the leaking is, too. There will be lots less mischief if we keep it in Washington.

From State (throughout years of Vietnamese bombing, north and south): It's ridiculous not to be able to get damage assessments on civilian casualties, non-military targets hit, and military targets missed. *From the Pentagon:* That's not intelligence—that's operations.

From the Air Force representative (to his State colleague after the meeting breaks up): I want you to know that I personally agree with every word in your dissenting footnote; the Air Force thinks otherwise.

From CIA: The DCI is statutorily charged with protection of intelligence methods and sources. Therefore he can override the National Security Council and take the matter directly to Capitol Hill. I doubt he will want to do so in this case.

From the Army: Back to our old friend cost-effectiveness—ignored by the Air Force as usual, for the usual good reasons.

From CIA: We are preparing a paper for the DCI in his personal capacity, since the President has asked him privately for his views. DIA is also preparing a paper for the Secretary of Defense in his personal capacity. However, the community as such has not been asked for its judgment, and should not render one unless and until it has.

From NSA: I see the State Department doesn't want me to go to Africa or Latin America these days. Actually, our record was very good except on the day it happened.

From CIA: We are entering a protracted period where the danger of nuclear war is subsiding, and the importance of the Third World is increasing. Yet our opportunities for information collection in the Third World are drying up with the State Department's connivance and approval.

From the Army: How did the White House expect us to predict what happened in Panama? Do they think we have the foresight to put Balboa High School students on the payroll?

From CIA: We were gratified to hear that the State Department is now keeping the indigenous cleaning force in ———— Embassy out of the restricted area. The President's advisers are preoccupied with the notion that significant espionage goes on there.

From FBI: The Attorney General is showing an intense personal interest in National Intelligence Estimates, and demanding the completion of this one at once. *Others:* If he wants it bad enough, he'll get it bad enough.

From AEC: Let's avoid the tidiness syndrome. I've never been one to split hairs on charters. Every case differs. CIA, for instance, is not a channel through which AEC must invariably deal.

From NSA: I'm sure we'd all have problems with the interpretation just given by the CIA representative. Let's let him continue to give the regulations his interpretation, and the rest of us will read them as written.

From Army: Is it only in Africa that ———— (civilian agency) refuses to cooperate in the national interest? *Chorus:* No, everywhere. *CIA:* Their cooperation has to be bought like any business transaction. *Army:* Apparently they are not for sale.

4. *Sometimes when the brass of the intelligence community went beyond their substantive depths, their interests were painfully plain:*

DIA: Shouldn't we say something about the Cultural Revolution?

CIA: We asked the Sinologists not to predict on this one. Their ignorance is so great that they would make us all look silly later.

Confronting an estimate on Angola. . . . *Defense:* Let's delete the sentence, "The day of colonialism in Africa is drawing to a close." *State:* Let's retain the sentence, inserting "has drawn." *CIA:* Let's remove these Political Science 101 statements. I am sure our policy-makers have these maxims well in mind. *State:* We should not be too sure how many of these maxims our policy-makers have in mind. *Navy:* We are destroying our remaining friends in Portugal and South Africa. The coaling stations. . . .

NSA: I confess I'm not at all sure what this means, but I find it very hard to oppose. . . . Do we ever consider the cost to the reader of taking up his time on irrelevant matters?

First CIA official: The Ambassador's primacy is, of course, unquestioned. But in ———— (Middle East capital) the ambassador was not witting; nor was the CIA station chief. Therefore Washington was misinformed.

Second CIA officer: We've dumped millions of dollars into that little country, and they still refuse to tell us what is going on.

General X: Outer space is free, just as free as the seas. Free seas, free space. *Admiral Y:* That may help on satellites, but it doesn't help make U-2's lawful. They fly in the atmosphere, not in space.

General Z: But we're flying U-2's over countries we don't recognize. So they're legal too.

AEC: The Soviet nuclear explosion is obviously embarrassing. The information points to a possible test ban treaty violation. We would not want our own Plowshare program to be endangered-by-analogy, nor would Capitol Hill. The Japanese Ambassador is seeing the Secretary of State. Let's hope they won't accuse the Soviets of violating.

CIA: This raises the question of who is going to say whether there is a violation of the treaty or not.

State: That judgment must remain an ultimate policy conclusion. We should go out of our way to avoid pre-empting it, and obviously should treat the matter as beyond our purview.

DIA: Who is better able to decide violations than we? Does State have someone in mind?

CIA: A damn good question.

State: The Committee of Principals might, not to mention the President.

CIA: I am the oldest living member of the Committee of Principals.

State: Perhaps the other members have an equally large view of their own role on that committee. The Director of ACDA, for example?

DIA: There are other influences, I am sure, which we can bring to bear.

FBI: All of us would be better off sticking to certitudes and not speculating about Communist intentions.

CIA: Estimating begins when certitude ends.

FBI: I disagree. (*Smothered laughter*)

Chairman: Let's take the marihuana out of this exercise.

5. *The use and abuse of international bureaucratic politics could sometimes add an extra dimension to interagency discussion.* Thus there were long-standing arguments over how and by whom foreign heads of state, Ministers, and NATO representatives should be briefed. Intricate competing networks of claims involved State, Defense, and CIA, complicating life at primary and secondary levels in several bureaucracies. Thus:

When State at first expressed doubts about the propriety of direct relations between the Director of CIA and foreign heads of state, the CIA head classified his way into the action: . . . The President wants me personally to go to the Head of State to brief him on matters which are too sensitive for his Foreign Minister. . . . The fact that I took the trouble to come personally made a deep impression on Erhard. . . . American *ambassadors* always welcome my visits—nothing personal, just a tribute to the advantage of dealing outside the rigidities of diplomatic channels. . . . The British, you know, had a complete misconception of Bobby Kennedy's trip to Malaysia. Luckily, I was able to explain all this to the Prime Minister. Our Ambassador didn't know. . . .

When a former Chairman of the British Joint Intelligence Committee was appointed U.K. Ambassador to NATO, there were intramural suspicions that he carried with him via his lines to London readier access to more U.S. intelligence than was available to his colleague, the U.S. Ambassador to NATO. Such speculation gave some members of the American intelligence community much pleasure. . . .

Alleged foreign dependence on receiving certain U.S. intelligence information was often used as a bureaucratic argument in Washington for preserving certain U.S. agency budgets. Similarly, arrangements with certain foreign governments for an agreed division of labor on information collection tended to sanctify certain U.S. budgetary levels. Only when disenchantment set in concerning lack of support from some of these same governments over Vietnam were reductions made in the intelligence flow on the American side. . . .

Once when the publisher Macmillan was about to bring out David Kahn's book *The Codebreakers,* a high-ranking American official became so carried away with his notion of the Special Relationship that he proposed that Prime Minister Macmillan be approached to intervene with his "family publishers" in behalf of the American national interest in keeping the material classified.

These glimpses of intelligence in motion suggest what might have occurred in the foreign policy free-for-all had centripetal elements not been present—i.e., what every-man-for-himself might have been like in the intelligence community of the New Frontier or the Great Society in the absence of serious efforts toward responsible coordination. The headier aspects of bureaucratic high life came down to earth because the intelligence community nevertheless had to focus on the steady and timely production of substantive National Intelligence Estimates. Their quality was infinitely better than the surrounding bureaucratic byplay might otherwise suggest.

For out of this unlikely and heterogeneous group of men and institutions, responsive in differing degrees to the bureaucracies surrounding them, there came a coherent, coordinated, high-quality product. The process of producing written NIE's was itself indispensable in bringing relative order out of relative chaos, in bridging civilian and military assessments, in telegraphing fundamental differences in the experts' views of the facts, in setting out disagreements in an orderly manner between two covers of the same paper, in documenting dissents, in winnowing, providing context, encapsulating, and highlighting estimative judgments in readable form. Set procedures regularly forced upward from said experts the drafts their superiors had to address prior to sending them on in finished form to policy echelons. In 1964–65 (to take a prime example) the intelligence community exercised its power to speak through a series of significant, timely, and prescient warnings contained in the majority and dissenting views in the National Intelligence Estimates on Vietnam. In retrospect, as we turn to consider the gravamen of those estimates, it can be regretted that the policymakers did not better exercise their own power to listen.

PRESENT AT THE ESCALATION

Well wired into the bureaucratic circuitry of Washington and the field, possessing indubitably both the power to listen and the power to speak, the U.S. intelligence community contemplated Vietnam. All in all, it must lament that it was not listened to. In retrospect, the intelligence community —especially its civilian components—more often than not turned out to be right. The community consistently recorded its own divisions and ventilated the fundamental issues in a manner that should have stimulated policy debate. Yet on balance, the most that intelligence can claim is that it was present at the escalation.

This phenomenon, already remarked upon by pundits and commentators, is bound to become even more striking in the future if and as hundreds and thousands of additional classified documents are released, and more reliable accounts are assembled especially of what civilian intelligence was actually saying on both an uncoordinated department basis and a coordinated community one. Enough is now available, however, for the serious researcher who has the time to piece it together to begin to discern with some insight the shape of national intelligence estimating on Vietnam.

Indeed, the disclosed literature is already so vast that even those of us whose personal predilections are to rush neither to judgment nor to the Xerox machine, can now comfortably refer to events in which we participated with the advantage of having already in the public domain a growing reference base of National Intelligence Estimates and Special National Intelligence Estimates in summary and occasionally documentary form. NIE's and SNIE's are perhaps not yet household words, but that is no fault of the subjective declassifiers, who have produced Presidential memoirs, Special Assistants' biographies, Assistant Secretary's autobiographies, scholars' studies, publicists' accounts, and journalists' best sellers, not to mention the hidden multitude of inners and outers who over the years have leaked or ghosted.

Since 1971 these efforts have been augmented by Daniel Ellsberg's and Senator Mike Gravel's massive initiatives in instant disclosure, so that the various compilations of the Pentagon Papers provide an unrivaled, if uneven, data base for everything else. The material itself is voluminous, spread sequentially over time, rich in its probative value, and historic in its setting. The cumulative result assures that Vietnam will inevitably be chosen as the subject matter for various illustrative purposes. In principle, however, if the material were publicly available, the central point I want to make about the potential relevance of the NIE system to the overarching issues of security, democracy, and Executive-Congressional relations, could be illustrated from the national estimative processes surrounding the other crises of the 1960's as well: Berlin, Cuba, the Congo, China-India, India-Pakistan, the Dominican Republic, Malaysia-Indonesia, and the Middle East. If in the future the full estimative picture surrounding these crises should likewise substantially enter the public domain, more or less comparable utilities will be apparent and a similar point could be made.

Focusing on the formal, coordinated NIE production defines boundaries in a useful way. Manageable in amount, usually significant in a specific historic context, written for Presidents and their chief advisors, NIE's have several enduring advantages over other contemporaneously written materials, both intrinsically on the merits and as a corrective to partial or faulty memories. For time itself is always a problem—an elusive one—in the reconstruction of events, the recollection of participants, the writing of memoirs. Comparatively speaking, NIE's are among the least fragmentary of bureaucratic assessments. Their procedures require that their parameters be as clear and their contexts as explicit as possible.

More than with other papers, estimates speak for themselves. Fewer interpretations are necessary at the time of writing or later. Whatever personal and bureaucratic politics go into them, whatever waffles, compromises, and ambiguities are present, the estimates are the products of many minds with the important safeguards numbers afford, and they are printed in cold type, placed between hard covers, and stamped with dates and signatures.

Special NIE's were often requested with urgent policy needs in mind. They frequently reflected strenuous arguments over the interpretation and evaluation of critical events and trends; they often mirrored fateful disagreements and contained explicit dissents. They regularly projected a more accurate reflection of the data base available to the experts at the time than did the contingency papers of the Pentagon or the arguments-in-interest of the policy proposers at Cabinet and sub-Cabinet levels.

Even more important, the serious reader of NIE's and SNIE's at the time could read them as an index to the separate estimative production of the contributing agencies, especially the dissenters. As such, national estimates could be an easy guide to the greater elaboration and sharper statements of conflicting positions to be found in the readily available separate products of the component organizations. These estimates too, more numerous than the NIE's, were distributed in a timely manner inside both the relevant intelligence and policy communities.

Likewise, the original all-source information data base was available to most of the working Vietnam analysts in Washington on an interagency basis. Curiously, however, except for a few INR estimates referred to in the Pentagon Papers—one reprinted in full, two or three others briefly noted—the vast bulk of these departmental estimates were ignored in that huge collection. They currently remain classified and unreachable, including scores of estimative documents consisting especially of thousands of pages of "Research Memoranda" and "Intelligence Notes"—nearly the total formal INR in-house production on Vietnam—issued by that Bureau alone from 1961 to 1969. All of these were regularly distributed to the White House, the Pentagon, and CIA, as well as inside the State Department. Also classified and unavailable are literally hundreds of daily informal INR items on Vietnam used in oral and written form to brief the Secretary of State, the Under Secretaries, and the ranking Far East/East Asia bureau officers throughout the decade. Apparently none of these briefing items found its way into the Pentagon Papers data base at all. The power not to listen may extend, it seems, to some of the authors of the Pentagon Papers.

The treatment of NIE's and SNIE's in the Pentagon Papers is anything but systematic, the coverage ranging from the rare reprint, to lengthy excerpts, to summaries of summaries. There are substantial differences in inclusions and exclusions between the Department of Defense edition and the Gravel volumes. Some references are specific, some vague. While occasionally it is appropriately emphasized that these estimates were coordinated documents, produced by the entire intelligence community and approved by USIB, frequently there are misleading references attributing them variously to CIA or "NIB" (*sic*).

Nevertheless, enough is stated and reprinted so that an over-all impression comes through. Thus there was NIE 50–61 warning on March 28, 1961, that the situation in South Vietnam was likely to become increasingly difficult, not only because of rising Communist guerrilla strength and declining internal security, but also because of widening dissatisfaction with Diem—the odds favoring a coup attempt by non-Communist elements in a year or so. There was NIE 14–3/53.61 warning on August 15, 1961, that Hanoi would increase the pace and scope of its paramilitary activity during the next few months, and that the outlook was for a "prolonged and difficult struggle."

There was SNIE 10–3–61, issued on October 10, 1961, when the National Security Council was considering a SEATO engagement in South Vietnam. After reviewing several paragraphs from this estimate, the commentator in the Pentagon Papers says:

> In this instance, and as we will see later, the Intelligence Community's estimates of the likely results of U.S. moves are conspicuously more pessimistic (and more realistic) than the other staff papers presented to the President. . . . It is hard to imagine a more sharp contrast than between this paper, which foresees no serious impact on the insurgency from proposed intervention, and . . . a JCS estimate . . . of the size of the American force needed "to clean up the Viet Cong threat."[4]

Following the Talyor-Rostow recommendations for the dispatch of a U.S. military task force, SNIE 10–4–61, issued November 5, 1961, warned that Hanoi would respond to an increased U.S. troop commitment by increasing support to the Viet Cong. The SNIE went on to estimate that air attacks against the North would not cause Hanoi to stop that support. The Pentagon Papers commentator states:

> This SNIE, incidentally, is the only staff paper found in the available record which treats communist reactions primarily in terms of the separate national interests of Hanoi, Moscow, and Peiping, rather than primarily in terms of an overall communist strategy for which Hanoi is acting as an agent.[5]

As the months went on and the Kennedy Administration's commitments were made, the intelligence community divided on the issue of whether progress was actually occurring. NIE 53–63 issued April 17, 1963, found no particular deterioration but noted that "Decisive campaigns have yet to be fought and no quick and easy end to the war is in sight. The situation remains fragile." The Pentagon, however, was trumpeting optimism. The anonymous writer in the Pentagon Papers writes:

> Mr. McNamara was told and believed that there had been "tremendous progress" in the past six months. . . . All the statistics and evaluations pointed to GVN improvement. . . . Even as late as July 1963 a rosy picture was being painted by DIA. . . . The first suggestion of a contrary evaluation within the bureaucracy came from INR. Noting disquieting statistical trends since July, an unpopular INR memo stated that the "pattern showed steady decline over a period of more than three months duration." It was greeted with a storm of disagreement. . . .[6]

---

4. Mike Gravel, ed., *The Senator Gravel Edition: The Pentagon Papers,* vol. 2 (Boston: Beacon Press, 1972), p. 78.
5. *Ibid.,* p. 107.
6. *Ibid.,* p. 164

In the four months between the appearance of that INR paper and the appearance of SNIE 50–64, issued February 12, 1964, most of the rest of the intelligence community had come around to the INR view, including an appreciation of the highly doctored Diem Government statistics against which INR had consistently warned. The SNIE stated that "South Vietnam has, at best, an even chance of withstanding the insurgency menace during the next few weeks or months."

In the meantime also, the coup against Diem had taken place, just as another SNIE, 53–2–63, issued July 10, 1963—and quoting large sections of INR language verbatim—had predicted. That estimate had warned that if Diem did not seek to conciliate the Buddhists, new disorders were likely and there would be better than even chances of coup or assassination attempts. The attempts were successful within four months.

It is worth examining in greater detail what now is known about the dozen or so SNIE's on Vietnam produced by USIB during 1964–65, the critical years of escalation considerations and moves. Such a survey sheds light not only on the substantive contrasts between intelligence and policy at the time, but also on the independence of viewpoint which characterized intelligence judgments of the day—even in the environment of politics, sensitivity, secrecy, and pressures for conformity which the public has usually come to associate with those two years.

The February 1964 SNIE has confirmed the pessimism now felt in all quarters of the intelligence community about the political and military situation in South Vietnam. In May there were policy discussions in Washington to consider low-scale actions—force deployments, serious threats, or South Vietnamese attacks on outlying targets in Communist-held Laos or North Vietnam. Significant divisions of opinion were again apparent in the intelligence community but were papered over in SNIE 50–2–64, adopted unanimously by USIB and issued May 25, 1964. This estimate stated that in response to the above actions, the insurrection might be reduced "for the moment." USIB noted, however, that if the hypothesized U.S. actions continued, no "meaningful odds" could be set on Hanoi's response. Lowered terms for a negotiated outcome were possible, but there was a "significant danger" that Hanoi would fight. Hanoi's *will* was the most that could be affected, the estimate noted; none of the actions forecast would affect their *capabilities,* since the "major sources of communist strength in South Vietnam are indigenous." The estimate warned that "retaliatory measures which Hanoi might take in Laos and South Vietnam might make it increasingly difficult for the U.S. to regard its objectives as attainable by limited means. Thus difficulties of comprehension might increase on both sides as the scale of action mounted."[7]

---

7. *Ibid.,* pp. 124–25.

On October 1, 1964, SNIE 53–2–64 painted a generally pessimistic view: USIB expected the political situation in South Vietnam to continue to decay, and the Saigon Government's morale and effectiveness to continue to deteriorate. For that reason, and in the wake of the events in the Gulf of Tonkin in August and September, it was natural that U.S. policy attention turned increasingly to the contingent question of whether pressures against the North offered any way out. On that issue the constituent elements of the intelligence community, in a series of critical estimates over the next fourteen months, set forth their differences in clear and unmistakable terms, directly relevant to the decisions confronting the policy makers. In general, during this period, the armed services estimators were optimistic about the possible effects of pressures on the North, INR was consistently pessimistic, and CIA fluctuated. The positions were well articulated, and the conflicting judgments clearly joined.

Beginning with SNIE 10–3–64, issued on October 9, 1964, USIB split in its estimates of probable Communist reactions to certain postulated U.S. courses of action, including non-retaliatory attacks on North Vietnamese targets. In writing this estimate, CIA, with majority support including DIA, discussed two alternative North Vietnamese reactions (i.e., to retrench or intensify) and "concluded that these would probably be limited to defensive and propaganda measures with possibly some scaling down of operations in the South."[8]

The USIB majority expressly doubted that Hanoi would attempt any overt invasion of South Vietnam. INR dissented, arguing that Hanoi would not wish to lose momentum, or lose face with the Viet Cong, or bolster South Vietnamese morale by buying time. Instead, INR predicted, Hanoi would carry on the fight and proceed to send its own armed forced on a large scale to Laos and South Vietnam. In a bold estimate bearing directly on the central issue facing Presidential decision in the weeks ahead, INR predicted that Hanoi would choose the aggressive response, considering that at this juncture it would have optimum provocation from Washington and Saigon as well as international acceptance for its own overt retaliation in the South.

Six weeks later, INR registered a similar dissent in the tripartite INR/CIA/DIA paper of November 26, 1964 (essentially a SNIE, although technically not approved by USIB), reacting to the famous "Option C or C-Prime Moves" of the Bundy-McNaughton scenarios described in the Pentagon Papers and elsewhere. The new paper noted that Washington would probably find itself progressively isolated in the event its sanctions did not soon achieve either a measurable reduction in Communist pressures in South Vietnam or some progress toward meaningful negotiations. While

---

8. *Ibid.*, vol. 3, p. 133.

CIA and DIA foresaw that certain medium-to-upper levels of escalation could create a situation wherein Hanoi would probably seek to negotiate as good a settlement as it could, INR in a footnote reasserted its conviction that Hanoi would fight on, with considerable risk of a North Vietnamese invasion of South Vietnam and of an entirely new war situation's developing.

All three elements of the intelligence community agreed in telling the policy-makers that bombing North Vietnam as contemplated in the contingency planning would fail to force Hanoi to cease its support of the Southern insurgency. The estimators did not believe that bombing would have a crucial effect on the daily lives of the population in the North, nor that striking industrial targets would create unmanageable control problems in Hanoi, nor that that regime would be unwilling to suffer bombing damage in a test of wills with the United States. These tripartite estimates were read and rejected by the contingency-paper writers, whose own quite different assumptions went into their policy papers—which in turn went forward from the State and Defense Departments to the White House.

With fateful policy decisions at hand, and within hours after the attack on the U.S. military advisers' compound at Pleiku, the policy-makers were warned once more by SNIE 10-3-65, issued on February 11, 1965, that initiation of the new U.S. bombing policy almost certainly would not lead Hanoi to restrain the Viet Cong. It was followed by SNIE 10-3/1-65 one week later, February 18, two days before the Rolling Thunder bombing program was scheduled to begin. Even though part of the rationale for going North was relief for the South, the SNIE predicted that Viet Cong attacks against U.S. air bases would continue at their existing level of intensity despite the new air action against North Vietnam.[9]

But once more the intelligence community split on the ultimately critical question of Hanoi's will to persist. With INR again dissenting, the majority led by CIA again considered Hanoi's alternatives of retrenchment or intensification, and concluded that the former was somewhat more likely. As summarized in the Pentagon Papers:

> The intelligence community gives its view that sustained attacks on the DRV would probably cause it to seek a respite rather than to intensify the struggle in the South.[10]

Once again the majority also discussed the possibility that Hanoi would launch a large-scale movement into the South, and once more they concluded that it was unlikely that Hanoi would do this in response to the American bombing of the North.

---

9. *Ibid.,* p. 400.
10. *Ibid.,* p. 277.

In this final estimate on the eve of escalation, INR dissented twice. First it repeated the conclusion and argumentation of its previous dissent of October 9, 1964, reaffirming its estimate that Hanoi would accept the bombing and intensify the struggle in the South. It pointed out in addition that Hanoi's persistence would be reinforced by the knowledge that concessions combined with a reduction of Viet Cong activity might only invite the United States to resume air strikes whenever Viet Cong activity increased. In its second dissent, INR argued that once U.S. attacks had destroyed major industrial and military targets, Hanoi would have substantially lost its hostage against greater incremental damage from the air, thus making it even more likely that Hanoi would fight on and proceed to send its own armed forces to the South on a large scale.

Six weeks of bombing later, the rest of the intelligence community came round to the INR view. In language unanimously agreed to in SNIE 10–5–65 on April 28, 1965, USIB concluded:

> The policies and tactics of the Communist powers have settled into a fairly definitive pattern. It appears that the DRV, with strong Chinese encouragement, is determined for the present to ride out the U.S. bombardment. Both the DRV and Communist China have hardened their attitude toward negotiations. . . . They apparently calculate that the DRV can afford further punishment. . . . Moreover, they consider that the tide is running in their favor in the South.[11]

SNIE 10–6–65 was issued on June 2, 1965, with American ground troops about to engage in their first large "search and destroy" mission. It unanimously restated a pessimistic analysis of the likelihood that Hanoi would seek a respite from the bombing through negotiations.[12]

With a major enlargement of U.S. ground involvement pending, USIB was asked in July 1965 to consider world reactions to a course of action including U.S. troop levels at 175,000 in Vietnam, the call-up of a quarter million U.S. reservists, extending duty tours and doubling the draft, and a step-up of U.S. air strikes against North Vietnamese land lines of communication with China. On July 23, in SNIE 10–9–65, USIB agreed that increases in the U.S. forces in South Vietnam would be offset by the introduction of 20-30,000 North Vietnamese regulars by the end of 1965. Hanoi would seek, and the Soviets provide, more air defense. American allies would find it increasingly difficult to give U.S. policy any public support. Hanoi and the Viet Cong appeared confident of ultimate and possibly early success without important concessions on their part. USIB did not believe

---

11. *Ibid.,* pp. 480–81.
12. *Ibid.,* pp. 283–84.

that the U.S. actions assumed for the SNIE would basically alter these expectations.[13]

INR moved from a dissenting position taken in the June estimate on the contingent eventuality of Chinese air involvement into an agreed majority position on the same point, with the military now dissenting. The change was due to a shift to the INR position by Admiral W. F. Raborn, Jr., then Director of CIA, taken despite the implicit unhappiness of CIA estimators who left their own disagreement unexpressed.

Another majority including CIA believed that the accumulated strains of prolonged bombing of lines of communication in North Vietnam would inhibit and might prevent an increase in large-scale Communist activity in the South. On this point INR and the Army dissented, believing that in spite of prospectively greater damage to lines of communication and other targets, it was impossible to do irreparable damage to communications. Given demonstrated Communist logistical resourcefulness, INR and the Army credited Hanoi with an ability to continue the war at the scale envisaged in the South.[14]

In mid-September of 1965, as the escalation continued to go forward, USIB was asked once more to address the probable reactions to new U.S. courses of action. This time air strikes were postulated against North Vietnamese missile sites, airfields, power plants, and prime rail, road, and traffic targets. INR reiterated its pessimistic viewpoint with its cautionary implications for policy. In a precedent-setting dissent from the entire estimate, INR estimated that Hanoi would regard the composite program as a watershed—i.e., a departure from the previous U.S. policy of graduated pressure, in favor of a broad assault on the chief elements of the economy, inevitably involving large industrial and civilian losses. Under the circumstances, INR estimated that it was unlikely that Hanoi would choose to compromise, or that Moscow would urge her to do so. Peking would press her to persevere. These positions would be mutually reinforcing and lead to militant prosecution of the war, increased Chinese and Soviet aid, and probable retaliation on the ground with additional North Vietnamese troops moving south. The majority position was more sanguine.

In early December the intelligence community was asked for its final estimate for the year of escalation. USIB complied on December 10, 1965, with SNIE 10–12–65. It was perhaps a fitting tribute, both to the stubborn independence of the community and to the intractabilities of the problems with which the prior year of estimating had dealt, that no fewer than seven separate sets of dissents were registered to this estimate. By now Chinese

13. *Ibid.,* pp. 484–85.
14. U.S., Department of Defense, *United States-Vietnam Relations 1945–67* (*Pentagon Papers*), vol. 6, sec. IV, c. 7 (a), p. 11.

capabilities and intentions were a source of brooding interest, and accounted for most of the disagreements. Thus the Army and INR joined in one dissent on Chinese capabilities; NSA and INR joined in another on unfolding patterns of Chinese border involvement; and NSA, INR, and the Army joined in still another—on Chinese air activity.

But the estimate inevitably returned to the underlying question regularly asked by policy-makers in one form or another: When would the "other side" relent? An author in the *Pentagon Papers* summarizes the SNIE results this time as follows:

> With the exception of State's INR, other intelligence agencies appeared to look with favor upon escalating the bombing. They agreed that intensified air attacks, beginning with POL facilities and key power plants and extending to other targets in the Hanoi/Haiphong area and mining the harbors, would not bring about any basic change in NVN policy but would in time hamper NVN's operations and set a lid on the war in the South. . . . DIA, NSA, and the 3 Service intelligence [agencies] even recorded a judgment that the intensified air strikes, combined with the projected build-up of U.S. ground forces in SVN to about 350,000 troops by the fall of 1966, might ultimately result in a change of heart in Hanoi. . . . INR dissented. Its Director, Thomas L. Hughes, wrote that the escalation would evoke stronger reactions than indicated in the SNIE, "because it would be widely assumed that we were initiating an effort to destroy the DRV's modest industrial establishment. . . . The distinction between such operations and all-out war would appear increasingly tenuous. As these attacks expanded, Hanoi would would be less and less likely to soften its opposition to negotiations and at some point it would come to feel that it had little left to lose by continuing the fighting. . . ."[15]

The intelligence community had been present at the escalation, and the fighting would continue.

THE POWER TO BE HEARD

The might-have-beens of the Vietnam tragedy are numerous, but one of them comes close to the present subject matter of secrecy and democracy. Had a serious bipartisan representation of the ranking and relevant Congressional leadership in key committees bearing on defense, the military, and foreign relations systematically enjoyed the power to listen—if only through regular and instant access to the NIE's and SNIE's of the period—they would have had a roughly reliable index to the central issues of the Vietnam escalation. Moreover, they would have been alerted at the time to

---

15. *The Senator Gravel Edition: The Pentagon Papers,* vol. 6, pp. 65–66.

the depth and seriousness of the differences in interpretation of key data among the Executive's own experts and to the emphasis all the experts were placing on the gravity of the problem and hence on the unlikelihood of American success in any reasonable time.

If the Congressional leadership had been not only systematically apprised of the National Intelligence Estimates but also systematically staffed to handle them, they would have been in position to probe further, had they so desired. The estimates themselves would have pointed the way across the mine-laden bureaucratic landscape, suggesting which further questions to pursue and where they might be pursued. Moreover, regular Congressional access and attention could easily have stimulated more Executive Branch attention to its own expertise. For if the Congress in this sense had had the power to listen, the Executive would have had less power not to listen, and the Congress itself would have had more power to speak. The Congressional power to listen would thereby have amplified the estimators' own power to be heard. In sum, had the Congress through this information been present also at the escalation, the discussion could have been different, the process would probably have changed, and the escalation itself might, just might, not have occurred.

Let us consider, then, the arguments for a Permanent Joint Committee on Intelligence Estimates, composed, say, of a membership of fourteen to consist of the Speaker of the House and the majority and minority leadership of both Houses, who in turn would agree on the choice of other members. While the others should be chosen with due deference to committee jurisdictions and responsibilities, they should not be limited to Foreign Affairs/Foreign Relations, Appropriations, Armed Services, or Atomic Energy. Flexibility should be clearly specified in the enabling resolution, to assure a desirable distribution of representation in terms of geography, party affiliation, length of service (with some representation also of newer members), substantive talent, and possible rotation of terms. It is imperative that the purpose be understood to be substantive and not the supervising, overseeing, or policing of Executive Branch machinery.

The rationale would flow directly from the National Security Act of 1947, in which the Congress provided by statute for "the appropriate dissemination of such intelligence within the government." Resisting the rumored intention of the Nixon Administration to reduce, eviscerate, or eliminate the National Estimates process, the purpose would be to feed the intelligence community's own estimates in an orderly and timely way into an institutionalized Executive-Legislative leadership relation. Perhaps even now such a move could promote fruitful consultation instead of destructive confrontation between the branches, while simultaneously enhancing the role of the National Estimates process as a servant to both. Security, staffing, and other modalities would have to be negotiated on a mutually acceptable basis between the Committee and the intelligence community.

Consider the apparent advantages:

—Structured in form, regularized in procedure, independent in view, guaranteed access, charged with disinterestedness, desiring relevance, and yet stopping short of policy advice of the kind that evokes legitimate Executive privilege, the vehicle of organized intelligence is almost ideal for making a serious multipurpose inroad on the secrecy/democracy issue in the Executive-Legislative framework.

—The Congress and the intelligence community have a similar stake in institutionalizing skepticism and in assuring that the products of an expensive and elaborate process are not ignored. Their joint countervailing power could help compel greater Executive articulation of its own rationale for proposed international action.

—With the supposed distillation of national intelligence vouchsafed to the Congress, the credible use of secrecy to undermine Constitutional checks and balances in other areas should decline.

—Once the NIE base is available to the Congressional leadership, some protection is afforded against organizations habitually manipulating partial information on Capitol Hill to protect their interests or promote their programs.

—Since NIE's and SNIE's are encapsulations and do not disclose sources, they are different in kind from, and more secure than, raw intelligence reports. Likewise, since no attribution is made to diplomatic or other official conversations, diplomatic discourse is protected and another of the normal arguments for minimum disclosure is overcome.

—Institutionalizing these arrangements with the Congress could have the accompanying effect of heightening attention to the NIE system within the Executive Branch and protecting it against further institutional erosion there.

—It would be perfectly consistent with the Joint Committee proposal to require Senatorial confirmation of all the ranking representatives of the various agencies on USIB—a step long overdue.

—The Joint Committee's access to National Estimates might serve as an indirect check and reference point against the selective and slanted intelligence often sped to the Appropriations and Armed Services Committees by means of end-runs around budget time.

—Focusing on intelligence estimates probably avoids the Executive privilege issue. Estimates are supposed to be expert evaluations and predictions. Until the Nixon Administration, they have been considered beyond policy control. Authors of estimates are not advisers to Presidents. Hence both they and their products should be outside the assertion or protection of a claim of Executive privilege.

—In scope, size, and manageability, in quantity and quality control, and in practicability for both Executive and Legislative branches of government, the proposed Joint Committee is logical and serious. It could work if both branches wished it to work. Self-enforcing, self-sustaining, and even self-enhancing elements could be built into the modalities to help assure that all parties would want to make the arrangements work and work better.

—The Congress would have the advantage, which it now lacks, of knowing that its leadership has access to the coordinated wisdom of the Executive Branch's own experts after those experts have sifted the Executive's information. The alternative of building a comparatively miniature but none-the-less expensive Congressional service of competitive experts, with all the consequent confrontations, duplications, and inconclusiveness, could be avoided.

—Emphatically involving the Congressional leadership in roles on the Joint Committee would mark a move away from the diffusion of Congressional power, helping assure that the men who may normally be expected to consult with the President when a crisis builds have been thoroughly introduced to the estimative background.

—The proposal goes very much to the question of the environment in which estimative intelligence is listened to, and hence the environment in which Presidential decisions are ultimately reached. By ending the Executive's current exclusive access to estimates, and converting them genuinely into what their name implies—*national* estimates—the President and Executive officials below him would be less able to turn off the estimative process in moments of dissatisfaction or embarrassment.

—Implicit from the start would be the possibility of growth and change. Experience alone would tend to set the tolerable boundaries for the Committee's further expansion of its role—e.g., into hearings, staff activities, expanded liaison functions, and affecting the terms of reference set for estimates themselves. At any rate the potential would be there for consolidating initial successes.

The risks of the proposal are also evident. The Executive-Legislative tensions surrounding such a relation might turn out to be simply too great for the system to bear. Despite all the protections of the formal Joint Committee structure, direct appointment of the membership by the Congressional leadership, and full-scale security clearances, the Executive Branch would still worry that the Congressional elements in the picture were adversaries in interest. It might be hoped both Executive and Legislative parties to the arrangement would be concerned enough about this predictable problem to make the process work.

New problems of classification might arise, including the jurisdictional relations between this Joint Committee on Estimates and committees engaged in. policing and overseeing functions on classification, intelligence operations, and perhaps others. While this proposal would not be inconsistent with current Congressional interest in a frontal approach to the de-classification problem, there are potential problems of overlap. For the new Joint Committee to do its job credibly and effectively, however, it would be necessary for the Congressional side to be fully cleared for the highest classifications. It would be essential for access to the estimates to be automatic and not discretionary. Otherwise, sooner or later the Executive Branch would inevitably be tempted to overclassify those items it wished to restrict. Limiting the Joint Committee to confidential and secret material, for example, could easily promote the "bumping" of classifications up to top secret when the Executive considered it important not to share the estimate. Executive policy itself, not to speak of Executive-Legislative relations, has long been victimized by the practice of restricting and withholding certain very special information which, when a policy is criticized, can then be said to have been critical to the decision. If a Joint Committee is to be considered, only comprehensive access to the full product of the National Estimative system makes any sense.

The privileged position of a new Joint Committee—with secure access to National Estimates that others on Capitol Hill would not ordinarily see—might, of course, set up new jurisdictional problems inside the Congress. But the Congress will sooner or later have to pay that price if it is serious about moving ahead in the area of sharing Executive secrets systematically. No President is going to co-operate with a system the end product of which is a Senator Gravel reading classified documents into the *Congressional Record*.

There is no magic formula in any institutionalized solution. Even if this proposal were adopted, after everything is said and the estimates are read, the participants could find that they are only in the thick of thin things. But that has often been the fate of proposals designed to make headway in the twilight zone of concurrent authority. At least it is possible to visualize an outcome of multiple benefits: to the Executive, to the Congress, to the function of estimating in government, and even, in a responsible way, to the democratization of secrecy.

3

Secrecy and Openness in Foreign Policy Decision-Making: a British Cabinet Perspective

THE RT. HON. PATRICK GORDON WALKER, M.P.

The balance between secrecy and openness in foreign policy will vary from one country to another according to three main factors. The first in importance is a country's Constitutional procedure and its concepts of public propriety.

Britain is by its Constitution (which in effect means the Cabinet system) more inclined to secrecy than the United States in foreign policy, defense, and cognate matters. The British Cabinet system presupposes secrecy about conclusions reached, in order to preserve the "collective responsibility" of its members. Its decisions are communicated to, and carried out by, an obedient civil service. It would be regarded as highly improper if one department of government leaked information or briefed the press in order to frustrate or prevail over another department or to challenge a Cabinet decision.

In matters of high secrecy the Cabinet Secretary does not enter the matter in the *Minutes* (which, though themselves secret, are fairly widely distributed in departments), but reserves it for a special *Annex*. That this has been done is mentioned in the Minutes, and a Cabinet Minister may, if he wishes, consult the Annex.

HOW SECRETS STAY SECRET

Secrecy is the easier to preserve because of the peculiar committee system of the British Parliament, which itself reflects the supreme authority of the

---

Mr. Gordon Walker, former British Foreign Secretary, is the author of *The Cabinet* and a member of the British House of Commons.

Cabinet. While in America one speaks of the three branches of government, in Britain "The Government" is roughly equivalent to the Executive Branch only. The Government—that is, the Prime Minister and his Ministers—is the servant of the House of Commons and can only go on so long as it has the support of the majority of members: but, given a majority, it is in a more important sense master of the House. The Government drafts, introduces, and puts through all major bills, including the Budget. There is therefore no need or place for committees of the kind needed under a Congressional system, to enable either House to collect information in preparation for the introduction of legislation. Committees in the House of Commons are primarily a device to speed up legislation and are therefore of benefit to the Government. These committees reflect the balance of parties in the House and take the committee stage of bills. Thus some half-dozen measures can go simultaneously through this often lengthy and time-consuming stage.

There are two committees that watch over government expenditure, and a few "subject" committees that consider one or another aspect of the work of a department and report to the House; but as yet there is no such committee on defence or foreign policy. In any event, there is a strong tradition that the House of Commons as a whole has the right to be informed first by the Government of any matter of importance. To inform a committee first would be met by great anger.

No British Parliamentary committee has inquisitorial powers. It follows that there is no way of telling the House anything about foreign policy that does not at once become known to the whole world. In consequence a Foreign Secretary tends to be cautious and reticent in foreign policy debates or when answering Parliamentary questions. Indeed, a Minister will often reply that it would not be in the public interest to give the information asked for: this applies, for instance, to questions about a meeting between the Prime Minister and the President of the United States.

Another cause and symptom of the British tendency to secretiveness is the Official Secrets Act—a fearsome enactment under which anyone who discloses State secrets can be severely punished by the courts. A case recently brought against the *Daily Telegraph* was lost by the prosecution. This led to renewed attempts to have the Act more narrowly drawn, and a committee of enquiry set up by the Government in power recommended that the more inclusive and loosely drawn section of the Act should be repealed. So far nothing has been done. The Act is convenient for the powers that be, and they tend to hold that an Act of this kind has to be widely drawn to be effective. Under it a number of spies have been punished.

The very strict libel laws and interpretation of contempt of court in Britain are characteristic of the view that there are things more important than freedom to report or comment, among them the protection of a person's character and the fairness of a court trial.

The maintenance of secrecy extends even to the Cabinet. Thus, some matters are disclosed to certain members only. Questions of internal and national security are always reserved to the Prime Minister, the Foreign Secretary, and the Home Secretary. The Cabinet could insist on being informed but never does so because security is a high matter of state and may well concern the secrets of other countries, and also because Ministers do not wish to be burdened with unnecessary secrets. But things are taken farther than that. Foreign Office telegrams have long been distributed on a discriminatory basis to Ministers. Salisbury and Grey themselves marked on the covers of telegrams the Ministers who were to see them. Today there are distribution lists arranged according to the degree of secrecy of the telegrams. On a number of occasions, including some within my own knowledge, Ministers in Cabinet have asked to see a telegram that had been mentioned in discussion but had not been sent to them.

The system of discrimination has never been challenged. Indeed, Ministers do not always welcome the receipt of Foreign Office telegrams, which are very numerous and often lengthy. As early as 1884 Sir Charles Wentworth Dilke, member of the Gladstone Cabinet responsible for local government, protested that his inclusion on the list of recipients of telegrams took up too much of his time. Ministers sometimes do not read the telegrams they receive: one Minister I knew told his private office not to put Foreign Office telegrams in his box of papers to read when he got home at night. In 1898 the Permanent Head of the Foreign Office complained that despatches "failed to distract Balfour from the pursuit of the golf ball or the Duke of Devonshire from his pheasants."

The Prime Minister and Foreign Secretary traditionally work very closely together, both having offices in Downing Street. They do not always disclose foreign policy matters of high importance to the whole Cabinet. No one would to-day go so far as Malmesbury, who in 1797 wrote false or "ostensible" despatches that could be circulated to Ministers, and another set to "be entirely suppressed" and seen only by Grenville and Pitt.

Foreign affairs figures as an item each week on the Cabinet agenda (as it is put, "to be raised orally"). The Foreign Secretary briefly informs his colleagues of matters in progress and answers questions. When I was Foreign Secretary I used to have a word beforehand with the Prime Minister about what I should disclose and what keep (for the time being, at least) to myself. I imagine that this is regularly done.

Secrecy, at any rate in the formative stages of foreign policy decisions, is aided by the Cabinet Committee system. A Cabinet committee, within the terms of its remit, has parallel and equal powers with the Cabinet itself. It is served in the same manner by the Cabinet secretariat, which prepares the agenda and records the conclusions. The most important of these committees is the Defence and Overseas Policy Committee. The Prime Minister presides and most major Ministers are members; and foreign policy questions of great import and secrecy are discussed. If positive conclusions are reached, the matter will be brought before the full Cabinet.

Sometimes an inner group of Ministers may discuss foreign political matters. From May 1918 till the end of World War I the Cabinet Secretary kept an "X" series of Minutes of specially secret discussions outside the War Cabinet. Similarly in September and October 1938, the Cabinet Secretary kept a special series of Minutes of meetings between Chamberlain, Simon, Halifax, and Hoare.

There is some discussion about the Constitutional propriety of proceedings such as these. To me they appear to fall within the proper flexibility of the Cabinet system. No ultimate decision may be taken save by the Cabinet: no other body has authority to issue instructions to departments. The consequence is that Cabinet committees or groups of Ministers must be so representative of the Cabinet and so influential within it that they can count on carrying the Cabinet with them. Otherwise they will be overruled.

There have been striking examples of the Cabinet's overruling the Prime Minister and his leading colleague. In 1863 the three most powerful men in the Cabinet, the Prime Minister (Palmerston), the Foreign Secretary (Russell), and the Chancellor of the Exchequer (Gladstone), were overruled by the Cabinet in their desire to recognise the Southern States in the American Civil War. In the Second World War the Cabinet overruled Churchill over the occupation of the Azores. In my own memory, Mr. Harold Wilson as Prime Minister and Mr. George Brown as Foreign Secretary were overruled by the Cabinet on a proposal to send naval ships to the Gulf of Akaba in an attempt to forestall the six-day war between Egypt and Israel.

HOW SECRETS BECOME KNOWN

In fact, of course, the strong tendency towards secrecy in Britain is mitigated in a number of ways. The Government of the day may well want to rally public opinion behind it on some issue of foreign policy and will then disclose what it would otherwise wish to keep secret. Every Government is sometimes defied and secrets are deliberately aired. Common sense must be used in such cases.

Sometimes the Official Secrets Act is not invoked if the prominence of the leaker would lead to undesirable publicity. This problem arises mainly in connexion with ex-Cabinet Ministers who publish their memoirs or an account of a particular episode. Every Minister is entitled to consult the Cabinet papers with which he was concerned while in office. Partly for this reason, partly because he must have many secrets in his memory, a Minister is expected to and, as far as I know, always does submit his intended publication to the Cabinet Secretary, who can if he wishes consult the Prime Minister of the day.

Anthony Nutting, who had been a middle-rank Minister during the Suez crisis of 1956 and resigned in disagreement, published his account of this affair in 1963. He had submitted his text in page-proof form, and though he altered some passages on request, he refused to accept many suggestions made to him. Although he may have been in breach of the Official Secrets Act, it was decided not to prosecute him. I submitted the manuscript of my book on the Cabinet to the Cabinet Secretary and made a number of deletions and alterations at his request. But some requests I refused. In the second edition, when more time had elapsed since the events I related, I reinstated some of the material omitted from the first edition. No one took the matter up with me. On some occasions, however, when the leakers are less protected by prominence, proceedings have been brought in order to deter disclosure of secrets.

The major mitigation of excessive secrecy in foreign policy consists of Cabinet leaks. These are peculiar to Britain, as they arise out of the Cabinet system. Since they conflict with the doctrine of collective responsibility, leaks are not meant to occur; and they are always deplored. Collective responsibility is indeed very important; it ensures that when the Cabinet has taken a decision, not only are Cabinet Ministers (some of whom may have opposed the decision) bound by it but also Ministers outside the Cabinet and junior Ministers who in all probability had no idea that the matter was even under discussion. All Ministers have to defend the decision in public, though of course they can be adept at manifesting varying degrees of enthusiasm in support of a Cabinet decision.

The doctrine of collective responsibility grew up slowly as the modern Cabinet emerged. In Prime Minister Sir Robert Walpole's time (1721–42), Ministers who disagreed with a Cabinet policy simply stayed away. In George III's time Ministers still sometimes spoke and even voted in Parliament against a policy determined by the Cabinet. With the rise of a two-party system such behaviour came increasingly to be regarded as improper. When, in the second half of the nineteenth century, a stable and mass two-party system arose, the doctrine of collective responsibility passed into the unwritten conventions of the Constitution, as something that everyone took for granted. The doctrine was by now necessary. Cabinet Ministers were national party leaders; accordingly both their leadership and the party itself would be weakened if the leaders openly attacked, or attributed views to, one another.

Here, however, I begin to take issue with our strict constructionists who defend Cabinet secrecy at all costs and in all instances. When I first advanced the views I am about to develop here, concerning Cabinet leaks, I was sharply attacked in many quarters. Yet I hold that an inevitable concomitant of collective responsibility is the unauthorized disclosure of internal Cabinet affairs. Such leaks must be distinguished from the disclosure of true state secrets, such as the details of a budget, a decision to alter the value of the currency, or security matters.

There have been only a few examples of a breach of state secrecy; and they have been severely punished. J. H. Thomas as a Minister betrayed budget secrets to some cronies. After enquiry by a tribunal that ultimately found against him, he had to resign office, and then disappeared from public life. Similarly, in 1945 Hugh Dalton, as Chancellor of the Exchequer, inadvertently let out the details of his budget to a lobby correspondent; and although no one could possibly have benefited from the disclosure, he immediately resigned office. These rare breaches of state secrecy must, however, be distinguished from the ordinary Cabinet leak, which involves the disclosure of matters that are secret only because of the doctrine of collective responsibility, such as the subject of Cabinet discussions, Cabinet decisions, divergent views of Ministers, and the like.

Of course, many decisions that are not state secrets are taken, and they are not leaked—either because they cause no controversy in the Cabinet or because no one, intentionally or unintentionally, leaks to the press. If there are positive decisions they have to be disclosed sooner or later so that they can be carried into effect. The only "political secrets" that do not see the light of day are decisions not to do something. Such decisions can be of importance, as for instance when the Wilson Cabinet decided not to cancel the *Polaris* submarine project and, later, not to accede to President Lyndon Johnson's request for a token military contribution to Vietnam. After a time both decisions were made public—by the Wilson Government.

An element of concealment is inherent in the very concept of collective responsibility. To say that the Cabinet must appear united presupposes divisions that have not been wholly reconciled; hence collective responsibility must to some extent be a mask worn by the Cabinet. The self-same conditions of mass democracy that gave rise to collective responsibility also produced the unattributable leak. Ministers are political creatures living in a political world. As party leaders they accept the need for the doctrine of collective responsibility; as political creatures they feel it sometimes necessary to let their political views be known. In their party they have followers whom they wish to convince of their consistency and their radicalism or their conservatism (as the case may be) when the Cabinet has taken a decision departing from these criteria. Also, a group of Ministers may leak to the press in an effort to get their policy accepted by the Cabinet.

At the same time a new kind of press has arisen in Britain, a press whose readers are increasingly interested in "secrets" felt to be of a political and not a security nature. Already by the mid-nineteenth century one newspaper kept a man stationed in Downing Street to report the length of Cabinet meetings and any persistent absentees. Today an elaborate organization of "lobby correspondents" has grown up; journalists who are given special privileges in the House of Commons and have fairly easy access to Members of Parliament. They are also bound by a very strict code of conduct never to attribute to a Member (unless he gives permission) any views that he expresses. It is thus very easy for a Member or a Minister to leak information to one or two newspapers in perfect safety.

From time to time the Prime Minister also holds press conferences in which, again, if he wishes he can speak without attribution. He is tempted, sometimes, to give a slant to what he says; and this, in turn, tempts other Ministers to put their different slant to the press.

The occurrence of the leak as a Constitutional convention, so to speak, may be dated from the Liberal administration of 1880–85, when it became generally known that various Ministers maintained special relations with particular newspapers and fed them information to prepare the ground for an argument in Cabinet. This was the first Government based on a mass national party. There have since been innumerable well-documented instances of leaks, many of them on matters of foreign policy. When, for instance, Prime Minister Neville Chamberlain's statement about Czechoslovakia to the House of Commons on 2 September 1939 met a very hostile reception, his Foreign Secretary Lord Halifax wrote: "I could not acquit some members of the Cabinet of having fed the flames of suspicion." Extensive leaking about divisions of opinion in the Cabinet occurred during the Suez crisis of 1956.

The one I remember best took place in December 1967 over the question whether the sale of arms to South Africa should be barred. The Cabinet, evenly divided, had angry argument over this issue, one that roused strong feelings in the Parliamentary party. Prime Minister Wilson and Foreign Secretary Brown indulged in competitive leaking that disclosed the Cabinet division to the whole world.

This was a case when a leak may have affected the Cabinet decision, for had there been no leak the Cabinet might have decided not to ban arms to South Africa. Another such example occurred before the First World War, when David Lloyd George, Chancellor of the Exchequer, leaked to the radical press his controversy with Winston Churchill over the Admiralty Estimates (of expenditures). This may well have helped the Chancellor to get them reduced. It is, however, impossible to prove such speculations.

Cabinets (including Ministers responsible for them) always deplore leaks when they occur, and efforts—usually futile—are sometimes made to trace their source. The only successful tracing of a leak occurred during one of Prime Minister Ramsay Macdonald's Governments, when he set detectives to work to discover its origin. Owing to the readiness of Mr. J. R. Clynes, the Home Secretary, to volunteer information, it was learned that the leak had been due to a quite inadvertent remark of his which had been ingeniously and accurately elaborated by a journalist. But leaks should not be suppressed, since, paradoxically, they are necessary to preserve the doctrine of collective responsibility: they are the mechanism by which the doctrine is reconciled with political reality. The unattributable leak is itself a recognition and acceptance of the rule that members of a Cabinet do not disagree in public.

Analogous to a leak—except that it is done openly—is the resignation speech of a Minister. Any senior Minister who resigns has the right to make a speech in the House explaining his reasons for leaving his colleagues—and such a speech cannot be questioned or answered. The Cabinet has no control over what this Minister says, and sometimes he makes embarrassing disclosures. In point of fact, rarely is a strong tradition of restraint seriously breached on such occasions.

A SUMMARY

In conclusion: first, the national tendency to secrecy in Britain is very strong and is part and parcel of the Cabinet system; and yet it is mitigated by leaks that are also part and parcel of the Cabinet system.

Second, the balance between secrecy and openness in foreign policy in any country will vary according to the moral authority of the government at any particular time. Thus, for example, after the experience of devaluation and of the open, competitive leaking about the sale of arms to South Africa, by January 1968 "the shock to morale and to Cabinet cohesion led to some weakening of Cabinet solidarity in the matter of unauthorized disclosures"—in the words of Mr. Wilson. While the Cabinet was discussing cuts in public expenditure following devaluation, "after each meeting, press stories appeared even with some degree of accuracy on how the Cabinet had divided." The phenomenon is not, of course, localized. The effect of the Vietnam war on American public opinion was in all probability what led to such occurrences as the leaking of the Pentagon Papers and Mr. Anderson's disclosures of confidential White House discussions concerning U.S. policy during the Bangla-Desh crisis.

Third, the attitude of countries to the balance between secrecy and openness in foreign policy may be affected by the world balance of power. When wars were manageable affairs, great diplomatic secrecy prevailed and sudden foreign policy coups were possible. Bismarck was the leading exponent of these devices. But in a nuclear world it becomes increasingly necessary, especially for the nuclear powers, to "signal" to one another by disclosing what would otherwise be secrets of the highest nature.

A CRITIQUE

The whole situation about openness and secrecy in foreign policy-making is not very satisfactory either in Britain or America.

On the one hand Governments in power undoubtedly keep secret the mistakes and errors or divisions of opinion in the Administration, the disclosure of which could not affect public security. This they do sincerely for the reason that such matters, as they see it, should be kept secret in order not to undermine the authority of the Administration and perhaps weaken its international standing. A Government that could not keep such secrets might well find that other nations became increasingly reluctant to confide their own secrets to it. Moreover it is not easy, in the hurly-burly of daily administration, to draw the line between true and false secrets. Nonetheless, Governments do undoubtedly abuse their right to determine what shall be kept secret and what disclosed.

On the other hand, we must not take too seriously the claims of the press and the TV networks to be the guardians of liberty and of the public's right to know. The media are unlikely to be the best judges of what is in the national interest. This is indeed not their principal goal, which is to increase circulation and ratings.

Should we in Britain now try to devise some machinery—say, an outside judge or commission—that could check on the Government's decisions about secrecy?

I think not. First, the Government would have to decide what to disclose. If the whole Cabinet is not to be given all the facts, why should some outside body be? It would be constitutionally improper to hand over to an unelected, unrepresentative body decisions that can properly be made only by an authority responsible to Parliament and people.

Then, too, it is generally assumed that foreign policy decision-making must be positive. But, as we observed above, some of the most important decisions are concerned with *not* doing something. An example was the aforementioned decision of the British Cabinet, in 1967, to overrule the Prime Minister and Foreign Secretary in their desire to send British naval vessels to the Gulf of Akaba. If there were an outside judge, should such negative decisions be disclosed to him?

It seems to me that no workable machinery could possibly be devised. There is nothing better (with all its defects) than the maintenance of a certain tension between those whose interest it is to disclose everything and those whose interest it is to disclose as little as possible.

4

Secrecy and Democratic Participation in the Formulation and Conduct of Canadian Foreign Policy

GEORGE IGNATIEFF

THE NEED FOR PUBLIC PARTICIPATION

Canada has been conventional in recognizing the need for secrecy in the conduct of diplomacy, while developing an unconventional approach in at least experimenting with public participation in its formulation.

It has long been a maxim of statecraft that foreign policy is distinct from diplomacy; but it is still perhaps insufficiently recognized that the formulation, and even the conduct, of foreign policy is something more than diplomacy. The formulation and conduct of foreign policy may involve not only diplomats but also politicians, propagandists, businessmen, soldiers, and academics. It does not necessarily follow even that the persons best qualified to coordinate all the activities involved in foreign policy are professional diplomats. This is an admission hard to make for one who has spent most of his career as a civil servant, a working diplomat; yet it is a necessary premise to the discussion which follows.

Diplomacy, in the sense of managing international relations through negotiations, is an instrument of policy employed in relations between nations. As such it calls for certain professional skills including tact, the ability to communicate orally and in writing with precision, persuasiveness, and infinite patience, preferably in more than one language, and especially with people of differing backgrounds. The diplomat must be able to establish personal rapport with the other side. To prepare for negotiations, he must be able to identify the key factors bearing on the success of the negotiations,

Mr. Ignatieff, Provost of Trinity College in Toronto, was formerly Ambassador and Permanent Representative of Canada to the United Nations in Geneva and New York; Canadian Permanent Representative to the North Atlantic Council; Canadian Representative to the Geneva Disarmament Conference; Ambassador to Yugoslavia; and Assistant Under Secretary of State, Department of External Affairs.

and make recommendations to his Government accordingly. ("Government" in Canadian, as in British, usage means the Prime Minister and his Cabinet.)

In the past, secret negotiation conducted by specially trained professional diplomats was the *only* instrument of foreign policy other than war. This is no longer so. Professional diplomats are still necessary for the conduct of negotiations, but they no longer enjoy a monopoly. Understandably, diplomats are reluctant to admit that times have changed. One might wish that they had not. In the age when professional diplomacy dominated the international scene, before the interdependence of nations and the intrusion of domestic politics into international affairs, international relations were perhaps more efficiently and less painfully conducted. Today, conferences and Parlimentary diplomacy, through international organizations, have replaced, to a considerable extent the personal relations that were the strongest point in the diplomat's role.

The erosion of personal diplomacy is, however, primarily reflective of a change in the subject matter of international relations. Impersonal factors such as security interests, trade rivalry, economic and social development, conflicts of class and nations, and the arms race underlie international disputes and inevitably touch upon an ever-growing spectrum of interests. These are subjects of direct concern to many citizens and many interest groups, and it is now often in the interest of the state to bring these groups along into the foreign policy process in order to win their co-operation and to draw on their expert knowledge.

THE LIMITS OF PUBLIC PARTICIPATION

There are, then, growing needs and opportunities for the non-professional to play a role in the formulation and even execution of foreign policy. A key concomitant of this is the necessity for at least a few "outsiders" to know enough of what the Government knows to be able to participate effectively. I shall return to this point.

There are also limits to the role the "outsider" can play, however, and precisely because there are still times when absolute secrecy is essential to success, even at the risk of excluding or perhaps alienating those excluded. Serious diplomatic negotiation, for one, can still take place only by secret diplomacy. Negotiation can be successful only when both parties wish to achieve an agreement, as for example, the negotiations with the People's Republic of China initiated and conducted in secret by the Canadian Government through diplomatic channels, and successfully concluded in 1970.

If, on the contrary, negotiation is regarded by one or the other of the parties simply as a part of a political manœuvre designed to gain an advantage in propaganda or in public posture while putting the other party in the wrong, then no agreement will be reached, and secrecy as well as mutual confidence is cast to the winds. The more publicity, the less serious negotiation. It is as well to know, before embarking on negotiations, which type of international activity is involved. Examples abound to illustrate the principle, among them certain phases of developments in Vietnam and the Middle East, and the failure to stop the arms race. Despite endless conferences these areas of negotiation demonstrate the difference between diplomatic manœuvering, with its public "breast-beating," and real but inevitably secret professional negotiations.

True enough, secret diplomacy, particularly as practised by totalitarian regimes, has brought secrecy in diplomatic practice into a degree of disrepute. But this does not make secrecy less necessary in situations where serious intention to reach agreement through compromise (with each side making sacrifices) has been established, usually through preparatory contracts. The classic example of secret diplomacy at its worst with disastrous historic consequences, was the series of parallel negotiations conducted in the summer of 1939 by the Soviet Union with England and France and with Germany, and ending in the Molotov-Ribbentrop Pact. The wartime conferences at Moscow, Teheran, and Yalta also included a good deal of notorious and deleterious secret diplomacy. In all these cases secret diplomacy was used to reach agreements, essentially at the expense of a third party.

In the Cold War following the breakup of the wartime alliance the situation became radically different. In the 1950's and 1960's there were no third parties against which to unite. Soviet leaders regarded the Western Powers as the enemies, and vice versa. During this period Soviet diplomacy aimed not so much to secure agreements based on give-and-take as to score propaganda points against their opponents at the United Nations and in various conferences, and thus to create a climate of opinion favourable to gaining concessions without having to fight for them. Thus the world went from the evils of the wrong kinds of secret diplomacy to the evil of open grandstanding, and that was not diplomacy at all.

With the 1970's we appear once more to have entered an era in which real negotiations are possible. Once again, the actual bargaining process will inevitably have to be primarily secret. This does not mean, however, that all aspects of the process of policy-making necessarily exclude the public.

THE SEARCH FOR A PUBLIC INPUT

Canada has been experimenting with public participation in aspects of foreign policy-making. It has moved rather slowly in this direction, in part for the reason that in order to have a policy discussion there must be a range of policy options. It has not always been clear (to speak realistically) that Canada has had options.

In the absence of a stable world order (which the United Nations had been established to provide but which, because of the Cold War confrontations, it was generally unable to offer[1]) postwar diplomacy has been concerned with the conduct of foreign affairs on a balance-of-power basis. This balance, in the atomic age, has in effect meant "nuclear balance," or "balance of deterrence." On it have depended world peace and world survival, in the absence of international authority and control over weaponry.

The maintenance of the nuclear balance being the prerogative of the nuclear powers, each of them has employed secrecy to help in its unending pursuit of equilibrium in an unstable and constantly changing world. A non-nuclear power like Canada has had to seek shelter under the "nuclear umbrella" of its ally and neighbour, but within the limitations of secrecy imposed by the McMahon Atomic Energy Act of 1946. Mutual defence arrangements under NATO or Continental defence arrangements under NORAD had to be taken on trust by the public; even government officials have had access to this kind of information only on a "need to know" basis. Under such circumstances, in which world peace had not been achieved by the United Nations, and major decisions relating to the nuclear balance constituted privileged information of the nuclear powers, there seemed little point to engaging in foreign policy planning on a national basis on the part of a "middle power" like Canada, which preferred to operate through multinational organizations.

The Canadian Department of External Affairs prepared position papers, some of which emerged in Ministerial statements to Parliament; but no general review of policy objectives was attempted at that time. When the author was brought back to Ottawa in 1955 from a course at the Imperial Defence College in London to engage in planning in conjunction with the Department of Defence, he ran into two kinds of difficulties. In the first place the military minds regarded strategic matters as a preserve exclusively of their own, despite the fact that the effects of missile-borne atomic weapons, if used, would likely be as destructive of civilian as of military targets—if not more so. They were not impressed with the argument of "no incineration without representation," and accordingly resented the interference of "longhaired intellectuals" as the Chief of the Defence Staff (then General Charles Foulkes) frankly informed External Affairs. Letters arguing the case for joint planning to deal with the nuclear weapons threat went unheeded during the fifties.

---

1. An exception of sorts is the United Nations mediation and peace-keeping activities in marginal disputes that did not engage the vital national interests of the Great Powers —except in Korea.

The other obstacles arose from a certain amount of indifference within the Department of External Affairs itself, on the grounds of the essential unpredictability of the future and hence the doubtful value of assigning the requisite staff to prepare hypothetical answers to unknown contingencies. A pragmatic approach, or "flying by the seat of your pants," seemed to serve our purposes better, as well as being economical in the use of manpower. Perhaps this scepticism arose from the career officer's concept of diplomatic negotiation as being the cutting edge of foreign policy. The diplomat has to be able to make the best of day-to-day developments over which he has little or no control. He is an artist; the planner, in contrast, borrowing from science, has to try to anticipate future situations and provide contingency plans to meet them.

The fact that Canadian foreign policy was dominated by a supreme practitioner of the art of diplomacy, Mr. Lester B. Pearson, then Secretary of State for External Affairs (and later Prime Minister of Canada), may have had something to do with this preference for the pragmatic approach, and made public participation appear less relevant.[2] With the ending of the era of Pearson's spectacular personal successes[3]—which ending coincided more or less with the defeat of the Saint Laurent Government in 1957—the problems of Canadian foreign policy began to increase and to focus on the unresolved issue of the risk of nuclear war, and the related question of Canada's dependence on the United States for nuclear protection. These concerns were highlighted by the Cuban missile crisis of 1962 and by events in Vietnam. Increasing public concern about Canada's relation with the United States, in regard to defence as well as economic policy, was not assuaged

---

2. Yet it should be noted that Lester Pearson himself favored forward-thinking in foreign affairs, both for himself as well as for others, and was meticulous in keeping the House of Commons informed of developments. This was well illustrated by the fact that not only did he sponsor the idea of joint-planning with the Department of Defence to seek solutions to the risks of nuclear war with a view to presenting a public report, but he also came to the rescue of NATO as one of the "Three Wise Men" (the others being H. Lange of Norway, and G. Martino of Italy) charged to consider ways of improving political consultation when co-operation had broken down among the principal NATO allies, following the Suez crisis of 1956. None saw more clearly than Mr. Pearson that military strategy and foreign policy are inseparable, and that effective foreign policy requires consensus as well as well-considered content. As the Suez crisis brought out only too clearly, national security policy among the allies lacked both unity and coherence. Decisions were still being made on an *ad hoc* basis, unguided by any over-all purposes. The resultant NATO report, which was mainly the product of Mr. Pearson's thinking and is in the public domain, contained two main prescriptions: first, more continuing political consultations among allies before decision-making, and more coordination in the planning of policies among the allies—military and political as well as economic.
3. These were due to some measure to his close teamwork with Prime Minister Saint Laurent.

by pleas for the exercise of "quiet diplomacy." In fact, a public assize on these issues, put off by the previous wide consensus in support of the Saint Laurent-Pearson emphasis on collective security, could no longer be postponed.

Public questioning had begun to be directed against Canada's commitment to internationalism. Divisive issues emerged, such as the deployment and control of nuclear warheads, Canadian involvement in Vietnam through membership in the International Commission of Control and Supervision, and the control over Canadian natural resources. Moreover, the proximity of Canada to its immense neighbour to the south had become profoundly troubling economically and culturally, as well as from a strategic and political standpoint. Finally, President Eisenhower's farewell warning about the growing influence of a "military-industrial complex" did not go unheeded across the border. It is to the credit of the Trudeau Government that in 1968 it publicly acknowledged that circumstances had changed, so that a new approach to the formulation and conduct of foreign policy was needed, with some participation by the growing number of critics of Canadian foreign policy.

It is not necessary to prove that popular discussion of foreign affairs is intrinsically desirable. In a democratic society it is essential that the people be informed and that their views be heeded. Reactions to the Vietnam War in the United States and elsewhere show that no foreign policy that does not have its roots in public opinion, that cannot be endorsed and sustained by the elected representatives in Parliament, can long endure. Hence it was not surprising that one of Prime Minister Trudeau's first acts as Leader of the Liberal Party in succession to Mr. Pearson was to commit his Government to a major review of Canada's foreign policy. This exercise implied two important changes in Executive thinking; first, a decision, in 1968, to conduct a thoroughgoing foreign policy review—virtually to unravel the strands of foreign policy and to test each one; and second, a decision to include a degree of public participation in certain aspects of the formulation of foreign policy.

Canada's foreign policy had been concerned largely with objectives and commitments arising out of active membership in multinational organizations like the United Nations and NATO, and so its international role, its influence, and its policies, had been formulated chiefly in the context of these institutions. As Prime Minister Trudeau explained in launching the review: "We wish to take a fresh look at the fundamentals of Canadian foreign policy to see whether there are ways in which we can serve more effectively Canadian interests, objectives, and priorities." Then for a period of over two years—from May 1968 to June 1970—the foreign policy of Canada was submitted to most intense public scrutiny. In this process, academics, journalists, businessmen, and representatives of labour joined government officials in the exchange of ideas about shifts in policy that should be made.

The discussions were addressed to aims and options rather than to a detailed scrutiny of past policies and events. Thus, the normal relation of confidentiality was maintained between civil servants and the Cabinet in the proffering of advice. These internal processes were neither interrupted nor made public while the consultation with "outsiders" went on. No significant departure from normal rules of secrecy within the government was involved. Members of the public, like members of the bureaucracy, were invited to propose; it was left to the Cabinet to do the disposing. The whole process of consultation between government and public through seminars and private meetings, as well as through the press media, proceeded alongside, but wholly separate from, the preparation of proposals and recommendations by government officials for the consideration of Ministers under the usual rules of confidentiality.

The Defence Review—and a Modest Proposal

The most controversial product of this review was the decision in 1969 to reduce substantially Canada's contribution to NATO. The question of Canada's participation in NATO was given priority over all other issues.[4] For this there were three reasons. First, it was the defence aspect of Canadian foreign policy that had aroused most interest among the critics as being most overdue for public debate and scrutiny. Second, it was the NATO issue that had apparently caused Prime Minister Trudeau himself to question the foreign policy he had inherited. Third, there were urgent financial implications that had to be resolved in time for budget preparation.

The author of this chapter had his part, in the capacity of a civil servant specializing in multinational organizations, in the discussions leading up to the formulation of policy recommendations on NATO as well as on the United Nations. For dealing with the NATO problem the Government organized its Interdepartmental Special Task Force on Relations with Europe (known as STAFFEUR). This staff, composed of civil servants, was required to examine not only the options in regard to NATO policy but also the broader question of Canada's relation to Europe in their political and economic as well as defence aspects. At the same time the Department of External Affairs and National Defence began a joint study of a more

---

4. The principal issues are discussed in six booklets published in 1970 and entitled *Foreign Policy for Canadians*. These booklets were made available to the public to serve as a basis of continuing discussion.

specialized nature and under conditions of strict secrecy, in which the various options relating to NATO were analyzed and the cost of these options as well as of Canada's commitments were taken into account.

In addition to these "collegiate" or "inside"-bureaucratic approaches, the Government also invited the appropriate political committee of the House of Commons to get into the act. This was a new departure for the House, one which is more fully discussed by Gordon Fairweather in Chapter 9 of this book. Thus, during the first three months of 1968, the House of Commons Standing Committee on External Affairs and National Defence undertook an extensive examination of Canada's NATO policy, holding hearings not only in Ottawa but in Europe as well. Experts in defence matters (including academics) were invited to testify at its hearings. The author stated his views to the Standing Committee in his capacity as Canadian representative to the Geneva Disarmament Conference as well as to NATO from 1961 to 1965.

In the course of his presentation to the Standing Committee on March 15, 1969, while it was in Geneva conducting hearings, the author stressed the need for Canada to participate in all international arrangements (including NATO and the United Nations) that would enable Canadians to exert influence over the course of international events affecting Canadian security. Recalling that Canada's geographical location between the two most powerfully armed nations on earth makes security, disarmament, and arms control matters of vital interest to all Canadians, he suggested that, in order to be in a better position to influence international events and to take independent initiatives in the direction of war prevention, as well as to reduce the risks of the on-going arms race, a continuing government panel on defence policy should be set up on which various interests—political, military, economic, scientific, and legal, as well as military—should be represented.

As the author said in explaining this proposal to the press,

> The essence of the proposal is that few people in Canada or elsewhere have the requisite scientific and technical information and competence to contribute to effective decision-making on the vital issues concerning the related problems of weaponry and disarmament.

Recalling that various ways had been found in other countries for continuing efforts involving Parliamentary as well as public participation—such as, for example, through the American Arms Control and Disarmament Agency in Washington and the Stockholm International Peace Research Institute in Sweden—the author concluded as follows:

> What is most required is that the complex problems connected with the reduction of the risks of war and preventing war, as well as the economic bur-

dens of armaments, should be made the subject of continuous study by the best brains available in Canada.

In this way some of the procedures employed in the foreign policy review could be perfected and put to work on a continuing, rather than merely an *ad hoc,* basis.

Could such a panel function on anything less than full possession of all defence information? It may well be that the ramparts of defence policy formulation will inevitably be the last to be breached, insofar as secrecy is concerned. But the stakes of the public are extremely high. In the atomic age the effects of mass-destruction weapons are likely to be catastrophic for the mass of the population—in terms of numbers, possibly even more so than for the military. Additional ways, therefore, have to be found to overcome rules of secrecy that protect defence and disarmament planning from participation by non-military experts; these rules must be overturned in the larger interests of survival and the control of military expenditures.

Admittedly there are matters concerning a nation's defence which cannot safely be divulged without imperiling relations with other nations, and which it may not be in the public interest to disclose. But secrecy is a relative, not an absolute, factor. In deciding whether a "secret" should be told to one, ten, twenty, or twenty million persons, a range of social trade-offs must be taken into account. To include a few more responsible persons may bring benefits disproportionately larger than the increase in risk entailed thereby. An admixture of experienced and responsible individuals—a small group of experts—with minds open to new thinking can, nevertheless, be a valuable corrective to merely treading familiar but misguided paths. A body such as this could also be expected to act as watchdog where vested interests of the military-industrial complex may diverge from the public interest, or where the motivation for secrecy may be related to political considerations rather than to those of national security. Ministerial accountability to Parliament under the Canadian system could be strengthened, if, before final decisions were made, the prevailing Government's plans were fully and openly submitted to the scrutiny of a panel of experts on which Parliament were represented.

The United Nations Policy Review:
The Politicians Prevail on Southern Africa

For obvious reasons the review dealing with the United Nations ran into less difficulty over secrecy. No other activity in the field of foreign affairs is conducted under such intense and continuing public scrutiny; thus the public hears more about the deliberations of the U.N. Security Council, for example, than of those of the Canadian Cabinet. But secrecy exists also at the United Nations. A distinction has to be drawn between, on the one hand, the United Nations' continuous multilateral Parliamentary diplomacy, conducted at conference and committee meetings open to the public, in which the member nations' positions and views are put on the record by the representatives of respective countries; and on the other the secret, behind-the-scenes efforts to arrive at a consensus on a resolution to enable an inter-governmental decision to be taken.

As regards the former type of diplomacy, the mass media and the modern developments in communications technology have expanded informational horizons to a degree undreamed of in the past. The reports submitted annually by the U.N. Secretary-General as well as by expert groups, even when based only on published statistics, usefully supplement the information provided regularly by the mass media. World public opinion based on such information has the potential of exercising direct influence on the conduct of national governments.

But the production of a consensus, such as on the important Resolution 242 of November 17, 1967, setting out guidelines for a settlement in the Middle East, could not have been achieved except through secret negotiations. The reason for this is that the U.N. Security Council, which adopted this resolution, has to act by consensus or not at all. The only chance of reaching a consensus among the Council's disparate, and often divergent, membership is to indulge in painstaking consultations and negotiations to arrive at a compromise based on identification of certain common interests. This responsibility to work out a consensus falls either on the President of the Council for the month, or on one or another of the constituent groups composing the Council. Public debate usually serves only to harden divergent national positions.

The foreign policy review of Canada's U.N. role focused on the question of the adequacy of information flow to the Canadian public. Beyond this, the review studied also the substantive role Canada had been playing at the United Nations and whether in the light of the shifting balance of power to the Third World a change in that policy was advisable.

In the General Assembly or in its committees, it is the Afro-Asian bloc that commands a majority—if it votes together, as it usually does on matters of common interest such as decolonization questions, race relations, or issues relating to economic assistance to developing nations. Among the issues on which public reaction was sought in the Canadian foreign policy review dealing with the United Nations was precisely what Canada's position should be in these circumstances; one of permanent minority among the Western nations? or should Canada aim at a greater degree of flexibility, and if so, on what issues?

It was mainly to overcome a widespread suspicion in Canada that the Government had not sufficiently investigated the options for, nor the limitations on, Canada's freedom of action at the United Nations, that a seminar was organized by the Canadian Institute for International Affairs for March 28–30, 1969, at Scarborough, Ontario. A widely representative group was invited, and the discussion, though based on a draft paper prepared by the author and other officials of the Department of External Affairs, actually ranged far and wide.

These draft proposals were approved in general by those participating, and then submitted to the Government for consideration. Several useful new suggestions were added by participants, among them greater use of educational institutions to spread knowledge of the limitations, as well as the functions, of the United Nations, the need for the communication of more facts underlying the positions taken by Canada at U.N. meetings, and greater use of mass media for keeping in touch with what was going on. The decrease of press and mass media coverage of U.N. activities was recognized as a partial cause of the problem of inadequate information, rather than any deliberate intention at concealment on the part of the Government.

The most controversial issue raised in the section of the foreign policy review dealing with the United Nations was that concerned with "establishing an effective dialogue with the Governments of Africa on the problems of Southern Africa"—a subject on which there were key U.N. resolutions concerning colonialism and racism. In his work on Trudeau's foreign policy, Bruce Thordarson gives a substantially correct account of what eventually happened in regard to this controversial matter.

> The decision [he writes] to continue commercial relations in order to increase Canada's economic growth, rather than end all trade in the interests of social justice, was made in Cabinet. The Department of External Affairs dealt primarily with the options available to Canada in its relations with South Africa and, in accordance with Mr. Trudeau's wishes, made no policy recommendations.

He adds that in this matter "the civil service influence was not dominant,"[5] nor was that of the outside experts.

I am in no position to know whether it was Mr. Trudeau or other members of his Government who were primarily responsible, but there is no doubt that political consideration prevailed over the views of some, at least, of the Civil Service members involved in this review, as well as their academic advisors gathered at Scarborough, so far as "reconciling Canadian objectives in Southern Africa" was concerned.

---

5. Bruce Thordarson, *Trudeau and Foreign Policy: A Study in Decision-Making* (Toronto-New York: Oxford University Press, 1972), p. 171.

The Results of the Review: The Growth of the
Objective-Oriented Approach

Although some significant foreign policy changes were laid out in the policy papers announced by the Canadian Government, there is little evidence that the conceptual framework set out in the general introductory paper was exposed to the participation of public opinion during its formulation. The seminars and discussions in which academics, businessmen, and others outside government service were involved during the foreign policy review had to do with sector-by-sector proposals and to choice of objectives, rather than to the over-all philosophy of Canadian foreign policy.

Moreover, most of the changes of policy were announced during, rather than after, the policy review. These changes included the 50 per cent reduction in Canada's contribution to NATO, the decision to establish diplomatic relations with the People's Republic of China and with the Vatican, and the increase of economic aid, especially to francophone countries.

The effect of this foreign policy review as a whole was a change of emphasis rather than of direction. The economic aspects of Canada's relations received greater attention. Canda's wealth in natural resources (including exportable surpluses), as well as its stake in foreign trade, no doubt promoted a necessary adaptation to changing circumstances. The emphasis in the general paper on the "hexagonal" scheme of objectives was to suggest that previous Canadian foreign policy had been too "reactive." Canadian foreign relations, as well as domestic policy, were now to be geared to objectives.

But to pursue an "objective-oriented" approach requires programme planning and a high degree of coordination among all the various departments and private interests concerned with foreign relations. This in turn requires new answers to the question of who participates in planning—and how. If economic objectives seem increasingly important at a time when so much of the world's diplomacy is occupied with fiscal and monetary matters, the problem is no less controversial than when the focus was almost wholly on defence. Rather than national security, private trade secrets affecting the competitive interests of firms are involved; but the guardians of these secrets are no less justified in their concern for security.

In the near future, for example, Canada will be facing preparations for negotiations in the General Agreement on Tariffs and Trade (GATT), a concerted effort to revise the international monetary system, as well as dialogues with its principal trading partners (and competitors): the United States, the enlarged European Economic Community (EEC), and Japan. In the formulation of policy and preparations for these discussions, all kinds of interests in the private sector of the Canadian economy are involved. Apart from any action that may be taken by the Canadian Government to consult, it will be for Canadian business, through such associations as Chambers of Commerce, the Canadian Manufacturers Association, the exporters and importers associations, and the banks to ensure that the interests of their clients and constituencies are protected. Input may also be sought by the less organized consumers. As yet, no formal machinery exists to ensure these interests a role, or the information necessary to play an effective role.

The New Public Debate on Canadian-U.S. Policy

Since the conclusion of Prime Minister Trudeau's foreign policy review, a new public debate has opened in Canada, on the extent of the country's economic, military, and cultural dependence on the United States and its implications for Canadian independence. To this debate the Government contributed a paper entitled "Canada-U.S. Relations—Options for the Future." This paper, which was published by the Department of External Affairs in a special issue of *International Perspectives* (Autumn 1972) designed to stimulate public discussion, offers three options:

1. Canada can seek to maintain more or less its present relationship with the United States with a minimum of policy adjustments;

2. Canada can move deliberately toward closer integration with the USA;

3. Canada can pursue a comprehensive long-term strategy to develop and strengthen the Canadian economy and other vital aspects of its national life and in the process to reduce the present Canadian vulnerability.

These questions are still being actively discussed throughout Canada, as part of the process of arriving at a public consensus on this all-important issue, and the results of the debate have yet to be reflected in political decisions by Parliament or the Government.

PUBLIC PARTICIPATION IN POLICY MAKING

With the proliferation of conferences and international contacts abroad, it is inevitable that members of the public should increasingly be consulted in the formulation and the conduct of foreign policy. Businessmen and lawyers as well as academics will have to be more extensively involved in the process, not only for purposes of consultation before negotiations but also in the process of negotiation itself. Examples of such participation in preparation and negotiation abound in recent times: as in the Stockholm Conference on the Environment, the 1973–74 U.N. Conference on the Law of the Sea, the GATT discussion on the removal of trade barriers, and the World Health Conference. These are some of the occasions that have brought members of the Canadian public and government representatives together in effective working relations in which problems of secrecy have not proved an obstacle to co-operation.

If the quality of public participation is to be ensured, the time has come for the process of consultation between governments and members of the concerned public to take place on a less improvised basis. Initially, this means the development of new guidelines for what must remain absolutely secret within the inner circle of the Government and what may be shared with those sectors of the public that may now be needed to help formulate, execute, and support new policy. If nothing is shared with anyone outside the inner circle, no meaningful help in the form of advice, review, or support will be forthcoming.

We have noted that secret negotiations must remain secret. There are other aspects of the policy-making and Executive process that must similarly remain hidden from the public. Preserving the confidentiality of relations between responsible Ministers and their advisors on policy matters remains essential to the protection of the individual official's right to give advice freely and to differ sharply. Without destroying its collective responsibility to the public and Parliament, the political Executive should be encouraged to examine various alternative courses of action before reaching a consensus. To disclose the discussions, disagreements, advice and counter-advice that enter into the process of arriving at a policy decision would obviously undermine the principle of collective responsibility on which Parliamentary government depends. It would also discourage forthright advisement and sharp differences of opinion. These are a valuable part of the process and should not be lost in co-opting outsiders to play a new role in helping the policy-making process to grow.

Another type of Executive secrecy that can obviously be justified relates to matters potentially damaging to a nation's relations with other nations if disclosed prematurely. It would not be beneficial for a government to gain greater input from its own public at the cost of being cut off from the important input that normally comes from allies.

In each of these instances, it seems to me, a distinction can be drawn between, on one hand, factual information required by one who needs to understand a foreign policy problem, and, on the other, the views, advice, and recommendations of Ministers and officials expressed privately in the "insiders'" process of decision-making. The facts relevant to understanding of a problem under review should, to the greatest possible degree, be made public. The degree, in each case, should depend on the extent to which a sector of the public, or an individual, is participating, or can participate, constructively in evolving a policy or implementing it. The discussions within the Executive and the conflicting advice and recommendations, on the contrary, should never be revealed. This distinction, on the whole, underlay the practice followed in the foreign policy review conducted by the Trudeau Government.

In conclusion it should be stressed that popular discussion of foreign affairs is something intrinsically desirable, especially at a time when complex issues can affect not only the livelihood but also the very lives of the people in whose name policy decisions are made. The public suffers from a lack of reliable and objective information on international issues. A common-sense distinction can be drawn between disclosing factual information and revealing the internal discussions and processes whereby a Government arrives at decisions or deals confidentially with other governments. But the public has to be satisfied that there is continuing and effective access to all relevant factual information if that public is to be expected to agree with the need for secrecy in these special areas.

How can factual information flow more freely from government to public? Under a system of Parliamentary democracy this requires, in the first place, continuous access to political leaders to obtain that information. The House of Commons, with its Question Period, is intended precisely to encourage the ferreting out of factual information from the responsible Ministers. The way this system works, however, depends not only on the ability of the questioner to press home his demands for information under Parliamentary rules, but also on whether the Minister resorts to evasive action. Franker and more factual answers from Ministers are essential for effective public understanding and discussion of foreign policy issues.

Committees of the House of Commons, especially the Standing Committee on External Affairs and National Defence, have regular discussion of policy questions with the responsible Ministers; they also examine officials on administrative detail and enquire into the manner in which policy is being implemented. The daily verbatim Reports of the House of Commons debates in Hansard, together with special reports of the Committees of the House of Commons and of the Senate, constitute an essential transmission line furnishing foreign policy information to the Canadian public.

Factual information made available through Parliament is supplemented by regular publications of the Department of External Affairs, including *International Perspectives,* which sometimes prints views that are "not necessarily those of the sponsor." The Canadian Institute for International Affairs, through its many publications and discussion groups, provides opportunities for critical commentary on the factual information made available by the Government. The Parliamentary Centre for Foreign Affairs and Foreign Trade, in Ottawa, supplements the Institute by providing liaison between government officials and the public. In all, there is no lack of machinery for providing factual information on foreign affairs to the public in Canada, especially when one adds to these official and semi-official channels the private enterprise of the communications media. It is not so much a matter of devising means as of the use to which these will be put.

An unresolved problem exists for all governments: that leaks and information obtained through other than official channels are more likely to provide headlines, as well as ammunition for the opposition and embarrassment for the Government. As Samuel Johnson said, "The vanity of being known to be trusted with a secret is generally one of the chief motives to disclose it." Here again, the remedy would seem to be greater use of existing official or above-board channels of fact dissemination. Frankness about facts is the best way to restrain the "vanity" of disclosure.

Experience with the foreign policy review in Canada showed that, despite certain limitations discussed above, it served as a timely means of deflating public pressure built up over differences of view (partly because of lack of factual information) on issues relating to Canada's commitments—particularly military commitments—through participation in multinational organizations and arrangements in the atomic age. This review served also to make the transition to an environment in which the implications of the interdependence of nations in economic and social matters, as the world continues to shrink in response to technological advancement and population growth, is increasingly claiming the public limelight.

Since the balance between secrecy and openness in foreign policy and defence matters is decided primarily on the basis of political considerations (whatever the law and regulations may be in respective countries), it is hoped that, as co-operation replaces confrontation in world affairs, there will be more chance for the balance to favor openness. As the United States, for instance, initiates policies of co-operation among formerly antagonistic states, could not this have a marked effect on every nation's penchant for secrecy? Surely the democratic societies can hardly expect the totalitarian societies of Russia or China to move toward openness, as we are urging them to do, unless we show them the way.

Part 2

The Legislators Confront the Security Managers

5

Executive Privilege
and Congressional Responsibility
in Foreign Affairs

SENATOR CHARLES McC. MATHIAS, JR.

"The Constitution," the distinguished scholar Dr. Edward S. Corwin once observed, "considered only for its affirmative grants of powers capable of affecting the issue, is an invitation to struggle for the privilege of directing American foreign policy."[1] Indeed, Professor Corwin need not have limited his remark to foreign policy, for the Constitution is in many respects an invitation to struggle—or, if you will, an opportunity for co-operation—between the Legislative and Executive branches of our national government in most major spheres of activity, domestic as well as foreign.

The Constitution was not, as it is sometimes pictured, a "scissors-and-paste job" put together out of the pages of Montesquieu and Locke, with sharp dividing lines and precise distributions of power among self-contained departments of government. It was above all a singularly pragmatic and eclectic document arising out of the fires of the colonial experience and reflecting the very real and very human problems and passions that the experience engendered. Its framers were extremely sensitive to human frailties and skeptical of utopias of any kind. They were not content, therefore, with a simple "separation of powers" among the three branches of the new national government. They insisted, instead, on further "hedging their bets" by giving each branch a hand in each other's business, with the possibility that over the years a given hand could exert a grip far stronger than anyone had originally imagined or intended. Although certain powers were peculiarly and pre-eminently reserved to each branch, there was a great deal

Senator Mathias (R–Maryland) is the ranking Republican on the Subcommittee on the Separation of Powers of the Senate Judiciary Committee.
1. Edward S. Corwin, *The President: Office and Powers 1787-1957* (4th rev. ed.; New York: New York University Press, 1957), p. 171.

of overlapping and intermingling of jurisdictions, a rather broad expanse of territory whose boundaries were, at best, blurred. The result, as Richard Neustadt has described it, is not a government of separate powers, but a "government of separated institutions sharing powers."[2] It is no accident, for example, that among the proposed Constitutional Amendments expressly rejected during Congressional consideration of what became known as the Bill of Rights, was an explicit declaration that the Legislative, Executive, and Judiciary powers are "separate and distinct."[3]

The history of the American national government can, in fact, legitimately be read as a series of boundary disputes, of advances and retreats, between the various branches of government. Even where the respective roles of the Legislative and Executive branches are explicitly stated in the Constitution, there is enormous room for variation in actually carrying out these roles. The Constitution declares, for example, that the President "shall have Power, by and with the Advice and Consent of the Senate, to make Treaties." President Washington interpreted that phrase "advice and consent" in the literal sense and rather astounded the Senate when on a humid Saturday in late August of 1789 (as Pennsylvania Senator William Barclay noted in his journal) he arrived at the Senate chambers, "was introduced, and took our Vice-President's chair . . . rose and told us bluntly that he had called on us for our advice and consent to some propositions respecting the treaty to be held with the Southern Indians."

The Senate, however, regarded this as an attempt to railroad the treaty through without giving it time to gather and examine the evidence on its own authority and to reach its own independent decision. Washington's reaction to the Senate's refusal to respond immediately to his request was what Barclay described as a "violent fret." He left, after detailing his displeasure, and never again appeared in person to ask the Senate for its "advice and consent." As Barclay summed up the apparent views of the Senate, "I can not now be mistaken. The President wishes to tread on the necks of Senate. . . . He wishes us to see with the eyes and hear with the ears of his Secretary only. The Secretary to advance the premises, the President to draw the conclusions, and to bear down our deliberations with his personal authority and presence. Form only will be left to us. This will not do with Americans. But let the matter work; it will soon cure itself."[4]

This incident is but one example of the very real possibilities during the first years under the Constitution for the establishment, in practice if not in theory, of an integrated relation between the Executive and Legislative

---

2. Richard E. Neustadt, *Presidential Power* (New York: Wiley, 1960), p. 33.
3. See the excellent discussion of this entire question in Louis Fisher's *President and Congress: Power and Policy* (New York: Collier-Macmillan Ltd., 1972), chap. 1.
4. Quoted in Corwin, pp. 210–11.

branches more or less resembling the Parliamentary system. There is no way of knowing how differently the role of the Senate in the conduct of foreign affairs might have developed had the Senate chosen to accede to Washington's effort to secure the Senate's "advice and consent" in person. Had the Senate done so, the practice might very well have become institutionalized and thus have ensured for the Senate a far more influential role in foreign affairs than it has today, when, in foreign as in other affairs, relations between the Legislative and Executive branches can so often and aptly be described as "foreign."

If, over the two centuries of national government, there have been periods of Congressional dominance, these have in fact proven to be primarily periods of respite in the expansion of Executive and the decline of Congressional power. There are undoubtedly a number of reasons for this. A collegial body like the Congress suffers from an inherent disadvantage in the face of the Executive assets summed up in *The Federalist* as unity, "decision, activity, secrecy, and dispatch."[5] And the Constitution, in some respects, "stacks the deck" in favor of the Executive Branch. In the words of Abel P. Upshur, President Tyler's Secretary of State and a close student of the Constitution:[6]

> The most defective part of the Federal Constitution, beyond all question, is that which relates to the executive department. It is impossible to read that instrument without being forcibly struck with the loose and unguarded terms in which the powers and duties of the President are pointed out. So far as the Legislature is concerned, the limitations of the Constitution are perhaps as precise and strict as they could safely have been made; but in regard to the Executive, the Convention seems to have studiously selected such loose and general expressions as would enable the President, by implication and construction, either to neglect his duties or to enlarge his powers. We have heard it gravely asserted in Congress that whatever power is neither legislative nor judicial is, of course, executive, and as such belongs to the President under the Constitution. Be this as it may, it is a reproach to the Constitution that the executive is so ill-defined as to leave any plausible pretense, even to the insane zeal of party devotion, for attributing to the President of the United States the powers of a despot—powers which are wholly unknown to any limited monarchy in the world.

The Executive Branch, at any rate, has taken full advantage of the latitude offered by the Constitution, the opportunities presented by events, the failures of the Congress to fulfill its responsibilities effectively. And the in-

---

5. *The Federalist* No. 70 (Modern Library ed.), p. 455.
6. Quoted in Wilfred E. Binkley, *President and Congress* (3rd rev. ed.; New York: Random House, Vintage Books, 1962), p. 32.

stitutional balance of powers has tipped decidedly, if not decisively, in favor of the Executive.

THE EXECUTIVE'S CLAIM OF "PRIVILEGE"

The whole vexed question of "executive privilege"—the alleged right of the Executive to deny information to the Congress—has its roots in the intermingling of jurisdictions among the branches of government, the open-ended grant of executive power (whether intended or not), and the growth of the Executive Branch into one of the most enormous information-gathering machines devised by man. The Constitution nowhere confers upon the Executive the power to deny information to the Congress, nor does it explicitly recognize the right of the Congress to require information from the Executive Branch.

Proponents of executive privilege have claimed that the concept of "executive Power" contained in the Constitution (Article 2, Section 1, clause 1 begins: "The executive Power shall be vested in a President of the United States") includes and implies the traditional privilege of monarchs to withhold information.[7] It seems quite clear, however, that the framers of the Constitution did not regard the figure of the monarch as precedent or prototype for the Chief Executive of the new republic. No one disagreed when James Wilson, a leader of those who favored a strong and independent Executive, declared during the Constitutional Convention that he "did not consider the Prerogative of the British Monarch as a proper guide in defining the Executive powers."[8] It was he, interestingly enough, who composed the draft in which the phrase "the executive Power of the United States shall be vested" first appeared. The debate made it obvious that, in wrestling with the language of this part of the Constitution, the delegates were at issue, not over the scope or content of executive power, but over whether or not the Executive should consist of a single or more than one person.

In the ultimate assertion of executive privilege, the then Attorney General William Rogers claimed during the Eisenhower Administration that the Executive had an "uncontrolled discretion"[9] to withhold information. He traced the privilege directly to two interrelated sources: the fact that the Constitution vests the "executive Power" in the President and charges him to "take care that the laws be faithfully executed," and the doctrine of the

---

7. Bernard Schwartz, "Executive Privilege and Congressional Investigatory Power," *California Law Rev.,* vol. 47, no. 1 (March 1959), pp. 7–8.
8. Max Farrand, ed., *The Records of the Federal Convention of 1787,* I (New Haven: Yale University Press, 1937), 65.
9. Raoul Berger, "Executive Privilege v. Congressional Inquiry," 12 *U.C.L.A. Law Review* (1965), 1045.

separation of powers. Since the Executive is supreme in the duties assigned to him by the Constitution, the Congress cannot "compel heads of department by law to give papers and information involved" if the President decides that they should be withheld.[10] The Executive, in other words, has exclusive and absolute ownership of the information in its possession. And while heads of departments, in Rogers's words, "have frequently obeyed congressional demands . . . and have furnished papers and information to congressional committees, they have done so only in a spirit of comity and good will, and not because there has been an effective legal means to compel them to do so."[11] Although the courts have not ruled on the question of executive privilege to withhold information from the Congress, they have considered several cases in which the Executive claimed the right to withhold information from the Judiciary. And they have made it very clear that the Executive does not have sole discretion as to whether or what information should be withheld. In the 1953 decision *United States* v. *Reynolds* the Supreme Court declared that "the Court itself must determine whether the circumstances are appropriate for the claim of privilege," and that "judicial control over the evidence in a case cannot be abdicated to the caprice of executive officers."[12]

THE CONGRESSIONAL POWER OF INQUIRY

The Constitution does not spell out any Congressional power to inquire into the administration of the laws it has passed, to acquire information for the making or changing or repeal of laws, or to investigate the conduct of Executive affairs. But, as Raoul Berger has pointed out, "The broad power of Congress to inquire into executive conduct is deeply rooted in parliamentary and colonial history and was immediately asserted by the first Congress."[13] In 1927, in *McGrain* v. *Daugherty* the Supreme Court declared:

> We are of the opinion that the power of inquiry—with process to enforce it —is an essential and appropriate auxiliary to the legislative function. It was so regarded and employed in American legislatures before the Constitution

10. *Ibid.,* p. 1067.
11. Cited in testimony by Alan C. Swan, Professorial Lecturer in Law, Graduate School of Business, University of Chicago, at a Hearing before the Subcommittee on the Separation of Powers of the Committee on the Judiciary, U.S. Senate, 92d Cong., 1st sess., on "Executive Privilege: The Withholding of Information by the Executive" (Washington, D.C.: U.S., Government Printing Office, 1971), p. 242. (Hereinafter referred to as *Hearing.*)
12. 345 U.S. 1 at 8-10 (1953). These are decisions of the U.S. (Federal) Supreme Court, hereinafter referred to by volume number and authorized citation "U.S.," followed by the page on which the case report begins.
13. Berger, p. 1053.

was framed and ratified. Both Houses of Congress took this view of it early in their history.[14]

Elsewhere in the same decision the Court wrote that "The power to legislate carries with it by implication ample authority to obtain information needed in the rightful exercise of that power and to employ compulsory process for the purpose."

The courts have not, however, ruled directly on executive privilege to withhold information from the Congress; neither have they ruled specifically on the powers of the Congress to require the Executive to supply requested information. Still, the legislative power of inquiry is firmly established in our law and in our history. And it is difficult to see how it can be exercised effectively if the Executive can, with absolute impunity, withhold from the Congress any information within its possession. As Joseph Story put it in his *Commentaries on the Constitution,* the President "must possess more extensive sources of information, as well in regard to domestic as foreign affairs, than can belong to the Congress. The true workings of the laws . . . are more readily seen, and more constantly under the view of the executive. There is great wisdom, therefore, . . . in requiring the President to lay before Congress all facts and information which may assist their deliberations."[15]

EVOLUTION OF THE ISSUE

In general the history of the executive privilege issue has been "that of the Executive Department asserting the right to withhold, Congress challenging . . . [its] assertion and the result determined by negotiation or political pressure, but without an authoritative decision of the validity of either position."[16] While there have been, since the early days of the Republic, differences between the Legislative and Executive branches over the disposition of information in the hands of the Executive, the emergence of executive privilege as a full-blown, formal doctrine did not occur until well within this century —not, in fact, until the 1950's, when the Eisenhower Administration invented it as a shield against the excesses of the McCarthy investigations.

Eminent legal scholars have examined the precedents cited by Attorney General Rogers[17] in his effort to argue the existence of an absolute "privi-

14. 273 U.S. 135, 174 (1927).
15. Joseph Story, *Commentaries on the Constitution of the United States,* II (Boston: Little, Brown, 1905), 367.
16. Report by the American Law Division of the Library of Congress in *Hearing,* p. 543.
17. William P. Rogers, "Constitutional Law: The Papers of the Executive Branch," in *Hearing,* pp. 551–66.

lege" and have concluded that they are "entirely equivocal" and, at best, "show ambiguous action accompanied by brave words in which the Congress never acquiesces."[18] The First Congress adopted and President Washington signed an Act creating a Department of the Treasury. That Act contained a provision (drafted by Alexander Hamilton himself) which declared it "the duty of the Secretary of the Treasury to make report, and give information to either branch of the legislature in person or in writing (as he may be required), respecting all matters referred to him by the Senate or House of Representatives, or which shall appertain to his office." Since this was an Act of the First Congress, many of whose members had taken part in the Constitutional Convention; since it was drafted by Alexander Hamilton, who was second to none in his assertion of the Executive's power and prerogative; since it was signed by the first President—this Act is strong evidence of the Constitutional power of the Congress to "require," at least in the form of statute, information from the Executive Branch.

In an instance cited by former Attorney General Rogers as evidence in favor of executive privilege, the House of Representatives set up a select committee on March 27, 1792, "to inquire into the failure of the late expedition under General St. Clair" and empowered it "to call for such persons, papers, and records as may be necessary to assist in their inquiries."[19] The President gave the House committee all the appropriate documents, and the Secretaries of War and Treasury both testified before the committee. At a Cabinet meeting to consider the request of the House committee, Jefferson recorded in informal, personal notes that the members were:

> of one mind 1. that the house was in inquest, therefore might institute inquiries. 2. that they might call for papers generally. 3. that the Executive ought to communicate such papers as the public good would permit, & ought to refuse those the disclosure of which would injure the public. Consequently were to exercise a discretion. 4. that neither the committee nor House had a right to call on the head of a department, who and whose papers were under the President alone, but that the committee should instruct their chairman to move the house to address the President. . . . It was agreed in this case that there was not a paper which might not be properly produced. . . .[20]

Nothing in these notes, so far as we know, was ever communicated to the Congress. Washington did not declare to the Congress that he had any right to withhold information—and in fact withheld nothing from the committee.

---

18. Swan, *Hearing*, p. 247.
19. Telford Taylor, *Grand Inquest: The Story of Congressional Investigations* (New York: Simon and Schuster, 1955), p. 38.
20. Quoted in the Berger article, p. 1079.

In 1796 President Washington did refuse a request by the House for correspondence, documents, and instructions to John Jay concerning the negotiation of the Jay Treaty. He did so mainly on the grounds that the House did not share in the treaty-making power assigned by the Constitution to the President and the Senate, and that he had, in fact, given the appropriate papers to the Senate. The House passed two resolutions affirming its power to review treaties and to require information without declaring its purpose for doing so. And Vice President Adams strongly disagreed with the President's decision. As he wrote in a letter to his wife: "I cannot deny the right of the House to ask for papers. . . . My ideas are very high of the rights and powers of the House of Representatives."[21]

In 1807 the House asked President Jefferson to supply all information on the Burr conspiracy "except such as he may deem the public welfare to require not to be disclosed." Jefferson did exercise the discretion the House thus granted him and withheld some papers while supplying others. As one authority has noted, this was a clear instance of a "congressional grant of discretion . . . [as] a matter of courtesy and not a recognition of right."[22]

It was not, in fact, until 1835 that President Jackson made what Professor Berger calls the "first unequivocal assertion of power to withhold information from the Congress." As Professor Berger goes on to say, "Coming 46 years after the Act of 1789, which itself is a reflection of parliamentary and colonial history, and the steadfast congressional insistence on the plenary power to require information, little weight need be attached to this belated Jacksonian claim on the issue of constitutional construction."[23]

As these examples suggest, the doctrine of executive privilege—as practice or principle—has only the flimsiest foundation in the first half-century of the republic.

FOREIGN AND MILITARY AFFAIRS

Although its exact origins are obscure, the Congress did adopt the practice fairly early in the nineteenth century of "regularly including a grant of discretion in requests to the President for documents concerning the Nation's foreign relations."[24] That "discretion" allowed the President sometimes to withhold documents in the interests of national security. Along with that discretion, which was clearly understood to be a matter of Congressional dispensation and not Constitutional right, the Senate developed the custom of reviewing these matters in executive (closed) session.[25] But during this

---

21. *Ibid.*, p. 1085.
22. Swan, *Hearing*, p. 246.
23. Berger, p. 1094.
24. Swan, *Hearing*, p. 247.
25. *Ibid.*, pp. 248–49.

century, in Professor Swan's words, as the Executive "has with increasing vigor asserted its claim to a plenary power to direct the Nation's foreign affairs," it "has been able without great difficulty to convert a historic courtesy into an unqualified claim of right, and to do so largely unchallenged by Congress."[26]

EXECUTIVE PRIVILEGE TODAY

During the 1950's, as I have said, executive privilege was raised by the Executive Branch to the level of an absolute, unqualified power. It could be exercised not only by the President himself, but by subordinate officials. It could apply to almost any kind of information. In March of 1962 President Kennedy responded to a request by Representative John E. Moss, chairman of the House Subcommittee on Government Information, for a clarification of his position on executive privilege.

> As you know [wrote Mr. Kennedy], this Administration has gone to great lengths to achieve full cooperation with the Congress in making available to it all appropriate documents, correspondence and information. That is the basic policy of this Administration, and it will continue to be so. Executive Privilege can be invoked only by the President and will not be used without specific Presidential approval. Your own interest in assuring the widest public accessibility to governmental information is, of course, well known, and I can assure you this Administration will continue to cooperate with your subcommittee and the entire Congress in achieving this objective.[27]

Presidents Johnson and Nixon have reaffirmed this basic policy. President Nixon has also spelled out detailed procedures to be followed before formal invocation of the privilege.

In the view of the Executive Branch, however, the privilege may still be employed to cover almost any category of information within its possession. A recent, dramatic instance is the President's extension of executive privilege to cover White House documents, files, and tape recordings even in a matter of such concern to the public political process and to the enforcement of the law of the land as that being investigated in the Senate Watergate hearings. Moreover, the Executive Branch has more or less dispensed with the formality of invoking the privilege by the expedient of simply denying or delaying information requested by the Congress. As Senator Stuart Symington has observed, "As a practical matter, in the long and tedious negotiations we have had in the Subcommittee on the United States Security

---

26. *Ibid.*
27. Quoted in Clark R. Mollenhoff, *Washington Cover-Up* (Garden City, New York: Doubleday, 1962), p. 239.

Agreements and Commitments Abroad, a formal claim of 'executive privilege' was rarely if ever lodged. Instead, first one reason and then another was asserted as to why the information requested was not to be supplied."[28] Similarly, Senator Sam Ervin, Jr., as chairman of the Senate Judiciary Subcommittee on Constitutional Rights, requested information and testimony concerning U.S. Army surveillance and data-bank programs. While he did secure some information and some witnesses, he was denied the most important of these for the following reasons, which he extracted from letters received from the Department of the Army:[29]

—. . . we are precluded by consistent Executive Branch policy from releasing to the public. (J. Fred Buzhardt, General Counsel, Department of Defense)

—Inappropriate to authorize the release of these documents. (Melvin Laird, Secretary of Defense)

—This information is solely for your use in conducting your inquiry. (R. Kenly Webster, Acting General Counsel, Department of Army)

—The records . . . cannot be obtained without an inordinate expenditure of time and effort. (R. Kenly Webster, Acting General Counsel, Department of Army)

—No useful purpose would be served by a public report on the materials. (J. Fred Buzhardt, General Counsel, Department of Defense)

—I do not believe it appropriate that the general officers in question appear before your subcommittee, but that any " 'desire' testimony" . . . should be furnished by my designated representative. (Melvin Laird, Secretary of Defense)

Section 313 of the 1921 Act setting up the General Accounting Office (GAO) directs every agency of the U.S. Government to furnish the Comptroller General with

Such information regarding the powers, duties, activities, organization, financial transactions, and methods of business of their respective offices as he may from time to time require of them.

In 1969 the Senate Foreign Relations Committee requested the GAO to conduct a review of the training of foreign military personnel under the Military Assistance Program. The GAO asked the Department of Defense for copies of its five-year plan for military assistance, of performance evaluation reports on Korea and possibly other countries, and of a Defense Department staff report on the status of foreign military training systems. All

---

28. *Hearing,* p. 220.
29. *Ibid.,* pp. 5–6.

were refused on various grounds. When submitting its report on the military training program in early 1971, the GAO pointed out that officials of both the State Department and the Defense Department had "withheld or delayed the release of Military Assistance Program reports and records essential to a full and complete review." It went on to say that this denial of access to records was nothing new but "a continuation of similar problems the General Accounting Office has encountered over the years in reviewing Department of Defense programs, particularly evaluations of military assistance programs."[30]

The ability of the Congress to obtain information from the Executive Branch has been especially undermined in recent years by the enormous growth in number and influence of the White House staff, which Presidents have long regarded as entirely immune to Congressional inquiry. Increasingly, in both foreign and domestic affairs, the crucial decisions and recommendations once made in the Cabinet departments—which, as creatures of the Congress, cannot with complete impunity escape Congressional scrutiny —are centered in the White House staff.

Over recent years, for example, a whole new bureau or department has emerged in the White House, and one that in fact exerts the most fundamental influence over the decisions of war and peace. Its core is the National Security Council (NSC), currently headed by Henry Kissinger, the President's Assistant for National Security Affairs. During 1971 Dr. Kissinger directed a total staff of at least one hundred forty employees, of whom fifty-four were substantive experts, and presided as well over a number of interagency committees and working groups covering the whole range of foreign and national security affairs. Yet the Congress is denied the opportunity to query Mr. Kissinger, in any formal way, concerning his activities or views or knowledge.

The Congress, as a consequence, is increasingly denied access to the critical information it must have if it is to exercise effectively its responsibilities for making laws and appropriating funds. The debilitating and destructive effect upon the Congress and the nation of this absolute and arbitrary Executive control over information was superbly stated by former Senate and White House aide George Reedy in testimony before the Senate Subcommittee on the Separation of Powers. His remarks are worth quoting at some length:

> In observing the two major divisions of the Government, the legislative and the executive, . . . one of the principal differences is that within the executive branch, there exists a virtual horror of public debate on issues.

---

30. *Ibid.,* pp. 26–27.

I do not think this is a question of venality; I do not think it is a question of executive officials who feel that they have to play fast and loose with the public trust and if Congress knows too much, it is going to catch them in wrong doing.

I think it is a feeling which has arisen over a long period of time that if the public debates these issues, then the debate is going to make government impossible.

Now, on the other hand, the legislative branch of government is one which basically exists on the need for public debate. I think that is one of the principal functions of Congress. . . . Senator Fulbright has already outlined . . . the difficulties that Congress encounters in transacting its business when it does not have sufficient information. But there is one other aspect of this. . . . That is the impossibility of Congress serving as a focal point for public debate if the Congress itself does not have the information upon which these issues should be debated and I believe that public debate on the major issues is one of the most important functions in sustaining the unity of the United States. If people feel that there has been a legitimate opportunity to discuss issues in advance of the actual commitment, if they believe they have had their say, then I think they are going to be quite willing to support their Government even when it makes mistakes.[31]

CONGRESSIONAL EFFORTS TO RESIST

The Congress has made a considered effort over recent years to reassert its right to any and all information which the Executive Branch possesses and which the Congress requires to perform its basic functions of oversight, legislation, and inquiry. In June 1955 the aforementioned Subcommittee on Government Information was created by Representative William L. Dawson, chairman of the House Committee on Government Operations. He appointed as chairman, Representative John E. Moss, who had suggested its creation. Since its inception that Subcommittee has conducted extensive hearings and investigations into the information policies and practices of the entire Federal Government and sponsored important legislation affecting those policies and practices. In 1963 that Subcommittee merged with another to form the Subcommittee on Foreign Operations and Government Information. In 1958 and 1959 the Senate Judiciary Subcommittee on Constitutional Rights held extensive hearings into the subject of Executive privilege. The Senate Judiciary Subcommittee on the Separation of Powers chaired by Senator Ervin held similar hearings in 1971 and approved legislation sponsored by Senator William Fulbright designed to clarify and curtail the use of the privilege.

31. *Ibid.*, pp. 455–56.

Congressional efforts to compel Executive compliance with its requests have generally failed—primarily because the means of compulsion at the disposal of the Congress are so crude as to be virtually unemployable and also because, in what is essentially a boundary dispute the courts have never ruled upon, the Executive has successfully ignored Congressional efforts at compulsion.

In the category of "crude means" are the power of impeachment and the power of subpoena. The power of impeachment is, in Lord Bryce's words, "the heaviest piece of artillery in the Congressional arsenal, but because it is so heavy it is unfit for ordinary use. It is like a hundred-ton gun which needs complex machinery to bring it into position, an enormous charge of powder to fire it, and a large mark to aim at."[32] The Congress has also the power to subpoena witness and documents both of public officials and private individuals and to cite an individual—public or private—for contempt for failure to comply. Nor does the Congress have to rely upon the Department of Justice to act on a contempt case. As one observer has written,

> Congress undoubtedly has power to punish contempts without invoking the aid of the executive and the judiciary, by the simple forthright process of causing the Sergeant at Arms to seize the offender and clap him in the common jail of the District of Columbia or the guardroom of the Capitol Police.[33]

But the use of this power against an official of the Executive Branch would, like the use of the power of impeachment, amount to nothing less than a declaration of war between the two branches and could conceivably lead to chaos and conflict whose outcome no one could control.

On several occasions—and with little success—the Congress has employed the power of the purse in attempts to pry information out of the Executive Branch. Section 533A(d) of the Mutual Security Act of 1959 arranged for the expenses of the Office of the Inspector General and Comptroller, on condition that all documents and papers relating to the operation and activities of the Office would be furnished to the General Accounting Office and to any committee of the Congress requesting such information. Section 534(b) imposed a similar duty upon the International Cooperation Administration (ICA). Upon signing this Mutual Security Act, however, President Eisenhower declared that he had

> signed this bill on the express premise that the . . . amendments relating to disclosure are not intended to alter and cannot alter the

32. Quoted in a Memorandum submitted by Prof. Arthur S. Miller, George Washington School of Law, in *Hearing*, p. 524.
33. Joseph W. Bishop, Jr., "The Executive's Right of Privacy: An Unresolved Constitutional Question," 66 *Yale Law Journal* 484 (1957).

recognized Constitutional duty and power of the Executive with respect to the disclosure of information, documents, and other materials. Indeed, any other construction of these amendments would raise grave Constitutional questions under the historic Separation of Powers Doctrine.[34]

The Mutual Security and Related Agencies Appropriations Act was revised by the Congress in 1960 to forbid any expenditures under the Act if after a set period of time the ICA had not delivered all information required of it to the GAO or duly authorized committee or subcommittee of the Congress or a certification by the President that we will not permit the deliverance of such information for this or that specific reason. A similar provision was added to the Mutual Security Act of 1960. Although the House had originally approved stronger language for this measure, the House-Senate conference decided "that the separation of powers under the Constitution makes it impossible for the Congress to infringe the prerogatives of the Executive by legislative action and that consequently this provision would serve to indicate the will of the Congress but that it could neither prescribe nor limit the constitutional powers of the Executive."[35]

The Mutual Security and Related Agencies Appropriations Act of 1961 included the same provision as the previous year. The President, however, continued to refuse Congressional requests for documents concerning ICA projects, certifying that for several reasons disclosure of the information was contrary to the national interest. The Comptroller General informed the Secretary of State on November 17, 1960, that, under the appropriate provision of the Mutual Security Act, funds would be cut off from the Office of the Inspector General unless the requested information was furnished. On December 8, 1960 the Comptroller General ordered all funds cut off effective the next day.

The White House, at the same time, asked the Attorney General for an opinion as to "whether, after the President forbids the furnishing of information . . . requested by a committee or subcommittee of Congress and issues a certificate reciting such action pursuant to section 101(d) of the Mutual Security and Related Agencies Appropriations Act, 1961, appropriations for the use of the Office of the Inspector General and Comptroller must, nevertheless, be cut off by virtue of the operation of section 533A(d) of the Mutual Security Act of 1954, as amended."[36] The Attorney General predictably concluded that "the Comptroller General's view that the proviso

---

34. *Public Papers of the Presidents,* Dwight D. Eisenhower, 1959, p. 549.
35. Cited in Robert Kramer and Herman Marcuse, "Executive Privilege—A Study of the Period 1953–1960," 29 *George Washington Law Review* 859 (1961).
36. William P. Rogers, Memorandum of December 9, 1960, in "Availability of Information from Federal Departments and Agencies: Progress of Study July–December 1960," Fifth Report of the House Committee on Government Operations, 87th Cong., 1st sess., House Report No. 818 (Washington, D.C.: U.S., Government Printing Office, 1961), p. 168. (Hereinafter referred to as *Fifth Report.*)

of section 533A(d) has cut off funds under the circumstances disclosed here is an erroneous interpretation of the meaning of this statute. I further conclude that if this view of the Comptroller General as to the meaning of this statute is correct, the proviso is unconstitutional."[37]

As a result, funds never were cut off. The President ordered the Secretaries of State and the Treasury to ignore the Comptroller General's order. Representative Porter Hardy, whose House Subcommittee on Foreign Operations had requested the documents, waited until after the change of administration and received the requested information from the State Department in March-April 1961 after the intercession of President Kennedy.[38] The Foreign Assistance Act of 1971 and the Foreign Assistance and Related Programs Appropriations Act, 1971, contain provisions nearly identical to those above.

There is another statute providing that "An Executive agency, on request of the Committee on Government Operations of the House of Representatives, or of any seven members thereof, or on request of the Committee on Government Operations of the Senate, or any five members thereof, shall submit any information requested of it relating to any matter within the jurisdiction of the committee."[39] This section is adapted from an Act approved in 1928 to discontinue the large number of reports being transmitted to the Congress and yet enable the Congress to secure the information it had been receiving in these reports when necessary. Representative Henry Reuss employed this statute in an attempt to obtain a copy of a report on the supersonic jet (SST) prepared in 1969 by a committee appointed by the Executive Branch. John Ehrlichman, then Assistant to the President for Domestic Affairs, informed Representative Reuss that the "report constitutes an internal governmental memorandum of a confidential nature which cannot be released."[40]

In sum, the Congress has had no success in using fiscal or other pressures to force the Executive Branch to supply information it requires. The one remaining recourse to which the Congress has not yet resorted, and to which it may have to turn in the future, is to bring the entire question of executive privilege before the courts.

REDRESSING THE BALANCE

During the Senate Subcommittee on the Separation of Powers 1971 hearings on the question of executive privilege, I engaged in the following ex-

---

37. *Fifth Report,* p. 193.
38. *Fifth Report,* pp. 157–59.
39. 5 U.S.C. 2954 (1970). The designation "U.S.C." is the authorized citation for the United States Code of Federal Laws.
40. *Congressional Record,* May 1, 1971, E6929 (daily edition).

change with the late former Secretary of State Dean Acheson concerning the "gulf" that had developed between the Executive and Legislative branches of our national Government:

> *Senator Mathias.* I think we have as fair men accepted the fact that there have been changes on both sides [of the national government]. But men of good will, I think, have to reach across the gulfs that have developed. And perhaps the fact is that . . . a gulf does exist today, and it is to the detriment of the United States of America.
>
> *Mr. Acheson.* I quite agree. . . . I don't believe this can be cured by law.
>
> *Senator Mathias.* How can we cure it? Because for the good of the country it ought to be cured.
>
> *Mr. Acheson.* It can be cured only by people. I don't think we need to go too deeply into that.[41]

There is no question but that relations between the Legislative and Executive branches of government, like all other institutional relations, cannot in reality be separated from the particular people who happen to inhabit these institutions and from the relations between them. If we really believe in a government of laws and rules, however, the role of any one branch of government, its ability to carry out its responsibilities, cannot be determined merely by the quality and character of the people who man it at any given time. In particular, the role of the Congress cannot continue to be—as it has increasingly become—a function of Executive "good will" and "generosity." In short, while relations between the two branches must, in some degree, depend upon and be determined by the good will that exists or does not exist between the humans involved, it must above all depend upon and be determined by a clear understanding and acceptance by both branches that each is a coordinate branch of government and that neither is superior nor subordinate to the other. And the time may well be at hand when the courts have to be called upon to settle the "boundary disputes" and clarify the ground rules governing relations between the two branches.

The Congress has recently begun to take steps to reassert its role under the Federal system on a variety of fronts: by legislation ending what it regards as Executive abuse or usurpation of the war-making power and subversion of the treaty-making power; by going to court on such matters as the Executive pocket veto and impoundment of funds; and by undertaking various internal reforms. It has also begun to move to set definite limits to the "privilege" of the Executive to withhold information from the Congress. Thus, during the 92nd Congress the Senate Judiciary Subcommittee on the Separation of Powers approved legislation sponsored by Senator Fulbright

---

41. *Hearing*, p. 263.

that could well set the stage for taking the whole question of executive privilege to the courts. Senator Fulbright's measure, as approved by the Subcommittee, contains the following provisions:

1. Employees of the Executive Branch—including members of the White House staff—would be required to appear in person before the Congress or appropriate Congressional committees when requested even if they intend to do no more than invoke executive privilege. When they appear they would be required to state, in effect, that: "I have been instructed in writing by the President to invoke executive privilege, and here is why. . . ."

2. Information could be withheld from the Congress only on the basis of a formal invocation of executive privilege on specific order of the President.

3. Procedures are spelled out by which agency heads wishing to withhold information must secure the approval of, first, the Attorney General and, then, the President before the privilege could be invoked.

4. The information must be supplied immediately if the Attorney General should fail to agree or the President decline to invoke executive privilege.

5. If within sixty days the Executive has neither provided the requested information nor invoked executive privilege, funds will be cut off from the agency concerned until either the information is provided or executive privilege invoked.[42]

There is, of course, no reason to believe that, if this measure is adopted and if funds are cut off under its authority, access to information will be secured. The response of the Executive may be precisely the response the Eisenhower Administration made to the effort to cut off funds under the Mutual Security Act of 1959: the Attorney General will declare that the Congress has no Constitutional power to do so, the President will order the Department of the Treasury and the agency in question to ignore the fund cut-off, and the issue will rest there unless the Congress decides to take it to the courts. In considering this measure, moreover, the Congress will undoubtedly want to be extremely careful in considering whether or not by insisting on a formal invocation of executive privilege it concedes far more than it should concerning the existence of and need for such a privilege. In contemplating whether or not, or how, to take this issue to the courts, the Congress must face some very difficult questions. There is, to begin with, the question of whether or not the issue is genuinely "justiciable," of whether or not the Congress has legal "standing" to take the issue before the courts, or whether it is simply a political matter that the Legislative and Executive branches must work out on their own as well as they can.

It would seem, on the face of it, that bringing the issue before the court is

---

42. *Ibid.,* pp. 20-21.

an acceptable and even desirable alternative to a naked confrontation between the Legislative and Executive branches in which the one withholds funds and the other withholds information. As James Madison declared in *Federalist* No. 49, neither of the departments "can pretend to an exclusive or superior right of settling the boundaries between their respective powers."[43] Several eminent legal scholars have declared that the Congress does have, or can confer upon itself, the requisite legal "standing" to take the issue to court.[44] They believe, as Professor Berger has put it, that "What we have here are two conflicting claims of constitutional power; a conflict respecting constitutional boundaries. And neither branch can settle those boundaries by itself. A boundary dispute has to be turned over to the courts."[45]

The Congress, for its part, would be perfectly willing to agree that the President has the right to "confidential" advice from his employees and that certain matters—involving, say, foreign or defense policy—should be kept secret. The Congress would insist, however, that what constitutes "confidential" or "personal" advice be very carefully defined and circumscribed, since these categories can and have, in fact, been used to cover almost any kind of information. It would further maintain that the Executive cannot reserve to itself alone, but must share equally with the Congress, the right and responsibility to decide whether and to what degree certain information should be kept secret. The Congress would, of course, have to develop more effective procedures than it now has of ensuring that its own members abide by any decision it might make concerning the secrecy of information.

It would seem, in short, that the courts may well be called upon to determine whether the Congress has the power to require from the Executive any and all the information it may need to do its job—whether the Congress can, in fact, function as the equal and coordinate branch of government that the Constitution intended it to be. The saving grace of this Republic has always been, however, the lubricant of good will that has kept the checks and balances from jamming, and the Government from stalemate. While it seems to each generation that such a vital ingredient is in short supply in its time, there has always been enough to keep the political wheels in motion. Let us hope we can prove in our day that the critical supply is not yet exhausted.

---

43. Cited in Berger, p. 1354.
44. Miller, *Hearing,* pp. 524–25.
45. *Hearing,* p. 274.

6

Operation and Reform
of the Classification System
in the United States

REPRESENTATIVE WILLIAM S. MOORHEAD

INTRODUCTION

In the United States in recent years we have seen violent political and legal controversies over the proper balance between the obvious need of the Federal Government to safeguard vitally important, sensitive classified information affecting our national defense and foreign policy interests, on the one hand, and the equally obvious requirement within an open, representative system of government for its citizenry to keep itself adequately informed of governmental policies so that it may make sound electoral judgments in the selection of its public officials.

This classic dilemma raises basic questions of major consequence that are constantly increasing in frequency and in their dimensional scope. Thus,

—How can a President be held accountable by the electorate if the major elements of his defense and foreign policies are kept hidden in "state secret" vaults during his term or terms in office?

—How can the Congress act responsibly as a co-equal branch of the Federal Government if such vital secrets are withheld so that it is forced to legislate and appropriate public funds for weapons systems, defense installations, or foreign policy programs with access to only part of the information it requires and has a Constitutional right to expect?

—How can the American public be expected to make the human and economic sacrifices necessary to maintain our military strength and preserve world peace if its Government must keep secret the very facts that would make such sacrifices politically palatable?

Congressman Moorhead (D–Pennsylvania) is Chairman, Foreign Operations and Government Information Subcommittee of the House Committee on Government Operations.

NEW AMERICAN EAGLE

—How can our Government maintain our own national security and the confidence of our global partners if its system of classification lacks integrity, is administratively unworkable, and is abused by overclassification to the point where patriotic Americans feel compelled to leak or otherwise compromise such information?

—How can the heralded open society of a democratic system of government operate effectively with the type of secrecy restrictions imposed because of global defense and foreign policy considerations involving closed, totalitarian systems of other world powers?

The Foreign Operations and Government Information Subcommittee of the House Government Operations Committee has been struggling with these and related questions of public policy during our many days of public hearings on freedom of information issues in the 92nd and 93rd sessions of Congress. They touch the most tender and vulnerable parts of the body politic. They are of immense complexity and of almost limitless ramifications. They involve such tough Constitutional questions as the separation of powers and First Amendment rights. They affect the most excruciatingly difficult decisions on which our defense and foreign policy strategies are based. And, as is natural under our system, these questions are among the most controversial and most politically dynamic with which any of us must deal.

By way of illustrating the dimensions of this problem, we might consider, in brief retrospect, some of the controversial cases of the past few years.

There was the newspaper publication of the famous Pentagon Papers and the Government's abortive efforts through the courts to enforce prior restraint on their publication.

There was the continuing controversy over events taking place in 1964 off the coast of Vietnam and resulting in Congressional enactment of the Gulf of Tonkin resolution and subsequent expansion of U.S. involvement in the Indo-China War.

There was the embarrassing leak of the so-called "Kissinger Papers" during the India-Pakistan War, with its revelation of our Government's secret "tilt" toward one of the participants.

There was the leak of information that triggered the public revelation of the hushed-up My Lai massacre in Vietnam.

There was the later leak exposing the role of General John D. Lavelle, former Commander of the U.S. 7th Air Force in Vietnam, in ordering unauthorized bombing strikes against "off-limits" targets in North Vietnam.

These incidents caused grave embarrassment in turn to the Johnson Administration and to the Nixon Administration, and occasioned deep concern on the part of some of our global allies, who wonder whether any joint defense or foreign policy secrets are now safe. They brought despair and disillusionment concerning U.S. war policies in Southeast Asia to many millions of Americans and other peoples in the world. They undermined the credibility of our national leaders, as well as the very institution of government, at a time of waning public confidence in virtually every established social, economic, and political institution.

Critics of the present system of handling classified information within the Executive Branch point to an obvious double standard. On one hand, the full power of the Government's legal system is exercised against certain newspapers for publishing portions of the Pentagon Papers and against someone like Daniel Ellsberg for his alleged role in their being made public. This is contrasted with other actions by top Executive officials who utilize the technique of "instant declassification" of information they *want* leaked. Sometimes it is an "off-the-record" press briefing or "backgrounder" that becomes "on-the-record" at the conclusion of the briefing or at some future politically strategic time. Such Executive Branch leaks may be planted with friendly news columnists. Or, the President himself may exercise his prerogative as Commander in Chief to declassify specific information in an address to the Nation or in a message to the Congress seeking additional funds for a weapons system.

Obviously, confidence in the integrity of the classification system—both within governmental agencies utilizing the system and by those outside government who are affected by its operations—is undermined by these double standards. These considerations are compounded by massive administrative shortcomings in the classification system, as will be discussed later in this chapter.

HISTORICAL AND CONSTITUTIONAL BACKGROUND

The Constitution uses the word "secrecy" only once, and then referring to the right of each House of Congress to keep secret portions of the "Journal of its Proceedings" as stated in Article I, section 5. Nowhere in the Constitution or any of its Amendments is there any other mention of the word or any specific basis for the secret conduct of government business by the Executive or Judicial branches.

Yet, from the earliest days of our Republic the President has exercised the provisions of Article II of the Constitution to limit the dissemination of information affecting our defense and foreign policy interests. President Washington presented to the Senate for its approval a "secret" article to be inserted into a 1790 treaty with the Creek Indians. Two years later, controversy with the Congress arose over "secret" reports on General St. Clair's abortive military campaign against the Indians on our Northwest frontier. "Secret" negotiations by Chief Justice John Jay with Great Britain's Baron

Grenville toward production of the Jay Treaty in 1796 stirred additional public controversy.

Section I of Article II of the Constitution vests executive power in the President; section 2 makes the President the Commander in Chief of the Army and Navy; and section 3 requires the President to "take care that the laws be faithfully executed." These Constitutional provisions and other, more recent statutes have been cited as authority for the President to exercise secrecy in his conduct of foreign affairs and in the area of national defense policy.

The oldest statutory authority cited as a basis to withhold information is the so-called "Housekeeping Statute," enacted by the first Congress in 1789 and giving Federal departments the authority to regulate the business of government, to set up filing systems, and to keep records.[1] This 1789 law was amended in 1958[2] at the urging of our subcommittee to prohibit its use to withhold from the public any information or government records that are otherwise subject to disclosure.

Legal authority for the operation of the security classification system, as it has functioned during the past twenty-two years under three separate Executive Orders, stems in part from the Constitutional authority of the President in Article II. In part it derives also from additional authority claimed by the Executive by virtue of provisions of the Espionage Acts (for discussion see Chapter 9 in this book), the National Security Act of 1947 (which created the National Security Council), the Internal Security Act of 1950, and section 142 of the Atomic Energy Act of 1954.[3]

SECURITY CLASSIFICATION AND THE
FREEDOM OF INFORMATION ACT

During the mid-1950's considerable attention was directed to relations between the nation's security classification system and the right of the Congress and the public to obtain information from the Executive Branch. Impetus outside government was sparked by the late Harold L. Cross, Freedom of Information Counsel for the American Society of Newspaper Editors.[4] In the Congress the fight was led by Representative John E. Moss of California and Senator Thomas Hennings of Missouri, and later by Senator Ed-

---

1. Now Title 5, sec. 301, U.S. Code.
2. Public Law No. 85–619.
3. U.S. Code: Title 18, sec. 793–98; Title 50, sec. 401; Title 50, sec. 781; Title 42, sec. 2162.
4. Harold L. Cross, *The People's Right to Know—Legal Access to Public Records and Proceedings* (New York: Columbia University Press, 1953).

ward Long of Missouri. In 1955 Moss became the first chairman of the Special Government Information Subcommittee (predecessor of our present Subcommittee) and served in this capacity through 1970. He is the principal author of the Freedom of Information Act (FOIA) of 1966,[5] the culmination of more than eleven years of effort in behalf of the people's right-to-know.

This Act, which became effective on July 4, 1967, is a unique effort by the U.S. Government to guarantee to all citizens the basic right to obtain information about governmental actions of interest and concern. The FOIA philosophy is based on the people's right to know about the activities of their Government, consistent with the need to afford protection to vital secrets affecting our national defense, foreign policy, and certain limited areas of normal governmental functions. President Lyndon Johnson described the basic purpose of the new law as follows:

> This legislation springs from one of our most essential principles: a democracy works best when the people have all the information that the security of the Nation permits. No one should be able to pull curtains of secrecy around decisions which can be revealed without injury to the public interest. . . . I signed this measure with a deep sense of pride that the United States is an open society in which the people's right to know is cherished and guarded.[6]

The key provisions of the Freedom of Information Act are:

1. that disclosure of information by government agencies be the general rule, not the exception;
2. that all individuals have equal rights of access;
3. that the burden be on the Government to justify the withholding of a document, not on the person requesting it;
4. that individuals improperly denied access to documents have a right to seek injunctive relief in the Federal courts;
5. that there be a change in government policy and attitude to further the objectives of the Freedom of Information Act, as the Congress clearly intended; and
6. that exemptions contained in 552(b) of the Act relating to national defense, foreign policy, personnel and medical files, trade secrets, investigatory files compiled for law enforcement purposes, interagency or intra-agency memoranda, and similar areas are *not mandatory* in their use to deny information, but are *only permissive* and should be used sparingly.

---

5. Title 5, sec. 552, U.S. Code.
6. U.S., Department of Justice, "Attorney General's Memorandum on the Public Information Section of the Administrative Procedure Act," June 1967, p. ii.

Although prior to action on the Freedom of Information legislation many of the hearings and reports of the Moss Subcommittee dealt with security classification abuses by Executive agencies, it is not accurate to conclude that the Act itself was directed at this aspect of the broader problem of citizen access to information and public records from our Federal Government. In fact, the first of the nine permissive exemptions contained in the FOIA applies to matters "specifically required by Executive Order to be kept secret in the interest of the national defense or foreign policy."[7] This language was cited in March 1972 as another statutory authority by President Nixon when he issued Executive Order 11652, making significant changes in the old security classification system.

DEVELOPMENT OF U.S. CLASSIFICATION SYSTEM

The history of the use of classification markings on government documents involving communications from military, naval, or other public officials has been traced almost continuously for more than a century by Dallas Irvine, a researcher at the National Archives.[8] His study reveals that secrecy in military and diplomatic affairs and the marking of defense and foreign affairs documents to provide for confidentiality has always been practiced to some degree by the Executive Branch. A formal classification system, however, did not develop until recent times by way of ensuring a more sophisticated mechanism to protect such types of sensitive information.

Origins of the present security classification system, according to the Irvine study, date to the World War I period, when a 1917 General Order of the American Expeditionary Force in France established classifications of "Confidential," "Secret," and "For Official Circulation Only," patterned after the British and French classification procedures. A more formal system was created by Army regulation in 1921 and amended in 1935. On the eve of World War II President Roosevelt issued the first Executive Order (E.O. 8381) governing the classification of certain "vital military and naval installations and equipment," including maps, photographs, drawings, models, plans, contracts or specifications, and similar types of defense information. President Truman issued Executive Order 10104 in 1950, updating the previous order.

A government-wide regulation dealing with security classification was issued in September 1942 by the Office of War Information (OWI) under au-

---

7. Title 5, Sec. 552(b) (1), U.S. Code.
8. See U.S., National Archives, "Origin of Defense-Information Markings in the Army and Former War Department," prepared by Dallas Irvine, December 23, 1964. The other historical examples cited below are taken from this study.

thority vested by Executive Orders 9103 and 9182.[9] The regulation, a fore-runner of subsequent classification Executive Orders, provided definitions of classified information—"Secret," "Confidential," and "Restricted"—and designated authority to classify. It contained provisions warning against overclassification and provided instructions for the identification of classified information, for its proper dissemination and handling. During the following year the OWI created the Security Advisory Board (SAB), consisting of Army and Navy officers charged with responsibilities as "an advisory and coordinating board in all matters relating to carrying out the provisions of OWI Regulation No. 4." An SAB coordinating committee, which included representation from the State Department as well, was later appointed.

It is important to emphasize that throughout this early period of the development of formal security classification procedures, such directives, regulations, or Executive Orders applied to the safeguarding of military secrets, rarely extending to either secrets affecting related non-military agencies or those involving foreign policy or diplomatic relations. Non-military agencies, as well as the State Department, relied mainly on their own internal procedures, and until 1958 had relied generally upon the 1789 Housekeeping Statute mentioned earlier as the basis for withholding vast amounts of classified and unclassified information from public disclosure.

Executive Order 10290, issued by President Truman in 1951, formalized and extended the security classification system to non-military agencies. Under its provisions *any* Executive department or agency was given authority to classify "official information the safeguarding of which is necessary in the interest of national security, and which is classified for such purposes by appropriate classifying authority." The Truman order was strongly criticized by some segments of the press and by Members of Congress because of its vagueness and its potential for imposing dangerous government censorship policies in violation of First Amendment rights under the Constitution. Legislation was introduced in the Congress to "prohibit unreasonable suppression of information by the Executive branch of the Government"—legislation which, if it had been enacted, would in effect have repealed the Executive Order.

This order was superseded in 1953 by President Eisenhower's issuance of Executive Order 10501. With the addition of several important amendments by President Kennedy in 1961, this order served as the basis for our classification system until March of 1972. The 1953 order reduced the number of agencies authorized to classify "national defense information" and redefined the use of the three classification categories—"Top Secret," "Se-

---

9. U.S., Office of War Information Regulation No. 4, issued September 28, 1942; amended November 13, 1942.

cret," and "Confidential." It also provided for a twelve-year "Top Secret" classification limit, with certain exceptions, and for declassification
procedures.

INITIAL INQUIRIES INTO CLASSIFICATION POLICIES

In July 1956 the newly created Special Subcommittee on Government Information, under the chairmanship of Representative Moss, began a two-
year series of hearings into all aspects of information policies and practices
of Federal departments and agencies. The Subcommittee concentrated
heavily on Defense Department information activities, which had been
the subject of considerable criticism by Members of Congress and the public media.

Soon after these hearings commenced, Defense Secretary C. E. Wilson
named a five-member Committee on Classified Information, headed by
Charles A. Coolidge, a former Assistant Secretary of Defense. Pentagon
leaks appearing in the press earlier that year revealed basic disagreements
among the various military services over their respective roles and missions
in the atomic-missile era, and had thus triggered the creation of the Coolidge Committee. This Committee was charged with reviewing "present
laws, Executive Orders, Department of Defense regulations and directives
pertaining to the classification of information and the safeguarding of classified information, to evaluate the adequacy and effectiveness of such documents."[10] At the urging of Chairman Moss the Committee was subsequently
directed also to examine such matters as overclassification and the arbitrary
withholding of information from the public and the Congress.

After a three-month study the Coolidge Committee concluded that the
two chief shortcomings in the operation of the security classification system
were "overclassification and deliberate unauthorized disclosures." The report stated also that it had found "a tendency on the part of Pentagon officials to 'play it safe' and overclassify"; also an abuse of security in the classification of administrative matters, attempts to "classify the unclassifiable,"
confusion from basing security on shifting foreign policy, and a failure to
declassify material which no longer required a secrecy label.[11] The committee also made a number of important recommendations for improving the
classification system but did not propose penalties or disciplinary action in

---

10. U.S., House of Representatives, 85th Cong., 1st sess., House Committee on Government Operations, Foreign Operations, and Government Information Subcommittee,
Hearings, "Availability of Information from Federal Departments and Agencies,"
Part 8, submitted by the Department of Defense, p. 2146.
11. For full text of Coolidge Committee report and recommendations cited here, see
the above *Hearings,* pp. 2133–46.

cases of misuse or abuse of classification procedures. This resulted in the issuance of newer, streamlined versions of Defense Department regulations implementing the provisions of Executive Order 10501.

Overlapping the work of the Coolidge Committee and the Subcommittee's hearings was that of another group established by the Congress in 1955: the Commission on Government Security. It became known as the Wright Commission for its chairman, attorney Loyd Wright of Los Angeles, former president of the American Bar Association. Its mandate— much broader than that of the Coolidge Committee—included the study of the entire national security program in all departments and agencies. In addition to the document classification system, it covered such areas as industrial security, government personnel security, immigration and nationality programs, port security, and related fields. It must be remembered that the Wright Commission was created immediately following Senator Joseph McCarthy's broadside attacks on alleged Communist infiltration of government agencies, which he claimed was caused, in part, by weaknesses in our military establishment and security system.

In its June 1957 report the Wright Commission stated that its review of the operation of Executive Order 10501 had revealed that some 1.5 million government employees were authorized to classify documents, and it recommended a reduction in such numbers. It found also that the overuse of the "Confidential" label restricted the free exchange of information in the scientific and technological areas, thus retarding progress necessary to our national security. Further, it recommended the creation of document classification training programs and a statutory "Central Security Office having review and advisory functions with respect to the Federal document classification program and to make recommendations for its improvement as needed."[12]

The most controversial portion of the Wright Commission recommendations was its proposal urging the Congress to "enact legislation making it a crime for any person willfully to disclose without proper authorization, for any purpose whatever, information classified Secret or Top Secret, knowing, or having reasonable grounds to believe, such information to have been so classified."[13] The recommended bill would impose a $10,000 fine and a jail term of up to five years on anyone convicted of violating its provisions. The Commission made it clear that its proposal was aimed at persons outside of government—newsmen, for example. The recommendation was soundly criticized by the press in articles and editorials. One pointed out

---

12. The complete text of Report of the Commission on Government Security was published in June 1957 by Washington, D.C.: U.S., Government Printing Office, 1957.
13. For full text of the proposed bill, see above Report, p. 737. The measure was never introduced or considered by the Congress.

that it would have resulted in the prosecution of even the reporter who uncovered the Teapot Dome scandal during the 1920's.

In June 1958 the Special Government Information Subcommittee issued its report on the hearings and investigations of Defense Department information practices.[14] The conclusions and recommendations made some fifteen years ago (at this writing) on the basis of this exhaustive study pinpointed the major problems that subsequently toppled the system established in Executive Order 10501. Had the Subcommittee's recommendations for overhaul of the classification system been heeded and properly implemented, chances are that the security classification "mess" condemned by President Nixon in 1972 could have long since been corrected. Many of the Subcommittee's conclusions could have been written today. Thus, for example, in discussing the handling of information by the military establishment, the Committee concluded:

> Never before in our democratic form of government has the need for candor been so great. The Nation can no longer afford the danger of withholding information merely because the facts fail to fit a predetermined "policy." Withholding for any reasons other than true military security inevitably results in the loss of public confidence—or a greater tragedy. Unfortunately, in no other part of our Government has it been so easy to substitute secrecy for candor and to equate suppression with security.
>
> . . . In a conflict between the right to know and the need to protect true military secrets from a potential enemy, there can be no valid argument against secrecy. The right to know has suffered, however, in the confusion over the demarcation between secrecy for true security reasons and secrecy for "policy" reasons. The proper imposition of secrecy in some situations is a matter of judgment. Although an official faces disciplinary action for the failure to classify information which should be secret, no instance has been found of an official being disciplined for classifying material which should have been made public. The tendency to "play it safe" and use the secrecy stamp, has, therefore, been virtually inevitable.
>
> Abuse of the security classifications under Executive Order 10501 has been only one part of the unnecessary secrecy in violation of the right to know. Equally important—although entirely distinct—have been restrictions on information about the day-to-day operations of government, ineligible by any stretch of the imagination for secrecy labels on grounds of military security.[15]

In this same report and those based on later investigations of the classification system, our Committee repeatedly called upon top Executive officials

14. U.S., House of Representatives, 85th Cong., 2d sess., House Committee on Government Operations, House Report No. 1884, "Availability of Information from Federal Departments and Agencies," in *Twenty-seventh Report,* June 16, 1958.
15. *Ibid.,* p. 152.

—both Republican and Democrat—to institute effective disciplinary action in cases of overclassification or misclassification, as a means of tightening up the effectiveness of Executive Order 10501. We recommended also—and in the strongest possible terms—other administrative changes in the order to improve classification procedures; to reduce the number of government agencies and individual employees authorized to classify; to require identification of the individual classifier on the document so that responsibility could be placed in cases of abuse; to speed up the downgrading and declassification machinery; and to implement the appeals procedures of the order against misclassification.

Unfortunately, little was done by the Executive Branch to put these Congressional recommendations into effect—or even to take them seriously. The classification system, as historically operated, has always been a pet Executive Branch preserve. Thus, the mountain of classified documents continued to grow as thousands upon thousands of middle- and lower-echelon government bureaucrats pursued their "stamp happy" game. The inevitable was finally recognized early in 1971, as massive overclassification and other abuses of the system created a classification crisis and the virtual breakdown of our system. This realization and the resulting actions during 1971 and 1972 will be discussed later in this chapter.

DIMENSIONS OF THE CLASSIFICATION PROBLEM

During the controversy over the publication of portions of the Pentagon Papers by *The New York Times, The Washington Post,* and other newspapers in June of 1971, our Subcommittee undertook hearings into the basic issues involved—including First Amendment rights under the Constitution, the so-called doctrine of executive privilege, and the operation of the security classification system. It was then revealed that six months earlier—in January 1971—President Nixon had secretly directed that a review be made within the Executive Branch of ongoing security classification procedures. The study was undertaken by an interagency committee headed by then Assistant Attorney General William H. Rehnquist, who served until his appointment to the Supreme Court in December 1971.

A draft Executive Order to supersede President Eisenhower's Executive Order 10501 was subsequently completed by the Rehnquist committee early in 1972 and circulated for comment among affected agencies. After articles describing the provisions of the draft order had been published in February 1972 by *The Washington Post,* our Subcommittee asked the White House for a copy of the draft for informal study and comment, but the request was turned down.

Several weeks later, in a speech on the House floor, I warned against the premature issuance of a defective Executive Order and questioned the timing of the White House plan.[16] It appeared to many in the Congress that the new order was being issued to try to head off action by our Subcommittee in this field. The hearing plan, announced in January 1972, included some three months of testimony beginning early in March on the administration of the FOIA during the five-year period it had been in effect, including an investigation of the relation between the Act and the security classification system.

President Nixon issued the new security classification Executive Order 11652 on March 8, 1972—just two days after the Subcommittee's hearings began. It carried a June 1, 1972, effective date.[17]

BASIC POLICY CONSIDERATIONS

President Nixon expressed eloquently the basic public policy and Constitutional issues involved in the security classification problem in his statement accompanying the new order.

> The many abuses of the security system [he wrote] can no longer be tolerated. Fundamental to our way of life is the belief that when information which properly belongs to the public is systematically withheld by those in power, the people soon become ignorant of their own affairs, distrustful of those who manage them, and—eventually—incapable of determining their own destinies.
>
> Yet since the early days of the Republic, Americans have also recognized that the Federal Government is obliged to protect certain information which might otherwise jeopardize the security of the country. That need has become particularly acute in recent years as the United States has assumed a powerful position in world affairs, and as world peace has come to depend in large part on how that position is safeguarded. We are also moving into an era of delicate negotiations in which it will be especially important that governments be able to communicate in confidence.
>
> Clearly, the two principles of an informed public and of confidentiality within the Government are irreconcilable in their purest forms, and a balance must be struck between them.[18]

---

16. *Congressional Record,* 92d Cong., 2d sess. (March 1, 1972), vol. 118, p. H1637.
17. 37 *Fed. Reg.,* no. 48 (March 10, 1972), pp. 5209-18.
18. The statement, the Executive Order 11652, the implementing directive by the National Security Council, and various departmental and agency regulations issued subsequently may be found in U.S., House of Representatives, 92d Congress, 2d session, House Committee on Government Operations, Foreign Operations, and Government Information Subcommittee, *Hearings,* Part 7, May 1972, "U.S. Government Information Policies and Practices—Security Classification Problems involving Subsection (b) (1) of the Freedom of Information Act," pp. 2309 *et seq.*

His statement included also a strong indictment of the classification system as it had operated for almost twenty years under Executive Order 10501. As he went on to assert:

> Unfortunately, the system of classification which has evolved in the United States has failed to meet the standards of an open and democratic society, allowing too many papers to be classified for too long a time. The controls which have been imposed on classification authority have proved unworkable, and classification has frequently served to conceal bureaucratic mistakes or to prevent embarrassment to officials and administration. . . .

VOLUME OF CLASSIFIED INFORMATION

Some insight can be gained concerning the dimension of the security classification mess by considering the tremendous volume of classified material that has accumulated over the years. No one really knows the precise volume, but a number of expert witnesses who testified before our Subcommittee provided revealing estimates.

William G. Florence, a retired Air Force security classification official, estimated that the Defense Department had at least twenty million classified documents, including reproduced copies, and that in his judgment more than 99 per cent of them did not warrant security classification protection under a strict interpretation of definitions of the Executive Order.[19] Another witness, former U.N. Ambassador and Supreme Court Justice Arthur J. Goldberg, testified that in his judgment and experience, "75 per cent of these documents should never have been classified in the first place; another 15 per cent quickly outlived the need for secrecy; and only about 10 per cent genuinely required restricted access over any significant period of time.[20]

A Defense Department witness could not verify Mr. Florence's twenty-million figure but estimated that there were perhaps some six million cubic feet of documents in Department of Defense files—both classified and unclassified. He said that an Air Force study showed that about 17 per cent of its total volume of documents were classified, so that if this same percentage estimate were applied generally, it would mean that Defense had about one million cubic feet of classified documents.[21] When translated into linear feet at two thousand pages per linear foot, the classified holdings would make eighteen stacks of classified document pages, *each as high as*

---

19. *Ibid., Hearings,* Part 1, June 1971, "U.S. Government Information Policies and Practices—The Pentagon Papers (Part 1)," p. 97.
20. *Ibid.,* p. 12.
21. *Ibid.,* Part 2, June 1971, p. 658.

the Washington Monument! A State Department witness estimated that his department had about 150 million documents in files and that about 35 million of them were classified. Dr. James B. Rhoads, Archivist of the United States, testified that the National Archives is responsible for the staggering total of *some 470 million pages of classified documents.* Some 172 million pages are from the World War II years, 150 million from the 1946–50 period, and another 148 million cover the 1950–54 years.[22]

A 1971 Subcommittee study revealed that some fifty-five thousand government officials were authorized to classify documents "Top Secret," "Secret," or "Confidential" under the provisions of the old Executive Order 10501.[23] This total represents employees of some thirty-eight Federal departments and agencies. The top official of another thirteen agencies not closely related to the national defense also had classification authority under the old order. The Department of Defense alone had some thirty-thousand officers and employees with classification authority.

LACK OF ENFORCEMENT

The Subcommittee's investigation showed also that existing administrative penalties against overclassification were ignored by Executive departments and agencies. Over a four-year period these agencies carried out 2,433 investigations of violations of regulations governing the security classification system under Executive Order 10501, and assessed administrative penalties—ranging from reprimands to loss of pay—against 2,504 individual employees involved in these investigations. But only two of the investigations involved cases of overclassification, and not a single administrative penalty was imposed against overclassification.[24]

This shocking failure to apply sanctions against overclassification—one of the most often mentioned causes of the breakdown of the classification system under Executive Order 10501, and the subject of repeated Committee recommendations—is also a direct violation of the basic intent of the order. Section 3 clearly specified that "Unnecessary classification and overclassification shall be scrupulously avoided." Similar language is found also in the new Executive Order 11652 issued by President Nixon; but if enforcement is as lax under the new order as under the old, it is already doomed to failure.

---

22. *Ibid.*, Part 7, May 1972, p. 2605.
23. *Ibid.*, pp. 2283–84; 2723–2820.
24. *Ibid., Hearings,* Part 4, March 1972, "U.S. Government Information Policies and Practices—Administration and Operation of the Freedom of Information Act," pp. 1332–43.

SECURITY CLASSIFICATION COSTS

At our Subcommittee's request the General Accounting Office undertook a study to determine the estimated costs of the security classification system. The study, completed early in 1972 (B-173474),[25] was based on estimated costs of four departments and agencies having extensive classified business— the Departments of State and Defense, the Atomic Energy Commission, and the National Aeronautics and Space Administration. Items included in the GAO cost study included all aspects of security classification: management and policy, classification and declassification procedures, training, transmitting, safeguarding, and enforcing security policies, counterintelligence activities related to document security, and the costs of personnel security investigations.

The total, as estimated by the GAO in this study, was $126.3 million annually, including some $66.1 million for personnel security investigations. But this total is only a fraction of the total expenditures since it covers only four departments and agencies out of the twenty-five authorized to classify and moreover did not include security costs associated with the performance of government-classified contracts, which costs the respondents said could not be isolated, but are estimated to be some $49,000,000 in the Defense Department alone. Others did not furnish GAO with all the cost data requested, so that the total for these four departments and agencies alone could conservatively be expected to reach about $200,000,000 a year.

MAJOR FEATURES OF EXECUTIVE ORDER 11652

As described in President Nixon's March 8, 1972, statement, the "most significant features" of the new order were the following:

—The rules for classifying documents are more restrictive.

—The number of departments and people who can originally classify information has been substantially reduced.

—Timetables ranging from six to ten years have been set for the automatic declassification of documents. Exceptions will be allowed only for such information as falls within four specifically defined categories.

—Any document exempted from automatic declassification will be subject to mandatory review after a ten-year period. Thus, for the first time, a private citizen is given a clear right to have national security information reviewed on the basis of specified criteria to determine if continued classification is

---

25. *Ibid., Hearings,* Part 7, May 1972, pp. 2286–93.

warranted, so long as the document can be adequately identified and obtained by the Government with a reasonable amount of effort.

—If information is still classified thirty years after origination, it will then be automatically declassified unless the head of the originating department determines in writing that its continued protection is still necessary and he sets a time for declassification.

—Sanctions may be imposed upon those who abuse the system.

—And a continuing monitoring process will be set up under the National Security Council and an Interagency Classification Review Committee, whose chairman is to be appointed by the President.

"MAJOR DEFECTS" IN NEW ORDER

A Subcommittee staff analysis, providing a detailed section-by-section comparison of the text of the old and new orders, pointed out what we characterized as "major defects and technical errors in the new order."[26] Executive Branch witnesses who subsequently testified in May 1972 on the provisions of the new order were asked to address their remarks in rebuttal to the allegations of defects and errors we had made in this analysis. Despite the fact that they had some six weeks to review the analysis, most of the witnesses did not choose to deal directly with these points of contention in their prepared statements. Nonetheless, a number of the most important of these disputed sections of the new order were discussed during cross-examination of the Executive Branch witnesses. They included controversy over such areas as the following:

—Lack of provisions to assure adequate Congressional oversight into the administration of the new order, since major responsibility for its operation and enforcement is vested in the National Security Council and the Interagency Classification Review Committee. In May 1972 NSC officials refused to testify before the Subcommittee on technical details of the new order, and such officials have been virtually immune to Congressional inquiry because of the exercise of so-called executive privilege.

—Reasons for the application of security-classification to matters involving "national defense and foreign relations," now defined as "national security." The old order used the term "national defense and foreign policy"—language identical to the exemption provision of the FOIA. Subcommittee Members questioned the intent of the terminology change, which some interpreted as broadening the coverage, and also raised legal questions because of its conflict with the statutory language of the FOIA.

---

26. *Congressional Record*, 92d Cong., 2d sess. (March 21, 1972), vol. 118, pp. E2774 *et seq.*

—Lack of specific sanctions against unnecessary classification or overclassification, which has been noted earlier to be a basic weakness in the operation of all previous Executive Orders.

—The potential of the new 10–8–6-year declassification schedule, with its
loopholes, to work to the political advantage of an incumbent Administration by hiding grievous mistakes in defense or foreign policy, thus protecting
any President for his full eight years in office—if re-elected—and then making it possible for these same mistakes to continue to be hidden well into
the first term of the successor (if he should be of the same political party).

—Legitimization of dozens of so-called "control or access" markings applied
heretofore without specific Executive Order authorization by most agencies
—stamped on both classified and unclassified documents. The encouragement of proliferation of such distribution-control markings may have the
effect of diluting the integrity of the entire system. The use of such stamps
as "For Official Use Only," "Nodis," "Limdis," "Crypto," or "Noforn" is intended to limit the distribution of documents to certain selected officials.[27]
It may also be used by political appointees in a department to deny information to career officials, thus abusing the need-to-know principle. It may likewise be an attempt by the Administration to get better control over information leaking outside of the Executive.

—Loopholes inherent in the language of the new Executive Order in the so-
called "ten-year mandatory review" provisions affecting classified information subject to the exemptions from downgrading because of its intelligence,
cryptographic, or other sensitivity. Under these provisions any individual
may request a "classification review" ten years after a document's date of
original classification. But the request for the document must describe it
"with sufficient particularity" to enable identification, and it must be obtain-
able by the affected department with only a "reasonable amount of effort."
Since the reviewing Executive department is both the judge and jury of
these requests, some Subcommittee members are skeptical about the
amounts of information that will be disclosed under this provision. Similar
loopholes or "escape clauses" in the thirty-year "automatic declassification"
procedures are viewed in the same manner.

This skepticism was reinforced by a November 1972 article in *The York
Times* summarizing the efforts of that newspaper and of various historians
and scholars who have sought access to classified materials more than ten
years old. As the article states,

> President Nixon's pledge "to lift the veil of secrecy" from needlessly classi-
> fied official papers is being throttled by bureaucratic confusion, timidity and
> prohibitive costs, in the opinion of historians, other scholars, and newsmen.

---

27. Such terms are abbreviations; for example, "Nodis" means no distribution;
"Limdis," limited distribution; "Crypto," cryptographic material; "Noforn," no distribution to officials of foreign governments.

Five months after the President's order on June 1, directing a freer flow of information to the public from secret and confidential papers more than 10 years old, the output is still no more than a trickle. More requests for documents have been denied or labeled "pending" than have been granted. . . .[28]

LAG IN IMPLEMENTATION

Another of the Subcommittee's criticisms was directed at the time lag in drafting the National Security Council's guideline directive to affected departments and agencies for the implementation of the new order. This lag caused a 64-day delay in the issuance of the first regulations to put the order into effect after its June 1, 1972, effective date. There was no "savings clause" in Executive Order 11652 under which the old order might continue to function until the new order could be fully implemented.

Our Subcommittee hearings in May 1972 on the implementation actions being taken by the NSC and by affected departments and agencies revealed serious problems occasioned by the hurried issuance of the new order. I therefore called upon President Nixon to suspend its effective date to assure adequate time to prepare implementing guidelines properly, to provide for the timely issuance of departmental regulations, to disseminate them to our military and diplomatic posts around the world, and to instruct officials on the new procedures to be followed.[29] The White House ignored this request also, and the first departmental regulations were not issued until August 3, 1972—more than two months after the effective date of the new order. As of the end of December 1972—six months after the effective date of the new order—twenty-one of the twenty-five affected departments, agencies, and offices possessing classification authority have issued their regulations. Eight of these were promulgated during the month of December.

Thus, a complex administrative and perhaps legal tangle has been allowed to develop. Questions have been raised concerning the legal effect of documents classified during this hiatus period—after June 1, the effective date of the new order, and before the issuance of regulations governing its implementation. During this period the Subcommittee has been furnished classified documents as part of its regular foreign operations oversight functions. We were surprised to see that the State Department was using *both* the new and old classification markings, classified under *different* procedures—*after* the legal authority had expired in one case and *before* the proper regulations had been issued to govern such classification in the other case.

---

28. *The New York Times,* November 22, 1972, p. 40.
29. *Congressional Record,* 92d Cong., 2d sess. (May 3, 1972), vol. 118, pp. H4096-97.

This confusion over the parallel operation of two separate classification systems during this hiatus period is obvious. We can only speculate about the effect of this blunder on the over-all security of our classification system and on the nature of the administrative jungle that has been created by the questionable classification status of perhaps hundreds of thousands of documents marked during this hiatus period. It may take months or even years to untangle—hardly an auspicious start for the new Executive Order.

HISTORICAL RESEARCH

The new Executive Order, along with President Nixon's collateral order to the State Department to update the publication of the *Foreign Relations* series of official diplomatic records and papers, has received considerable attention in the academic community. This valuable series, heavily relied upon by scholars for source material, is now published through 1946, and the President gave instructions to reduce the time lag to twenty years by 1975. The Department subsequently requested additional funds from the Congress to speed up the job.

The importance of scholarly research access to historical classified information cannot be overemphasized. One Subcommittee witness, Lloyd C. Gardner, chairman of the history department at Rutgers University, outlined the important service performed by historians and other scholars in our democratic society. As he observed,

> Nations, like individuals, depend in part upon memory in order to be able to function rationally in the present. Historians are to a degree responsible for what stands out in a nation's memory: they supply experience longer than one generation's lifespan, and broader than that of any group of individuals.
>
> As one approaches the present, the historian's most valuable asset, perspective, is diminished chronologically, and in a secrecy-conscious nation, by the lack of available evidence as well.
>
> The Nation's memory is thus weakest for the years of the recent past, a serious defect, unless one is prepared to concede that the public should reach its conclusions on the basis of little or no information, or that the policymaker is the only one who needs the memory.[30]

During the past several years the secrecy policies of the U.S. Government have become more and more a matter of public attention and concern. As historians, political scientists, journalists, and others have become more interested in the study and analysis of contemporary foreign policy and recent

---

30. Foreign Operations and Government Information Subcommittee, *Hearings, op. cit.,* Part 7, May 1972, p. 2657.

diplomatic history, they have protested governmental restrictions on study and research of official records. A recent report by Carol M. Baker and Matthew H. Fox, dealing with scholars' access to government documents, describes the broad scope of the problem in some detail:

> In essence, the security classification system and other restrictions on access to records permit government officials to control the flow of information to the public. The executive departments, particularly the presidency, can dominate the headlines with official pronouncements, news releases, press conferences, and publication of documents. An administration can even "blow the lid" on its own secrecy, as shown by President Nixon's recent disclosure of the secret negotiations with the North Vietnamese. Off-the-record briefings and leaks to the press permit officials to discuss policy and events—often without taking responsibility for what they reveal. Former officials publish memoirs of their years in office; government departments issue their own histories of significant events; favored scholars and journalists are sometimes given access to official records that remain off limits to others.
>
> In each case, officials or former officials exercise discretion in choosing what to reveal and what to conceal. As a consequence, the public must rely on sources that have some vested interest in the information that is given out.
>
> What the public has not received—or has waited decades for—are accounts of government operations based on firsthand records and commentaries by detached observers. The State Department, which has maintained a thirty-year limit on classification of its files, did not make the official record of American diplomacy in World War II available to the general public until January 1972. The documents on most of our Cold War diplomacy remain in closed files. The Joint Chiefs of Staff have only recently opened segments of their World War II records, and their postwar files are unavailable for any non-official purpose. Few Army records from the post-1945 period are available to unofficial researchers even on a restricted basis. Researchers at the Truman Library in Independence, Missouri, still cannot use some of the secret documents on which Mr. Truman based his memoirs, published in 1958.[31]

Few would argue with the general premise concerning the Government's general obligation to avoid carrying out its sensitive operations in a "goldfish bowl," particularly in these days of international tension. Certainly there can be overwhelming public support for the President's broad policy statement:

> Within the Federal Government there is some official information and material which, because it bears directly on the effectiveness of our national de-

---

31. Carol Baker and Matthew Fox, *Classified Files: The Yellowing Pages* (New York: Twentieth Century Fund, 1972), pp. 4-5.

fense and the conduct of our foreign relations, must be subject to some constraints for the security of our Nation and the safety of our people and our allies. To protect against actions hostile to the United States, of both overt and covert nature, it is essential that such official information and material be given only limited dissemination.[32]

Such a statement is even more readily acceptable when it is placed within the context of the first paragraph of Executive Order 11652:

> The interests of the United States and its citizens are best served by making information regarding the affairs of Government readily available to the public. This concept of an informed citizenry is reflected in the Freedom of Information Act and in the current public information policies of the executive branch.

As the historian Arthur Schlesinger, Jr., pointed out in a recent article, "The functioning of democracy requires some rough but rational balance between secrecy and disclosure, between official control of information and public need for it." Mr. Schlesinger also cited Supreme Court Justice Potter Stewart's view that "secrecy can be preserved only when credibility is truly maintained."[33]

SECURITY CLASSIFICATION REFORM PRINCIPLES

On the basis of our Subcommittee's long experience in oversight functions involving the security classification system, there emerge certain basic principles that should serve as a guide for any effective reform of security classification procedures, whether by statute or by Executive Order. Such a system must be designed to protect our vital national defense secrets and the confidentiality of our dealings with foreign nations, and also must safeguard the right of the Congress and of the public to be fully informed on the policies of our Government.

A basic guiding principle is that our nation is strengthened wherever and whenever the people are informed on matters involving our international commitments and defense posture to the maximum extent consistent with overriding security requirements. Our fundamental liberties are endangered when abuses occur in the classification system. Information is essential to knowledge about the real impact of governmental decisions—nationally and internationally—and knowledge is the basis for political power, which must,

---

32. Foreign Operations and Government Information Subcommittee, *Hearings, ibid.,* p. 2297.
33. 37 *Fed. Reg.,* no. 48 (March 10, 1972), p. 5209.

in our representative system, always reside firmly in the hands of the American people.

Another basic principle involves the integrity and efficiency of any classification system. Any such system ultimately rests in large part on the proper use of classification definition categories (sparsely utilizing the higher category when a lower one will suffice). Good classification judgment can make certain that unnecessary classification of marginal information, and overclassification of all other information, will be strictly avoided. Obviously, when the mass of classified information reaches the staggering total of billions of pages, there can no longer be the degree of respect or selectivity upon which classification markings depend for their integrity. To the extent that any classification system does not severely punish those of its participating officials who abuse the system, who classify unnecessarily, or who "play it safe" by overclassifying, it adds immeasurably to the proliferation of classified documents. This gradually but surely weakens and eventually destroys the integrity and effectiveness of the system.

Another essential principle for the efficient operation of the system is the procedures established for downgrading and rapid declassification of all classified information when the need for its protection has ceased to exist. Such circumstances are not so much measurable in time periods as they are geared to the rapidly moving sequence of events involving scientific development, defense technology, weapons systems, diplomatic situations, and the like. Vast amounts of classified information fall into these categories, which often have relatively short periods of security safeguard requirements. For example, scientific data connected with the operational characteristics of the radar system on an Air Force night fighter-plane might not require the same level of classification protection if our intelligence sources confirm that such equipment had fallen undamaged into the hands of the North Vietnamese during the late hostilities.

An effective system must likewise have a sound mechanism for strictly limiting classification authority among Federal agencies involved in national defense and foreign policy matters, and among the key policy-making officials of those agencies. These officials must be identified on documents they classify, must be held strictly accountable for their classification judgments, and must be subject to discipline for abuse of their authority. Otherwise the system will be compromised and the volume of needlessly classified information will overwhelm those who stamp it.

Finally, an effective classification system must certainly have a sound and vigorously enforced mechanism for reviewing and policing its own operations to assure that the system does not abuse the people's right to know, compromise vital defense and foreign policy secrets, or founder in its own bureaucratic excesses. In the past administration of Executive Order versions of security classification systems, these and other basic criteria for successful operation of the system have been notably absent or have not been properly implemented or enforced.

The Atomic Energy Commission has, for many years, been the only agency of the Federal Government to have its own statutory classification system. It has operated in conjunction with the Executive Orders in an efficient manner and has provided for a maximum degree of continuing review of classified information of a highly sensitive nature for declassification purposes. The result has been the systematic declassification of some 650,000 classified documents in the past year alone.[34] I submit that if such an agency as the AEC can operate under a statutory system—and operate well—then the Congress can, in its wisdom, devise a broader statutory classification system to apply to all Executive departments and agencies.

CLASSIFICATION LAW PROPOSED

It is my considered judgment that the only ultimate solution of the classification dilemma—both administratively and philosophically—is the enactment of a workable, efficient, enforceable law to create a new system that meets the basic criteria I have described above. At the conclusion of the Subcommittee's classification hearings in 1972, I introduced legislation based on such principles. After review by a number of leading classification authorities, the measure was improved and reintroduced in 1973. The bill would establish what I feel is a sound and workable statutory system to govern our security classification procedures, operations, and enforcement, replacing the present Executive Order system. It strives to strike that delicate balance between the conflicting needs of the Executive in the conduct of sensitive defense and foreign policy affairs, the Congress in the carrying out of its Constitutional duties in these areas, and the public as a whole in its need to be informed to the maximum extent consistent with our national interest.

A key feature of the legislation is the creation of an independent, nine-member Classification Review Commission with broad regulatory and quasi-adjudicatory authority over the operation of the nation's security classification system. It would have also the responsibility of settling disputes between the Congress and the Executive over access to classified information requested by the Congress or the Comptroller General of the United States. Other provisions of the classification bill may be summarized as follows:

---

34. Foreign Operations and Government Information Subcommittee, *ibid.*, p. 2577.

—It strictly confines classification of national defense information to "Top Secret," "Secret," and "Confidential," depending on the level of damage to the national defense that would be caused by its unauthorized disclosure.

—It limits original "Top Secret" classification to only the Departments of State, Defense (including the Army, Navy, and Air Force), the Central Intelligence Agency, the Atomic Energy Commission, and designated offices within the Executive Office of the President.

—It limits original "Secret" classification to only departments and agencies listed above and the Departments of Justice, Treasury, and Transportation.

—It limits original "Confidential" classification to the departments and agencies listed above and the Department of Commerce and the National Aeronautics and Space Administration.

—It provides for a strict limitation upon those top officials in each of the departments and agencies listed above as to who can exercise the authority to classify information. Such officials shall be held fully accountable and shall be subject to reprimand and other disciplinary action for overclassification or other violations of regulations.

—It requires a three-year downgrading procedure for most types of classified national defense information: one year from "Top Secret" to "Secret," one year from "Secret" to "Confidential," and one year from "Confidential" to a declassified state and transfer to the National Archives, where it would then be subject to disclosure provisions of the FOIA.

—It authorizes a procedural "savings clause" that could be applied narrowly to certain types of highly sensitive national defense information when invoked by the Executive department or the President, subject to the approval of the independent Classification Review Commission created under the legislation.

—It provides that national defense information previously classified is subject to an automatic declassification procedure after a period of fifteen years, except for highly sensitive data subject to the "savings clause" procedure.

This legislation, if enacted, would establish a sound, flexible statutory system to deal effectively with the dual need to safeguard our truly vital defense and foreign policy secrets, while assuring the Congress and the public access to information required to preserve our representative system of government. The mechanism created by the independent Classification Review Commission would guarantee that the "tilt" would always be toward disclosure.

SUMMARY

To summarize the basic aspects of this complex subject:

Government secrecy is not a new problem nor was it invented by the present Administration. Some confidentiality in the affairs of government, particularly involving the diplomatic and defense areas, has always been necessary. But the emerging global U.S. leadership role since World War II and the periods of international tension during the past twenty-five years have created a new dimensional scope in U.S. secrety requirements. It has spawned a new level of more formalized classification systems, has resulted in an increasingly complex maze of administrative problems, and has caused new pressures in the seemingly irreconcilable area of secrecy requirements vis-à-vis the public's right to know.

In our representative democracy, the classification system must achieve a proper balance between adequate protection of our truly vital security needs, and a sufficient flow of information to the Congress and the public. Such a flow is necessary to maintain the essential degree of credibility toward our governmental system and our elected and appointed officials. Down through our history, no national Administration has been able to resist the overwhelming political pressures to classify information in order to withhold it from the public and the Congress. The tendency of Administrations in power to use every means to prevent embarrassment, scandal, blunders, and the resulting political consequences is a bipartisan one. Yet no President has totally escaped the political embarrassment of leaked information thought safely hidden away in the dark corners of the Federal bureaucracy. The public's confidence in government at all levels is currently at its lowest ebb in our history. Terms such as the "credibility gap," "government secrecy abuses," "news management," or "the government propaganda machine" have been used over the past few years to describe this increasing trend toward the people's disbelief in government information and in statements by government officials.

Past efforts to construct and operate a workable, flexible, and administratively sound security classification system through an Executive Order mechanism that would also fulfill the basic objectives of our representative system have been made during the past four Administrations and they have failed. While the new Executive Order 11652 has been touted as "the first major overhaul of our classification system since 1953," and does attempt to deal with some of the worst defects in the system, there are serious doubts in the minds of many experts that this or any Executive Order can possibly do the job necessary. As has been discussed earlier, a number of its key provisions have been subject to considerable question because of their design, problems of interpretation, and procedural shortcomings.

Some progress, however, has been claimed for the new Executive Order 11652. In Executive departments and agencies there has been an announced reduction of some twenty-seven thousand persons who are authorized to classify under the new order—a drop of 63 per cent. The number of departments, agencies, and offices authorized to classify has been cut to twenty-five, and the Interagency Classification Review Committee, headed by Ambassador John Eisenhower, has been created to monitor the administration of the new order.

The new order itself makes an effort to tighten up the security classification categories and to promote the speedier downgrading and declassification of information; it also makes a slight reduction—from twelve to ten years—in the length of the normal declassification schedule from the "Top Secret" level. But oversight work undertaken thus far by the Subcommittee on the operation of the new order confirms other public observations that it was oversold and that it has already bogged down in the same administrative morass as its predecessors.

It is my view, as well as that of experts in the classification field, that the Congress must ultimately assert its authority to enact legislation providing clear legal guidelines in the classification, declassification, and safeguarding of information vital to our national defense and foreign policy interests. The Congress has the overriding Constitutional responsibility to take such action, as well as the duty to ensure that fundamental guarantees of the public's right-to-know are written into any such legislation.

7

The Cannikin Papers:
A Case Study
in Freedom of Information

REPRESENTATIVE PATSY T. MINK

On November 9, 1972, the United States Supreme Court made legal history by hearing oral arguments in a relatively obscure case with the potential for drastically curbing the Executive Branch's ability to withhold embarrassing or dangerous data. The case, now popularly dubbed the "Mink case," involved attempts by Congressmen to obtain government information on the 1971 nuclear test "Cannikin."[1]

This was the first time a case invoking the Freedom of Information Act had reached the nation's highest tribunal. The Congressmen hoped that ultimately a favorable disposition of the case would put new teeth into the 1966 Act, which generally requires the disclosure of government information but exempts some data from mandatory release on national security and other grounds. These exemptions have been interpreted so broadly by the Executive Branch as to render the Act almost meaningless. Indeed, in the *Mink* case, the Executive made the rather frightening assertion that the President has the sole, absolute right to specify which data are protected from disclosure by the Act's exemptions. In effect the President enunciated a new doctrine of immunity from judicial scrutiny equal to the Fifth Amendment protection against self-incrimination but not actually written into the Constitution. This claim that the courts lack authority to examine

Congresswoman Mink (D–Hawaii) is a member of the Committee on Education and Labor and Members of Congress for Peace Through Law (Chairman of U.S. China Committee). She was the litigant in an action before the Supreme Court in which she claimed the right by way of the Freedom of Information Act to secure information from the Executive Branch concerning certain effects of the Amchitka nuclear tests.
1. Mink *et al.* v. Environmental Protection Agency *et al.*, 464 F.2d 742 (D.C. Cir. 1971), 410 U.S. 73 (1973).

the Executive's actions is a key issue in the legal dispute. In advancing their arguments, the plaintiffs felt that if a Presidential dictum such as this did not sit well with the Justices, they might remind the President that the Executive is not the only branch of government and that even he must endure restraints on his powers.

Thus, while Cannikin's reverberations have long since ceased on the remote, windswept island of Amchitka in the Aleutian chain off Alaska, the aftereffects are still all-too-present for Washington officials who see a potent threat to their power to cover up mistakes or misdeeds under a cloak of official secrecy. Potentially, the strategy of conducting the test under hushed-up circumstances could backfire on the President even though Cannikin's success showed that there never was a need for concealment of adverse information or views.

EFFORTS OF CONGRESS TO FIND OUT ABOUT CANNIKIN

Apparently involved in the Executive's decision to withhold information on Cannikin were environmental questions as well as foreign policy considerations such as the objections of Japan and Canada to the uncomfortably close detonation of a nuclear blast having two hundred fifty times the explosive force of the first atomic bomb dropped on Hiroshima twenty-seven years earlier. There is, of course, an international treaty against atomic tests, but that did not cover underground explosions. In 1966 the Atomic Energy Commission decided that its Nevada test grounds were no longer suitable for the larger "events" planned in the future testing program. New sites were investigated; and finally in faraway Amchitka the AEC found what it wanted. The island, forty miles long and three to five miles wide, is in a sparsely populated region fourteen hundred miles southwest of Anchorage, Alaska, and seven hundred miles from Russia. An explosion of practically any size could be touched off at this remote location with no effect on anybody except the sea otters and other indigenous wildlife in the area.

The presence of considerable wildlife was, however, the cause of one small problem. By reason of the uniqueness of the natural ecosystem, Amchitka is part of the Aleutian Wildlife Refuge created by President Taft in 1913 in which, accordingly, small handguns were barred. But examination of Executive Order 1733 (which created the Refuge) disclosed a provision that "The establishment of this reservation shall not interfere with the use of the islands for . . . military . . . purposes."[2] The AEC declared that

---

2. U.S., National Archives, Executive Order 1733 of President William Howard Taft, March 3, 1913.

its plans for Amchitka were "fully in accord" with the basic charter of the Refuge.[3] Cannikin was designed to test a warhead for the ABM system, and that was definitely a military purpose. The U.S. Interior Department, the Federal agency responsible for administering the wildlife area, gave its concurrence.

There matters stood for several years while an army of more than a thousand construction workers and technicians was assembled on Amchitka for a remarkable engineering project. Hundreds of cylindrical steel casings up to ten feet in diameter were brought in from Seattle by barge while a huge drill rig labored night and day for many months to dig a hole straight down more than a mile into the earth. The steel casings were lowered in, one by one, to form a perfectly round shaft, an accomplishment that would have been a technical impossibility only a few years before. In October 1969 a "calibration experiment" of one megaton was touched off four thousand feet under Amchitka in a similar hole, and the lack of a major disaster was interpreted by the AEC as sufficient proof that the five-times-larger Cannikin could be safely detonated. Finally, all was in readiness to lower the Cannikin nuclear charge into its mile-deep hole, plug it with concrete, and touch off the blast while instruments measured the results.

Environmental and public officials, and concerned people of other nations joined in protest. Cannikin foes decried the threat to Amchitka's sea otters, bald eagles, Dolly Varden trout, and other wildlife. Commercial fishing interests warned of possible radioactive contamination of important fisheries in the nearby North Pacific and Bering Sea, used by the Japanese, Koreans, and Russians. Formal diplomatic protests were lodged by the Governments of Canada and Japan, which feared radioactive venting as a threat to their populations near by.

My opposition centered on the danger to the State of Hawaii from Cannikin. Amchitka Island is in a dangerous earthquake zone. It lies athwart a great earth fault running all along the Pacific Coast to California—where it is known as the San Andreas Fault—and beyond. By the AEC's own admission, Amchitka "is located near one of the earth's most seismically active regions." Many earthquakes have occured there, and the tension energy for another one might be building slowly within the earth, like a coiled spring poised for release. Would the detonation of a force of such great magnitude upset a delicate balance deep within the earth's crust? Unfortunately, there could be no way of predicting such a result until it had happened. Said the AEC: "Inasmuch as earthquake mechanisms are not completely understood, no absolute statement can be made about the possibility of triggering an earthquake of large magnitude in this area."[4] In other

---

3. U.S., Atomic Energy Commission, report, "Underground Nuclear Testing," September, 1969, p. 3.
4. *Ibid.,* p. 21.

words, the AEC could only hope for the best—an attitude which I did not feel was an adequate measure of our responsibility to the public interest.

The danger to Hawaii was not only in an earthquake, however, but also in a great ocean wave, or *tsunami,* that might be launched by it. Tsunamis occur when an earthquake shifts a great land mass on the ocean floor. This produces a large ripple of water on the ocean surface, and this can surge for thousands of miles across the open sea, often at speeds in excess of one hundred miles an hour. When channeled by certain coastal configurations such as exist in Hawaii, these waves or tsunamis can reach great heights and impact.

In the past, earthquakes occurring naturally in the Aleutian chain have spawned waves that inflicted massive destruction and loss of life. In 1964 an Aleutian earthquake triggered a tsunami that rolled across the Pacific and killed 173 persons in Hawaii and destroyed $25,000,000 in property. This happened again in 1967, and caused $3,000,000 damage to Hawaii. In 1964 a similar earthquake in Alaska touched off a tidal wave that killed twelve persons in Crescent City, California, and left four hundred families homeless. The people of my State could justifiably have deep apprehension about any deliberate human action that might reap such consequences. A 1968 report to the President on the safety of underground testing contained this warning: "The hazards of triggering an earthquake in the Aleutians are different from [the hazards of doing so in] Nevada. The triggered event may be larger in the Aleutians and it may excite a tsunami which could be destructive at great distances."[5]

Fueled by such statements by responsible scientists and experts as came to public attention, the opposition to Cannikin grew fiercer as the rumored time for the blast approached. Petitions began cascading into the White House. In Canada, thousands of protestors blocked border crossings. A coalition of environmental groups brought a suit to block the test. Pushed on an emergency basis, it went all the way to the U.S. Supreme Court, where it was rejected by a split vote on the morning of November 6, 1971, the day of the blast.

The fact that a government project of the size and multi-million-dollar cost of Cannikin requires at least a perfunctory degree of Congressional involvement gave opponents another chance at preventing the explosion. Authority for Cannikin operations had been routinely handled in legislation shepherded through the Congress under the tender care of the Joint Committee on Atomic Energy. Ordinarily, secret military projects like Cannikin are not fully disclosed to the Congress general membership. Despite this, when the AEC's authorization bill for fiscal year 1972 was to be voted on

---

5. *Ibid.,* "Report of the Ad Hoc Panel on the Safety of Underground Testing" (Dr. Kenneth S. Pitzer, Chairman; November 27, 1968), reproduced on p. 53.

July 15, 1971, I offered an amendment to the bill (H.R. 9388) to eliminate authority for the Cannikin test. The amendment was defeated by a vote of 27 to 70. A similar effort failed in the Senate, and the bill was enacted into law. Thus, the test program was authorized, and all that remained was to provide the appropriations, which requires separate legislation.

I resolved to offer another amendment against Cannikin when the AEC-Public Works appropriation bill carrying $19,700,000 in funds for the test was taken up in the House. This bill, H.R. 10090, was scheduled for floor action on July 29, 1971. Regrettably, there appeared little chance that a majority of members would change their minds from the vote taken on July 15. I had been unable to marshal sufficient evidence to document our concerns. All we had been able to do was state our fears and the opinions of the few scientists who had spoken out on the issue. In the face of a united stand in support of Cannikin by all the experts of the AEC, and stymied up by the unavailability of any compelling critical data, we were—to say the least—handicapped.

THE NEWS LEAK

It was at this rather unpromising juncture that we were given new hope by a venerable Washington institution known as the "news leak." On Monday, July 26, 1971, just three days before the second vote on Cannikin was to be taken on the House floor, the (Washington) *Evening Star* carried an article under the headline, "Agencies' Views Differ on Amchitka Blast."[6] Quoting anonymous sources, the article reported that "The White House has received conflicting recommendations from various government agencies on whether to go ahead this fall with an underground nuclear test on remote Amchitka Island," and further, that two agencies, the Department of Defense and AEC, favored a go-ahead for the test. Five others, the State Department, Office of Science and Technology, U.S. Information Agency, Environmental Protection Agency, and the Council on Environmental Quality, were described as recommending that Cannikin be either canceled or postponed. The Office of Science and Technology was said to feel that the nuclear warhead to be tested by Cannikin was already obsolete. All these recommendations were a product of a departmental Under Secretary-level committee named to investigate the controversy, the article said. The recommendations had reportedly gone directly to Dr. Henry Kissinger, the President's chief foreign policy adviser, and to Mr. John Ehrlichman, his chief domestic adviser.

---

6. News article, "Agencies' Views Differ on Amchitka Blast," *Evening Star* (Washington), July 26, 1971, p. B-10.

On reading the article I was shocked that criticism or opposition by five Federal agencies had been kept from public knowledge. These were not mere independent critics, but major branches of the U.S. Government itself, including the two agencies specifically created to protect the public environment. Apparently, someone within the Executive Branch felt obliged by conscience to "blow the whistle" on Cannikin just before the House vote, but could not do so officially. If these agencies, presumably having access to all the information denied to those of us on the "outside," had strong views against the test, this was indeed compelling reason why the issue should be re-examined by Congress.

I immediately began all efforts to obtain the documents or reports on which the article was based. I contacted each agency mentioned in the article as questioning Cannikin, requesting a copy of the materials, but in each case the answer was negative. One of the five agencies, the Department of State, sent a written reply to my telephone inquiry, stating that "it would not be appropriate for the Department of State or any other agency to make available to anyone outside the Executive Branch an internal study that was prepared for the President." Finally, on July 28, the day before the vote, I sent the following telegram directly to President Richard Nixon:

> Urgently request that Administration honor its many promises and obey law by providing Congress with vitally needed information so it can properly legislate. Need immediate release of recommendations and report by inter-departmental committee urging cancellation or postponement of under-ground nuclear test on Amchitka Island. Administration currently in violation of Freedom of Information Act by claiming material is classified as basis for refusal. Believe strongly that Congress entitled to know why the Environmental Protection Agency and Council on Environmental Quality opposed test. Continued secrecy on this aspect only helps to intensify public distrust of government.

No reply was received by the following day, and all I was able to do in debate on the appropriation bill was to quote from the news article about agency doubts on Cannikin. Offering my amendment to delete funds for the test, I told my colleagues, "All this week I have besieged all five of these departments plus the White House for the release of this important report. We are entitled to know the full official recommendations of these agencies. . . . This is another instance of the Administration's refusal to accord the right of Congress to know all the facts when considering legislation such as H.R. 10090 which is before us today."[7] Nevertheless, a majority remained unconvinced by a mere leaked news article. My amendment was de-

---

7. *Congressional Record,* 92d Cong., 1st sess. (July 29, 1971), vol. 117, pt. 21, 28081.

feated, although with a larger vote of 108 for and 275 opposed. And the bill moved on to the Senate.

On August 2, one John W. Dean III, then Counsel to the President, replied to my telegram with the following letter:

> This is to thank you and reply to the request which you made on July 28 for the release of agency recommendations on the proposed underground nuclear test at Amchitka Island in Alaska.
>
> These recommendations were prepared for the advice of the President and involve highly sensitive matter that is vital to our national defense and foreign policy. Therefore, I regret to inform you that they are not available for release.
>
> We appreciate your interest in this matter.

Plainly, this reply from the President exhausted the administrative remedies available to those who might want to see what were by now called the Cannikin Papers. It was at this point that I began contemplating the possibility of seeking court action to force release of these documents.

In the interim, on July 31 the Senate took up H.R. 10090, and efforts were made in that body to restrict the use of funds for Cannikin. Ultimately a compromise amendment was adopted by the Senate to prohibit the use of funds appropriated by the bill to finance the scheduled Amchitka test "unless the President gives his direct approval for such test." The compromise thus placed the responsibility squarely on the President for assuring the safety of Cannikin before allowing it to proceed. The Senate amendment—to which the House was asked to concur—also gave Cannikin foes another opportunity to raise the issue in the House.

The House scheduled a summer recess from August 6 to September 8, and prior to the departure of the members, I talked with a number of my colleagues about filing a court suit for release of the Cannikin Papers. We decided to proceed with a suit, and the Honorable Ramsey Clark, former U.S. Attorney General, agreed to provide legal services on a *pro bono* basis.

THE LAW SUIT

On August 11 the suit on behalf of thirty-three other Members of Congress, was filed in U.S. District Court for the District of Columbia. It sought to compel four agencies (the U.S. Information Agency and part of the State Department not included) and their heads to release the Cannikin Papers as required by the Freedom of Information Act. We pressed for expeditious action by the court since the Senate provision placing responsibility on the

President was still a legislative issue. (The provision was later enacted into law, and the President approved Cannikin without a public announcement.)

The FOIA itself had been signed into law on July 4, 1966, to take effect a year later, and is now codified in 5 U.S. Code, section 552. By its enactment the Congress sought to revise section 3 of the Administrative Procedure Act (5 U.S.C. 1002) "to provide a true Federal public records statute by requiring the availability, to any member of the public, of all the Executive Branch records described in its requirements except those involving matters which are within nine stated exemptions," according to the House Report accompanying the legislation.[8] Thus, the purpose of the Act is to prevent government agencies from unjustifiably withholding information that should be reasonably available to a person having some basis for seeking it. The U.S. District Courts are given jurisdiction to enjoin an agency from withholding records as well as to order the production of any agency records improperly impounded.

In our suit we contended that as Members of Congress we were entitled to disclosure of the Cannikin data without regard to the exemptions from disclosure on national security or other grounds. The Justice Department, acting for the Executive, moved to dismiss the action or, in the alternative, asked for summary judgment, on the ground that the requested materials were specifically exempted from disclosure under exemption 1 and 5 of the Act. Exemption 1 excludes from disclosure matters "specifically required by Executive order to be kept secret in the interest of the national defense or foreign policy." Exemption 5 exempts from disclosure "inter-agency or intra-agency memorandums or letters which would not be available by law to a party other than an agency in litigation with the agency." This exemption was described in the House Report as covering "any internal memorandums which would routinely be disclosed to a private party through the discovery process in litigation with the agency."[9] The legislative history indicates that only staff advice and opinions, and not factual matters, are exempted.

In support of its motion the Executive filed an affidavit from Mr. John N. Irwin II, the Under Secretary of State. The Irwin affidavit states that in January 1969 the President established an "Under Secretaries Committee" of which Mr. Irwin was Chairman, under the National Security Council. According to this affidavit,

> On June 27, 1969, the President directed the Under Secretaries Committee to review the annual underground nuclear test program and to encompass within this review requests for authorization of specific scheduled tests. He

---

8. *Ibid.,* p. 10.
9. U.S., House of Representatives Report 1497, 89th Cong., 2d sess. (1966), p. 10.

directed that the Committee consider the policy and technical justification for the proposed tests to determine whether they are consistent with the requirements of national security and foreign policy. He requested that the results of the Committee's review of the underground nuclear tests be transmitted to him in time to allow him to give them full consideration before the scheduled events.

Mr. Irwin then listed for the first time the documents comprising the Cannikin Papers. They included a memorandum from Mr. Irwin to the President, a report of the Committee on Cannikin to which several documents pertaining to the test were attached, and letters concerning Cannikin from the two environmental agencies and the Office of Science and Technology. Although the affidavit noted that a number of documents included in with the report were "separately classified" as "Top Secret" or otherwise, Mr. Irwin said of the three letters only that each "is classified." It could therefore be assumed that these letters were classified solely because they were physically attached to other documents separately classified in their own right.

In addition to claiming exemption from disclosure, the Government's response contended that Members of Congress could not sue Executive officials because of the "separation of powers provisions" of the Constitution. In essence the Government seemed to argue that if the Executive Branch repudiated a lawful duty toward the Legislative Branch, the Executive could not be held accountable by the Judiciary. The District Court, without an *in camera* inspection of the papers in question, accepted the Government's contentions, and ruled that the documents were "exempted from compelled disclosure" by exemptions 1 and 5 of the Act. Accordingly, it granted the Government's motion for summary judgment, and dismissed the action.

An emergency appeal was taken to the Court of Appeals for the District of Columbia Circuit. Several reasons were urged in support of reversal of the trial court's judgment. First, we contended that Members of Congress were entitled to sue as such and that such suits were not barred by any "separation of powers" principle. Actually, a careful reading of records in the case discloses that the Government has not offered the sanction of executive privilege as a basis for withholding the Cannikin Papers. A memorandum to the heads of Executive departments and agencies, signed by the President on March 24, 1969, provides for a specific procedure under which this privilege must be invoked. That procedure was never used to justify withholding the Cannikin Papers. Instead, the Government's strategy involved defending its secrecy as within the scope of the FOIA. Obviously, a judicial decision upholding this would deal a body blow to the FOIA's effectiveness. In our appeal we pointed out that, since the issue of executive privilege was not raised, the case did not present a conflict between the Legislative and Executive branches.

Secondly, we argued that Members of Congress are not subject to the restrictions on disclosure contained in the FOIA. In section 552(c) of the Act it is stated that "This section does not authorize withholding of information or limit the availability of records to the public, except as specifically stated in this section." This is an obvious reference to the nine exemptions set forth in the immediately preceding section 552(b). The next sentence of section 552(c) reads: "This section is not authority to withhold information from Congress." Here no reference at all is made to the statutory exemptions, and thus the exemptions spelled out in 552(b) do not apply to the Congress. The intent behind this clause was described in House Report 89–1497:

> Members of Congress have all the rights of access guaranteed to "any person" by S. 1160 [the Act], and the Congress has additional rights of access to all government information which it deems necessary to carry out its functions.

Clearly, the Act does not reduce Congressmen's right to data—a right extending even beyond the rights spelled out for all citizens under the Act. Instead, as we contended in our suit, the Act grants greater information rights to Congressmen.

Third, our appeal contended that the Executive had not sustained the burden placed on it by the FOIA to justify non-disclosure and that the trial court had not conducted the *de novo* hearing required by the Act. The Act provides that in disputes over which information should be released, the courts will not be bound by traditional principles of deference to determinations by the agencies involved, but that, on the contrary, "the court shall determine the matter *de novo* and the burden is on the agency to sustain its action [in denying the records sought]." We maintained that the obligation of the District Court was either to direct the disclosure of materials, or to examine them *in camera* and release the maximum information possible.

Fourth, we contended that the "classification" and "internal memoranda" exemptions of the FOIA did not apply to the documents in question. Exemption 1 in the Act applies to matters "specifically required by Executive Order to be kept secret in the interest of the national defense or foreign policy." Yet no Executive Order relates specifically to the Cannikin Papers. Rather, they are classified "Secret" under Executive Order 10501 (November 5, 1953), which establishes a general classification system for all government materials. Most of the Cannikin Papers were "classified" derivatively—that is, because of the way they are filed. According to the Government's reasoning, by attaching one classified page to a volume or series of volumes of innocuous materials the entire mass of material becomes immune from disclosure. Under this kind of extreme interpretation of the Act, the first exemption becomes a bottomless canyon capable of safeguarding from disclosure virtually all information the Government prefers to conceal. We felt that the Court was obliged to prevent such a misuse of the Act by inspecting the papers *in camera* to determine which parts are releasable. Moreover, we asserted that the Act requires a specific Executive Order for the witholding of any requested data, just as the President has voluntarily established a system for his specific action each time executive privilege is invoked.

Insofar as the fifth exemption, on interagency memoranda, was claimed, we pointed out that the only evidence offered by the Government was the Irwin affidavit, supplemented by passages from two reports in which the President described to the Congress the Irwin Committee.[10] But these exhibits themselves refuted the Executive contention that the Committee's role was solely to provide recommendations rather than factual information to the President. One of the Government's exhibits revealed that the National Security Council had been implemented in part to provide a system "which would summon and gather the best ideas, the best analyses, and the best information available to the government and the nation." Because "intelligent discussions and decisions at the highest level demand the fullest possible information," it is an "essential function" of the Council "to bring together all the agencies of the government concerned with foreign affairs to elicit, assess, and present to [the President] and the Council all the pertinent knowledge available."[11] If much of the Cannikin Papers consisted of factual information rather than recommendations to the President, clearly the Congress was just as entitled to have such information as the President. The only way to determine the extent to which the reports were factual information instead of confidential advice is by actual examination. Again, we felt that this was the Court's obligation.

Our fifth ground for appealing the lower court decision was basically that the District Court had failed to explore fully the facts behind the witholding by way of determining the legality of the agency action. Without such judicial intervention the Executive Branch would be able to take virtually any action withholding information with absolute immunity from the need to justify such deeds. All it would need do is dispatch an affidavit,

---

10. "U.S. Foreign Policy for the 1970's—A New Strategy for Peace," a report to the Congress by Richard Nixon, President of the United States, February 18, 1970. "U.S. Foreign Policy for the 1970's—Building for Peace," a report to the Congress by Richard Nixon, President of the United States, February 25, 1971. Washington, D.C.: U.S., Government Printing Office, 1970, 1971.
11. *Ibid.,* Report of February 18, 1970.

beyond which the court could not question. This assuredly seems a threat to our democratic process—a process that depends on citizen involvement and necessarily requires dissemination of information to the citizenry.

THE APPEAL

The Court of Appeals did not pass on all our contentions, but did reverse and remand the case to the District Court for further consideration. This was a major victory for the plaintiffs. The Appeals Court "conclude[d] that summary disposition [of certain issues] is inappropriate," and that several issues "should be the subject of a full consideration on the merits by this court if the appeal is continued following the disposition on remand."[12] It did not resolve the question of whether the FOIA confers any greater rights to disclosure on Congressmen than it does on the public generally. Neither did the court pass on our assertion that the first exemption to the publication requirement (for "national defense or foreign policy" interest) requires that each document sought to be thus withheld must be classified by a separate Executive Order.

The Court of Appeals did, however, decide two issues in a way favorable to the plaintiffs. The first related to the Executive's claim under the first exemption. Here the court noted the inadequacies of the Irwin affidavit, holding that a matter as important as one involving the first exemption should not be determined on the basis of such an unexamined claim by one of the parties in a dispute. It directed the District Court to "take evidence on whether, and to what extent, the file [of withheld documents] contains documents that are now within the umbrella of a secret file but which would not have been independently classified as secret."[13] On the same reasoning, it directed the trial court to determine whether "non-secret components [of documents] are separable from the secret remainder and may be read separately without distortion of meaning."

The second part of the Court of Appeals' decision directed similar treatment with respect to the Executive's claim under the fifth exemption. The court noted that "the exemption protects the decisional processes of the President, or other policy-making executive officials," and ruled that it would extend that protection to factual information wherever "it is inextricably intertwined with policy-making processes."[14] To protect whatever documents would ultimately be ruled to need protection among the dis-

---

12. *Per curiam* order in Mink *et al.* v. Environmental Protection Agency *et al.*, 71-1708, U.S. Ct. of App., D.C., October 15, 1971.
13. *Ibid.*
14. *Ibid.*

puted materials, the court ordered that the trial judge should conduct his own *in camera* inspection of the documents. Thus a court inspection of the Cannikin Papers was intended to protect the rights of the Government from arbitrary disclosure that might otherwise have been required by the Appeals Court on the basis of the Government's failure to produce the required proof that the materials should be withheld. Apparently, however, the Government felt that even an *in camera* inspection for its own protection was too much of an infringement on its secrecy prerogatives. Without waiting for the District Court to conduct such an examination, the Government abruptly sought Supreme Court review of the Appeals Court decision. The thrust of its petition for *certiorari* was that the court's judgment raised an important and recurring problem in the administration of the Freedom of Information Act.

The Executive asked the Supreme Court to review the propriety of *in camera* inspections with respect to both the first and fifth exemptions in the Act. Significantly, it did not challenge the Appeals Court ruling with respect to the first exemption—i.e., that an inspection was required to ensure that no documents were "derivatively" classified. Indeed, on March 8, 1972, two days after the Supreme Court agreed to hear its case, the Government replaced the 1953 Executive Order, which held that "The classification of a file or group of physically connected documents shall be at least as high as that of the most highly classified document therein." The President's new Executive Order 11652 established a new system of portion-by-portion classification of documents:

> Each classified document shall . . . to the extent practicable, be so marked as to indicate which portions are classified, at what level, and which portions are not classified in order to facilitate excerpting and other use.

This was the very procedure called for by the Appeals Court in its decision, which read:

> This court sees no basis for withholding on security grounds a document that, although separately unclassified, is regarded secret merely because it has been incorporated into a secret file. To the extent that our position in this respect is inconsistent with . . . Executive Order 10501, we deem it required by the terms and purposes of the [Freedom of Information Act], enacted subsequently to the Executive Order.

If our court suit was a factor in this revision of the Government's classification system to ease the task of releasing non-classified portions of documents, it is a significant victory. Nevertheless, there remained a need for continuing the court effort on the Cannikin Papers.

While dropping its contentions that "derivative" classification prevented release of some of the documents, the Executive in its Supreme Court petition still argued that the Court of Appeals erred in calling upon the District Court to determine whether passages, paragraphs, or components of documents classified secret as a whole may be excised for disclosure. As to the fifth exemption, the Government objected to the court's position that the District Court should disclose all facts contained in agency reports unless inextricably intertwined with agency opinion and recommendation. In effect, the Government seemed to be attempting to reform its own procedures so that the courts could remain excluded from involvement in informational policy.

Unfortunately, the Supreme Court ruling on January 22, 1973, was against us, in effect shattering our once-lofty hopes for the FOIA.[15] The majority opinion, written by Mr. Justice White with the concurrence of Associate Justices Burger, Stewart, Blackmun, and Powell, held that exemption 1 of the Act does not permit compelled disclosure of the classified documents or *in camera* inspection to sift out "non-secret components." The majority stated that the Executive had met its burden of demonstrating that the documents were entitled to protection under exemption 1 by the simple expedient of filing an affidavit.

With respect to exemption 5, the majority held that this exemption does not require that otherwise confidential documents be made available for a District Court's *in camera* inspection regardless of how little, if any, purely factual material they contain. In implying that such an inspection be automatic, the Court of Appeals order was overly rigid, the majority said; the Government should have an opportunity of showing a court by lesser means that the documents sought are clearly beyond the range of material that would be available to a private party in litigation with a government agency. As Mr. Justice White noted, "An agency should be given the opportunity, by means of detailed affidavits or oral testimony, to establish to the satisfaction of the District Court" that the documents sought are covered by exemption 5. If the agency fails to do so to the satisfaction of the Court, the Court may order an inspection, or select a representative document for inspection. The majority opinion did remand the case to the Appeals Court to permit the Executive to show "by means short of submitting them for an *in camera* inspection" that the Cannikin Papers were immune from disclosure under exemption 5, but this still left the power of withholding in the Executive Branch and reduced the court to a passive role.

Since the issue of whether a Member of Congress has standing to sue did not reach the Supreme Court, there was no determination of whether the

---

15. *Supra,* Note 1.

FOIA's nine exemptions restrict the rights of Congressmen to government data. Neither did the Appeals Court ruling with respect to exemption 1 reach the Supreme Court, since the Executive did not appeal this portion of the decision. Consequently, at least some progress was made toward a concept of making available non-secret portions of classified documents. Yet the Supreme Court decision threatened even this non-appealed ruling by giving blanket approval to an otherwise unsupported agency assertion of the right to withhold. In effect, the Supreme Court said that the FOIA's wording as adopted by the Congress left no alternative but to accept the Executive's determination. The ruling thus left it up to the Congress to revise the Act to permit judicial scrutiny of Presidential actions. In a dissenting opinion Mr. Justice Douglas commented: "Unless Federal courts can be trusted, the Executive will hold complete sway and by *ipse dixit* make even the time of day 'top secret.' "

Naturally, I agree with Justice Douglas. Before a final decision can be made on the merits of any claim for sole Executive authority to conceal under sections 1 and 5 of the FOIA, it seems to me that the factual basis of any suit should be expanded through court inspection. Otherwise, the Executive will remain free to raise the specter of alleged damaging disclosure of this nation's secrets without proper proof. After District Court examination of the papers, it would then be possible for higher courts to have complete information on which to base subsequent reviews of the issues raised in the case, should such reviews become necessary.

THE STAKES FOR THE FUTURE

What is really at stake is whether the courts have the right to hold the Government accountable for actions taken under the FOIA to withhold data. If the Executive Branch is adjudged to have an absolute power to determine what may be concealed, with only its own affidavit offered as substantiation, the Act will have been dealt a severe blow. Indeed, its adoption will have accomplished little.

If Congressional adoption of the Act is to have any meaning, it will be necessary for procedures, including judicial ones, to be established for assuring that its intent becomes a reality. Had we been able to entrust the Executive with total discretionary power, after all, there would have been no need for the Congress to legislate toward such a goal. For the Executive to come back now and claim the Act does not really have an impact on its right to conceal information amounts to unilateral repeal of its provisions by one branch of the Government. This must not be allowed to happen.

This case symbolizes what is fast becoming an information crisis in this country. More than ever before, information is power. Those who have the most direct access to, and control over, the information needed to make decisions in our complex society are the ones who are truly in command. The President has recognized this by his own attempts to form an organization—the National Security Council—charged with obtaining the best information on crucial issues and presenting it directly to him. A decision-maker does not need advice and recommendations as much as he needs complete and accurate information on which to base his own judgments. This is why it is folly to claim that the Under Secretaries group involved in the Cannikin case exists only to supply advice. Obviously this cannot be supplied to the President in a vacuum, with no background information for him to check.

The power of information is seen in private industry, where boards of directors are becoming outdated appendages. The management of corporations has become the superior power, because of its direct and continuing access to the information needed to make wise decisions in the marketplace. Through this control over data, management is readily able to manipulate ill-informed and dependent directors, not to mention stockholders. We can only hope that this same phenomenon is not transferred to the equivalent governmental institution, the Legislature.

It is my firm belief that a democratic society cannot survive the suppression of information such as revealed by the Cannikin episode. Unless we are to abandon our concept of the separation of powers, the Congress must have equal access to the information necessary to make wise and informed decisions on governmental policy. The Congress could, of course, establish a bureaucracy equal in size to the Executive Branch, devoted solely to gathering duplicative information. But this expense and waste should not be necessary.

The Congress has also the power to withhold appropriations from an agency or agencies, including the Office of the President, for instances of refusal to supply information. Yet this is an equally drastic solution. If the functions of government have any value to the people, they should not be terminated. There must exist a better system for the Congress to obtain the data it needs from the governmental branch that has the task of collecting it. This is where I feel such a law as the FOIA has a positive role.

Further, to be meaningful, the Act's provisions must be applied to requests for information from individual Congressmen rather than from committees or from the Congress as a whole. In the course of arguments on our court case the Executive attempted to draw a distinction between requests by the Congress as an institution and those on the part of individual members—presumably believing that individual members have less right to affirmative response. I do not wish to disparage the right of the Congress as a whole to information; yet on inquiry to the Congressional Research Service

I was advised that the Service was unable to discover any instances where the Congress in its official capacity has sought information under the FOIA. Thus, if this is the only avenue by which the Congress can benefit from the Act, it is an unconscionable restriction of each Member's right to information. If a majority must ask, it would be virtually meaningless. The issue is one of access to information, and each Member of Congress must have an equal right to information so that such a right is not concentrated in committees or the Legislature as a whole. The right to disagree will be seriously compromised if information can be secured only through collective request.

It is hoped that the courts will eventually construe the FOIA along these lines. Even so, it may be necessary to seek changes in the Act to strengthen the power of individual legislators. Some of us in the Congress are working on ways to offset the Supreme Court decision in the *Mink* case. One change might be to write into statutory law the requirement that any Executive refusal of information to the Congress must follow certain guidelines. This would apply whether the claim was made on the basis of executive privilege, FOIA exemptions, or other cause. Presidents have already issued their own guidelines at least in the case of executive privilege, but these should apply to all forms of suppression and should be written into law so that they will not be arbitrarily abandoned in the future. (Such a step would not recognize or endorse the doctrine of executive privilege, whose Constitutional basis is dubious at best.)

The purpose of such guidelines would be to ensure that only the President himself could refuse information, and in each specific instance it would have to be in writing. The guidelines should specify that a reply would have to be made promptly to each Congressional request, whether approval or claim of privilege. In any case of refusal the matter would automatically be referred to a U.S. District Court, where the court would have the final decision on whether the materials sought should be released. The courts would decide on a case-by-case basis under expedited procedures, with their rulings forming a body of precedents binding on future Executive disclosures. The courts would also be authorized to require a Member of Congress receiving information under court direction to treat it with confidentiality.

It seems to me that such a procedure is vital if we are to preserve the essential elements of our democratic process. There have been too many recent attempts to centralize information in one branch of government. Traditionally, knowledge (and therefore, power) have been diffused among such institutions as the Congress, the press, and the academic community. Each was able, through utilization of information, to influence public opinion and the course of national events.

In time, I feel, this nation will come to realize that in order for freedom to be real there must exist a body of public information freely available to all citizens, not the exclusive province of any select institution. Neither the Executive Branch nor the Legislative Branch can assume arbitrary control over this public data. It must be made available to all, in order to preserve our freedoms intact. We have not yet reached full awareness of the importance of such a total information policy, but it is really the only way to safeguard our cherished principles of government by the consent of the governed. The apathy and distrust of a faraway government operating in secrecy is building to the extent that our very institutions of government are in danger of crumbling. Until we realize that the reason for this decay is distrust of the people, and act accordingly to correct our policies, we must endure increasing opposition, blind or otherwise. But when we recognize the enduring value of the frankest dissemination of knowledge, we will have immeasurably strengthened the security and the confidence of a united people.

8

Secrecy and the Right of Parliament
To Know and Participate
in Foreign Affairs

R. A. R. MACLENNAN, M.P.

In the United Kingdom, Parliament very rarely intervenes effectively to alter the course and conduct of foreign policy. Indeed, the attention that Parliament as a whole chooses to give to the external relations of the country is sporadic and infrequent. The few foreign affairs debates tend to be in the form of a series of low-key contributions by those who are considered to be specialists in a particular area, or *parti pris* in a particular international dispute. The clangour of Party controversy seldom disturbs these peaceful, almost private exchanges.

Parliament, it seems, has come to accept for itself a limited role in the formation and scrutiny of foreign policy. There is, in consequence, little disposition in Parliament to press Governments for more official information about the conduct of foreign affairs. Although Members of Parliament do from time to time criticize Ministers with foreign affairs responsibilities for their policies, they rarely criticize them for their reticence. Foreign Ministers are usually not forthcoming with Parliament, but Members of Parliament are mostly untroubled by any concern that their effectiveness might be unnecessarily diminished by official secrecy.

Ministers are responsible for the formation of foreign policy, for overseeing its administration, for managing international crises, and for conducting or directing international negotiations on Britain's behalf. But they tend to prefer not to unravel before Parliament the strands of their foreign policy thinking. Consequently the advice upon which governments rely is not that of Parliament but that which is tendered within the machinery of govern-

Mr. Maclennan is a Member of the British Parliament and former Parliamentary Private Secretary to the Secretary of State for Commonwealth Affairs in the Wilson (Labour) Government. He has specialized in foreign affairs.

ment itself, and this is usually based on better information than is available to Parliament. This can be disadvantageous even to the Government.

WHEN SECRECY MAY BE HARMFUL

The functioning of the British Parliament often appears less like an inquest on the affairs of the nation than like extended adversarial proceedings in which Government and Opposition each present a case before the bar of public opinion. The persuasiveness of the case does not always depend upon the degree of penetration of official secrecy nor upon the stripping bare of the actual workings of the governmental machine. Yet in the field of foreign affairs, although Parliament may appear to be engaged in a dialectic between Government and Opposition just as in domestic affairs, in reality the debate is much less than equal.

Members of Parliament outside the Government rarely bring to these debates the weight of personal knowledge or recent experience that they collectively bring to bear upon domestic issues. Governments make little effort to provide the information that would help to correct this deficiency. In consequence, when a Government's foreign policy does come under fire in Parliament it cannot assume that its motivations will be understood, far less accepted, by Parliament or by the public. Thus, when the Labour Government was roundly attacked for supporting the Federal side in the Nigerian Civil War, a factor contributing to the lack of Parliamentary sympathy for the Government's position was its choice not to make fully explicit its knowledge of the role of France in Biafra.[1] Reasons for this were of course pressed upon the Government by its advisers, but the Government paid a price in loss of support for its lack of frankness.

Similarly, successive Governments have presented their decision to Parliament to seek membership in the European Communities when very little of the groundwork done by the Civil Service had been made known to Members of Parliament. The existing degree of public opposition to entry might have been significantly reduced if, over the period of more than a decade during which these Governments were persuaded to seek entry to the EEC, the detailed appraisals being received by these Governments themselves had been made available for scrutiny and debate in Parliament.

The natural tendency to caution and conservatism marking the civil servant's advice is potentially harmful to the conduct of foreign policy. In domestic affairs this caution is to some extent offset by the pressure of informed Parliamentary opinion. This is less true of foreign affairs. The great-

---

1. Great Britain, House of Commons, *The Parliamentary Debates (official reports)* (hereinafter: *Hansard,* H.C. Deb.), 766, 12 June 1968, c. 243.

est weakness of British foreign policy has been the repeated failure to recognise, and to act upon the recognition, that circumstances have changed.

A recent example of this was Britain's attempt to sustain a military role in Southeast Asia long after such a course had ceased to be reasonably justifiable. The responsibility for sticking to the policy lay squarely with the Ministers concerned. Their pursuance of the policy may or may not have been in reliance upon advice proffered by their civil servants. Certainly Ministers did not look to Parliament for advice. But when the decision to withdraw from "East of Suez" was finally taken, the advice of the Foreign and Commonwealth Office does not appear to have played a significant part. It was, in fact, a precipitate decision dictated not by considerations of foreign policy but of economic necessity, and because of its manner and timing it smacked of national defeat. Had Parliament earlier made its voice heard, the decision might have been taken sooner and been seen as a natural progression. But the Government had never had from Parliament a coherent critique of the policy such as to make it reconsider the assumptions on which the policy was based.

In part this failure of Parliament was due to the weakness of its own institutional arrangements for probing foreign policy. Since Parliament is not so well informed about the day-to-day developments as the officials of the Foreign and Commonwealth Office and moreover lacks the means to acquire the necessary information, it cannot hope to carry great authority when it questions a Government's over-all assessments. Indeed, the very lack of a body such as the Public Accounts Committee operating within the field of foreign affairs means that Members of Parliament cannot even present a collective judgment on a particular line of foreign policy; yet if they disagree with it individually they are forced to act on *francs-tireurs*. The actual weakness of the Members' position vis-à-vis the Government may contribute to their lack of interest in the field of foreign affairs.

Governments usually try to present their foreign policies to Parliament in such a manner as to enlist the maximum support from all sides, as they recognize that disagreements about a policy in Parliament will make it harder to sell it abroad. Opposition leaders for their part frequently acquiesce in the general direction of a Government's foreign policy, contenting themselves with criticisms of detail. In part this stems from the Opposition's natural wish to appear responsible, in the sense that they recognise that there is and must be an element of continuity in the conduct of foreign policy to safeguard the stability of Britain's relations with foreign governments. But Opposition leaders in their role as party managers recognise also that foreign policy issues tend to divide parties internally, as in the 1950's the issue of German rearmament divided the Labour Party, and more recently the issue of economic sanctions against Rhodesia has divided the

Conservative Party[2]; and for this reason they seek to avoid treating foreign affairs as a central ground upon which to attack the Government. Moreover, it is commonly believed in Parliament that foreign affairs only rarely provides parties with such vote-winning issues as arise from domestic controversies.

The importance of foreign affairs to Britain is acknowledged, but the connexion between the current issues of foreign policy and the immediate interests that Members of Parliament feel called upon to defend in Parliament is not always seen to be intimate. If Governments go badly wrong abroad then Oppositions can capitalize on their mistakes *ex post facto*. If, however, a Government error can be revealed only by deep probing, then most Members of Parliament are inclined to think that the issue will appear to the public as arcane and remote from its interests. Hence there is little disposition in Parliament to investigate continuously and deeply the process of the Government's diplomacy; and although Governments are nowadays involved almost constantly in international negotiations, Parliament is usually content to have a brief post-conference statement from the responsible Minister and a short exchange of question and answer on the statement.

On occasion, when the Government surmises that there is virtual Parliamentary unanimity on some issue—as, for example, when Iceland threatened British fishermen's livelihood by altering the limits of her territorial waters,[3] or when President Amin of Uganda announced a takeover of British businesses,[4]—then a statement will be made to Parliament to allow Parliament to trumpet its disapproval of the foreign country's action. Normally, however, the practice of Foreign Secretaries in describing to Parliament their contacts and exchanges with foreign countries is to refer to the talks as "useful" but, where an agreed communiqué has not been issued, to indicate that it is not customary to reveal the content of the talks. Parliament does not usually cavil at this. Foreign Ministers are of course aware of the expectations of Members of Parliament—particularly those of their supporters—and will take them into account in presenting their decisions and views to Parliament. But once a Cabinet has decided upon a course of action in the foreign affairs field, only rarely does Parliament consciously stand as an obstacle in the way of its fulfillment.

The general government practice as to providing information to Parliament in the foreign affairs field does, of course, have exceptions. The Labour Government, for example, chose to make available to Parliament the fullest

---

2. *Sunday Times,* "Tories and Mr. Smith," 1 March 1970; *The Times,* "Backbench Tories' threat over Rhodesia," 4 November 1970.
3. *Hansard,* H.C. Deb. 840, 13 July 1972, c. 1850; *Hansard,* H.C. Deb. 847, 30 November 1972, c. 636.
4. *Hansard,* H.C. Deb. 848, 19 December 1972, c. 1126.

information, in a series of White Papers, on the conduct of negotiations with the illegal régime in Rhodesia.[5] The reasons for these unusually detailed revelations were at least two. For one thing, the rebel Prime Minister of Rhodesia, Ian Smith, notoriously produced his own versions of the talks —and they were travesties of what had happened. Then, too, the British Government was anxious to show not only how it had struggled to obtain what it thought fair-minded people might regard as a reasonable settlement but also that their efforts had been frustrated by the devious and obdurate Smith. This, however, was clearly a special case. The same Government was much less forthcoming, for example, regarding details of its talks with the Argentine Government on the future of the Falkland Islands[6] and on its exchanges with the Spanish Government over Gibraltar.[7]

The most striking exception to the norm of reticence is seen in the attitude of successive British Governments from Harold Macmillan's to Edward Heath's toward providing information about negotiations for the accession of Britain to the European Communities. In this case it was recognised that Members of Parliament were more than usually interested not only in the outcome of negotiations but also in ensuring that no vital British interest was conceded by the Government in the course of negotiations. Thus the Wilson Government not only promised to follow the practice of the Macmillan Government in giving detailed periodic statements to Parliament describing the progress of negotiations, but also sought in a series of White Papers to spell out in advance both the problems the Government would face in the negotiations and its general objectives.[8]

The case of the EEC negotiations is the best example since the Suez invasion of 1956 of that rare phenomenon in which Members of Parliament acknowledge almost to a man that an important issue of foreign policy profoundly and directly affects their own constituents' interests. It was also recognised by successive Governments that not only would anodyne statements tend to provoke Parliament, but moreover that the calculated leak from Brussels or some other European capital was a weapon of diplomacy that could be blunted only by Britain's giving a fairly full and factual account of her objectives in the negotiations.

Notwithstanding the continuing interest of Parliament in these negoti-

---

5. Southern Rhodesia, Cmnd. 2807; Rhodesia, Proposals for a Settlement, 1966, Cmnd. 3159; Rhodesia, Report on the Discussions held on board H.M.S. *Fearless,* October 1968, Cmnd. 3793.
6. E.g., *Hansard,* H.C. Deb. 791, 20 November 1969, c. 1522.
7. E.g., *Hansard,* H.C. Deb. 788, 13 October 1969, c. 9.
8. Membership of the European Communities, Cmnd. 3269; Common Agricultural Policy of the European Economic Community, Cmnd. 3274; Legal and Constitutional Implications of United Kingdom Membership of the European Communities, Cmnd. 3301.

ations over a ten-year period, it may be doubted whether Parliament showed itself to be institutionally equipped to probe into the validity of government assumptions about the issues to be negotiated. For example, Parliament drew attention to the remarkable and generally unhelpful revelation in the White Paper of February 1970, to the effect that the adverse balance of payments impact on Britain of Common Market membership could be between £100,000,000 and £1,000,000,000.[9] Parliament failed, however, to lift the veil of official secrecy over the way these figures had been arrived at and failed to ascertain from either Government or civil servants whether or not a more precise estimate was possible. Neither could Parliament learn whether the figures quoted were the consensus of opinion within all the Departments of State, or (as was hinted at the time) only the opinion of a small but powerful group whose views were not widely shared even within the Civil Service. This example, however, illustrates not so much a failure of the Parliamentary will to penetrate official secrecy as the shortcomings of the techniques of obtaining official information in the foreign affairs field.

THE QUEST FOR INFORMATION

By what techniques does Parliament seek to inform itself about foreign affairs? In his evidence to the Franks Committee on section 2 of the Official Secrets Act 1911, Sir Denis Greenhill, Permanent Under Secretary of State at the Foreign and Commonwealth Office, said: "I think it is fair to say that foreign affairs debates in the House of Commons attract less attention than they used to, and it was foreign affairs debates which were very often the source of information about policy."[10] Sir Denis was undoubtedly right; but the information made available in such debates was, of course, the information that Governments were willing or eager to make available and not necessarily the information Members of Parliament would like to have had. Indeed, the very discursive nature of such debates enables the Minister to pick and choose the subjects he will expatiate upon and those he will not find time to discuss in depth. When in December 1972 Parliament held a general foreign affairs debate it was the first such debate for thirteen months.[11] And yet, although Parliament may have been even less vocal than usual on foreign affairs (other than those affecting Europe), it is doubtful

---

9. Assessment by Her Majesty's Government of Economic Effects of Membership of the E.E.C., Cmnd. 4289.
10. Departmental Committee 1972 on Section 2 of the Official Secrets Act, 1911, vol. 3, p. 132 (The "Franks Report"), Cmnd. 5104.
11. *Hansard,* H.C. Deb. 848, 14 December 1972, c. 645.

if, in consequence of this long gap between debates, it was seriously less well informed than usual.

Likewise, the use of the Parliamentary Question is of extremely limited value in penetrating the veil of official secrecy. Individual Members of Parliament are customarily permitted to ask one supplementary question of a Minister after their tabled question has been answered. Even when a group of Members of Parliament seeks to orchestrate their questioning, this limitation tends to prevent in-depth cross-examination. Indeed any Minister worth his salt can avoid answering the penetrating question by offering information for which he was not asked, by repeating a well-worn and well-known formula that expresses government policy, by an irrelevant witticism, by invoking a practice of non-disclosure of the information sought, or by one of a hundred similar devices. It is a definite mark of incompetence if a Minister has to take refuge in an excuse for not answering a question, such as that it is not in the national interest to reveal the information sought. Ministers rarely need to offer such excuses.

In practice tenacious questioning of a Minister on a particular subject is used by Members of Parliament not to obtain hitherto secret information but to publicize their own points of view. The *locus classicus* of this technique was the questioning of the (Conservative) Government about the alleged existence of a collusive agreement with the French and the Israelis to invade Suez in 1956.[12] After the invasion was halted and the troops were withdrawn, it was of great historical interest to establish the truth about the putative agreement between the French and the British. But the political purpose of the persistent questioning of Ministers on the subject was to establish the Opposition's disapprobation of the whole venture and, if possible, to discredit the Ministers most deeply involved by demonstrating their unwillingness to make a clean breast of the whole affair. It could not have been expected either that Ministers would reveal the facts or that, if they had, that the disclosure could have undone what had been done.

A more recent example of the technique of publicizing an issue through the use of Question Time was the persistent bombardment of the Labour Government's Secretary of State for Defence about the Government's intended use for defence purposes of the ecologically significant island of Aldabra in the Indian Ocean.[13] The purpose of the questioner was not so much to wring from the Minister information of a secret or even sensitive nature (granted that the Minister was not completely forthright about the Government's intentions—perhaps because a policy had not been decided upon), but rather to arouse public interest in and support for the conserva-

---

12. *Hansard,* H.C. Deb. 562, 20 December 1956, c. 1456.
13. E.g., *Hansard,* H.C. Deb. 753, 8 November 1967, c. 1018.

tionists' viewpoint. Similarly, questions to Ministers as to whether British arms supplied to Portugal for NATO purposes are being used by Portugal against guerrillas in Portugal's African colonies[14] are not intended so much to ascertain what in fact happens to the arms as to demonstrate hostility to Portugal's African policies and to express the view that the Government should wholly disassociate Britain from these policies.

In the case of the Suez affair, Members of Parliament sought an official enquiry into the past events. In the case of British arms sold to Portugal the questions related to current and continuing government policy. In the case of Aldabra the Member of Parliament concerned sought to influence an imminent policy decision. But in none of the cases does it appear that the evident Ministerial reluctance to reveal official secrets seriously affected the political impact of the questioning. In fact the very reticence of Ministers about events past, present, and to come tended to confirm the worst construction the questioner wished to have put upon government action. What all three cases also show, however, is that Ministers cannot be forced by Parliamentary questions to reveal secrets if they do not wish to do so.

The application of the Official Secrets Acts to Members of Parliament themselves has not been reviewed since 1938. In that year Duncan Sandys, a young Conservative Member of Parliament, showed a Minister the draft of a Parliamentary Question based on confidential information on the country's defences. When Sandys revealed that he had been subjected to pressure to disclose his source of information, a Select Committee of the House of Commons then set up reported that Members of Parliament were not entitled to solicit the disclosure of secret information; but that if they did obtain such information then the Acts should not be used to impede Members from carrying out their Parliamentary activities.

Although it has not been put to the test since then, it appears that Members of Parliament who choose to use, in the House of Commons, information obtained from a government source are protected from prosecution by Parliamentary privilege. If, however, the information is communicated without authorization to a person outside the House, this might constitute an offence under section 2 of the Official Secrets Act of 1911. On the other hand, in a case in which official information is made available to a Select Committee of the House of Commons but has not been reported to the whole House, its unauthorized communication is regarded as a contempt of the House, and the Member of Parliament responsible is subject to its penal jurisdiction.[15]

In one small respect Members of Parliament have received a useful addi-

---

14. E.g., *Hansard,* H.C. Deb. 828, 13 December 1971, c. 6 W.
15. Official Secrets Acts. Select Committee Report, 1938-39 (101) viii.

tion to their armoury for the penetration of government secrets. The Parliamentary Commissioner for Administration—the Ombudsman—is permitted to look at all the relevant government documents when a Member of Parliament alleges to him that there has been maladministration on the part of the Government or Civil Service and that this has damaged the particular interest of a constituent. Thus the Foreign Office was criticized by the Ombudsman for its handling of the claim of a number of prisoners held at Sachsenhausen concentration camp to a right to share in the compensation funds made available by the West German Government for distribution among British victims.[16] The then Foreign Secretary, while disagreeing with the Ombudsman's findings and arguing that the disagreement was about policy and not administration, nonetheless agreed to the compensation of the prisoners involved.[17] The Ombudsman, however, is required to establish the existence of a close nexus between the maladministration he uncovers and the particular interest of the individual affected. It was not intended through the Ombudsman to provide Members of Parliament with a means of obtaining information of general interest on the conduct of policy.

It is a purpose of the Official Secrets Acts to prevent unauthorized revelation of information about government conduct of policy. The Acts are, however, increasingly criticized in Britain, as it is doubted that the sanction of the criminal law is necessary to ensure official discretion. But as Sir Denis Greenhill stated in his evidence to the Franks Committee, he felt that "a special measure of protection" was needed in foreign relations;[18] and although he was speaking specifically of legal protection against unauthorized disclosures, his answer, when considered in the context of his entire evidence, implied protection for the whole range of foreign affairs. It is the view of the Foreign and Commonwealth Office that virtually all information about its activities is potentially sensitive and requires special protection. This is illustrated by the reply of Sir Denis that although much of the work of the educational and cultural attachés is "perfectly open," even this activity "should not be advertised."[19]

The Franks Committee Report recommended that where relations between nations were involved, the unauthorized revelation of official information should attract the possibility of criminal sanctions.[20] But the Committee was also strongly critical of over-secretiveness in foreign affairs, concluding that "a democratic government should not use the plea of secrecy to hide from the people its aims and policies in foreign any more than in

---

16. House of Commons Paper No. 54, 20 December 1967.
17. *Hansard,* H.C. Deb. 758, 5 February 1968, c. 107.
18. Franks Report (v.s.), vol. 3, p. 136.
19. *Ibid.,* p. 148.
20. *Ibid.,* vol. 1, p. 103.

domestic matters."[21] Nonetheless, Members of Parliament in their attempts to obtain just such information are all too frequently confronted by Ministers who plainly share the predisposition of the Foreign and Commonwealth Office to regard even the most innocent activities as matters that "should not be advertised."

The strongest argument the Foreign and Commonwealth Office can produce against giving information to Parliament is the touchiness of other nations that share the information or might be embarrassed by its disclosure. By and large, Governments are not prepared to shrug off such revelations as part of the normal democratic process. But within the EEC the practice of leaking information about current proposals and other Common Market matters is already accepted. Member countries and the Commission in Brussels have developed the "leak" as a tool of diplomacy. For example, the text of the proposed communiqué of the EEC Summit Conference of October 1972 was made public and published in *Le Monde* even before the heads of governments had assembled in Paris.[22] Indeed, Article 17 of the *Statute de Fonctionnaire* provides only that their civil servants must not publish texts without authority, which authority can be refused only if the envisaged publication is of such a nature as to jeopardize the interests of the Community.

There is some doubt as to how this will be construed and applied in the future, and the Foreign and Commonwealth Office appears to want the strictest construction to ensure non-publication of such official materials. But experience suggests that the Foreign and Commonwealth Office may not find it easy to prevent the practice of leaking from continuing. Unauthorized leaking is less desirable than authorized briefing; yet if leaking induces a gradual relaxation of attitude towards the revelation of official information, it will be a welcome development. The very openness of EEC diplomacy may enable Members of Parliament to participate in the formation of government attitudes toward proposed EEC policy. Indeed, Britain's membership could open up to scrutiny many foreign policy questions hitherto little considered by Parliament.

WHAT PARLIAMENT CAN DO ABOUT NON-DISCLOSURE

How should Members of Parliament seek to overcome the handicap of lack of information? There are several complementary possibilities. If they had access to better general information they would have a more critical understanding of the need for better official information. The existence of the

---

21. *Ibid.*, p. 49.
22. *The Times*, 21 October 1972.

International Institute for Strategic Studies has immensely improved the quality of the Parliamentary contribution to the continuing debate on Britain's defence needs. Independent bodies of experts such as this can at least help to identify some of the questions that ought to be put to Governments. Members of Parliament should be expected and financially assisted to travel. They would be helped by acquiring foreign languages and more frequently participating as observers at international conferences.

Parliamentary time for foreign affairs is inevitably short, but it could be better used. Debates would be more revealing and effective if they were less geographically and politically extensive. Parliament is at its most effective when it is most pointed. Governments do brief newspapers and broadcasting correspondents on current issues and the Government's attitude to them. They should do no less for Members of Parliament. These press-type conferences could be held in public as a rule and only exceptionally in private. The Government publishes an annual white paper on Defence. The foreign relations of the country deserve similar treatment. White papers should not merely reproduce already available texts of agreed communiqués and treaties but should present as well the premises upon which government policy is based and the objectives they consider it reasonable to seek.

Above all, Parliament needs the opportunity to cross-examine Ministers systematically about policy, and for this the specialist Select Committee is the only possible instrument. A Defence and External Affairs Sub-Committee of the Expenditure Committee has recently been established. Its functions are "to consider any papers on public expenditure presented to the House and such of the estimates as may seem fit to the Committee and in particular to consider how, if at all, the policies implied in the figures of expenditure and in the estimates may be carried out more economically, and to examine the form of the papers and of the estimates present to the House."[23]

With its concentration on the details of expenditure and economy this falls far short of the scope of the needed specialist committee which would range over the whole field of foreign affairs. The experience of the Canadian House of Commons discussed in Chapter 9 is enlightening in this respect. Now naturally, Ministers would not always be willing to reveal all the available information about foreign policy to such a committee. Parliament would need to show some reasonable forbearance about this if the experiment were to succeed. But the existence of such a committee would help to ensure that there would be within the House of Commons a body of Members fully conversant with the current issues and with the Government's detailed reasons for a particular policy. It could not be assumed that

---

23. House of Commons, 126 Sess. 1971–72, Standing Order No. 87.

such a committee would be radically at odds with Government policy. Indeed, the experience of such committees in other fields tends to suggest that there is some danger that committees of this kind may become stodgily establishment-minded. But it need not be so; and its success in dispelling ignorance, even if it did not—as it could not—reveal all the Government's secret information, would enhance Parliament's authority in the field of foreign affairs.

9

The Role of Parliament in the Review
and Planning of Canadian National Defence
and External Affairs

R. GORDON L. FAIRWEATHER, M.P.

Two decisions made within the past ten years, the first by the Canadian House of Commons for the reform of its procedures and the second by the Government of Canada to review its foreign policy, provide a convenient juxtaposition for considering whether Parliament had both the information and the opportunity to play a meaningful role in a thorough foreign policy review. For convenience I shall divide my chapter into four topics: first, the situation as it was before the 1965 rule changes, which were made permanent, with modifications, in 1968; second, a discussion of the 1965–68 reorganization of the House of Commons, which was the most fundamental since 1867; third, how the rule changes have worked; and fourth, suggestions for further reforms of the House of Commons organization and the work of its committees. The fourth part will include also a plea for accessibility of government information and less secrecy.

THE SITUATION BEFORE 1965

The 1965–68 reforms are the most important and far-reaching since Confederation in 1867. I will not be diverted into yet another polemic on Parliamentary reform. Cornucopias of this nature are available in great numbers elsewhere. Everyone who has thought about Parliament, including the high-school teacher who hurriedly shepherds her wards from the Visitors' Gallery lest they all turn into incorrigible cynics, has a hat full of pet reforms

---

Mr. Fairweather, Q.C., M.P., is a member of the Progressive Conservative Party of Canada. He was Attorney General of New Brunswick and is Opposition Parliamentary Spokesman for matters pertaining to the Ministry of Justice.

for these solemn sessions. Harold Laski once wrote that if all the criticisms of Parliament were added up, one might easily conclude that the institution ought to be abolished.

Procedural reform was one of the dominant issues of Canada's 26th Parliament, and even managed to compete for public attention with highly controversial matters such as the decision to have a national flag and charges of scandal in high places. Public interest in the subject was stimulated by the image of incompetence that the House of Commons presented to the nation throughout the marathon session of 1964–65. This session, which extended over fifteen months with only one recess, received less publicity for its achievements than for the sterile debates and interminable wrangling that continually obstructed its progress. Public confidence in Parliamentary democracy was severely shaken. It is my thesis that the public's frustration was vented also on the Prime Minister of the day, Lester Pearson, and accounted for his inability to lead his Liberal party to a majority of the seats in the general election of 1965.

The procedure of the Canadian House of Commons was inherited from the British Parliament at the time of Confederation in 1867. Canada made an inevitable progression through the various evolutionary stages from colony to independence, but, paradoxically, it experienced no such evolution of its Parliamentary rules and procedures. These remained largely as they had been in the British Parliament prior to the reforms of the 1880's. The British had been pushed to reform by the crisis in Ireland. Canada had no such motivation, and the pressure for procedural reform was not felt here until eighty years later.

A key to reform was the developing of a functional committee system. The report of our Special Committee on Procedure and Organization expressed the view "that the potential value of the committee system of the House of Commons is not being exploited to the full," and that "the structure of the Standing Committees tends to be cumbersome and, in some respects, archaic." The Committee stated its conviction "that a fundamental reorganization of Standing Committees is necessary if they are to be revitalized and their effectiveness and prestige enhanced."

A Parliamentary committee system must be considered in relation to the institution of which it forms a part. One often hears suggestions that Canada should look to the United States Congressional system, but these suggestions overlook the fact that the Congressional system and the Parliamentary system are entirely different forms of government. Under the Parliamentary system the Executive governs and is responsible to Parliament. Parliament has no executive power but it can influence, criticize, and in the final analysis, uphold or dismiss a Government. A Parliamentary committee system must, therefore, reflect the functions of the parent body.

Until 1965 Canada's Parliamentary committees were few in number, infrequently assembled, and then carefully controlled by the Government (which in Canada, as in Britain, is roughly equivalent to the Executive in the United States and is usually taken to mean the Cabinet, any Junior ministers, and their Parliamentary aides). The announced purpose of the reforms was to provide what history seems to have denied most Parliamentary committees. They were to "save the time of the whole house" and in the words of Prime Minister Pearson, to "make a thorough-going examination of the administration of government in all its forms." Because Canadian procedure failed to keep pace with the changing requirements and growing complexity of modern Parliamentary government, the public was treated to prolonged sessions of the House of Commons, where obstruction was master and irrelevancy swamped most debates, depriving them of theme and meaning.

Canadian legislators, sensing the public mood, took the first of a series of actions which would culminate in the reforms of December 1968. A number of changes that radically altered the substantive procedure were implemented on a provisional basis during the years 1964–67, some deriving from the recommendations of Procedure Committees and others from resolutions initiated by the Government. Being provisional, they depended upon renewal at each session. Meanwhile, the fundamental task of devising new permanent procedures acceptable to all parties remained to be accomplished. Another complicating feature was that there were general elections in Canada in June 1962, April 1963, November 1965, and June 1968, so that Parliamentarians had preoccupations other than those of procedural reform.

THE 1968 REORGANIZATION OF
THE HOUSE OF COMMONS

Under the new rules of procedure the work and significance of the Standing Committees of the House have been greatly increased. Eighteen Standing Committees are provided for by Standing Order, and most of them specialize in a particular subject area. With certain exceptions each of these committees combines the three functions of legislation, finance, and *ad hoc* inquiry; bills, estimates, and specific investigations are all referred to the same committees in accordance with the subject areas they cover. The intention of this new procedure is to remove as much detailed work as possible from the floor of the House; to enable members to develop a subject expertise through service on committees; and to give to committees an important new role in the parliamentary process.

The Standing Committee on External Affairs and National Defence consists of thirty members and, like other Standing Committees, is empowered to examine and enquire into all such matters as are referred to it by the House. This Committee can send for persons, papers, and records and print papers as evidence. It can delegate to subcommittees all or any of its powers except that of reporting directly to the House. Although the Committee technically cannot go beyond the terms of reference granted by the House, in practice the subject matter of enquiries or studies is developed by the Committee and, after consultation with House leadership, is granted by the House without debate.

These Committees are instruments of the House that appoints them, and they can have no powers that the House itself does not have. They report directly to the House, and the final outcome of any committee investigation is normally a set of recommendations that the House can debate, accept, reject, refer back, or even ignore. Thus the ultimate power of a Parliamentary committee is one of recommendation only. It is completely responsible to the House that appoints it. The House defines its terms of reference, and only the House can alter them.

The recommendations of a committee do not necessarily have to be debated in order to be acted upon. Parliament uses its committees in order to relieve its own workload, and if it did not act on the advice of its committees to a great extent, the system would be self-defeating. The prestige of a committee can add weight to its recommendations, and if the work of a particular committee is well regarded by the Government, its advice may be considered and acted upon even though its report is not formally adopted on a motion for concurrence. Committees seem to be more effective when the subject being investigated is of a specialized nature; thus, for example, the Justice and Legal Affairs Standing Committee was able to scuttle an ill-conceived bill on young offenders because most members of that committee had knowledge of the law as well as professional experience in dealing firmly and wisely with juveniles. The Committee was able to prevent officials from doing extraordinarily impractical things. As we shall see, the Standing Committee on External Affairs and National Defence, in its first major effort, the NATO review, fared less well.

The committees have representation from the various parties in the House of Commons in proportion to their strength there. For example, in the 29th Parliament there are one hundred nine Liberals, one hundred seven Progressive Conservatives, thirty-one New Democrats, fifteen Social Creditors, and two Independents, one of whom is the Speaker. Thus the membership of the Standing Committee on External Affairs and National Defence is: twelve Liberals, twelve Progressive Conservatives, four New Democrats, two Social Credit. The Senate also has a Standing Committee on

Foreign Affairs, but in view of the unrepresentative nature of the Canadian Senate, I have not considered here its rules or committee structure. The Senate Foreign Affairs report on Canadian Caribbean relations, for example, provided useful recommendations, but its work has very little public impact because it is seldom well publicized.

The Standing Committee has subpoena powers that are rarely used; an invitation to appear is invariably enough. Ministers come to the committees with prepared statements and are examined on matters of policy, leaving more mundane details of administration of the Department of External Affairs or Defence to be accounted for by Civil Service officials. Technically, a failure to respond to an order to appear could result in the gaoling of a recalcitrant witness. I am unclear as to whether the offender would be put away in some storeroom in the bowels of the Parliament Building or if relations between Parliament and the civic officials of Ottawa are sufficiently cordial as to permit the use of the local gaol. The technique would be for the committee to report the contempt to the House, and the House would then determine the penalty. There is a civility about responses to requests to testify before Canadian Parliamentary Committees which is a welcome acknowledgement that we are up to some good after all!

To be effective, the reorganized Standing Committees required some new means by which information could be made available to members serving on them. Partly as a consequence of the reorganization of committees and the reform of procedures, the following collateral changes also took place: the Parliamentary Centre for Foreign Affairs and Foreign Trade was established; funds were provided for research staffs for political parties represented in Parliament; and a separate Research Branch was organized within the Parliamentary Library.

The Parliamentary Centre for Foreign Affairs and Foreign Trade is the brainchild of Peter Dobell, the present director, who assumed the position with a background of sixteen years in the Canadian Foreign Service. The Centre, which has offices near but not on Parliament Hill, is funded in a unique way by a vote in the estimates of Mr. Speaker, from a grant from the Canadian Institute of International Affairs (which is itself the recipient of some government funds but in such a way as to ensure the neutrality and independence of its judgement and action), and from subscriptions from Canadian corporations and trade unions. The Centre staff is small but expert, and relations with the Standing Committee on External Affairs and Defence are excellent. The Centre assists the Standing Committee by suggesting possible witnesses for committee hearings, providing background data, and arranging for briefings for Parliamentarians who take part in international conferences. Since the founding of the Centre I have not heard a word of suspicion about bias; this speaks well for the sensitivity of the director and staff and suggests that the method chosen to finance the operation has merit.

A *quid pro quo* for getting Parliament's acceptance of the changes in the rules and procedures was that the Government placed a grant of $195,000 in the estimates so that the opposition parties could hire research staffs. Later, the sum of $130,000 was added to provide research for the Parliament supporters of the Government. A noticeable improvement in content of speeches and questions has resulted;[1] this is particularly true (I add gratuitously) when the issues involved have a low emotion-quotient. Debates on abolishing capital punishment continue to be a series of statements taken from firmly fixed positions, whereas a bill to provide a measure of control of Canadian business takeovers by foreign corporations was discussed largely on its merits—thanks to the new research component.

The Research Branch of the Library of Parliament is another fruit of the rule changes and is used by members requiring a longer look at implications of policy or forecasts of things to come.

HOW THE NEW REFORMS HAVE WORKED

Notice was given by Prime Minister Trudeau during the 1968 election campaign that a review of foreign policy was contemplated. The review was needed, as he said, "because of the changing nature of Canada and the world around us." What was sought was policies that would "accord with our national needs and resources, with our ability to discharge Canada's legitimate responsibilities in world affairs." The study of so recent an event as the foreign policy review conducted between 1968 and 1970 poses many problems for a researcher, chief among them a lack of available written material. My membership on the Standing Committee on External Affairs and National Defence gives me some status as a witness to what happened on Parliament's side of the review, and yet obviously I, too, suffer frustration because of lack of material in attempting to analyse how the review developed and reached its final form.

The Standing Committee on External Affairs and National Defence was

---

1. Ten Parliamentary Interns—graduate students spread among the two hundred and sixty-four Members of Parliament—might seem too insignificant a number to effect the study and scrutiny of legislation and policy. This is not so, as I have reason to know. Professor Paul Thomas, now of the University of Manitoba, was of immeasurable assistance to me during his six-month internship in 1972.

Bruce Thordarson, who specialized in International Affairs at Carleton University in Ottawa, also served as a Parliamentary Intern and is now on the staff of the Parliamentary Centre. Mr. Thordarson's book *Trudeau and Foreign Policy* complements Peter Dobell's *Canada's Search for New Roles* and gives evidence of the resources available to Members of Parliament.

not immune to the public expectations aroused by the election rhetoric and subsequent government announcement that a review of foreign policy and defence commitment was under way.

The terms of reference of the Standing Committee were direct enough. The House of Commons on 16 January, 1969 "Ordered,—That the Standing Committee on External Affairs and National Defence be instructed, to hear evidence on and consider Canada's policy with reference to defence and external affairs." A later order permitted this Committee to travel outside Canada "for the purpose of furthering their work." During the twenty-four meetings held in Canada during January, February, and March of 1969, the Committee heard sixteen witnesses ranging from the Deputy Chief of Operations of the Canadian Armed Forces and the chairman of the Science Council of Canada, to Professor Adam Yarmolinsky, then of Harvard Law School and formerly an adviser to President John F. Kennedy, as well as two senior staff members of the Hudson Institute of New York. A cross section of Canadian political scientists, historians, and economists was also heard.

The Committee visited Europe, making stops in Cyprus, the Federal Republic of Germany, Great Britain, Switzerland, Sweden, France, and Belgium. Discussions were held with NATO civilian and military personnel, including the Supreme Allied Commander in Europe. European politicians and officials of foreign and defence ministries also participated in discussions with Committee members, though usually not in a formal way. The fact that a committee of the Canadian House of Commons was convening meetings in various countries of Europe was said to have caused a flutter among those who worry about the propriety of such events.

The Committee had hoped to present a report and recommendations to Parliament with regard to Canadian participation in the North Atlantic Treaty Organization before the Government announced its NATO policy on or before 10 April, 1969, at the North Atlantic Council meeting in Washington. As the Committeemen left Europe to return to Canada on 22 March, they were under a severe handicap as to time for the preparation and submission of the report, but finally accomplished this on 26 March, thus beating the Government's deadline by a few days. Among its recommendations were the following:

1. Canada should continue to play an effective role in the preservation of peace through membership in NATO.

2. Canada should continue to maintain forces in Europe as a contribution to the collective defence arrangements of NATO.

3. Canada should continue its present roles in Europe until such time as the main items of equipment for its Air Division and Mechanized Brigade require replacement.

4. The future long-term military roles of Canadian forces assigned to NATO should be reviewed promptly and kept under periodic review in the future by the Government and this Committee, bearing in mind (a) the desirability that our NATO forces should be as compatible as possible with our other forces; (b) that decisions on roles must be arrived at in sufficient time to negotiate with our allies and, if necessary, to acquire new equipment and to retrain forces.

5. Through NATO, Canada should use its influence to seek detente in Europe and, while maintaining security, negotiate balanced force reductions.

There were also promises of separate reports on the subject of Canada's Maritime forces earmarked for NATO and for peacekeeping, civil defence, and disarmament.

The priority given the NATO defence review had its incongruous aspects. Prime Minister Trudeau had frequently expressed a desire to ensure that Canada's defence policy would flow out of its foreign policy. Yet the decision to revise Canada's military contribution to NATO and to set new defence priorities preceded, by fourteen months, the publication in 1970 of a government paper outlining a new approach to foreign policy. The first reason for this was to be found in the exigencies of fiscal planning. The Cabinet needed to know as quickly as possible the size of the defence budget for the fiscal year 1969–70, and only after a thorough review of defence policy could the Government decide whether this budget should be reduced, increased, or frozen.

Moreover, the annual review of NATO by all its members was approaching, when Canada and the other member countries would be required to make firm military commitments for one year and tentative forecasts for the next five years. Mr. Trudeau acknowledged that the need to meet this 10 April, 1969, deadline had influenced the order in which the components of Canada's external policy had been reviewed. As he said, "It is more difficult, and not easier, for us to have to make a decision on NATO before we have made a decision on other aspects of our foreign and defence policy." Yet that is exactly what we had to do.

Finally, it can be surmised that the defence review was given priority because NATO was the issue that seemed to arouse the greatest interest among critics of Canadian foreign policy, and because it was one of the areas in which Mr. Trudeau himself appeared critical of existing policy. I would add that many M.P.'s had special reasons for being interested in the outcome of the Government's review. Some had previous experience as Ministers of National Defence; others were members of the NATO Parliamentary Association—known around Parliament Hill as the most "gung-ho" of all of the Parliament groupings; and still others were representing constituents recently arrived from Europe with understandably inflexible attitudes about *détente* and the North Atlantic Alliance. Yet, as many observers pointed out, NATO was symbolic of the detested *status quo*.[2]

The NATO review process included several new departures on the part of the Government. One was to seek advice beyond the public service and another was the Prime Minister's encouragement of Cabinet Ministers to express publicly their own differing views on NATO. It is a pity that our Parliamentary Standing Committee on External Affairs and National Defence did not also avail itself of the opportunity of having the outside experts testify before it as they did before the group preparing the foreign policy review. It is also a pity that the review process inside the Government did not have better liaison with the Parliamentary Committee. For example, no M.P.'s were included in the list of invitations to a weekend seminar in Hull in January 1969, at which academics and a large number of officials from the Departments of Defence, External Affairs, and Industry, Trade and Commerce foregathered.

To stimulate discussion at that meeting, the Government distributed six background papers covering such topics as Canada's relations with Eastern Europe, Canadian-European economic relations, Europe and national unity, and Europe as a counterweight to the United States. It was the paper dealing with Canada's defence relations with Europe, however, that dominated the discussions. It soon became clear that academics had come to talk about NATO. Assessments of the success of the seminar vary; some called it a dialogue of the deaf, and others thought there had been no real conflict of ideas. If the seminar was a valuable learning experience—which in itself is no mean achievement—Members of Parliament might have profited from

---

2. Other diplomatic initiatives of both Canada and the United States, such as recognition of the People's Republic of China and its succession to the U.N. Security Council seat formerly held by Nationalist China, President Nixon's journeys to Peking and to Moscow, have long since dampened down the restlessness of that part of the public that sought new direction in foreign policy. The truth is that foreign affairs had no impact on the Canadian General Election of October 1972, and it is becoming increasingly difficult to arouse interest in broad international policy issues. Such preoccupations as the role of Canada in a supervisory mission in Vietnam give rise to parliamentary questions, and a one-day debate on arrangements for sending the force to Vietnam, and extricating it should the need arise, but the wire services and the correspondents of the several large-circulation Canadian newspapers reported only the two or three lead speeches, and these only sparingly. Or to put it another way, the impact of Parliament on such decisions is as usual, very little indeed.

Despite this somewhat jaundiced comment, I continue to believe that it is essential to have a core of M.P.'s who are knowledgeable about the broad implications of Canada's foreign commitments. Foreign affairs may be considered by some to be non-partisan but I, for one, get nervous when Canadian international involvement is debated in a sort of never-never land where it is *infra dig* to challenge the authorized version. Prime Minister Edward Heath might have got away with his ill-conceived plan to provide arms to the Republic of South Africa had it not been for the cries of outrage from Labour, Liberal, and Conservative M.P.'s. Who knows how much earlier the tragedy of Vietnam could have ended had the issue of U.S. involvement been joined much earlier than it was.

being there. But—come now—despite a change in rules and an overturning of all the old accepted truths about Canada's role in foreign affairs, we must not go to the extreme of permitting M.P.'s to share a learning experience![3]

Perhaps the problem was the multiplicity of contending reviews that got under way in this first Canadian experiment with "open" policy-planning. The Trudeau Cabinet had to contend with a series of reports as they prepared to make their NATO decision. There was the report of our Parliamentary Committee, one prepared by the public service departments involved in foreign activities, one by an interdepartmental Special Task Force on Relations with Europe that became known by the code name STAFFEUR. There was also a report of a more specialized nature known as the External-Defence Report and classified as "Secret, for Canadian Eyes Only." This dealt with the problems and costs of maintaining and replacing military equipment and with the international obligations to which Canada was committed, and analyzed all possible options ranging from neutrality to increased support of NATO. "Secret, for Canadian Eyes Only" did not include the eyes of Canadian Members of Parliament.

To complete the record we must refer to one final report prepared by the Prime Minister's own advisers, a committee chaired by Ivan Head. The report is known as "Canadian Defence Policy—a Study" but referred to by a few in the Prime Minister's Office and the Privy Council Office as the "non-group report." This is perhaps a somewhat derisive allusion to the large bureaucratic and Parliamentary committees or "groups" that had prepared the other NATO studies. Yet some of us "groupies" may have some satisfaction reflecting that, as it turned out, we seem to have been more closely in tune with the realities of the Government's options than was the "non-group."

The time factor pressed the Government relentlessly. The Parliamentary Standing Committee began work at a very late date; yet the Government could hardly avoid considering the Committee's report even though it was not tabled until March 26, 1969. The Cabinet met to decide Canada's defence policy with respect to NATO the following weekend, but no statement was made until Parliament rose for the Easter recess. Thus the House of Commons did not have an opportunity to hear or discuss the Government's NATO decision. The leader of the New Democratic Party summed up the belief of many of us when he said, "I say the only reason he [the Prime Minister] is not making the statement in the House today is that he has no respect for the House of Commons and for Parliament and wishes to make the statement outside."

---

3. The incident reminds me of the Defence Department official who told me I could not have a certain piece of information because I had "not been cleared for NATO secrets." I am still not cleared for NATO secrets but I have a much better idea about how to go about getting the data I require and I do believe that government departments are slowly becoming more forthcoming about sharing what they know.

The Prime Minister announced the decision the very next day.

Before leaving the topic of Canada's NATO involvement, I must make some general observations. The chronology of events points up the dilemma faced by a strong committee that must conduct its affairs within the limitations of the Parliamentary system. In the case of our Standing Committee on External Affairs and National Defence, the frustrations were accentuated by lack of sufficient time and the fact that the new rules and procedures had only recently been accepted by Parliament (in December 1968). The Government, having pressed the House to agree on the new committee structure, was duty bound to go through the motions of awaiting the committee report before making its final decision. It stretches credulity, however, to believe that the Committee's report had any significant impact on the ultimate policy decision of the Government.

Yet there were dividends from this first, weak-kneed attempt to make a Standing Committee contribute to policy-making and exert influence. The hearings produced a group of M.P.'s who were in general much better informed than the majority of the Cabinet members. Undoubtedly when the Government considered whether to withdraw or reduce the number of Canadian forces the opinions of its followers in Parliament were canvassed.[4] I am sure that the Prime Minister and Government realized that their Liberal caucus would not approve of the Government's decision to withdraw all Canadian troops from Europe. To this extent, then, the process had not been in vain. In the Opposition caucus, too, the M.P.'s who had served on the Committee played a role in urging their views on fellow Members.

It might be thought that the Standing Committee had cause to be discouraged by the result of its first major attempt to influence policy. Most politicians are realists and accepted limitations imposed upon them by the Parliamentary system. The tension between the Executive and Parliament will continue, and I am optimistic enough to believe that the tension will be of a productive rather than a negative variety.

Essentially, then, the foreign policy review was conducted by four groups all of which were under the aegis of either the Parliamentary or Executive structure. Invitations to academics and other experts to appear before the Standing Committee or the committee of officials meant some opinion mix; yet most of the studies were conducted independently of one another. This technique is part of the Prime Minister's well publicized wish to get inputs from outside the established structure. Insofar as I am aware, the "non-group" chaired by Ivan Head functioned in secret, and its existence was not known to the Departments of External Affairs or National Defence.

---

4. One Liberal M.P. observed that the great weight of opinion in the party was in favour of continuing a strong relation with NATO, and this cannot be ignored. Another member predicted that if the Government decided on the immediate withdrawal of troops from Europe it would split the party wide open.

The Standing Committee on External Affairs and National Defence has had several other opportunities to review government policy since the new rules gave it a wider mandate and a better defined status. Subcommittees considered the subjects of international development assistance, the role of the Maritime force, peace-keeping. The full Committee studied and reported on Canada-U.S. relations and also heard evidence and made a report on the Canadian Foreign Policy Review.

On the whole, the Committee's reports have been well-balanced, perhaps more so than the Government's own position papers and statements of policy. The report on NATO added to the Prime Minister's problems (as we have seen) by advocating the maintenance of existing force levels. The Committee also gave a more balanced view of the Canadian role in international affairs in the postwar years. The Government's foreign policy review took a rather strong new line in suggesting that the nation's foreign policy should and would in future be "the extension abroad of national policies." This apparent rejection of the more internationalist-minded postwar years—a source of pride to many Canadians—inevitably gave rise to concern within the country that Canadian policy was to be significantly reoriented and was in future to be more self-serving. This unease has revealed itself in particular in some of the testimony before the House of Commons Standing Committee which conducted hearings from November 1970 to June 1971 on the first (or general) volume of the Government's "Foreign Policy for Canadians" and is reflected in the more balanced report of this committee.

The Committee, directly, through its individual members' role in the party caucus, and by the mere fact of its existence, has also played a role in the refining of U.S.-Canadian relations. Many Canadians are apprehensive about the possible mortgaging of Canada's capacity for independent decision-making. This point alarmed the Standing Committee. As its eleventh report on Canada-U.S. relations, prepared in 1970, concluded,

> The danger facing Canada is not one of political absorption by the United States: the danger which Canada must guard against is that it will drift into such a position of dependency in relation to the United States that it will be unable, in practice, to adopt policies displeasing to the United States because of the fear of the American reaction which would involve consequences unacceptable to Canadians.

The Committee can influence government policy not only through its hearings and reports but also by merely threatening to conduct a study or force a debate. In at least one important case, this caused the Cabinet to act more decisively and quickly than it otherwise might. Discovery of oil on the north slope of Alaska set in motion a chain of events in Canadian-U.S. relations centering on the issue of sovereignty in the Arctic. The slow passage of the *Manhattan,* a supertanker converted into an icebreaker, evoked great interest in Canada. But some members of the Standing Committee on Indian Affairs and Northern Development were alarmed that the transit of the Northwest Passage might generate an internationally-accepted presumption that this ice-covered route was an international waterway. They pressed the Government to assert Canadian claims but the Government was not ready to do so; its hand was forced because committee members asked for a debate on an emergency basis at an awkward time in Parliament's timetable. The pressure was kept up, and finally a Progressive Conservative member of the Committee on the floor of the Commons moved concurrence in the committee report, and his right to do so was upheld by the Speaker. The Government talked out the report but could no longer avoid the issue, and a series of tough measures followed, among them amendments to the Territorial Sea and Fishing Zones Act extending the breadth of the territorial sea to twelve miles, and the introduction and passage of the Arctic Waters Pollution Prevention Act.

The implications of the Government's handling of the issue are fascinating. For example, the bill was given unanimous consent as a result of the initiative of an Opposition party leader, and thus the Government was protected from further political criticism on a subject on which, until that moment, the Opposition had been effectively attacking it. In this instance a Standing Committee had had the information and the chance to play a vital role in making policy. The evaluation of that policy is an ongoing enterprise, but in future the Standing Committee will be taken seriously by the Government.

During the 1960's Canadians were yearning for an independent role in world affairs. The Prime Minister responded to the mood, and the foreign policy review was set in motion. A cynic might suggest that the act of having the review was enough in itself and that the actual content was of lesser importance. Fortunately, Members of Parliament are not immune to public opinion and they accordingly responded to cross-currents, one for an increased status and role for themselves within the parliamentary system, and the other, a need to assert Canadian independence in foreign affairs. Canadian nationalism is a prevailing element of our ethic; it was the cement of the Canadian founding statute—the British North America Act—and in contemporary terms could be the element strengthening the forces of internal cohesion that must prevail if Canada is to survive and grow.

FURTHER REFORMS AND ACCESS TO
GOVERNMENT INFORMATION

It is improbable that Canada will return to a situation in which the Legislature is itself able to generate a significant proportion of the policy decisions of Government. Yet the result of our new structure of committees and their increased research support is more public understanding of the issues underlying policy options. There are also opportunities for committee members to use the expertise and information gained in committee to outline policy directions either to the full caucus of their party in Parliament or the relevant caucus committees. Begun early enough, this process can influence policy-making and the form in which Parliament does, or does not, ratify government initiatives.

If we cannot have government by Parliament, neither can there be, on the other hand, any going back to the days of a wholly docile government majority accepting without question the authority of the whip as legislation is pushed through the Committee of the Whole House. Indeed, there will be more reforms, which will include a deadline for the convening of committees once a new Parliament begins its term; more access by committee members to classified or secret information; a panel of "cross-party" chairmen from whom can be drawn the chairman of a particular Standing Committee (as is now the case at Westminster); and more freedom on the part of standing committees to initiate their own program and agenda.

Other aspects of Parliamentary reform included a fundamental change in the way the Government's spending estimates were considered. Happily this work is now done by the appropriate standing committee rather than by the unwieldy Committee of the Whole (House) on Supply. Yet despite welcome changes in the committee system, the system is still imperfect. To begin with, the new Standing Orders do not guarantee that the Standing Committee will begin work on the estimates (or any other matter) early each session, but only "with all convenient speed," a not inconvenient phrase for allowing dilatory referrals.

In general, however, the trend towards committee effectiveness and independence is clearly set. There can be little doubt that the Government now has less effective control of standing committees. Many times, of course, broad views adopted by the Government can be submerged as Members of Parliament tend to grind their own axes. But this was a risk that the Government took in agreeing to the latest reforms in rules and procedures, and it is a small cost. Several Standing Committees are equipping themselves with expert staffs, if not on a permanent basis, then at least during the consideration of a particular bill or report.

There was no way, for example, that the Standing Committee on Transport and Communications could hope to meet on equal terms the railways' freight-rate experts, who make a lifetime profession of the vagaries of railway rate structures. The Committee quite properly had to get help when the new Canadian Transportation Bill was before it. So, too, the Special Joint Committee of the Senate and House of Commons on the Constitution had essential and invaluable assistance from a Constitutional lawyer and an economist, as it considered ways to make the Constitution—now a British statute—into a wholly-Canadian instrument and amend its provisions relative to power-sharing in a federal state. Actually both committees are examples of a neat blending of the theoretical and the practical. A constructive tension resulted from the interplay between views pressed upon us by the experts, and their challenge by those who have the added responsibility of representing the often conflicting interests of the public.

SOME THOUGHTS ON SECRECY

Here are my tentative thoughts about this matter of government secrecy.

First, we should be told much more about the background against which decisions are taken.

Second, there is a vast shaded area about which most of us know nothing and generally suspect the worst. Flitting in and out of the penumbra are the cognoscenti and those who wish to appear to be of that number. The nearer we are to the source of truth, the more we will hear—though not necessarily the more truths. Foreign affairs and defence are the deepest in the shadow. We accept the necessity for some of this, but surely it is grossly overdone.

Third, when the Government consults with private interests before finally taking decisions, could we not be told something of the bargains struck, the compromises reached, the promises given?

Fourth—and most generally—the Cabinet, its individual members, and its supporting bureaucracy, could afford to be much more open about policy objectives and national goals. Ministers seem to be genuinely fearful of being specific about even the ends they are seeking to achieve.

In an article entitled "on Telling People" in *Essays on Reform 1967* (edited by Bernard Crick, Professor J. A. G. Griffith writes:

> The wish to take the lid off the machinery of government, to see how it works, who says what to whom, at what level decisions are taken, what private criteria are used, how far 'politics' is allowed to override those criteria, on what statistical and other 'facts' the decisions are based: this wish does not derive only from curiosity or from party animosity but also from self-interest, from *quis custodiet,* and from a feeling (by some) that Governments represent another group interest.

Professor Griffith's piece concludes with a plea—one I applaud—for "telling people." Although written for British readers, it applies with equal aptness to Canada. We read in the newspapers, we listen to and look at political commentators, and then we hear Ministerial statements; the differences between what we are told by unofficial and by official sources make us conscious of the existence of another, hidden, world, the other side of the moon. So we become cynical to the point of switching off radio and television during general election broadcasts because, simply, we do not believe what is being said. The evasions, the half-truths, the falsities shine through the words and we are angered because we are treated like children. So politicians are laughed at—and remain powerful. Can all this play-acting really be necessary for the management of fifty million people? Only if politicians trust the people can they expect to be trusted. If politicians wish to be trusted, they must take us into their confidence.

I am by no means sanguine about the Canadian scene, but I do suggest that our recently adopted rules relative to standing committees go a long way toward meeting some of the public disquiet and frustration. While the play-acting is still woefully very much part of the scene, more and more of the right questions are being asked. The mask of Civil Service anonymity is slipping slightly and there is a greater disposition to answer questions. More of the right questions are being asked—thanks to the much better research facilities available. I myself would prefer a much more concentrated examination of the spending estimates to see whether past policies are still relevant to changing conditions.

If Parliaments could be persuaded to exercise some self-discipline and agree to concentrate their examination on three or four departments per year, the results might be surprising to public and politician both. It would be easier to ask the "correct questions" if one knew in advance that in 1973 the estimates of the Department of Indian Affairs and Northern Development, the Post Office, and the Ministry of Transport were earmarked for careful scrutiny. Other departments could be given a more routine check but always forewarned that their day will come.

The truth is that if anything useful and significant is to be done in a free society, it must be done publicly and in such a way as to consult, involve, and carry with it those affected. We are in an age where the legislator has assumed a new role, that of building acceptance of government policy. This is an age where the twin uglies of dehumanization and depersonalization make it more important than ever that the legislator understand the purpose and thrust of government policy and be able to interpret to a bemused and confused constituency. Understanding and consent in this instance do not spring from some previous interaction of Government and voter at a general election, but is the constantly renewed product of a continual exchange of communications.

While there are no procedures in the Canadian Parliament that would permit a core of M.P.'s with "some competence in a substantive field of government" to "control" or manage any subsequent debate on the subject in Parliament, they do become a force: one with disproportionate power based on the competence and information they have gained through their committee work on a defined issue. For example, the Standing Committee on Broadcasting, Films and Assistance to the Arts gained special knowledge of the rationale behind the Broadcasting Act of 1968. Committee members worked closely on the bill and also studied a government report on the future of public and private broadcasting. Close contact between M.P.'s meant that partisan suspicion was lessened, so that when the bill returned to the House of Commons, the debate was not so much one between Government and Opposition as between those who had been on the committee and those who had not.

Standing Committees "covering" certain departments of state can exercise a role in public education, provide a focus for the debate of particular issues, and provide a forum for finding out what the Government is doing. Committees must have the facilities for scrutiny, investigation, and publication; and these essentials are well on their way to being met in Canada.

A concomitant of the improved committee system is a lessening of the Government's predilection for secrecy. The equilibrium to be maintained among publicity, secrecy, and privacy in governmental affairs is impossible to define in the abstract with any precision. The reconciliation of the competing claims of publicity, secrecy, and privacy must be approached on an individual case basis. Yet no society can attain an appropriate balance before there has been an intelligent debate on the theoretical, Constitutional, and practical issues involved. It is to be hoped that from within the chapters of this book some of the answers can be found. I am sure it is not sufficient to keep repeating with boring regularity slogans like "open access" or "executive privilege."

We must avoid what Harold Laski once described as the "trained incompetence of the specialist"—that narrowness of vision that often comes with immersion in a program or a policy field. Breadth of view must be combined with technical skill in effective policy-making. In general, the training of information technologists does not overcome their limited social and political sensitivities. Harold L. Wilensky makes the point well: "The danger of technicism is in direct proportion to the shortage of educated men. Too often the new technologists are methodological and exact in their specialized fields, but impressionable, naive and opinionated on broader issues of policy."

One means of attaining an appropriate balance is through the Standing Committees of Parliament, which might be receptive to assistance from those possessing special technical skills. The Report of the Task Force on Government Information states that: "One way to check apathy, alienation and disaffection toward government is to ensure that the flow of information, back and forth between government and people, is fast, accurate, credible, open and relevant to the public issues of the time."

It is now possible to arrive more efficiently at wrong decisions, based upon poor judgement and buttressed by awesome statistics than ever before. Ignorance cannot be the basis of sound policy-making; so also must we be sure our definition of knowledge is not dangerously narrow. Bemoaning the decline of meaningful action, T. S. Eliot once spoke of a world that ends "not with a bang but a whimper." What we have to fear is that the bang will come, preceded by the contemporary equivalent of a whimper—a faint rustle of paper as some self-convinced chief of state, reviewing a secret memo full of comfortable rationalizations just repeated at the final conference, fails to muster the necessary intelligence and wit, and miscalculates the power and intent of his adversaries.

As Bernard Crick reminds us, "If doubt goes with a genuine scepticism, that is an asset not to be despised." Santayana once called scepticism "the chastity of intellect—one does not give oneself to the first set of new ideas that come along." But scepticism is not to be confused with cynicism, for the true sceptic has standards and he has hopes even if purely secular and usually disappointed.

Although it is acknowledged that Canadian M.P.'s did not make a significant contribution to the Government's review of foreign policy in general and the NATO commitment in particular, the basis for evaluating future government policy was laid down. A restructured committee system backed with a variety of aids for research so that the right questions will be asked, has helped develop better informed and more competent Members of Parliament. Parliament must convince the Cabinet that this is to its advantage: that Parliament is the great mediator between people and executive power, informing and listening to the people and legitimating the use of power. The key element in this process is a more continuous, intimate interaction between authority and those subject to authority. And to be able to have this, the Member of Parliament, and hence the public, must be subjected to far less secrecy than is now the case.

BIBLIOGRAPHY

Books

Crick, Bernard. *The Reform of Parliament.* London: Weidenfeld & Nicolson, 1964.

Dobell, Peter C. *Canada's Search for New Roles: Foreign Policy in the Trudeau Era.* Toronto-New York: Oxford University Press, 1972.

Laski, Harold. *Reflections on the Constitution*. London: N.U.P., 1951.

Thordarson, Bruce. *Trudeau and Foreign Policy: A Study in Decision-Making*. Toronto-New York: Oxford University Press, 1972.

Wilensky, Harold. *Organizational Intelligence: Knowledge and Policy in Government and Industry*. New York: Basic Books, 1967.

Essays and Periodical Articles

Beer, Samuel H. "The British Legislature and the Problem of Nobilizing Consent," in *Essays on Reform: A Centenary Tribute*, ed. Bernard Crick Toronto-New York: Oxford University Press, 1967.

Griffith, J. A. G. "On Telling People," *ibid.*

Head, Ivan. "The Foreign Policy of the New Canada," in 50 *Foreign Affairs: An American Quarterly Review*, January 1972.

Laundy, Philip. "The Visit of the Canadian Procedure Committee to Westminster" in *The Table* (London: Butterworth & Co.), vol. 36 (1967).

———. The Current State of Procedure in the Canadian House of Commons," *ibid.*, vol. 39 (1970).

———. "Procedural Reform in the Canadian House of Commons," vol. 34 (1965).

Papers

Hockin, T. A. *The 1965 Parliamentary Reforms and the Future of Canada's House of Commons*. A Paper presented to the meeting of the Canadian Political Science Association, Sherbrooke, Que., June 8–10, 1966.

Laundy, Philip. *Parliamentary Committees in the Canadian House of Commons*. Unpublished paper, 1973.

Thomas, Paul. *House of Commons Committees and Legislative Oversight*. Unpublished paper, 1972.

———. *The Problem of Administrative Secrecy*. Unpublished paper, 1972.

Official Publications

Canada, Parliament. House of Commons. *Debates*. Ottawa: Queen's Printer, April 2, 1969.

Canada, Parliament. Standing Committee on External Affairs and National Defence. *Report*. Ottawa: Queen's Printer, 1971.

Canada, Task Force on Government Information. *Report*. Ottawa: Queen's Printer, 1969.

United Kingdom, Departmental Committee on Section 2 of the Official Secrets Act 1911. *Report*, vol. 1. London: Her Majesty's Stationery Office, September 1972.

Part 3

The Media Confronts the News Managers

10

The Irreconcilable Conflict Between Press and Government: "Whose Side Are You On?"

HAYNES JOHNSON

In a moment of frustration and pique, Dean Rusk once snapped to a group of journalists: "There gets to be a point when the question is, 'Whose side are you on?' Now, I'm Secretary of State of the United States, and I'm on *our* side."[1]

To those who see the increasingly serious and bitter conflict between press and government as stemming solely from the Vietnam era, Rusk's remark sounded a familiar refrain. It was "us" and "them," the patriots and the enemy, and there was little doubt about which side the Government thought the press was assisting. As the longest war in American history extended on into the 1970's, it became sadly common to hear once again that old and ugly phrase "giving aid and comfort to the enemy" applied by the Government to members of the American press. In Vietnam the favorite journalistic story, told and retold elaborately down through the years, dealt with a similarly rigid and combative state of mind: the celebrated time when a high-ranking American military commander sternly advised a group of newsmen "to get on the team"—the Government's team, of course.

On the part of the press, and particularly that portion of the American press dealing most intimately with the Government in Washington, it is now popular to cite all the old journalistic chestnuts about the virtues of rugged independence and the people's right to know and the special adversary role that exists—and must exist—between journalists and public officials. These are constants in the American experience, it is argued, and they are in danger of becoming casualties of the Vietnam War.

Mr. Johnson is a Pulitzer Prize winning correspondent of *The Washington Post,* author of *The Bay of Pigs, Dusk at the Mountain,* and other works on U.S. foreign policy.
1. Cited in Arthur Schlesinger, Jr., *The Crisis of Confidence* (New York: Houghton Mifflin Co., 1969), pp. 175–76. The Rusk statement was made on February 9, 1968.

As James Reston of *The New York Times* has said, in spelling out the old creed, "The United States had a press before it had a foreign policy. This is a large part of the trouble between its writers and its officials today. The American press was telling the country and the world where to get off before there was a State Department. The eighteenth-century American pamphleteers not only helped write the Constitution but thought—with considerable justification—that they created the Union. They believed that government power was potentially if not inevitably wicked and had to be watched, especially when applied in secret and abroad, and they wrote the rules so that the press would be among the watchers. In their more amiable moods, they no doubt conceded that the press should serve the country, but they insisted that the best way to serve it was to criticize its every act and thought, and something of this pugnacious spirit has persisted until now."[2]

THE CONFLICT IN HISTORICAL PERSPECTIVE

Naturally there are examples in abundance of the inevitable, indeed irreconcilable, conflict that has always existed between press and government. Every President from George Washington to Richard Nixon has had his difficulties in this area. Often they have been of a most serious nature. In historical perspective, the experience of America's first three leaders is worth recalling. Even before he became President, Washington (who went to his grave despising the excesses of the press) was bitterly complaining about published information that was endangering the operations of his Continental Army. "It is much to be wished," he wrote in 1777, "that our Printers were most discreet in many of their Publications. We see almost in every Paper, Proclamations or accounts transmitted by the Enemy, of an injurious nature. If some hint or caution could be given them on the subject, it might be of material Service."[3]

John Adams was more doleful on the subject of the press. "If there is ever to be an amelioration of the condition of mankind," he wrote, "philosophers, theologians, legislators, politicians, and moralists will find that the regulation of the press is the most difficult, dangerous, and important problem they have to resolve. Mankind cannot now be governed without it, nor at present with it."[4]

And Jefferson, that symbol of liberty, whom the pooh-bahs of the press

2. James Reston, *Sketches in the Sand* (New York: Alfred A. Knopf, 1967), pp. 178–79.
3. Cited in *The Washington Post,* June 27, 1971.
4. Cited in Reston, p. 199.

never cease quoting approvingly for saying "Were it left to me to decide whether we should have a government without newspapers, or newspapers without a government, I should not hesitate a moment to prefer the latter,"[5] had a quite different view of the press once he became President. "The abuses of the freedom of the press here have been carried to a length never before known or borne by any civilized nation," he said at one point while in the White House.[6] And while still President:

> During the course of this administration, and in order to disturb it, the artillery of the press has been levelled against us, charged with whatsoever its licentiousness could devise or dare. These abuses of an institution so important to freedom and science, are deeply to be regretted, inasmuch as they tend to lessen its usefulness and to sap its safety; they might, indeed, have been corrected by the wholesome punishments reserved and provided by the laws of the several states against falsehood and defamation, but public duties more urgent press upon the time of public servants, and the offenders have therefore been left to find their punishment in the public indignation.[7]

THE CONTEMPORARY CRISIS

Despite these examples from a contentious past, I am prepared to argue that never before in our history has the delicate relation between press and government become so difficult as at present, that, indeed, the very concept of a free press is under attack in America. And I would further argue that the Vietnam War—the longest, most controversial, and most divisive in our history—is primarily responsible for the profound challenges now confronting the press and its role in American society. The War, and the bitter recriminations it has engendered, have altered the working conditions and even the laws pertaining to the journalist's profession. In the process a historic switch has occurred. Now it is the press, not the Government, that is under attack and on the defensive. Now it is the press, not the Government, that bears the burden of proving its right to free expression. Now it is the press that is in danger of becoming an investigative arm of the state.

The evidence of these threats is extensive, and recent. In the Pentagon Papers case of 1971 the U.S. Government, for the first time since the founding of the Republic, succeeded (if only briefly) in imposing the doctrine of prior restraint on the press and halting publication of current news of vital importance to the American people. In a growing number of legal cases the

---

5. *The Writings of Thomas Jefferson,* vol. 18 (Washington, D.C.: The Thomas Jefferson Memorial Association, 1904), p. 1.
6. *Ibid.,* vol. 10, p. 357.
7. *Ibid.,* vol. 3, pp. 380–81.

courts have been upholding the issuance of subpoenas served on the news media and rejecting protests that such subpoenas constitute a violation of the First Amendment guarantee of freedom of the press. These subpoenas have demanded that newsmen reveal secret sources, or disclose what they have been told in confidence, or relate what they have seen in private encounters, or vouch for the truth of their news reports.

Now, the Supreme Court has ruled that newsmen have no right under the First Amendment to protect their sources when called before a grand jury. In one case in New York a Federal judge ordered a newspaper reporter not to publish anything except what goes on in a courtroom during a trial. The judge threatened to punish the paper's editors, as well as the reporter, for contempt if they continued to publish material in connection with the trial that was not brought out in open court. In a number of instances across America, government law enforcement agents have posed as members of the press, complete with false press credentials, to gather information leading to possible criminal prosecution. In recurring attacks on radio and television broadcasters, the Government has conducted a deliberate campaign to discredit the mass media in the mind of the public, and has, as a corollary of this attack, warned of prospective legislation to revoke broadcast licenses if it is decided that stations have failed, by *government* definition, to present among other things "objective news and public affairs programs."

Again, the Government places the burden of proof on the press. As the White House representative said in outlining that thesis at the end of 1972:

> First, the broadcaster must demonstrate he has been substantially attuned to the needs and interests of the communities he serves. . . . Second, the broadcaster must show that he has afforded reasonable, realistic, and practical opportunities for the presentation and discussion of conflicting views on controversial issues.

And, in a startling passage, the official, Clay T. Whitehead, director of the President's Office of Telecommunications Policy, made the following philosophical statement about freedom of the press:

> The First Amendment's guarantee of a free press was not supposed to create a privileged class of men called journalists, who are immune from criticism by government or restraint by publishers and editors. To the contrary, the working journalist, if he follows a professional code of ethics, gives up the right to present his personal point of view when he is on the job. He takes on a higher responsibility to the institutions of a free press, and he cannot be insulated from the management of that institution.[8]

---

8. Clay Whitehead speech before Indianapolis (Ind.) chapter, Sigma Delta Chi, December 18, 1972. Text available from the White House.

In other words, the journalist has no right to express a point of view, to dare to dissent, to differ. He has, thus, lost perhaps the most precious right of free expression—the right to be wrong. The day the Government has the power to decide what is right and what is wrong, what is fair and what is objective, is the day a free press ceases to exist in America. As Mr. Whitehead said: "I think that my remarks today leave no doubt that this Administration comes out on the side of a responsible free press."[9] The question, of course, is: "responsible" by whose standards? Clearly, if that view prevails, the Government will be the final arbiter of standards, taste, responsibility—and expression.

These are not isolated cases, nor are they by any means all that could be cited. They do help to explain, however, the near-venomous state that so often characterizes present relations between the working press and the Washington foreign policy and Executive Branch establishment. On both sides, the ill will growing out of mutual charges of deception, irresponsibility, lying, inaccuracy, sensationalism, news management, and lack of credibility and trust have driven the working press and government officials into separate camps. The newsman is now virtually a member of what passes for the American official Opposition, an Opposition whose loyalty the Government questions.

I believe these conditions are among the terrible prices of the war in Vietnam. That is hardly an unusual position for a Washington journalist to take these days. But here is a heretic's view. I also believe much of the problem rests with the press itself. In spite of its rather breast-beating public stance of independence and unrelenting government criticism, for years the Washington press corps was a willing accomplice of government secrecy, official trial balloons, and justifications for policy failures. To some extent, it still is. My basic criticism of the press is that it was not critical enough—and I mean intelligent, sophisticated criticism, not mere name-calling. The press allowed itself to be used by the Government. By and large, it was a staunch supporter of government policies, particularly in foreign affairs. (It is hard to realize now, but as late as August 8, 1967, Senator J. William Fulbright was describing *The Washington Post,* the present *bête noire* of the Government, as "a newspaper which has obsequiously supported the Administration's policy in Vietnam,"[10] and President Lyndon Johnson was telling the editor of that newspaper that his editorials were worth a division to him.)

---

9. *Ibid.*
10. Haynes Johnson and Bernard Gwertzman, *Fulbright: the Dissenter* (New York: Doubleday, 1968), p. 309.
11. Private remark by President Lyndon Johnson to J. Russell Wiggins, then editor of *The Washington Post.*

GROWTH OF THE BUDDY SYSTEM

Until Vietnam finally changed the equation, a cozy and comfortable relation had developed between the working press and Washington officials. The press co-operated—indeed, it often helped draft the rules—in mutually advantageous private meetings in which the press permitted public officials to advance positions—many dubious, many purely political—under a cloak of anonymity. These background meetings, as they came to be known, were both the grist for the Washington press and the vehicle for Washington officials. Here, it seems clear, the habit of operating secretly in this area eventually was harmful to both press and government.

Over the years these background sessions grew in importance and scope. During World War II, for instance, Fleet Admiral Ernest King met regularly with selected journalists at the home of Phelps Adams, Washington bureau chief of *The New York Sun,* to give elaborate, detailed briefings on military progress and future engagements. Not a single breach of confidence occurred during that period. There were no bitter accusations then about the press's being on the "wrong side," no doubts about patriotism or disloyalty. It was a popular war; the press backed it whole-heartedly.

The immediate postwar era and the advent of the Cold War brought a change in the background briefings. Instead of a forum for a privileged few in the press, the background sessions became institutionalized. Diplomats, generals, admirals, Cabinet officers, and White House officials (including the President), conducted the sessions for an ever larger group of Washington correspondents. All of these operated under rules first promulgated in the 1930's by Ernest K. Lindley, then a *Newsweek* magazine correspondent and later a State Department consultant. The Lindley Rule, as it came to be known, required the journalists not to attribute the things they were told. "It was a system of compulsory plagiarism and it served us well,"[12] Lindley later recalled.

Before long the "backgrounder" became a way of life and an accepted means of transacting business between the press and the Government. As the practice spread and the sessions proliferated, the character of the backgrounder changed. It ceased to be an academic seminar for the philosophers of the press and became instead a form of news conference conducted in private. Officials learned that they could promote pet projects and policies anonymously, and pass on tidbits of gossip for which they would not be held accountable. Journalists came to like the informality and the close association with the cream of Washington officialdom. They could even glory

12. Quoted in *The Washington Post,* April 30, 1967.

in the social relations they were able to develop. It was heady wine to be able to call the eminent Cabinet member or famous ambassador by his first name, and even more gratifying and seductive to be referred to in turn on a first-name basis. (Even now, I hardly know a prominent Washington journalist who does not say, with casual and familiar pride, "Henry" when referring to Henry Kissinger.)

Useful as these sessions often were (and are), essentially they were corrupting. They led both the press and the Government to forget their basic roles and responsibilities. I happen to agree with the view of Benjamin C. Bradlee, editor of *The Washington Post,* that backgrounders are a mutual conspiracy on the part of the press and the Government in restraint of public truth.[13] But it was not until the Vietnam War so soured the relations between press and officials that the general public became vaguely aware of the insidious practice. Even now, many newsmen are embarrassed to acknowledge how deeply they were involved in a process that deceived the public. In late 1964, for example, at a critical moment when decisions were being taken to change the character of the Vietnam intervention from a limited advisory role to a full-scale land combat operation involving American troops, background foreign policy briefings were being conducted all over Washington. These private appearances fortified the public belief that the United States would not become involved in a major land war in Asia. Dean Rusk, then Secretary of State, was central among the top men in the Lyndon Johnson Administration who conducted those briefings.

In those days Rusk was arguing with what appeared to be great personal conviction that it would serve no useful purpose to bomb North Vietnam or to send in American fighting men. In his "bottle club" sessions with newsmen on the eighth floor of the State Department, at which drinks were always served, Rusk would say that white men should not fight an Asian nation's war; that large numbers of U.S. troops would only lead to future and serious hostility with the Vietnamese. On the question of bombing, Rusk would always say, "The war must be won in the South." When pressed to be more specific he would beg the question, for, as he remarked, the President had said that he was not "going North" but was undecided about what action he might take to counter specific situations. Rusk's public appearances backed up many of his private remarks. On January 3, 1965, for instance, when interviewed on a television program, he stated that an expansion of the Vietnamese war would lead to a multiplication of casualties and subject the people to devastation.[14]

Such remarks contributed to what eventually came to be known in Wash-

13. *The Washington Post,* January 2, 1972.
14. Johnson and Gwertzman, *Fulbright,* p. 201.

ington as the "credibility gap" between the Government and its citizens. But really it was the press, rightly or wrongly, that felt it had been betrayed. As the war expanded and lengthened, the press found itself reporting more and more information that proved to be wrong. Much of this information came from the background briefings with top officials, and it was particularly galling for a journalist to have written authoritatively, but without giving his source, and then find that he was totally in error. But it was *his* reputation that suffered, not that of the anonymous official. It was during this period that the phrase "news management" was resurrected and increasingly applied by the press to government activities. The phrase stemmed from a statement by Assistant Secretary of Defense Arthur Sylvester, formerly a leading Washington journalist, in the aftermath of the 1962 Cuban missile crisis. Sylvester stated that news "generated" by the American Government was used, and used successfully, in that crisis and that his department would continue that policy. Management of the news, he said, was "part of the arsenal of weaponry"; and he also uttered the now-famous phrase that he believed in "the inherent right of the Government to lie."[15] Not surprisingly, mutual hostility and suspicion soon became the normal climate between press and officials as the Vietnam War proceeded and aroused such strong emotions.

I recall vividly, for instance, the embarrassment—and anger—of a colleague who returned from a tour in Vietnam in the fall of 1967 after having been briefed extensively by leading American diplomatic and military officials throughout that country. "The war—the military war—in Vietnam is nearly won," he began the first of a series of articles on the situation at the time. "It is nearly won in the sense that the major, readily identifiable military problem that existed when American troops were committed on a large scale in mid-1965 is very close to solution.[16]

It was during the same period of growing involvement that the American press reported, again and again, the glowing words of optimism from government and military officials. Take, for example, the public assessments of General William C. Westmoreland on the Vietnam problem:

July 8, 1964: "I believe the whole operation is moving in our favor."

July 9, 1965: "It is doubtful if we will ever have anything in the way of opposing land forces as in the Korean War."

July 13, 1967: "We have achieved all our objectives, while the enemy has failed dismally."

November 22, 1967: "I am absolutely certain that, whereas in 1945 the

---

15. *Facts on File,* vol. 23, no. 1150 (November 8–14, 1962), p. 397; *The Washington Post,* December 7, 1962.
16. *The Evening Star* (Washington), November 7, 1967.

enemy was winning, today he is certainly losing. . . . In general he can fight his large forces only at the edges of his sanctuaries. . . . His guerrilla force is declining at a steady rate. . . . I see progress as I travel all over Vietnam. . . . The enemy's hopes are bankrupt."

January 1, 1968: "Through careful exploitation of the enemy's vulnerabilities and application of our superior firepower and mobility, we should expect our gains of 1967 to be increased manyfold in 1968."

February 26, 1968: "I do not believe Hanoi can hold up under a long war."

April 8, 1968: "Militarily we have never been in a better relative position in South Vietnam. . . . The spirit of the offensive is now prevalent throughout Vietnam."

June 9, 1968: "The enemy is getting nowhere militarily. . . . He is frustrated to the point where he is desperate."[17]

THE BITTER HARVEST OF VIETNAM

Step by step, statement by statement, the Government's involvement in Vietnam led to further conflict with the press. The official public explanations for the Gulf of Tonkin crisis in 1964, for the combat mission of American ground troops in 1965 (first, the stated goal of protecting U.S. installations, and later the concession that American forces were in fact seeking out and destroying the enemy), for the bombing missions launched secretly from Laos and Thailand in 1966 and 1967, for the handling of the Mylai massacres story in 1968, for the failure to produce the secret "plan to end the war" in 1969, for the Cambodian invasion in 1970 and the stated goal of capturing the enemy's secret command center, for the on-again-off-again "peace is at hand" claims of late 1972, followed by the massive resumption of the bombing of the North in the most savage attacks to that time—all these deepened an already bitter controversy between press and government until the working relation deteriorated to probably the worst in U.S. history. The controversy between *The Washington Post* and the Nixon Administration over the Watergate break-in provides the domestic counterpart to this Vietnam-bred hostility.

The real questions growing out of this unhappy experience are not concerned with the Government's proper, and necessary, role of operating in secret, nor with a fallible daily press's errors of omission and commission. The tragedy of Vietnam is that it has created among American citizens a loss of faith in both their press and their public officials. It has sowed a bitter harvest of distrust and cynicism that corrupts and poisons the fabric

17. Cited in Schlesinger, *Crisis of Confidence*, pp. 173–74.

of a democracy. From the press's standpoint the Government is now viewed as something like Ibsen's "enemy of the people"; the press now is not only suspicious and distrustful of the Government, it tends to believe the worst in advance of the facts. From the Government's side the press is pernicious if not vicious, a destroyer of reputations and a wrecker of policies, an unbridled power that is damaging to the public good.

Small wonder that many Americans today believe neither what is reported in the press nor what is stated by public officials. That may sound like a sweeping generalization, but on the basis of my own experience of traveling extensively throughout the country over a period of many years and talking to Americans in all walks of life, I am convinced of its truth. In a democracy a government that has lost the respect of its citizens has lost the ability to govern effectively. The concern, thus, is not with public secrecy so much as it is with public candor and trustworthiness.

SELECTIVE SECRECY AND SELECTIVE CANDOR

No journalist I know would contend seriously that the Government does not have a right to operate in secrecy. That this right is often abused, that it is often excessive, that it often serves to hide mistakes and protect reputations, that it contributes to the lessening of faith among citizens, are not the main points either. Much of the basic relation between press and government is, of necessity, predicated on secrecy. To me one of the most painful aspects of the Pentagon Papers case was the public admission on the part of so many Washington journalists that they have been playing—and extensively—the secrecy game. As a writer, I myself have had access to extremely sensitive material bearing the highest secrecy classification. Thus, in the course of my research for a book on the Bay of Pigs invasion, the contents of the Government's top secret "Taylor Report" investigation of the affair, including the role of the Central Intelligence Agency and the names of agents, was made available to me. (Allen Dulles, the CIA director, later accused me publicly of coming close to being a traitor for the disclosures, which he conceded were accurate.[18]) Now, more than a decade later, not a line of that top-secret report has yet been published officially. It still bears the highest classification.

The New York Times was made the recipient of the top-secret Yalta Report. *The Washington Post* was given the contents of the top-secret Gaither Report on U.S. military preparedness. And at the time of the Pentagon Papers case, a number of other Washington journalists testified to occasions when they were given access to the most secret and sensitive government

---

18. See the article in *The New York Times,* June 8, 1964, quoting Allen Dulles.

material. "I can testify that President John F. Kennedy once read to me portions of a highly classified memorandum of a conversation between him and Nikita Khrushchev in Vienna in 1961," said Benjamin C. Bradlee of *The Washington Post*. "I received his permission to use this material, which is still highly classified, and it appeared in *Newsweek*. His stated purpose was to convince the American public that the Soviet Union was taking an extremely hard, belligerent line on Berlin."[19]

Journalists have been given access to secret inside information on the Cuban missile crisis, on the intervention of American forces in Santo Domingo in 1965, on too numerous occasions to recite here during the course of the Vietnam War. The point is that almost invariably these secret documents are given to the journalist by an official of the U.S. Government to promote a certain point of view. Max Frankel of *The New York Times* describes the practice best. As he stated during the Pentagon Papers period,

> Without the use of secrets, . . . there could be no adequate, diplomatic, military or political reporting of the kind our people take for granted, either abroad or in Washington, and there could be no mature system of communication between the government and the people. That is one reason why the sudden complaint by one party to these regular dealings strikes us as monstrous and hypocritical—unless it is essentially perfunctory, for the purpose of retaining some discipline over the federal bureaucracy.[20]

Frankel also understands as well as anyone the complex and differing motives that sometimes compel a public official to reveal secrets. "Presidents make 'secret' decisions only to reveal them for the purposes of frightening an adversary nation, wooing a friendly electorate, protecting their reputations," he said. "The military services conduct 'secret' research in weaponry only to reveal it for the purpose of enhancing their budgets, appearing superior or inferior to a foreign army, gaining the vote of a congressman or the favor of a contractor."[21]

THE BASIC PROBLEM; AND AN ANSWER
THAT IS NOT A SOLUTION

These practices are not the basic problem between press and government. Neither are abstract theories about American democracy and freedom of the press the central dilemma. The dilemma today, for press and government alike, is the same that Lincoln posed more than a century ago: "Must

---

19. *The Washington Post,* June 22, 1971.
20. *The New York Times,* June 19, 1971.
21. *Ibid.*

a government of necessity be too strong for the liberties of its people, or too weak to maintain its own existence?"[22] Now, as then, no final answer exists to that question.

We all know that in theory press and government are supposed to be allies. Both are supposed to serve the same master—the public. The fact is that they are natural adversaries rather than allies. They are now, always will be, and probably always should be in some form of conflict (creative and, we would hope positive, conflict). Despite nearly two hundred years of experience with each other, neither seem to understand or fully appreciate the other's role. The public official who equates criticism or error with unpatriotism—or treason—and the member of the press who believes that *per se* he has the right to examine every secret action of government are equally wrong.

It hardly need be repeated that relations between press and government are now in a parlous state, to the detriment of the nation. Basically these problems do not stem from secrecy in government, although secrecy is a contributing factor. Just as surely as secrecy in Washington is essential to the operation of government, so is it certain that secrecy in government is being seriously abused. The classification stamps applied so freely by officials are, too often, a cover for mistakes and an insurance against legitimate public inquiry. The background briefings that have for so long been the staple for much of reporting from Washington are to a large extent archaic. I know of few that could not be held in public, just as I know of no public official who should not be held accountable for his actions. In private sessions of this kind it is the public, not press or government, that is the loser. But these practices will not change unless the press itself reasserts its once vaunted independence and refuses to participate in them. It is an old, and perhaps naïve, conviction of mine that the Government needs us more than we need it. Strangely, that is not an article of faith among members of the American press at this moment.

These questions, though, are only incidental to my larger concern about the present relations of press and government. Most disturbing to me, and dangerous, is the present climate that permeates the entire intricate network of journalist and official. I am afraid I must say that the smell of censorship and repression is in the air. We witnessed in the Vietnam era a deliberate, aggressive, and unprecedented campaign by the Executive Branch to discredit publicly, threaten privately, and attempt to bring into line through dull and stupid conformity major elements of the American press. This assault already has had a chilling effect on the press. The failure of the media, other than *The Washington Post* and a very few newspapers, to take Water-

---

22. J. C. Wahlke, ed., *Loyalty in a Democratic State.* Problems in American Civilization (Boston: D. C. Heath & Co., 1952), p. 1.

gate as a serious subject for investigative reporting after the 1972 Presidential elections reflects this. Intimidation threatens, if sustained by public indifference or lack of understanding of the stakes involved, to become more serious in the future.

By the end of 1972, the lines of communications between official Washington and journalistic Washington had seriously diminished. The channels of information were becoming more closed than ever. Criticism was taken more seriously and personally; the government reaction became increasingly sharper, and there existed genuine concern about the use of governmental police powers to suppress the press. Agents of the Federal Bureau of Investigation and the Pentagon, for instance, began to compile secret dossiers on members of the press. White House "Enemies Lists" featured media correspondents.

It remains to be seen whether President Nixon genuinely meant his handsome apology to the press after the Watergate affair showed that the journalists investigating the case had been right and the White House wrong. But after years of Vietnam-caused antagonism between White House and media, the role of the press in blowing the lid off Watergate can help only if a lot of Washington politicians are willing to be almost superhumanly wise and generous in helping to rebuild bridges between government and media.

In saying this I am not trying to paint an Orwellian portrait of America in the first part of the 1970's. Nor am I suggesting, chauvinistically, that the press is perfect, all-wise, all-seeing, all-virtuous. Nonsense! The press has not always exercised its freedom well or wisely or responsibly. Worse, from my perspective, is that it has not been critical enough; that it lacks sophistication; that it still dwells more on the superficial and sensational than on questions of moment. I subscribe entirely to the complaint lodged by Senator Fulbright.

> The problem for a Senator or Senate committee is not simply one of being heard. [Fulbright said]. Anything that has the color of scandal, sensation, accusation or prediction will command eager attention from the media. What you cannot easily interest them in is an idea, or a carefully exposited point of view, or an unfamiliar perspective, or a reasoned rebuttal to a highly controversial Presidential statement. During the years of the Vietnam war, the Foreign Relations Committee has heard thoughtful and significant statements on the war by scholars, professors, journalists, businessmen, theologians, and political and military leaders, but owing to the lack of interest of the media, many of the most enlightening of these proceedings have remained a well-kept secret between the witnesses and the members of the committee. Why this is so is beyond my understanding. All I do know is that the only reliable way of getting the media to swallow an idea is by

candy-coating it with a prediction or accusation or by drowning it in the spectacle of a "head-to-head confrontation" with some prominent executive-branch official.[23]

Yet for all the imperfections and failures of the press—and they are many and serious—the experience of the Vietnam era and its impact on the workings of the press have taught this one journalist to be thankful for those shrewd, tough, flinty men who drafted the Constitution and the Bill of Rights, those innately cautious men who had such a healthy suspicion of power and the might of the state.

We do not need, in the relations between press and government, more secrecy. We do not need, in this country, an Official Secrets Act, or press councils, or public censors, or any other moves that are now being discussed to restrict further the flow of information from government to citizen. We do need a better understanding of the process by which both press and government function, and an appreciation of the roles of each. But most of all we need to recall the reasons that a free press was established in America.

No one ever gave more expressive, eloquent voice to those reasons and principles than James Madison. In his great plea Madison acknowledged that freedom of the press is a mixed blessing, that, as he said, "this liberty is often carried to excess; that it has sometimes degenerated into licentiousness, is seen and lamented." Then he added: "But the remedy has not yet been discovered. Perhaps it is an evil inseparable from the good with which it is allied; perhaps it is a shoot which cannot be stripped from the stalk without wounding vitally the plant from which it is torn. However desirable those measures might be which might correct without enslaving the press, they have never yet been devised in America."

---

23. J. William Fulbright, *The Crippled Giant* (New York: Random House, 1972), p. 56.

11

The American Espionage Statutes
and Publication
of Defense Information

BENNO C. SCHMIDT, JR.

INTRODUCTION

One issue currently stands out in assessing legal restrictions in the United
States on the right of journalists to gather and publish information likely to
be of prime political importance. This is the extent to which persons may
legally gather for publication or actually publish information relating to the
national defense. The Pentagon Papers decision and the prosecutions of
Daniel Ellsberg and Anthony J. Russo, Jr., are dramatic manifestations of
this problem; but, quite apart from these two cases, some accommodation
of security and the fundamental public interest in free expression on matters of political concern is clearly a continuing problem of basic practical
and theoretical significance to our society. My aim is to consider in general
the legal status of publication of defense-related information.

Despite an understandable impulse to treat this problem as mainly one
of Constitutional dimension, I believe it is fundamentally a statutory issue,
in two senses. First, the state of our present law on the subject is better
understood as a matter of interpretation of the Espionage Statutes—despite
the great difficulties of that analysis—than of application of First Amendment principles. Second, given the confused state of present statutes,
changes in our law on this vexing problem of public policy seem to me close
at hand. These changes will take place, in my opinion, on a legislative rather
than a judicial level—that is, by statute rather than by evolution of Constitutional principle. If viewing publication of information relating to national
defense in statutory perspective is proper, as I shall try to demonstrate, such
an approach entails some special difficulties. The issues are not measured

Mr. Schmidt is Professor at Columbia University School of Law. He was formerly
Law Clerk to Chief Justice Earl Warren and Special Assistant to the Assistant Attorney General, Office of Legal Counsel, Department of Justice.

against the relatively familiar, if somewhat amorphous, principles of the First Amendment. Instead, analysis focuses on the unfamiliar conceptions of a difficult and archaic body of statute law.

THE NEW YORK TIMES CASE

The Pentagon Papers decision is typical of "great" Constitutional cases in that the Supreme Court terminated the litigation leaving more questions open than answered. Among the ten opinions produced in *New York Times Company* v. *United States*[1] the only proposition commanding a majority of the Court was the naked and uninformative conclusion that the Government had not made a record adequate to justify injunctive relief against publication. But chilling the satisfaction that might otherwise have been released by that victory for freedom of the press, was *dicta* amounting to an admonition, loosely endorsed by four Justices, that the present Espionage Statutes may authorize criminal sanctions against the newspapers and their reporters for their role in the affair. The warnings of criminal liability under the Espionage Statutes for publication as such have not materialized. The prosecutions of Daniel Ellsberg and Anthony Russo, however, proceeded on statutory premises that would in effect criminalize publication by subjecting to liability communication and retention activities that necessarily are preliminary to publication. Since the dismissal of the Ellsberg case for reasons irrelevant to these issues, the questions raised remain unanswered but important.

Justice White was the principal author of the warnings. His opinion, joined by Justice Stewart, detailed a construction of section 793 of Title 18 that would impose criminal liability on newspapers for retaining defense secrets, a necessary step in publishing them. He noted, moreover, that "the issue of guilt or innocence would be determined by procedures and standards quite different from those that have purported to govern these injunctive proceedings"[2]—a clear reference to the traditional wisdom viewing the First Amendment as less a restraint to sending authors to jail than it is to the issuance of injunctive relief against publications.

Justice Stewart, besides joining Justice White's opinion, wrote for himself that the criminal statutes are "of very colorable relevance to the apparent circumstances of these cases."[3] Chief Justice Burger and Justice Blackmun respectively registered "general agreement"[4] and "substantial ac-

---

1. 403 U.S. 713 (1971).
2. *Id.* at 740.
3. *Id.* at 730.
4. *Id.* at 752.

cord"[5] with Justice White's views, evidencing a surprising willingness to speculate about matters completely unattended to in a litigation which, as they complained in dissent, had proceeded too hurriedly for careful judgment on the relatively narrow questions briefed and argued. Justice Marshall, while not approving the construction, noted its plausibility.[6]

Aside from these significant, if *obiter,* statutory speculations, the central theme sounded throughout the opinions of the six Justices joining the *per curiam* resolution of the case is an unwillingness to venture very far, particularly in regard to injunctive relief, without Legislative authorization. That reluctance necessarily lost the case for the Government, which had chosen to press the theory that, without regard to legislation, the President's Constitutional powers as Commander in Chief and foreign relations steward entitled him to injunctive relief to prevent "grave and irreparable danger" to the public interest. The Government's brief in the Supreme Court, amazingly enough, did not even cite the Espionage Statutes, let alone take a position on whether *The New York Times* and *The Washington Post* had violated criminal laws by publishing the Pentagon Papers, or by their conduct in obtaining and retaining the alleged national defense information contained in the Papers. The Government apparently decided to ignore the statutes on the ground that they did not authorize injunctive relief, whether or not the statutes made the publication criminal.

The Government's aversion to the statutes, however, did not succeed in deflecting judicial focus from the legislative materials. All the Justices concurring in the judgment—including even Justice Black, who in any event found the First Amendment dispositive—relied to some extent on the Government's failure to premise its case on legislative authority. Thus, as decided, the case resembles most closely a similar defeat in court suffered by another unadorned claim of executive power made by the Truman Administration in defense of its seizure of the steel industry in the *Youngstown Steel* case.[7] Whether or not an alternative strategy would have succeeded, the Government might well have fared better with arguments directed to interstitial power to seek injunctions against contemplated criminal behavior, testing head-on the issue whether the Espionage Statutes were in fact being violated.

Given the lack of any statutory basis for the Government's position, a number of factors support the Supreme Court's refusal to take upon itself the fashioning of rules governing publication of defense secrets with tools no better suited for the task than First Amendment language and gloss. First, the spacious generalities of the First Amendment text provide only

---

5. *Id.* at 759.
6. *Id.* at 745.
7. Youngstown Sheet & Tube Co. v. Sawyer, 343 U.S. 579 (1952).

vague standards if, as surely will be the case, absolutist construction is not adopted. Second, no body of judicial precedents even remotely analogous is available from which the Court could have drawn a body of developed and tested principles amounting to more than question-begging oversimplifications.

For one thing, street demonstrations, apocalyptic rhetoric, obscenity, libel, and the rest of the usual First Amendment judicial fare are poor materials from which to fashion permissions and restraints on publication of national security secrets. Furthermore, even if standards could be formulated, the judicial process is not well suited to test the factual basis of Executive claims of the risks inherent in releasing particular secrets. The line between appropriate and unjustified prior restraint cannot be drawn *ad hoc* without an overview of the substance and interrelations of military and diplomatic policy that the judicial process cannot provide. A secret may be disclosed to demonstrate the futility of current policy, and one's assessment of the disclosure's impact will depend on one's reaction to the policy.

Again, individual breaches of secrecy by publication will usually arise as a result of heated policy disagreements. Official efforts to suppress will therefore trigger political debate on the policy question, and generate extensive publicity and political pressures, these in turn threatening the detached and deliberate judgment that is the basis for public acceptance of judicial law-making. Finally, as Justice White notes in his opinion, it would be particularly hazardous to build a judge-made system of rules in the secrecy area, when of necessity much of the litigation must be done *in camera* (behind closed doors). For an understanding of governing principles, judicial decisions defining the scope of the First Amendment are especially dependent upon full elaboration of the facts on which judgment has turned. For judge-made law to dominate official policy in this area would produce little more than a series of *ipse dixits* as unenlightening as the *per curiam* (unattributed) opinion in the Pentagon Papers case.

The best hope in a nuclear age for accommodating the need for secrecy with the public's right to know lies in the Legislative process, where general rules about specific categories of defense-related information can be fashioned farther from the pressures of determining the outcome of a particular, politically sensitive case. The problems are too important and subtle to be left to the courts.

While the Court was right to decline the Executive Branch's invitation to fashion judicial rules without statutory guidance, it is surprising that the Executive found it necessary to proceed without a clear statutory basis. Few problems have had a greater claim to postwar legislative concern than the issue of national security. Surely, public revelation of defense information is one of the major problems. Security is, by and large, equally compromised by publication of secrets in newspapers or magazines available to all as by their transfer to foreign spies in encoded microdots. Since the danger to national security in publication of defense secrets is obvious, one would expect that a security-minded Congress would have dealt with the problem in some reasonably clear-cut way. The facts are quite the reverse. The legislation controlling public revelation of "defense secrets" poses forbidding problems of interpretation. The Espionage Statutes are hardly adequate to inform, much less to reconcile sensibly, the competing demands of national security and public debate about matters of prime political importance.

THE ESPIONAGE STATUTES

Legislative history strongly supports the conclusion that the Congress, despite its use of broad language in several sections, has chosen not to subject publication of general defense information to any restraint.[8]

An Overview

The Espionage Statutes are codified in sections 793-98 of Title 18 of the United States Code. The basic provisions are sections 793 and 794. Section 794 contains the most comprehensive provisions bearing on transfer of defense information to foreigners. Section 794(a) punishes actual or attempted communication to any foreign citizen of any document or information "relating to the national defense," if the communication is "with intent or reason to believe that it [the information] is to be used to the injury of the United States or to the advantage of a foreign nation." Section 794(b) deals also with transfer of information to foreigners, and expressly covers publishing, though in other respects it is narrower. Applicable only in time of war, it covers collecting, recording, publishing, or communicating certain relatively specific information about troop movements and military plans, "with intent that the same shall be communicated to the enemy." Sections 794(a) and 794(b) thus are offenses directed at intentional transmission of information into foreign hands.

Despite section 794's seemingly comprehensive coverage of espionage situations, section 793 defines six additional offenses, each involving conduct preliminary to information coming into foreign hands. Sections 793(a)

---

8. Professor Harold Edgar and I have found it necessary, elsewhere, to treat the Espionage Statutes at what I fear may be forbidding length to do justice to the problems of interpretation that arise. Our study appears in 73 *Columbia Law Review*, 929 (May 1973).

and 793(b) cover entering an installation or copying a document "connected with the national defense" for "the purpose of obtaining information respecting the national defense with intent or reason to believe that the information is to be used to the injury of the United States, or to the advantage of any foreign nation." Subsections (c), (d), and (e) of section 793 are even more sweeping, criminalizing respectively receipt of material in the knowledge that it has been obtained in violation of other provisions, communication of defense-related material or information to any person not entitled to receive it, and retention of information. On their face, these provisions seem to make criminal nearly all acquisition by newspapers of properly classified information, despite the fact that the provisions have never been so employed, and the Congress, as we shall see, did not understand them to have that effect.

Other important provisions of Title 18 directed at breaches of security are section 798, which prohibits publication of information dealing with the special category of cryptographic information—codes, interception operations, code-breaking, and the like—and section 795, which prohibits photographing or making any graphic representation of any vital military equipment or installation the President has defined "as requiring protection against the general dissemination of information relative thereto," without first obtaining permission from the appropriate military authority. The President has greatly expanded the scope apparently intended for section 795 by defining all documents classified by the Defense Department as vital military equipment within the meaning of the section.[9]

Central questions of coverage under these statutes cannot be satisfactorily resolved by analysis of statutory language and judicial constructions. Legislative history must be a prime interpretive resource in construing the espionage statutes. At the same time, the history of these statutes is more than usually confused, ambiguous, and just plain lengthy. One of the major failings of the Espionage Statutes is that they pose so many questions that turn on arduous analysis of complex and disorderly legislative materials.

The basic provisions of sections 794 and 793 dealing with the disclosure of defense-related information were enacted in the Espionage Act of 1917,[10] and have remained almost unchanged since that time. The Espionage Act was introduced in the Sixty-fourth Congress two days after President Wilson had announced to a joint session of Congress the severance of diplomatic relations with Germany. Over three hundred pages of the *Congressional Record* attest to the attention given to the Act. Heated debate on the subject stretched over two frenetic sessions of the Congress, and encom-

---

9. Executive Order No. 10107, February 1, 1950.
10. 40 Stat. 217 *et seq.* (1917).

passed four bills and two conference reports. Concern about enemy spying, triggered by American entry into World War I, accounted for some of the Congress's consideration. Most of the significant debate, however, was not provoked by worry over classical espionage. The Wilson Administration proposed to censor, or make punishable after the fact (exactly which option was never made clear), publication of defense information in violation of Presidential regulations, without any limiting culpability requirement.

The desirability of such a measure was seen by its adherents to flow logically from the obvious harm that could result to military interests from untimely publications that would certainly fall into enemy hands. The proponents of the measure reached back to Civil War experience, in which the Union cause had been hindered by newspaper retailing of military plans prior to their execution. Sponsors of the Espionage Act were eager to carry over to the new law certain broad prescriptions on information-gathering contained in a 1911 Act. They were content to rely on prosecutorial discretion to ensure that these would not be invoked against the activities of innocent citizens whose only motive was to secure information about military policy.[11]

In response to this proposal, the Congress engaged in its most extensive debate over freedom of speech and the press since the Alien and Sedition Acts. The preoccupation was not an academic one. Opponents feared that President Wilson or his subordinates would impede, or even suppress, informed criticism of his Administration's war effort and foreign policy under the guise of protecting military secrets. The 1917 debates were thus highly partisan. Important votes repeatedly broke along party lines. The aggrandizing of Presidential power during wartime was a recurrent fear of Republicans, especially Senate progressives such as Borah, La Follette, Norris, and Hiram Johnson.

The proposal was ultimately defeated. A close vote of Senate and House rejected controls on publication that did not require the Executive first to prove an intent to injure the nation. After preliminary maneuvering a Conference Report reinstating the control provision was rejected. The only prohibition directed expressly at publication to survive was that now found in section 794(b), which covers wartime publication of military information "with intent that the same shall be communicated to the enemy." Equally important, the broadly drawn information-gathering activities brought forward from an earlier statute were made criminal in the 1917 Act under sections 793(a) and (b), for the most part, only when done with "intent or reason to believe that the information is to be used to the injury of the United States or to the advantage of any foreign nation."

---

11. The Defense Secrets Act 1911 is found at 36 Stat. 1804 (1911).

Despite the rejection of the proposed flat ban on publication, the meaning of the legislative history of the Espionage Act of 1917 on the problem of publication is not simple, and as to preliminary information-gathering the statutes are in a dreadful mess. The result of Congressional action was not to leave the law utterly without impact on such activities, but rather to make them illegal when done with certain states of mind such as "intent" and "reason to believe." Ascertaining the meaning of such phrases is thus a central task. Furthermore, in a state of almost unbelievable confusion, the Congress included in the 1917 Act a provision—now codified as sections 793(d) and (e)—that made criminal mere communication or retention of defense documents not conditioned on any specific intent requirement. This provision, if construed in its literal sweep, would make completely meaningless the insistence on tight culpability standards in the other sections, and yet finding a satisfactory narrower meaning is exceedingly problematic.

The problem of regulating publication in the interest of national security was again debated in 1933, when the Congress, in response to the publishing activities of a former State Department code-breaker, made criminal the publication by Federal employees of any matter originally transmitted in foreign code.[12] Broader controls on publication were considered in 1950 with the passage of section 798 dealing with publication of information concerning domestic codes and communications intelligence operations.[13] The 1932 and 1951 debates indicate that the Congress and the Executive Branch considered the 1917 Espionage Act inapplicable to publication of general defense information that would subsume the narrower categories of information. Other retrospective views of the 1917 Act have been reflected in debates on the Internal Security Act of 1950, when one subsection of 793 was extended in a confused effort to make the statute reach activities like those of Whitaker Chambers,[14] and in the (unadopted) recommendation in 1957 of the Commission on Government Security that publication of anything classified be made a crime.[15]

With these overviews of the Espionage Statutes and their legislative history in mind, the individual provisions and their impact on publication of defense information may be examined.

Section 794

Section 794 contains the most comprehensive provisions in the Espionage Statutes bearing on the transfer of information to foreigners. The section consists of two subsections, with a third added to cover conspiracies.

Subsection 794(a), the more inclusive of the two, provides that:

---

12. 48 Stat. 122 (1933).
13. 64 Stat. 159 (1950).
14. *Id.* at 1003.
15. See 103 *Congressional Record* 10447 *et seq.*

Whoever, with intent or reason to believe that it is to be used to the injury of the United States or to the advantage of a foreign nation, communicates, delivers, or transmits, or attempts to communicate, deliver, or transmit, to any foreign government, or to any faction or party or military or naval force within a foreign country, whether recognized or unrecognized by the United States, or to any representative, officer, agent, employee, subject, or citizen thereof, either directly or indirectly, any document, writing, code book, signal book, sketch, photograph, photographic negative, blueprint, plan, map, model, note, instrument, appliance, or information relating to the national defense, shall be punished by death or by imprisonment for any term of years or for life.

The major question of interpretation concerning the impact of this provision is whether publication of defense information by a newspaper certain to reach foreign hands is within the scope of the language "communicates, delivers, or transmits . . . to any foreign government, or to any . . . citizen thereof." Both the language of 794(a) and the clear intent of the Congress confirm that the provision does not reach public speech. Two aspects of the language of 794 as a whole imply that a difference is intended between publishing—used in the dictionary sense of "to make publicly (generally) known"—and communicating, even though the latter term might in ordinary speech be thought to comprehend all transmissions of information, including publication. First, while 794(a) covers "communicates, delivers, or transmits," the word "publishes" appears in section 794(b), where both "communicates" and "publishes" are used. By implication, the drafters saw a difference. Second, under section 794(a), the proscribed behavior is communication *to* a foreign recipient. A person who publishes a fact does not communicate it *to* foreigners in the statutory sense simply because foreigners are among the many readers of his journals.

Legislative history virtually demands this conclusion. When the Congress enacted 794(a) and 794(b) as part of the Espionage Act of 1917, the proposed legislation reported by the Judiciary Committees of both House and Senate contained a third provision, one that would have allowed the President to issue regulations to prohibit publication of any information about the armed forces or military plans, without any limiting mental requirement whatever. This potential blanket restriction on publication received the lion's share of attention in the debates on the Espionage Act, and was soundly defeated in both House and Senate despite a last-minute personal appeal by President Wilson. What is significant about the rejection of this general prohibition on publication for purposes of construing subsection 794(a) was that opponents of the general prohibition argued that the *only* controls on publication consistent with sound public policy were accomplished by what is now 794(b). Supporters of the blanket prohibition argued that 794(b) was not a sufficient control on publication, because that measure prohibited publication only with intent to communicate to the enemy; they urged the necessity of the general prohibition not conditioned or any such mental requirement. But neither the supporters nor the opponents in the voluminous debates on the Espionage Act asserted that the prohibition on communication to a foreign recipient codified in 794(a) had any bearing whatever on the problem posed by publication of defense information.

The second provision of section 794, subsection (b), is in form applicable to public speech about military matters, since it covers explicitly publication as well as communication.

Subsection 794(b) provides that:

> Whoever, in time of war, with intent that the same shall be communicated to the enemy, collects, records, publishes, or communicates, or attempts to elicit any information with respect to the movement, numbers, description, condition, or disposition of any of the Armed Forces, ships, aircraft, or war materials of the United States, or with respect to the plans or conduct, or supposed plans or conduct of any naval or military operations, or with respect to any works or measures undertaken for or connected with, or intended for the fortification or defense of any place, or any other information relating to the public defense, which might be useful to the enemy, shall be punished by death or by imprisonment for any term of years or for life.

Apart from its coverage of publication, section 794(b) is in most respects narrower than section 794(a). First, it is applicable only in time of war. Second, the quantity of information made subject to restraint is considerably smaller than that described by 794(a)'s "relating to the national defense" standard, assuming that "any other information related to the public defense" as used in 794(b) is limited to matters of the same genus as the items specifically described therein. Third, only communications to enemies violate the statute; subsection 794(a)'s proscription extends to transfers intended or likely to advantage "any" foreign nation.

A first issue of section 794(b)'s coverage concerns its present applicability. Although the statute on its face applies only in time of war, in 1953 the Congress enacted a second section (§798) of Title 18, providing that "acts which would give rise to legal consequences and penalties under section 794 when performed during a state of war shall give rise to the same legal consequences and penalties when performed" throughout the Presidentially proclaimed state of national emergency or until concurrent resolution of the Congress declares otherwise.[16] Insofar as the declared state of

---

16. The Congress inadvertently enacted two sections 798 of Title 18. The "emergency" provision is at 67 Stat. 133 (1953).

national emergency continues to this day (1974), section 794(b) is purportedly in force.

Whether the sentiment moving the Congress in 1953 has been successfully implemented is, however, questionable. Section 794(b) requires communication to the "enemy"—and, in the absence of declared war, who is the enemy? The statute itself gives the Executive no power to make the determination, nor do any Executive Orders purport to do so. Is it based on "common sense" notions? The complexities of current international politics argue against such a reading. In 1972 we were bombing Chinese ships in Hanoi at the same time as playing host to their ping-pong team. In 1973 we were at peace with North Vietnam in South Vietnam but *de facto* at war with Hanoi in Cambodia. Because of the increasing interrelations among nations, co-operation in some problems while pursuing violent solutions to others is likely to be the pattern in which such fighting as occurs takes place. To ask the citizen to determine when hostilities are sufficiently intense to make another nation "the enemy" is unrealistic. Does it occur when United States military equipment is given to resist foreign advances; when "advisers" are sent; or only when all-out military activity is commenced?

Passing the question of its present applicability, section 794(b) is significantly broader than section 794(a) in that it makes "publishing" criminal, thereby bringing newspapers under the statute. Here, however, is the first of many striking paradoxes under the espionage laws. Publication is criminal, as is all other conduct under 794(b), only if done with an intent to communicate to the enemy. If this intent requirement is read to mean conscious purpose—a construction suggested by the absence of the "reason to believe" standard used in the culpability formulation of 794(a)—then prosecution of normal publication under section 794(b) is a virtual impossibility. The purpose underlying publication will almost always be to inform the public, affect national policy, and sell newspapers. That foreigners will become aware of the information is an inevitable, but not a desired, side effect. Yet it seems an obvious anomaly to include "publishing" under the statute, and then condition the offense on a mental requirement that will almost never be present—thus leaving the statute applicable only to the coded classified advertisement or the disloyal newspaper that can be shown to have a purpose to promote the enemy cause by using its pages as a medium for communicating to foreigners. Anomalous or not, it seems clear that this is what the Congress intended.

I have earlier noted the proposal by the Wilson Administration in 1917 of what would, if enacted, have been a third provision of section 794, one authorizing a blanket restriction on publication of defense-related information, without any limiting mental requirement. The successful critics of the censorship provision attacked its failure to include any intent requirement. Yet they did not oppose the prohibition on publication contained in 794(b), since they were satisfied that this provision was conditioned on intent to communicate with the enemy. This is most revealing of what they understood by 794(b)'s intent requirement. General publication, of course, can be assumed to lead to receipt of information by an enemy. If knowledge of this expected consequence satisfied an intent requirement, it would have been redundant to insist on this requirement in a prohibition on publication. The opponents of the censorship provision therefore must have understood intent in 794(b) to require *conscious purpose to inform the enemy,* and not merely constructive proof to the effect that the usual and predictable consequence of general publication of information is that the enemy will learn of it.

Speaking from the opposite point of view, supporters of the blanket prohibition also understood 794(b)'s intent requirement to require a showing of *purpose* rather than *knowledge.* They repeatedly pointed out that newspaper disclosures of defense information could aid the enemy even though the newspaper and its reporter were entirely lacking in any bad purpose. The provision now codified as 794(b) does not deal with this problem—as they insisted in arguing for the blanket prohibition—since it affected only persons who published defense information with the treasonable purpose of aiding the enemy.[17]

The inferences to be drawn about the impact of 794(b) on publication of defense information are clear if the pattern of Congressional action is kept in view. That statute is violated only if the actor's purpose in publishing information about troop movements and ship sailings is to communicate it to an enemy. A newspaper publishing such detailed information—even if it is headlined "Normandy to Be Invaded Tomorrow"—simply to satisfy its readers' curiosity and fill its own coffers, does not breach this law. The result, however, as indicated earlier, is that the statute is in effect a prohibition on publication that is without real content. The nation's only general prohibition on publication of information—even as specific as, for example, when and how troops will be moved in time of war—turns out to be so limited as to be, in actual practice, insignificant.

Section 793

When we move to §793's treatment of information-gathering, the Espionage Statutes become exceedingly difficult. Section 793 creates six offenses, each entailing a maximum of ten years' imprisonment and involving among

---

17. See, e.g., the statements of Senator T. J. Walsh at 54 *Cong. Rec.* 3998–99, and Senator Adolphus P. Nelson, *id.* at 3488.

them various activities with respect to defense information—activities that augment the probability that such information will come into foreign hands. The problem is, of course, that these same activities are likely to occur also in preparation for publication of any information the Government tries to keep secret. And since the crimes under §793 are not defined in terms of the actor's intent to transfer information to foreigners, the overriding question in interpreting §793 is whether it reaches newspapers, their reporters, their informants, and anyone else who investigates, accumulates, informs about, or retains information as a prelude to public speech about national security. They are shielded neither by the communication/publication distinction found in 794(a) nor by 794(b)'s requirement that they be found to have acted with intent to communicate to the enemy.

Subsections 793(a) and 793(b) provide that:

(a) Whoever, for the purpose of obtaining information respecting the national defense with intent or reason to believe that the information is to be used to the injury of the United States, or to the advantage of any foreign nation, goes upon, enters, flies over, or otherwise obtains information concerning any vessel, aircraft, work of defense, navy yard, naval station, dockyard, canal, railroad, arsenal, camp, factory, mine, telegraph, telephone, wireless, or signal station, building, office, research laboratory or station or other place connected with the national defense owned or constructed, or in progress of construction by the United States or under the control of the United States, or of any of its officers, departments, or agencies, or within the exclusive jurisdiction of the United States, or any place in which any vessel, aircraft, arms, munitions, or other materials or instruments for use in time of war are being made, prepared, repaired, stored, or are the subject of research or development, under any contract or agreement with the United States, or any department or agency thereof, or with any person on behalf of the United States, or otherwise on behalf of the United States, or any prohibited place so designated by the President by proclamation in time of war or in case of national emergency in which anything for the use of the Army, Navy, or Air Force is being prepared or constructed or stored, information as to which prohibited place the President has determined would be prejudicial to the national defense; or

(b) Whoever, for the purpose aforesaid, and with like intent or reason to believe, copies, takes, makes, or obtains, or attempts to copy, take, make, or obtain, any sketch, photograph, photographic negative, blueprint, plan, map, model, instrument, appliance, document, writing, or note of anything connected with the national defense; . . . shall be fined not more than $10,000 or imprisoned not more than ten years, or both.

Two formulations common to these two subsections are basic to an understanding of their impact on public speech. First, what is the "information respecting the national defense," the places and the documents "connected with the national defense" to which the prohibitions on entering and obtaining relate? Do these subsections cover a broad or narrow range of information relevant to the national security? Second, what is the meaning of the phrase "intent or reason to believe that the information is to be used to the injury of the United States, or to the advantage of any foreign nation"? These two concepts are basic not only to sections 793(a) and (b) but throughout the Espionage Statutes as well. Comparable language appears in section 794(a), and the other subsections of §793 utilize the same concepts or derivations thereof.

The principle problem in construing the term "connected with the national defense" is to find its limits in an era when the nation's potential for waging war of any duration calls for evaluation of virtually every facet of civilian life. The problem did not go unseen in debates over the passage of the Espionage Act of 1917: numerous speakers in both Houses of Congress remarked the dangerous breadth of the phrase. And yet no consensus for a narrow definition emerged. In the end a majority of Congressmen was willing to accept the breadth, and, depending on their political predilections, to rely either on prosecutorial discretion or the culpability requirements to avoid harassment for innocent activities.

As is so frequently the case, the courts were left to grapple with the amorphous phrase. The efforts of the courts to find limits on this statutory conception is an interesting story in itself.[18] The fundamental question is whether national defense is to be restricted to concrete military affairs such as specific battle plans, weapons capabilities, troop conditions, and enemy capacities, or does it spill over to encompass broader issues such as overall national policy, the state of civilian defense readiness, economic capacities, and the like? Other key questions with which the courts have struggled are whether information in the public domain can possibly relate to the national defense in the statutory sense,[19] and—in a sense the opposite problem—what the effect of classification should be.[20]

For present purposes, however, I wish to turn away from these intriguing problems, since the focus of this chapter is on the controls that do exist in American statutes on publication of information (assuming its relation to the national defense). In brief (at least as I read the cases), after some sixty years in the statute books, the meaning of the phrase "related to the

---

18. See, e.g., Gorin v. United States, 312 U.S. 19 (1941); United States v. Heine, 151 F.2d 813 (2nd Cir. 1945); United States v. Soblen, 301 F.2d 236 (2nd Cir. 1962).
19. The leading case on this point is Heine, *supra*. But see, Gros v. United States, 138 F. 2d, 261 (9th Cir. 1943).
20. The cases dealing with classification are United States v. Drummond, 354 F.2d 132 (2nd Cir. 1965); Soblen, *supra;* and Gorin, *supra*.

national defense" is not much clearer now than it was on the date of its passage. Judicial gloss has not restrained the phrase's tendency to encompass nearly all facets of policy-making related to potential use of armed forces. Oddly enough, the courts' efforts to give content to the term follow— unwittingly, no doubt—the pattern of the Congressional debates. Unable to find satisfactory limits inherent in the term itself, the courts also turned to the culpability requirements to seek the degree of concreteness necessary to save the statute from being held unconstitutionally vague.

Conduct covered by section 793(a) and (b) must be done "with intent or reason to believe that [the defense-related item obtained] is to be used to the injury of the United States, or to the advantage of any foreign nation." The statutes make no effort to define what is meant by the key terms "intent," "reason to believe," "injury," and "advantage." In this respect the Espionage Laws share the characteristic ills of Federal criminal law resulting from use of both undefined and exceedingly complex culpability standards to mark the boundaries of Federal offenses. Moreover, these espionage provisions have been the subject of few judicial decisions that might set limits on the literal language of the law. The courts have not had to face up to defining the meaning of the culpability formulation in the context of public speech. Worse, the fact that prosecutions have been directed at clandestine transfer of information to foreign agents has pushed courts to construe rather broadly the culpability terms.

On the face of it, sections 793(a) and (b) define offenses of data-procurement rather than of communication. Nonetheless, except in the oddest sort of situation, culpability can be proven only when the act of obtaining is shown to have been committed with the intention of revealing the information to someone else. Thus, if the actor's sole intended use of information obtained is to contemplate alone the state of America's defense posture, he does not run afoul of these two laws. Mere satisfaction of individual curiosity cannot be said to injure the United States or give an advantage to other nations.

In most instances, however, people who go to great trouble to obtain defense-related information do so because they envision telling certain other people what they have learned. The proposition is true for newspapermen as well as for spies. In such cases—in which the actor expects to tell others— the statute purports to make the acquisition criminal depending upon the intended or predictable consequences of revelation: that the information will subsequently be used to injure the United States or to give advantage to a foreign nation. And yet, by establishing the predictable consequences as the test of criminality these statutes ignore, on their face, the questions that so concerned the Congress in rejecting direct publication controls in section 794: To whom, and for what reason, is the revelation made?

If words are given their usual meanings, a reporter who obtains secret defense documents with the intent that they be published must have reason to believe that the information subsequently will be used to injure the United States or to give advantage to a foreign nation. Foreigners keep up with our journals, just as we keep up with theirs. As a consequence of making public the formerly secret, foreign agents will gain information the obtaining of which in a clandestine manner would be clearly criminal.

Perhaps the situation may be concretized by recollection of the Bay of Pigs affair. Had *The New York Times* published that our invasion of Cuba was imminent, as President Kennedy retrospectively thought it should have done, is it not pretty clear that Cuba would have benefited? Is it not clear also that the *Times* would have had reason to believe that such advantage would accrue? Thus the plain meaning of sections 793(a) and 793(b) would impose severe criminal penalties upon information-gathering activities that are demonstrably a frequent, and perhaps a typical, prelude to publication of defense information. Can the Congress in 1917 have intended to make a rule in 793(a) and (b), so apparently at odds with 794 which rejects a general prohibitions on publication? If not, did the Congress simply overlook the problem for public speech posed by these provisions, or does legislative history support a narrower construction that can be applied to 793 without doing violence to its actual language?

While the legislative materials permit no indubitable conclusions as to the Congress's understanding of this cumbersome culpability standard, my tentative judgment is that the legislative history of the Espionage Statutes, taken as a whole, suggests that the Congress understood that the culpability requirement of the "gathering" offenses of 793(a) and (b) were not met merely by a showing that the gatherer had the intention to engage in public debate.

As originally proposed in the Senate in 1917, the 793 provisions did not condition criminal responsibility on any culpability requirement, other than having "the purpose of obtaining information respecting the national defense." Opponents concentrated their attack on the absence of any intent requirement and successfully urged that it be amended to require intent to injure the United States or advantage a foreign country as an element of the various offenses defined. Senator A. B. Cummins of Iowa, the leading critic of sweeping espionage proposals, was the most determined advocate of this position. One Cummins statement bears quoting because it is typical of the criticisms of the proposal during the Senate debates:

> I am . . . anxious . . . to prevent the revelation . . . in a time of war to
> an enemy or to a foreign country of things that are connected with the
> movements of our Army and our Navy. But I am not willing in order to

bring about that state of efficiency, if it be a state of efficiency, to close the mouths of the hundred million of American people upon all subjects at all times relating to the national defense. I think that if we must allow this one man, however unfortunate it may be, to go unpunished in order that these millions may preserve the liberties which they have acquired through long and arduous labors, we had better allow the one man to go unpunished. But I see no reason for permitting that. It is not hard, I am sure, to prescribe the terms of a statute which will punish any man who attempts to reveal to an enemy or even to a foreign country or who gathers information for the purpose of revealing to an enemy or a foreign country information that ought to be confined to American shores.[21]

Senator Cummins' approval of subsections 793(a) and (b) after the culpability standard was added—largely in response to his objections—must have signified that he considered the information-gathering offenses adequately limited by a requirement that there be a proven purpose to reveal the gathered information to a foreign country. I suspect that this was the general understanding in the Senate. The issue involving publication of defense information, as all must have assumed, would be resolved by the defeat or passage of the Wilson Administration's proposed blanket prohibition on publication.

The House debates are clearer that the "gathering" offenses were not meant to cover activities contemplating public speech. There is other clear evidence that the House understood the culpability formulation to require a purpose to injure the United States. Congressman George S. Graham, the dominant influence on the espionage legislation in the House, was the chief opponent of the proposed blanket prohibition on publication so long as it was *not conditioned on a purpose standard*—and took this position because of his concern that public speech about defense matters not be stymied. Despite his opposition, Graham still could warmly embrace 793(a) and (b) in the following terms:

. . . The Committee has carefully guarded innocent people who might communicate, who might obtain a photograph of some public work connected with the defense of the country, from being held liable for a criminal act, because the Government must prove affirmatively . . . that the person obtaining it had a guilty purpose, to wit, to injure the United States. Now, that applies to the first two sections.[22]

The best way to give effect to Congressional understanding of the scope

---

21. *54 Cong. Rec.* 3487–88.
22. *55 Cong. Rec.* 1717–18.

of the bill is to focus on the middle phrase of the culpability formulation: the actor's state of mind with respect to whether the defense material "is to be used" to bring about injury to the United States or advantage to a foreign nation. A person contemplating clandestine espionage intends or has reason to believe that the primary—indeed, in most cases the only—use to which the information he has gathered will be put is attempted advantage for foreigners or injury to the United States. By contrast, while the reporter is aware that some will put published defense materials to that use, he intends other, and predominant, uses contributing to consequences precisely opposite to those envisioned in the statutory formulation. It is consistent with Congressional purpose to focus on what the obtainer thinks will be the principal use of the materials.

If this reading of the culpability provisions of 793(a) and (b) is accepted, those sections do not apply to the activities of reporters, newspapers, and others who gather information with the intention of engaging in public speech about defense matters.

Sections 793(d) and 793(e)

These two provisions are undoubtedly the most confusing and complex of all the federal Espionage Statutes. They are also the statutes posing the greatest potential threat to newspapers' and reporters' obtaining and printing of national defense information. The legislative drafting is at its shotgun worst precisely where greatest caution should have been exercised. Moreover, legislative history suggests a basic and continuing Congressional misunderstanding of the effects actually achieved.

The subsections are a radical (if apparently unnoticed) departure from the general pattern of conditioning all espionage offenses upon a showing of culpable purpose. The results are most regrettable. The statute promises almost certain conflict with the First Amendment in its literal application to newspapers, reporters, and other participants in public debate on national security. Because of excessive broadness and vagueness in several fundamental elements, it is subject to challenge—even if prosecutors should act with careful discretion—under the accepted rule that overbreadth in statutes bearing on First Amendment freedoms may be attacked as unconstitutional even by a defendant whose own activities could constitutionally be the subject of a narrower statutory prohibition.

Sections 793(d) and 793(e) cover:

> (d) Whoever, lawfully having possession of, access to, control over, or being entrusted with any document, writing, code book, signal book, sketch, photograph, photographic negative, blueprint, plan, map, model, instrument,

appliance, or note relating to the national defense, or information relating to the national defense which information the possessor has reason to believe could be used to the injury of the United States or to the advantage of any foreign nation, willfully communicates, delivers, transmits, or causes to be communicated, delivered, or transmitted or attempts to communicate, deliver, transmit or cause to be communicated, delivered or transmitted the same to any person not entitled to receive it, or willfully retains the same and fails to deliver it on demand to the officer or employee of the United States entitled to receive it; or

(e) Whoever having unauthorized possession of, access to, or control over any document, writing, code book, signal book, sketch, photograph, photographic negative, blueprint, plan, map, model, instrument, appliance, or note relating to the national defense, or information relating to the national defense which information the possessor has reason to believe could be used to the injury of the United States or to the advantage of any foreign nation, willfully communicates, delivers, transmits or causes to be communicated, delivered, or transmitted, or attempts to communicate, deliver, transmit or cause to be communicated, delivered, or transmitted the same to any person not entitled to receive it, or willfully retains the same and fails to deliver it to the officer or employee of the United States entitled to receive it.

Both sections create two offenses: one involving willful communication of national defense information to those not entitled to receive it, the other criminalizing retention of the material. Neither offense is conditional on any requirement of culpable intent; the communication or retention need only have been done "willfully." The two provisions are identical but for slightly differing treatment of the retention offense, as turning on whether possession of national defense-related material is "lawful" on the one hand or "unauthorized" on the other. In the first instance the possessor is obligated to return the material only on demand; in the second, the obligation to return commences upon receipt. Their differentiation of the obligation-to-return as depending upon what type of possession is involved came into the law in 1950, at which time the offense created in section 1(d) of the Espionage Act of 1917 was split into two separate sections in order to accomplish that variation.[23]

The legislative history of 793(d) and (e) is incredibly confused and can only be summarized here. These provisions are successors to section 1(d) of the Espionage Act of 1917, which was understood, despite aimless drafting, to apply only to government employees. This narrow reach had been thought to justify the absence of any culpability requirement, on the ground that it was appropriate to exact a higher standard of loyalty—and a denial of

---

23. See Note 13, *supra.*

right to engage in public speech about defense information in their keeping —from government workers.

Whatever one may think about the Congress's wisdom in imposing these liabilities on government employees in 1917, the extraordinary feature of the 1950 rearrangement into the present subsections 793(d) and 793(e) is that the same liabilities were extended to all persons, but without the slightest indication that the Congress knew what a radical break it thereby accomplished. This oversight came about for the reason that the 1950 Amendment occurred as a little-attended aspect of the Internal Security Act of 1950, a massive legislative effort to deal with what was in those days perceived to be the substantial threat of domestic Communism.

Greater confusion than mere oversight was involved, however. The reason subsection 793(e) was extended to non-government workers was as a response to the notorious Whitaker Chambers "pumpkin papers" episode. The purpose was to make mere retention of national defense materials a crime. Of course, apart from the "pumpkin papers," Chambers had been involved in activities which, according to his own admission, would have easily been encompassed within the culpability framework of the 1917 Act. Subsection 793(e) is thus a radical extension of the basic coverage of the Espionage Statutes, and was passed in response to a particular activity that was part and parcel of an over-all design of clandestine espionage easily encompassed within the earlier statutes.

The Congress, in a state of both confusion and preoccupation with other matters, has in 793(d) and 793(e) enacted communication and retention offenses that raise a host of troublesome challenges to public speech about defense matters. Let us look first to the communication offense. Insofar as both subsections cover communication without any limiting culpability standard other than that the communication must be "willful," several difficult questions emerge.

First, in this statutory context, should the prohibition on communication encompass publication? Of course, insofar as newsmen are involved, they might avoid liability for themselves by pointing to the absence of the magic word "publish" in (d) and (e). It is also true, however, that elsewhere in the espionage statutes prohibitions on communication are invariably conditioned on a specific intent. The absence of any intent requirement in 793(d) and 793(e) might warrant a broader construction of communication than is appropriate in the other provisions. Even if (d) and (e) do not reach acts of publication as such, are they applicable to preliminary communications and retentions that necessarily take place prior to actual publication?

Second, the communication provision is violated only if the intended recipient is someone not "entitled to receive the information." But who is "entitled to receive information"? On the surface, one might think this a reference to the classification system established pursuant to a series of Executive Orders. Thus, a person is "entitled to receive" information if he has a security clearance appropriate to the particular item. There are some serious drawbacks to such a reading, however.

In the first place, the "entitled to receive" language appeared first in a predecessor statute, the Defense Secrets Act of 1911, and then was re-enacted in section 1(d) of the Espionage Act of 1917. At neither time was there a classification system pursuant to Executive Order, and it seems difficult to infuse language that has not changed since 1917 with a meaning that the initial draftsmen could not possibly have intended.

Second, such a construction flies in the face of persistent Congressional refusal over the years to place general criminal sanctions behind the Executive classification system. The consequence of such a construction is to make it a criminal offense, subject only to propriety of classification, to reveal such documents—and this is precisely what the Congress has hitherto shied away from doing. Finally, the 1917 Act included a provision—section 6—that would have expressly authorized the President to determine by Executive Order who was and was not "entitled to receive" defense information. This provision was deleted from the bill in Conference, without any attention to what the entitlement phrase might mean without it. These considerations suggest the odd conclusion that the key phrase "entitled to receive" may be meaningless, leaving the communication and retention offenses of 793(d) and 793(e) a dead letter.

Third, what materials and information will be deemed within the scope of the 793(d) and 793(e) offenses? One's initial assumption is that the answer is the same as it is for 793(a) and 793(b); after all, the key phrase "relating to the national defense" is common to the four subsections. But with respect to 793(a) and (b), the courts chose a broad construction of the phrase because the culpability standard of those subsections provided a *scienter* (guilty intent) element to help resolve otherwise powerful constitutional doubts on grounds of vagueness. Since 793(d) and 793(e) lack any explicit basis for a *scienter* requirement, is there a limited construction of "related to the national defense" that could save these subsections from either unconstitutional vagueness or overbreadth?

Fourth (and related), what meaning will be given to the term "willfully," the only mental requisite of the communication offenses? The absence of a more specific culpability standard in a statute otherwise so full of them seems to warrant a very liberal construction of the word. Yet the need to find a *scienter* requirement to render Constitutionally definite the range of materials covered by the statute, no less than the tradition of requiring specific intent in statutes bearing on freedom of expression, suggests that courts might give "willfully" a very narrow construction.

The retention offenses raise all but the second of these problems. While publication as such is obviously not reached, any publisher necessarily holds on to material before it can be published—as Justice White pointed out with such telling force in the Pentagon Papers decision. The problems with the meaning of the terms "related to the national defense" and "willfully" are parallel to the difficulties with the communication offenses. An additional question about the retention offenses is that they are nonsensical as applied to non-documentary information. It is clear from the legislative history of these provisions that this category, added in the 1950 Amendments, was intended to cover "oral communications." Yet how can one "turn over" such oral information to an official entitled to receive it? The legislative history appears to be one of definite and basic misunderstanding, coupled with a degree of carelessness that would be inexplicable but for the fact—characteristic of all the section 793 offenses—that invariably these provisions have been acted upon at times when the focus of legislative attention was directed to quite different yet overriding concerns.

We do have one hint lodged in the statutes themselves. A different provision—section 798—makes it criminal knowingly to communicate or publish classified information concerning the communications intelligence and cryptographic systems used by the United States.[24] This statute, which bars publication, for whatever reason, of a narrow class of highly sensitive defense information, was passed virtually contemporaneously with the 1950 enactment of sections 793(d) and (e). The clear assumption behind the passage of section 798 was that no other, more general, statutes barred publication of this information. Thus the passage of section 798 constitutes further strong evidence that the Congress did not realize that in subsections 793(d) and (e) it had enacted an effective prohibition on publication of all information relating to the national defense, by criminalizing communication and retention activities necessarily precedent to publication.

The confusion in the legislative history constitutes, in my judgment, a clear invitation for the courts to declare subsections 793(d) and (e) unconstitutional on grounds of vagueness and overbreadth. Their inclination to do so—which in any event should be strong, given that provision's literal sweep—should be bolstered by the fact that the Congress seems neither to have intended, nor even to have understood, the potential of sections 793(d) and (e) to prohibit publication of defense information. These two subsections are virtually incomprehensible. Judges must sometimes overlook this, and accept the proposition that the statutory draftsman was an artist with a complex vision, whose canvas is coherent if only brooded upon long enough. But the presumption is demonstrably false with respect to 793(d)

---

24. 65 Stat. 719 (1951).

and (e), and the courts should insist that the Congress provide a more understandable legislative direction before using these statutes as a barrier to free speech.

CONCLUSION

In my reading of the Espionage Statutes, publication of defense information not animated by a purpose to communicate to a foreign country is not prohibited, except for the narrow range of cryptographic information covered by sections 952 and 798. This reading admittedly makes heavy use of legislative history in construing the culpability provisions of subsections 794(b), 793(a), and 793(b). My conclusion rests also on the belief—perhaps speculation would be a better word—that courts will refuse to apply sections 793(d) and (e) to acts preparatory to publication, either by finding some very narrow reading that conforms the provision to the pattern of the other Espionage Statutes, or—preferably as it seems to me—by striking the provisions from Title 18 on grounds of vagueness and overbreadth.

Whether my interpretations are warranted or not, it is clear that the Espionage Statutes are hopelessly complex and confused with respect to publication of information in the area of national defense. The confusion may have been acceptable in an era when the press and the Government were in substantial agreement upon the ends, if not always the means, of foreign policy. But *The New York Times* decision to print the results of the most spectacular security break in our history signals the passing of the period when newspapers could be expected to play by tacit rules in treating matters that government leaders deem confidential. Our statutes governing publication of defense information are an unacceptable morass, and we must soon face up to basic policy questions not confronted since 1917: questions concerning our freedom to know about vital government decisions.

12

Cabinet Secrecy, Collective Responsibility, and the British Public's Right To Know about and Participate in Foreign Policy Making

WILLIAM CLARK

The facts of life under the Official Secrets Act of Britain were first thrust under my astonished nose in my twenties when, by an odd series of chances, I had been working for nearly a year towards the end of World War II as Press Attaché in Washington. In the course of duty I naturally saw many of the War Cabinet papers sent to Lord Halifax, Ambassador to Washington and member of that super-select body.

It all happened accidentally. Just after V-J Day the very efficient Head of Chancery was whisked away to bring order out of Indonesia's chaos, and a new broom was put in his place. So, quite early in the new regime I was summoned to the Head of Chancery's room for the purpose (as his secretary put it) of having my security talk. I had not been so excited since a dozen years earlier, my housemaster had given me (similarly belatedly) my obligatory talk on sex.

I was kept waiting only a very short time and then ushered in.

"Good morning, William."

"Good morning, Donald." (Though we knew each other only slightly we of course observed the proper Foreign Office familiarity.)

"I find you've never done the Official Secrets thing, and so I thought we ought to clear it up. Could you just sign this."

I was handed a slip of paper on which I was asked to acknowledge that

Mr. Clark is Director of External Relations for the International Bank for Reconstruction and Development (World Bank). He was formerly Director of the Overseas Development Institute; Public Relations Adviser to Prime Minister Sir Anthony Eden; a diplomatic correspondent; editor of "The Week" in the (London) *Observer,* and a television interviewer.

the terms of the Official Secrets Act had been drawn to my attention. I asked if I could see a copy of the famous Act whose terms had been drawn to my attention, but was told a trifle testily that this was quite unnecessary, though if I insisted there was probably a copy in the British Information Services Library in New York.

I must have looked crestfallen because the Head of Chancery unbent and said: "Look, honestly, it's just a formality saying you must never pass information gained in the course of your work to unauthorised persons."

"Are journalists unauthorised persons? Because if they are, I seem to have taken a Trappist vow of silence which would not suit my temperament."

"Don't be frivolous, William. Of course you should talk to *good* journalists. It's not them we're after, it's people who might make use of the information. For instance . . ."—and he carefully disconnected his phone by pulling out the jack on his desk—"I would always disconnect the phone when talking to business men, because of course our phones are tapped by the U.S. Government, and we don't want them to get all our trade plans. And one last thing, William, don't ever tell secrets to the French, they leak like sieves. Goodbye now, and be discreet."

"Goodbye and many thinks, Donald."

I went away pensive and a little puzzled, but I always feel I was lucky to have had my security talk from one so well qualified as Donald Maclean.[1]

INITIATION RITES AND RITUALS OF THE SECRECY FRATERNITY

What I discovered about security in my time in Washington was not all learned at Donald Maclean's knee. This was an active period: the end-of-war summits (Yalta and Potsdam), the post-war negotiations over nuclear weapons, and over the economic settlement that began with the Anglo-American loan and was fulfilled with the Marshall Plan. It saw the beginnings of the Cold War, and the spy scare resulting from Soviet cypher clerk Igor Gouzenko's defection. All these events involved problems of secrecy and problems of publicity—the mirror image of secrecy.

What I came to learn was that in any democracy there is no such thing as absolute secrecy because it is always *necessary* for some to know, and *desirable* for many more to be informed. There is really no important argument about those with "a need to know" (a phrase that became a security category) except the determination of who does indeed need to know. A rough rule of thumb is that it is 1 per cent of those who claim a vital necessity to know. Even so, great inconvenience can arise from excluding lowly but decisive persons; I shall long remember the awkwardness of a Minis-

---

1. Maclean was later found to have been a Soviet agent in British Intelligence.

ter's luggage arriving—in strict accordance with the cover story—in Rio de Janeiro, while the Minister fumed and shivered in Ottawa.

I should add parenthetically that in most of my information jobs I established the need to know most secrets on the true grounds that you can only keep secrets which you know. As a result, at the Embassy I was given the last copy of "Green Registry" telegrams—which, in that pre-Xerox Age of Innocence, were usually illegible, being written in invisible carbon. For these I added two files to my safe: for the very difficult to read there was a file (behind that called "Eyes only" and next to "British Most Secret/American Top Secret") labelled "X-Ray eyes only." For the totally illegible I invented a special category: "Burn before reading."

As we moved beyond war, dominated by military security, towards peace negotiations dominated by diplomatic secrecy, we became aware that a new element was entering in to all our security/secrecy calculations, and that was the desirability of carrying the politicians (and so ultimately the electorates) with our policies. Not just our own British electorate, but also, we reluctantly realised, the electorate, or at least the elected, of our dominant ally.

The question of security and official secrets became a question of who was authorised to receive secret information, and that turned on the meaning of the word "authorised," which I interpreted to mean that it was in the interests of H.M.G.[2] I should add that I was myself never "authorised" to do this, but I had one long conversation with Lord Halifax in which I satisfied myself that I was doing right. My argument was that postwar Britain was extremely weak in any argument or bargaining with the United States; our greatest strength was the goodwill that we enjoyed in America, and the generosity of spirit that the American people then displayed. If Roosevelt and Churchill, and the Foreign Office and State Department, could be utterly frank with each other, should not we be much more frank than was customary with the columnists and radio commentators who did so much to mould American and Congressional opinion? In briefing them on secrets, we would be doing no more than the State Department and White House did, from the American point of view, to their own favourites.

This was agreed, or at least not disagreed at the top, though I suspect it was disapproved of in lower echelons, where more regular diplomacy was practised by more regular diplomats. I have often wondered in later years whether Donald Maclean approved or disapproved of my activities (about which he knew in fair detail); as we now know he was at this time clandestinely passing diplomatic telegrams *in toto* to the Russians, just as he did openly to the American State Department. Both Russia and America were

---

2. His (Her) Majesty's Government.

wartime allies of Britain; why in the eyes of the law was one action treachery, and the other, loyal diplomacy? If that question cannot be easily answered, then indeed the law is an ass.

I was not, of course, *giving* diplomatic documents to anyone but I was showing them to journalists because that was the best way of overcoming an American *idée fixe* that they are always tricked in diplomatic bargaining. For instance, after Roosevelt's death there was a rumour that Churchill and Stalin had divided up Europe at Yalta, that the dying Roosevelt had been tricked into accepting this betrayal, which was only recorded because Mr. Byrnes (who was along for the ride) had been a court reporter and so kept the sole record of this nefarious deal at the Summit. Since the rumour got a lot of publicity, and led to a lot of recrimination against Britain, it seemed necessary to do something about it. I therefore asked Lindsay Hoben, the respected editor of the *Milwaukee Journal* and an old friend, who was in Washington for an editors' meeting, to come to my office. There I presented him, somewhat to his surprise, with the full printed record of the Yalta meetings that the Foreign Office had produced immediately afterwards. I told Lindsay he could have two hours to read it through, on condition he did not make notes or reveal that he had seen it. I do not know just what Lindsay said to his fellow editors, but there was no leak and the rumours began to die on the vine. About a decade later, as I recollect, Mr. Dulles leaked the whole record to *The New York Times*.

I did not think then, nor do I now, that negotiations are best held in a glare of publicity, but total secrecy on one side may be very deleterious. This was the case with negotiations for the post-war loan which was expected to start Britain and so Europe on the path to recovery. Britain's case was couched in terms of a high moral appeal from a country which had fought alone, to an ally which had won the war that Britain alone, by an enormous expenditure of blood and treasure, had prevented being lost. This was exactly the wrong approach, as the new Labour Government would have known if they had read our despatches from Washington. Churchill could have made such an appeal to Roosevelt and Morgenthau, but Dalton and Attlee could not get away with using it on Vinson and Truman. As a result of this miscalculation, Keynes found himself, in his phrase, talking poetry to people who wished to hear the prose of a sound company report.

Worse still from my point of view, in spite of an extremely able Press Officer (Paul Bareau) attached to the Keynes mission, agreed conditions of secrecy led to suppression of the British case, while the British demands (or requests) became gradually and exaggeratedly well known. Eventually the British delegation decided (in consultation with London) that they were being pressed too far (in terms of trade concessions and the removal of protection for the pound sterling) for too little. Accordingly, Lord Halifax spoke frankly at the regular afternoon bargaining session, concluding gently but firmly by saying that perhaps Britain would have to break off the talks and "go it alone."

This created a sensation in the conference room but, as I realised from the subsequent joint press briefing, it would not be heard outside. It seemed to me (and probably to others whom I consulted—but I have no record, so I write in the first person *solo*) that it was necessary that the American public should be aware of how serious was the situation with their main ally. So I rang Raymond Swing (then still at the height of his fame as a radio commentator) and gave him the gist of Lord Halifax's speech. This was probably a breach of several conventions, rules, laws, and understandings; but whether *propter* or only *post,* the talks resumed with considerable American concessions, all supported by a wide section of the columnists and commentators.

I must add for the record, however, that in my belief the general and agreed secrecy surrounding these immediate postwar economic talks, screened the American people from the realities of the trans-Atlantic situation and thus delayed for three or four vital years the necessary decisions on the part of the United States, which were eventually taken by General Marshall in his historic Harvard speech and carried through the Congress by Senator Vandenberg and his colleagues.

To sum up these wartime and early postwar recollections, I would say simply that we learnt the necessity, in dealing with allies whose people have a large measure of control over foreign policy, for revealing a great deal of "secret" diplomatic activity to those opinion formers who are quite outside the official round of diplomatic contacts.

Before I left the British Embassy in Washington late in 1946 I left a record of my views on these topics, and told of my experience and practice in revealing "secrets" to the media. My successor (Philip Jordan, who later became my predecessor at No. 10 Downing Street) told me that this document was read by one of H.M. Inspectors of the Foreign Service, who minuted it thus (to my rough recollection):

> This seems to set out everything a prudent Press Attaché should *not* do. It will *not* be done in future. We should be thankful that Clark has gone into journalism, where he can do little harm to the processes of diplomacy and foreign policy.

He little knew.

TO OPEN DIPLOMACY AND BACK AGAIN

It was true, though, that for most of the next decade I was working on the other side of the fence as Diplomatic Correspondent of *The Observer,* and

as a commentator on the BBC. The beginning of this period was dominated, for diplomatic correspondents, by the long series of meetings of the
Council of Foreign Ministers, which was charged with negotiating peace
treaties to end World War II. Since the Cold War was at its height, the negotiations turned out to be not between Victors and Vanquished, but between Russia and its former Western allies. For the Western governments
the most difficult task was keeping the peoples of their democracies firm in
their opposition to (or containment of) the Soviet Union, which had many
admirers for its wartime sacrifices.

As a result, a new form of "open diplomacy" was evolved in which members of the press were cast in the role of the Greek Chorus, commenting
sadly to the public audience about the fearful tragedy being enacted off
stage. Whenever the Foreign Ministers, or their deputies, met we of the
Chorus were there also. At the end of the day we were summoned to the
presence of the briefing officer of our choice (there were always British and
American briefings, usually French and sometimes Russian), who "strictly
for background" read their notes of the day's proceedings, with particular
attention to their own national star. We journalists then had hurried consultations with friends and colleagues who had been to the other briefings,
and finally sent despatches beginning "Today's meeting of the Big Four remained deadlocked, I learned from unimpeachable sources. . . ." It was
as easy, and as useful, as falling off a log.

In this period the need to hold together the Western alliance, and to keep
their public's support for a tough policy, led the Governments of Britain
and the United States to go to unusual lengths to play their cards face up-
wards. Each day the diplomatic correspondents would descend on the Foreign Office for a thorough briefing. They were divided into two groups: "the
Circus," representing the popular journals, and "the Trusties," correspondents of the quality press, who saw the head of the News Department. About
three times a year we were all herded in to see the Foreign Secretary, on an
off-the-record basis, and given a chance to ask him a few questions.

My recollection is that all these briefings were of a very high order. It is
quite possible to criticise the policy of Cold War containment, but the presentation of it to the British people through their press was done with skill,
and produced a very large measure of national unity in support and understanding of the Government's basic policies. There can be no criticism of
the Government for keeping secrets from the public; it did not do so. By its
control of the sources of information, however, and by the implied threat
that criticism of policies would lead to a less full flow to that correspondent; by co-opting all of us diplomatic correspondents into a cosy club of
those in the know, I fear that the Government (under both parties) did
manage the news of our foreign policy, so that the public got a smug and

insular view of the world and our place in it. For Britain this meant a failure to realise how comparatively weak we were, how fragile the Empire/
Commonwealth was, how far Europe was prepared to go without us, and
how little our "Special Relationship" meant to America.

Secrecy is not the only way of fooling most of the people most of the
time; it can be done by open disclosure, too.

I would suggest that, looking back at the Cold War (Berlin blockade to
Geneva Summit), it was a classic example of the disadvantages and the in-
appropriateness of open, popular diplomacy—if you regard the object of diplomacy as being to arrive at settlements of disputes. The inevitable result
of popular diplomacy is to mould clear, hard positions ultimately baked by
moral fervour into a brittle solidity that cannot be bent or adapted without
disaster. The advantage, of course—and it should not be underestimated—is
that it rallies a democracy to firmness when it believes that it could only
lose in any negotiation. That was exactly the position that the Western democracies believed they were in during the immediate postwar years. The
policy of open disagreements openly arrived at vis-à-vis the Soviet Union
was arguably a legitimate tactic to freeze the situation until an opportunity
for real negotiation appeared on the horizon.

The new era was signalised by Sir Winston Churchill's memorable phrase
that he "would seek a meeting at the summit" to negotiate with the new
leaders of Russia after Stalin's death. But his vision was to remain like
Moses' view of Palestine from Mount Pisgah; because of the arthritic state
of Western diplomatic activity, Churchill himself never got to the Summit,
which was first scaled at Geneva in 1955, after Anthony Eden had succeeded him in the Premiership.

But the whole international atmosphere was changed in 1952 by the arrival of the Churchill-Eden team. Churchill, who had no chink in his armour
whereby he could be called soft on Communism, or weak in the defence of
British interests, did not fear to say that the current confrontation could and
should not last and that we must negotiate. He had as his lieutenant Anthony Eden, probably the best negotiator ever to hold the post of Foreign
Secretary.

The change in style was immediately apparent to the Press Corps and, in
my recollection, was quite welcome. We became aware that the old-style
conferences—in which every Minister was accompanied by a phalanx of advisers, experts, retainers, and (we suspected) restrainers, so that there
would be a hundred present at a restricted session, and up to four hundred at plenaries—that these leaky mass meetings were being replaced by
committees of Ministers with one adviser apiece. The old briefings with
their endless repetitions of national lines, were replaced by shorter communiqués outlining the topics discussed, and leaving fuzzy during the negotiations the points of agreement and disagreement.

THE VIEW FROM NO. 10 DOWNING STREET

It was during this period that I changed back from poacher to gamekeeper, and my views must be discounted accordingly. But it is my impression that the press and the public were happy to resume a meaningful diplomatic game, even if they could not watch every move.

Two negotiations which Eden undertook as Foreign Secretary seem models of the new diplomacy—the patching up of Europe after the collapse of the proposals for a European Army, and the Geneva accords on Indo-China in 1954. Both had disastrous side effects: the European effort, because it intentionally left Britain outside Europe; the Indo-China settlement, because it offended Mr. Dulles' peculiar sensibilities and caused him, more or less single-handedly, to involve the United States in the Vietnam War. But the limited objectives—the avoidance of the breakup of the Franco-German rapprochement; the end of the French war in Indo-China—were achieved. And they were achieved by negotiation carried on in considerable secrecy as to detail, but with broad public understanding and sympathy. It is worth examining how the British system works when it works well.

First of all, when a crisis arises—such as that caused by the French Chamber's rejection of the European Army agreements—the Foreign Office goes to work immediately on preparing papers for the Foreign Secretary, setting out options and their consequences. As a rule, all that the press is told at the time is that the Foreign Secretary is studying the situation, and the diplomatic correspondents are kept fairly happy by being given a series of uninformative facts: e.g., the Foreign Secretary saw the Ambassadors of France and Italy, he spoke to our Ambassador in Bonn, and also had communications from our Ambassadors in Rome and Brussels. All this helps to pad out an intrinsically dramatic story.

If there is time (more than twenty-four hours) the Foreign Secretary will write a Cabinet Paper setting forth the position and his intentions in about fifteen hundred very succinct words. That is secret and remains so. There follows the Cabinet discussion (usually about thirty minutes, very rarely more than an hour), led by the Foreign Secretary and summed up as a rule by the Prime Minister. The discussion is absolutely free, and Ministers do not feel that they can be called to account for views they express there—views that often differ widely from their public persona (Aneurin Bevan is said to have argued strongly in Cabinet *for* Britain's building its own hydrogen bomb). The Secretary of the Cabinet, who is present unless—very rarely—the Cabinet discusses party political affairs, keeps a detailed record of Cabinets, but this is not circulated (except sometimes to the Monarch). What is circulated to a very limited group is "Cab. Con." (Cabinet

Conclusion), which records what was agreed finally, and only mentions the debate in which it had direct impact on the final decision.[3]

This is what the Cabinet is collectively responsible for; this is the policy of H.M.G. All the debate, all the qualifications, all the reluctancies are swept under the carpet. Which is why Ministers who resign often seem to do so on some very slight scruple, straining at a gnat after swallowing a camel, and prevented by Cabinet secrecy from explaining in their resignation statement how far they had been dragged from their original purposes and principles. But I would argue, strongly, that the secrecy of the Cabinet is well worth preserving if it is done really effectively, as it has been. The secrecy is maintained by tradition rather than by law or rules. In theory Cabinet Ministers are bound by their Privy Councillor's oath, not by the Official Secrets Act; yet it is the lively tradition that "it is not done to leak Cabinet secrets" which really ensures that even the most publicity-seeking Minister thinks twice before revealing the gist of any Cabinet discussion.

Furthermore, the Civil Service, few of whom know what does go on in Cabinet, protect its secrecy absolutely. I, for instance, always knew what was on the Cabinet Agenda, but as Press Secretary I would never confirm or deny that any item had come up. As a curious result the press felt free to say "It is understood that such and such an item was raised at to-day's Cabinet," secure in the knowledge that it would never be officially denied. On one occasion when the Cabinet met till nearly 1:30 P.M. (thus breaking a dozen lunch appointments) the press universally declared that the Cabinet had been discussing the critical issue of Burgess and Maclean, when in fact it had been discussing the Oxford ring road plan. As a footnote let me say (putting myself at risk of prosecution) that the Cab. Con. in the autumn of 1955 was that the road should be built as soon as possible across Christ Church Meadows; almost twenty years later the debate continues and no road is built.

The basic reason for maintaining Cabinet secrecy in foreign affairs is that it enables the Government to discuss with absolute candor what is the best policy for them to pursue, without the risk that its disadvantages, which are seen and faced, can be used and exaggerated by its critics. At the same time the doctrine of collective responsibility ensures that the doubts and difficulties of colleagues are subordinated to an agreed line. Nothing of this, however, ensures that it will be a good policy—collective insanity is not unknown—nor that it will be a policy, that appeals to the people.

Once a policy is decided, the question remains as to how far shall it be made public and how far debated. It has little to do with the secrecy sur-

---

3. The style of Cabinet records varies from time to time, from Secretary to Secretary, and from Prime Minister to Prime Minister. Before 1939 the Cabinet Minutes of Lord Hankey were much longer and more revealing.

rounding the Cabinet debate. When the British system is working well the discussion of foreign policy begins, or reaches its first climax, in Parliament. This is an institution designed for the purpose of examining the Executive's actions, and it still can do so better than television, radio, the newspapers, or the periodicals. For one thing it has time; a foreign policy debate will last from 4 P.M. till 10 P.M.; the chief speakers will have forty-five minutes to make their points. The Foreign Secretary can use the Cabinet Paper he prepared, as the basis for a speech that will be the most thorough and extensive exposition of H.M.G.'s policy that could be produced by an able bureaucracy serving an experienced Minister. With luck the second speaker (leading for the Opposition) will be an ex-Foreign Secretary who will probe the weak spots and elucidate what is unclear, but will not—with the experience of office recently behind him—press the Foreign Secretary beyond the bounds of discretion. It is in this way that, it seems to me, the Parliamentary debate is far superior to the Press Conference as an instrument of national democratic policy.

In spite of complaints that Parliament is not televised or broadcast, it is still (I think, and I am certain was in the 1950's) an admirable platform for addressing the nation. The substance of the debate is carried by the media, and all the commentators at least have available to them the presentation of the Government's case in extenso, and the Parliamentary questions and answers which followed it. Yet the Government does have the advantage of choosing its own terrain; the Foreign Secretary does not have to deal all his cards face up before he goes into the Conference Chamber, and he is allowed considerable freedom of manoeuvre in negotiation, if he has convinced the House and the public that his broad policies are correct.

To sum up: when the machine works well in Britain it has a great deal going for it. There is first a careful and secret study by expert officials; there is then an examination of this by an elected political figure—the Foreign Secretary, who submits his analysis and conclusions to a Cabinet composed of all the political leaders of the Government. There it is examined again in secret, but once agreement is reached, the Government case is put at length to the people's elected representatives, who usually include in their number several experts in the subject matter. The Government has the advantage of presenting its case first and on its own terms; that I believe is a proper privilege of responsibility. This Parliamentary system has the added advantage (particularly over press conferences) that, in general, the Government does not have to reply to questions on the spur of the moment but can give a considered reply in the winding-up speech. And there is the strong tradition that when a Government is about to enter negotiations its hands are not too tightly bound. This tradition is kept lively by the presence on both sides of the House of many men with experience of Ministerial responsibility.

THE SUEZ CRISIS

I have argued that the system of Cabinet secrecy and controlled disclosure to Parliament is a good form of governance, superior to communication by press conference, for instance. But lots of things can go wrong, of which the simplest is that Parliament is on vacation, as it always is during the diplomatic hurricane season lasting from August to October! This leads me to examine (rather superficially and without access to papers) what went wrong in the Suez crisis of 1956, which Mr. R. A. Butler, sometime Chancellor of the Exchequer, later described as essentially a failure of the Government's public relations. I was rather cross at this statement, since I was supposedly in charge of the Government's public relations at the time and suspected that some other things had gone wrong as well. But it is certainly true that the Suez crisis is a classic example of the failure (for whatever reason) of communication between government and people, and it is on this that I wish to concentrate.

The nationalisation of the Suez Canal by President Nasser on 26 July 1956 was the culmination of a series of rebuffs Anthony Eden had suffered in the Middle East, where he had pursued a pro-Arab and pro-Egyptian policy culminating in the withdrawal of British troops from the Zone. Part of the right wing of the Conservative party, including many close to Churchill, had regarded this at the time as a dangerous scuttle; and when the policy did not pay off in any agreed Middle East defence organisation, but resulted in a humiliating dismissal of Glubb Pasha from Jordan and finally in the seizure of the Canal, they were lusting for blood. At the same time Eden's patience snapped, and he saw Arab nationalism as a threat to British vital interests, just as German nationalism had been twenty years before. He therefore decided that Nasser must be forced to disgorge by any means, including force if necessary.

In all of this the Prime Minister was very close to ordinary British public opinion. He carried the Cabinet with little discussion, and in a debate in Parliament the day before it rose for the summer recess it seemed that both sides of the House were agreed that Nasser was a new Hitler and must be dealt with accordingly. At Number 10 it seemed to us (I use the first person plural to indicate that my own opinion was derived from what I believed to be the opinion of the Prime Minister and his closest colleagues) that if we could display this national unity and determination we might well bring diplomatic pressure to bear on Nasser to agree to a settlement, or alternatively rouse opinion in Egypt to overthrow him as a dangerous adventurer. What was essential was that the bulldog should continue to growl and show its teeth, as it had done so convincingly at the beginning of August.

But Parliament, which the Prime Minister could address in person, had gone on holiday. How was the nation to be brought to the mood of fighting on the beaches when it was in fact sunbathing on them? We tried a television address, which was not a great success because the Prime Minister had not the sureness of touch he had in the House, and moreover the BBC felt bound to balance the Ministerial statement by subsequent discussions displaying the growing doubts in the country about Britain's warlike posture. The mood of resolution shown in Parliament on August 2 began to fade as the holiday month wore on.

To make things worse, Mr. Dulles came across to see the Prime Minister and made it quite clear that while he sympathised with British indignation at the loss of the Canal he could not approve any use of force to win it back. Pressure, *yes,* but force, *no;* and of course he let the American press, and so the world including Nasser, know of his warnings to Britain. But the decision had been taken that Britain could not accept the loss of the Canal; it was a vital national interest, which Mr. Dulles could not give away for us. Furthermore, there was always a sneaking feeling that if it came to a crunch Mr. Dulles could not bear to see an ally of the Soviets win a major diplomatic victory in the Middle East.

And so it came about in that curious August and early September of 1956 Britain and America were both trying to persuade each other of their unyielding determinations. In the absence of Parliament our main salvos were fired by the Press Officers at Number 10 and at the Foreign Office. Certain eminent journalists used to shuttle between Sir George Young's office in the Foreign Office and mine in Number 10 to see if they could detect differences in emphasis between us. They were foiled because Sir George and I always spoke on the intercom while they were crossing Downing Street.

But I did loyally and fairly openly warn the press (especially the American press) that we were serious and meant business. This had the somewhat bizarre result that some politicians began to believe that this was a reflection of my own personal bellicosity. One of them coined the phrase "Clark's Cold War," and Dick Crossman—an ex-colleague from my *New Statesman* days—described me as "a sort of Burgess and Maclean for Nasser." I never quite found out what he meant, but it was clear that he felt I was being far tougher in words than the Government meant to be in action, in a journalistic-diplomatic attempt to scare Nasser.

What was perfectly true was that the British Government was trying to maintain the credibility of its menace to Nasser, so as to bring pressure on him to disgorge the Canal. In a democracy threats are credible only if they are publicly voiced and publicly supported. In the temporary absence of the proper Constitutional means for voicing the Government's views and establishing the nation's reaction, we were forced to use, rather amateurishly, the Government spokesmen and the press.

In mid-September there was a short emergency meeting of Parliament, during which the Government demonstrated its determination not to settle for less than the re-establishment of international control of the Canal; but it also showed that there was deep anxiety in the country about the possibility of our using force to achieve this objective. The Opposition, which had been (through Hugh Gaitskell) strong in its denunciation of Nasser in August, now openly opposed any use of force. But, looking back on it, I believe that the Prime Minister gained by having a chance to put his views to Parliament and the nation.

A few weeks later, however, when I took soundings amongst my British press friends, particularly those working outside London, I found that they were more or less unanimously opposed personally and editorially to any military attack on Egypt. I reported my findings to the Prime Minister, and he was not surprised since he had had a number of contacts with editors singly and in groups over the preceding weeks. Shortly afterwards he held another meeting for the editors of the main national papers and explained very frankly and reasonably how hampered he was in negotiation with Nasser by signs of weakness at home. What especially irked him, and others, was the knowledge that the daily BBC *Press Review,* widely listened to in the Arab world, gave full weight to the attacks on his policy made by the *Manchester Guardian* and the *Observer* in particular. It was in an attempt to deal with this running sore that various attempts were made to control the BBC, chiefly in its external services.

By the end of September it was clear to the British Government that diplomatic pressure and international negotiation were not going to dislodge Nasser. It was equally apparent that the British people had not fully been persuaded of the necessity of recovering control over the Canal "by force if necessary." They needed, or the Government needed on their behalf, at least some pretext for action—such as the incompetence of the Egyptians to run the Canal themselves (which proved a vain hope), or some overt act of aggression against our ships in the Canal (which the Egyptians were too smart to commit).

As a result the Cabinet policy of August 2 lay in ruins. It may have been an unwise or old-fashioned policy, but it had been pursued quite honorably, attempting to use the threat of force as the *ultima ratio* in negotiations designed to undo what was regarded (old-fashionedly) as the seizure by force of a vital national and international asset. The policy failed because the threat of force did not seem credible from a divided Britain, faced with American antagonism and general international coolness. In the light of history the policy failed because the era in which Great Powers controlled parts of the territory of weaker powers was coming to an end. This was not perceived by the generation of men at the top of the British Government, but it was dimly understood by a large minority of the British people, and not all the news management and briefing by Government officials could shake their doubts.

In early October there was a lot of talk of the failure of the Government's policy, and serious consideration of ways of getting out from under without too much humiliation. Something tipped the balance the other way, and the disasters of Suez followed. I do not want to discuss them except in relation to Government policies of disclosure to the public.

The situation with which the Government was faced in October 1956 was the failure of its attempt to rally the country behind a strong and clearly defined policy. Probably a bare majority of the populace favoured the use of force against Nasser, but a democracy needs more than a bare majority to take an effective, bellicose line—at least if the hostilities are going to last for more than a few days. Overwhelming and immediately effective power may provide its own justification.

Could the British Government exercise overwhelming and immediately effective power in the Canal Zone? There was debate and disagreement within the Cabinet and within the Defence Committee. Eventually, it now appears, the decision was reached that, with allies, the Canal could be seized, but it must be done before opposition could be mobilised in the United Nations, the United States, and amongst the British public. The element of surprise was essential, not against the enemy, but against public opinion at home and abroad. Thus, foreign policy had to be made without any of the usual consultation with Parliament, the public, or even the bureaucracy. What was worse, Parliament, the public, and the bureaucracy were not only unconsulted, not only surprised, they were deceived. They had to be; because the secrecy was not the proper security of a military operation, it was the conspiratorial concealment of a political *trompe d'oeil*. Public opinion at home and particularly abroad was sufficiently potent that it could not be ignored, it had to be fooled. News management became news invention.

THE LESSON OF SUEZ FOR THE STUDY OF SECRECY

It was without precedent in history, but it was the lessons of history, I believe, that moved the Prime Minister—a very honorable man—to act in this extraordinary way. He felt strongly that the lessons of the 1930's showed that to save the world from disaster Governments must move ahead of lethargic public opinion. As he argued, if Britain and France had stopped Hitler when he reoccupied the Rhineland, we should have been spared the horrors of the Second World War. As a politician of the period, Eden knew very well that public opinion favoured our vacillation at the time of the Rhineland occupation, and supported Chamberlain's betrayal of Czechoslovakia at the time of Munich. He was determined that Britain should not again lay herself at the proud feet of a conqueror by her own misguided folly.

He failed, and he has written his apologia.

What are the lessons of history that future Prime Ministers should learn from the Suez episode? I am tempted to say that future Prime Ministers should learn that in a democracy such as Britain one cannot successfully lead the country into a military adventure without preparing public opinion; that in the modern world secret diplomacy cannot be backed by force, for the public will not accept the risks of a war about which they have not been openly and endlessly consulted. But I fear that someone who was clever enough to become Prime Minister would also be clever enough to see through this argument. Britain, in the final analysis, was *not* stopped in Suez by its domestic public opinion, which, despite vociferous critics, generally rallied round the flag; this was even more true of France and Israel. Britain and the two temporary allies *were* stopped by the force of external, world public opinion, which was made effective by the fluke that America and Russia were for once united.

The Machiavellian lesson of Suez is that such a deed must be done so quickly that world opinion *cannot* be mobilised in time to prevent it. The world will accept a *fait accompli* before long. This was the lesson Israel learnt in 1956 and applied in 1967. On the other hand, both the superpowers have shown that they can successfully defy world opinion; *quod licet Iovi non licet bovi*. Yet I hope that future British Prime Ministers will not be pupils only of Machiavelli; there is much more to learn from Suez. The Suez adventure was wrong because:

1. It failed.

2. It was bound to fail in the long run because it was against one of the most powerful of historic trends (now generally accepted, but not so in 1956) — the anti-colonialist trend where Great Powers should not (and usually could not) assert their sovereignty over parts of other sovereign countries, even under cover of ancient agreements.

3. It was not according to the rules of the democratic game to trick the British people into a major foreign policy decision.

Number 3 is perhaps the most debatable judgment, and it is what this paper is all about. Do the (British) people have a right to know and approve or reject the foreign policy of their Government? The strongest argument against this seemingly obvious truism is one that was always in Eden's mind: Suppose the people are wrong? Suppose that British Governments in the 1930's had not followed popular enthusiasm for disarmament and peace but had stood up to Hitler in 1936; would it not have been nobler of the Government and better for the people?

More recently, the man who in 1956 had been Eden's Chief Whip, has taken Britain into Europe—perhaps the most important decision in foreign policy since Attlee took Britain out of India in 1947—with the support of only a minority of the people. Is Heath to be condemned as Eden has been for tricking the British people?

The answer to the basic question of the British peoples' right to know and approve is not simple, nor obvious. Clearly any Government will try to rally popular support for its policies, and, particularly with foreign policy, this involves explaining it to the people by all possible means. But H.M. Government is responsible to Parliament, not to the press nor to the opinion polls. If Parliament can be persuaded, as it has been over British entry into Europe, then the Government has every right to act, even against public opinion. It also has the right to "persuade" Parliament by all the usual tricks of the political trade—such as threats of calling an election or of withdrawing the whip from a Member, exiting him from the party caucus.

What is not permissible under the only rules of the game which make democratic politics possible is that the Government should try to fool all of the people and Parliament by a false prospectus on major action. This is not just a moral judgment about deception; it is based on the knowledge that the power of Government to deceive is so immense that fooling all of the people some of the time can successfully and easily lead to fooling them all of the time. That is why a Press Officer who is being used for fooling the press should break the rules of the Civil Service and resign.

13

Secrecy, News Management, and the British Press

ANTHONY SAMPSON

The discretion of British newspapers, and their reluctance or inability to uncover official secrets, has often been commented on by visiting journalists, particularly Americans. To quote one recent critic, James Michael of "Nader's Raiders," who has been undertaking an enquiry into British secrecy in government: "The rule here seems to be that everything is kept secret unless and until the government decides it wants the public to know what is going on."[1]

There are several spectacular examples of information that is not printed in Britain, of the kind that would be expected to be available in America. The events preceding the Suez crisis of 1956 remain shrouded in secrecy in spite of a succession of memoirs by leading characters, including Harold Macmillan, R. A. Butler, and Anthony Nutting, Minister of State at the Foreign Office, who resigned at the time. The proof copies of Mr. Nutting's book included an account of the crucial Cabinet meeting of 15 October 1956, which was then expunged from the manuscript at the insistence of the Cabinet office. More recently, the arguments for and against the use of force in Rhodesia in 1965 have not yet been revealed. Perhaps most consistently surprising to visiting journalists is the fact that the name of the Director-General of the Security Services (MI5)—roughly equivalent to the Director of the FBI—is never printed, even though he has emerged to give detailed evidence to the recent Franks Commission on Official Secrets.

Most British journalists, I think, would agree that our newspapers are too reluctant either to uncover or to reveal government secrets. It was the great

---

Mr. Sampson is a well-known British journalist, author of *Anatomy of Britain* and other books, and currently Washington correspondent for the (London) *Observer.*
1. Public Interest Research Centre, London. Press release 1 October 1962.

nineteenth-century editor of *The Times,* John Thaddeus Delane, who wrote that "newspapers live by disclosure"; but it is difficult to imagine this as the motto of *The Times* today. Perhaps more relevant to the twentieth-century British press is the slogan of Lord Northcliffe, in 1918: "The power of the press is very great, but not so great as the power of suppress." There has been a saying on *The Times,* that if readers knew how much of their subscription went to keeping information from them, they would demand their money back. But it is hard to say where they would do better—except perhaps in the *Sunday Times,* whose editor, Harold Evans, has emerged as the closest heir to the Delane tradition (if we except *Private Eye,* the fortnightly scandal-sheet, which lives, like its eighteenth-century forebears, by a combination of disclosure and invective).

For this discretion, most journalists are inclined to blame the law—the law of libel, and more relevant to this discussion, the Official Secrets Act, which since 1911 has been the chief legal instrument for preventing governmental disclosure. On the surface, certainly, section 2 of the Act appears a powerful deterrent. Its most recent application in 1971 became a *cause célèbre* that revealed all the vagueness and omnipotence of the Act. The *Sunday Telegraph* was prosecuted for publishing a secret report on the Nigerian Army by the British Military Advisor, and after a year's delay, the four defendants were acquitted by Mr. Justice Caulfield, who suggested that section 2 of the Act, being sixty years old, had reached retirement age and should be pensioned off. Two months afterwards (though not, the Government insisted, as a result of the case), a committee was appointed under Lord Franks to report on the notorious section 2; and eighteen months later they reported that the "catch-all" section 2 should be repealed and replaced by narrower provisions—though not so much narrower—limiting prosecution to questions of defence, security, and foreign relations.

But at this writing the Franks Report has not yet been accepted; the existing legislation continues to be enforced. A current investigation has drawn attention, once again, to the "catch-all" powers of section 2. The *Sunday Times* published details of a government review of railway policy recommending large-scale closure of lines, and this had reached them through the *Railway Gazette.*[2] Detectives later raided the *Gazette* offices and questioned both editors, apparently invoking the powers of the Official Secrets Act to do so. The use of the Act was the more bizarre in this case in that it was mobilised against the kind of disclosure of the decision-making process that many would regard as being an important part of "open government"—to use the phrase coined by Edward Heath in Opposition.

Such uses of an all-powerful Act encourage the view that the law is the

---

2. *Sunday Times,* October 8, 1972.

chief deterrent to a revelatory and indiscreet press; and certainly the press of the early nineteenth century, when newspapers had many fewer legal restraints, gives support to this assumption. But I believe nevertheless that the law is only part—and not necessarily the key part—of a deeper tendency towards discretion in British newspapers. This discretion is rooted not just in the Constitution but also in the politico-social relations between journalists and government. A respect for secrecy is more than the enforcement of a law; it has become a habit of mind, both among the potential providers of secrets—the civil servants and Ministers—and among the journalists themselves.

The Franks Committee members, having investigated the treatment of secrecy in other countries, including the United States, themselves emphasised that laws were only part of the difference. "Too much emphasis," they commented, "should not be placed on the nature of a country's laws when considering openness in government. In each of the four overseas countries which we visited, as in this country, there is a variety of factors affecting openness. Constitutional arrangements, political tradition, and national character, habits and ways of thought, all have their influence. . . . In the United States the Constitution incorporates a series of checks and balances, and the right of access to certain official documents can be seen as a natural part of this system."[3]

NEWS SOURCES AND CENTRALISATION

The basic structural weakness of British journalism in its attempts at disclosure is its dependence on relatively few sources of information—a dependence that in turn flows from the non-separation of powers. All correspondents who are concerned with central areas of administration—whether political, foreign, defence, or even environmental—find themselves relying heavily on the few people inside the relevant government department who are authorised, or feel themselves free, to provide information; and the more frequently a correspondent has to write, the more reliant he is on these easily available sources, so that the correspondent of an evening paper with several editions, or of a television programme, has little time for more than these official briefings. The premium of ever-changing news, which is now so characteristic of television and radio, thus tends to strengthen the hand of the government news-machine.

The most extreme and most criticised example of the journalists' depend-

---

3. United Kingdom, Home Office, Departmental Committee on Section 2 of the Official Secrets Act 1911, Cmnd. 5104, September 1972 (hereafter referred to as the *Franks Report*), vol. 1, p. 34.

ence is that of the lobby correspondents, who are allowed free access to the Members' lobby in Parliament and given off-the-record briefings by the Prime Minister and others, on condition that they do not disclose their sources. The lobby correspondents personify the ambivalence of the journalistic profession in encounters with government. On the one hand they have considerable prestige and seniority within their newspapers; on the other they are highly vulnerable to Ministerial pressure and sanctions—a vulnerability of which Harold Wilson, in his first years as Prime Minister, made full use to ensure favourable reporting of his "hundred days." Such newsmen can easily come to believe that their success depends on maintaining the closest relations with the ruling Government, and that this would be jeopardised by disclosing secrets, even if such secrets came from some quite separate source.

Any President or Prime Minister in a democracy will, of course, attempt to secure a good press by favouring certain journalists; but the British journalists have fewer alternative sources than the Americans, outside the government machine. The Congress committees, with their large staffs geared to publicity, have no real equivalent in Britain. No Opposition leader since World War II has been able to command his own effective intelligence system, as Churchill could before the War through his own contacts and staff. Moreover, the centralisation and concentration of government departments has tended further to exclude journalists and Opposition members from areas of controversy, and thus from leaks.

To take the most important example: before 1964 sporadic arguments and leaks escaped out of the Admiralty, the War Office, the Air Ministry, from irate admirals or testy generals who played out the battle between the Army and Navy in public; but since the ministries were merged in the mammoth Ministry of Defence, far less has been heard about these disputes—though they certainly remain as important as ever—for the reason that the new ministry is able to present a much more united front to the journalists and politicians. Likewise, the new Department of the Environment, embracing the old Ministries of Transport, Housing and Local Government, while having the advantages of coordinating policies, can also more effectively cover-up from the public the conflicts among road, rail, land, and housing interests.

The most effective centralisation of news has been achieved in a quarter where I believe it is least desirable, the Foreign Office. The News Department of the Foreign Office provides daily or weekly briefings, and controls the doors to the Foreign Secretary's office; so that no diplomatic correspondent dare consistently offend the official channels. Few diplomats will risk their careers by providing alternative information; for diplomatic leaks are often easily traced. As a result, even on issues where the Government goes against prevalent Foreign Office thinking—as on arms to South Africa in 1970—very little detailed hard evidence of opposition is available to the press.

The success of the Foreign Office's control of the news can be seen most dramatically in the reporting of Anglo-American encounters, particularly of successive Prime Ministers' visits to Washington. A great deal of the energy of the Foreign Office is devoted to ensuring that disputes between Britain and other nations do not come out into the open, even though this suppression may not be in the best interests of either country. An important historical example was the ability of Harold Wilson, at the height of Vietnam War in 1967, to persuade his party to moderate their criticism of President Johnson's policy, on the grounds that he was exerting effective pressure on the President in private. As it turned out, from the evidence of Wilson's own subsequent memoirs, that private pressure was futile, and was known to be futile by many British diplomats. If that secret had been less well kept, British foreign policy at that time might have been more honourable, and public protest over Vietnam might have had more effect on the President. It could not have had less.

There is nothing surprising about the reluctance of civil servants to leak information. As Max Weber wrote,

> The concept of the "official secret" is the specific invention of the bureaucracy, and nothing is so fanatically defended by bureaucracy as this attitude.
> . . . In facing a parliament, the bureaucracy, out of a sure power instinct, fights every attempt of the parliament to gain knowledge by means of its own experts or from interest groups.

A Foreign Office witness in the *Sunday Telegraph* case, John Welser, explained that "it is no business of any official to allow the government to be embarrassed. That is who we are working for." Embarrassment and security are not really two different things. The word *embarrass* is, I think, very characteristic of the British attitude; the sense that even if a disclosure were to be in the public interest, it would disturb the delicate relations of trust within the department and the government. Lord Franks' committee acknowledged that "civil servants are noted for their discretion rather than the reverse," and suggested that their discretion was influenced less by the Official Secrets Act than by informal sanctions:

> A civil servant who is regarded as unreliable, or who tends to overstep the mark and to talk too freely, will not enjoy such a satisfactory career as colleagues with better judgement and greater discretion.[4]

---

4. Franks Report, vol. 1, p. 28.

It may be that this sanction may become less effective in the future, as it seems to have done in America. Thus, for example, the First Division Association (the trades union of senior British civil servants) has recently held much discussion as to where its members' ultimate duty and responsibility should lie, and some have suggested that they should sometimes choose the public interest rather than that of their current political master. But there is not much indication of a rush of leaks from Whitehall; and the fact that the Director of Public Prosecutions should be so concerned about a disclosure of railway plans suggests a lack of more serious causes for worry.

The secretiveness of British civil servants may have the most high-minded motives, and be based on a genuine belief that disclosure can only damage and politicise the decisions; but it is also closely linked with the power instinct, as Weber suggests. The authority and influence of senior civil servants with politicians is likely to be the greater, the more the arguments are protected from the public domain. Compared to that of the Ministers, the continuity of the Permanent Secretaries, who are civil servants, is itself reinforced by the tradition of secrecy. An incoming Minister, after a change of Government, will not be shown any of the previous Government's "politically sensitive" decisions files—for instance, the detailed arguments about Rhodesia in 1965, or about devaluation in 1964. It is part of the unspoken Constitutional theory that each Government leaves its secrets with the civil servants, on the understanding that they will not be disclosed to their successors. This unique knowledge of "what happened last time" can give a Permanent Secretary a useful edge over his political master.

At the very top, the Secretary of the Cabinet—coequal with the head of the Civil Service—is the ultimate guardian of the nation's secrets, from the indiscretions of politicians as much as any other's. Each Secretary of the Cabinet since Lord Hankey—the original "man of secrets" when the post was invented during the First World War—has maintained a stern control over disclosures, and the last two Secretaries, the late Lord Normanbrook and Sir Burke Trend, have upheld the tradition. Their effective discipline has become more dramatic since the spate of politicians' memoirs in the last decade, coming ever closer to being contemporary chronicles. Lord Kilmuir, Lord George-Brown, Lord Butler, have each had to endure the censorship of the Cabinet office, which in each instance insisted on important excisions. One junior Minister in the Labour Government, Jeremy Bray, was even compelled to resign (on the advice, it is understood, of Sir Burke Trend) before publishing a very discreet book called *Decision in Government*. Only ex-Prime Ministers enjoy a special license, which derives ultimately from their right to appeal to the current Prime Minister (who may, of course, have autobiographical ambitions of his own); and since Churchill's massive plundering of secret files for his memoirs, it has been difficult to deny successive autobiographers—Attlee, Eden, and Wilson—some latitude in their revelations. It may even have become tacitly accepted that income from memoirs is now a major contribution to any Prime Minister's pension, and that this income depends on some relaxation of secrecy.

THE D NOTICES AND THE STRUGGLE OF THE PRESS

Faced with such a secretive and centralised bureaucracy, with so few points of contact, British journalists might be forgiven for their lack of disclosures. Their natural allies, the Opposition Members of Parliament, are almost equally in the dark; and both groups lack the kind of counter-bureaucracy that is provided by the staffs of committees and Congressmen in Washington. The difficulty is not merely in finding specific information; it is also in knowing what kind of information to look for; as Harold Wilson said (in his more rebellious days as chairman of the Public Accounts Committee), "It's easy to find the answers to the questions: what's difficult is to find the questions to the answers." Within the citadel of the Ministry of Defence, for example, the basic arguments involving hundreds of millions of pounds can be concealed until they emerge as apparently unanimous decisions.

The most spectacular triumph of British secrecy (and perhaps the most justifiable one) is in the non-publicity given to the Security Services, which have carried out the dictum of Thomas Carlyle: "He that has a secret should not only hide it, but hide that he has it to hide." The anonymity of the head of MI5 (Security Services) marks the evident success of this policy: since no one knows who he is, no one asks questions about him. The Director-General of MI5, giving evidence to the Franks Committee, was able to boast: "I can say with absolute assurance that information about my own affairs which appears in the newspapers is ninety percent inaccurate. . . . In this sense leakage of information which appears in public prints must be a pretty unreliable source of intelligence for, say, the Russians, or South Africans, or whoever may be thought our principal enemy." He later explained:

> My name has been published once or twice, and my address has been published, and photographs of my house. Happily, it is not my address and it is not my house. . . . I have no direct relations with the press. Where does one stop? If my name is published, why not my deputy's name? If my deputy's name is published why not my directors'? And before you know where you are, you are publishing the name of someone who is running agents, and his photograph appears in the press.[5]

5. Franks Report, vol. 3, pp. 246 and 254.

Such a smokescreen of secrecy, whether concerning the Security Services or railway closing, is certainly discouraging to the journalist bent on disclosure. Yet I believe that much of the discretion of British journalists must be traced to their own profession, and its relations with the Government of the day. A large number of secrets do come into newspaper offices, and are never printed; and most of this suppression is voluntary, not legally, enforced. The Government's chief instrument for preventing publication is not the official Secrets Act, but the system of "D Notices," which are notices addressed to editors, asking them not to mention certain general areas of defence and related subjects. The D Notices were devised a year after the Official Secrets Act, in 1912. They are issued by the "Defence, Press and Broadcasting Committee" composed of defence civil servants and journalists, and they are (as Lord Franks stressed), entirely voluntary and have no legal authority. Yet they are very effective. It is a D Notice, for instance, that forbids mention of the names of the heads of MI5 and MI6.

The system of D Notices came under scrutiny during Harold Wilson's Government when Chapman Pincher of the *Daily Express*—probably the most effective revealer of defence secrets over the last decade—published some details of the Government's surveillance of cables, something proscribed by a D Notice. Wilson attacked the *Daily Express* in Parliament, and provoked a crisis he later described as "in personal terms one of my costliest mistakes."[6] The *Express* counterattacked, and a committee of enquiry that had been appointed eventually supported the *Express*, on the grounds that Mr. Pincher had not been convincingly dissuaded from publishing by Colonel Sammy Logan, Secretary of the D Notices Committee, with whom he had lunched beforehand. What was interesting about the incident was not so much the single case of disclosure (of a not very serious kind) as it was the evidence of how scrupulously the press normally obeyed these voluntary requests; no newspaper in the course of the enquiry suggested that the system should be abolished.

The D Notices are only the most formal part of the newspapers' own unwritten code of non-disclosure. Every journalist dealing with any branch of politics has a body of knowledge accumulated from off-the-record conversations with Ministers and civil servants, none of which would he ever attribute, some of which he would never disclose. Every politician knows that he can use indiscretion to silence a journalist, and to lure him towards his own point of view; the invitation to share a secret is an essential part of a special relation that depends on the exclusion of others. The relation between a subtle Cabinet Minister and a subtle political correspondent is a complex

---

6. Harold Wilson: *The Labour Government 1964–1970* (London: Weidenfeld & Nicolson, 1971), p. 373.

one going beyond any expectation of the printed word. Both sides need each other, for reassurance and self-justification as well as for expediency; and in this relation the balance between indiscretion and secrecy is crucial. If the journalist becomes over-attracted by this intimate relation he can cease to be a reporter in any real sense at all. Every newspaper has one or two men on its staff who know so much that they feel they cannot disclose anything.

Within the context of this delicate relation there is often, of course, a deliberate leak by a Minister as his means of starting his dissent from his colleagues—a concomitant of the principle of the Cabinet's collective responsibility, which has been well analysed by Patrick Gordon Walker in his chapter in this book. Although in any Cabinet, leaks may be deplored, even condemned, paradoxically, they are necessary to the preservation of the doctrine of collective responsibility. Through such indiscretions, for instance (it can now, I hope, be revealed) did William Whitelaw, Leader of the House of Commons, and Lord Carrington, Minister of Defence, indicate their disapproval of Edward Heath's insistence on selling arms to South Africa in 1970. This use of the press to influence Cabinet decisions might appear to increase the scope and influence of journalists. But the disclosures are very limited, and thoroughly shrouded; and they remind us of how well kept are the rest of the Cabinet secrets.

Most serious journalists are constantly torn between disclosure and non-disclosure. As they become more senior and established, however, the temptations of non-disclosure tend to become greater; and much of their social life will depend on extreme caution in their use of information. There are dining clubs where specialist journalists exchange views with diplomats or Treasury men. There are the Reform Club, the Travellers, the Beefsteak, where journalists mingle with politicians or academics. There are editors' lunches, where Cabinet ministers enjoy major indiscretions in the safe knowledge that they will not be printed. There are the meetings at Chatham House, where the rule of non-attribution is scrupulously obeyed. In such gatherings the journalist can have the agreeable feeling of sharing some of the secrets and burdens of government, providing he does not break the rules.

It may not be an accident that the editors and journalists best known for disclosure keep their distance from these traditional charmed circles. But the most obvious battering ram against this enclosed world—the popular press—has not been notably effective in breaking down secrecy. The profession of muckraking in the tradition of Drew Pearson and Jack Anderson in Washington does not have the same prestige in London, and its would-be practitioners do not find the same multiplicity of sources. With a few notable exceptions (like Chapman Pincher of the *Daily Express* and Walter Terry of the *Daily Mail*) the popular press prefers political bluster to serious disclosure.

All this is, perhaps, no more than to say that the traditions of secrecy among Britain's rulers have survived the threats and invasions of democracy, and that the Administration, in spite of the pretensions of Parliament, still regards itself as "the secret garden of the Crown." The system, argues Bernard Crick, should nowadays be called "Old Secrecy," in place of "Old Corruption";[7] and Old Secrecy still seems to have some tribal magic around him, as he initiates new acolytes into the world of red Cabinet boxes where secret State papers are kept, combination locks, and Her Majesty's Service.

How much does it matter? The traditional justification of secrecy, outside the most obvious justification of national security, is that decisions are likely to be fairer and more objective and far-sighted, if uninterrupted by the crude simplifications of disclosure; and that democracy can only be made to work, as Bagehot explained a century ago, if its real rulers are protected from vulgar enquiries.[8] As it is often said, if Cabinet Ministers and civil servants are constantly worrying about how their words may be misrepresented, they will be far more cautious and dishonest in their interventions, and will become preoccupied by self-justification.

Much of this argument would still be accepted, I think, by most English commentators. The extreme case of a Cabinet's holding its deliberations in public is difficult to defend; and in real questions of security the tradition of voluntary non-disclosure of the names of the directors has obvious advantages. But in the more general application, part of this justification for secrecy has already been undermined not by the journalists but by the politicians themselves. The succession of memoirs published soon after the events they describe, all of them inevitably shot through with special pleading, must have some effect on the candour of colleagues and civil servants who know that their outspoken statements may in two or three years' time appear as evidence against them. The most recent example, the published diaries of Cecil King, former chairman of the *Daily Mirror,* can in this respect be classified as the memoirs of a politician rather than of a journalist, and it raises the question: If Mr. King was so prepared to break the unwritten rules of discretion five years later, why did he not do so at the time, when his contempt for most Labour politicians might have had some effect on contemporary policies?

The diary writers are not very helpful as a corrective to government secrecy. They maintain their own discretion at the time, while encouraging mealy-mouthedness among colleagues (*"What will Harold write afterwards,*

---

7. Bernard Crick: *The Reform of Parliament* (2nd ed.; Gloucester [Mass.]: Peter Smith, 1968), p. 253.
8. *The English Constitution* (London: Collins/Fontana, 1963), p. 248.

if I say what I really think?"). For contemporary historians the self-serving reminiscences of politicians can be very misleading, and the sources that would be most valuable—the memoirs of the civil servants who served under both parties—are notably absent.

It is in foreign affairs that the breaking of secrets is considered to be specially damaging, as interfering with the delicate relations between nations, between whom offence can so easily be caused. It was the fury of the Nigerian Government at reading the secret British report about their army which encouraged the Labour government to prosecute the *Sunday Telegraph* under the Official Secrets Act. And the Franks Committee decided that information affecting foreign relations should remain safeguarded by the law. "The field of international relations is full of difficult, sensitive and contentious issues," stated the Report, "some of them long-enduring. It is a fact of international life that the resolution of such issues without resort to force, and the maintenance of our national position and interests, often depend upon a measure of secrecy."[9] But arguments about the need for secrecy and extreme delicacy in foreign relations can be taken too far, as they can in personal relations: there comes a time when it is the duty of a friend to say openly what he thinks. There have been times in Anglo-American diplomacy, I believe, when the negotiations have become altogether too delicate, and where more plain speaking would have benefited both sides. This was true, I think—and remains true—over Britain's attitude toward Vietnam; and it was true of America's attitude toward Suez. A well-timed leak of Eisenhower's true feelings and intentions in 1956—as emerge, for instance, in his outspoken letter to Eden on September 8—might have prevented a disastrous misapprehension.

It would be absurd to suggest that "Old Secrecy" is so deeply entrenched in Britain that no reform could diminish his power. A change in legislation, going further than Franks proposed, would certainly help. Even a single court case, like the trial of the *Sunday Telegraph,* can affect the climate of opinion. Most important, I believe, is the development of effective and well-financed institutions to counterbalance and if necessary defy the blandishments and threats of the central government. This means not only strong newspapers and broadcasting services, with the resources to enable them to build up their own intelligence service, and to risk prosecution. It also means more effective Parliamentary select committees, with their own permanent staffs, and more independent research institutions, to furnish the Opposition and the press with sources of information alternative to Whitehall. For "Old Secrecy" depends above all on centralisation for his power.

"Old Secrecy" must be broken down, I believe not only because secret

---

9. Franks Report, vol. 1, p. 49.

government becomes arbitrary and undemocratic, but also because secret government is unable to provide the material for the serious discussion of contemporary issues that can involve Parliament and hence the public. Secrecy will not necessarily result in anything so dramatic as stolen documents and imprisonments; it is more likely to lead—as it is now I believe leading—to a general withdrawal of public interest from the activities both of Parliament and of Whitehall. The debates on national defence, for instance, are now so jejune that it is hard to expect anyone to follow them with sustained interest. The natural extension of Carlyle's dictum, that the keeper of a secret must hide that he has it to hide, is that the safest form of government is one that bores people so much that people stop asking questions about it; and that way lies the end of democracy.

14

Disclosure, Discretion, and Dissemblement: Broadcasting and the National Interest in the Perspective of a Publicly Owned Medium

KENNETH LAMB

The BBC is in every proper sense of the word a national broadcasting service, but it is not and never has been government-controlled or government-run. It is because John Reith, our first Director-General, recognised from the beginning the importance of establishing the BBC's independence, and because his successors through the years saw how essential it was to maintain it, that the BBC's news services have been able to command world-wide credibility.

But independence can never be absolute, so perhaps I had better begin by explaining briefly the BBC's Constitutional position before going on to consider various occasions on which there has been some element of conflict between on the one hand the BBC's overriding duty to inform, and on the other the national interest or what the Government of the day or some section of the public conceived to be the national interest. The distinction is an important one, because the occasions when it is not in the national interest for the facts to be known are surely very rare indeed. As I ought to make clear from the outset, the BBC is not in the business of dissembling; government inescapably is.

In its earliest days the BBC was a company whose main aim was to sell the wireless sets made by the manufacturers who formed it. But largely as a result of Reith's influence, a government committee, set up in 1926 to consider the future of broadcasting in the United Kingdom, recommended that the company should be replaced by a public corporation established by

Mr. Lamb is Director of Public Affairs and member of Board of Management of the BBC. He has been involved in radio and television current affairs broadcasting over many years, and is continuingly concerned with political broadcasting and the BBC's relations with the world of politics.

Royal Charter and financed by licence fees. The Corporation's independence was recognised by the appointment of a number of public figures as a Board of Governors who would constitute the ultimate authority within the BBC and also act as trustees for the public interest. The Governors—now twelve in number—are appointed in effect by the Government of the day on a broadly representative basis, and serve for a period of five years, but since the date of the original appointment of each varies, there is seldom any question of a Government's being in a position to appoint more than one or two at any time. Responsibility for BBC's day-to-day management rests with the Director-General, who is appointed by the Board of Governors, as chief executive.

The BBC's constitutional position has remained broadly unchanged since the granting of the first charter in 1927. Under the charter's terms the BBC is required to obtain a licence from the Minister of Posts and Telecommunications, and this gives the Minister certain powers in relation to programmes. One clause states that the Minister "may from time to time by notice in writing require the Corporation to refrain at any specified time or at all times from sending any matter or matters of any class specified in such notice."[1] In principle this confers on the Government a formally absolute power of veto over BBC programmes (it is significant in this context that the Corporation has the discretionary right to announce that such a notice has been given). In practice the veto has never been used, and the BBC enjoys complete freedom in its handling of day-to-day programme activities.

The same clause places a number of specific obligations on the BBC. It is required to broadcast an impartial day-to-day account of the proceedings of both Houses of Parliament, but as a news organisation this is something it was already doing before the obligation was imposed. It is also required to broadcast government announcements whenever called on to do so by a Minister. But government announcements of any importance naturally find a place in news bulletins, while more routine announcements such as police messages are arranged informally between the government department concerned and BBC newsrooms.

There are two other restrictions on the BBC (one self-imposed) that are of some relevance to the obligations incumbent upon the BBC in regard to its reporting of political events. A number of memoranda serve as an unpublished appendix to the charter and licence, and one of these requires the BBC to "refrain from expressing its own opinion on current affairs or on matters of public policy." In the same memorandum the Minister took notice of assurances given by the then Chairman concerning the BBC's duty

---

1. Great Britain, British Broadcasting Corporation, *BBC Handbook 1973* (London, 1973).

to treat controversial subjects with due impartiality. But the principle of impartiality was not imposed by the Minister; it had been the BBC's policy from the beginning. Moreover, as will become clear later, this principle has been on more than one occasion inconvenient to the Government of the day which would have had the BBC abandon its objective stance and simply reflect that Government's opinions.

Of course, in its very early days, when it had little power and few resources, the BBC had a variety of restrictions imposed on it by nervous Governments, sometimes responding to pressure from groups that saw broadcasting as a threat to their interests. Much of the BBC's history is the narrative of the way in which it rid itself of such limitations. There was, for example, the ban on controversy imposed by the licence; or, worse still, the ban on broadcasting news before 7 P.M., imposed under pressure from the newspaper industry. As people became accustomed to the idea of broadcasting, however, and as the BBC itself became accepted as a part of national life, it grew easier to cast off such shackles. Looking back, it seems that the BBC was sometimes timid in pressing its claim for full editorial freedom, though at other times one can only admire the ingenuity with which changes were brought about.

Take the case of the "fourteen-day rule," which for a time during the 1950's barred the BBC from treating any subject that Parliament was to discuss within a fortnight. The rule persisted until eventually it was exposed to ridicule as a result of the clever stage-management of an edition of "Any Questions?", a radio programme in which members of an invited audience put questions on matters of opinion to a panel of public figures. On this particular occasion the four panel members announced at their pre-broadcast dinner that they intended to discuss a topic then very much in the news and down for immediate Parliamentary debate. They made it clear that if the BBC ruled out questions on this subject they would nevertheless drag it into the discussion of some other topic. The producer rang his head of programmes, Frank Gillard, and they agreed between them to allow any such discussion to run long enough for listeners to get the drift of it, and then to fade it out dramatically. The continuity staff in Broadcasting House was tipped off, and a series of announcements prepared with the aim of drawing maximum attention to the incident. Things worked out exactly as planned. The rule had been observed. At the same time public indignation was aroused, and within weeks Parliament decided to lift the ban.

POLITICAL PRESSURES ON THE BBC

Nowadays, the only way in which the BBC's treatment of news and comment differs in principle from that of a responsible newspaper's lies in its general obligation to be impartial and the particular obligation to avoid the expression of any opinion of its own. The conditions under which BBC journalists work are virtually the same as those of newspapermen. Naturally, our Parliamentary and diplomatic correspondents have to observe the confidentiality of Ministerial and Foreign Office briefings, but the fact that they are accredited to the BBC does not confer any special status on them. They do not on that account receive confidential information withheld from other journalists; nor are they expected to abide by stricter rules. Indeed, like all good newsmen they are required to watch out for attempts to manage news and to respond to such attempts with wary good sense. A good example is the BBC's handling of what became known as "the Soames affair."

At a time when Franco-British relations were at their coolest, Christopher Soames, then British Ambassador in Paris, was invited to lunch by President de Gaulle, who put to him a plan for a new European alliance. Apparently De Gaulle's idea was for an enlarged European economic association, with a smaller inner council made up of France, Britain, Germany, and Italy. But, he said, it would first be necessary to find out whether Britain and France saw things sufficiently in common, and accordingly he proposed that Britain make a gesture by asking for talks and that he would welcome such talks. It was, of course, the Ambassador's duty to send a full report of this conversation back to Whitehall, where it was seen as a trap intended to drive a wedge between Britain and her partners in NATO and the Western European Union. The details of the plan and the British response are not relevant here. What is of interest is the British decision to inform the other NATO countries and to make the whole business public.

Christopher Serpell (who has recently retired as our diplomatic correspondent) had just arrived at Broadcasting House from one of his regular calls at the Foreign Office when he received a telephoned invitation to return there at once. He found the head of the Foreign Office News Department in a room crammed with every journalist in London who could conceivably claim to write on diplomatic affairs—including some journalists he had never seen before. The F.O. man then proceeded to read aloud the text of the confidential telegram in which the British Ambassador in Paris reported to the home Government on his conversation with President de Gaulle. It was an unprecedented action on the part of the F.O. staff, and underlined their concern to make known the British version of the story. But when the whole text had been read out, the Foreign Office spokesman added: "The usual unattributable rule applies."

So the Foreign Office wanted the publicity without wishing to be associated with it. But while it is possible for a journalist to work a particular fact, or the expression of a particular point of view, into a story without attribution, it is really not sensible to give a detailed and circumstantial account of a highly confidential conversation without giving some indication of the source. So on this occasion Christopher Serpell thought it right to break the rules and make it clear to his listeners that the remarkable story he had to tell had been "learned officially" in London.

Indeed, anyone who imagines that our correspondents and reporters are unduly inhibited by their necessary contacts with officialdom would do well to read a piece called "Listen to Amin" in *The Listener* for 4 January 1973. The author is Peter Stewart, who has done a lot of reporting on East African affairs for the BBC and who set out in this instance to trace the course of recent differences between Britain and Uganda. "That these misunderstandings should have deepened over the last four years," he writes, "can be seen more as the fault of successive British Governments than of those of Presidents Obote and Amin."[2] He then sets out factually recent failures on the part of British diplomacy. As this makes evident, the ban on BBC's expression of opinions does not extend to informed analysis by experienced and knowledgeable correspondents, or to their comment set out as an inescapable conclusion from a series of undisputed facts.

There is, however, one part of the BBC which might be thought peculiarly vulnerable to government pressure. Our External Service is financed by a grant-in-aid from the Treasury and not, like the rest of the BBC, from licence fee revenue. The Constitutional position is that the Government of the day decides which languages shall be used in External Service broadcasts and the amount of time to be devoted to each of them, while the BBC has complete control over programme content. It is clearly open to a Government that is displeased with our broadcasts overseas to cut or end programmes in some languages and reduce or even slash the grant-in-aid. Yet I doubt if any part of the BBC's output has a higher reputation for accuracy and truth than the External Service news broadcasts. Indeed, it is this very reputation which is their safeguard. As the summary report of the government-appointed Drogheda Committee put it in 1954:

> . . . the popularity of the BBC External Service depends above all on its
> high reputation for objective and honest reporting. We believe this to be a
> priceless asset which sets the BBC apart from other national broadcasting
> systems. This high reputation for objectivity must be maintained at all costs
> and we would deplore any attempt to use the BBC for anything in the way
> of direct propaganda of the more obvious kind. This is not to suggest that
> the BBC External Services are not, in fact, a weapon of propaganda. The
> best and most effective propaganda to many countries consists of a factual
> presentation of the news and of British views concerning the news.[3]

---

2. Peter Stewart, "Listen to Amin," *The Listener,* 78 (4 January, 1973).
3. Great Britain, Summary of the Report of the Independent Committee of Enquiry into the Overseas Information Services, April 1954. Cmnd. 9138.

A similar view was taken by the Review Committee on Overseas Representation, set up more recently under Sir Val Duncan. Reporting in 1969, it had this to say:

> As an instrument of communication the BBC has the decisive advantage that it has a world wide reputation for telling the truth. Its overseas broadcast bulletins are, therefore, widely believed to give true and objective accounts of world events and they provide a sure basis for influential comment.[4]

But what about the reporting of opinion? Well, the BBC has always taken the view that the External Services must reflect all significant opinion in the country, and not just the Government or Foreign Office line. As Sir Beresford Clark, a former Director of External Broadcasting, saw it: "There are times when the reflection of responsible but different views seems to us to be absolutely inherent in the British way of life. We would be entirely false to the principles which we claim to observe if we suppressed views on any subject, political or otherwise, which were held by substantial elements in this country."[5] Yet it was on this very issue that the BBC and the Government clashed head on at the time of the Suez crisis.

Undoubtedly the Suez matter presented exceptional problems. For the first time we were faced with a policy issue of great national and international importance, one that might well have led to war and did in the event lead to military action, and one on which the country was deeply and sharply divided. Yet at an early stage the BBC Governors decided that our normal policy should in general apply, and they reaffirmed that decision at a crucial point later. There is no doubt that in doing so they had the full support of the Executive and indeed of the whole staff of the BBC.

Inevitably, perhaps, the Government took a different view. As they saw it, our job in broadcasts overseas was to show a united country, whereas we believed we had no alternative but to reflect the clear division that existed, and to report not only the policy of the Government but also the strong criticisms of this policy by the Opposition parties. We could not mislead listeners overseas into thinking that there was only one British view. Let me make it absolutely clear, however, that there was no question of the BBC's having a foreign policy of its own or opposing the Suez action in its broadcasts. We simply reported the views of those opposed to the action, just as we reported the Government's reasons for doing what it did. Indeed, it was the opinion of at least one Foreign Office official that the best defence of the

---

4. Report of the Review Committee on Overseas Representation 1968–1969. Cmnd. 4107.
5. Beresford Clark, *The BBC's External Services* (London: Royal Institute of International Affairs, 1973).

Government's policy was given in a commentary broadcast in our External Services.

In general, however, our broadcasts at the time came in for little praise, especially in official quarters, though this lack of approbation did nothing to lessen our determination to report the facts as fully and objectively as we could. Let me give an example. At one point reports of a bombing raid on Port Said were denied by a British military spokesman. Eventually, under pressure from correspondents covering the landings, he admitted that though Port Said had not been bombed, it *had* come under rocket attack. But the casualties, he said, had been very slight. The correspondents continued to press and probe as—fortunately for us all—newsmen will. Finally, the military spokesman gave in. The total number of dead, he said—and here I am drawing on the memories of the people concerned—was no more than, say, twenty. The BBC's correspondent quoted him in his dispatch. He then went on to report that this could not be true, as he had counted more than twenty bodies himself.

The Government and Conservative backbenchers (members of Commons who belong to the party in power but are not Ministers) were highly critical of our domestic broadcasts, but it was our broadcasts overseas that drew most of the fire. There was particular criticism of our program "Press Review," doubtless because it reflected the fact that most of the British press was against the Government's policy. This opposition was forcefully expressed in the *Manchester Guardian*. In one editorial it denounced the Suez decision as "an act of folly without justification in any terms but brief expediency." And on the following day it declared the Suez action "wrong on every count—moral, military and political." We took the view that no honest press review could ignore the *Guardian* editorials, and that it was unthinkable not to quote harsh phrases that gave the tone of the whole. A source of anxiety to many Conservatives was the possible effect such broadcasts might have on troops about to go into action.

As we saw it, there could be no question of suppressing in our overseas broadcasts the reports we would carry in our broadcasts at home. We could not allow listeners at home to hear the views of Mr. Gaitskell and the *Manchester Guardian* and yet ban these views from listeners overseas. Moreover, we knew that troops had access to the BBC mainly through local forces' stations under military control and that they must, in any case, have been aware of the domestic political conflict. Indeed, it emerged later that during the campaign troops had access to the *Daily Mirror,* which was strongly opposed to the Government's policy.

The BBC came under pressure at an early stage, and this pressure took a variety of forms at different times. We were made aware of the Prime Minister's dissatisfaction and anger over certain aspects of our broadcasts, and of the Foreign Office view that in the situation then existing it was not necessary to tell the whole truth. We were informed of a proposal—to which we reluctantly agreed—to appoint a Foreign Office liaison officer who would work at Bush House, where the External Services are based. This appointment (which was to be on an experimental basis) was inplemented on 1 November, five days before the Suez landings. The scope of the appointment had never been discussed with the BBC, and in the view of staff at Bush House it succeeded in confusing previously established lines of communication with the Foreign Office without yielding any compensatory advantage. The liaison officer had no editorial function or powers, and could only intervene—in the words of one senior BBC man—"intermittently and undesirably." At the same time and more seriously, the BBC was abruptly informed that the grant-in-aid would be cut substantially and the External Services reorganised so that they would accord more closely with the Government's policies abroad. Neither of these intentions was carried out.

Finally, there was also talk of a "takeover." In his autobiography *One Thing at a Time* Harman Grisewood, who, as Chief Assistant to the Director-General at the time of Suez, was in the midst of the toings and froings between Broadcasting House and Number 10 Downing Street, recalls being told that Sir Anthony Eden had instructed the Lord Chancellor, Lord Kilmuir, to draw up an "instrument" to take over the BBC. Indeed, as Mr. Grisewood recollects having heard it, Kilmuir did prepare such a draft for the Prime Minister, who found it inadequate and asked him to draft something stronger. It is possible that Mr. Grisewood may have misunderstood or have misinterpreted what he heard—and in an article in *The Listener* of 18 December, 1969, F. R. Mackenzie gives reasons for looking at the matter differently.[6] Whatever the whole truth may eventually turn out to have been, the fact that a senior, experienced, and politically sophisticated BBC official believed, on the evidence available to him, that there was such a threat is itself indicative of the atmosphere and tension of the time.

Further pressure on the BBC came not from the Government itself but from Conservative backbenchers. On 14 November, Mr. Peter Rawlinson (now, as Sir Peter, Attorney General) raised in the House of Commons on the motion for the adjournment the question of the BBC charter and the political balance of BBC broadcasts. There were cheers from the Government benches when he said he shared what he called "a widespread impression" that the BBC had not maintained its standards of impartiality during the past few weeks over the crisis in the Middle East. After criticising BBC broadcasts on a number of points, he said he thought that overseas broad-

---

6. F. R. MacKenzie, "Eden, Suez and the BBC: A Reassessment," *The Listener,* 74 (18 December 1969).

casts must speak "in the name of the Government of the day."[7] A number of other speakers—almost entirely from the Conservative side—also attacked the BBC, accusing it of bias or blatant bias.

Replying for the Government, Assistant Postmaster General Cuthbert Alport stated that the BBC was examining the methods of presentation of the various aspects of the controversy, bearing in mind the importance of not only being impartial but of also being seen to be impartial by the listening public. It would be possible, therefore, for the BBC to judge what action, if any, was needed to safeguard its vital tradition of impartiality. Eight days later the Board of Governors met under the chairmanship of Sir Alexander Cadogan (formerly the most senior official at the Foreign Office) to consider the allegations of bias made during the debate. After examining the evidence of what had been broadcast beside what was alleged, they concluded that the allegations were groundless. Recognising that the period had been one of great difficulty, the Board considered that in the face of that difficulty a successful and creditable result had been generally achieved; and that this result fulfilled the BBC's obligations for impartiality, objectivity, and truth-telling.

Another inquiry into the Overseas Services was carried out about six months later by the Chancellor of the Duchy of Lancaster, Dr. Charles Hill, who later, as Lord Hill of Luton, was appointed during a Labour Government to be Chairman of the BBC. The secretary to his committee was Burke Trend, later Secretary to the Cabinet. Their report recommended an increase of £58,000 in the total annual revenue for Bush House, and moreover declared unequivocally: "In the Government's view, the impartiality and objectivity of the BBC is a national asset of great value and the independence which the Corporation now enjoys should be maintained."[8] Shortly before this report was published, new arrangements had been made —satisfactory to the BBC—for liaison with the Foreign Office. At the same time the Foreign Office appointed a new Assistant Undersecretary with responsibility for information matters, a former member of the BBC staff and future member of the Board of Governors.

There are a number of important aspects of the Suez affair not touched on here, since this account is obviously not intended to be comprehensive. Nevertheless I think I have said enough to show that the External Services maintained the highest traditions of objective news reporting at a time when they were under severe and constant pressure from the Government on which they were dependent for their total income. While their success in doing so is a remarkable tribute to the senior BBC men of the time, I doubt whether it would have been possible but for the established reputation of our

7. *Hansard,* H.C. Deb. 1023–31, November 14, 1956.
8. Great Britain, Overseas Information Services, vol. 26, 1956–57, Cmnd. 225.

overseas broadcasts for telling the truth, together with the safeguard provided by the organic relations between the External Services and the BBC as a whole.

IMPARTIALITY AMID CRISIS AND CONFLICT

It is, of course, always right to listen to what Government says and to weigh it carefully, and there are even occasions—though they are rare—when it is right to follow it. Let me cite the example of the acquisition by our Russian Service of exclusive rights to broadcast the original Russian version of Svetlana Alleluieva's "Only One Year," a letter to a friend that was later published in the *Atlantic Monthly*. It was intended to put it out on the day the *Atlantic* was to appear. On that day, however, the then Foreign Secretary, Mr. George Brown, was in Moscow talking to the Soviet leaders about the issue of war and peace in the Middle East. It was represented to us that the broadcasting of this item on that day could be seen by the Soviet authorities as proof of the untrustworthiness of the British Government and therefore as an argument for rejecting whatever overtures the Foreign Secretary might be making to preserve the chance of peace in the Middle East and possibly the world.

We at the BBC thought it more likely that the Russians would do what they wanted to do regardless of what we broadcast, but we also had to recognise that there might be something in the Foreign Office argument. Moreover, the topicality of the Svetlana Alleluieva article—as between one day and the next—could hardly be said to be an issue of the utmost importance. So when it was put to us at a very high level that the Prime Minister wished us to give the most careful consideration to a postponement of the broadcast until Mr. Brown had left Moscow, we eventually agreed that this should be done. But a postponement of a day or two was all that was agreed or asked for; there was no question of a cancellation.

International crises are not of course the only occasions on which the BBC—like any responsible newspaper—must take proper account of the possible effect of what it says. In our coverage of industrial stories we clearly cannot be unaware of the possibility of damage to the sales of British products both at home and overseas. In any case the industries concerned are very quick to draw our attention to anything they regard as harmful to their interests. But here again the BBC has always regarded it as its duty to state the facts whatever they may happen to be. It is certainly no part of its job to cover up for any shortcomings existing in some sectors of British industry or deliberately to play down success stories about industry overseas. Our adherence to this policy has led to a number of rows with the motor industry, which sometimes seems to be unduly sensitive to any suggestion that there may be something to be said for foreign cars.

Others have taken us to task, too. I remember an occasion some years ago when turning to the editorial page of the *Sunday Express* I found we were in trouble for using a foreign-made car—a Mercedes—in a sequence illustrating the merits of colour television. But when I turned a few pages I found that the *Express*'s own motoring correspondent had devoted his column to the Fiat! We have also been criticised from time to time for our coverage of the *Concorde* (British-French superjet) project. An item in the television current-affairs programme "24 Hours," which had attempted a fair assessment of the sales prospects for the *Concorde,* led to complaints from two Members of Parliament and a reference to a (non-existent) body of people in the BBC who, it was said, "took a delight in denigrating British projects." Of course, the M.P.'s concerned had been acting well within their rights in drawing attention to what they saw as a defect in our output, but we were also within our rights in setting out—along with the selling points of the *Concorde*—the reasons why at that stage world airlines seemed hesitant about buying it.

But issues such as these are seen at their starkest when it comes to covering a major financial crisis of the kind which, in November 1967, led to devaluation of the pound. The announcement came late on a Saturday evening after a week of rumour and speculation during which the BBC secured a remarkable financial scoop. The previous Wednesday, November 15, our then economics correspondent learned in Paris that the British Government was negotiating with foreign bankers for another huge loan. The implications were at once apparent to him, as were the possible effects of broadcasting such a story at that time. So he telephoned the editor in charge of our whole News and Current Affairs operation, and put it to him. The editor considered the matter for a moment and then told our correspondent that since his source was a reliable one he should go ahead. In other words, the possible effects of such a disclosure on the financial situation were taken into account at a senior level in the BBC, and it was decided that the duty to inform must come first.

Our correspondent's subsequent dispatch spelled out the significance of the story in full. He pointed out that an additional loan of one thousand million dollars—£357,000,000 at the then rate of exchange—coming on top of the £37,000,000 borrowed from the Swiss the previous month and the £90,000,000 secured from a number of foreign banks earlier in the week, made it only too plain just how severely the pound had been battered and how serious were the fears for its future without further support. He also pointed out, however, that the loan made it plain how strongly most overseas bankers were prepared to back Britain, and added that he had been told firmly from Paris that there was no sign of Britain's considering devaluation. The following day there was a row in the House of Commons over the refusal of the Chancellor of the Exchequer to confirm or deny the report. Some M.P.'s were saying that the issue was whether Britain got the loan or had to devalue the pound. Speculation continued on Friday, with the pound under intense pressure, and then late on Saturday the announcement was made. Shortly afterwards it was arranged that the Prime Minister, Mr. Wilson, should make a Ministerial broadcast on Sunday at 6 P.M.

This is a special category of broadcast that from time to time allows the Government of the day to make important statements of a factual nature or to explain legislation approved by Parliament or to appeal to the public to co-operate in national policies. Ministers making such broadcasts are under an obligation to be as impartial as possible, but in the event that the content is controversial the Opposition can claim a right of reply. On this occasion the Opposition had exercised that right, and Mr. Heath was to broadcast at 8 P.M. on Monday. But the situation was complicated by the fact that on the previous Tuesday, several days before devaluation, the Opposition's "Shadow" Chancellor, Mr. Iain Macleod, had accepted an invitation to take part in the Sunday lunchtime radio programme "The World This Weekend." The BBC was thus faced with the possibility that before the Prime Minister had had a chance to explain his decision to devalue, the Shadow Chancellor would have had his opportunity of mounting an attack on it. Moreover, since the BBC had invited Mr. Macleod to take part in the programme, the BBC would be seen as initiating the attack. This was very different from reporting in news bulletins—as of course it had done—Opposition criticism of devaluation.

Normally, the BBC seeks to maintain its impartiality in matters of opinion by striking a balance over a period. But on issues of acute and immediate political controversy—of which devaluation was undoubtedly one —we think it necessary to strike a balance within the framework of each individual programme or item. As things stood, "The World This Weekend" found itself in danger of presenting a wholly unbalanced item on a politically superheated subject. On Sunday morning, therefore, the Director-General ruled that should the Chancellor of the Exchequer not agree to take part in the programme then Mr. Macleod should not be allowed to broadcast either. An invitation to the Chancellor, Mr. Callaghan, had been issued shortly after the announcement of devaluation the previous evening, but by the time it was clear that he would not be taking part, Mr. Macleod (who had been staying in the country) had already left for London and Broadcasting House. On his arrival he was taken to the offices of "The World This Weekend," where the unenviable task of telling him he was not to be permitted to broadcast fell to our editor of News and Current Affairs. Not unnaturally, Mr. Macleod was very angry; the interesting point, though, is that when he asked whose decision this was and was told it was the BBC's, he replied that he didn't believe it. To his mind such a decision could have been taken only under Government pressure. He was wrong—quite wrong.

I suppose that those whose own actions are frequently motivated politically find it hard to understand the absence of such motives in others, and this may go some way towards explaining the constant suspicion with which some politicians, at least, regard the BBC. Subsequently, the "Peterborough" column in the *Daily Telegraph* carried the comment that the BBC's attitude "seems to have been conditioned by the Prime Minister's wish that no politician except himself should appear immediately after devaluation," and the Director-General, Sir Hugh Greene, had to point out to the *Telegraph* that no wish of this kind had been conveyed to the BBC in any way by the Prime Minister. "The BBC's attitude," wrote Sir Hugh, "was conditioned by our concern to give full information about what was happening and to preserve a proper political impartiality."

Of all the events of postwar years, none has provided the BBC with more difficult problems than the conflict in Northern Ireland. Of course, experience in reporting the fighting between India and Pakistan, the Nigerian Civil War, and the conflict in the Middle East has made us familiar with situations in which any attempt to present an objective account of events based on the ascertainable facts is interpreted by partisans on one side or another as a blatant display of bias in favour of their opponents. But in these cases the criticisms were at long range. In Northern Ireland the range shortened dramatically.

We were broadcasting to the combatants themselves and their fully-committed supporters, and we found ourselves the targets not of criticism but of bitter and irrational anger. At the same time we were broadcasting to the audience in the rest of the United Kingdom, with a need and a right to be informed, and a strong attachment to the tradition of free comment and fair debate. Even here, however, we found ourselves under attack from some quarters. Anything that showed the Army in an unflattering light was particularly resented. Our efforts to give the facts even led two Members of Parliament to use the phrase "the BBC sniping at the Army." There was also a tendency on the part of one section of the audience to regard all Catholics living in Northern Ireland as supporters of the Irish Republican Army and to think of them as "the enemy." It was forgotten that they, too—whether they liked it or not—were citizens of the United Kingdom and had an equal right with Protestants and Unionists to have their voices heard.

From the beginning the BBC took the view that it had a duty to tell the truth—or as much of the truth as could be ascertained—to both sides in Northern Ireland and to the rest of the United Kingdom, where responsibility ultimately lies. It has stuck to that view throughout. But one of the real difficulties facing reporters in Northern Ireland is the readiness of people on both sides to say anything they believe will further their cause. This makes peculiarly difficult the reporting of shooting incidents in which the Army is involved. The chances are that any eyewitness who is willing to talk will himself be highly committed one way or another. Some people have taken the view that in such circumstances we ought to broadcast only the Army or official account of the incident. This is a suggestion we are wholly unable to accept—and for what we regard as very good reasons.

First, anyone may be mistaken about what actually happened at such a time—and especially those who were themselves involved. There have, indeed, been occasions (including "Bloody Sunday") on which the official version of what happened has later been amended by the authorities themselves or has been shown to be inaccurate or incomplete in some respect. Second, in Northern Ireland what people believe to have happened can often be almost as important as the facts themselves. It can both reveal and explain people's attitude towards the security forces and towards authority in general. Last—but by no means least important—if the BBC were to report only the official account of such events, it would be taken to be the mouthpiece of Government and would swiftly lose credibility in Northern Ireland and elsewhere. In those circumstances, of course, rumour would take over. Advocates of what is sometimes, ironically, mistermed "responsible" broadcasting fail to recognise the value of free reporting in discrediting false rumour. There was an occasion, for example, when our cameras showed people in Londonderry affirming with total conviction that a 14-year-old Catholic boy arrested after a scuffle with the police had had his head split open and was dripping with blood. Seconds later we were able to show in close-up the boy himself bruised, but without any trace of blood and with no sign of a wound on his head.

Nevertheless, we have had to consider on occasion the possibility that television reports—by the nature of the medium—might inflame the hatred of one section of the community for the other. So at the outset of the sectarian strife in August 1969, after whole streets of houses in Belfast inhabited exclusively by Catholics were set on fire by a crowd of Protestants, we decided to give the most provocative utterances only unfilmed news reports. We placed a restriction on filmed interviews either with the people who had been burnt out or with those who had done the burning. We also reported speeches by extremist leaders on one side and the other without televising the film that might have brought the scene of ranting into every house or pub in Northern Ireland and throughout the United Kingdom. This restriction was in force for only a couple of days, and during those days we continued—as we never at any time ceased—to report everything we regarded as news. There were no omissions and no fiddling with the facts. There are of course some people who hold that in reporting Northern Ireland we ought always to avoid anything that could raise the temperature. And yet to report events in the Province as though problems there are being considered and discussed rationally is to miss the whole point of what is happening. The anger and hysteria in people's faces and voices have to be reflected if the audience outside Northern Ireland is to have a chance of understanding the situation.

We made one other departure from our normal practice, and it had to do with interviewing members of the IRA. We took—and still take—the view that the IRA, like any other organisation that works outside the accepted system of Parliamentary democracy and uses force for political ends, cannot be afforded the same treatment as organisations working within that system. Moreover, we have had to recognise that the IRA has a very keen appreciation of the value of propaganda, and we are naturally anxious to ensure that it does not use the BBC for its own ends. For those reasons we introduced a requirement that any reporter seeking to film or record an interview with an IRA member must first obtain permission at the highest editorial level within the BBC. That permission is granted only when we believe that an appearance in the flesh by an IRA man is necessary to a proper understanding of the facts. There have been quite a number of occasions when we concluded that this was the case. One was an interview with David O'Connell in "Panorama" (a regularly scheduled program of news analysis) on the Monday evening in June 1972 when the IRA truce was about to come into effect. Many people had doubts about the sincerity of the IRA in agreeing to this truce and we felt that a television interview with one of its leaders would help the audience to form an independent judgement on this point. But I must emphasise that at no time has there been anything to stop our correspondents and reporters from talking to IRA members and reporting in news bulletins anything of significance that might emerge. Throughout the Northern Ireland conflict we have sought to reflect the full range of political views held by people in the Province. Every significant body of opinion without a gun in its hand has been talked to at length.

Early on we took another important decision, and have only once made an exception to it. The decision was that we would not take the easy way out by transmitting to England, Wales, and Scotland reports on Northern Ireland which we would not carry also in Northern Ireland itself. This, we felt, would be failing in our duty to the people of the Province. It would also have destroyed our credibility in Northern Ireland if people there had learned that we were saying to the rest of the United Kingdom what we dared not say to them. The one exception was an edition of "Panorama" scheduled to go out on Monday, 6 July 1970. There had been rioting and fighting with troops over the weekend, and the "Panorama" item included film in which hatred was expressed first by a political leader and then by the widow of a man who had been killed a few days before. A brief preview of the programme was shown on Sunday, and afterwards the switchboard at Broadcasting House in Belfast was jammed by callers protesting that to show the film could only inflame an already tense situation. Our Controller in Northen Ireland was himself deeply concerned over possible reaction to such a film if shown at this time.

The matter was discussed at the weekly meeting of Board of Management on Monday afternoon, and our Editor of News and Current Affairs then went to the Current Affairs television studios at Lime Grove to see for himself the raw material for the film, being edited at the time. Exercising editorial control in a broadcasting organisation is a much more complex business than doing so in a newspaper, and it is in the nature of television that at that stage there was no completed film for him to view. Thus he saw only the sequence of which a part had been used for the trailer, and another sequence that had not yet been dubbed. In addition he was briefed on an interview that had been completed and was at that moment being flown over from Belfast. It was enough to convince him that if the programme were to be shown in its entirety in Northern Ireland the possibility that it might lead to more killing could not be ruled out. At the same time he was satisfied that any attempt to cut the film would ruin a very fine report. He believed that it would tell people in England, Scotland, and Wales something they needed to know about the emotions current in Northern Ireland and so would add to their understanding of the situation. It was under these circumstances that he recommended to our Director-General, Charles Curran (who agreed), that Northern Ireland should be allowed to "opt out." In other words, the film would be seen in all parts of the United Kingdom except Northern Ireland.

All day long angry telephone calls, containing threats of what might happen if we showed the film, continued to reach Broadcasting House in Belfast. It wasn't until 8 o'clock that evening—the time "Panorama" starts—that viewers in Ireland were told that they would not be seeing the film. Instead, by an act of unintentional irony, they were shown an old and sentimental film with the title "If You're Irish." Still the telephone calls did not cease; they continued right up to close-down, though their burden now was different. This time they were abusing us for letting viewers in other parts of the United Kingdom see a programme about Northern Ireland we were not showing in the Province itself.

Undoubtedly the most interesting and probably the most important problems faced by the BBC in its coverage of Northern Ireland arose from our decision towards the end of 1971 to mount a programme to explain to the

British public the views held by those sections of Irish opinion likely to be involved in any political settlement. We felt it was time to look below the surface of violence and confrontation and to examine the solutions offered from 'round the spectrum of politics in Northern Ireland and the Republic. By early November an outline had been drawn up. An enquiry format was chosen approximating the model of a United States Senate committee hearing. The aim was to bring information before the public and to rule out the element of debate between the interested witnesses. The programme would also have to be open-ended so that it could not be accused of skimming superficially over the issues or of depriving any important faction of a reasonable voice in it.

There were to be eight Irish speakers—two from the Republic and the rest from the North—and the programme was to be prefaced by statements from the Home Secretary, Mr. Reginald Maudling, who then carried responsibility for Northern Irish affairs, and from the Opposition Leader, Mr. Wilson. Then each of the Irish speakers would make a statement. After each statement the speaker would be questioned by a three-man panel to clarify or perhaps elicit the implications of his policy. It was essential to the whole concept of the programme that the questioning should be carried out by distinguished men of known independence and character. Eventually invitations were accepted by Sir John Foster, a Conservative Member of Parliament and a leading international lawyer, and Lord Caradon, a former Labour Minister and Colonial Governor. The third member and President of the panel was Lord Devlin, a former judge of the High Court and Lord of Appeal, who had also been chairman of the Press Council. It was not intended that the panel should make any sort of adjudication. Their role was to be limited to summing up their views in turn on the propositions they had heard; not judging between them, but setting them in perspective in the light of what had been said.

Proposals for casting the eight Irish speakers were complete by early December, and the first invitation was sent to Mr. Robin Bailie, Minister of Commerce in Mr. Brian Faulkner's Stormont Government. Although he expressed reservations about doing such a programme at that time, he agreed to refer the proposal to Mr. Faulkner as well as an invitation to Mr. Faulkner himself to make an opening statement. At this point invitations were sent out also to the other proposed participants, among them a Minister in Mr. Jack Lynch's Dublin Government.

The first difficulty we ran into was the expression of doubts by Mr. Faulkner about the wisdom of the programme while the killing was going on. He was also critical of the proposed casting on the grounds that the eight Irish speakers suggested included only one Ulster Unionist. We recognised that the question of balance was a difficult one and were ready to discuss possible adjustments to it. But we were not prepared to accept the argument that because there was violence in Northern Ireland we should not seek to represent to the British public the opinions that sustained the violence and would have to be taken into account in any settlement. Still, at this stage we were nevertheless hopeful that the Stormont Government would allow a Minister to take part.

The next difficulty was an objection from the Home Secretary, Mr. Maudling. At a meeting he had requested with the BBC Chairman, Lord Hill, and Director-General Curran, he expressed serious disquiet about the project. He feared that the programme might lead some of the participants to express more rigid views than they had done previously, and so prevent them from taking part in discussions that he hoped to arrange at the political level. He objected also to what he thought was an attempt to sit in judgement on the Government's performance. When told clearly that this was not the BBC's intention, he remained unconvinced. We, for our part, could not accept his argument that the programme should not take place on the ground that the situation was too difficult to explain to the people. (This meeting was private; but since an account of it—not from a BBC source— was published in the *Daily Telegraph* later that month, no confidentiality remains.)

All the remaining intended participants agreed to appear, provided that the others took part, and that there was no editing—that the programme went out live. There even seemed good reason to expect that a Stormont Minister would take part, but on Christmas Eve it was learned that no representative of Mr. Faulkner's Government would be allowed to do so. It was after this, when we had made it clear that we still intended to go ahead, that the *Daily Telegraph* published its account of the programme, identifying its objectives as those the Home Secretary attributed to the BBC. It also denounced us for "rampant irresponsibility and cold impartiality."

It was now clear in public that political pressure was being brought to bear on us to prevent the production of a programme that we believed to be right and proper to show. We took the view that, provided we could secure a spokesman for the Unionist cause, we should go ahead; and we took this view in part because we realised that if we gave way to this pressure we should never again be trusted by the public to be a voice independent of Government. At the same time it became clear also that Conservative and Ulster Unionist pressure was being applied to prevent any spokesman of the Unionist view from taking part—and it very nearly succeeded. Shortly after Christmas, when it looked as though the programme might have to be abandoned, the BBC issued a statement to make it clear that, if this happened, immediate thought would be given to the preparation of the programme for a later showing. In the words of the statement,

The BBC recognises the formidable difficulties of producing such a programme but is confident of its ability to do so. What the BBC cannot accept
is that it should be diverted from its purpose of presenting all points of view
by a campaign of pressure by a newspaper or anyone else.

This statement was widely reported and commented on, and press opinions about it were divided. *The Times* and the *Guardian* urged us to go
ahead, but the *Sun* sided with the *Daily Telegraph* in opposing our plan.
Said the *Telegraph:* "The project in its present form is demonstrably ridiculous. The BBC should scrap its original ideas and start again." It was only
three days before the programme was due to go out that we finally succeeded
in finding an Ulster Unionist spokesman—a relatively little known Unionist
M.P. at Westminster, Mr. Jack Maginnis. His reason for taking part was
that it was a function of the Unionists M.P.'s at Westminster to explain to
the British electorate why the Unionists take the point of view they do. He
was clearly a courageous man to defy his party, and it may well be thought
that on this occasion he had a better understanding of the democratic process than his colleagues.

The day before the broadcast the Home Secretary took the unprecedented
step of sending the BBC a letter (released later to the press) in which he repeated his opposition to the programme and confirmed his own earlier refusal to take part in it. In his belief, he said, the programme "in the form in
which it had been devised could do no good and could do serious harm."
The Chairman replied at once in these words:

If we shared your fears that such a programme would worsen the situation
in Ulster we would not dream of proceeding with it. On the contrary we
hope and believe that it will be of value in widening understanding of the
issues involved. No good purpose can be solved by our declining to air conflicting views as to the future.

So the programme went ahead and as a result of all the publicity it got a
much bigger audience than would normally have been expected. When it
began at 9:20 P.M. it drew an audience of seven and one-half million viewers, including nearly two-thirds of the population of Northern Ireland. In
addition Telefis Eireann relayed it live throughout the Republic. Lord Caradon said on the programme: "We may have been dull, but not dangerous."
However that may be, more than half the viewers who started stayed to the
end at a quarter past midnight—a bigger proportion than had stayed with
previous political programmes of this length. Ironically, perhaps, one benefit of a programme whose critics had said could do no good was that, with so
many people at their TV sets, Northern Ireland had one of its quietest nights
for weeks.

The programme proved to be what it was planned to be: a sober and low-key examination of eight different proposals for the future of Northern Ireland, with no attempt by Lord Devlin or his two colleagues to give judgement. Whereas telephone calls to the BBC had been 10 to 1 against the programme beforehand, they were 5 to 1 in favour afterwards. Letters that beforehand had been 7 to 1 against us, ran 3 to 1 in our favour afterwards—an unprecedented phenomenon. Moreover, after the broadcast, roughly 80 per cent of the press comment took the line that we were right to have done what we did. In general, the position was now reversed, and the complaints were directed at the Government for trying to stop the programme and not at the BBC for broadcasting it. Even so, the Home Secretary still contended that the programme might yet have done harm, since it could serve only to harden attitudes. He was apparently referring to a statement in it by Gerry Fitt, M.P., of the Social Democratic and Labour Party of Northern Ireland, who had said that he would not take part in any talks before internment was ended. But Mr. Fitt had said that same thing in the House of Commons five weeks earlier.

One of the benefits of the programme was its demonstration of the technique of veto by abstention. Without a genuine representative of the Ulster Unionist voice it could not have been produced in the form in which it had been devised. To begin with, at least one other participant would have withdrawn, and the whole structure would subsequently have collapsed. In any case, the BBC would not have wished to proceed with the programme in a form that would manifestly have failed to give the Ulster Unionist view at first hand in the way opposing views were given. Anyone—and any government—has the right to decline to take part in a television programme. Whether it is right for a Government and a party to extend that right to the point of deterring individual elected members from appearing is another matter. The programme was of particular importance in illustrating the will of the BBC to back its judgement against any pressure—and in this instance the pressure was considerable. It also demonstrated again the independence of the BBC, even though there was a price to be paid—that of a heightened feeling of resentment in the Government and among many Conservative M.P.'s toward the BBC, for acting in a way they regarded as characteristic of an over-mighty subject.

In the long run, however, perhaps the most important aspect of our clash with the Government over "The Question of Ulster" is the fact that at no time was it suggested that the final decision could rest with anyone other than ourselves. Clearly the Government was doing everything it legitimately could to stop the programme, even to the extent of allowing itself to be seen to apply pressure in public. Yet it never questioned our right to make up our own BBC mind. A former editor of News and Current Affairs, Donald

Edwards, has said that he would have been sacked long before reaching retirement age if the BBC had been controlled by the Government. And so, he added, would every Director-General from Reith onwards. Actually, he said, he had made news decisions under six Prime Ministers without a single order to keep an item out or to put one in. Of course he had had requests, hints, pressures—but the ultimate decision always rested with the BBC.

Making such decisions is never easy. It means assuming national responsibility, serving as a trustee for the national interest. Clearly, it requires a full understanding of what the issues are and that understanding can be based only on knowledge. Hence, if the BBC is to make the right judgements on such occasions, it must know without a shadow of doubt what is in the Government's mind; it must be fully aware of what the Government conceives the national interest to be. Our experience at the time of Suez underlined the importance of establishing and maintaining links and channels of communication with Government. They can never rule out misunderstandings or even clashes, but they can at least help us to avoid unnecessary ones. Of course, all this calls for frankness not only on the part of Government but also on the part of the BBC. There must be a readiness, on both sides, to put one's cards on the table, even when risks are involved. Information imparted in confidence may leak out and be used to cause us embarrassment; but this may be part of the price one has to pay for fruitful dialogue. If broadcasters are to exercise their right to go against the wishes of Government, they must be quite sure that they know what those wishes are and that they have valid reasons for deciding to disregard them.

The BBC is independent, and its independence is vital to its credibility. But it is also a corporate citizen. It is not above or outside the nation, but a part of it.

15

Access to News
in a Small Capital: Ottawa

ANTHONY WESTELL

INTRODUCTION

In his recently published memoirs[1] Lester Pearson described his first experience at managing the news. He was at the time a young Canadian
official at the Imperial Economic Conference in Ottawa in 1932, and was
assigned to assist the Minister in charge of press and information matters,
Dr. R. J. Manion. As Pearson recalls it,

> As the Prime Minister alone decided what should be given to the press and
> kept most of the information on Canadian policy to himself, Dr. Manion's
> role at a press conference was an unenviable one. . . . He told me, there-
> fore, to look after press conferences and press enquiries. I knew even less
> than Dr. Manion, but Malcolm Macdonald, who was a friend, was my op-
> posite number on the British side. They did things differently in that delega-
> tion. He was always well briefed and was kind enough to give me about as
> much confidential information as he gave to British journalists. Therefore I
> was able to hold Canadian press briefings which were not entirely useless
> but certainly not entirely Canadian.[2]

Things are different in Ottawa today, of course, but not that much different. The Canadian Government has a machine for dispensing news, but
it is small in scale, often amateurish in operation, and certainly does not
compare with the British system of management that I knew in the 1950's.
As a diplomatic reporter for a London evening paper, I went every day
to the news conference at the Foreign Office. There the official spokesman

---

Mr. Westell, Ottawa Editor, *Toronto Star,* is Sessional Lecturer at Carleton University, Ottawa. He is also the author of *Paradox: Trudeau as Prime Minister.*
1. *Mike: The Memoirs of the Rt. Hon. Lester B. Pearson,* vol. 1 (Toronto: University
of Toronto Press, 1972).
2. *Ibid.,* p. 78.

read statements giving the British Government's reaction to the news of the day and evaded all questions except those he was carefully briefed to answer. Usually the spokesman said very little of interest because this was an open, on-the-record conference. We, the British reporters and the trusted foreigners, had to wait patiently for the official business to end and then we divided quickly into small groups for private, not-for-attribution briefings by the staff of the Foreign Office news department.

I had almost no other sources of news about the conduct of foreign affairs and no real way of checking whether the information I was being given day by day was accurate or not. From what I read in other papers, I believe my colleagues and competitors were in much the same boat. This system of news management did not strike me as curious at the time. I was employed to report on the conduct of foreign affairs by the British ·Government, and the F.O. officials kindly provided me with a steady flow of information to use at my discretion, provided I did not actually attribute it to them. The system was much the same for political correspondents. For several years in London, I was a member of the Lobby Correspondents' association—so-called because we had access to the M.P.'s in the lobby outside the entrance to the chamber of the House of Commons. Every day we went to Number 10 Downing Street to be briefed by the Prime Minister's spokesman, again on a not-for-attribution basis. There were also private briefings by Ministers and officials in a room discreetly tucked away in a remote tower of the Parliament buildings.

It did not follow that every recipient of official news wrote it in such a way as to reflect favor on the source, the Government. The essential point was that there was very little hard information which did not come through official channels.

This was the system in which I trained as a reporter, and it hardly occurred to me that another world might exist. But in 1956 I emigrated to Canada and discovered to my surprise, indeed my alarm, on my first assignment to Ottawa, that no established system for channeling news or briefing reporters existed— or rather, was evident to a newcomer.

I do not mean to suggest that either the Canadian Government or the Canadian press was possessed of some superior virtue inspiring them to eschew news management in favor of the free flow of information. There was simply a different political tradition, different political and press imperatives than those obtaining in London. To understand news in Ottawa it is helpful to look briefly at history.

PAST PRIME MINISTERS AND THE PRESS

From Confederation in 1867 to about the end of the Mackenzie King era in 1948, Prime Ministers generally dealt with a few chosen newsmen who were not only journalists but often influential advisers to the Government.[3] These reporter-politicians served as ambassadors from their editors—who were powers in their own provinces and regions of Canada—to the Prime Minister in Ottawa. They reported the views of the Government to their editors and readers, and conveyed to the Prime Minister the opinions of their editors and their interpretations of local opinion. Some of these men were so well trusted, it is said, that they were admitted on occasions to Cabinet meetings. Less-favored reporters often had to rely on what the insiders wrote for their news of what was happening deep within the Government. Thus, in a real sense, the trusted reporters served as spokesmen for the Government.

As the number of political reporters in Ottawa began to grow rapidly during the postwar years, and the newspapers became less partisan and more independent in their attitudes, this tradition of press relations gradually declined. The transition from a highly personalized to a more formal structure of press relations and news management seems to have begun in the time of Prime Minister Louis St. Laurent (1948–57). It was during this period, incidentally, that Pearson, as External Affairs Minister, developed the practice of inviting groups of correspondents for weekly background briefings on his conduct of foreign affairs, and developed the warm fellowship with the press which was a trademark of his career.

After John Diefenbaker became Prime Minister in 1957 he appointed a well-known Ottawa journalist as press secretary—the first Prime Ministerial press officer in Canadian experience. But he never gave the man much of his confidence, and preferred, in reality, to conduct his own press relations. As a backbench M.P. and later as Leader of the Opposition, he had many friends and admirers in the press gallery, and in his successful 1957 and 1958 election campaigns he was assisted by a warmly enthusiastic press. No doubt he believed that he could continue this relation, but of course the rules of the game changed when he became Prime Minister, and the press became more critical. Diefenbaker seems to have regarded this as a personal betrayal, and his press relations became worse and worse over the years. Toward the end of his time in power he made contemptuous speeches about the "servile press."

Nonetheless, he retained close relations with a few reporters, and used them to manipulate opinion—although, unlike his predecessors, he seldom if ever took their advice. Peter Dempson, who was in the press gallery for seventeen years, mainly for the (Tory) *Toronto Telegram,* has described the arrangement.[4] He and Richard Jackson, from the (Tory) *Ottawa Jour-*

---

3. My colleague at Carleton University's School of Journalism, Joel Weiner, is completing a research project on relations between Prime Ministers and the press and has kindly let me see some of his material.
4. Peter Dempson, *Assignment Ottawa* (Toronto: General Publishing Co., Ltd., 1968).

nal, used to see Diefenbaker almost every week to ask questions about government policy, check rumors, and discuss the politics of the day.

Dempson recalls that on several occasions Diefenbaker used them to test public reaction to his ideas. For example, after the sudden death of External Affairs Minister Sidney Smith in 1959, he encouraged the two reporters to speculate on the possibility that Finance Minister Donald Fleming would be moved into the Department of External Affairs. "Two weeks later," Dempson relates, "Jackson and I were again in Diefenbaker's office. Before either of us could say anything, the Prime Minister pointed to a stack of letters on his desk [and] said: 'Forget about Fleming, I'd like to let you read these, but I can't. Anyway, they've given me my answer.' "[5] The business community had apparently made it clear to the Prime Minister that it wanted Fleming to remain in Finance.

Dempson and Jackson apparently did not object to being used in this way —perhaps because they were occasionally rewarded with important exclusives. Dempson, for example, deduced from some of Diefenbaker's comments that he had finally made up his mind to appoint Howard Green to the External Affairs post. Diefenbaker refused to confirm the fact directly, but: "Finally, he got out of his chair and walked to one of the windows overlooking the lush lawns in front of the Parliament Buildings. He stood silent, his hands on his hips. After what seemed like an interminable time, he beckoned me to his side. 'Those lawns,' he said wryly, pointing out the window, 'they sure are nice and green, aren't they.' He was smiling. That was all he said. I knew then it was Howard Green."[6]

The point of this brief history has been to show that relations between the Government and the press were traditionally managed on a selective and highly personal basis in Ottawa. While there was very little official machinery for controlling and directing the flow of news, certainly there was management for political ends.

It was into this different and mystifying world that I came in 1958 on my first major assignment in Ottawa. I was preparing to cover a Commonwealth trade and economic conference in Montreal and, fresh from my background as diplomatic reporter for a London evening newspaper, I made like a homing pigeon for Prime Minister Diefenbaker's press secretary—the approved London procedure—only to discover that he knew almost nothing. It was the same at the press office in the Department of External Affairs; the spokesman was polite but useless for all except issuing credentials. His British counterpart would have been a prime source of such information as I was intended to have.

---

5. *Ibid.,* pp. 103–4.
6. *Ibid.,* pp. 104–5.

In Montreal, I began to discover how the Canadian system worked. I discovered that Ministers could be approached individually; they were not the lofty and remote figures of my British experience. And when Ministers were not available, they had invaluable aides known as Executive Assistants, combined speech writers-advisers and public relations men who were very often former newsmen. If one could catch an Executive Assistant on the run, he would rummage through his briefcase and produce an answer to a question or a tip about some upcoming event to provide material for a story.

It was not as smooth as the British system for dispensing news, but at least it provided a supply of information, and that's what reporters are in the business of obtaining. And if it was sometimes alarmingly haphazard, and left one in danger of being scooped by more energetic or better connected rivals, it also had advantages. Often one could check with two or three Ministers or their assistants, or compare notes with other reporters who had been using different sources. Because the Canadian Government had no professional machinery for controlling and coordinating the stream of news, one was likely to get different interpretations of what was happening, and thus arrive at a more accurate view of reality.

From the point of view of the Canadian Government, the lack of an efficient system could be a severe disadvantage in the conduct of international negotiations. In 1962 I was one of the newsmen who went to London with Diefenbaker and External Affairs Minister Green, who were attending the conference of Commonwealth Prime Ministers. They wanted to press Canada's case against Britain's desire to enter the European Common Market, and they hoped to win support in Britain and in other Commonwealth countries.

The conference was in private, of course, so that a great deal depended on how the press was briefed on the proceedings and presented the arguments to the public. There was a very general public briefing for all correspondents, and beyond that each delegation was supposed to confine itself to talking to the press about its own position, and not that of other countries. Typically, the principal Canadian briefing officer, Bob Bryce, was not a professional press officer but the Cabinet Secretary and chief of staff for the delegation. He generally played by the rules, as did Diefenbaker and Green when they talked to Canadian reporters. But almost from the outset of the private meetings, the British papers, guided by their private briefings on the British point of view, began to cut up Diefenbaker's performance behind the closed doors of the meetings.

I do not wish to argue here whether the critical reporting of Diefenbaker was accurate, whether the British spokesmen were presenting a fair account of the conference or one reflecting the British Government's annoyance with Diefenbaker when he opposed its plans. The important fact is that the

Canadian Prime Minister was wounded and bewildered by the reports in the British press. He could not believe that British officials whom he so deeply admired were playing by a different set of rules. Green was moved in the end to complain that "Statements in the British press are completely inaccurate and unfair."[7] Because at that time I still had many friends in the British press, understood how the British system worked, and was privy on occasions to what was being said at the British briefings, I was astonished by the naïveté of the Canadians, who were by then my chosen fellow citizens.

I pause in my narrative to underline: (1) Reporters can never consent to suppression of the news. But they are often willing (or unthinking) recipients of managed news. Their primary interest is in getting a story and in not being scooped by rivals; the source of the news and the fact that it may be angled is of secondary importance. (2) In London, in my experience, the news was smoothly managed to serve the interests of the British Government. In Ottawa, up to this stage in my story, it had been managed and angled by individual politicians rather than by Government, with indifferent success.

There may be many reasons contributing to the difference in practice in the two capitals, but the principal one, I believe, was a function of size and importance. London was the seat of a powerful Government which had to be careful how it spoke to other countries. It was reported by newsmen who were often separated by class barriers from the decision-makers in politics and bureaucracy and who tended, with the population at large, to back their Government in its dealings with foreigners.

Ottawa was a small capital, and the news it generated was of little importance outside the country. Ministers and civil servants knew personally the leading members of the press corps. Because Canada was a large, federal state, the national interest was not as well defined, and Ministers and newsmen might often see questions of policy from regional points of view so that there was no "right" or "wrong" interpretation. This brings me to recent times and the significant changes which occurred in Ottawa when Lester Pearson became Prime Minister.

THE PEARSON PERIOD

Mr. Pearson, who became Prime Minister in 1963, made far more sophisticated use of the press than had his predecessors. Perhaps this was because he had served as a diplomat in London, Washington, and the United Nations, and thus knew how things were done elsewhere; perhaps because, as he often said, he enjoyed the company of newsmen and found them useful sources of information; perhaps simply because the media—now that it

---

7. John T. Saywell, ed., *Canadian Annual Review for 1962* (Toronto: University of Toronto Press, 1962), p. 118.

included TV and radio as well as newspaper writers—were more sophisticated, demanding, and politically important in the new era of electronic communication.

In any event, Pearson established the first effective press department in the Prime Minister's office and designated as his spokesman a professional "P.R. man" who had assistants and a small support staff. Informal question-and-answer sessions outside the Cabinet room after a meeting gradually gave way to more structured press conferences. The spokesman rather than the Prime Minister became the most important source of daily information and background briefing—if only because he was always available.

This is not to say that Pearson was remote from the press. Far from it. He entertained groups of reporters regularly at his official home for a drink and an off-the-record chat, and when he was traveling out of Ottawa he often invited the accompanying newsmen to his room for a nightcap and a discussion of the events of the day. Although he was capable of using these occasions to manage the news, his methods were sometimes so subtle that there is still argument as to whether some of his results were achieved by design or by accident. For instance, in the spring of 1964 he suddenly announced to a surprised group of reporters invited to his home for a drink that he intended to give Canada its distinctive national flag, replacing the Red Ensign of British heritage. He even showed his guests the design he preferred and gave them permission to write about his intentions as long as they did not attribute the news directly to him. There was of course great excitement in Parliament and the country, and the incident has often been cited as a classic example of floating a trial balloon.

My own interpretation is different, and it is based on another of those quiet chats with Pearson, on this occasion explaining a theory of leadership-by-crisis. When times are settled and secure, he said, it is extremely difficult to change the course of events. People with power are too comfortable and complacent to risk major reform. But at times of crisis, when the familiar world is threatened, it is possible for a skillful operator to suggest a solution embodying a great reform, and thus to be welcomed on all sides as a statesman and a savior. For example, as he continued, he had been trying to interest the United Nations in peace-keeping long before the Suez crisis, but he got nowhere until the crisis raised the threat of a confrontation between the Great Powers. His proposal for a peace-keeping force was suddenly acceptable. As for the flag issue, I believe that Pearson deliberately used the press to stir up a political crisis so that in time he could—and did—offer a compromise: not the flag design he had specified but in any case a national flag that proved acceptable to a country and a Parliament deadlocked on the issue, frustrated, and looking for a settlement. This, I suggest, was an unusual form of news management as a means of manipulating opinion.

Under the Pearson Government there was also a great change in the press relations office of the External Affairs department. The Minister, Paul Martin, wanted an effective spokesman to promote both his own image and that of the foreign policy of the Government. His first intention had been to appoint a senior journalist, but he was persuaded by officials that an outsider would never be accepted with confidence in the tight little world of a department that regarded itself as an Ottawa elite. So Martin approved the appointment of a Foreign Service officer who had had experience as a spokesman at NATO.

This officer, a first-rate choice, immediately set about opening channels between the department and the press. I was one of those invited by him to serve on a committee to advise the department on how to improve its press relations. The problem was not how to get managed news into the press; it was how to win the attention of hard-worked reporters in the press gallery for any sort of news of foreign affairs except during occasional crises. One device was a weekly background briefing session to which the spokesman might invite a senior official whose area of specialization happened to be in the news. One such event I remember was the return of a Canadian officer who had been serving on the International Control Commission in Vietnam and who had some interesting and very pro-American views on the situation. We were invited to write (on a not-for-attribution basis) about the information we gleaned at these sessions.

For me it was almost like being back at the Foreign Office, but for some of my colleagues it was altogether too much like managed news, suspiciously selective and underhand. They began to write about the briefing system, and there were questions in Parliament, for there the Opposition—far more than in Britain—is always jealous of its claim to hear first about the views and intentions of the Government. It was not this, however, that led quite soon to the abandonment of regular briefing sessions. The truth was that there just was not enough news to sustain a weekly event. The briefing had become to some extent an exercise in manufacturing news where none existed.

Briefing has of course continued, but on an occasional basis. This raises the second major point I wish to make in this chapter. In Canada foreign policy is of importance and news value only from time to time in special circumstances, such as when the Government is engaged in some major initiative or has a role in an international crisis. Most of the time there isn't much news worth suppressing or managing in the area of External Affairs.

SOME CASE STUDIES

That is why I found it difficult while researching this chapter to document interesting examples of news management or suppression. I asked a number of people inside and outside the External Affairs department to recall, in the conduct of foreign affairs, any unusual event that had been hidden entirely from public view or presented in such a way as to create a misleading impression. Very few ideas were forthcoming. Of course, if a matter has been successfully kept secret, then my informants and I may simply be blissfully ignorant. But I doubt that there are many interesting skeletons buried in the basement of External Affairs. If the examples I now offer are not exciting or controversial, that probably reflects reality.

Suppression

In 1948 Canada was experiencing severe economic difficulties and had to raise a loan in the United States and also impose quotas on imports from the United States. During discussions in Washington about these arrangements, the U.S. officials suddenly threw out the idea of a free-trade treaty on terms generous to Canada. Prime Minister Mackenzie King and some of his senior Cabinet colleagues were intrigued, and so exploratory negotiations were authorized. A draft treaty was in fact negotiated, under conditions of great secrecy at the official level. But then, prompted by what he felt was "guidance from beyond," Mr. King began to get political cold feet.

Although the United States was pushing for action the Canadians held back; and eventually the scheme simply died. This was an important turning point in Canadian affairs, for a free-trade arrangement would probably have led to some form of North American political association. Very few people knew anything about it at the time, however, and the story had been told in detail only in recent years.[8]

Misinformation

In an address at Temple University in Philadelphia in April 1965, Prime Minister Pearson advocated a pause in the U.S. bombing of North Vietnam. It was a polite but unmistakable criticism of U.S. policy by a foreign head of government visiting the United States. President Johnson invited—perhaps summoned would be a better word—Pearson to Camp David for a private talk.

After the meeting the U.S. briefing officer indicated that the President had made his displeasure very plain to the Prime Minister, and Canadian reporters clamored for a Canadian account of the event. When Pearson's press secretary briefed them on the plane flying back to Ottawa, he tended to play down the President's annoyance, suggesting that while the meeting had been frank and forthright, it had not been unfriendly. A day or so later, an

---

8. Pearson, *op. cit.,* p. 292.

American column carried what was obviously an accurate and informed account of the meeting and made it plain that Johnson had been sharp, if not downright offensive, in scolding Pearson.

The Canadian reporters had been misled. The question is whether Pearson (or his press spokesman) deliberately gave the reporters a distorted version of events in order to preserve the dignity and political image of the Prime Minister by concealing the fact that he had been treated by the President rather as though he were a naughty child. The truth, so far as I can ascertain it now, is that Pearson, being an unpretentious man, did not take Johnson's blunt language very much to heart. He was not shocked or offended (although, perhaps, he should have been, in view of the dignity of his office), and he gave a complacent account of the meeting to his press secretary, who then passed it along to the reporters.

This incident will perhaps illustrate that on some occasions when there is interference with the free and accurate flow of the news it may be an accident or breakdown in internal communications rather than calculated management. I am tempted to believe that this is frequently the case, for I do not take a conspiratorial view of politics and maintain that more things happen by accident than by design. Of course I may simply be naïve or credulous, and my more suspicious colleagues who see news manipulators everywhere may be more realistic. In any event, my next case is that of an incident widely said to have involved media manipulation at its most sinister. Yet in my view this imputation is almost wholly a myth.

Alleged Manipulation

The Diefenbaker Cabinet was sharply split between the External Affairs Minister and his supporters, who wanted to repudiate nuclear weapons and pursue the goal of disarmament, and the Defence Minister and his colleagues, who considered that Canada was bound by commitments to NATO and NORAD allies to accept nuclear warheads from the United States for weapons already in place in Canada and Europe. By January of 1963 the row was coming to a head, and the Opposition and the press were steadily increasing pressure on the Government to make up its mind and declare a policy. At this critical juncture General Lauris Norstad, retiring U.S. commander of NATO forces in Europe, arrived in Ottawa and held a press conference. When questioned by reporters he said, Yes, Canada would be reneging on its NATO commitment if it failed to acquire nuclear warheads. The statement created a political sensation and contributed toward the weakening of the Government and its defeat in the Commons the following month. No less an authority than Donald Creighton, perhaps Canada's most distinguished historian, has written of the event in these terms:

The Kennedy Administration regarded Canada with a cold fury of impatience. If the Canadians could not make up their minds on this vital subject [nuclear policy], they must be taught to do so! On the 3rd of January, General Lauris Norstad, the American officer who had just resigned his post as commander-in-chief of NATO forces in Europe, arrived in Ottawa and frankly informed Canadian newspapermen that, if Canada did not equip her Starfighter squadrons with nuclear ammunition, she would not be fulfilling her NATO commitments.[9]

Thus Creighton implies that Norstad was an agent of Kennedy's policy and that Canadian newsmen were the instruments used to help destroy the Diefenbaker Government. This view is apparently shared by Diefenbaker and by many other people. It is a splendid scenario, a perfect example of how to manufacture news and manipulate the media for political ends— but so far as I can make out, it is a mistaken view of what really happened.

Norstad was not sent to Ottawa by Kennedy. He was on a farewell tour of all the NATO capitals. When he was questioned in Ottawa about nuclear policy, he was not briefed with a ready reply and was unaware that it was politically explosive. He merely repeated a familiar NATO view, and one that was in fact shared by Diefenbaker's own Defence Minister, who shortly resigned from the Cabinet. In short, it was not at all a U.S.-managed affair but an accident.

As a footnote to this story I might add that the Defence Department at that time did indeed attempt to influence public opinion on the issue of nuclear weapons, but its efforts took an unusual form. The department concluded that it was not succeeding in telling its story to the public about Canada's commitments, since the press tended to favor the disarmament position advocated by External Affairs. Defence therefore decided to make an end-run around the press by organizing a series of trips for opinion leaders—such as businessmen and members of the Canadian Institute of International Affairs—to NORAD headquarters at Colorado Springs to be briefed on Canada's role in continental defence. This tactic was deemed successful in influencing opinion despite the press.

I have mentioned specific cases of news management or alleged management and none of them is particularly sinister. This does not mean, however, that the flow of all news in Ottawa is free and unpolluted. Foreign affairs, as I have said, are not often a sensitive political issue in Canada, and it might be easier to document suppression or distortion in areas of policy of more urgent concern to our Government. I must also record my impression that if anyone had the fortitude to review the hundreds of statements made about Vietnam by Prime Minister Pearson and External Affairs Minister

---

9. Donald Creighton, *Canada's First Century* (Toronto: Macmillan, 1970), p. 326.

Martin during the years 1963–68, he would find that cumulatively they gave an altogether too rosy view of Canada's role and a quite unwarranted defence of the U.S. position. I doubt, however, that this was the result of a deliberate decision to mislead; more likely, it was a natural tendency to put the best face on unpleasant facts, to avoid controversy with the United States, and to gain whatever credit there was to be had as peacemakers.

My conclusion at this stage of the story, therefore, is that while there was during the Diefenbaker and Pearson years a certain degree of manipulation of the news for political ends, it existed only on a small scale and did not reflect a policy of calculated censorship. There was probably more news and less management of news than in earlier times, and perhaps no more management than is inevitable.

TRUDEAU AND INFORMATION

When Pierre Trudeau became Prime Minister in 1968, his views about political privacy and public information appeared to some people to be in conflict and have, I think, given rise to considerable confusion.

The Pearson Cabinet had been notoriously leaky. Once the Prime Minister gave his colleagues a severe warning about the importance of Cabinet secrecy, and a full account was published in the press within a few hours. Trudeau was determined to stop these leaks, as he thought they were undermining a system of government that depended on free exchange of views in private and collective responsibility for the final decision. He warned that he would fire, perhaps even prosecute, any Ministers who breached their Privy Council oath of secrecy.

Trudeau also enlarged the press office organized by Pearson. Instead of serving as a facility for making the Prime Minister and his opinions available to the press, the new office became in some ways a shield between him and reporters. In my view a trend toward more formal relations between the Prime Minister and the press was evident during the Pearson years and probably inevitable, but Trudeau speeded it up—and this for several reasons. For one thing, he was a media figure who attracted crowds of newsmen, and his press relations had to be organized to avoid chaos. For another, he did not like or respect the mass media. As he wrote in 1967,

> There is thus the danger that mass media—to the extent that they claim to reflect public opinion—constitute a vehicle for error, if not indeed an instrument of oppression. For my part, I have never been able to read newspapers without a sense of uneasiness, especially newspapers of opinion. They follow their customers and are therefore always lagging behind reality.[10]

10. Pierre Elliott Trudeau, *Federalism and the French Canadians* (Toronto: Macmillan, 1968), p. xxii.

Then, too, he was the first Canadian Prime Minister to be a master of television, a medium of communication he much preferred to the press.

This is not to say that Trudeau cut himself off from the press. He was often available after Question Period in the Commons to elaborate on answers he had given in the House. Yet he was prone to give tart answers to what he regarded as stupid or unfair questions, and he did not hesitate to tell reporters that they were guilty of "crummy" behavior when they intruded on what he regarded as his right to a private life. He gave press conferences at irregular intervals and, in the months leading up to the 1972 election, a remarkable number of exclusive interviews. Still, his insistence on Cabinet secrecy and his sometimes high-handed dealings with the press gave rise to the widely held view that his era was one of "paranoid secrecy."

On the other hand, on coming to power Trudeau invited the people to plug in to Ottawa so that they could participate in decision-making.[11] He was concerned to bridge the credibility gap between the public and the Government in modern society, to moderate impossible expectations by showing people what the choices really were. He recognized that, in order to participate, people needed information; and one of his early acts as Prime Minister was to appoint a Task Force on Information. The Task Force quickly documented what it called "the mess in government information" and recommended, among other things, a new agency—to be called Information Canada—that would help to improve the flow of information between government departments and the public.[12]

Recognizing that "since any strengthening of the government's information apparatus involves the possibility of a government manipulating public opinion," the Task Force recommended also strengthening Parliamentary control of information programs, and it declared as a principle of public policy that "The Government has an obligation to provide full, objective and timely information; and that citizens have a right to such information."[13] These assurances were ignored by the press and by Parliament Opposition, which persisted in viewing Information Canada, when it was set up, as a sinister propaganda agency. For its part the Government made grave mistakes in the way the agency was organized, so that it has never functioned effectively.

---

11. See also Bruce Thordarson, *Trudeau and Foreign Policy: A Study in Decision-Making* (Toronto-New York: Oxford University Press, 1972), pp. 158–60, 176–91.
12. *The Report of the Task Force on Information* (Ottawa: The Queen's Printer, Ottawa, 1969).
13. *Ibid.,* p. 49.

TRUDEAU AND THE GRAY REPORT

During the 1960's there was rising public concern about foreign ownership of Canadian industry and resources, and the danger that it was undermining cultural distinctions and political independence. In the spring of 1970 the Cabinet appointed one of its junior members, Herbert Gray, to study the problem. Gray assembled a small working group, and in May 1971 a first draft of his study was submitted to a Cabinet committee. Members of Parliament and the press were continuously pressing for information as to how the study was progressing, if and when it was to be published, and when the Cabinet would declare a policy.

Trudeau was equivocal in his answers, not to say misleading. Sometimes he suggested that the full report would be published; at other times he alluded to a White Paper on Government policy; on yet other occasions he indicated that no decision had been made to publish anything. There were grounds for wondering whether Trudeau's final decision would be governed by the public's right to know what Gray had discovered, or by the political considerations of the Cabinet.

In November 1971, the decision was taken out of the hands of the Government when the *Canadian Forum,* a small magazine of opinion and the arts published in Toronto, announced that it had received a copy of the Gray Report and was publishing a condensed version. As the editors rationalized their action, "Our impression is that the Cabinet is now deadlocked on the question of releasing the Gray Report and that a decision has been taken against its release. Our sympathy lies with those ministers in the Cabinet who wish the report to be made available to the Canadian people."[14]

The Government made an embarrassed reply to the effect that (a) the *Forum* document was only part of an early draft of the study prepared by Gray's group; and (b) the actual Gray Report—that is, the recommendations Gray had made to the Cabinet on the basis of the study—remained confidential. Within a few days there was another leak, this time of a Cabinet Minute that actually recorded the Cabinet's agreement (in principle) with the Gray Report proposal of a board to review foreign takeovers of Canadian companies. Another Cabinet document bearing on the Gray Report was subsequently leaked; and so, when the Government finally published the Report in February 1972,[15] it was not clear whether it was done voluntarily or because there was really no alternative.

---

14. *Canadian Forum: An Independent Journal* 61 (November, 1971).
15. Canada, Information Canada, *Foreign Direct Investment in Canada* (Ottawa, 1972).

In view of the Government's predilection for publishing white papers and draft legislation on other issues, it is reasonable to assume that there was from the outset an intention to publish at least a part of the information arising from the Gray study. My enquiries indicate that the Cabinet had not decided what form the publication should take by August 1971, when President Nixon's new economic policy suddenly put the future of U.S. investment and of Canada-U.S. relations in a new light. This dramatic shift in policy interrupted the Cabinet's consideration of the Gray Report and raised doubts about the wisdom of publishing a paper that might be offensive to the United States at a critical time. This issue had not been resolved by November 1971, when the *Forum* published its version.

I should add that the Gray Report and accompanying Cabinet documents were only part of a steady trickle of Government documents to leak in recent years. In addition to a branch-plant economy, Canada appears to have branch-plant Ellsbergs—that is, government employees who have decided that their private responsibility to make information available to the public is greater than any obligation they owe to their Government.

Some of the information leaked was interesting, if not vitally important. Other documents achieved fame only because they were marked secret; if they had been issued as handouts, they would have attracted little attention. This did in fact happen during the 1972 Canadian election campaign. External Affairs Minister Sharp published a long article in an official journal discussing alternative policies for Canada to follow in relations with the United States, and opting for a deliberate strategy of increasing economic and cultural independence from the United States.[16] The article was in fact approved by the Prime Minister and other members of Cabinet, but because it appeared as an article during an election and the contents were not dramatic or surprising, it attracted almost no interest. If the paper had been marked "secret," labeled as a Cabinet decision, and leaked, it would no doubt have received wide publicity. (For a fuller discussion of the legal implications of leaks in Canada see Maxwell Cohen's contribution in Chapter 21.)

THE PROBLEM AND SOME SUGGESTIONS

When we complain about secrecy and suppression or management of news, what precisely are we criticising? Or, to put it another way, to what extent is Government entitled to privacy and to control of information about its activities?

---

16. Canada, Department of External Relations, Mitchell Sharp, "Canada-U.S. Relations, Options for the Future," *International Perspectives* (Ottawa, 1972).

Everyone can agree on the proposition that eventually all the information in possession of Government should become public property. For example, the Canadian Government has recently instituted a thirty-year rule for release of private files to the public archives, and the External Affairs Department in particular prides itself on giving reasonable access to its files within this closed thirty-year period. So the essential question is not whether government information should be released but how soon.

The press is primarily concerned with news—and news, I suggest, consists of one or more of the following elements: *urgency*—something is just happening; *relevance*—the event is of immediate importance to the reader; *human interest*—the information satisfies curiosity about public personalities and the exercise of power in its many forms. In our approach to government, therefore, we political reporters are interested primarily in day-to-day happenings and decisions: we demand to know right now, today, what decisions are being made. Tomorrow won't do. We are intrigued by conflict between men of power, by the clash of political personalities and ideas. We believe as a general principle that the more and the sooner the public knows of the inside workings of their Government, the better. When we are denied answers to questions or access to documents, we say that news is being suppressed; when the Government releases less than the truth, the whole truth, and nothing but the truth about its activities and decisions, we say that news is being manipulated.

The interests of Government are quite different—at least in the short term. Government seeks to protect the privacy of the Cabinet discussion until tomorrow, or next week or next year, when Ministers have finally arrived at a decision that all of them can support. It wants to safeguard the confidentiality of advice civil servants give to Ministers, so as to preserve at least the appearance of Ministerial leadership and responsibility. Less legitimately perhaps, Government tries to conceal internal doubts and divisions in order to present a united front against its political opponents until after the next election. Illegitimately, it may attempt to hide indefinitely any evidence of wrongdoing that will besmirch its reputation.

In my view, no general law can be written or enforced to resolve this natural conflict between the demand of the press to know and to publish now, today, and the desire of Government to time the release of information. We have to leave to Parliament the task of deciding day-by-day what information can and should be made public, beyond that volunteered by the Cabinet. I am not implying that the press should not probe, explore, and analyse. Certainly I am not arguing that the press should refrain from publishing any information that comes into its hands, whether by enterprise or by the accident of receiving a leak from an anonymous source. The mandate of the press is to publish, and a reporter or an editor would have to be a very competent judge of the public interest to decide to suppress news of importance.

I am saying that the way to increase the flow of information is not to give special powers or rights of access to the press, but to increase the effective powers of Parliament. The Canadian Parliament, of course, already has the power to remove a Government it considers to be too secretive; and this can be an effective weapon when the Government has only minority support in the Commons, as is the case with the second Trudeau Government. But there are other, less Draconian ways of opening Government to Parliamentary and public scrutiny. Some of these are discussed in Gordon Fairweather's chapter.

The development of the Parliamentary Committee system permits M.P.'s to examine Ministers and their advisers more closely than is possible in the full House; the publication of white papers in which the Government makes known its intentions and arguments before making a final decision, encourages the flow of information and argument. Both trends should be strengthened. Then too, the Parliamentary Centre for Foreign Affairs and Foreign Trade, while operating on a small scale (on funds from the Speaker of the Commons and from private sources), is already providing important aid and advice to Parliamentary committees. Members of Parliament might well consider financing similar Centres to cover other areas of policy. Likewise, Royal commissions, task forces, Parliamentary committees of enquiry, and permanent semi-official institutions such as the Economic Council of Canada have a certain access to Government information. Very often the information they assemble is more valuable than the recommendations they make.

The Commons has a procedure under which an M.P. can move for the production of papers—that is, for example, of a Government document he wishes to see. In theory, if the Government declines, the motion is transferred for debate and vote. Unfortunately, there is seldom time to debate motions and bring them to decision. The rules of procedure should be changed so that the motions become effective, and the Government required to produce every document demanded or give convincing reasons why it will not.

Early in 1971 the Task Force on Information considered recommending appointment of an Information Ombudsman. Where requested information was denied to a newsman or a member of the public, an appeal could be made to the Ombudsman, who would in turn require the governmental department to show cause why it was keeping the matter secret. As I understand it, objection was taken within the Government to this idea, and the Task Force finally settled on a much more modest idea which was, anyway, never implemented. But the concept of an Information Ombudsman responding to public request and reporting to Parliament seems to me worth reviving.

It will be said of course that Parliament and press and public can demand only documents and information they know to exist within the Government. What about the millions of documents—reports, studies, recommendations, letters, analyses—generated within the bureaucracy every year and routinely stamped "Confidential" or "Secret" so that no word of their existence ever reaches the public? It is now admitted on all sides that this process conceals a mass of information that could and should be made public. Indeed, when Trudeau was asked how he intended to deal with leaks, he replied that the answer was to publish most of the documents before anyone was tempted to leak them.

Various explanations are offered for the excessive degree of administrative secrecy. A friend of mine in the Government suggests cynically that in the matter of studies commissioned from outside experts, very often the reason for keeping them secret is not that they are revealing but that the Government is ashamed of having paid so much for so little of value. Another friend, an American journalist who worked in Washington before spending some years in Ottawa, assures me that U.S. officials are far more willing to release information than Canadian officials raised in a different and perhaps more disciplined political tradition. Generally speaking, it is easier for a bureaucrat to stamp a document "Secret" than to take the responsibility for releasing it.

Professor Donald Rowat, of Carleton University, has argued persuasively for the adoption in Canada of the Swedish policy that reverses the onus by declaring all documents to be public unless they can be declared to be secret under the provisions of the law protecting such matters as national security or privacy of individuals.[17] While I certainly have no objection to this idea, I doubt that it would be a cure-all for the problem of secrecy. The long tradition of administrative secrecy in Canada would be hard to break, and bureaucrats would find ways of placing documents under confidential classifications.

FINAL OBSERVATIONS

Governments have always sought to suppress or manage information damaging to their political prospects, and I expect they will always do so. But in Ottawa over the years there seems to have been an increase in the flow of information, and this trend is continuing and perhaps accelerating. In such

---

17. Donald C. Rowat, "How Much Administrative Secrecy?" 31 *Canadian Journal of Economics and Political Science* 4 (November, 1965), pp. 479–98.

a small and intimate capital it is extremely difficult for Governments to hide important news for any length of time, and I have no evidence that there are great secrets of state waiting to be uncovered. I doubt in fact that in Ottawa there is much worth knowing that is not already public property.

Finally, as a working newsman, I am convinced that the greatest contribution that could be made to improve the flow of news would be for editors to commit more and better reporters to the job of covering the Government and communicating to the public the information already available.

Part 4

The Individual Confronts the State

16

Enforcing the Public's Right to Openness in the Foreign Affairs Decision-Making Process

RICHARD A. FRANK

That the U.S. Government, with respect to domestic affairs, must follow open administrative procedures, allow interested citizens an opportunity to participate, and disclose relevant information and the reasons for decisions is judicially axiomatic. Yet these natural qualities of democracy are commonly dispensed with by government agencies if the subject under consideration can be said to embrace, albeit indirectly, "foreign affairs."

In this chapter I want to discuss some of the means that may be available in administrative or judicial forums to compel disclosure and citizen participation in the foreign affairs decision-making process. While it focuses on one area—international trade—and on three contemporary cases in which a closed process is being challenged, the issues and answers have a more extensive application. In addition to casting light on possible methods of combating secrecy, the cases bring into question whether the Executive, even if entitled to claim confidentiality on problems of war and peace, should exercise that same prerogative for other matters, merely because they involve discourse with, or action affecting, alien governments or persons.

THE CLOSED PROCESS

Before considering specific ways in which foreign affairs secrecy may be challenged, it is important to understand on what grounds a closed process is generally justified and what forms it usually takes.

Mr. Frank, former Assistant Legal Adviser of the U.S. Department of State and in private practice in Washington, D.C., is presently Director of the International Project of the Center for Law and Social Policy, a public interest law firm that provides legal counsel to previously unrepresented segments of the public. The International Project represents consumers in the trade area, and environmental groups in the international environmental area, and is counsel to the plaintiffs in the cases referred to in this chapter.

Whenever the Department of State is compelled before the judiciary to articulate why foreign affairs must not be impeded by openness, it resorts to an old stand-by, the extensive language of the Supreme Court in *United States* v. *Curtiss-Wright Export Corp. et al.*[1] Even in 1936, during the only era in which delegation of authority in the domestic area was being found unconstitutional, the Court was prepared, in most generous terms, to grant the Executive great latitude in foreign affairs. According to this decision,

> In this vast external realm, with its important, complicated, delicate and manifold problems, the President alone has the power to speak or listen as the representative of the nation. . . . [He] must necessarily be most competent to determine when, how, and upon what subjects negotiation may be urged with the greatest prospect of success. . . . The nature of transactions with foreign nations, moreover, requires caution and unity of design, and their success frequently depends on secrecy and dispatch. . . . He has his agents in the form of diplomats, consular and other officials. Secrecy in respect of information gathered by them may be highly necessary, and the premature disclosure of it productive of harmful results. . . .[2]

To accommodate this alleged need for speed, secrecy, unity, and deference to the President's expertise, foreign affairs becomes a closed process in the following ways:

Failure to conduct administrative proceedings

Under the Administrative Procedure Act (APA),[3] government agencies are required, in implementing law and policy, to follow specified rule-making or adjudication procedures. An agency must give notice through the Federal Register or otherwise; describe the proposed rule and its underlying authority; give interested persons an opportunity to participate through submission of written views and, in some instances, an oral hearing; render a decision supported by a record; and state the basis and purpose of the decision. These procedural requirements do not apply "to the extent that there is involved a military or foreign affairs function of the United States."[4]

The Department of State interprets this exclusion to exempt all of its activities, since all of them to some extent have a nexus to foreign affairs. Consequently, the Department does not have generally applicable regulations prescribing these or similar procedures. When a particular matter arises, no examination is made whether public procedures could or should

---

1. 299 U.S. 304 (1936).
2. *Id.* at 319–20.
3. 5 U.S.C. §511 *et seq.* (1970).
4. *Id.* §553(a) (1), §554(a) (4).

be applied; the Department has automatically exempted all of its activities, even those that substantially affect the economic or other rights of persons, from the APA. The sole significant area subject to public proceedings is the environment; and the Department succumbed in this instance only because of the special requirements of the National Environmental Policy Act of 1969[5] and only after intense pressure from environmental groups and Members of Congress.

Failure to disclose information

The Freedom of Information Act[6] establishes the general rule that government agencies should make all information available to the public upon demand. This requirement, however, does not apply in nine enumerated categories, including "matters that are . . . specifically required by Executive order to be kept secret in the interest of national defense or foreign policy."[7] Executive Order 11652 of March 8, 1972,[8] advertised as an attempt to reduce the confidentiality sanctioned by its predecessor, classifies information concerning "national defense or the foreign relations of the United States" when disclosure would damage "national security." The Freedom of Information Act seems to contemplate less secrecy than the Administrative Procedure Act, since under the FOIA the subject must both Order 11652 is so broad, as drafted and interpreted, however, that this dual qualification is rendered essentially meaningless.

Failure to include citizens on advisory committees or on delegations

The Department of State and other foreign affairs agencies invite certain persons to advise on the making or implementation of policy through appointments to advisory committees and to negotiating delegations. Meetings or sessions of delegations are subject to no regulations and are always closed to the public. In the Federal Advisory Committee Act,[9] which became effective on January 5, 1973, the Congress stated the policy that "the public should be kept informed with respect to the . . . activities of advisory committees." The Act requires that membership of the advisory committees be "fairly balanced." Meetings and committee records are to be open to the public unless the committee is concerned with a matter listed in the exemption section of the FOIA—e.g., a matter specifically required by Executive Order to be kept secret in the interest of foreign policy. (Under Ex-

5. 42 U.S.C. §4321 et seq. (1970).
6. 5 U.S.C. §552 (1970).
7. Id. §552(b) (1) (1970).
8. 37 Fed. Reg. 5209 (1972).
9. Pub. L. No. 92-463, 86 Stat. 770.

276 SECRECY AND FOREIGN POLICY

ecutive Order 11671 of June 5, 1972[10]—predecessor to the Act—the criteria were essentially the same—that is, secrecy was permitted for matters "analogous" to the FOIA exceptions.) Certain public interests may be totally precluded from participating in these processes if the Government merely declines to appoint their representatives to the delegations or advisory committees, and then labels committee activities as involving the foreign affairs function.

The procedures mentioned above assume an increased significance in that foreign affairs decisions are often not subject to the ultimate safeguard: judicial review. The Supreme Court eschewed responsibility to adjudicate the legality of a Presidential grant of an international airline permit in 1948 in the oft-cited case, *Chicago and Southern Airlines* v. *Waterman,* by stating in sweeping language:

> It would be intolerable that courts, without the relevant information, should review and perhaps nullify actions of the Executive taken on information properly held secret. But even if the courts could require full disclosure, the very nature of executive decisions as to foreign policy is political, not judicial. . . . They are delicate, complex, and involve large amounts of prophecy. They are decisions of a kind for which the judiciary has neither aptitude, facilities nor responsibility and which has long been held to belong in the domain of political power not subject to judicial intrusion or inquiry.[11]

Later, in *Baker* v. *Carr,*[12] when the Supreme Court took the bold step of assuming jurisdiction over apportionment of electoral districts, it incidentally articulated a more balanced approach:

> Yet it is error to suppose that every case or controversy which touches on foreign relations lies beyond judicial cognizance. Our cases in this field seem invariably to show a discriminating analysis of the particular question posed . . . of its susceptibility to judicial handling. . . .[13]

By and large, while the courts have granted more deference to Executive Branch judgments relating to foreign affairs matters, they have not declined to scrutinize whether the Executive has followed statutorily prescribed procedures, for example in various trade laws.

THE STEEL QUOTA SYSTEM

Foreign policy world-wide is being increasingly influenced or determined by economics. As opposed to general or political foreign policy, economic de-

10. 37 Fed. Reg. 11307 (1972).
11. 333 U.S. 103, 111 (1948).
12. 369 U.S. 186 (1962).
13. *Id.* at 211.

cisions tend to have a direct, foreseeable impact on individuals and identifiable public segments—the industries involved, labor, the consumers. In the following trade-related cases, the decision-making process was closed to the most diffuse and politically impotent of these groups—consumers; and that secrecy is being challenged.

During the years between 1956 and 1967 various types of less expensive steel imports from modernized plants in Japan and Europe constituted a major source of competition to U.S. steel producers. Consumers, of course, were a beneficiary through lower prices. The domestic companies, saddled with lethargic management and archaic milling techniques, attempted to remove this thorn, not by effective modernization or aggressive marketing, but through pressure on the Congress to pass quota legislation, and on the Executive Branch to have restraints imposed in a quicker, more informal fashion. The Department of State, so it later claimed, made the independent judgment that sharply increased steel imports would have been undesirable in an industry of such importance to the over-all economy and to the national security. The Department was prepared to take measures to prevent injury to the domestic industry.

During 1967, while steel quota legislation was encountering sizable opposition, the Department of State undertook extensive discussions with representatives of the Japanese and European steel industries in the hope of reaching an understanding under which the foreign producers would limit their steel exports to the United States. At the same time, the Department consulted with domestic producers' representatives, conveying to them the foreign representatives' offers respecting voluntary restraints and obtaining their views, reactions, and concerns. The Department and the domestic industry discussed data on imports, domestic capacity, and the injury increased imports would cause to U.S. producers. As a result of these parallel discussions, representatives of Japanese and European producers ultimately in 1968 conveyed to the Secretary of State letters of intent, agreeing to restrain their steel exports to the United States through 1971 at given levels and specified annual growth rates.

The Department of State initiated similar meetings and discussions in 1971 to modify and to extend for three additional years the restraint agreements. In May 1972 the same foreign industries, joined by the British Steel Corporation, again signed letters of intent, this time agreeing to additional and more restrictive limitations.

Consumers Union, the largest consumer organization in the country and the publisher of *Consumer Reports,* had become concerned by 1971 about the adverse cost effects of this reduced marketing competition in the United States. During the three years of restraints, steel prices had increased five times as much as during the previous eight years. Steel is pervasive in the economy, with price rises affecting virtually every sector, either directly through cost push by raw materials, or indirectly through—for example—higher transportation costs.

Although the views of consumers had not been solicited by the Government, Consumers Union approached Department of State officials, expressed displeasure with the restraints, and presented arguments against concluding the new agreements. While the diplomats who were to negotiate the agreements listened courteously, they were unwilling to provide, either informally or in formal proceedings, the statistics or analyses behind their decision that limitations were necessary, or to be specific about the status or objectives of the negotiations.

The Department of State had never formally announced that it was investigating whether increased imports would adversely affect the domestic industry or that it was considering restraint arrangements. The Department had not made public the data on which it based its conclusion that domestic industry was entitled to protection. It did not call for written comments from interested persons or groups or hold a hearing. To be sure, the Department responded to general inquiries during open Congressional hearings; a smattering of facts became available by way of newspaper coverage, and Department officials did not refuse to meet with and listen to importers or—on one occasion—with consumers. But these sketchy newspaper accounts and *ex gratia,* informal chats with competing public interests were hardly comparable to the intimate collaboration and extensive exchanges of information with producers (including a meeting between the President and the industry), nor could they provide the safeguards inherent in traditional formal procedures.

Unable to convince the Department of State to remove this veil of secrecy or to have facts and views subjected to the test of formal proceedings, Consumers Union, on behalf of itself and its 350,000 members, commenced a lawsuit, *Consumers Union* v. *Rogers et al.,* in May 1972 in the Federal District Court in the District of Columbia, for the purpose of challenging the restraint arrangements.[14]

In essence the lawsuit rested on the simple principle that in foreign affairs the President does not have unlimited and unrestrained authority allowing him, in this case, to avoid all procedures. The Constitution explicitly provides that the Congress is to regulate foreign commerce, and grants the President no express authority in the area. The plaintiffs pointed out that, even if the President has inherent power to regulate foreign commerce emanating from vague Constitutional language, the enactment of both comprehensive trade laws and the Sherman Antitrust Act pre-empt his concurrent

---

14. Civil No. 1029-72 (D.D.C., decided January 8, 1973).

authority. Any restraint of trade, at least, would be subject to those laws. The President could, to be sure, act pursuant to legislation. For instance, section 352 of the Trade Expansion Act of 1962[15]–the "escape clause"– authorizes the negotiation of voluntary restraints to alleviate the type of injury complained of by the U.S. steel industry. But section 352 requires the Tariff Commission to conduct an investigation and determination of injury, with a record and hearings–a process allowing public participation on which the Department of State declined to embark.

The primary count in the suit charges the Secretary of State and Deputy Assistant Secretary for Economic Affairs (now, perhaps appropriately, changed to "Economic and Business Affairs") with acting in excess of their authority to regulate commerce, with violating section 352 of the Trade Expansion Act and Article I of the Constitution, and with depriving plaintiffs (and other interested parties) of the assurance in that statute that restraints could be adopted as policy only on the basis of specified criteria and in conformity with certain open procedures (or after the public process entailed in the passage of new legislation). The activities of the Department officials and the foreign and domestic steel producers are also claimed to be subject to, and in violation of, the Sherman Antitrust Act.

The Government attempted in this case, as it has in numerous others brought by public groups, to prevent an adjudication of the merits by alleging that Consumers Union had no standing to sue. The argument was that the relevant provisions of the Trade Expansion Act were designed to protect industries and labor and that while consumers are ultimately affected, they do not fall within the statute's "zone of interest." (We should note here that the public will often be forced to clear this initial hurdle of standing, since most laws are intended to benefit special interests.)

On January 8, 1973, the District Court handed down an unusual decision in the form of a declaratory judgment. The court first found that the plaintiffs had standing. With regard to the merits, Judge Gesell declared that

> the Executive has no authority under the Constitution or acts of Congress to exempt the Voluntary Restraint Arrangements on Steel from the antitrust laws and that such arrangements are not exempt.

The steel companies, fearful of treble damage actions under the antitrust laws, and the U.S. Government have both appealed.

On the other hand, the court indicated that the President possessed inherent power to negotiate with foreign companies and that this power had not been totally pre-empted by trade or other laws. Judge Gesell's reluctance to limit Executive power was expressed thus:

---

15. 18 U.S.C. §1982 (1965).

Obviously this litigation raises novel and difficult constitutional questions which have wide import. The Court recognizes that it will be well advised to avoid any decision that reaches beyond the specific dispute presented. Some observers note a gradual erosion of congressional authority in favor of the Executive, which is said to reflect the growing complexity of our society and widening involvement in foreign affairs. Others suggest the trend reflects stultifying inhibitions built into congressional processes and other factors. The courts have no general role in this shifting emphasis between competing branches of government. It is only when a distinct aspect of the struggle surfaces into a clearly justiciable controversy that a court must act. When this occurs, the Court should apply well-settled legal principles to the limited dispute presented, leaving ultimate solutions to our democratic processes.

While the District Court did not focus on the issue of secrecy, it was obviously hesitant to direct the President to follow specific, open procedures in the exercise of his inherent authority. The decision notwithstanding, the question persists: Should the Government be permitted to make this kind of economic policy, which may ultimately bear on foreign negotiations and trade, in the back room behind doors open to U.S. producers but closed to consumers and other interested public segments? The following factors lead to a negative conclusion.

The traditional excuses for the foreign affairs exemption simply do not apply. The relevant issues and facts (injury to a domestic industry or labor force, and the causes thereof) would not contain sensitive communications from foreign governments. Speed was not a prerequisite; no particular time frame existed, and each set of negotiations ultimately took more than a year in 1967–68 and in 1971–72. The Department of State had no more expertise than the Tariff Commission—or, indeed, than private economists—at evaluating the cause of injury to the industry or the legitimacy of its cry for protection. And unity of purpose would hardly be necessary before negotiations began. The issues in similar cases had been subjected to formal analysis time and time again during investigations and hearings under the Trade Expansion Act and its predecessors. In sum, the economic decisions preceding the ultimate determination to negotiate the steel restraint arrangements did not, in the terms of *Curtiss-Wright,* require "secrecy and dispatch" or involve a "vast external realm, with its important, complicated, delicate and manifold problems."[16]

The Administrative Procedure Act does not imply a contrary Congressional will. According to Senate and House Committee reports, the "foreign affairs function" exemption of that Act was never intended to "be loosely interpreted to mean any function extending beyond the borders of

---

16. 229 U.S. at 319-20.

the United States but only those 'affairs' which so affect relations with other governments that, for example, public rule making provisions would clearly provoke definitely undesirable international consequences."[17] The U.S. Government negotiated the steel restraint arrangements with foreign companies, not with foreign governments. Relations with those governments could, no doubt, be effected; yet presumably such rule-making procedures prior to the restraint negotiations would create no more undesirable international consequences than those resulting from section 352 procedures.

Indeed, the Congress has shown a constant and definitive predilection for openness with regard to trade decisions. The various trade laws permitting the Executive to impose trade barriers require in almost every instance that threshold decisions be made only after public, sometimes elaborate, procedures. Various combinations of investigations, determinations, review of comments, and hearings are prescribed. The 1934 Trade Agreements Act, a cornerstone of modern trade laws, included a provision that:

> Before any foreign trade agreement is concluded with any foreign government or instrumentality thereof under the provisions of the Act, reasonable public notice of the intention to negotiate an agreement with such government or instrumentality shall be given in order that any interested person may have the opportunity to present his views to the President, or to such agency as the President may designate, under such rules and regulations as the President may prescribe. . . .[18]

This philosophy has carried over to the Trade Expansion Act of 1962, which exacts open hearings before any product may be added to the tariff list, any concession granted, or any retaliation taken against a foreign country. Even when import adjustments are necessitated by national security, an investigation and determination must be made and a public report published under the "national security provision"—section 232 of the Trade Expansion Act.[19] In the agricultural field, for example, under section 22 of the Agricultural Adjustment Act of 1933,[20] the President can restrain imports that render domestic programs ineffective—but only after a determination by the Secretary of Agriculture and an investigation by the Tariff Commission, including a hearing.

The Government, as defendant, argued that disclosure and procedural safeguards were not a prerequisite to the steel negotiations. This has far-reaching implications. In a brief accompanying a motion to dismiss, it was contended that the President has implied inherent Constitutional authority

---

17. S. Doc. No. 248, 79th Cong., 2nd sess. 199 (1946).
18. Ch. 474, §4, 48 Stat. 945.
19. 19 U.S.C. §1862 (1965).
20. 7 U.S.C. §624 (1964).

to regulate foreign commerce; that this authority was not infringed when the Congress exercised its concurrent authority to establish a trade regime requiring safeguards or antitrust laws, since an explicit prohibition to Executive action was not included; and that the Executive need not follow any procedures when exercising its inherent foreign-commerce power. Apparently in any matter that can somehow be clothed in a foreign affairs cloak, the Executive will assert "inherent" authority that may be exercised with unrestrained secrecy, regardless of what the Congress may have said.

This conclusion is even more disturbing in the light of the alternatives considered by the Government and its motives for following the route of voluntary restraint negotiations outside the purview of a statute. In an affidavit submitted to the court, the Department of State professed that a solution to the steel problem was needed because of national security, but in the same breath rejected the use of section 232 of the Trade Expansion Act on the grounds that the provision was "inappropriate" when national security was only one reason for action, and that its use forebode "broad implications for our trade policy." Under section 352 the President could impose voluntary restraints only if injury was caused in major part by trade concessions. The State Department, however, took upon itself, without hearing opposing views, to decide that the alleged injuries were caused principally by excess U.S. capacity, improved foreign technology, and cheaper foreign labor (as opposed, for example, to domestic mismanagement), and as such were due only in part to concessions. Finally, the Department was concerned that the legislative process—the will of Congress expressed after open hearings—might not result in a law containing those precise restraints the Department considered sound, and might afford other domestic industries, excluded from the Department's processes, the opportunity to seek similar quotas on the import of competing products.

Such analysis aside, should the President be able to formulate trade policy unimpeded by checks and balances? In 1929 Secretary of State Cordell Hull, then a member of the House of Representatives, commented as follows on President Hoover's request for broad authority to fashion trade restraints without procedural safeguards: "That was too much power for a bad man to have or for a good man to want."[21]

OIL IMPORT PROGRAM

For the last thirteen years the import of oil into the United States has been limited by this country's most fully developed quota scheme, the Mandatory

---

21. Reported in *Hearings* on Reciprocal Trade Agreements, Before the Senate Committee on Finance, 73d Cong., 2nd sess., at 9 (1934).

Oil Import Program. The program was promulgated pursuant to section 8 of the Trade Agreements Extension Act of 1958, precursor to section 232 of the Trade Expansion Act of 1962. Section 8 provision stipulates that import restraints may be imposed for national security reasons. As noted above, however, specific procedures are spelled out in the statute, and the Director of the Office of Emergency Preparedness must conduct an investigation to determine the effects on national security of imports of the article in question. If he determines that the import threatens to impair the national security, he must so inform the President; and the President, if he concurs in that judgment, may "adjust" the imports. The statute requires that a report be made and published on the disposition of each request for an adjustment. The Director must publish procedural regulations, and the regulations now in effect provide for hearings.

In 1959 President Eisenhower, acting on the basis of a determination by the Director and the recommendation of a government-business advisory committee, found that oil imports threatened to impair the national security, and set quotas through the issuance of a Proclamation. The theory was that unrestrained imports of inexpensive oil would reduce domestic exploration and exploitation, thus making the country ultimately dependent on foreign sources that might be cut off in an emergency. As it turned out, the program has caused the national security threat it allegedly was created to avoid, by encouraging protected domestic exploiters to deplete limited U.S. resources and making the nation more dependent on foreign production.

The President and Attorney General were at that time quite properly concerned about the inflationary pressures that might attend oil controls. Consequently, the Presidential Proclamation contained a requirement that the Director of the Office of Emergency Preparedness maintain constant surveillance and, in particular, make a determination as to whether each price increase of oil or oil products, by an industry now relieved of serious competition, is "necessary to accomplish the national security objectives of the Act" and Proclamation.

The oil import program forces consumers to purchase products derived from high-priced domestic oil rather than from oil at lower world-market prices. According to the Government, the program cost consumers $5.26 billion in 1969.[22] According to a Presidentially appointed Cabinet Task Force that studied the program comprehensively, the cost will rise to $8.4 billion by 1980.[23] And yet the implementation of the program was a process closed to the public though open to the oil industry. This is how it operated.

22. "The Oil Import Question," A Report on the Relationship of Oil Imports to the National Security, by the Cabinet Task Force on Oil Import Control, February 1970, at 26.
23. *Id.*

When instituting changes in the program, the Government would discuss proposals with industry, but would not comply with TEA section 232 requirements, nor follow the Administrative Procedure Act, nor conduct public rule-makings, nor disclose the basis for decisions except in the most general terms. It avoided the Act by turning upside down the usual progression of agency decision-making. The agency should have conducted open proceedings under the Administrative Procedure Act and then forward the result to the President for final decision. Instead, the President (who is thought to be exempted from the Act) would amend the Proclamation, without the benefit of public advice. Insignificant implementing regulations might or might not be published in the Federal Register for comment, but, either way, the submission of consumers' views on these would be irrelevant, since the critical decisions had already been predetermined by the original, covert recommendation to the President, and his action on that recommendation.

As a case in point, there had always been some question as to whether oil imports from Canada could be said to threaten national security. Canada, after all, is an ally, and transport of oil by pipeline to the United States is less subject to physical disruption by hostile forces than tanker transport from the Virgin Islands or Alaska. Between 1959 and 1967 imports from Canada were not restrained, the President having found that the national security did not necessitate quotas. Between 1967 and 1970 imports were restrained by a secret (and probably illegal) intergovernmental agreement between the Department of State and the Government of Canada. Section 232 procedures were avoided, and the State Department did not even comply with its own internal regulations when seeking the Secretary of State's approval to negotiate; the agreement's very existence was not admitted. It was finally discarded as a consequence of inquiries from the Congress and legal challenge by a U.S. importer to the administration of the agreement.

In 1970 for the first time a quota under the oil import program was placed upon Canadian imports into the eastern part of the United States. When questioned by the Congress, the Director of the Office of Emergency Preparedness admitted that a national security finding had not been made and that the requirements of the Administrative Procedure Act had been neglected—but excused this on the ground that foreign affairs was involved and an emergency situation existed. This imperviousness to safeguards was not uncommon in the program's administration and was not reserved to emergencies. The above-mentioned Cabinet Task Force revealed that on many occasions regulations had been issued without prior public notice or opportunity to comment, and warned that the APA standards "should be more nearly adhered to in the future."

No wonder, given the way the law was being implemented, that the Governors of the New England States—an area on which the program has an especially severe impact—had constantly failed in their petitions to the Federal Government for increased imports to meet demand and reduce prices.

In April 1972 a lawsuit challenging the oil import program, *New England Governors Conference et al.* v. *Morton et al.*,[24] was filed in the Federal District Court in Maine by the New England Governors and their states, Consumers Union, and Public Citizen, an organization founded by Ralph Nader. The complaint contends that the oil program violates the Constitution and section 232 of the Trade Expansion Act by establishing separate and discriminating quota systems for two parts of the country, and violates the statute by allocating imports and regulating marketing within the United States without authorization. It also points to the procedural irregularities that inhibit plaintiffs' rights to an open process. One count maintains that quotas on oil imports from Canada violate section 232 since the required finding on national security, preceded by an investigation with public participation, was omitted. Failure of the Director to make price determinations, with public participation, was claimed to violate the Proclamation.

The Government, in submissions to the court, provides an interesting insight into its conception of its procedural responsibilities. In response to this last contention on price determinations, the Director has stated in answers to interrogatories that he has, indeed, made such determinations, but that they were not made in writing, that no record was kept of price increases studied or of the determinations or their conclusions, and that no estimate of their number or dates could be made. The defendants contend that neither the national security nor the price determinations need be documented, let alone released to the public.

In April 1973, a year after the suit was filed and just before a court decision was expected, the President issued Presidential Proclamation 4210, which substantially modified the oil import program. Import quotas were eliminated; thus, the plaintiffs achieved one of their major objectives. The new program was promulgated without the public investigation required by section 232; its development involved intimate collaboration with industry, but virtually no contact with the plaintiffs or other consumers. Certain aspects of the program will permit increased consumer prices, added concentration in the oil industry, and higher profits in the major oil companies. Whether or not the consumers will challenge these aspects remains to be seen.

TEXTILE POLICY

One of the few trade laws that empower the Executive Branch to negotiate restraint agreements without expressly providing for pre-negotiation public

---

24. Civil No. 13-59 (D. Me., filed April 27, 1972).

procedures is section 204 of the Agricultural Act of 1956.[25] That statute authorizes the President, "whenever he determines such action appropriate," to negotiate with foreign governments agreements limiting the export from such countries into the United States of textiles or other agricultural products.

Pursuant to this law, the President in 1962 negotiated a multilateral Long Term Arrangement Regarding International Trade in Cotton Textiles[26] to which thirty other governments are now signatory. Articles 3 and 6 of that agreement authorize unilateral action by a party to limit imports of textiles "causing or threatening to cause market disruption"; and the United States has taken such unilateral action numerous times. In addition the United States has negotiated thirty bilateral cotton textile agreements and five bilateral agreements on wool and man-made fiber textile products, pursuant to section 204. The President, in Executive Order 11651, has assigned to the Committee for the Implementation of Textile Agreements (CITA) the responsibility to take action under section 204 and the Long Term Arrangement. CITA consists of representatives of the Departments of State, the Treasury, Commerce, and Labor, and is chaired by Commerce.

Section 204, unlike most trade laws, neglects reference to safeguards. Consequently, whether any open implementation process is effected will depend on whether the implementors apply safeguard provisions of statutes that relate in general to procedures, information, and advisory committees.

Formulating textile policy is a somewhat complex process that includes a decision as to whether market disruption (and how much) has occurred, and if so, whether to seek quotas, either bilaterally or unilaterally. According to the Long Term Arrangement, market disruption contains such elements as a substantial increase in imports of particular products from particular sources; offering of imports at prices substantially lower than prices for similar goods in the importing country; serious damage to producers of domestic goods or threat thereof; and price differentials that are not the result of governmental intervention or dumping. Determinations of import prices and injury to domestic industry at least involve no foreign affairs considerations, and such determinations are of course subject to procedural safeguards under different restraint provisions of the Trade Expansion Act.

Yet, neither the Department of Commerce, the Department of State, nor CITA has followed any rule-making procedures in reaching decisions connected with those matters. The Committee has determined that all actions—even determinations of injury—relating to the imposition of unilateral restraints or the negotiation of bilateral agreements "involve" the foreign af-

---

25. 7 U.S.C. §1854 (1964).
26. October 1, 1962, 13 U.S.T. 2672, T.I.A.S. No. 5240.

fairs function and are therefore exempted from the rule-making provisions of the Administrative Procedure Act.

One principal focus of the textile decision-making process has been the Management-Labor Textile Advisory Committee. This Committee was established by Executive Order in 1962 and is composed of forty or so representatives of producers and labor (including, until his appointment as Secretary of Commerce, Frederick Dent, formerly President of Mayfair Mills). The Committee meets regularly to provide advice and information to the Government on conditions in the textile industry and on trade in textiles and apparel.

As noted before, under Executive Order 11671, advisory committee meetings had to be open to the public, unless the meeting was concerned with matters "analogous" to an excepted category in the FOIA, e.g., specifically required by Executive Order to be kept secret in the interest of foreign policy. Yet even though the Executive Order had been promulgated two months earlier, in August 1972, the advisory committee met secretly, shutting out the public and the press as was its wont. No announcement of the meeting was made, although the order required such notice. An official at the Office of Management and Budget stated to the press that the Department of Commerce's Office of Textiles had "just ignored" and violated the Executive Order.

In September 1972 the Department of Commerce announced that the public-participation provisions of the Executive Order would be inapplicable to another committee session because of the foreign policy exemption. Counsel representing consumers protested the closed meeting and asked the Department for the requisite detailed statement of reasons. Although the Department of Commerce would not open the meeting to the consumer counsel or to the public, the Secretary of Commerce's statement was released and provides as follows:

> In the development of the Government's negotiating position for these [possible bilateral textile] agreements it is essential that the Government understand conditions in the domestic industry since the objective of these agreements is to avoid disruption to the domestic textile market. The Government receives from members of the Committee sensitive information which they receive from various sources on the attitude of foreign governments in the negotiations which the Government is undertaking. The Government discusses with the members of the Committee possible negotiating positions as to specific levels of restraint in order to receive their evaluation of the effect of such proposed levels on the domestic industry. The development of negotiating positions and certain sensitive aspects in the implementation of some of the agreements are scheduled to be discussed at the September 7 meeting. If the meeting were open to the public, the foreign policy interest of the

United States Government would be substantially compromised. It would not be possible to have the kind of candid discussion that has existed at meetings of this Committee over the last decade. Public participation at the meeting would reduce its effectiveness to the point where it would be meaningless to hold the meeting.[27]

Although it invokes the so-called "foreign policy exemption," the Secretary's memorandum does not indicate that any of the matters to be discussed at the meeting are matters "specifically required by executive order to be kept secret in the interest of national defense or foreign policy"—the only permissible justification for the foreign policy exemption under the Freedom of Information Act; and none of the matters mentioned by the Secretary falls within this rubric. To the extent that industry members may reveal information they receive on the attitude of foreign Governments regarding United States trade negotiations, serious questions arise concerning the unauthorized participation of private individuals in what is properly an intergovernmental process.

Furthermore, the information, if initially communicated to private parties, is clearly not so "sensitive" as to preclude its revelation to representatives of concerned consumer or public groups when, at the same time, it is being revealed to forty-odd representatives of labor and management with presumably diverse interests. Similarly, evaluations of the potential effect on industry of possible levels of restraint relate to general domestic industrial conditions, not to the subject of the "foreign policy exemption," and, if again revealed to all members of the Committee, not matters that can even be characterized as "privileged or confidential commercial or financial information"—another possible exception to the general rule of free access to information. Finally, incidental effects on candor or effectiveness of committee meetings—effects that the Secretary of Commerce may consider undesirable—clearly cannot justify non-compliance with the law.

Despite repeated petitions for openness by counsel for consumers, the Department of Commerce continued the policy of *in camera* meetings and declined to make public the records of the meetings and memoranda discussed, or to provide them to consumer representatives on a restricted basis. The same language cited above, apparently window-dressing, has been presented as justification in later determinations by the Secretary.

As all administrative remedies have been exhausted by the consumer groups, further closed sessions of the Labor-Management Textile Advisory Committee are being challenged in court on the grounds that such sessions

---

27. U.S., Department of Commerce, Internal Memorandum of Secretary of Commerce Peterson, "Exemption of the Management-Labor Textile Advisory Committee from the Public Participation and Record Keeping Requirements of Executive Order 11671," August 31, 1972.

violate the Federal Advisory Committee Act.[28] All denials of relevant data, including records of meetings, are being contested as contrary to the Freedom of Information Act. And the decision-making process regarding market disruption as a prelude to possible action under the Long Term Arrangement is being challenged as a violation of the rule-making provisions of the Administrative Procedure Act, inasmuch as the decisions are not accompanied by administrative proceedings. The courts are being asked to hold that wholly domestic decisions—e.g., whether injury has occurred—resolved by a committee chaired by a domestic agency are not exempt from the above laws.

Shortly after the law suit relating to the Federal Advisory Committee Act and the Freedom of Information Act was filed, the Government indicated a willingness to settle. The Department of Commerce has agreed to make the advisory committee open to the public and to provide plaintiffs with its market disruption criteria, and plaintiffs have agreed to dismiss the suit.

Another inequity—and one that is more difficult to question judicially—is the habit of the Departments of State and Commerce to include industry advisers on delegations negotiating restraint agreements. This practice is neither unique in history nor unique to the textitle area. During the early days of Athenian democracy, diplomatic missions were composed of several persons representing different parties and points of view: the Greeks were suspicious of diplomats. The Department of State conducts dozens of negotiations annually, and interested industry representatives—but not persons reflecting other viewpoints—are often asked to join the delegation.

For example, during the late 1960's and early 1970's the Department of State negotiated several conventions involving oil or other marine pollution, most often before the Inter-Governmental Maritime Consultative Organization, a United Nations specialized agency. These matters were of evident concern to the oil and tanker industries, but were no less so to environmental organizations. Yet when representatives of the industries were dutifully asked to serve on virtually each delegation, environmental representatives were never given that opportunity.

Finally, during a conference in late 1971 to conclude an accord on a compensation fund for oil pollution damage, several environmental groups formally protested the inclusion of persons representing the industries on the delegation. The petition argued that these persons would be privy to official instructions, would be able to influence on-the-spot decisions at the conference, and would engage in lobbying with foreign delegates and other activities calculated to promote their special interest. The groups contended that this involvement was improper, and demanded that either industry

---

28. Consumers Union v. Dent, Civil No. 133-73 (D.D.C., filed January 22, 1973).

representatives be removed from the delegation or other public segments added. The Department ultimately responded by excluding industry participation on the delegation, but also by affirming its right to include persons associated with affected industries in the future.

The chairman of the Council on Environmental Quality later proclaimed a more balanced attitude—that environmental groups should be permitted to participate in conferences considering the environment. But he has implemented his promise by inviting environmentalists to join delegations that do not grapple with hard problems (such, e.g., as a team attending a 1972 social meeting with the Soviets—a meeting that negotiated nothing), and by excluding them from meetings focusing on domestically controversial issues (e.g., the conference to conclude an ocean-dump convention).

In the economic area the Government has never indicated any willingness to balance industry participation with consumer representatives. In seeking to compel their inclusion in important negotiations, these consumer groups are up against the problem that the composition of negotiating terms may seem to the courts to be close to the heart of the foreign affairs function, and public segments unfairly excluded may therefore not be able to utilize judicial redress.

DOMESTIC OR FOREIGN AFFAIRS?

During the early days of the Republic and the nineteenth century, foreign countries were far away in more ways than one. Foreign affairs assumed a cachet of mysticism. Diplomats, not the citizenry, spoke foreign languages and dealt with aliens. That situation engendered an Executive Branch predilection—reinforced by the laxity of a Congress, and courts apparently more comfortable with domestic issues—for playing diplomacy close to the chest.

Technological advances in transportation and communications have metamorphized our relations with foreign countries. Americans have access to massive amounts of timely information and can visually monitor the world stage. No longer are such areas the private domain of diplomats. Indeed, the State Department's traditional diplomat is fast becoming an endangered species, inexorably losing ground to the domestic-oriented agencies because the internal impact of these issues is being seen in government, and out, to be more important than their foreign consequences.

While more public groups are now equipped to participate in the decision-making process, the Government seems even more inward and arcane. Instead of using their normal rule-making procedures for their new duties, domestic agencies such as the Department of Commerce borrow habits of secrecy from the Department of State. The Department of State, in its publication *Our Foreign Policy,* has declared that there is "no longer any real distinction between 'domestic' and 'foreign affairs.' "[29] Almost all issues today have a transnational component, and the Government finds it convenient, when evaluating its administrative responsibilities, to let that tail wag the dog.

Yet even so, statutes bearing on matters susceptible to standards often specify procedures, and the courts, it is hoped, will require reasonable compliance. The foreign affairs exemption in the general procedure, as well as the disclosure statutes, should be appropriately narrowed to fall in line with the original intent of the Congress: to be applicable only when truly needed, not merely because foreign affairs is implicated. And, the more often public groups challenge unreasonably secretive foreign affairs decision-making, the sooner that exemption will be placed by the courts in proper perspective.

---

29. U.S., Department of State, General Foreign Policy Series 26, Department of State Publication 3972, September 1950 at 4.

17

The Ellsberg Case:
Citizen Disclosure

LEONARD B. BOUDIN

INTRODUCTION

The Ellsberg case was the first criminal prosecution in American history for disclosure to the American public of information classified as secret by the U.S. Government. It is the criminal analogue of the Government's injunction suit against *The New York Times* to prevent it from publishing excerpts from the Pentagon Papers[1] and an attempt to incorporate into American law the doctrines of the British Official Secrets Act, which Lord Franks' committee has proposed amending.[2] (This Report is discussed in Chapters 18, 19, and 20 of this book.)

The factual background of the case is not seriously disputed. The Department of Defense of the United States retained a number of experts and researchers in and out of the Government to study the Government's decision-making process in the Vietnam War. The result was a forty-seven-volume study entitled *United States-Vietnam Relations 1945–1967,* popularly known as the Pentagon Papers. Marked "Top Secret" under the Government's classification system, it was distributed in early 1969 to a number of former government officials and to the Rand Corporation, a privately owned think-tank originally working primarily for the Air Force and based in

Mr. Boudin, General Counsel to the National Emergency Civil Liberties Committee, has been counsel in the conspiracy trials of Benjamin Spock, Eqbal Ahmed, and Daniel Ellsberg, and was Visiting Professor of Law at Harvard Law School 1970-71. He is presently Senior Fellow at the Center for Criminal Justice, Harvard Law School, and is a frequent contributor to legal journals.
1. New York Times Company v. United States, 403 U.S. 713 (1971).
2. United Kingdom, Home Office, Departmental Committee on Section 2 of the Official Secrets Acts 1911, Cmnd. 5104, September 1972, vol. 1; commonly referred to as the Franks Report. See also Jonathan Aitken, *Officially Secret* (London: Weidenfeld and Nicolson, 1971).

Santa Monica, California. When parts of it were published in *The New York Times* and other newspapers, the Government sought unsuccessfully to enjoin its further publication. Literally upon the eve of the Supreme Court hearing of the *Times* case, the Justice Department filed a criminal complaint against Dr. Daniel Ellsberg, a former Rand staff member, charging violations of the laws on espionage and theft of Government property. There followed an indictment by a Federal grand jury charging Dr. Ellsberg and Mr. Anthony Joseph Russo, Jr. (another former Rand employee) with having conspired with others to violate three sets of Federal statutes claimed to protect the Government against the release of the Pentagon Papers.

The first charge was that of conspiracy to defraud the United States of a claimed governmental function—the non-disclosure of *classified* information; the second was a violation of the Espionage Laws which make it a crime to retain or transfer to unauthorized persons material relating to the *national defense;* the third was the stealing of *government property* (although it is not clear whether the Government regarded the information or documents as property).[3] Strangely, none of these charges was keyed to the publication of the Papers in *The New York Times* or other newspapers, since the indictment period ended eight months prior to their publication in those papers. Instead, the Government relied upon earlier events, principally the Xeroxing of the Pentagon Papers outside the Rand property. The charges were brought primarily under three provisions of the U.S. Code: 18 U.S.C. 371, 18 U.S.C. 641, and 18 U.S.C. 793.

A MORE DETAILED VIEW OF THE INDICTMENT

It may be of some value to discuss more specifically the allegations of the indictments in the Ellsberg case. The first, filed two days before the Supreme Court's decision in the *New York Times Company* v. *United States* case, was a rather simple two-count indictment. Count 1 charged a violation of the Espionage Laws, 18 U.S.C. §793(e), in that in September and October 1969 Dr. Ellsberg, having "unauthorized possession" of Xerox copies of the Pentagon Papers, unlawfully retained them and failed to deliver them "to the officer or employee of the United States entitled to receive them." Count 2 charged a violation of the Theft of Government Property Statute, 18 U.S.C. §641, in that he "converted" to his own use the study described as "being things of value of the United States."

Again, upon the eve of an important event, the argument of pre-trial mo-

---

3. The Government's bill of particulars named both information and documents as the subject of the theft.

tions, the Government in December 1971 filed a 15-count superseding indictment. Mr. Anthony Joseph Russo, Jr., was named as co-defendant. Two other persons, Mr. Vu Van Thai, former South Vietnamese Ambassador to the United States, and Miss Lynda Sinay were named unindicted co-conspirators. The first count of the indictment alleged conspiracy among these four persons, first, to defraud the United States and, second, to commit offenses against it.

The conspiracy to defraud the United States is the most interesting part of the indictment, for it alleges that the defendants conspired "to defraud the United States . . . by impairing . . . its lawful governmental function of controlling the dissemination of classified government studies." This charge is not based upon the fact either that the studies involved national defense (counts 8-15), or that it necessarily involved property of the U.S. Government (counts 2-7).

The second part of the conspiracy charge described the offenses (subsequently set forth in substantive counts) as involving the conversion, receipt, concealment and retention of "classified government studies" in violation of 18 U.S.C. §641 and the receipt, transmittal, retention, and failure to deliver to the Government, documents "relating to the national defense" in violation of 18 U.S.C. §793(c) (d). Ellsberg was charged with eleven substantive crimes, Russo with three.

THE FACTUAL BASIS FOR THE GOVERNMENT'S CASE

It is well known, even judicially recognized,[4] that by 1967 there was considerable division inside the Government, as well as outside it, over the Vietnam War. In June 1967 Secretary of Defense Robert S. McNamara commissioned a history of U.S. involvement in Vietnam. He wanted the important documents assembled and a narrative written so that those who came after him could assess the history of Vietnam and perhaps avoid repeating its mistakes.

Dr. Morton S. Halperin, a former Harvard professor then serving as a Deputy Assistant Secretary of Defense, was placed in charge of the project; under him was a task force headed by Dr. Leslie Gelb, also a former teacher at Harvard and Wesleyan, but at the time working in the Defense Department. A team was assembled to write the narrative, and it included a number of military officers on active duty, together with researchers and scholars both from government research centers and from universities. Several of the participants were drawn from Rand Corporation, among them

---

4. United States v. Spock, 416 F. 2d 165 (1st cir. 1969); United States v. Dellinger, 41 L.W. 2283 (7th cir. 1972) (Sept. term 1971, No. 18295, Nov. 21, 1972).

Dr. Daniel Ellsberg, who had had a long history of employment by Rand as well as by the Department of Defense, where he had been Special Assistant to the Assistant Secretary for International Security Affairs working on high-level Vietnam policy; he had also been Special Assistant to the Deputy Ambassador in Vietnam and a Marine officer.

The history was written over a period of a year and one-half, during which time President Johnson moved Mr. McNamara to the presidency of the World Bank and appointed Clark Clifford in his place. Clifford in turn designated Paul Warnke to be in charge of the history, and Halperin and Gelb worked under him.

By January 1969, when the Johnson Administration came to an end, officials throughout the Government were gathering together their private or personal papers connected with their service, including copies of studies and memoranda produced either by them or under their supervision. The best-known example, of course, is President Johnson, who removed tons of material to the Johnson Library in Texas. Messrs. Warnke, Halperin, and Gelb, in collecting their private papers, decided to include Xerox copies of the thirty-eight volumes—of what became a forty-seven-volume history—still in typescript at the time. The Rand Corporation agreed to store these private papers in an arrangement that gave Warnke, Halperin, and Gelb control of access to them, and they were deposited in a private safe in the Rand Washington office.

Rand next commissioned Ellsberg to do a study for the Defense Department on the lessons of Vietnam, and to this end obtained approval from Warnke, Gelb, and Halperin for Ellsberg to take the documents to Rand's Santa Monica office and to read them. Ellsberg received ten volumes in March of 1969, and eight in August of 1969, and carried them to Rand's Santa Monica headquarters, where they were placed in a special safe installed by Rand in Ellsberg's office. Ellsberg read the volumes, which covered events classified and concealed from the public although they were in some instances twenty-five years old. Thus, Volume I was entitled *Vietnam and the United States 1940–1950*. Volume VIc involved negotiations between the United States and North Vietnam.

When Ellsberg completed his reading in September 1969, he concluded that the volumes unfolded a record of duplicity by Executive Branch officials and a story that, if read by others, would help them understand that the United States must get out of Vietnam and avoid future Vietnams. Believing that it was in the interest of the United States that the Congress and the public know the history, he decided that the material should be given to Senator J. W. Fulbright, Chairman of the Senate Foreign Relations Committee, and through him to the Congress and the American public.

In order to do this, Ellsberg and Russo proceeded to Xerox some of these documents. Mr. Russo in his capacity as a Rand staff member had conducted investigations in Vietnam and thus was aware of the existence of the study. He procured the facilities of a Xerox machine at the advertising office of Lynda Sinay (later named a co-conspirator), and a number of the volumes were copied by the defendants and Miss Sinay. Vu Van Thai, a former South Vietnamese Ambassador to the United States, was also named co-conspirator solely because his fingerprints were found on certain volumes of the study.

Dr. Ellsberg transmitted this material to Senator Fulbright and made parts of it available to other members of the Congress. Senator Fulbright was apparently unwilling to disclose the particular materials he had received —a reasonably cautious approach in view of the subsequent indictment of Ellsberg. Instead, he wrote repeatedly to Secretary of Defense Laird, requesting that the full report be made available to him; all of these requests were rejected.[5] With the Congressional avenue thus blocked, the only possibility of widespread disclosure was through the press. *The New York Times* received a copy of these papers and proceeded to publish them, as did other newspapers—a course of action that led to the Supreme Court's decision in the *New York Times Company* v. *United States* case, described in Professor Schmidt's chapter in this volume.

While that case was not a criminal case and was decided upon the basis of the First Amendment's proscription on prior restraint, the Government did claim that *The New York Times* and the other newspapers had violated the Espionage Laws (not the Theft of Government Property or Conspiracy to Defraud Laws). Some members of the Court proceeded also to interpret 18 U.S.C. §793 in a manner obviously prejudicial to Ellsberg's subsequent criminal case.[6] This was unfortunate, particularly since the Court was aware of the fact that Ellsberg had been indicted and since neither counsel for the Government nor counsel for the newspapers had made a thorough study of the Espionage Laws or the other statutes involved in the Ellsberg criminal litigation.

Dr. Ellsberg was not indicted for having disclosed the materials to *The New York Times;* if he had been, it might have raised a question as to why the Government had decided not to proceed criminally against the *Times.* Instead, the Government's indictment in the Russo-Ellsberg case covers a period from March 1, 1969, to September 30, 1970, and its case was based upon the theory that when Ellsberg obtained the ten volumes of the mate-

---

5. See U.S., Senate, 92d Cong., 2d sess., *Hearings,* Senate Judiciary Committee, Hearings, July and August 1971, "Executive Privilege: The Withholding of Information by the Executive," pp. 37–47.
6. See, e.g., 403 U.S. 713 at 736–37 (White, J., concurring). See also Branzburg v. Hayes, 408 U.S. 665 at 691 (1972).

rials from Rand's Washington office with the approval of the Department of Defense and of Rand, he did so pursuant to a conspiracy with Russo, Vu Van Thai, and Sinay to defraud the United States and to violate the laws on espionage and theft of government property. The Government claims were based upon the failure of Ellsberg to deposit the materials in the Rand Security System, the removal of the materials from Rand overnight, the Xeroxing of the materials, and the fact that Miss Sinay had a copy of one of the volumes in her possession while doing the duplicating, and by the fact that Vu Van Thai may have looked at some of the pages (since his fingerprints were found on it).

The indictment refers also to two other documents: one a study of the 1954 Geneva Conference, and eight pages of a memorandum of February 27, 1968—a report by General Earle Wheeler, then chairman of the Joint Chiefs of Staff. These additional documents are quite subsidiary to the Pentagon Papers study, and will not be referred to specifically in this chapter.

THE ESPIONAGE LAWS

In Chapter 11 Professor Benno Schmidt has analyzed the state of the U.S. Espionage Statutes as they pertain to journalists and newspapers. The attempted use of these laws to punish the revelations of "national defense" information by an individual like Ellsberg brings us, in a different situation, to examine the data in the light of: statutory language,[7] legislative history,[8] judicial and administrative implementation,[9] Constitutional problems,[10] the British Official Secrets Act[11] and the U.S. Congress disapproval of that Act.[12]

The British Act, which was first passed in 1889, penalizes revelations of any "official" information regardless of its relevance to national defense. Criminal intent is presumed from the fact of revelation. Neither of these is characteristic of the American Espionage Act of 1911, which was intended "to protect the nation against spying in wartime,"[13] was limited to "national defense," and whose draftsmen viewed the presumption of criminal intent as "not fair."[14]

In 1917 the Justice Department, concluding that the 1911 Act was "in-

---

7. F. Frankfurter, *Some Reflections on the Reading of Statutes* (New York: The Association of the Bar of the City of New York, 1947).
8. *Ex parte* Collett, 337 U.S. 55 (1949).
9. United States v. Laub, 385 U.S. 475 (1967).
10. United States v. Rumely, 345 U.S. 41 (1953).
11. 1 and 2 Geo. V, c. 28.
12. See, e.g., comments of Congressman Parker during the debates over the 1911 Espionage Act, 46 *Congressional Record* 2030 (1911).
13. U.S., House of Representatives, 1942, 61st Cong., 3d sess. 2 (1911).
14. See Note 12, *supra*.

complete and defective," proposed new legislation.[15] The Congress, however, was concerned about the dangers to the Republic of secrecy and censorship of issues of major national importance, about the evils of vagueness
and overbreadth[16] inherent in the proposed bill, and about the potential
for Executive abuse in the broad delegations of authority sought for the
Executive Branch. The debate placed special emphasis upon the public's
right to know the truth about the vital national issues.[17] As a result, Congress included an explicit specific-intent requirement which read: "whoever,
for the purpose of obtaining information respecting the national defense
with intent or reason to believe that the information is to be used to the injury of the United States, or to the advantage of any foreign nation, goes
upon. . . ."[18] While other provisions of the statute did not repeat the
phrase *in haec verba,* the use of the word "willfully" suggests that the Congress intended to impose the requirement of bad purpose, evil or criminal
intent, or reckless disregard of the best interests of the United States.[19]
Hence it is not surprising that Assistant General Counsel Miskovsky of
the CIA wrote in 1961:

> While inadequacy of the 1911 Act was said to be the basis of changes sought
> in 1917, espionage provisions of the statute enacted by the 65th Congress, as
> it turned out, were made less effective for the protection of national defense
> information than the provisions of the 1911 Act.[20]

This view of 18 U.S.C. §793, the Espionage Act provisions, is supported
by the construction of other legislation relating to secrets and by the un-
ceasing and unsuccessful efforts of Administration officials to improve the
legislation and by authoritative governmental commentators. Most dramatic
proof comes from 18 U.S.C. §794, entitled "Gathering or delivering defense information to aid foreign governments." Although the Congress was
dealing with an even more sensitive problem than in 18 U.S.C. §793, the
statute begins with the significant condition, "whoever, with intent or
reason to believe that it is to be used to the injury of the United States
or to the advantage of a foreign nation, communicates, delivers or
transmits. . . ."

On the legislative front, Congressman Lyndon B. Johnson in a House re-

---

15. Report of Attorney General for 1916; S. 8148 (64th Cong.) introduced Feb. 5,
1917; see also House Report 1591, 64th Cong.
16. 54 *Congressional Record* 3486, 3489, 3492, 3498, 3591.
17. 54 *Congressional Record,* 3585, 3667; 55 *Congressional Record,* 779, 780, 847.
18. Espionage Act of 1917, 40 Stat 217, 65th Cong., sess. 1, ch. 30.
19. Hartzel v. United States, 322 U.S. 680, 686 (1944). See also "Willfulness," Extended Note B, 1 Working Papers of the National Commission on Reform of Federal Criminal Laws 148 (1970).
20. M. G. Miskovsky, CIA Memorandum, *The Espionage Laws,* p. 4 (1961).

port[21] on a related statute (18 U.S.C. §798) described 18 U.S.C. §793 in the following significant words:

> . . . unauthorized revelation of information of this kind can be penalized only if it can be proved that the person making the revelation did so with an intent to injure the United States.[22]

Dissatisfaction with this construction led the Commission on Government Security, in June 1957, to recommend legislation eliminating specific intent.[23] Similar views were expressed by another Assistant General Counsel of CIA, John Morrison, and by an interdepartmental Intelligence Committee urging a statutory amendment so that the offenses "shall not be construed to require proof of any intent or reason to believe that the information is to be used to the injury of the United States."[24]

All these efforts failed.[25] Indeed, when §793 was again amended in 1950, Senator McCarran obtained from the Federal Law Section of the Legislative Reference Service of the Library of Congress a statement that the new legislation also required such specific intent.[26] This was confirmed by Attorney General Tom C. Clark's comment that "nobody other than a spy, saboteur, or other person who would weaken the internal security of the Nation need have any fear of prosecution under either existing law or the provisions of this bill."[27] Every indictment under 18 U.S.C. §793 following the amendments of 1950 contains an allegation that the disclosures of the information either would, or were intended to, injure the United States or aid a foreign power.[28] When the National Commission on Reform of Criminal Law recently proposed the codification of pertinent laws under the title "Mishandling National Security Information," it recommended that one condition of criminality be "reckless disregard of potential injury to the national security of the United States."[29]

---

21. House Report No. 1895, Cryptographic Systems and Communications Intelligence Activities–Prevention of Disclosure of Information, 1950 U.S. Code Congressional Service, p. 2297.
22. *Id.* at p. 2298.
23. Wright Commission on Government Security Report, p. 619, June, 1957.
24. *Studies in Intelligence* at p. 9–12, 37.
25. *See,* Miskovsky *supra,* p. 23.
26. 95 *Congressional Record* 9747–48 (1949). See also 96 *Congressional Record* 12069 (1950) (Senator P. A. McCarran).
27. 95 *Congressional Record* 9749 (1949).
28. Assistant Attorney General (now Mr. Justice) Rehnquist testified before a Congressional committee that subsections (a), (b), and (c) of 18 U.S.C. §793 required an "intent or reason to believe that the material is to be used to the injury of the United States or to the advantage of a foreign power." See U.S., House of Representatives, 92d Cong., 1st sess., House Committee on Government Operations, Foreign Operations, and Government Information Subcommittee, *Hearings,* Part 2, June 1971, "U.S. Government Information Policies and Practices–The Pentagon Papers," p. 386.
29. §1113 in *Hearings* before the Subcommittee on Criminal Laws and Procedures of the Senate Committee on the Judiciary, U.S., Senate, 92d Cong. (1971), p. 240.

In considering the statute's application, one very important criterion must not be forgotten: that the information must relate to national defense. In *Gorin* v. *United States*,[30] Gorin claimed that the phrase "relating to the national defense" was unconstitutionally vague and overly broad. The Court approved the conception of "national defense" urged by the Government in the following language:

> National defense, the Government maintains, "is a generic concept of broad connotations, referring to the military and naval establishments and the related activities of national preparedness." We agree that the words "national defense" in the Espionage Act carry that meaning.[31]

The Court avoided finding the statute unconstitutionally vague by the device of emphasizing that the defendant acted with intent to injure the United States or aid a foreign nation. *"This requires those prosecuted to have acted in bad faith. The sanctions apply only when* scienter *is established."*[32] As we have seen, in the Ellsberg case the Government sought to have its cake and eat it too—i.e., it urged this very broad definition of national defense while claiming that specific intent is not required by the subsections involved.

There is, of course, serious doubt whether the Pentagon Papers do relate to the national defense. Certainly the oldness of most of the materials suggests the contrary; they are a far cry from the *Gorin* case, in which the defendant had obtained from an employee in the Navy Department the contents of over fifty intelligence reports relating chiefly to the activity of Japanese officials and citizens. Gorin was indicted in 1939, a critical year in our history. Moreover, much of the material (even if not the official documentation), set forth in the Pentagon Papers was disclosed by government officials, newspapers, and others both prior and subsequent to the acts charged in the indictment. After all, the literature of the Vietnam War is very extensive, and once-well-known government officials such as Roger Hilsman, Townsend Hoopes, Chester Cooper, and indeed the late President Johnson have written recollections based upon government papers, just as such commentators outside Government as David Halberstam, Jean Lacouture, Bernard Fall, and I. F. Stone have written extensively on the subject.

The key here may be found in Chief Judge Learned Hand's opinion in *United States* v. *Heine*,[33] adopting a narrowing construction of "related to the national defense" to exclude information in the public domain so as to save the statute from overbreadth. No matter what Heine's intent may have been, according to Judge Hand, "that motive did not make the spread of

---

30. Gorin v. United States, 312 U.S. 19 (1941).
31. *Id*. at 28.
32. *Id*. at 25, 27, 28; italics added.
33. 151 F. 2d 813 (2d Cir. 1945)

information criminal, which it would not have been criminal to spread, if he had got it fairly."[34] Another question is whether material of this kind is not to be treated as though it were in the public domain where it is published by the Government (either officially or through leaks) *subsequent* to the acts charged in the indictment. In short, do the Government's own revelations constitute an admission that the material does not fall within the category of national defense?

The trial of the Ellsberg case revealed the Constitutional morass into which citizens are plunged by the vagueness of the term "national defense," particularly when it is not limited by the specific military items appearing in the first sections of 18 U.S.C. §793. The Government's principal witness testified that the revelation of military information as well as of diplomatic information—even if previously publicized—could be "of use" to a foreign nation since it carried the imprimatur of the Defense Department and was marked "top secret." The witness stated further that if the materials were revealed to a hypothetical foreign analyst, they could be of use for propaganda purposes, with the consequence of affecting the United States-North Vietnam negotiations in Paris and thus prolonging the war. Ironically, the defense discovered official Defense Department and State Department studies prepared as a guide to the Justice Department in this very case which concluded that most of the materials did *not* relate to national defense. The Government had been secreting such studies for almost a year prior to their discovery.

What is so fascinating about the problem is that Ellsberg did not give this information to the hypothetical foreign nation and that its publication in 1971 in *The New York Times* had no adverse effect upon our national defense. Yet the defense was not permitted to go into the actualities of the situation and to inquire of the Government's expert whether his mind had not been changed by the evident absence of any adverse effects discernible from the actual publication.

The legislative and judicial history discussed above shows a concern for the threats posed in a democratic society by restrictions upon the free flow of information and upon criticisms of government policy and actions. That history reveals a deep popular suspicion of information control by the Executive Branch and a concern that innocent and patriotic actions and criticism—biting, embarrassing, and revealing though they may be—of Executive misjudgments and miscalculations should not be suppressed by application of laws meant to control espionage.

This concern is of course based upon a recognition of the requirements of a democratic society under our Constitutional form of government. In

---

34. *Id.* at 815.

more recent years the Supreme Court has repeatedly articulated the Constitutional support under the First Amendment in particular for this concern by two kinds of Constitutional principles: the first is the right of people to express themselves, particularly upon matters of public interest.[35] In this respect the work of Alexander Meikeljohn on freedom of speech in governmental matters stands out as an admitted inspiration to the Supreme Court.[36] The second principle involves not the right of the speaker but of his audience, and is most frequently described as "the people's right to know." This right was recently upheld in *Lamont* v. *the Postmaster General*,[37] in which the Court held unconstitutional on First Amendment grounds a statute restricting the entry into the U.S. of so-called "communist propaganda."

The Ellsberg indictment seeks to turn the clock back to pre-*Lamont* days. As indicated, alone among all post-1950 cases, it omits any allegation of injury to the United States or of aid to a foreign power. For the first time the Government seeks to punish under the Espionage Laws certain actions directed toward the revelation to the Congress and the public of information that many people believe they both have a right to know—if citizens are to be in a position to exercise their right of petition and to vote intelligently, and if the Congress is to hold its place in our tripartite democratic system.

The Ellsberg case revealed most dramatically the necessity for the public to know, by reason of both the subject matter of the Pentagon Papers and the particular disclosures therein made. This country was never so divided—except during the Civil War: a melancholy precedent—as it has been on the issues in the Vietnam War. This division caused the retirement of President Johnson and a change in Administration; among young people it led to disaffection resulting in a massive change of attitude toward government, and a change in society itself; an extraordinary number of criminal prosecutions relating to the War and an exodus to other countries of thousands of young men and women; it created an economic crisis. And of course all this led ultimately to the Paris peace negotiations and the ending of the war. The tragedy is that the revelations of the Pentagon Papers were not made public until 1971.

What did the Pentagon Papers themselves reveal? While numerous scholars had been writing with knowledge and perception about the Government and the War, it is fair to say that the Pentagon Papers added a new dimension: they documented by reference to government papers the scholars'

35. New York Times Company v. Sullivan, 376 U.S. 254 (1964).
36. A. Meikeljohn, "The First Amendment Is an Absolute," *1961 Supreme Court Review*, 245. William J. Brennan, "The Supreme Court and the Meikeljohn Interpretation of the First Amendment," 79 Harv. L. R. 1 (1965).
37. 381 U.S. 301 (1965); but see Kleindienst v. Mandel, 408 U.S. 753 (1972), limiting the right of an American audience to secure the entry of a Belgian Marxist scholar.

charges and conclusions, and revealed deception and self-deception on the part of government officials. The documentation shows clear duplicity on the part of the Executive Branch and a determination to manipulate the opinion of the public and the Congress; in the view of many it revealed also conduct that was not only immoral but also very possibly illegal under the governing principles of international law: indifference toward the requirements of the United Nations Charter, determination to engage in aggressive war, particularly through the bombing of North Vietnam; determination to undercut the Geneva Accords of 1954; and a policy of bombing that in the belief of many commentators violates the Hague and the Geneva agreements on international warfare.[38]

Secrecy in government has been a subject of concern in this country for many years. The House Committee on Government Operations has issued a score of reports on the subject.[39] Secrecy with respect to a war that has so affected the country is, however, a far more serious matter. Senator Symington has repeatedly emphasized his concern over Executive refusal to disclose facts necessary for the Congress if it is to legislate and to appropriate funds.[40] Senator Fulbright, as we have seen, failed in his attempt to secure a copy of the Pentagon Papers.

The aftermath of the acts alleged in the indictment is not without significance. After all, only four persons are alleged in the indictment to have come into possession of any of the documents or information revealed in the Pentagon Papers, and none of them represented a foreign country, much less an enemy country, at the time of the disclosures. But in 1971—almost a year after the last act referred to in the indictment—*The New York Times* published considerable parts of the Papers; as did other newspapers. Beacon Press published the *Gravel Edition* of the Papers, and the Government then published a slightly expurgated version—this time in twelve volumes at a price of $50. Thus, all three sets of the publications were broadcast, not to four people, but to the world. One has to ask whether such widespread distribution to the entire world by the Government—albeit reluctantly—has in any way injured the interests of the people of the United States. On the contrary, it would seem that such publication well fulfills the purposes of those who ordered and those who produced the Papers:

---

38. See R. Falk, *Crimes of War* (New York: Random House, 1971), *passim,* and R. Falk, ed., *The Vietnam War and International Law* (Princeton, N.J.: Princeton University Press, 1972).
39. See e.g., *Hearings* as in Note 28; also U.S., Senate, 88th Cong., 1st sess., "Report on Availability of Information from Federal Departments and Agencies, Progress of Study," September 1961–December 1962 (1963).
40. U.S., Senate Committee on Foreign Relations, Symington Subcommittee on Security Agreements and Commitments Abroad, *Report,* 91st Cong., 2d sess. (December 21, 1970), p. 3.

namely, to guide future Governments and the people in their conduct of domestic and foreign affairs on a more informed basis.

THEFT OF GOVERNMENT PROPERTY

Not since the larceny prosecution of Charles Marvin in England in 1878[41] has it ever been thought that copying a government document or revealing its contents constitutes a larceny, theft, conversion, or embezzlement, such as the Ellsberg indictment alleged. Marvin, a temporary copyist in the British Foreign Office's treaty department, frustrated by his meager earnings and propelled by journalistic ambitions, memorized the salient points of an Anglo-Russian agreement regarding the negotiating positions to be taken by the two countries at the Berlin Congress on the controversial "Eastern Question," and proceeded to the offices of the London *Globe*. The next day a special edition of the *Globe* summarized, under banner headlines, the agreement's terms, subjecting the British Government to heated demands for an explanation from representatives of those nations about to participate in the Berlin Congress. Annoyed when the Foreign Secretary disavowed the story's revelations, Marvin again obtained access to the agreement in the Foreign Office, memorized every word in it, and, returning to the *Globe,* wrote out the full text for its editor. The day after the Congress convened, the *Globe* published the agreement *verbatim* on its front page, and again caused the British Government acute embarrassment.

Marvin was charged under the Larceny Acts with theft of the treaty document from the Foreign Office and with theft of the paper on which he copied the treaty for the *Globe*. The chief magistrate of Bow Street dismissed the case without waiting to hear from the defense because "it was only [through] an effort of memory that the defendant was able to supply the articles which were printed," and the Foreign Office had not been deprived of any documents. Marvin's conduct violated governmental interests in non-disclosure of sensitive information, but that was not a crime until 1889, when Britain's first information-control law was enacted.

Although 18 U.S.C. §641 makes it a crime to steal, embezzle, or convert government property, until the Ellsberg case no prosecutor, grand jury, or judge ever claimed that information constituted government property. For one thing, information appears to be too tenuous to be the subject of ownership—or at least, of a larceny statute; for this reason a large body of industrial-secrets law and of copyright law (which gives very little protection to the Government) has been created (principally by statute) for the pur-

---

41. H. Street, *Freedom, the Individual and the Law* (Gloucester, Mass.: Peter Smith, 1963), p. 201.

pose of protecting ideas and formulae and writings that have pecuniary or business value. But with these exceptions, the courts have not infringed upon the area of information and ideas, and only recently the Supreme Court rejected the claim that a computer program was patentable.[42]

The second difficulty in applying the property concept to information lies in the question of ownership. Can it be said that information—assuming it is susceptible of ownership—is owned by the Government as against the electorate? Here we see another aspect of what is called the public's right to know.

The unusual theft charge made in the Ellsberg case is not made in the *Coplon*[43] or other leading espionage cases based upon 18 U.S.C. §§793 and 794. Indeed, when the U.S. Government sought not only to restrain *The New York Times* from publishing the Pentagon Papers but also to recover those Papers, it relied upon only one criminal statute; this was not 18 U.S.C. §641, but 18 U.S.C. §793(e). It is a tribute to the ingenuity—if not the soundness—of the government lawyers that §641 made its appearance in the Ellsberg case. As indicated above, it was not clear whether the property allegedly stolen in the Ellsberg case was information, or the documents themselves. While the indictment suggested that it was information, the Government's bill of particulars included both.

Passing over our reservations as to whether information is susceptible of theft, we turn to a consideration of how documents in the Ellsberg case can be said to have been stolen. The Government argued that they were stolen by not having been delivered promptly to Rand; by having been removed overnight from its premises; by having been Xeroxed; and by having been shown to Russo and the two co-conspirators.

The difficulty with the government approach is that 18 U.S.C. §641 appears—for statutory and Constitutional reasons—not to prohibit *misuse* of governmental documents incidental to the disclosure of their contents. As the U.S. Supreme Court declared in *Morisette* v. *United States*,[44] it collects "crimes so kindred as to belong in one category," and applies only "to acts which constituted larceny or embezzlement at common law and also acts which shade into those crimes but which, most strictly considered, might not be found to fit their fixed definitions." As such, the section's scope seems to be limited to conduct that permanently or substantially deprives the Government of the use, benefit or value of tangible property, that involves a likelihood of such deprivation, or that is infected with an intent to

---

42. Gottschalk v. Benson, 41 L.W. 4015 (Nov. 20, 1972).
43. See United States v. Coplon, 185 F. 2d 629 (2d Cir. 1951), *cert. den.* 342 U.S. 920; United States v. Coplon, 191 F. 2d 749 (D.C. Civ. 1951), *cert. den.* 342 U.S. 926 (1952).
44. 342 U.S. 246, 266 n.28 (1952).

accomplish that deprivation.[45] As Marvin's case demonstrates, the defendants' limited unauthorized use of government documents does not fall within that prohibited category of conduct. Moreover—and Marvin's case is illustrative again—any intangible governmental interests in non-disclosure of the information do not constitute property of the sort §641 protects.

It would appear that the only governmental interests in the acts ascribed to the defendants in the Ellsberg case arise from the limited disclosure of sensitive information. To make such disclosure criminal under 18 U.S.C. §641 would turn the law pertaining to theft of government property into a sweepingly crude and awkward instrument of information control. Such a construction poses three serious problems. First, a construction insensitive to the important interests at stake would cover misuse of any governmental documents regardless of subject matter and the intent behind the disclosure. It would allow the Government to enforce criminally its own conception of information control policy free of the intent and subject matter limitations of the explicit information control laws enacted by the Congress. Second, the Congress, having thoroughly considered the need to protect information relating to the national security, has enacted a comprehensive scheme of law barring the injection of the general provisions of §641 into that special field. Third, the construction urged by the Government would reach the most innocuous conduct, carrying an absurdly drastic impact on the flow of information to the people.

Construed to reach the disclosure of government information, §641 suffers from First Amendment overbreadth and vagueness. In enacting §641 the Congress did not specifically address itself to the expressive interests in dissemination of governmental documentary information, nor weigh them against governmental interests in controlling the use of its documents or in non-disclosure of sensitive information. Nor is the Government's interest in controlling the disclosure of information in Government documents sufficiently compelling or substantial to warrant felony limitation of expressive conduct, particularly when that construction is not narrowly and specifically tailored to serve the valid governmental interest in non-disclosure of sensitive information. Because the interest in preventing limited misuse of documents is so negligible, the Government could prosecute only on the basis that the disclosure embarrassed or annoyed government officials. The statute thus construed would be an invalid prior restraint of expressive conduct, lacking narrow, objective, and definitive standards.

The most spectacular refutation to such construction of §641 is found in a case celebrated because of the litigants—*Pearson* v. *Dodd*.[46] Two members

---

45. R. Perkins, *Criminal Law*, 234 *et seq.* (1969).
46. 410 F. 2d 701 (D.C. Civ. 1969). *Cert. den.* 395 U.S. 947 (1969).

of Senator Thomas Dodd's staff had entered his office without authority, removed numerous documents from his files, made copies of them, replaced the originals, and turned over the copies to the defendant columnist Drew Pearson, who, aware of the manner in which the copies had been obtained, published articles containing information and actual excerpts gleaned from the documents. The Court of Appeals for the District of Columbia held that this conduct did not constitute conversion:

> It has long been recognized that not every wrongful interference with the personal property of another is conversion. Where the intermeddling falls short of the complete or very substantial deprivation of possessory rights in the property, the tort committed is not conversion, but the lesser wrong of trespass to chattels.[47]

Construed to extend to the mere unauthorized use of governmental documents incidental to dissemination of the information they contain, §641 would drastically constrict the free flow of governmental information to the people and to their representatives in the Congress, sweeping overbroadly across, and casting an unduly vague burden on, expressive interests. It would encompass many of the vital avenues by which the American people learn what truly happens in the Government and what its policies are, as opposed to the versions offered in sanitized information releases, formal press conferences, and white papers. These avenues include, for example, books by memoirists and interviews by officials who use government documents for non-attribution press leaks and Congressional briefings. It would give the U.S. Government, as employer, the power not merely to dismiss an employee who disobeys its house rules of file control but also to imprison him. And it would delegate to the Executive the power to define the scope of control, unlimited by any substantive standard. The people of this country as the Supreme Court has stated,

> may not be regarded as closed-circuit recipients of only that which the State chooses to communicate. They may not be confined to the expression of those sentiments that are officially approved.[48]

As Justice Douglas declared in the *New York Times Company* v. *United States* case:

> The dominant purpose of the First Amendment was to prohibit the widespread practice of governmental suppression of embarrassing information. It

---

47. *Id.* at 706.
48. Tinker v. Des Moines Independent Community School District, 393 U.S. 503, 511 (1969).

is common knowledge that the First Amendment was adopted against the widespread use of the common law of seditious libel to punish the dissemination of material that is embarrassing to the powers-that-be. . . .

Secrecy in government is fundamentally anti-democratic, perpetuating bureaucratic errors. Open debate and discussion of public issues are vital to our national health.[49]

THE CONSPIRACY TO DEFRAUD

As previously indicated, the third string to the Government's bow was the most interesting: conspiracy to defraud the United States of its lawful governmental function of "controlling the dissemination of classified government studies, reports, memoranda and communications." This provision, too, has never been used against persons engaged in revealing information to the public; indeed, it has not even been used against persons giving classified defense information to foreign governments. Since it is not mentioned by the Government in the *New York Times Company* v. *United States* or in the first complaint or indictment against Ellsberg, it is clearly a brilliant afterthought. That, of course, does not dispose of the problem, because even an afterthought can be correct.

At the outset it must be recognized that the attempt to use the Conspiracy to Defraud Statute in this manner turns it into a form of information control which appears to be inconsistent with Congressional opposition from the beginnings of our Espionage Laws to the concepts underlying the British Official Secrets Act. The Espionage Laws were directed against information affecting the national defense—but no one, either at the time of the enactment of 18 U.S.C. §371 or subsequently (prior to the Ellsberg case) suggested that the statute could be used as a form of information control.

There have, of course, been numerous prosecutions under 18 U.S.C §371, and many of these have been criticized in a well-known article by Dean A. Goldstein of the Yale Law School.[50] But all of those cases involved actual fraud upon the Government, whether by filing false claims to government lands or false non-Communist affidavits under the Taft-Hartley Law or by suborning government prosecuting officials. None of them involved leaks of information.

Is "controlling the dissemination of classified government studies" a lawful governmental function? One might well question this claim, both in terms of the people's right to know and in terms of the total legislative structure. It is, after all, the Congress that must determine what conduct con-

---

49. *Supra,* Note 1 at 723–24 (concurring opinion).
50. Goldstein, *Conspiracy to Defraud the United States,* 68 Yale L.J. 405 (1959).

stitutes a crime. There is no Federal statute providing for a general system of information control of classified documents. On the contrary, the statutes dealing with classified information are limited to very specific areas.

Thus, in 1933 the Congress made it a crime for one who "by virtue of his employment by the United States" secures access to an official diplomatic code or to matter prepared in such code, and willfully furnishes to another any such code or matter obtained while in the possession of, or in transmission between, any foreign government and its diplomatic mission in the United States.[51] In 1951 the Congress made it a crime to willfully disclose classified information pertaining to codes, ciphers, and cryptographic systems.[52] In 1950 the Congress passed 50 U.S.C. §783(d), which makes it a crime for government employees to communicate classified information to foreign governments or communist organizations or their agents.[53] The Congress also passed legislation to protect "restricted data" relating to atomic information.[54] The passage of these four statutes protecting classified information in limited categories appears to be inconsistent with the attempt to protect all classified information by means of criminal sanctions.

The fact is, the system of classifying documents has been created by Executive Order, not by statute. Its purpose is to control the conduct of government employees and/or government contractors and their employees by the use of administrative sanctions—such as dismissal—except where the material released met the national-defense standards of the Espionage Statutes. It is very doubtful, Constitutional considerations aside, whether the creation of a system of classified documents by Executive Order may be said to be a "governmental function" protected by the general criminal laws. But even if this were theoretically possible, the implementation of the Executive Order was so anarchic as to justify applying the term "lawless" rather than "lawful" to this governmental function. Thousands of governmental officials are engaged in classifying documents, often without any knowledge of the appropriate standards to follow. For more than a decade the House Government Operations Committee has complained about the overclassification of documents and the failure to declassify them—a bureaucratic deficiency not limited to any specific Administration.[55] Although one President after another, including President Nixon, seemed to promise an improvement in the situation, none has succeeded—as is illustrated by recent analyses of President Nixon's Executive Order on the subject.[56] Sub-

---

51. 18 U.S.C. §952.
52. 18 U.S.C. §798 (1951).
53. 50 U.S.C. §783(d).
54. 42 U.S.C. §§2271–77.
55. See the hearings referred to in Note 29 *supra*.
56. Executive Order 11652. For a fuller discussion see Chapter 6, by Congressman Moorhead.

sequent to the release of the Pentagon Papers, the House Committee conducted elaborate hearings at which experts testified that as much as 99 per cent of classified material should never have been classified.[57] But classification, like state secrets and Executive privilege, has continued to be a substantial barrier to Congressional efforts to learn the truth.

DISCRIMINATORY ENFORCEMENT OR
ADMINISTRATIVE INTERPRETATION

The revelation of classified information or that relating to national defense and the leaking of documents are familiar practices in government. Indeed, the Franks Committee Report specifically approved the view that Ministers and senior civil servants should have the right to make disclosures to selected newspapermen.[58]

In the United States, where everything is done on a large scale, the same applies to the system of leaks. Persons on all government levels from the President down leak information and show documents to favored members of the press. President Johnson—following his term of office—"declassified" a document in the course of a television interview with a selected reporter. Some of these leaks were made in support of the government policy; some by officials in disagreement with established policy.

There are two other effective vehicles for disclosure of so-called classified information: the form of memoir or autobiography, and the library deposit. Recollections involving the Vietnam War are the most recent of that category, and President Johnson's and Roger Hilsman's the most spectacular in their reference to secret National Security Council proceedings. Again, when government officials leave office they may take with them numerous documents used in the course of their office or employment; and these materials often land in library collections. The Truman and Johnson libraries are two monuments to this fact; similarly, in the larger university libraries of the country may be found classified documents deposited there by former government officials. Now these leaks, whether in books, in newspapers, or as "backgrounders," have never been regarded as a conspiracy to defraud the United States. That they may have other undesirable consequences is discussed by Haynes Johnson in Chapter 10, but such selective disclosure has never been considered criminal. It was not until the *New York Times* case that the Government raised the specter of 18 U.S.C. §793—and then did not pursue *The New York Times* with criminal sanctions. It was not until the

---

57. See p. 104 of the hearings referred to in Note 29, *supra,* U.S. Government Information Policies and Practices.
58. *Supra,* Note 2.

Ellsberg case that the Government sought to employ the law pertaining to conspiracy to defraud.

The Ellsberg case contains elaborate documentation of the foregoing system of leaks, disclosures, memoirs, and library deposits. Detailed affidavits submitted by former Ambassador John Kenneth Galbraith, by Robert Manning (former Assistant Secretary of State and now editor of *The Atlantic Monthly*), and by others set forth the relevant facts. Indeed, an affidavit of Professor Abraham Chayes of Harvard Law School stated that during his tenure as legal advisor to the Secretary of State, such leaks of classified information repeatedly occurred and were recognized by government law officers as not constituting a basis for criminal proceedings.

The District Judge in the Ellsberg case declined to dismiss the indictment for selective prosecution. In so doing, of course, he seemed to give support to the Government's use of its system of information control for partisan purposes—i.e., for punishing those who make disclosures embarrassing to the Government.

Should we not interpret the three statutory schemes here under discussion in the light of a system of unabashed leaking to the press for partisan purposes? In other words, the long American history of giving "backgrounders" of making documents available to selected newspapermen when it suits the governmental purpose, these support the argument that we do not have a system of information control and that the consistent Congressional concern over censorship since 1911 has been vindicated by the implicit recognition that the First Amendment permits such revelations. Such an argument urges that the release of such information does *not* violate the criminal laws. The Ellsberg case thus has been the first judicial vehicle for presentation of evidence of a system of administrative practices which habitually treats as noncriminal the historic tradition of leaking government information to the press.

CONCLUSION

It is ironical that the Ellsberg case should have arisen at the very time that the English Government began considering a major revision of its Official Secrets Act. The Ellsberg case was an incident of the *New York Times* litigation; there is no other way to explain the timing, uniqueness, and shifting governmental theories of its case. It is idle to speculate why the Government persisted in litigation so utterly without precedent and contrary to the opinions of its experts. On the other hand the Ellsberg case cannot be isolated from the assault upon the First Amendment that has occurred in so many other areas during the Nixon Administration: the attacks made upon the

media by Vice President Agnew, the use of grand juries against newspapermen and scholars,[59] and indeed the attempt to enjoin the publication of the
Pentagon Papers—to mention only a few. Whatever may be said of the
prosecution of the Ellsberg case, it did present a unique opportunity to determine what powers of information controls, if any, the Congress or the
Executive possesses under the First Amendment.

Due to a particularly aggressive transgression by persons in the Government in the pursuit of evidence against Ellsberg, the case was dismissed and,
so, has not been the vehicle for resolving the crucial questions it raised. So
long as the law remains unclear in its defense of the individual's right to
speak up, governments will likely be tempted to use concepts like "theft of
property" and "espionage" to embrace communication of embarrassing
information to the American people.

No doubt there are matters which, even in a democracy, may for a time
be kept secret from the public. But the Congress should now ensure that the
definition of these matters is so clear and so narrow that no Ellsberg in a future and comparable situation need again be put to the financial and psychological ordeal of demonstrating his rights. In any case, Ellsberg's actions, their
impact on the American public consciousness, and the collapse of the Government's case against him, may make it less likely—even if the statutory
ambiguities are not resolved in favor of clearly stated liberties of the citizen
—that there will in future be so much government lying to the public or that
those who expose official lying when it occurs will be treated as though they,
rather than the dissemblers, were the criminals.

---

59. See e.g., Branzburg v. Hayes, 408 U.S. 665 (1972).

18

Official Secrecy
and External Relations in Britain:
The Law and Its Context

STANLEY DE SMITH

THE ENGLISH ADDICTION

In 1970 the Rt. Hon. Richard Crossman, leader of the House of Commons
in the Wilson Government, delivering the Godkin Lectures at Harvard, referred to the "English addiction to secrecy."[1] A few months later the Secretary
of State for Social Services had become the editor of the *New Statesman,* and
in his less inhibited journalistic capacity was proclaiming: "A delight in
secrecy and a passion for keeping the public in the dark still dominates
Whitehall."[2]

His was no voice in the wilderness. In 1968 the Fulton Committee on the
Civil Service had concluded more circumspectly that "the administrative
process is surrounded by too much secrecy"; that "civil servants, and perhaps also Ministers, are apt to give great and sometimes excessive weight to
the difficulties and problems which would undoubtedly arise from more open
processes of administration and policy-making"; and that "the Government
should set up an inquiry to make recommendations for getting rid of unnecessary secrecy"—an inquiry that, added the authors, ought to embrace the
Official Secrets Acts.[3]

The Government's reaction was to issue a white paper entitled *Information and the Public Interest*[4] that explained how matters were improving and

Professor de Smith is Downing Professor of the Laws of England, University of
Cambridge, and author of *Judicial Review of Administrative Action, Constitutional
and Administrative Law, The New Commonwealth and its Constitutions,* and *Microstates and Micronesia.*

1. *Inside View* (London: Jonathan Cape, 1972), p. 99.
2. Writing as "Crux," 67 *New Statesman* (February 11, 1971). See also issue of September 24, 1971.
3. U.K. Parliamentary Papers, Cmnd. 3638 (1968), vol. 1, paras. 277, 280.
4. Cmnd. 4089 (1969).

promising to try harder. No commitment to review the Official Secrets Acts was offered. But in 1970 the Conservative election manifesto did include such an undertaking, and in 1971 a Committee under Lord Franks was appointed to review section 2 of the Official Secrets Act 1911. Its report, recommending not very far-reaching reforms, was published in September 1972.[5] No Government decision as to implementing the recommendations was immediately forthcoming.[5a]

Radical critics of official secrecy in British administration—and the critics cover a very wide political spectrum[6]—have found little to cheer about in this Report. I happen to think that it is on the whole a rather good report. On such matters, however, I have often been an odd-man-out, murmuring soothing words to embattled bureaucrats,[7] words lost amid the thunderous denunciations surging from my fellow academic lawyers, from political scientists, journalists, and other libertarians. Sometimes I wonder whether I am really Establishment-minded, and if so why. But I am usually able to console myself with the reflection that I view these matters in proper perspective. The others must therefore be out of step.

A PERSONAL NOTE

Over twenty years ago I decided to investigate the way in which a particular kind of issue affecting individual rights was decided within a government department. The matter was politically sensitive only insofar as the department (which was concerned neither with security questions nor with external relations) was being severely criticised for undue secretiveness in its procedures and for making harsh decisions. I suspected that much of the criticism was misconceived, even unfair, but I wanted to know how the system worked in practice.

A senior official in the department agreed to see me. He was very helpful and supplied me with hitherto unpublished information; this proved to be

---

5. Great Britain, Home Office, Departmental Committee on Section 2 of the Official Secrets Act 1911, Cmnd. 5104, September 1972 (referred to as the Franks Report).

5a. For the Government's first cautious reactions, see 858 House of Commons Debates (5th Series), cols. 1885–1973 (29 June 1973).

6. The most important general studies are David Williams, *Not in the Public Interest* (London: Hutchinson, 1965); Harry Street, *Freedom, the Individual and the Law* (London: Penguin, 3rd ed., 1972); Paul O'Higgins, *Censorship in Britain* (London: Nelson, 1972). See also Max Nicholson, *The System* (London: Hodder & Stoughton, 1967); Jonathan Aitken, *Officially Secret* (London: Weidenfeld & Nicolson, 1971). Many critical comments, with documentation, are to be found in the Minutes of Evidence submitted to the Franks Committee and published in three volumes simultaneously with the report.

7. See, e.g., my comments on the doctrine of "Crown Privilege" (executive privilege) in *Constitutional and Administrative Law* (London: Penguin, 1971), pp. 598–603.

quite interesting but wholly undramatic. He also introduced me to two senior technical officers in the department. They showed no apparent comprehension of any ground for public disquiet. I decided to incorporate in an article some of the factual material obtained from these interviews. As a matter of courtesy I showed the draft to my informant. He was outraged (*"If you publish this I'll be shot"*). An American lawyer who had trodden the same corridors was more fortunate; his material was duly published. Less than ten years after this ludicrous experience, all the information disclosed to me, and a good deal more, was being made available to the general public.

In this type of context official secrecy has significantly diminished. Senior civil servants are more accessible and less apprehensive. Nowadays I seldom find difficulty in obtaining from civil servants factual material of this kind, or interpretations of departmental announcements or even departmental policies, provided that I put my questions to a highly placed official. Belatedly the British Civil Service has become interested in cultivating good public relations, even with inquisitive academics. I believe that this change of attitude is traceable to the 1957 publication of the other Franks Report, on Administrative Tribunals and Enquiries,[8] which made out an irresistible case for more openness in particular areas of decision-making.

My experience in dealing with American officials in 1967 and 1968 is not especially useful for the purpose of comparing the two systems, since as I understand it American Federal Government has always been more "open" than central administration in Britain. Under the auspices of the New York University Center for International Studies I was undertaking a survey of American dependencies, with particular reference to the Trust Territory of the Pacific Islands (Micronesia). I found no difficulty at all in obtaining personal interviews with senior and middle-grade officials in the Office of Territories of the Department of the Interior and in the State Department, and with the Governors of two territories. Only once during this period was I refused access to relevant information. Possibly the official concerned was unaware that the material was in fact available, but if he was putting me off the scent I harbour no ill feeling.

After I had published my study,[9] which was mildly critical of some aspects of U.S. policy towards Micronesia—a policy that has since veered towards the position I had tentatively advocated—the Office of Territories continued to comply with my occasional requests for factual information. The only overtly hostile reaction[10] came from the Chairman of the House of Repre-

---

8. Cmnd. 218 (1957). Nearly all the Committee's detailed recommendations were implemented quite rapidly by legislation or administrative action. See Professor Street's contribution to this volume (Chapter 19) for an illustration.

9. *Microstates and Micronesia* (New York: New York University Press, 1970).

10. Apart from an irate personal letter from an official, who justifiably complained of a snide footnote allusion.

sentatives Subcommittee on Territorial and Insular Affairs, who enshrined my name in the *Congressional Record* amid columns of obloquy, spiced with a suggestion that Bernadette Devlin might usefully be called to testify about the iniquity of British colonial rule in Ireland.[11]

I may have been lucky in that in 1968 the U.S. Government had probably not yet formulated any clear policy for the ultimate political status of Micronesia. I doubt whether even the National Security Council had precise ideas about American strategic needs in Micronesia. And so, except at Eniwetok and Kwajalein in the Marshalls, there was little to hide from me. Moreover, the climate of American opinion had just engendered the Freedom of Information Act. Micronesia lay at the margin of national defense and foreign policy. A strategic trust territory, it was nevertheless primarily the responsibility of the Department of the Interior—not in the same way as Northern Ireland, the Isle of Man, and the Channel Islands came under the jurisdiction of the Home Office, but rather as dependent territories were a matter for the Colonial Office before it was merged with other departments. This having been said, I doubt whether any department of the United Kingdom Government responsible for politically sensitive overseas affairs would have afforded a foreign research worker such generous facilities.

My involvement with British external affairs has been exclusively in the colonial field. I spent three months in Uganda in 1954 as personal assistant and Constitutional aide to Professor Sir Keith Hancock in a complex and broadly successful negotiation, designed to prepare the ground for a rapprochement between the British Government and the Baganda following the temporary deportation of the Kabaka of Buganda.[12] In the late 1950's I acted as a Constitutional adviser or consultant to various colonial nationalist groups seeking self-government by negotiation with the British Government; these fascinating exercises taught me a little about politicians and civil servants, but they were irrelevant to the general theme of this paper, save in one respect. Such controls as the British Government maintains over the flow of news affecting external policies are largely ineffective to prevent information or misinformation from percolating through to the media from overseas governments, politicians, and journalists.

In 1961 I became constitutional adviser to the Secretary of State for the Colonies in connection with Mauritius. Intermittently I resumed this role over the next few years. More briefly, I occupied a similar position in respect of Fiji.[13] I had to read "Secret" and "Confidential" files. During the

---

11. *Congressional Record*, 91st Cong., 1st sess. (December 18, 1969), vol. 115, pp. 39864–66.
12. The story has been told by Professor D. A. Low, *Buganda in Modern History* (London: Weidenfeld & Nicolson, 1971); and discreetly but over-optimistically by myself in 26 *Political Quarterly* 4 (1955).
13. Mauritius became independent in 1968, and Fiji, in 1970.

formal Constitutional conferences and informal discussions I had the opportunity of observing the interaction of Ministers and senior civil servants thrashing out questions of policy and tactics; and I played a guarded part in those deliberations. If I have an Establishmentarian bias it must have been acquired during that period, for it was glaringly obvious to me that many things having to be stated bluntly and placed on record presupposed that complete confidentiality would be maintained. Nothing is at all likely to shake that conviction, a conviction that colours my approach to the issues we are now considering.

THE CONTEXT

Other contributors have dealt with the background to the law of official secrecy in Britain, but I offer my own sketch.

The Cabinet

Ministers are collectively responsible to Parliament. This means (1) that if the Government is defeated on a vote of confidence in the House of Commons, the Prime Minister must either submit the resignation of his Government or advise a dissolution of Parliament; no such occasion has arisen since 1924; and (2) that the Cabinet must present a united front to the world, even if some members in fact disagree with a particular decision. A Minister who is unable to acquiesce in a Cabinet decision of which he disapproves ought to resign, even if he is not himself in the (inner) Cabinet.

Anthony Nutting, a Minister of State at the Foreign Office but not a Cabinet Minister, resigned at the beginning of the Suez venture because he was fundamentally opposed to it. He was persuaded by the Prime Minister (Eden) to defer announcing his resignation until military operations were under way, and by Macmillan (soon to be Eden's successor), not to disclose the full reasons for it until after the Conservative Government had lost office.[14] If Nutting had publicly dissociated himself from the Government's policy while he still held office, the Prime Minister would have been compelled to dismiss him. But in practice a Prime Minister will sometimes acquiesce in breaches of the convention of public unanimity for reasons of expediency. Indeed, collective responsibility is apt to be a mask, a disguise

---

14. Anthony Nutting, *No End of a Lesson* (London: Constable, 1967), chaps. 13–17. Macmillan said to him: "Why say anything at all? You have already been proved right and we have been proved wrong. You have done the right thing by resigning and, if you keep silent now, you will be revered and rewarded. You will lead the Party one day" (p. 169). Nutting was disowned by his constituency association, resigned his seat in the House of Commons, and has never come back into politics.

conceding differences of opinion so strong that individual Ministers will covertly initiate unattributable leaks to fortify their own positions or merely to blow off steam.[15]

The Rt. Hon. Patrick Gordon Walker has justified the occasional unattributable leak as a device necessary for supporting the strain of maintaining an ostensibly united front;[16] the metaphor that springs to mind is the acceptance of discreet adultery as a means of preserving the state of holy matrimony. Some draw halfhearted distinctions between leaking to the media (a bad thing) and briefing the media (which may be a good thing). The Rt. Hon. James Callaghan, Home Secretary in the Labour Government, said to the Franks Committee: "You know the difference between leaking and briefing: briefing is what I do and leaking is what you do."[17]

Secrecy applies not only to the substance but also to the procedure of Cabinet. The Cabinet committee system is crucial to an understanding of how top-level decisions are made. But we are not told the composition, powers, or even the names of existing Cabinet committees, with the incongruous exception of the Defence and Overseas Policy Committee. This blanket of secrecy was recently justified by the Secretary of the Cabinet as a time-honoured safeguard of collective responsibility and the maintenance of confidentiality.[18] Many of us remain unconvinced.

Collective responsibility to Parliament implies that the Government must control the House of Commons. But in practice it will be extremely difficult for the Government to hoodwink the Opposition on a politically controversial issue once the basic facts are known or suspected. The Eden Government was able to conceal its intentions about the Suez intervention in the first instance, but the Parliamentary storms that followed blew away the Prime Minister. Backbenchers' allegations of duplicity might, on the other hand, be brushed aside if they were not taken up by the Opposition front bench that constitutes the "Shadow Cabinet."

Former Cabinet Ministers are supposed to accept collective responsibility for past decisions, but we have been offered so many Ministerial revelations

---

15. Differences of opinion within the Labour Cabinet in 1967 over the question whether to resume arms supplies to South Africa were thus disclosed by the Prime Minister and others; see Patrick Gordon Walker, *The Cabinet* (rev. ed.; London: Collins/Fontana, 1972), pp. 29–30, and also his chapter in the present volume; George Brown, *In My Way* (London: Penguin, 1972), pp. 163–67; Harold Wilson, *The Labour Government 1964–1970* (London: Michael Joseph, 1971), pp. 470–76.
16. *Op. cit.,* pp. 26–33.
17. Franks Report, vol. 4, p. 187. Mr. Callaghan hastened to add: "I believe very much in the doctrine of collective responsibility, and I think it would be very foolish and good government would be bad government if people were *regularly* to depart from it" (italics supplied).
18. Franks Report, vol. 3, pp. 324–26. See also Written Evidence by the Cabinet Office (vol. 2, pp. 9–10).

of disagreements within the Wilson Labour Government[19] (notably in connection with the decision to re-apply for membership of the European Economic Communities (EEC) in 1967) that the very existence of this Constitutional convention is now questionable. Disclosures in Ministerial memoirs are directly relevant to a consideration of the scope of the Official Secrets Acts.[20]

Of the many aspects of the individual responsibility of Ministers, two may be singled out. First, a Minister is expected to answer questions in Parliament on matters within the sphere of his responsibility, but it is not uncommon for a Minister to refuse to answer a question on security grounds without specifying any reason.[21] The circumstances in which Commander L. K. P. Crabb was drowned during the Bulganin and Khrushchev visit to Britain in 1956—in fact he lost his life as a frogman investigating a Soviet warship in Portsmouth Harbour[22]—were not disclosed despite Parliamentary interrogation of the Prime Minister.[23] Second, the political responsibility accepted by Ministers for acts done by their departmental officials is of crucial importance in maintaining the loyalty of the Civil Service to successive Governments.

The Civil Service

Recent reforms have done much to open up areas of departmental decision-making. Thus, civil servants have had to appear before inquires to explain departmental policies, and the Parliamentary Commissioner for Administration (the Ombudsman) has challenged the sacrosanctity of departmental files when investigating complaints of injustice caused by maladministration on the part of central Government departments. But the Parliamentary Commissioner is precluded[24] from investigating any matter concerning external relations apart from administrative action raising no issue of security or national policy. Nevertheless, he scored his most heavily publicised success in exposing a minor case of maladministration by Foreign Office offi-

---

19. A few are to be found in the memoirs of Mr. Wilson and Lord George-Brown (Note 15, above); see also Lord Wigg, *George Wigg* (London: Michael Joseph, 1972). Several disclosures have been made by Richard Crossman in his journalistic writings.
20. See Part V, below.
21. For a list of matters about which successive Governments have refused to answer questions, see Report from the Select Committee on Parliamentary Questions (House of Commons Paper 393 (1971–72), pp. 114–17); the list ranges well beyond security matters.
22. Wigg, *op. cit.,* pp. 190–91.
23. Eden did, however, concede that what had occurred had not been authorised by or known to Ministers; see Geoffrey Marshall & Graeme C. Moodie, *Some Problems of the Constitution* (5th ed.; London: Hutchinson, 1971), p. 141.
24. Parliamentary Commissioner Act 1967, ss. 5(1), 8(4), Sched. 2, Note 6, Sched. 3, paras. 1–5, 10. See further, Professor Street's contribution in this volume.

cials in a case where *ex gratia* payments of compensation had been refused
to former prisoners of war incarcerated in Sachsenhausen concentration
camp. The Foreign Secretary, though complaining bitterly of an encroach-
ment on Ministerial responsibility, agreed to pay up.[25] In practice the Parliamentary Commissioner has been at pains to avoid identifying erring officials
where possible.

The House of Commons

Specialised select committees of the House with power to scrutinise central
administration outside the field of national expenditure have existed only
since 1967. None has yet been established for defence or external affairs,
though accession to the EEC will necessarily involve an extension of the
committee system. Although the British select committees interrogate civil
servants and occasionally Ministers and have power to subpoena, they lack
the status, prestige, and staff of Congressional committees in the United
States. They have no autonomous power base, and the specialised committees exist from one session to the next at the will of the Government. Their
members, moreover, are chosen by the party whips, and some members are
liable to pull their punches for fear of losing the prospect of Ministerial
preferment.[26]

Their committee reports have often been constructive and informative,
but only the long-established Public Accounts Committee has as yet proved
a heavyweight. The inadequacy of the factual information made available
to Members of Parliament about external affairs handicaps them at question time and in debate.[27] Although civil servants have undoubtedly become
more forthcoming in their dealings with non-political investigators, there is
still a general impression that they are extremely reluctant to talk to M.P.'s
on politically sensitive issues affecting external relations. Setting up a Parliamentary Committee would not necessarily overcome this obstacle, but it
could help to find a way around it.

The Media

Of the constraints imposed on the information media, others have written
with a degree of authority that I cannot approach. Journalists have repeat-

---

25. House of Commons Paper 54 (1967–68); 758 House of Commons Debates (5th
series), cols. 107–70 (February 5, 1968); Geoffrey K. Fry (1970), Public Law 336–
58.
26. Crossman, *Inside View,* pp. 103–104. This factor should not, however, be exaggerated. In December 1972 the House of Commons Select Committee on Science and
Technology defied precedent by publishing a suppressed departmental report on the
development of inventions.
27. Peter G. Richards, *Parliament and Foreign Affairs* (London: Allen & Unwin,
1967), *passim.*

edly asserted that they are unduly inhibited by the laws of libel and contempt of court, by Parliamentary privilege, and by the Official Secrets Acts. I cannot pretend to be especially sympathetic towards their complaints about the law of libel. In particular, I should not welcome the introduction into English law of the rule in *New York Times Company* v. *Sullivan*,[28] affording immunity to the publication of any defamatory falsehood relating to the conduct of a public officer, provided that the statement was made in good faith. We have, of course, no First Amendment; but if we decide to adopt a Constitutional bill of rights, I hope it would not lend itself to such an interpretation.

The English law of contempt of court is perhaps too strict in precluding prejudicial comment on imminent or *sub judice* civil proceedings before a judge sitting without a jury[29]; but on balance I prefer the law of contempt in Britain to the more permissive regime in the United States. The rule that a journalist refusing to disclose his sources of information in judicial proceedings may be committed to prison for contempt in the face of the court[30] has naturally incurred a great deal of criticism in both countries. As to the position regarding breach of Parliamentary privilege: this is unsatisfactory in Britain, because (1) the House of Commons has asserted exclusive jurisdiction to determine whether aspersions cast on its members in their Parliamentary capacities constitute contempts of the House; (2) the courts recognise in effect (though not in form) that the House has exclusive jurisdiction in this matter; (3) the House has sometimes proved more hypersensitive to slurs on its reputation than are judges to attacks on their own conduct[31]; (4) when the Committee of Privilege inquires into a complaint of breach of privilege it not only acts as "judge" in its own cause but fails to observe judicial-type procedures[32]; and (5) justification and fair comment are not accepted as defences to breaches of privilege. It could be held to be a breach of privilege or contempt to assert that a Minister had misled the House, or that a Member's advocacy of a particular point of view had been influenced by the hospitality extended to him by a foreign government.

---

28. 376 U.S. 255 (1964).
29. For the most recent review of the law on this matter, see Att.-Gen. v. Times Newspapers Ltd. [1973] 3 W.L.R. 298.
30. See Att.-Gen. v. Clough [1963] 1 Q.B. 775. Principle applies to judicial tribunals of enquiry as well as courts.
31. Compare the findings by the House in 1956 that John Junor, editor of the *Sunday Express,* was guilty of contempt for publishing an article during the Suez crisis complaining that M.P.'s were getting an excessive allocation of petrol—he was ordered to be severely reprimanded by the Speaker—with the relatively indulgent attitude of the Court of Appeal towards harsh criticism of itself in R. v. Metropolitan Police Commissioner, ex p. Blackburn (No. 2) [1968] 2 Q.B. 150.
32. Recommendations for procedural reform made in 1967 (Report from the Select Committee on Parliamentary Privilege; House of Commons Paper 34, 1967–68) had not been adopted five years later.

That section 2 of the Official Secrets Act 1911 has an inhibiting effect on the media (see below) can readily be conceded. Journalists giving evidence before the Franks Committee were almost unanimous in arguing that the section should be repealed and not replaced.

Special rules apply to the broadcasting media. The governors of the British Broadcasting Corporation and the members of the Independent Broadcasting Authority are appointed and removable on Ministerial advice; and the Minister of Posts and Telecommunications may require these bodies to refrain from broadcasting any specified matter or class of matter. Disobedience to such a direction might entail the summary removal of the governors or members—such action was taken by the Dublin Government in November 1972 in relation to RTE, the Irish equivalent of BBC—but in fact British Ministers have been very circumspect in exercising their powers.[33]

I accept, in principle, the need for a free and fearless press; and I should be adamantly opposed to the imposition of legal controls similar to those applicable to the broadcasting media. I recognise that the press has a duty to expose embarrassing and discreditable facts that men in places of power or trust would wish to stifle. But my attitude is ambivalent. I become incensed at the use of high-flown liberal platitudes to excuse offensive intrusions on personal privacy motivated only by a zeal for achieving or maintaining a mass circulation. I have every reason for being cynical about the standards of accuracy in reporting events in which I have been personally involved. So perhaps I ought to lean over backwards to commend the sense of responsibility often shown by the press in censoring itself and adopting double standards.

The Westminster lobby correspondents appear to maintain strict standards of confidentiality when entrusted by politicians with private briefings or leaks; if they publish the information at all they will not attribute it to their source. The system is institutionalised, regulated by a written code of rules.[34] Information is thus divulged and published which might never have got into the press at all; but is the information too hygienically packaged, and is the cutting edge of criticism blunted by these confidential relations? (Diplomatic correspondents, like the editor of *The Times,* are perhaps under still stronger pressures to be "responsible" commentators.[35]) If a political journalist sets himself apart from the press Establishment (e.g., by attributing advocacy of specific policies to named civil servants) he is liable to be

---

33. See also Chapter 14 by Kenneth Lamb in this volume. For the reluctance of courts to restrain by injunction the broadcasting of marginally offensive programmes, see Att.-Gen., *ex rel.* McWhirter v. Independent Broadcasting Authority [1973] Q.B. 629, which concerns the right to broadcast a film on the life of Andy Warhol.
34. See Jeremy Tunstall, *The Westminster Lobby Correspondents* (London: Routledge & Kegan Paul, 1970); Colin Seymour-Ure, *The Press, Politics and the Public* (London: Methuen, 1968), esp. chap. 6.
35. See Seymour-Ure, *op. cit.,* 259–63.

denied access to confidential information. In 1965 the *Sunday Times* appointed Anthony Howard (now editor of the *New Statesman*) its "Whitehall Correspondent." Within a few weeks Ministers were told not to speak to Howard except in the presence of their press officers, who were to report to the Minister in charge of Government Information Services; and civil servants were apparently instructed not to speak to him at all.[36]

Institutionalised self-censorship on a limited scale appears in two other forms. The Press Council, a worthy body of newsmen with a judicial chairman and a small minority of laymen, receives complaints about misreporting and intrusions on privacy, and administers publicised rebukes. In the absence of adequate remedies in the courts for breach of privacy, this can at least be said to be better than nothing.[37] A more important non-statutory body is the Defence, Press and Broadcasting Committee, presided over by a senior civil servant but with a majority of representatives of the media; its functions in connection with D Notices (Defence Notices) are considered elsewhere. For a journal to disregard a D Notice is to risk the possibility of prosecution under the Official Secrets Acts, or at least to court a first-class political row. The fact that official information may be outside the ambit of current D Notices does not guarantee immunity from prosecution under the Official Secrets Acts, as Mr. Brian Roberts, editor of the *Sunday Telegraph*, discovered in 1970.[38]

Much of the foregoing *tour d'horizon* has but remote bearing on the central question: How much information is made available in Britain for meaningful discussions of foreign policy issues? My own general impression is that the factors inducing confidentiality are more pervasive than those inducing openness. But we have had no Vietnam—not even in Northern Ireland—and no clear-cut comparison with the American scene is feasible. Factual information about other countries is obviously available in the quality press; yet in the second half of 1972 I read only a handful of items about my far-away true love, Mauritius—items on tourist facilities, the association agreement with the Common Market, an infinitely depressing impressionistic feature article by V. S. Naipaul, and a note on the brush-off given the Foreign Minister by Brigitte Bardot on her arrival at Plaisance Airport. Of Micronesia I have read nothing at all in a British journal. Who wants to exercise his right to know?

There are, however, random indications that relevant and important

---

36. *Ibid.*, 176–85.
37. See the Report of the Committee on Privacy (Cmnd. 5012, 1972, chap. 7) for description and evaluation.
38. See further on D Notices, Franks Report, vol. 1, para. 65; vol. 2, pp. 241–45; vol. 3, pp. 51–68; and Professor Street's contribution in this volume. For an account of this case and its history by a participant, see Jonathan Aitken's *Officially Secret.*

information is often withheld. How did the British public get to know about official wire-tapping practices, for example, or the very existence of D Notices, the misuse of "interrogation" in depth by the security forces? *Answer:* From reports on *ad hoc* enquiries conducted by or under the chairmanship of eminent Establishment figures appointed by the Prime Minister for the purpose, following pressures from Parliament and the media. This is one of the most curious phenomena of the British political system.

On giving publicity to official information the United States appears to score significantly higher marks than Britain. For the journalist and the modern diplomatic historian, the United States—at least since the Freedom of Information Act—offers better prospects. And yet decisions like *Epstein* v. *Resor*[39] and the *Mink* case show how Executive classification of highly embarrassing foreign policy information will still be upheld by the courts, even in the United States.

EXTERNAL AFFAIRS, SECURITY, AND THE LAW

The conduct of foreign relations lies pre-eminently within the scope of the Royal prerogative. The courts have held many times that they will not review the exercise of prerogative discretionary powers. Even the withholding or withdrawal of a United Kingdom passport is a prerogative matter. So, indeed, is arbitrary executive action in a protectorate. (So is the disposition of the armed forces, and so too—if we are to accept the opinion of a committee of Privy Councillors[40]—is the power to tap telephones, though the prerogative is supposed to be a residue of inherent Royal attributes extant since time immemorial, when, presumably, there were no telephones to tap.) In instances in which an aspect of external affairs has to be restated on a statutory basis, the Government and Parliament generally do their best to keep the matter within the area of conclusive Executive determination.

When the concept of associated statehood was devised for Eastern Caribbean island colonies unable to form a federation and too weak in population and resources to sustain meaningful independence, the West Indies Act 1967 was passed to implement the concept. The United Kingdom Government and Parliament would retain full control over defence and external affairs (apart from minor non-political aspects of external affairs delegated to the local governments); the associated states would have full control over their internal affairs. When Anguilla purported to sever itself from the associated state of St. Kitts-Nevis-Anguilla, the United Kingdom at first refused

---

39. 421 F. 2d 930 (9th Cir. 1970), certiorari denied 398 U.S. 965 (1970). Top Secret classification sustained, since neither arbitrary nor capricious.
40. Cmnd. 283 (1957).

to comply with the request of the associated state's Government to intervene and subdue the rebellion, taking the view that it was an internal matter. In 1969 the U.K. Government changed its mind; having decided that the rebellion prejudiced Britain's responsibilities for the defence and external affairs of the associated state, it sent in troops and imposed direct rule on Anguilla.[41] In 1971, unable to persuade the Anguillans to return to the bosom of St. Kitts, the U.K. Government (in the interests of its responsibilities for defence and external affairs) secured the passage of legislation which in substance, though not in form, detached Anguilla from the associated state against the wishes of the Government of that state.[42]

None of these measures was tested in the courts; but if they had been, my presumption is that any challenge would have failed, because under the West Indies Act a declaration that a matter relates to, or is necessary for, the discharge of Britain's responsibilities for defence and external affairs is conclusive;[43] and it would be quite uncharacteristic for a British court to go beyond such an assertion.

During the last few years there has been a marked resurgence of judicial activism in English administrative law;[44] yet none of the leading decisions has had anything to do with national security or external affairs. In *Conway v. Rimmer and Another* (1968) the House of Lords jettisoned the doctrine of absolute Crown privilege[45] according to which a Minister could withhold relevant evidence from disclosure in legal proceedings merely by certifying that its production would be injurious to the national interest.[46] There is, however, nothing to suggest to me that the courts would require disclosure of, or even inspect, documents relating to matters of policy in the fields of defence and external affairs.

Since 1968 the House of Lords has upheld the validity of an order extraditing an alien to Greece as a fugitive offender although he had been convicted in his absence and claimed that the ulterior purpose of seeking his extradition was to penalise him for his political opinions;[47] and the legality of a fixed rule excluding alien "Scientology" disciples and refusing exten-

---

41. Anguilla (Temporary Provision) Order 1969 (Statutory Instruments 1969 No. 371). This Order was made with the agreement of the Government of the associated state.
42. Anguilla Act 1971; Anguilla (Administration) Order 1971 (S.I. 1971 No. 1235).
43. 1967 Act, ss. 3(2), 7(2), 18.
44. The leading cases are Ridge v. Baldwin [1964] A.C.40; Conway v. Rimmer and Another [1968] A.C.910; Padfield v. Minister of Agriculture Fisheries and Food [1968] A.C. 997; Anisminic Ltd. v. Foreign Compensation Commission [1969] 2 A.C. 147.
45. Propounded in Duncan v. Cammell Laird & Co. [1942] A.C. 624.
46. Thus bringing the law more into harmony with the American doctrine of Executive privilege; cf. United States v. Reynolds 345 U.S. 1 (1953), and see Professor Street's chapter in this volume.
47. R. v. Brixton Prison Governor, ex p. Kotronis [1971] A.C. 250.

sions of entry permits to those already in the country was sustained.[48] A few years earlier the deportation of Sobell to the United States was held to have been validly ordered, although this was clearly a case of disguised extradition for a non-extraditable offence. The Crown successfully claimed privilege (in a habeas corpus proceeding) for communications on the matter between the American and British Governments.[49] The summing up by the trial judge in the *Sunday Telegraph* case (an unsuccessful prosecution of journalists for breach of the Official Secrets Acts involving publication of a confidential memorandum that impaired friendly relations between Britain and Nigeria) was perhaps atypical—but then the judge was atypical, the public policy considerations in that case were finely balanced, and the section under which the proceedings were brought was singularly ambiguous.

English judges have generally manifested a keen sense of obligation to serve the interests of the State, not only in their judicial capacity but extra-judicially as well, readily agreeing to conduct inquiries into alleged security failures, public scandals, industrial disputes, and problems of law reform. Despite the historical antagonism between Bar and bureaucracy, Judiciary and Executive, this sense of obligation to a higher interest does not stop short at the frontier of adjudication.

How, for example, would English law have coped with a Pentagon Papers case? Since we have no First Amendment, the Government would have been in a much better legal position to prevent publication. If the authorities were willing to admit the authenticity of the documents, and the newspapers were proposing to publish *verbatim* extracts, the Attorney General could have obtained an interim injunction to restrain a breach of Crown copyright. If the newspapers were proposing merely to paraphrase and comment on the documents, I believe (though there is no authority directly in point) that the Attorney General might have been awarded an injunction to restrain this "breach of confidence," notwithstanding that the courts have never asserted a general equitable jurisdiction to restrain the commission of crimes[50] and that the relation between the newspaper and the Government would not have been of a typically fiduciary character.

THE OFFICIAL SECRETS ACTS

Until 1889, when the first Official Secrets Act was passed, there was no criminal sanction against peace-time espionage, or the unauthorised leak-

---

48. Schmidt v. Secretary of State for the Home Department [1969] 2 Ch. 149.
49. R. v. Brixton Prison Governor, ex p. Soblen [1963] 2 Q.B. 243.
50. But civil courts do have jurisdiction to restrain certain forms of criminal conduct, e.g., the commission of public nuisances and criminal contempts of court.

age—or even the sale—of official secrets by Crown servants and contractors. The Act of 1889 penalised such conduct, but it was thought to be too narrowly drafted; thus, for instance, it said nothing of the recipient of unauthorised disclosures. It was therefore replaced by the Official Secrets Act 1911, which attracted hardly a snore of animation during its passage through Parliament. This remains the principal Act. Its scope was slightly extended in 1920, and the 1920 Act was modified in 1939. For purposes of this study, the important statutory provisions are sections 1 and 2 of the 1911 Act, as amended.

The sidenote to section 1 reads: "Penalties for spying." The maximum penalty is fourteen years' imprisonment; sentences of up to forty-two years have in fact been imposed by sentencing defendants to consecutive terms on separate counts or charging them with conspiracy to contravene section 1— the penalty for conspiracy being indeterminate.

The section does not deal exclusively with spying. In 1961 nuclear disarmers organised a protest march designed to occupy a military airfield and immobilise it for a few hours. The leaders were convicted under section 1 of conspiring to incite persons to commit a breach of section 1, the offence being "for a purpose prejudicial to the safety or interests of the State" to enter a "prohibited place" within the meaning of the 1911 Act. It was held (1) that the defence dispositions of the State fell within the scope of the Royal prerogative, and the Crown's decisions as to their appropriateness were not reviewable by a court; (2) that the direct intention of the defendants was to do what the Act prohibited; and (3) that they were not entitled to argue that their motive was to promote the interests of the State.[51]

There is a real possibility that a British Daniel Ellsberg would have been convicted under section 1 of having, for a purpose prejudicial to the interests of the State, communicated "to any other person . . . any document or other information which is calculated to be or might be useful to an enemy." "Enemy" includes a potential enemy;[52] he would not have had lawful authority to communicate the documents; and although I doubt whether the existence of a prejudicial purpose would be held to be a non-triable issue in such a context, it is difficult to imagine a British court holding that the unauthorised communication of top-level foreign policy and defence discussions was not prejudicial to the interests of the State. He would doubtless, however, have been charged under section 2 in order to ensure a conviction.

Section 2 has an engaging charm about it. A masterpiece of convoluted

---

51. Chandler v. Director of Public Prosecutions [1964] A.C. 763. Lord Devlin in that case was not prepared to accept the mere assertion of the Crown as to the existence of a prejudicial purpose as being conclusive or even admissible; but he concurred in the result.
52. R. v. Parrott (1913) 8 Cr. App. Rep. 186.

draftsmanship, it creates 2,324 separate offences.[53] Civil servants and certain other persons entrusted with confidential government information are required to sign an Official Secrets declaration, which sets out the text of section 2 and other relevant provisions of the Acts, and draws attention to the serious consequences of divulging information without express authority. In its present form this minatory exercise is an indefensible charade. Not only is section 2 almost unintelligible but, as the Franks Committee pointed out, the warning set out in the most common form of this declaration includes two misleading statements about the effects of the Acts.[54]

Briefly, section 2 makes it an offence for any person having information *obtained in contravention of the Act,* or *entrusted to him in confidence* by a person holding office under Her Majesty (this term includes police officers), or obtained *by virtue of his present or former office under the Crown,* or as a contractor or as an employee of a Crown Officer or government contractor, to *communicate* that information to *any person other than (a) one to whom he is authorised to communicate it* or *(b) one to whom it is in the interest of the State his duty to communicate it.* It is also an offence for a person to *receive* such information knowing, or having reasonable ground to believe, that it has been communicated to him in contravention of the Act —unless he proves that the communication was contrary to his desire; or to fail to take reasonable care of such information. Prosecutions cannot be instituted save by or with the consent of the Attorney General. The main criticisms of section 2 are these:

—Its ambit is not confined to classified information—it is a catch-all;
—Its scope is singularly uncertain, so that its effect has been misstated not only in the Official Secrets Act declarations but also by at least two law officers of the Crown.

Among its many obscurities, three may be singled out. In the first place, how is one to know when a person is "authorised" to communicate official information; and how is authorisation conveyed? Government witnesses before the Franks Committee expounded a doctrine of implied authorisation. Ministers "authorise" themselves; civil servants have implied authority to communicate information to outsiders if this can fairly be regarded as part of their job. The Franks Committee accepted these propositions; and the concept of implied authority in the case of civil servants could reasonably be accepted by the courts (e.g. by analogy with the doctrine of implied agency), though it increases rather than diminishes the area of uncertainty.

Moreover, in the absence of authorisation, when is a person under a duty in the interests of the State to communicate to another person officially ac-

---

53. Franks Report, vol. 2, p. 262 (Appendix to Evidence of the General Council of the Bar).
54. Franks Report, vol. 1, paras. 34–36, and pp. 134–35.

quired information? How is the journalist to know, if his briefing has been an off-the-record one? And take a former Constitutional adviser like myself. During a Constitutional conference I have to act as a go-between and mediator. For this purpose I must convey and interpret the provisional views of the United Kingdom delegation to the local delegation, and *vice versa,* having been implicitly authorised to use my discretion in deciding what to disclose and withhold. But what if, some time afterwards, a former member of the local delegation asserts that civil servants in the U.K. delegation were dominated by certain preconceived views, which they successfully pressed on the Minister? I can only correct his misapprehension by giving him a slightly fuller interpretation of the facts than I should normally feel it desirable to give.

Such a conversation did in fact take place on one occasion between a local politician and me. My acquaintance went back home and apparently repeated his allegation, indicating that I had supported it. Had I then been threatened with prosecution under section 2, I should have pleaded that I was performing (or trying to perform) my duty in the interest of the State. I hope that in the end a court would have agreed with me, but I should be disinclined to bet on the outcome. This kind of problem pervades section 2, and its pervasiveness cannot but inhibit the diffusion of relevant information.

Finally, although section 2 does purport to define the *mens rea* (guilty mind or guilty knowledge) that must be established before X can be convicted of having *received* confidential information from Y, it does not even specify that *mens rea* needs to be proved at all before X can be convicted of *communicating* to Z or to the general public information received from Y, who has communicated it to X in contravention of the Act. This was one of the main issues in the *Sunday Telegraph* case.

In that case Colonel Robert Scott, defence adviser to the British High Commission in Nigeria, had prepared a report entitled "An Appreciation of the Nigerian Conflict" during the late stages of the Nigerian civil war, and sent out fifty copies of it. The report, while generally favorable to the Nigerian federal cause, included criticisms of the federal forces. One recipient was Colonel Douglas Cairns, senior British member of an international observer mission in Nigeria. Cairns sent his copy to a friend, Major-General Henry Alexander, living in retirement in England and a supporter of the federal cause. Alexander showed it to Jonathan Aitken, a young journalist and aspirant politician who was a supporter of the Biafran cause. Aitken privately took a copy and sold the report to the *Sunday Telegraph,* whose editor made some inconclusive enquiries of officials in London and then published it.

Cairns, Aitken, Brian Roberts, the editor, and the *Sunday Telegraph* were subsequently prosecuted under section 2. Alexander was not, and gave evidence for the prosecution. The trial judge, Mr. Justice Caulfield, directed the jury that they had to find that, if the journalists were to be convicted, each of the links in the chain of communication had *mens rea,* in the sense of knowledge that they were contravening the Act. He also spoke of a "political trial" and suggested that section 2 should be "pensioned off" and replaced. The accused were duly acquitted and yet the judge's direction may well have been wrong, and the law remains as obscure as ever.

—It is no defence to a prosecution under the Act to establish that the communication was made in good faith or for the public benefit (subject to the vague but limited exceptions already indicated) or that no harm was done by the unauthorised communication.

—Decisions as to whom to prosecute are unfair or look unfair. The Attorney General as a politician is not insulated from political pressures. He may be induced to prosecute because a Minister colleague is incensed by a revelation of his own incompetence or duplicity. No Minister or ex-Minister has ever been prosecuted under the Act. Some prosecutions under section 2 have been for trivial offences, and no discernible body of principles regulates the exercise of the Attorney General's discretion. Civil servants who contravene section 2 for reasons other than personal gain are hardly ever prosecuted; they are disciplined or dismissed, unless the case is thought to have serious repercussions.

These criticisms raise difficult issues. The publication in the *Sunday Telegraph* of the confidential memorandum from Nigeria led to Colonel Scott's being declared *persona non grata* by the Nigerian Government; but it also revealed that the quantity of British arms supplies to the Nigerian forces in that civil war had been publicly understated by Ministers. The prosecution could, therefore, have been politically motivated. The Attorney General had indeed consulted the Foreign Secretary before setting the proceedings in motion. But it would have been remiss of him *not* to do so in a case with international political implications. I accept the assurances of everyone concerned in the matter that the Attorney General exercised his own independent judgement—not wisely but in good faith. This is, however, a key assumption on my part. It would be entirely unacceptable for the Attorney General to have decided to prosecute as an exercise in party politics or under political instructions.[55]

Section 2 is tolerable only because prosecutions have been so few—only one a year on average. But such a degree of selectivity suggests that there is something wrong with the law. It cannot be right to hold a sword of Damocles over the heads of so many recipients of official information. And the possibility of prosecution under the Act is used to suppress or amputate books and articles by civil servants and ex-civil servants, while their former political masters remain ostensibly immune.

---

55. The only known modern instance of the Attorney General's using his discretion in the field of criminal law on the basis of a Cabinet decision was in 1924, when he stopped the prosecution of a Communist for a seditious offence.

This is yet another curious Constitutional phenomenon. True, it ought not to be necessary to flourish section 2 at an indiscreet Minister; the Prime Minister has political sanctions at his disposal. No such sanction is operative against a *former* Minister (unless he hopes for a return to office), but no section 2 prosecution has ever been launched, or, as far as I am aware, even threatened. As a case in point, in 1934 Edgar Lansbury was convicted of using Cabinet documents when he was writing his father's biography. No proceedings were taken against George Lansbury himself, though he, a former Minister, had supplied the documents.

Former Ministers are theoretically still bound by a convention of collective responsibility. If they have been Cabinet Ministers they are also (according to the orthodox though questionable doctrine) bound by their Privy Counsellors' oath not to divulge Cabinet secrets.[56] They can be released from that oath of secrecy by the Sovereign's permission conveyed by the Prime Minister of the day through the medium of the Cabinet Office. But it seems that in practice ex-Ministers' memoirs are given merely a selective vetting by the Cabinet Office to eliminate references damaging to security or international relations,[57] and that a formal grant of permission to publish is neither sought nor accorded. The only reason they are in practice exempt from the operation of section 2 appears to be the "long and honourable convention in our public life, that anybody who has held a public office which makes him accountable to public opinion in his own person for what he says and does is entitled before he dies to put on record his own version of the events in which he has played a part." The Secretary of the Cabinet, having offered this explanation to the Franks Committee, prudently added: "Do not ask me, please, whether this is consistent or inconsistent with the Official Secrets Act."[58] Clearly it is not. The concepts of self-authorisation and implied authorisation can be stretched so far that they snap. Reading the revelations of former Ministers is one of my few remaining pastimes, but I should prefer not to have to indulge it in an atmosphere of Constitutional cant.

Then there is the question whether the threat of prosecution is needed at all to induce civil servants to keep state secrets. Are *esprit de corps,* official disapproval and disciplinary sanctions not enough? Nobody can quantify intangibles, and one's answer must be coloured by value judgements. My own feeling is that for some people a penal deterrent is necessary, and that an acceptable substitute for section 2 ought to be devised. Admittedly, it does

---

56. I have serious doubts about the validity of the orthodox doctrine. The oath is not to disclose what passed in the Privy Council. In my view the Cabinet is not to be regarded as a Committee of the Privy Council.
57. Franks Report, vol. 3, pp. 330–32 (evidence of Sir Burke Trend, Secretary of the Cabinet).
58. *Ibid.,* p. 329.

not follow that authors, journalists, politicians, and other commentators who publish official information or reveal and criticise Government policies ought to be subject to similar sanctions. There is a public interest in freedom to make revelations.

But at this point I must reveal one of my cloven hooves. For I broadly agree with the Franks Committee's view that "[i]f a civil servant has failed to protect a secret, . . . a citizen who thereby comes into possession of that secret, and who knows that it is a secret, should [not] be free to compound the failure of the civil servant, and to harm the nation, by passing on the secret as he pleases."[59] Of course, this rather pompous sentence presupposes (1) that disclosure of the secret in question would really be harmful, and (2) that somebody has made an informed and sound judgement that the harm done by unauthorised disclosure would outweigh the public interest in diffusion of information. If these two conditions are present, I am not prepared to concede that the news media are entitled to special privileges.

---

59. *Ibid.*, para. 230.

19

Secrecy and the Citizen's Right to Know: A British Civil Libertarian Perspective

HARRY STREET

> Some of us would like to see further developments in what is published. We would like, for example, to see a deeper analysis of foreign policy. This is a sphere in which the Government can set an example. There should be much greater freedom of discussion about the issues that arise and the alternative courses open to the Government to follow in dealing with them.
>
> *Edward Heath*   HOUSE OF COMMONS, 8 FEBRUARY 1967

THE RIGHT TO KNOW

English law rarely recognises in a formal way an individual's legal right to anything abstract. There is of course no written Constitutional document to set out any citizens' rights. Nothing in the experience of judges conditions them to speak of human rights. The case law is as silent as Parliament about such matters. We can therefore say confidently that English law does not support any "right to know" as such. I should be surprised if the expression has ever been used in a reported case. It is significant that when in the 1960's a British statesman published a book entitled *Communication and Political Power*[1] in which one chapter was captioned "The Right to Know," not a word in that chapter was about the United Kingdom—it was solely about the United States. The author did not find it necessary to explain why in a book largely about the United Kingdom this chapter never referred to Britain.

Of course rights that are expressly protected in other legal systems may, in English law, be secured indirectly or even by the provision of remedies. Yet not even in this sense can we find help in English law. Only one statute intrudes in this area: the Public Records Acts 1958–67.[2] It is enacted that public records shall not be available for public inspection until the expiration of thirty years or such either longer or shorter period as the Lord Chancellor may prescribe as respects any particular class of public records. The

---

Mr. Street is Professor of English Law at the University of Manchester (England) and author of leading works on British civil rights.

1. Lord Windlesham, *Communication and Political Power* (London: Jonathan Cape, 1966).

2. 6 & 7 Elizabeth II, c. 51; 15 & 16 Eliz. II, c. 44.

Lord Chancellor has prescribed longer periods in respect of, for example, exceptionally sensitive papers affecting the security of the State. Subject to all those matters "it shall be the duty of the Keeper of Public Records to arrange that reasonable facilities are available to the public for inspecting and obtaining copies of public records in the Public Records Office."[3] It is doubtful whether this restricted obligation could be enforced in court by a citizen aggrieved by the Keeper's failure to give him access to particular documents. The law then gives virtually no help in any circumstances to a citizen who seeks access to state documents, whether contemporary or historical. And the press has the same legal rights—no more, no less—as the private individual.

The next question is to what extent Parliamentary processes assist the citizen to gain information. I consider here not the general question of Parliamentary participation but how the individual can utilise Parliamentary procedures to find out what he wishes to know. The short answer is that he has no rights vested in himself; he is totally dependent on co-operation from his Members of Parliament.

It might be thought that the Parliamentary Commissioner Act 1967[4] would be important here. This is not so. It is true that the Act enables a citizen to ask a Member of Parliament to request that the Parliamentary Commissioner (British version of the Ombudsman) investigate particular Government action. It is also significant that he has the authority to obtain access to all relevant documents including internal Minutes (but excluding Cabinet papers). A Minister may, however, veto in the Commissioner's report the disclosure of documents or information in instances in which he deems disclosure to be "prejudicial to the safety of the State or otherwise contrary to the public interest."[5] Section 5 restricts the scope of the Act to situations in which the individual member of the public has sustained injustice in consequence of maladministration. It is an Act the sole purpose of which is to redress individual grievances.

In addition, the third schedule forbids the Commissioner to investigate "action taken in matters certified by a Secretary of State or other Minister of the Crown to affect relations or dealings between the Government of the United Kingdom and any other Government or any international organisation of States or Governments." In 1963, Morton Sobell, an American citizen convicted of espionage, had been granted bail pending his appeal. He decided to leave the country. While in transit out of the United States by air, he had to be taken to hospital in England. Following that the Home Secretary ordered his deportation on an aircraft bound back to the United States. Sobell's allegation that the Government had extradited him because

---

3. Sec. 5(3).
4. 15 & 16 Eliz. II, c. 13.
5. Sec. 11(3).

President Kennedy had asked Mr. Macmillan to do so could not be investigated by the Parliamentary Commissioner.

In the House of Commons any Member of Parliament is free to ask a question of the appropriate Minister about aspects of the work of a department under the control of that Minister. On every Parliamentary day except Friday, time is set aside for oral questions; and those for which time is not available may be answered in writing and fully reported in "Hansard," the official record of Parliamentary debates. Many of these questions are suggested to M.P.'s by their constituents. So stated, this looks a valuable counter indeed to excessive secrecy. Yet there are long lists of subjects about which the Government will always refuse to supply information. As a means of obtaining information, say, about Suez at the time of the crisis or afterwards, or any current aspects of foreign policy, the Parliamentary question is ineffective. Even if Parliament officials allow the question to be put, no adequate answer will be forthcoming.

In recent years the House of Commons has come to recognise that backbench M.P.'s might be able to scrutinise policy through newly instituted select committees of the House empowered to interrogate Ministers and their civil servants. This is an important new development, but none of these specialist committees has yet been set up in the foreign affairs area. Potentially the most important of them is the Expenditure Committee, which might influence policy in planning the use of national resources. Although it is true that its title is misleading when it suggests (contrary to the fact) a concern with limited economic issues, it is difficult for an observer outside Westminster to see it emerging as an instrument for surveying and participating in the making of foreign policy. As early as 1918 Ponsonby and his Union of Democratic Control were pressing for a foreign affairs committee; it is as far off as ever.

When the individual citizen is an actual party in judicial proceedings his right to obtain information from government sources are better now than ever before. It might be thought that the law on this topic is irrelevant to the issue of secrecy between State and public. What it does indicate is the possibility of acceptable lines for future judicial development. The House of Lords once held that if a litigant needed any public document in litigation, whether or not the Crown was a party to the proceedings, a Minister could always refuse to produce it or to allow it to be produced; and this he did merely by stating that its production would be contrary to the public interest. Ministerial refusal was conclusive; the court could not inquire whether the public interest would be prejudiced.[6]

In 1968 the House of Lords reversed this principle without legislative in-

---

6. Duncan v. Cammell Laird & Co. [1942], A.C. 624.

tervention.[7] Five separate judgments were given, and it is impossible to derive a set of clear rules from them. What is significant is the courts' own voluntary conclusion that they are competent to decide whether the public interest is prejudiced by disclosure. Absolute Executive discretion is replaced by judicial discretion. The courts have asserted their right to balance the Executive claim to secrecy in the national interest against the hardship caused to individual litigants by withholding the evidence.

It is difficult to say how significant this decision could be in the field of foreign affairs. Two judges in Britain's highest court have stated that there are some areas, like that of Foreign Office disputes, where the Minister's reasons should prevail inasmuch as the document is of a character that judicial experience is not competent to weigh. Other judges suggested that in such cases the competing interests would rarely be finely balanced. There was a general unwillingness to seek to examine Cabinet papers. One judge maintained that all departmental documents concerned with policy-making should be free from judicial scrutiny. Taking the judgements as a whole, they do not preclude the courts in future from exercising their discretion untrammelled in those aspects of foreign affairs not concerned with foreign office despatches or despatches from ambassadors abroad.

This House of Lords decision is quite out of line with the courts' centuries-old approach to questions of national interest raised before them by a Government. No doubt the courts were driven to this change by the harsh way in which the Executive exercised their discretion regardless of the hardship they inflicted on particular citizens; indeed, the Executive's policy was to refuse to disclose virtually everything without taking account at all of injustices thereby perpetrated on individuals. Yet the door has been opened, and later we must speculate on what reforms are made feasible concerning the citizen's right to know, as an effect of this change of judicial attitudes. It would not be the first time that blind Executive intransigence has paved the way to changes without which a more tolerant approach would never have occurred.

Another straw in the wind is furnished by town planning. The power to decide whether to permit land development or compulsorily to acquire land rests under statute in the Minister. One of his inspectors normally holds a public local enquiry and sends in a written report to the Ministry, where a decision is made in the light of that report and any other relevant facts and policy considerations. The Minister had always refused to disclose to objectors the contents of the inspector's report. This issue was one referred to the Departmental Committee on Administrative Tribunals and Enquiries in the 1950's. In evidence before the Committee the Ministry adduced about a

---

7. Conway v. Rimmer And Another [1968], A.C. 910.

dozen reasons why objectors should not see these reports. The Committee was not impressed, and its recommendation that they be published has been implemented by legislation,[8] with none of the evil consequences so confidently predicted by the Administration.

LEGAL RESTRICTIONS ON FREEDOM TO OBTAIN AND DISCUSS INFORMATION

As important as the right to know is the right to divulge. A legal system may restrict that freedom and with it the freedom to acquire information. Restraints of both kinds are contained in section 2 of the Official Secrets Act 1911, which Professor de Smith has examined in his paper. As his account shows, the deficiencies of that Act bear much harder on the press than on civil servants.

The sanction of prosecution is indeed rarely invoked against civil servants. There is a detailed code of discipline governing the official conduct of civil servants and the procedures and penalties for breaches of discipline. This code is not derived from statute; yet despite its extra-legal quality it is uniformly applied. Its sanction rests on the fact that no civil servant has legal security of tenure. Evidence before the Franks Committee showed that civil servants who transgressed section 2 were dismissed under this code, but not prosecuted under the Act. Thus, a social security official who explained in an anonymous article in *The Spectator* how the supplementary benefits scheme operated was chastised for this unauthorised article, but not prosecuted. There is no disciplinary sanction against a former civil servant; it is no longer possible to withdraw his pension.

Of course there are vetting procedures to check the suitability of persons with access to sensitive information. The Government also uses various systems of identification for official information requiring special protection. Security classifications are:

Top Secret: exceptionally grave damage to the nation
Secret: serious injury to the interests of the nation
Confidential: prejudicial to the interests of the nation
Restricted: undesirable in the interests of the nation

Contrary to common belief, these classifications have no legal significance; they are merely an administrative system for determining the precautions to be taken in handling a document.

---

8. Compulsory Purchase by Local Authorities (Enquiry Procedure) Rules 1962 (S.I. 1962 No. 1424); Town and Country Planning (Enquiries Procedure) Rules 1969 (S.I. 1969 No. 1092).

The D Notice

This is a purely administrative system for protecting official information, and without legal authority. The D Notice is issued only on the authority of the Defence, Press and Broadcasting Committee, a non-statutory body composed of officials from government departments concerned with defence and national security, together with representatives of the press and broadcasting authorities. The Notices are addressed to newspaper editors and to broadcasting authorities, with the advice that the Government regards the categories of information defined in them as being secret for reasons of national security, and hence requests the media not to publish. Perhaps the most significant feature is that the system has functioned since 1912, and yet was unknown to the public until circumstances forced its disclosure a few years ago. The press was content to obey in secret, perhaps because in practice though not in law D Notices guided it about the risk of prosecution under the Official Secrets Acts. But D Notices will never be quite the same again after the events of 1967.

In that year the *Daily Express* published an article claiming that the security authorities regularly sifted and scrutinised cables and telegrams sent out of the country. Prime Minister Wilson denounced this as "a sensationalised and inaccurate story," published in breach of D Notices. The Government set up a Committee of Privy Councillors to investigate. This Committee reported that the *Express* story was substantially true and that no D Notices were violated. The Government refused to accept the Committee's report and published a white paper designed to prove its case. Mr. Wilson subsequently wrote that the Committee had reached erroneous conclusions, since the Government was not legally represented before the Committee. Yet, it could have been.

The D Notice system continues, but with a tarnished reputation. The Privy Council Report, the Government, and the Services, Press and Broadcasting Committee have all said that all D Notices should be treated as confidential. All this is depressing when the Privy Council Report and subsequently the evidence given before the Franks Committee show that civil servants are not content to lean only on D Notices in their attempts to muzzle the press. They regularly try to suppress information outside the D Notice system: whether it was the attempt of Profumo as Defence Minister to keep the Keeler affair quiet, or preventing the *Daily Express* from revealing negligence in the construction of a nuclear reactor. Editors still receive confidential letters outside the system. This would be frightening enough if D Notices themselves were always connected with national security in the strict sense; the Privy Council Report has destroyed that myth. Within its limits the D Notice system serves the Government's purposes just as well as any compulsory legal censorship could, and of course much less odium attaches to an arrangement to which press and broadcasting authorities are freely consenting and participating parties.

Other Deterrents

The British press is much less successful than the American at obtaining government secrets. The Official Secrets Acts and D Notices are not the only deterrents. The theory of Ministerial responsibility for all that occurs within a department entails the rule that civil servants are to be anonymous. Although the press is gradually breaking down this anonymity, it is still largely true that the press finds it difficult to get at anyone between the Minister at the top and the press officer at the bottom. This suits civil servants, who have then almost a monopoly of the Minister's ear, who upon a change of Government find no difficulty with their dissociation from policy, and who find it little disadvantageous that it is then harder for them to obtain help from the press when needed.

Another factor is the lobby, about which journalists have been extremely silent until an academic opened it up for public examination in a recent book.[9] A select few Westminster reporters are set apart as lobby correspondents, and collectively given regular off-the-record briefings by Ministers and officials. They are bound to keep secret even the fact that the briefings are held, as well as the sources of this information when they use it. The value of the lobby to Ministers is obvious. It is equally clear that it helps to preserve government secrecy, and handicaps investigative journalism. The fact that the press fully co-operates is the clearest proof of its inability to prise out on its own what happens in the Government.

In 1965 the *Sunday Times* announced: "National security alone excepted, it is the job of newspapers to publish the secret matters of politics, whether the secrets are the secrets of the Cabinet, of Parliament, or of the Civil Service." For this purpose Anthony Howard was appointed Whitehall correspondent. The Cabinet's response was immediate and effective. Civil servants were ordered not to speak to Howard, so that the newspaper soon had to abandon the project.

The *Sunday Telegraph* affair of 1971, discussed in Professor de Smith's chapter above, illustrates the pressures on the press. As narrated by Mr. de Smith, the principals Aitken, Cairns, the *Sunday Telegraph* and its editor, Brian Roberts, stood trial at the Old Bailey on Official Secrets Act charges; but Colonel Alexander turned witness for the prosecution. The

---

9. Jeremy Tunstall, *The Westminster Lobby Correspondents* (London: Routledge and Kegan Paul, 1970).

news value of Colonel Scott's report lay in its disclosure that Government Ministers had given inaccurate information to the House of Commons about their arms supplies to the Nigerian Federal Government. It was generally believed that this was why the Government prosecuted. The judge, Mr. Justice Caulfield, summed up favourably for the accused. This is a typical extract:

> The 1911 Act achieves its sixtieth birthday on 22 August this year. This case, if it does nothing more, may well alert those who govern us at least to consider, if they have the time, whether or not Section 2 of this Act has reached retirement age and should be pensioned off, being replaced by a section that will enable men like Colonel Cairns, Mr Aitken and Mr Roberts and other editors of journals to determine without any great difficulty whether a communication by any one of them or a certain piece of information originating from an official source, and not concerned in the slightest with national security, is going to put them in peril of being enclosed in a dock and facing a criminal charge.

The jury acquitted, and the creation of the Franks Committee was the upshot. The accused were fortunate in their judge, and the trial understandably disturbed journalists.

GOVERNMENT ATTITUDES

The structure of British Government is devised to protect the policy-making function of the Government from public scrutiny; to suppress information has long been part of its ideology. Has there been a recent change of heart?

The Report of the Committee on the Civil Service (the Fulton Report) in 1968 devoted two paragraphs of its long presentation to a plea for open processes of administration. It complained that inadequate consultation impaired the quality of decision-taking and reduced public understanding of policies. The Government was stung into publishing a white paper the following year in order to demonstrate how much more defence and budgetary information the Government was now giving than ever before. Predictably its authors hastened to agree with the Fulton Report that discussions at the formative stage of policy-making must remain confidential. The usual justification was given: collective responsibility is a fundamental of the British Constitution, and the confidential basis of relations between civil servant and Minister must not be breached. Only Government can assess what is in the public interest to disclose; specifically this is true in defence and foreign policy matters. In his Foreword to the subsequent General Election Programme, Mr. Heath said:

I want to see a fresh approach to the taking of decisions. The Government
should seek the best advice and listen carefully to it. It means dealing
honestly and openly with the Press and the public.

One change may be discerned: a welcome tendency for the Government
to issue Green Papers setting out its provisional thoughts on policy matters
and inviting discussion and comment. Beyond that, matters seem much the
same at this writing. The Government protests loudly when the *Sunday
Times* reveals one proposal under consideration for closing railways, then
interrogates the editor and threatens him with prosecution under the Official
Secrets Acts, and the police execute search warrants to trace the leak. A local governing board is threatened with a cut-off of future information from
Government because it disclosed to its electorate the route of a proposed
motorway through its area. The Government would not tell a Select Committee of the medium-term economic assessments that would clarify its already disclosed five-year public expenditure projections. The Cabinet Office says that even to disclose the existence of Cabinet Committees is out of
the question as this would impair collective responsibility.

The Government takes the view that to report internal disagreement in
Government must remain a crime, so serious would be the damage to its
"corporate integrity." Lord Gardiner, Lord Chancellor in the Wilson Cabinet, knowing that the Government had sounded out magistrates about their
attitude to a proposal that their administration be transferred to central government control, asked the Government to publish the confidential views received from the magistrates. Only after pressure did the Home Office agree
to give him the information personally, in confidence, and on condition that
he would tell no one else.

A SURVEY OF DEVELOPMENTS IN FOREIGN AFFAIRS

It is easy to understand why there is so much pessimism about prospects for
openness in Britain with regard to foreign affairs. Governments persuade
the Opposition to accept a bipartisan policy with the carrot that they will be
kept informed. Let Opposition *oppose,* and they will be told that their criticisms are conceived in ignorance, and worse, that they are unpatriotic. The
line between national security and public morale is deliberately blurred. The
most recent example of Foreign Office attitudes is found in its evidence to
the Franks Committee. Safeguarding of virtually all Foreign Office activities
was demanded: messages between missions and the archives of all offices,
exchanges with other nations, information received in confidence, all assessments of policy in foreign affairs. Otherwise Britain's national security
would be damaged, her standing abroad impaired, and her negotiating po-

sition weakened. Fortunately, however, there was no cause for concern: according to its Memorandum,

> The Foreign Office, in the interests of stimulating informal public discussion of foreign affairs, constantly promotes through its News Departments, Information Departments and in many other ways, the highest possible degree of authorised disclosure consistent with the requirements of security.[10]

Law Officers' opinions too are inviolate. The Speaker of the House of Commons has ruled that neither a Minister nor the Attorney General can be compelled to disclose the Law Officers' advice.

There are few successes to record in the battle against secrecy since Ponsonby and his crusade against secret diplomacy. When he became a Socialist Minister in 1924 he was able to make one positive contribution, in what is now known as the Ponsonby Rule. Treaties were to be laid on the table of both Houses of Parliament for at least twenty-one days before ratifying. Conservative Governments did not accept this "no secret treaty" line at once, but in the 1960's it secured general recognition by both parties, together with the accolade of being quoted for the first time in the 1964 edition of Erskine May, the authoritative work on Parliamentary practice.

The Suez crisis of 1956 is the most revealing of recent British experiences. A reversal of traditional pro-Arab, anti-Israel Middle Eastern policy took place, concealed from all. Concerted military action against Egypt was concealed even from Sir Gerald Fitzmaurice, Legal Adviser at the Foreign Office; in fact some say that the almost total exclusion of lawyers from policy-making posts in the Civil Service is the reason for much of the secrecy. Cabinet members were in the dark until late in the day. (This was no new phenomenon in foreign affairs: Lloyd George complained that the Cabinet of 1914 was not informed of major decisions by the Prime Minister and Foreign Secretary, and Foreign Minister George Brown was to make complaint about lack of consultation with Cabinet colleagues in Mr. Wilson's administration of the 1960's.) The Foreign Office archives will never help, as no written records were kept. During Parliamentary debates at the height of the campaign, Parliament was kept in total ignorance of collusion; as Foreign Secretary Selwyn Lloyd observed, "It is quite wrong to state that Israel was incited to this action by Her Majesty's Government. There was no prior agreement between us about it."[11] Attempts to organise a Parliamentary Select Committee on Suez came to nothing. Secrecy is reinforced

---

10. Memorandum of Foreign Office, Evidence to Franks Committee, in Home Office, Departmental Committee on Section 2 of the Official Secrets Act 1911, Cmnd. 5104, September 1972, vol. 2, pp. 69ff.
11. Anthony Nutting, *No End of a Lesson* (London: Constable, 1967), p. 126.

by the rigid convention that the incoming Government never sees the policy documents of its predecessor. No doubt each set of front benchers or members of the Cabinet has a selfish interest in the continuance of this convention.

The South African arms ban provides an interesting example of the confusions arising from the way foreign policy is conducted. Since 1964 the Labour Government's policy was to ban arms to South Africa, but it continued to honour existing contracts till 1967. Then South Africa pressed for new contracts. Foreign Secretary Brown led South Africa to expect a continuance of supplies; he believed that was Cabinet policy. In the end the first public announcement turned out to be one of unconditional ban. The suggestion has been made that this affair revealed several facets of what is wrong with our policy-making: presidential government by the Prime Minister; secret policy formation regarding matters that could have been openly ventilated; half-leaks and briefings for the press lobby, preventing a balanced presentation to the public on decisions by the Cabinet.

Where in the contemporary scene can one pick up a few crumbs for the optimists? For one thing, the Foreign Office cannot pursue its traditional course of extreme secrecy at the United Nations. Too many other countries do not play the same game, and Britain, too, has to "meet the press," even if with reluctance, or else fail to present its own case. The Brussels of EEC, too, is likely to be like New York; and it is not too fanciful to hope that what U.K. civil servants and Ministers will be forced to endure in the European Communities they may grudgingly come to accept as not unthinkable in London as well. Too much should not be made of Article 223 1(a) of the Treaty of Rome establishing the EEC: "No member State shall be obliged to supply information the disclosure of which it considers contrary to the essential interests of its security."

It is well that one might look for something beneficial to emerge from the EEC, for the negotiations preceding it, back to the Conservative rebuff of the sixties, were correspondingly depressing. No doubt the Conservative Government consulted interest groups and informed opinion in Westminster, Whitehall, and the City before deciding to negotiate for entry; but not until the Prime Minister announced that decision to the House of Commons did the general public know anything of it: i.e., the public debate opened only when the crucial final step of decision-taking closed.

THE FRANKS COMMITTEE REPORT

The Franks Committee recommended the repeal of section 2 of the Official Secrets Act 1911[12] and its replacement by a new separate statute, the Offi-

---

12. 1 & 2 George V, c. 28.

cial Information Act.[13] This was done because the Committee wished criminal sanctions to be retained only to protect what is of real importance. That protection would extend to four types of official information:

1. Classified information relating to defence or internal security, or to foreign relations, or to the currency or to the reserves, the unauthorised disclosure of which would cause serious injury to the interests of the nation. The Committee used the expression "foreign relations" deliberately. Its scope was to be relations between the U.K. Government and any other power or any international body the members of which are Governments. It instanced information shared between the U.K. Government and other Governments, and information involving U.K. relations with other Governments. It excluded the field of trade and consular affairs when these are not being handled between Governments.

2. Information likely to assist criminal activities or to impede law enforcement.

3. Cabinet documents, including all documents marked as Cabinet documents circulated to Ministers, whether for the purpose of a meeting of the Cabinet itself or a meeting of any Cabinet committee of which a Minister was a member.

4. Any document entrusted to the Government by a private individual or concern.

The Act would apply to information within the first category (including foreign affairs), only if it had been classified. The relevant classification would be one containing the word "Secret" or, in the case of military equipment, one marked "Defence—Confidential." On the process of classification the Report said only this:

The Secretary of State should make regulations about the classification and declassification of documents, which should include provisions on levels of authority at which decisions on classification may be taken and on arrangements for review and classification.

The Report says nothing more about who will classify, but the implication is that it will be done entirely within Government departments.

Before a decision is taken whether to institute a prosecution for the disclosure of classified information within one of the three categories, there should be a classification review of the information allegedly disclosed without authority. This review should be carried out by the responsible Minister himself. He should be required to consider whether, at the time of the alleged disclosure as distinct from the time of classification, that information

---

13. Franks Report, vol. 6.

was properly classified "Secret" or "Defence—Confidential," in the sense that its unauthorised disclosure would cause serious injury to the interests of the nation. No prosecution would be possible unless he gave a certificate to the court of his satisfaction on that point; that certificate would be conclusive evidence that the information was classified within the meaning of the Act.

It should be an offence for a Crown servant or government contractor to communicate official information, on proof by the prosecution that the communication was contrary to his official duty. One defence might be that he believed on reasonable grounds that he was not acting contrary to his official duty, or that it was not classified, but not that the classification was incorrect or unjustified in the circumstances.

Of particular concern to the media are the offences proposed for those who receive classified information. Thus, it should be an offence for a citizen to disclose official information entrusted to him in confidence by a Crown servant if this citizen's attention had been drawn to the relevant provisions of the Act, and the disclosure was made contrary to restrictions imposed on behalf of the Crown. It should also be an offence, for a person who knows, or has reasonable ground to believe, that information in his possession has been communicated in contravention of the Act, to communicate that information otherwise than in accordance with an authorisation given on behalf of the Crown. The mere receipt of information would no longer be an offence. These provisions have a wide scope. They would cover the correspondent who disclosed non-attributable information along with its source, and the lobby correspondent who broke the lobby code. The consent of the Attorney General would be necessary for prosecution of these offences. The maximum penalty on conviction on indictment would be two years' imprisonment.

A CRITIQUE OF THE FRANKS REPORT

It is a merit of the Franks Report that the breadth of section 2 of the Official Secrets Act would be curtailed and defined with more precision. The effect of that change on prosecutions would be very slight; I can think of no successful prosecution in the last twenty-five years which would not have been covered by the restricted definition now proposed. This is a meagre benefit indeed for four volumes of Report and Evidence.

The proposed amendments to the Act are subject to one overriding criticism: they leave far too much discretion in the hands of Ministers and senior civil servants. The impression given is that the Committee addressed themselves to a narrow problem: What changes can we make to which Ministers—today's and tomorrow's—and senior civil servants will not object too strenuously? They appear to have abandoned altogether the attempt to make constructive proposals which by their own arguments and demonstration would be seen to be fair and workable. No doubt this is why the proposals have received such general and widespread public disapproval.

In the first place, all prosecutions are to be in the hands of the Attorney General. We are asked to believe that although the Attorney General is a politician and a member of the Government he will never give a thought to his hopes of political advancement at the hands of the Prime Minister, that all his decisions will be taken independently and solely on his own responsibility. It is expecting too much of an Attorney General to behave like this. It is asking even more of the press and public to believe that decisions such as that to prosecute in the *Sunday Telegraph* Biafra affair were taken entirely without consideration of political factors and the feelings of individual members of the Government. There was telling evidence from the Foreign Office witness at that trial: "Embarrassment and security are not really two different things."[14] If the task is one to be discharged in so judicial a spirit, why entrust it to a politician not yet in the Cabinet but always hoping to get in soon? The Committee insisted on the Attorney General's retaining control because he alone is qualified to determine the questions of public policy and because he, as the decision-taker, is accountable to Parliament. The latter point would have been more convincing had the Report produced a list of cases in which Parliament exerted any control over his discretion. The cynic will say that this accountability is a myth.

For another thing, many witnesses opposed so extensive a scope of official information as the Committee has proposed. Their common viewpoint —and they were supported by Mr. Justice Caulfield's written evidence—was that the Act should be concerned with espionage and nothing else. Beyond that, lock and key, disciplinary action against civil servants, and the law of corruption would suffice.

Take the Report's inclusion of foreign relations. The writers make great play with the fact that they are not including all foreign affairs. Yet they mention only two foreign items that will be outside the criminal range: "the work of a commercial section of a British Embassy in helping British firms with their overseas business . . . or the work of a British consul in helping British citizens." There is not a word about the way the Foreign Office is trying to clamp down on disclosure of information about European affairs through Brussels, no comparison of the postmortem on the Bay of Pigs with the veil over Suez. Have they read, for example, the passage in Lloyd George's War Memoirs in which he shows that most of the despatches from

---

14. Mr. Johann Welser, cited in Jonathan Aitken, *Officially Secret*, p. 142.

our representatives were quite harmless, since anything that mattered was conveyed to the Foreign Secretary personally and, likely as not, never even communicated to the Cabinet? Taken in conjunction with the extremely wide claims for secrecy made in the Foreign Office evidence, the Report must be seen to support the inclusion of the whole of foreign affairs except "trade and consular affairs." Its failure to analyse this area in detail with a view to keeping the crime within reasonable bounds merits criticism.

As a third objection, even if one found the list of classified information acceptable, the method of classification proposed is completely unsatisfactory. All we get is one sentence, to the effect that the Secretary of State shall make regulations. At the very least the practice followed with other forms of delegated legislation (such as social security) should be adhered to: the practice of mandating a Minister to submit draft regulations to a statutory committee outside Parliament and preventing him from laying these regulations before Parliament in a form with which the Committee disagrees, without first informing Parliament in detail of the differences between him and the Committee.

Elsewhere the Report does propose a consultative Committee of Government and media representatives with limited functions.[15] But this is not sufficient. What is really required here is that a committee be set up to consist only of representatives of the media and of the public; that draft regulations be submitted to the Committee for consideration; that if dissatisfied the Committee should be empowered to require the Minister or senior civil servant to justify them; and that if the Committee is still not satisfied, the Minister should have to lay its objections before Parliament along with his draft regulations. A safeguard of this kind is necessary to prevent automatic acceptance of the Foreign Office viewpoint. The Foreign Office in their Memorandum of Evidence to the Franks Committee presented a very long list of matters that in their view demanded protection. It may well be that the Franks Committee took this list for granted without further ado. That is to leave too much uncontrolled discretion to the Foreign Office. To take an extreme but important example: in war time the Foreign Office would certainly not distinguish national security from national morale any more than did Churchill and his advisers when they kept back bad news in the Second World War.

Finally, in our critique: the Committee has been shown to be evasive about specifying who should have the power to classify documents. Their reaction to the obvious criticism—that civil servants always overclassify—is to require a Minister to certify, before any criminal prosecution for passing along a classified document, that its disclosure would be injurious to the na-

15. Paragraphs 165 and 166.

tion—i.e., that it was correctly classified. Predictably, this proposal has met with universal rejection outside Whitehall. Equally predictably, the only justification advanced by the Committee is Ministerial accountability—the old argument that the only person qualified to assess the public interest is a member of the Government. This line of reasoning is at the heart of the whole Report and must be examined at greater length.

We are told that it is all right for judges in the United States to consider public interest, but because they are different animals from the British breed; their Constitutions, too, are so different. But the nature of the judicial process today, whether in England or in the United States, is such that judges are policy-makers who interpret and apply the public interest. As we have seen, in *Conway* v. *Rimmer* the Civil Service has already lost its battle over the production of government documents in litigation generally. British judges have successfully asserted their right to decide this issue of public interest. Within the Constitutional area there are many other examples: thus, e.g., the freedom of the press to publish free from risk of libel actions hinges on public interest (determined solely by the judges) when fair comment is pleaded. The contrast with the 1972 Younger Report on Privacy[16] is striking. The reporting Committee proposed a new offence—that of disclosing information acquired confidentially or unlawfully, and yet recommended that it would be a defence to establish public interest before the court in such publication.

The Attorney General told the Franks Committee that a jury was not to be trusted with the power to decide what was in the public interest, nor with the right to see evidence on this point. (The Committee had refrained from making the seemingly concomitant proposal that trials on espionage should be without jury.) But there would be no difficulty in keeping the issue from the jury and reserving it for a judge. A trial within a trial on admissibility of evidence is commonplace in the courts. It would be perfectly simple to have the judge alone, in the absence of the jury, decide on the issue of public interest.

In my view, if a case does not amount to espionage within other criminal enactments, and the Government is unwilling to satisfy a judge that disclosure has caused injury to public interest, there should be no criminal conviction under an amended section 2. And if the person in the case is under threat of imprisonment, key issues making for guilt or innocence are not to be decided by a politician with a direct interest in the matter, particularly one whose political future is at stake, and whose decisions, given without reasons, are unreviewable anywhere.

What experience, after all, has the politician in evaluating the public in-

16. Report of the Committee on Privacy. Cmnd. 5012 (1972).

terest in the press's informing the public of some act of Government mismanagement? At a time when on their own initiative British courts are reviewing more and more exercises of governmental discretion because of their claim to balance the larger public interest against the narrow element of administrative and political convenience, it would be setting back the clock to write into a new statute—one designed to "reform" the law, at that —a rule prohibiting the courts from interfering in any circumstances with governmental determinations of public interest.

What the Franks Committee refused to recognise is that one public interest has to be weighed against another and that judges do this regularly in other areas—e.g., in requests in court for the production of government documents. Nowhere does the Committee ever advert to this balancing process. It admits the public interest in knowing about foreign affairs but assumes without any discussion that because there is a governmental interest in secrecy, it follows that secrecy is, therefore, essential. The Franks Committee scarcely seems to recognise that there is a deep conflict between diplomacy with its demand for privacy, and democracy with its insistence on publicity and information. The question whether foreign policy can be effective without democratic procedures to reach it, is never ventilated by the Committee.

This critique of the Franks Committee has so far centred on one aspect of the problem considered in this book: When should the freedom of the press and of others to inform the public and discuss matters of governmental policy be interfered with by criminal law? Important though it is to citizens' participation in policy formation that the media should have as few legal restraints as possible when transmitting information in their possession, this is obviously only one aspect of the problem for lawyers.

THE RIGHT TO KNOW

Early in this paper it was shown that the Englishman's right to know is virtually non-existent. It is in respect of this problem that the Franks Report is quite extraordinary. The Committee took evidence on Swedish and American legislation supporting the right; visits were made to both countries specifically to see how those systems work; witnesses suggested adoption of something similar. And this is all the Report has to say:

> It seemed to us that this suggestion raised important constitutional questions going beyond our terms of reference. Accordingly, we have not gone fully into the possibility of such legislation in the United Kingdom, in the sense of treating it as if it fell within our terms of reference.[17]

---

17. Paragraphs 85 and 86.

And that is all; the Report does not even identify these "important constitutional questions," let alone explain why they make impossible a "right to know" in Britain. I can only assume that the explanation here is the same as I have offered earlier. To wit: If a citizen or the media were to have a right to know, it would displease Ministers and civil servants; therefore it raises an unacceptable Constitutional issue which it was not the policy of the Committee to ventilate. There is plainly no Constitutional objection to contemporary disclosure in foreign relations, by means of leaks, answers to Parliamentary questions, or memoirs. How is the "right to know" Constitutionally different from the "right to disclose"?

It is difficult for an English lawyer without any experience of those systems in which the private citizen can exert legal remedies in obtaining governmental information to make concrete proposals. Yet to me it seems feasible for Britain to protect a right to know. Legislation on the lines of the American Freedom of Information Act of 1966 would seem appropriate to Britain. The obligation on Government to produce would have to be mandatory. Some have thought that a citizen aggrieved by failure to inform should have his remedy in a complaint to the Parliamentary Commissioner (otherwise Ombudsman). I disagree. That official has been too deferential to the Civil Service in the discharge of his present functions. Particular instances are not called for here; it will be enough to mention one general matter.

Frequently what is at issue is the validity of a government department's action. Right from the start the Parliamentary Commissioner has refused to employ any lawyers on his staff. If he wishes to find out whether the challenged conduct of a department is lawful he relies on the Treasury Solicitor (the senior lawyer in Civil Service departments) for the answer! It is significant that the Act under which he operates makes the Minister, not himself, the sole arbiter of what, on the grounds of harm to the national interest, he is not to make public.[18] No, the Parliamentary Commissioner is not the answer. Enforcement of a right to know should lie with the ordinary courts through an order of *mandamus*. The courts in recent years have shown a refreshing readiness to invoke mandamus against Ministers unwilling to exercise their discretion in a reasonable manner.[19] One would therefore have more confidence in the courts than in the Parliamentary Commissioner to enforce Ministerial compliance.

18. Sec. 11 (3), Parliamentary Commissioner Act 1967.
19. E.g., Padfield v. Minister of Agriculture [1968] A.D. 997. The Act provided that "if the Minister so directs," a committee would be set up to investigate milk pricing for farms in particular regions. When the Minister refused so to direct, upon a complaint, the House of Lords held that his refusal was contrary to the implied purpose of the Act and issued mandamus to direct him to consider the complaint according to law.

It would be desirable that a check be made as to whether a scheme of this kind, once in operation, is actually achieving its aims. Britain acknowledges in other areas the consumer's need to have a watchdog, whether it be over broadcasting, the press, the Post Office, or British Rail. Here, too, it would be useful to have a committee composed of the media, academics from the universities, and perhaps backbench M.P.'s to look into complaints about the working of a new system. Perhaps this could be tied in with the consultative committee for classification advocated earlier.

The whole of this critique may be attacked on the grounds that it shows undue confidence in the capacity of the law to improve public participation in policy-forming. I do not believe that the law alone can put matters right. On the other hand I reject the Franks Committee conclusion that "the law is not one of the most important influences on openness in government." In Britain we have a governmental system thoroughly wedded to secrecy. Only a very sharp jolt will disturb this ideology. Unless Ministers and civil servants are compelled by legal sanction to change their ways, they never will. Legal reform is therefore the first step. We are a law-abiding people, and the hope must be that a change in law will gradually induce a change of attitude in the Government. Of course, without such a change, without genuine co-operation from senior officials, openness in the Government is unattainable. The Franks Committee believes that without legislative prodding Ministers and civil servants can be relied on to be dedicated henceforth to abolish governmental secrecy. I do not share that view. I believe that legal changes are necessary to condition the Government to a new state of affairs.

Action is demanded from the media as well. If they could put aside their competitive jostling with one another and look collectively to the greater good of better communication, their present mediocre performance might improve. They should renounce both the lobby system and the D Notice system, and eschew the anonymous inspired leak. The press has no business having cosy conventions with the Government. If all members of the media refused henceforth to take non-attributable statements from Ministers and senior officials, Government's hand would be forced. The lobby system is seen by Government as a necessity for them. But they need the media more than the media need them, and the media, collectively, could use this "clout" to change some of the ground rules.

In my view, the Official Secrets Act should be greatly restricted, so that none of the basic decisions, whether to prosecute people or to classify paper, could be taken by Ministers or civil servants alone. This restriction should be coupled with a right to know, enforceable in the courts, supervised in its working by a non-governmental public body, and supported by press and broadcasting bodies that steadfastly refused to obey the non-legal directives and wishes of Government. Such legislation would point the way towards what we need in Britain.

20

Reform of the British Law
Pertaining to Secrecy:
A Rejoinder to Professor Street

STANLEY DE SMITH

The Franks Report is a meaty, indigestible document. Its main recommendations, insofar as they concern external relations, have been summarised by Professor Street in his chapter of this volume. I shall confine this rejoinder to comment on the Report and its implications, and on some of Professor Street's own comments.

1. I was disappointed, as was Professor Street, at the Franks Committee's peremptory dismissal of experience in Sweden and the United States regarding the disclosure of official information. Although I am extremely sceptical of the desirability of following the Swedish example, the American Freedom of Information Act deserves far more careful scrutiny. I suspect, though, that it would be of limited use in the field of secrecy with which this volume is concerned. There is a fair amount of dissatisfaction in the United States with the way FOIA is operating, and with its demonstrated inability to deal with two more fundamental problems: overclassification and the suppression of the very fact that a secret exists at all.

2. Assuming that people will still be prosecuted for types of disclosures in the field of external relations that fall short of espionage, I am quite clear that the Committee was right in recommending that the decision to prosecute should rest with the Attorney General. It would sometimes be wrong for the decision to be taken *without* consideration of its political implications. The Attorney General can take soundings more readily than the Director of Public Prosecutions, who is a permanent official under his control. The Attorney General is at least potentially vulnerable to damaging political and professional criticism, and for an aspiring judge or Lord Chancellor this is not an insignificant deterrent. I thought I was more cynical than Professor Street; perhaps I was mistaken. Conceivably the present state of affairs might command greater confidence if we had an Attorney General who

was not a politician but an autonomous official with judicial security of tenure; but that idea may have been considered by the Royal Commission on the Constitution.

3. I cringed when reading the passage in the Report asserting that "Ministers have the same public duty to protect official information as their civil servants, and *should continue to be subject to the law as at present*"[1] (my italics). As I indicated in my chapter of this volume, Ministers are remarkably exempt in practice from section 2 of the Official Secrets Act. Is it only in Britain that a body of honourable and exceptionally well-informed men would concur in such a statement?

4. The crucial questions involve classification, and the scope of legal defences and judicial inquiry when a prosecution is brought. I do not pretend to be happy about the Committee's proposals on these matters, but I am not confident that I have yet read, heard, or thought up really satisfactory alternative answers.

I agree with Professor Street's suggestion for publicising disagreements between the Minister and the advisory committee about the content of regulations governing classification. But what, realistically, can one expect such regulations to say about the classification of information in foreign relations? The Permanent Under-Secretary of State to the Foreign and Commonwealth Office had said in evidence[2] that 95 per cent of the papers crossing the desks of senior officers were "classified in one way or another." One suspects that most were classified as "Confidential." The matters in respect of which the Franks Committee thought that secrecy needed to be protected by criminal sanctions fell into two main groups: certain forms of intergovernmental information; and United Kingdom information concerning other nations, which is based to a large extent on reports from British representatives overseas.

> The value of reports of this [latter] kind is limited if they cannot be completely frank, and in this context secrecy is an essential condition of frankness. They include information and reports of all kinds on the situation in other countries, including, for instance, comment on leading political and other personalities.[3]

I reluctantly agree that *this* type of material must normally be classified as "Secret"—or upgraded to "Secret" from "Confidential" in the first place—to come within the protection of the proposed Act. Why is secrecy in the conduct of foreign affairs so repugnant to so many people? Why have several

---

1. Franks Report, para. 210.
2. *Ibid.*, vol. 3, p. 134.
3. *Ibid.*, para. 134.

English judges and other people who ought to know better poured ridicule on the obvious fact that the prospect of publicity inhibits frankness? And would the Vietnam War have been over sooner if Kissinger had followed Woodrow Wilson's First Point calling for "open covenants of peace, openly arrived at"?

Still, overclassification is a real danger. If the material is documentary, then apparently the only significant legal function assigned to a court by the Committee is determination of the question whether the material initially fell within the description of a Secret category—a category that might be and probably would be loosely defined. I incline to the view that it should be open to a judge to determine, not whether it was properly or reasonably classified at the time when the decision to prosecute was taken, or whether publication was nevertheless in the public interest, but whether a reasonable man, not misdirecting himself as to the issues, *could* have arrived at the Minister's conclusion. This is an imperfect compromise between *de novo* review and the absolute conclusiveness of a Minister's decision recommended by the Committee, but it is a test of legality not unfamiliar in English law.

For this purpose a judge would exercise limited discretion involving some consideration of the question whether publication might be in the public interest. And if the unauthorised communication were oral, his discretion would be wider. But I cannot agree that certain analogies with other branches of the law are helpful. Of course a judge is competent to determine independently whether a defamatory statement was made in the public interest. Judges have also made a fair job of assessing the compatibility of restrictive trade practices with the public interest. And few issues are intrinsically non-justiciable. Yet I still entertain real doubt as to whether judges are appropriately equipped to balance (1) the public interest in *non-disclosure* of evidence against (2) public and private interests in *disclosure* where "Crown privilege" is claimed. Courts already carry out this task, but it is too early to say how badly they are performing it. There are some things that English judges are poorly equipped to do. I have already indicated their reluctance to encroach on the preserves of the Executive in matters touching on the conduct of external relations; and on the whole their reluctance (though carried to excess) seems to me to be not unreasonable. What they have to maintain is a residual jurisdiction to correct (and deter) *manifest* abuses of power in the context of the Franks scheme and, indeed, elsewhere.

Under the Franks scheme, if a report such as the one emanating from Colonel Scott in Nigeria had been classified as "Confidential," no question of prosecution would have arisen. If it had been classified as "Secret," then its recipients would have been placed on notice, and it would be essential for them to have a reasonably reliable means of discovering whether communication to them had been "authorised." The Franks proposal offers no real help with that problem. Of course, some material classified as "Secret" or even "Top secret" ought, in the public interest, to be disclosed. But I am certain that Daniel Ellsberg would not have been so easily rescued from his predicament in a British legal and Constitutional context as he was from the very beginning in the United States. His only vindication in England would have had to have been moral and political. Nor could we have a decision analogous to *New York Times Company* v. *United States of America.*[4] The editors of our *Daily Mirror* and *Private Eye* could publish and be canonised, damned, or simply ignored.

I do not believe that any liberalisation of the law of official secrecy can possibly eliminate all abuses of administrative power. The area of criminality, however, must be substantially reduced. The Franks proposals are a cautious step in the right direction though they still give too much weight to Executive discretion on crucial issues. Britain now needs an invigoration of the House of Commons committee system and a quicker movement towards a style of government in which the voluntary diffusion of public information is given a higher priority than ever before.

---

4. 403 U.S. 713 (1971).

21

Secrecy in Law and Policy: The Canadian Experience and International Relations

MAXWELL COHEN

SECRECY IN CANADA: THE NATIONAL SECURITY ASPECT

As a matter of technical origin, the Canadian tradition of secrecy in government has much the same lineage as its British counterpart, particularly as to its form and range. Historical perspective makes apparent how far back in antiquity secrets of "state"—and the concomitant efforts to spy them out in support of civil or military purposes—have been part of the process of organized societies. Alexander the Great is allegedly one of the fathers of codes and ciphers and instituted their concealment by his couriers.[1] English political and Constitutional terminology took the work "privy" (*privé*) and applied it to such classic institutions as the Privy Council. It seems to have been Lord Burleigh, Elizabeth's Treasurer, who encouraged her Secretary of State, Sir Francis Walsingham, to organize the earliest English secret service in a systematic form that was eventually updated by the Protector Oliver Cromwell but not revived effectively after him until the nineteenth century—although doubtless spying and counterspying by diplomats, agents, and "traitors" was the happy business of the intervening courts, as Pepys' Diary makes clear.[2] From the legal point of view, however, much of the early criminal law on disclosing state secrets seems to have been related to the various applications of the general law of treason, at least in the nations adhering to the common law.

The modern period in English law begins with the Official Secrets Act of 1889, itself partly a product of *Marvin's Case,* in which a civil servant was prosecuted (and later acquitted) for using his unconcealed relations with the (London) *Globe* to reveal—by memorizing, not by stealing—the

---

1. Brian Innes, *The Book of Spies* (New York: Grosset and Dunlap, 1966), *passim*.
2. *Ibid.*

contents of a secret Anglo-Russian agreement prepared in anticipation of the Congress of Berlin of 1878.[3] The British Government of the day realized that legal protection was required, and the Official Secrets Act of 1889[4] was the first effort to deal with the problem. But over the years it was felt that the Act emphasized espionage and treason, and as such could not cover mere disclosures of secret and/or confidential information, especially for non-treasonous purposes and to recipients who were not agents of a foreign power. Hence the much broader scope given to the Official Secrets Act of 1911,[5] introducing as it did not only activities involving disclosure of the espionage type but also a far more extensive range of activities involving improper acquisition of any official information.

The 1911 Act not only extended the range of the definition but also shifted the burden of proof to the accused, once a *prima facie* case on the facts had been made out. The onus fell on the defendant to exculpate himself from the charges. The British Act was not enacted separately in Canada but simply made to apply to the "Dominion," a process Constitutionally appropriate at a time when Canada was still not fully independent.[6] Some weaknesses were found in the 1911 Act and, in view of the Irish troubles and the continuing postwar fear of German espionage, the United Kingdom enacted the 1920 Official Secrets Act.[7] But this time the British law was not made applicable to Canada.[8] Consequently, the 1911 Act remained part of the law of Canada until it was displaced by a Canadian legislative enactment: the Official Secrets Act of Canada of 1939.[9]

In addition there is the Criminal Code of Canada, which defined such further related offenses as treason, sabotage, sedition, bribery of officials, breach of trust by a public officer, intimidation of Parliament, unlawful assembly or rioting, unlawful military training, false statements to secure a passport, fraudulent use of a citizenship certificate, spreading false news, making use of official papers, personation or mischief, hate propaganda, conspiracy to perform any of these acts, and preparation to commit an offence under the Official Secrets Act. Finally, certain important provisions in

---

3. For the story of these events see Jonathan Aitken, *Officially Secret* (London: Weidenfeld and Nicolson, 1971), pp. 7–14.
4. 52 & 53 Victoria, c. 52 (1889).
5. 1 & 2 George V, c. 28 (1911).
6. This incorporation of British law into the Canadian system was appropriate in the days before Constitutional Convention, and later the Statute of Westminster ended that practice forever—although *de facto* it had ceased, except with the consent of the Government of Canada, probably during the first quarter of the twentieth century for all practical purposes; good examples of its rare applicability were the Imperial Acts with respect to shipping and citizenship.
7. 10 & 11 Geo. V, c. 75 (1920).
8. Sec. 11.
9. Statutes of Canada (hereinafter: Stats. Can.), 1939, c. 49.

Schedule B of the Canadian Forces Reorganization Act of 1967 deal with
matters related to actions that come within the scope of the Official Secrets
Act.[10]

With some changes in definitions and sentencing, the Canadian Act of
1939[11] (as amended and revised) is much the same as the U.K. legislation
of 1911 together with that of 1920. Both the U.K. and the Canadian statutes are designed to cover spying in its generally understood sense of obtaining information not otherwise in the public domain in order to make it
available to a foreign government or agent. Perhaps more important, section 2 of the British Act and section 4 of the Canadian Act embrace in intent almost any form of information obtained in the course of service or
contract of employment, or otherwise, and then passed on without authority to any other person whatever his status and whatever the purposes of
the transfer of information may be, however unclassified the information
may be, if obtained from sources available because of holding a government position or having a government contract.

As in Britain, the law effects a deliberate shift of the onus of proof to the
accused when a certain limited case on the facts has been made out by the
Crown. And, as in Britain, the Court has power to order the proceedings
held so that the public is excluded from the trial, though not from the passing of sentences.[12] The Canadian statute, like its English counterpart, allows a defendant's "purpose" in revealing information to be implied from
his conduct or known character. Thus, any evidence of communication and
attempts at communication with a foreign agent are *prima facie* evidence of
"purpose."[13]

There are two important differences, however. Unlike the British statute,
the Canadian contains the phrase "secret official" qualifying the more gen-

---

10. Stats. Can., 1966–67, c. 96.
11. Stats. Can., 1939, c. 49; Revised Statutes of Canada (hereinafter: R.S.C.) 1952,
c. 198; R.S.C. 1970, c. 0–3.
12. The phrase in the Canadian statute justifying the exclusion of the public reads,
" . . . proceedings could be prejudicial to the interest of the state," in contrast to
the U.K. language in the 1920 Act, which reads ". . . proceedings would be prejudicial to the national safety. . . ."
13. There are some interesting differences in the definitions to be found in the
Canadian and United Kingdom statutes. These include the definition of "prohibitive
place," more detailed and wide-ranging in the Canadian statute; and the use of the
words "enemy" in sec. 1 of the U.K. Act in contrast to the use of the phrase "foreign
power" in the corresponding provisions of sec. 3 of the Canadian Act. Similarly the
lesser offence of a misdemeanor is provided for in the U.K. statute, sec. 2, in addition
to the felony provisions in sec. 1. By contrast the Canadian language provides generally for an indictable offence, a longer prison term (originally seven years, now
fourteen) than the 1911 U.K. Act, yet parallels the United Kingdom arrangements
for summary prosecution ("summary conviction" in the United Kingdom); but, as in
the United Kingdom, this is at the discretion of the Attorney General, with a modest
penalty in Canada in these cases, of $500 or twelve months' imprisonment, or both.

eral phrase "document or information" the communication of which is illegal under section 4. The British statute (section 2) has been so drafted and interpreted as to establish that the communication of any official information is illegal. The phrase "secret official" is used in the British section solely for the limited purpose of qualifying the words "code word or pass word" but not "document or information." In the preliminary hearings involving R. (*Beglaki, Informant*) *and Biernacki,* an unreported judgment of Judge Shorteno of the Court of Sessions of Peace in Québec,[14] held, among other things, that the phrase "secret official" determined and qualified the kinds of information whose disclosure the Act makes criminal. The other difference is in the punishment. The maximum sentence under section 2 of the British Act (the non-espionage crime of unauthorized communicating) is only two years' imprisonment, whereas in Canada, under the parallel section 4, the maximum is fourteen—the same as under the espionage section. Prosecutions under the Canadian section have, however, been much fewer than in Britain during the years since World War II.

To this list of provisions, of course, must be added the general theory of criminal "conspiracy." Indeed, through the doctrine of conspiracy as well as by other provisions, the Act apparently intended to embrace any "preparation" for undertaking prohibited acts. Hence it is that, both in the United Kingdom and in Canada, in several reported cases dealing with Official Secrets situations, there is a tendency to include the crime of "conspiracy" in the charge; and this would seem to differ very little from the additional concept of an "attempt" or "preparation" with the objective of committing an offence. As Lord Goddard, the Chief Justice, stated in *Gardner* v. *Akeroyd,*

> . . . leaving aside what it is necessary to prove in a charge of conspiracy to commit an act absolutely prohibited, we now come to the offences of attempting and of doing act preparatory to the commission of an offence against the regulations. I am by no means clear about the difference between these two offences. . . .[15]

Nevertheless, a review of the reported Canadian prosecutions arising out of the Gouzenko Papers disclosures of 1945[16] (see below) and following the report of the Royal Commission on Espionage,[17] indicates that the additional charge of conspiracy was brought in almost every case.

---

14. Case No. 5626, 1962, Court of Preliminary Enquiry, District of Montréal; see also R. v. Biernacki (1962) 37 C.R. 266, concerned with the quashing of a Preferred Indictment proceeding against the same accused.
15. [1952] 2 Q.B. 743.
16. M. Cohen, "Espionage and Immunity: Some Recent Problems and Developments," 25 *British Yearbook of International Law* (1948), 404.
17. Report of the Royal Commission, "Investigating the Communication of Secret and Confidential Information to Agents of a Foreign Power" (Ottawa: H.M.S.O., 1946). (Hereinafter: Royal Commission on Espionage.)

Finally, during World War II Canada promulgated the very extensive Defence of Canada Regulations[18] and passed the Treachery Act of 1940[19]; there was the further possibility of prosecution under military law by court-martial. While Sections 85 and 86 of the Canadian Criminal Code, before World War II, dealt with the passing of official secrets, these were repealed by the Official Secrets Act of 1939.

This brief legislative history should be viewed in the light of the actual administration of Canadian policy concerning official information over the past three decades. Because of the Parliamentary system, the Cabinet is less able than its American counterpart to cut itself off from day-to-day legislative cross-examination. Questions raised in Parliament which seem to require more disclosures than are there made, may give rise to the appointment of a Commission of Enquiry. Although the decision to appoint such a commission rests with the Government Ministers, as does appointment of its members, these commissions have been a valuable additional vehicle for public disclosure.

In late 1941 and early 1942 George Drew, then counsel to the Opposition Leader in the House of Commons and later Leader of the Conservative Party, charged that Canadian troops had been sent, ill-equipped and ill-trained, to reinforce Hong Kong, and had been caught by the Japanese in a lightning conquest of the area. Drew's allegations led to the appointment of a Royal Commission under the Chief Justice of Canada to enquire into such matters. Inevitably, the ensuing investigation involved the disclosure of "confidential" information with respect to the training and despatch of the troops concerned.[20] Colonel Drew was a prominent and powerful politician, with strong Army associations. The Liberal Government could not leave his charges unexamined or unanswered. From the point of view of the history of secrecy in Canada, the Report stands as an illustration of the extent to which the Parliamentary system can force a public review of secret government policies, even in wartime.

During almost the same period, charges of maladministration in the manufacturing of Bren guns, an important small weapon with which the Canadian Army was being equipped, led to the Bren Gun Enquiry of 1939.[21] Here again a good deal of information about matériel, otherwise highly classified, had to be disclosed. Under the circumstances of war, both enquiries were embarrassing to the Government. In his published diaries

---

18. Canadian Report, *passim, supra,* Preface, Note 1.
19. Stats. Can. 1940, c. 43; for the Defence of Canada Regulations see the Privy Council Order, 2483, September 3, 1939; Proclamations and Orders-in-Council passed under the authority of the War Measures Act, 8 vols, 1940–42.
20. Report on the Canadian Expeditionary Force to the Crown Colony of Hong Kong (Ottawa: H.M.S.O., 1942).
21. Royal Commission on the Bren Machine Gun Contract (1939), p. 51.

covering that period, the then Prime Minister, Mackenzie King, made the point that disclosure was embarrassing inasmuch as the documentation involved other nations and exchanges with them.[22] But the enquiry also contributed to public knowledge of the operations of government and tightened up the administrative process, engendering reform in the training and despatch of troops, manpower planning and, certainly—in the case of the Bren Gun—in the organization of wartime procurement procedures.

World War II produced also the most dramatic and serious of all Canadian Official Secrets offences, in consequence of which a Royal Commission was used not to examine government secrets but to impose secret procedures of its own on Canadian citizens. In September 1945 a Soviet cipher clerk named Igor Gouzenko defected with a large quantity of material from his Embassy's archives in Ottawa. Among his trophies was evidence of the Russian spy network in Canada.

For two or three days he had difficulty persuading anyone in the Canadian Government that he should be taken seriously. These were still the last months of the wartime alliance, and so, for Canada to have to expose a massive Soviet espionage program, employing several networks and using a considerable number of Canadians recruited from both private life and the public service (including a Member of Parliament, Fred Rose), was a traumatic experience for the Government. But soon a Royal Commission was appointed, comprising two judges of the Supreme Court of Canada, with very wide and unusual powers to enquire into the entire affair.[23]

Among these powers was the authority to hold persons *incommunicado,* to take their evidence *in camera* and without presence of counsel. The Commission was exempted from notifying witnesses that, under section 5 of the Canada Evidence Act, they could claim not to have their testimony used against them in any subsequent criminal proceedings. Rounded up in secrecy, held quietly until they were brought before an *in camera* enquiry, at first not even given the right to counsel, the detainees did not know about or invoke their section 5 protection.[24] As a result, several of those investigated were later prosecuted on the basis of the very evidence they had given to this Royal Commission. This procedure of compelled self-incrimination provoked objections from segments of the Bar, from the law schools, and from the public as well.[25]

From the point of view of the Official Secrets Act, the Royal Commission enquiry and the trials that followed remain the centerpiece of present Cana-

22. J. W. Pickersgill, ed., *The Mackenzie King Record,* I: *1939–1944* (Toronto: University of Toronto Press, 1960), pp. 352–54.
23. Report of the Royal Commission on Espionage, pp. 7–9.
24. R. v. Mazerall [1946] 2 C.R. 261.
25. Fyfe, "Some Legal Aspects of the Report of the Royal Commission on Espionage" 24 *Can. Bar Rev.* 777 (1946).

dian espionage experience and jurisprudence, demonstrating what an authentic espionage situation may offer as a challenge to security. Most of the
prosecutions were based on charges of "conspiracy" and specific violations
of the Official Secrets Act.[26] The trial of the Member of Parliament raised
especially important issues.[27]

Since the Gouzenko trials, Canadian experience with espionage and related questions of subversion has probably not been much different from
that of most countries beset by the intelligence problems generated by the
Cold War. Two other Royal Commission enquiries took place in 1966. One
dealt with a postal clerk who gathered generally unclassified information
and allegedly passed it to agents of a foreign power.[28] This was found not to
constitute an Official Secrets offence, although it was very "close to the
line."[29] Another involved an investigation into the behaviour of a German
woman who had interesting political connexions among certain former

---

26. See Cohen, *op. cit.*, Note 23 above, for a summary of these cases.
27. R. v. Rose [1946] 2 C.R. 107; [1947] 3 C.R. 277. The most interesting aspect of
the Gouzenko case was the attempt in almost all the defences to deny the admissibility of Gouzenko's evidence and particularly his documentation from Soviet Embassy
files—which also linked the accused Member of Parliament to the events charged—on
the grounds that these documents were archives of the embassy of a foreign State
and, therefore, as with all embassy archives, absolutely immune from the jurisdiction
of the host State. This issue was dealt with extensively in R. v. Rose, particularly in
the judgment of the Court of Appeal; see judgment of trial court, Judge Lazure, in
[1946] 2 C.R. at 108–109; and of the Court of Appeal (K.B. Appeal Side) Judge
Bissonette [1947] 3 C.R. at 288. But it is worth noting that the trial court Judge,
Lazure, disposed of the matter by the short finding that embassy documents brought
before a Canadian court, no matter how they reached the court, *are admissible* since
whatever immunity attaches to them is not absolute in itself but must be claimed by
the sovereign whose documents allegedly they are. And since the Soviet Embassy did
not—for obvious reasons—come into court to claim the documents as its own, the trial
judge seemed to have had no difficulty in finding the documents admissible when relevant. And relevant they certainly were. There is some doubt whether the judgment is
entirely sound because it permits stolen but otherwise immune embassy documents to lose
their immunity if not properly identified by a claiming foreign sovereign state. Clearly in
the *Rose* Case, the very fact that the prosecution relied upon them as Soviet documents
was an admission by the Crown that they were, in fact, parts of the "Archives" of the
Embassy—although there was the subordinate question whether espionage information is "diplomatic" and therefore within the privileges of immunity. See Cohen,
op. cit., for the debate on this issue. Yet, even under these conditions, why should
the court have accepted these materials as validly identified Soviet documents for the
purposes of the prosecution and then denied their status as embassy documents for
the purposes of the defence? This case has an indirect bearing on the policy problems
of the present chapter, for it is suggestive of some of the difficulties even in free
societies in a world of continuing espionage and it might be viewed in the light also of
the provisions dealing with embassy archives to be found in the more recent law as set
out in the Vienna Convention on Diplomatic Relations, 500 *United Nations Treaty
Series* 95. Art. 24: "The archives and documents of the Mission shall be inviolable at
any time and wherever they may be."
28. Commission of Enquiry into Complaints made by George Victor Spencer (1966).
29. See above Spencer Enquiry, p. 57.

Cabinet Ministers and was suspected also of having contacts with an agent or agents of a foreign power.[30] While these reports added to the scandal and spice of Federal politics of that year, neither enquiry was of great significance for the evolution of security policy.

Canada has also experienced the rather special security problems of nationalism in Québec, possibly with overseas connections. With considerable prescience, the 1969 Royal Commission on Security[31] in its analysis of separatism in Québec, seemed to forecast the possibility of seditious violence. Indeed, the Commission ranked this security problem as important as any posed by the Cold War, and within two years of their report's completion its predictions were grimly fulfilled when in October 1970 James Cross, the U.K. Trade Commissioner in Montréal, and Pierre Laporte, the Québec Minister of Labour, were kidnapped. Mr Laporte was murdered within a few days. These events led to an intensive search for the kidnappers and assassins and to the proclamation by the Federal Government of the War Measures Act on 16 October, 1970.[32]

Under this law and its subsidiary regulations, the Governor in Council, faced with an "insurrection, real or apprehended," had very broad powers of arrest without warrant, and detention without bail for a limited period. Over four hundred persons, most of them in Québec, were arrested, detained, and questioned. While many were released after some days, a few were retained for longer periods until discharged at the end of police enquiries. The War Measures Act was replaced later by the Public Order Temporary Measures Act, which incorporated the same regulations.[33] These measures reflected a policy of determined and vigorous policing, with the Canadian Army patrolling many sectors of Québec (particularly the cities of Montréal and Québec) as well as of eastern Ontario, with emphasis on Ottawa. Except in one or two other special situations such as the Great Strike of 1919 in Winnipeg, the Army had never before been called out in peace time under the War Measures Act.

During this time, too, censorship was imposed under the regulations prohibiting media publication of anything that threatened security or in any way gave a platform to statements or publications by the F.L.Q. (Front Libération de Québec), the organization regarded as primarily responsible for the kidnappings, murder, and other acts of violence.

---

30. Report of the Commission of Enquiry into Matters Relating to One Gerda Munsinger (1966).
31. The Year of the Report's submission was 1968, but publication was in 1969.
32. R.S.C. 1970 W-2, proclaimed October 16, 1970; for the Regulations see SOR 70/444, October 28, 1970. For the story of these days in Québec see 96 *Time* 116 (October 19, 1970), pp. 10–12.
33. The Public Order Temporary Measures Act, Stats. Can. 1970–71–72, c. 2 (now expired).

Nothing in postwar Canada provided such drama or seemed to pose such threats to order as these almost "revolutionary" events. They affected the very image of societal stability in the Province of Québec and particularly in Montréal. The Provincial authorities invited the "co-operation" of the national Government—or were compelled to accept it—and the air was filled with fear, enough to have influenced calculations by either the national or the Québec Government. Anyone living in the Montréal area at the time, with some "feel" for the psychological realities, must admit to the sense of physical fear that haunted the region. It was fear, personal and institutional, fear for self and fear for society.

Serious debate has since taken place both among students of politics and public law, and among political parties and the public in general, as to the significance of this recourse to maximum force—unusual for Canada—and the suspension in substantial part of the role of the civil authority during a period of the crisis. Coming as the kidnappings and murder did, as climax to almost a decade of mounting violence and intense nationalist fervour (especially among the intellectuals and the youth in Québec), the crimes at the time were not easy to evaluate for purposes of determining objectively the amount of force needed to meet the challenge. There are some, particularly on the left, who now argue that panic caused both Governments to resort to extravagant measures of control. This assessment has gained momentum since the actual number of revolutionary cell members involved was revealed to be not the three or four thousand terrorists estimated by one Federal Cabinet Minister, but only, at most, a few hundred.

This debate, with its advantage of hindsight, has not been very profitable. That there were abuses and mistakes in the course of the arrests and detentions is undoubtedly true. Many of these have been rectified, at least in part, by the findings of the Québec Ombudsman and his reports to the Provincial Government. And while pain inflicted on the innocent can never be wholly compensated, on balance the situation seems to have been handled with courage and firmness, and a minimum of rough dealing with persons and liberty in an authentic crisis.

THE CONTEMPORARY PROBLEM OF INFORMATION LEAKAGE

Censorship during the Québec crisis marked the high point in the use of government power to enforce secrecy in the postwar era. The trend, however, has been in the opposite direction, and during recent years there has been a marked increase in information leaks to the media. On the whole a strong tradition of respecting the integrity and confidentiality of government documents has been maintained by civil servants. There have been several exceptions, however, within the past three years,[34] involving disclosure of reports and studies prepared for committees of Parliament, or for Ministers and their colleagues to aid in policy formulation. Some leaks seem to have been deliberate efforts on the part of officials to influence policy; others were private ventures on the part of as yet unidentified sources. Among the more important Cabinet documents recently leaked to the public through the press was the paper on a proposal to transfer from the Queen to the Canadian Governor General the signing of Canadian diplomatic envoys' credentials, Letters of Credence, and Letters of Recall. Among research works leaked are the Foreign Investment and Takeover study and a study for the Royal Commission on Bilingualism and Biculturalism dealing with the policies of English-language employers in Québec toward the French language in plants and offices.

Thus there are some traces in Canada today of a breakdown, however modest it may still be, in the traditionally scrupulous regard for the letter as well as the spirit of confidentiality in government. This change in the atmosphere seems to be allied with the mood of challenge pervading many Western democracies toward government in general and the questioning of its actions. While this challenge tends to avoid revolutionary confrontation with constituted authority,[35] there appears a marked posture of disaffection—supported by the media—on the part of certain sections of the intelligentsia, of students, minorities, and those generally disenchanted with contemporary values or dissatisfied with their own place in the scheme of things. Together these constitute a formidable group, and they question the right of Government to exercise authority in open societies without giving good reasons for its decisions as well as adequate data to allow those decisions to be properly debated. Decisions, it is asserted, must not only be made but must be legitimated by the informed participation of the public in the making of them.

The most comprehensive statement of the issues both of theory and of practice is that made in June 1972 by a distinguished Canadian public servant, Mr. Gordon Robertson, Clerk of the Privy Council and Secretary of the Cabinet, in addressing the annual meeting of the Royal Society of Canada in St. John's, Newfoundland.[36] His thoughtful, balanced presentation concludes with a sense of regret at the mounting number of breaches of confidentiality within the operations of the Federal Government, and he makes the serious assertion that the democratic process and in particular

---

34. For a short outline of these leaks see the paper presented to the Royal Society of Canada by Gordon Robertson, Clerk of the Privy Council, June 6, 1972 (mimeo.), pp. 2–5.
35. The Robertson paper, *ibid.*, stresses this change of attitude.
36. *Ibid.*

the mechanisms of responsible and Cabinet government "much more than systems involving a single, presidential executive," is "dependent on confidentiality, not simply for national security, but also for its very operation." As he continues,

> If we believe that representative and responsible government is the best way we have so far been able to work out to provide a degree of participation that is consistent with effective action and to give expression and reality to the general will in determination of the interests and wishes of the people as a whole, we cannot accept as permissible a liberty by those in the service of the state to place their convictions about policy, or about the public right to know ahead of their official responsibility.[37]

No one will quarrel with Mr. Robertson's general statement of the proposition, for on the surface it is virtually unassailable. But that is only the beginning. The next question is whether the mechanisms of the democratic process in Canada provide enough safety valves to permit those who ought to know, to know what they ought to know. This is not a question each civil servant, or each professor working on government contract, ought to determine for himself, as though the law were non-existent. On the other hand, when citizens observe their Government making decisions that do not affect national security, and still without allowing the public or Parliament to play a role, then the temptation to do what is perceived to be "moral" may triumph over what is "legal."

Indeed, under present Canadian legislation it is not clear that a journalist or a scholar speaking to a civil servant is not in breach of the Official Secrets Act in the ordinary exchange of any confidences at all between them —and this may apply to civil servant and Cabinet Minister as well. When are journalists or scholars persons "authorized" to receive confidential information within the meaning of the Canadian Act? There is very little discretionary language in the present statute except for the safeguarding phrase "secret *official*" (italics added) in section 4. In practice some disclosure to journalists and scholars is tolerated up to a point, and indeed encouraged in some cases; yet the civil servant or adviser to the Executive is generally on his own in trying to assess the propriety of any particular disclosure he might make. It is not surprising that he finds himself developing guidelines of his own. Nor is it wholly surprising that some seem willing to disclose information in areas where no foreign powers, no vital national security interest, or any other inherently confidential national matter is involved, but where the information is important for informed domestic debate.

It may be answered, of course, that no such disclosure should ever be

---

37. *Ibid.*, p. 25.

tolerated if effective administration is to be maintained, that in any case it is a simple breach of the civil servant's oath to disclose any information without permission from the proper authority. Perhaps, on the other hand, a better approach to the problem would be to redefine the law so as to distinguish between minor and major breaches of secrecy, between those that harm national security and those that merely embarrass political interests. Should there not be some less Draconian rule for protecting significant foreign policy information, fiscal information, defence and national security information from unauthorized disclosures that could harm the nation: a rule that would not also discourage useful public dialogue and the disclosure necessary to democratic government?

Secrecy is a valuable means to effective administration; it should not become a worshiped end. And the more complex a society becomes—while at the same time more promises of a "participatory democracy" are made— the greater is the urgency for Governments to find new criteria for disclosure: criteria balancing the right to know with the necessity of confidentiality—and with the argument increasingly weighted, wherever possible, on the side of public knowledge in aid of effective public debate.

THE UNSTABLE BALANCE: AMENDING O.S.A.

The problem of finding a balance is one that Canada must resolve within its own Constitutional framework. The U.S. doctrine of separation of powers has no equivalent in Canada. The great power of Congressional Committees in the United States, abetted by Constitutional standards set by the Supreme Court, places the question of secrecy in a quite different institutional context. The approach to Cabinet government is quite different. Moreover, Canada has constitutional traditions and processes without equivalent in the United States. The House of Commons Question Period, discussed above, is one custom relevant to the "right to know." Each system has different Civil Service sanctions and discipline, recruitment and training procedures, and security classifications. Perhaps Canada, having taken its Official Secrets Act from Britain, ought now also to adopt the general conclusion of the Franks Report, which comes down on the side of replacing section 2—the "catch-all" section—by "narrower provisions."[38] As the Report recognizes,

> . . . a catch-all provision goes too far towards the protection of secrecy.
> Yet repeal of section 2, without replacement, would go too far in reducing
> the protection of necessary secrecy. A proper balance between openness and
> secrecy requires a reformed law in place of the present section.[39]

---

38. Franks Report, vol. 1, pp. 31–36; Robertson, *op. cit.*
39. Franks Report, *ibid.*, pp. 37–40, 102.

Some of this same spirit is to be found in the Canadian Report of the Royal Commission on Security of 1969. After stating in paragraph 208 that in their opinion the provisions of the Canadian Act "appear extraordinarily onerous," the Commissioners go on to say,

> . . . we have given some thought to the ideal content of an Official Secrets Act. . . . In our opinion such an Act should in the first place protect all classified information from any unauthorized dissemination, whether or not the purpose of such dissemination is prejudicial to the interest of the state and whether or not the information is intended to be directly or indirectly useful to a foreign power; possibly (as in the British Act) offences due to carelessness should be treated as misdemeanors (summary conviction offences) rather than as felonies (indictable offences) and thus carry reduced penalties, but the Act should have general application as far as classified material is concerned. A certificate from a responsible Minister that the classification of given material was necessary and appropriate in the national interest should be accepted by the Courts.
>
> 210. Secondly, the Act should protect unclassified information from attempts at collection and dissemination which are prejudicial to the interest of the state or intended to be useful to a foreign power. The fact that such attempts are systematic, clandestine, conducted for payment or carried out under the direction of foreign agents should be evidence that they are prejudicial to the state or intended to be useful to a foreign power.
>
> 211. Apart from the supervision we have mentioned (relating to classification in cases involving classified information, and relating to purpose in cases involving unclassified material), we see no reason for other major unusual evidential or procedural arrangements. . . . We think there is a good deal to be said for the view that conspiracy to commit offences against an Official Secrets Act amended as we suggest should be included in the Act itself.
>
> 212. Some countries manage without a formal Official Secrets Act. . . . Nevertheless, it is possible that an Official Secrets Act may have some deterrent effect. . . . On balance, we think that in the Canadian circumstances on Official Secrets Act is desirable.
>
> 213. . . . The present Act is unsatisfactory from a number of points of view. . . . There may be no urgency about the matter, but we nevertheless think that consideration should be given to a complete revision of the Canadian Official Secrets Act. . . .[40]

The combined effect of the Canadian Royal Commission Report and the Franks Report would seem to suggest that the severity of the "catch-all" in both countries is well recognized and should be modified; surprisingly, however, the Canadian Commission is less anxious about the problem than is

---

40. Canadian Report, pp. 76–78.

the Franks. The reasons are likely to be found in the infrequent use of the Act in Canada as a general policy, and also that the *Biernacki Case,* previously discussed, renders successful prosecution more difficult because of the way the words "secret official" were interpreted by Judge Shorteno.[41]

Whatever may be the effect of these small differences in law, probably the reason why the Canadian OSA is used less than the British is to be found not in the law itself but in the more aggressive role of the media in North America, as well as in the nature of North American society in general and of Canadian politics in particular. The attitude toward authority and elites may be less respectful than in the United Kingdom. But the fact that the Canadian Act is used less than the British does not mean that the statute should be left unreformed. Although largely unused, the law undoubtedly has a "chilling effect" on legitimate exchanges between scholars or journalists and the Cabinet and Civil Service. The very uncertainty it creates causes those who wish to be law-abiding to err on the side of exaggerated caution. Thus the public is probably deprived of a good deal of useful information, and the structures of government are probably more secretive than the necessities of confidential and effective administration may require. This is the conclusion of the Franks Report, and it applies equally to Canada.

AMENDING CROWN PRIVILEGE

The Canadian Government (the Crown) from time to time asserts its right to withhold information from courts or from litigants. Crown Immunity to Discovery and Crown Privilege—on the Federal level at least—are dealt with in section 41 of the Federal Court Act,[42] which gives a high degree of judicial discretion to the presiding judge in order to compel the admission of documents or information claimed by the Crown to be privileged. But this discretion does not apply where the interests of national security or the concerns of foreign Governments are involved.

This approximates the situation in Britain since the recent successful attack by the United Kingdom's highest court, the House of Lords, upon the former rule that had treated as absolute a Minister's statement that—on grounds of public interest[43]—a government document or testimony should

---

41. *Supra,* Note 14.
42. Stats. Can. 1970–71–72, c.1; see the recent case of Churchill Falls (Labrador) Corp., Ltd. v. The Queen (1972) 28 D.L.R. (3d) 493.
43. For a comprehensive review and analysis of Canadian Law in this area see Linstead, "The Law of Crown Privilege in Canada and Elsewhere" 3 Ottawa L. Rev. 79, 449 (1968–69) and see, particularly, for the recent U.K. position, Conway v. Rimmer and Another [1968] 2 W.L.R. 998 [1968], All E.R. 874 (H.L.).

not be disclosed to litigants or given to a defendant. Both the new Federal Court Act of 1970 and the evolving Canadian common law even before 1970, are now likely to produce fairer disclosure standards in both civil and criminal litigation between the Crown and a subject.

An old and rankling problem is the difficulty surrounding the position of Statutory Instruments (delegated legislation), enacted, in effect, by the Cabinet in closed session under a general grant of authority by Parliament, many of which were either never published or else were specifically made unavailable on grounds of security. New legislation to correct this abuse-prone situation and the regulations made in pursuance of it, were in large part the work of a committee of the House of Commons—the Standing Committee on Statutory Instruments.[44] In introducing the Statutory Instruments Bill on 25 January, 1971, the then Minister of Justice stated his opinion that it was "a significant step toward a more open society in Canada and constituted a major legal reform in the area that lawyers and parliamentarians have called subordinate or delegated legislation."[45] As he explained, the Bill sought to ensure that any regulations issued pursuant to a statute meet four tests: that they were authorized by the Statute; that they do not amount to an unusual or unexpected use of authority; that they do not trespass unduly on existing rights and freedoms, and particularly on the Canadian Bill of Rights; and, finally, that in their draftsmanship they were in accordance with established standards.[46]

These objectives may soon be largely achieved. Equally important, of course, they have clarified the types of, and access to, regulations that remain unpublished or secret, or published only in part.[47] Finally, they have provided a more systematic mechanism for Parliamentary scrutiny,[48] and, through the Federal Court Act, a means of judicial review. It remains difficult, however, to judge at this time the precise effect of the provisions dealing with those regulations that do not have to be registered with the Clerk of the Privy Council. No Parliamentary scrutiny is provided for these. Presumably only the good judgment of the Clerk of the Privy Council, guided by the Act's provisions describing such non-registerable regulations, are available as a check on secrecy and non-disclosure.[49]

---

44. Debates, House of Commons, January 25, 1971, p. 2734, quoted by the Minister of Justice.
45. *Ibid.*, pp. 2734–36.
46. *Ibid.*, p. 2375.
47. 19–20 Eliz. II, c. 38, sec. 27; SOR/71–592, 14–21.
48. *Ibid.*, sec. 26.
49. For an indication of the law pertaining to secrecy at the Provincial level of Canadian government, see: Wright et al. v. Her Majesty the Queen [1964] S.C.R. 192; see also Re Thodas [1970] 10 C.R.N.S. 290 (B.C.C.A.).

SECRECY AND THE INTERNATIONAL RELATIONS SCHOLAR

Following English practice, Canada had originally adopted the fifty-years rule for release of External Affairs documents. In 1968–69 the United Kingdom adopted the thirty-years rule, and so in 1969 did Canada.[50] The editorial beginning of the documentary series "Documents on Canadian External Relations" predates the thirty-years rule—but, otherwise, there had been very little regular official publication as long as the fifty-years rule was in effect.[51] Six volumes now cover the period 1909–39, to take the publication of Canadian foreign policy documents to pre-World War II days. Plans are in the making, as of 1974, to bring the series forward to 1945, but it will be several years before the task is completed.[52]

The obstacles, at least until recently, have been formidable. Indeed, even as late as 1959–60, when this writer attempted to develop a series on international legal decisions by the Government of Canada comparable to Hackworth's Digest in the United States—which includes much State Department and other contemporary U.S. legal opinion—there was great difficulty in finding an acceptable formula. Not until an annual summary of policies and statements of importance to international law began to appear in the Canadian Year Book of International Law in 1964 was there some effort towards systematic and relatively current disclosure of actions in that area. Collections of documents privately produced by academics have appeared over the years;[53] and here former members of the Department of External Affairs, such as John Holmes of the Canadian Institute of International Affairs and R. A. Mackay of Carleton University have been influential. Equally valuable are the efforts of Colonel C. P. Stacey, former official historian of the Department of National Defence who has become general editor of the series "Historical Documents of Canada, 1608–1968." Stacey has already completed his own volume, No. 5, dealing with documents of the period 1914–45.

Access by scholars and journalists to foreign relations materials more cur-

---

50. See Statement by Prime Minister Trudeau, House of Commons, May 1, 1969, "Release to Archives of Records in Existence for Thirty Years"; see also Communiqué No. 10, February 22, 1972, Department of External Affairs, "Transfer of Records to the Public Archives."

51. But see the valuable collections published in 1962 by Walter A. Riddell, *Documents on Canadian Foreign Policy 1917–1939* (Toronto: Oxford University Press, 1962).

52. I am indebted to Mr. A. E. Blanchette of the Historical Division of the Department of External Affairs for indicating the pattern of the expected publication.

53. See above, Note 51; see also the early effort of the writer here in Cohen, "International Law and Canadian Practice," in Edward McWhinney, ed., *Canadian Jurisprudence* (Toronto: Carswell, 1958).

rent in content has been encouraged increasingly by the Department of External Affairs. The Department is willing to discuss current information (sometimes of a sensitive nature), and even to disclose documents themselves to researchers, under conditions of mutually accepted restraints. The same ground rules are applied to members of the National Press Gallery, which has made only modest use, so far, of the new privilege. Obviously some difficulties arise out of this policy of controlled access.[54]

In actual operation, the system depends upon the degree of sensitivity of the subject and, too, upon the availability of personnel and other resources in the Historical Division of the Department of External Affairs. Preferential treatment naturally is given to senior scholars over their juniors. Perhaps more important is the fact that a responsible academic or journalist who has been given such access to, or a briefing about, an otherwise classified file, frequently finds himself in the difficult position of not being able to write about an entire subject with the same sense of freedom he might have enjoyed without such privileged access. Quotations from documents must be cleared with the Department, but there are other, subtle restrictions that may have even more inhibiting effect on scholarly or journalistic activities.

Five years ago a Parliamentary Centre for Foreign Affairs and Foreign Trade was created as an educational institution under the Canadian Companies Act to provide research and information services to committees of the House and Senate and to individual Members of Parliament. It is subsidized by grants from both Houses of Parliament and elsewhere, but is wholly independent in its operations: the Director and his small staff are not civil servants. The Centre has been instrumental in helping the House Standing Committee on External Affairs and National Defence, as well as the Senate Committee on Foreign Affairs, to organize enquiries. It has provided information and witnesses, arranged briefings and visits, prepared confidential reports for these Committees. Even so, the Centre apparently cannot yet provide the aggressive, independent research support for House or Senate committees that they could expect if they had research staffs of their own, or that the Legislative Reference Service provides the U.S. Congress.

Finally, the Department of External Affairs publishes the "Canadian Treaty Series," an Annual Report, another series entitled "Statement and Speeches", and the bimonthly periodical *International Perspectives*. These are useful sources for official government statements made in Parliament and elsewhere, and by Ministers or departments with a policy to explain. The Bureau of Legal Affairs also has had a useful program of distributing occasional information of interest to International Law teachers.

---

54. See above, Note 50.

Viewing all of this together, one may conclude that Canada is probably not yet so well served by the output of public or published *contemporary* international relations documentation as is the United States or Sweden— judging by the scholarship, journalism, and public debate in those countries. But is it access, or lack of it, that makes the difference? How important is it to require more disclosure than is now available? There is some evidence to suggest that the persistent reader of newspapers of record like the *Globe and Mail* of Toronto and *The New York Times,* of journals of opinion and scholarship, and of the reports of Parliamentary Committees, can come up with his own profile of a problem really not much less complete than one based upon access to the telegrams or the memoranda of the Foreign Office. The outlines of an emerging policy—preparations for the Law of the Sea Conference, alterations in Canadian-U.S. relations, Canada's future role in NATO—these can be understood and commented on intelligently by interested journalists, scholars, and politicians who have studied unclassified sources exclusively.

What may be missed is a better understanding of the *reasons* for a policy—which omission is to the disadvantage of the Government. Also, the lag between the time when a policy is still fluid and its discussion in the public or scholarly media may be too great for the reader dependent solely on these sources to be able to comment before the matter has hardened into a fully-made policy.

THE CLASSIFICATION PROBLEM

This brings our analysis to the final issue involved in secrecy policy—the classification of data. Even if the Official Secrets Act were modified to meet the objections of the Franks Committee and the lesser objections of the Royal Commission on Security in Canada, there would still remain the problem of deciding what documentation or information must be protected by criminal sanctions.

Broadly speaking, according to the Royal Commission on Security, it is only classified information that gives rise to problems of disclosure[55]—although the Canadian Report suggests that gathering unclassified information for transmittal to a foreign power may also come within the prohibitions of the Act, if that is the "intention" of the person so charged.[56] The Canadian classification categories are "Top Secret," "Secret," "Confidential," and "Restricted." The United Kingdom classifications, according to the Franks Report, are similar, but in addition there are "private markings"

---

55. Canadian Report, pp. 68–73.
56. *Ibid.,* p. 77.

used by departments "to identify information which does not warrant a security classification [but] which nevertheless needs protection."[57]

The Canadian Report suggests that there is a tendency—especially on the part of more junior officials—to overclassify in order to play it safe. The Report further states that overclassification is "a general current problem."[58] It recommends systematic efforts to declassify documents, including files-stripping programs, and concludes that in general "departments should be constantly reminded of the value of downgrading documents and that officers should seek any opportunity to amend the classification of papers that come to their attention in the course of their duties."[59]

There is no easy answer to this problem of classifying, overclassifying, and searches for more reasonable standards of declassification and disclosure, as the United States also is discovering.[60] But classification and secrecy go hand in hand, and the most liberal policy among senior officials of access or of disclosure may be frustrated by excessive classification by lower level bureaucrats. The Canadian public needs a "freedom of information" approach to the liberalization of classification as much as the Government needs classification to maintain its essential secrets and confidences. But even a more liberal law of access can still be frustrated by over-diligent bureaucracy, and so some system of effective internal control on overclassification is probably part of the answer.

CONCLUSIONS

The Canadian topography of secrecy and society does not disclose a flat plain of simple practice or description. Rather there are contours, some expressing the classical preoccupation with secrecy in government as though affairs of state were the personal business of officials and politicians alone, mandarins in their garden, surrounded by high walls of law and power. Yet Canada is essentially an open society, filled with the din of public debate, some of it very knowledgeable; and foreign policy does have its day in the give-and-take of national dialogue.

If *our* din is modulated, compared to America's, it is at least in part not because our government is more democratic or our people less energetic in asserting their rights, but because a middle power does not have thrust upon it the special burden of deciding great issues; and without great decisions to be made, Canadian secrets, although important, do not have the

---

57. Franks Report, p. 29, paras. 62, 63.
58. See pp. 71–72, paras. 190–93.
59. *Ibid.*, p. 73, para. 198.
60. *The New York Times,* December 31, 1972, sec. E, p. 9.

same aura that surrounds high policy in the capitals of the superpowers. This does not mean that there have not been and will not be pressures from the public, the scholars, the journalists, and Opposition politicians to have greater disclosure of facts on all fronts and in the foreign-policy arena in particular, so that better understanding can lead to better debate and to Canadian commitments more knowledgeably undertaken by the community as a whole.

Probably we are approaching in Canada—as elsewhere—a minor crisis in the art of government itself, accelerated by the complexity of problems, the refinements in analytical skills, and the deluge of data. The Canadian elections of October 1972, leading to a minority Government; the continuing debates over federalism and the French-English fact; the struggle to reshape Canadian relations with the United States; the search for a place amid the trading giants of the world; and the overriding duty of an affluent Canada to share in the many burdens of a much burdened mankind—all these are placing new stresses upon Government and demanding an open choice of priorities. It will not be an easy task, therefore, to reconcile the increasing public demand for knowledge and participation with Government's preference for confidentiality (at least until policy is made). If the art of the open society is always the art of balance, the pressures now to be kept in equilibrium are becoming more numerous than ever before.

Taking into account, therefore, the foregoing review of Canadian law and policy, together with analogous developments in the United States, the United Kingdom, and Sweden, we may state that Canada is ready for modernization of its general approach toward official secrets and freedom of access to information. We should heed the cautious encouragement of the 1969 Royal Commission on Security for a revision of the Official Secrets Act. The approach outlined below would seem to suggest a general formula for improving the balance between the flow of information from the Executive to public and the need of confidentiality in so much of its operations.

First, and basically, a good deal would seem to be gained from the passage of a statute combining a liberal concept of access to government information; a modernized official-secrets policy with provisions less awkwardly and repressively worded than in the present Canadian legislation; guidelines, in such a statute, for standards in classification of documents and with regulations promulgated to provide better rules than now exist; provisions also for a classification review mechanism not made up of personnel from the same operating level in the departments concerned; a system of time scales for the release of materials to the public through the national archives or otherwise and based on the degree of sensitivity of each item or the involvement of other nations; shifting of the onus of proof in criminal prosecutions from the accused to the prosecution; and, finally, the creation of an Ombudsman or analogous institution, to which appeals could be made for access to information that is refused when under new rules it ought to be provided, or for revision of faulty classification.

A single statute thus could incorporate (1) the right to information that it is not necessary to keep secret, and—after a period of years—virtually all information; (2) the criminal law prohibitions on disclosure of information that it is necessary to keep secret; (3) a classification system to distinguish between what must, and what need not, be kept secret; and (4) an independent body to review the way this distinction is applied in practice. This proposal has the virtue of combining complementary ideas within a single legislative project. It would also have to reconcile clearly antagonistic positions, and would moreover require considerable skill in draftsmanship to incorporate statements that liberalize the disclosure of information with the subsequent sections dealing with prohibitions on communication and disclosure. The virtues outweigh the difficulties. In a single statute the public, the bureaucracy, and the courts could all see more readily the balancing of interests: the liberalizing provisions regarding access, and the restrictive rules for the protection of confidentiality.

Such legislation would have to include effective appellate machinery, outside the often cumbersome and delaying process of the courts, to deal with the day-to-day claims for interpretation and action—particularly in cases of refusal to disclose or declassify. Including provision for this machinery in the same statute would further reinforce the network of standards and procedures.

Finally, the statute should include criminal law provisions carried over, reformed, from the Official Secrets Act. In allegations of serious breaches of confidentiality, the new law should shift the onus of proof in any criminal prosecution back to the Crown. This would remove from the accused a burden that is clearly inconsistent with fair administration of justice. There is no reason to believe that effective prevention of illegal disclosures requires the present arrangement, that it is necessary to force an accused to extricate himself from the vague and remote evidence which, under present legislation, may create a sufficient *prima facie* case to shift the difficult burden of exculpation to him.

Moreover, the reformed provisions of the criminal law ought to recognize a lesser degree of culpability when disclosure is made of documents or information that do not endanger any vital national interest, domestic or foreign, but actually contribute to public debate and equilibrium between the Government and the public in circumstances of unreasonable secrecy. Even under these conditions disclosure cannot be made "legal," but such circumstances should be weighed when determining the penalty. Hence there would be much merit in including in such a statute a theory of mitigation for application by the Court when conscience is involved and no vital national security or foreign-policy interest has been injured by disclosure.

This chapter now comes full circle. There is no escape from confidentiality in the exercise of power. It is the degree, the timing, and the correlative disclosures that marks the difference between a "free" political order where debate determines policy, and a silent tyranny where secrecy stands as a high barrier to any public share in, or surveillance over, decisions and their making.

22

The Protest Resignation in Britain:
Trap Door to Oblivion
or Back Stairs to Success?

LORD CARADON

At all events, I must have some consciousness of being somewhere near right. I must have some standard of principle fixed within myself.

Abraham Lincoln

Nearly every politician at some time in his career faces the prospect of resignation. Most officials holding responsible posts must do so too.

The circumstances may be confused. The motives may be mixed. But there comes a time for most men and women in prominent positions in public life when a vital individual decision must be taken—a decision of courage or cowardice, a decision of selfless defiance or calculating cunning, a decision of loyalty or betrayal, a decision likely to break or make a career.

While a resignation may be the result of a mixture of these various and conflicting circumstances and motives, above all it must involve a decision which is personal, and the decision must usually be made alone.

Resignation thus brings the impact of the person into politics. The human factor is predominant. The resigner may face the pit of political oblivion and personal hardship. Or he may dream that he will be free to scale the heights of power by a daring leap. He may ponder those two possibilities at the same time.

For once, whatever the complications and temptations, it is the personal judgement and personal choice that must prevail. It is a personal drama in a moment of lonely truth.

On what kind of issues is resignation justified? To what extent can a threat of resignation be fairly used? Does resignation usually lead to subsequent frustration, or to advantage? To what extent may or must a resigna-

Lord Caradon was Minister of State for Foreign and Commonwealth Affairs and Permanent Representative of the United Kingdom at the United Nations from 1964 to 1970. He is now a member of the Advisory Panel on the United Nations Development Programme and a member of the UN Advisory Board on Population. Previously he served for many years in the Middle East and Africa, and was later Governor of Jamaica and Governor of Cyprus.

tion be publicly explained and justified? What official or Cabinet secrets must be kept? Do different rules apply to politicians and to officials?

MY RESIGNATION

In considering such questions I myself can give some personal testimony. I very nearly resigned as a Minister of State a few years ago. I had made my position clear to my Government in advance and in writing that if the so-called "Tiger" or "Fearless" proposals (named after the ships on which they were negotiated) for a settlement with Rhodesia were adopted by the British Cabinet I would resign. I was saved by the rejection of the proposals by the rebel regime in Rhodesia. In 1962 I actually did resign as Ambassador to the United Nations, also on a matter pertaining to Rhodesia.

I do not pretend that the circumstances of my own decisions were of any particular importance, but I have had to put the awkward questions to myself, and I have had to think out my own conclusions. So I shall speak from my own experience and my own conviction.

First, one minor incident. In 1957, when I was Governor of Jamaica, I received (during a short speaking tour in Canada) a secret and personal telegram from the Colonial Office in London saying that I was being considered for the Governorship of Cyprus—which was then torn by violence. I was asked in the telegram to give assurance that if appointed Governor of Cyprus I would not resign on grounds of policy.

I had been in Cyprus before. I was devoted to the Island and its people. I was eager to go back to see whether I could help towards a peaceful solution of the Island's destructive troubles. But I could not bind myself for the future. I didn't know what the policy of the British Government in Cyprus was. I didn't even know if there was one. So I had to send back a telegram to London that I couldn't give the assurance about resignation. Sadly I continued my speaking engagements, but then I was summoned hurriedly to London. In the end I was appointed as Governor of Cyprus after all. But I had started off by confirming one useful lesson. The choice of resignation must never be blocked. To put it at its lowest, the escape hatch must never be locked. One must be free, to protest, to object, if necessary, to go.

I did in fact offer my resignation when my first efforts to find a solution to the Cyprus problem had not succeeded. It was not because I wanted to go. On the contrary, I was more than eager to take another initiative. But I thought it right to enable my Government to find someone else if they had lost confidence in me. They said they had not. And a year or so later we had a settlement.

In 1962 I resigned from my post as Ambassador in the United Kingdom Delegation to the United Nations.

The issue of my resignation in New York was the question of Rhodesia and specifically my contention that the Africans should be brought into consultation about the Constitutional future of their country. I need not now go into detail about this major difference of opinion between me and my Government. But at the time I restated the principle that the civil servant has no right even on resignation to disclose information he previously obtained in confidence in his official position—that is, unless he is given specific aproval to do so.

As I wrote some little time after I resigned:

> I have been an official for nearly a third of a century. I know the rules very well. When an official takes the extreme step of resigning his post he has no right, without permission, to publish information which he acquired in the confidence of his official position. The rule is important. I do not question it. Were this not well understood all confidence between Ministers and officials would be destroyed. And so, when I faced a crowded Press conference in the United Nations on the day after my resignation I refused to say anything at all about Southern Rhodesia. Again, I refused to say anything about the reasons for my resignation on my arrival back in England. *But this well-established rule does not prevent me, now that I am no longer an official, from expressing my own opinions. I have very strong views on the problems of Africa in general and on Southern Rhodesia, the Portuguese territories of Angola and Mozambique, and South Africa in particular. I have been free to state them in America and in England. I have not hesitated to do so.*

The distinction is important. I defend the rule that neither before nor after resignation may a civil servant disclose information given to him in confidence while he held an official position. In particular he must not disclose without specific permission what was said in exchanges between him and Ministers. But, subject to those rules, he is of course perfectly free—once he has resigned—to take a full part in public controversy.

When I later obtained permission to say why I had resigned, I made public what I had said to the leader of my delegation in New York at the time:

> My conclusion is, I greatly regret to say, that I do not feel able to speak in the UN or elsewhere in defence of our position in this matter [Rhodesia]. I simply cannot do it.
>
> If this were an isolated or minor disagreement my feelings would not matter. But, as I have emphasised, this is the main African question before the UN in which we are directly concerned, and no other subject I deal with now has anything like comparable importance. If, therefore, on this issue I am in disagreement and consequently unable to defend our policy, I fear that I must become a liability to the delegation.
>
> I am most sincerely sorry to create this difficulty, and to cause incon-

venience at this time to our delegation in which it has been a privilege and a joy to work, but in view of what I have said I think that it would be best for me to be replaced as soon as possible.

I had put my own proposal forward to my Government in a memorandum which ended in the following words:

> Might not the British Government declare that we are in favour of progressive steps towards full participation of all the people of the territory in the Government, and that following the forthcoming elections we shall invite the leaders of all parties to participate in a conference on future constitutional advance? Above all, could we not now make it plain that independence will not be granted to Southern Rhodesia until a new constitution has been worked out at such a conference?
>
> Neither Her Majesty's Government nor the Southern Rhodesian Government would be abandoning the course already set. Both Governments would be confirming that course but also offering hope for the future and confounding our enemies. We should have required the initiative both in Africa and in the United Nations.

But when my recommendation had been rejected by the Government, and when it was all over, I tried to sum up what I had learnt:

> I have learnt two principal lessons in my overseas service. First that self-government must be built on consultation and co-operation; it cannot be built on the dictatorship of one race, or the domination of one people over another. The second lesson I have learnt—and this lesson applied in such widely different territories as Nigeria, Jamaica and Cyprus—is that the initiative is all-important. To find the way out of difficulties and disagreements you must take and keep the initiative.
>
> Within the obvious limitations, which I well knew, I thought that the British Government in co-operation with the Government of Southern Rhodesia should take a new initiative last summer. I made my specific proposals accordingly at that time. When these proposals were not accepted I reluctantly came to the conclusion that I could no longer speak as an advocate of a policy which I didn't agree with. That was no hasty decision; I had made my views and my proposals and my position clear over a period of months.
>
> I have been an official for a long time, and the work of which I am most proud has been the work of training civil servants in the Near East and Africa and the West Indies.
>
> I told the civil servants who worked with me that *it is the duty of each fearlessly to advocate the policy he thinks right. And when a final decision is taken by the highest authority the official must carry it out—and he must carry it out whole-heartedly. Only one exception is possible. If the question·

is one of main principle, and is a continuing major issue, and one in which
he himself is directly involved, he has the right to say "I am sorry, I cannot
do it." I maintain that that is not only a right: it is a duty.

I could not go on for month after month speaking to a policy which I
didn't believe in, and I have no doubt that I was right to say so.

There was some controversy about my resignation and some people
maintained that an official should never resign on a question of policy.
There was correspondence on the subject in *The Times,* and a letter from
Kenneth Younger brought the debate to a conclusion. He said that

> . . . civil servants are likely to take the extreme step of resignation only if
> deep convictions are at stake. If one denies them this elementary right, where
> can one stop, short of condoning Eichmann's sustained obedience to high
> political authority.

As a footnote to this, I heard that Mr. Duncan Sandys, a Minister of
Government at that time, was asked what he had to say about my resignation. He replied that he was "not interested in the private opinions of civil
servants." Nor should he be. He was quite right. I said at the time that I
had no doubt that he would go further and agree that he would not wish
his Government to be represented in a world assembly by a spokesman convinced that his Government was drifting to disaster.

I have set out the circumstances of my own resignation ten years ago in
some detail because I believe that by so doing it is possible to bring out the
principles which apply to the resignation of a civil servant. They are very
clear, and certainly in my country would not be brought into any serious
dispute. Civil servants should not resign except in extreme circumstances.
More than that, they must be prepared to carry out policies they don't agree
with, and even to defend them. It is impossible to run a democratic government if action depends on the personal opinions of the civil servants serving
such a government. But if the three conditions I have mentioned are satisfied, then, as I say, I think that a civil servant in those extreme circumstances has not only a right but also a duty to resign. And when he does so
he must be prepared to go silent.

RULES OF RESIGNATION: WHAT MAY BE SAID

From these clear conclusions (my experience is limited to British practice
and principles) I turn to the much more complicated problem of the rules
that should apply to Ministers and particularly to Members of the Cabinet,
and it may be worthwhile to consider those questions by a comparison be-

tween the rules which should apply to a civil servant on the one hand and to a politician, on the other.

Two types or categories of resignation should be quickly dismissed from our discussion. First is the resignation due to some personal failure or scandal, and on this it may be sufficient to say (with a temptation to smugness perhaps) that the British record is admirable. British Ministers are not obstinate about staying when their personal conduct is open to public censure. The second category that need not delay us is resignation in a fit of pique. There may be an element of pique in some of the noblest sacrifices. Let us confine ourselves, however, to deliberate, principled resignations; and let us consider the rules that should govern those who contemplate such a move. For civil servants there are four of these:

> *First.* Never resign on a secondary issue.
> *Second.* Never resign unless the issue is continuing, don't insist on leaving on a matter that is over and done with, however angry it made you.
> *Third.* Never resign unless you are personally involved in presenting and promoting the policy in question—as I was, for instance, when asked to defend British policy in the United Nations over Rhodesia.
> *Fourth.* Never on resignation disclose information obtained in confidence as a result of your official position.

Those are the rules for civil servants, and it is on the last two of them that the position of the politician is somewhat different from that of Ministers.

With regard to the third—the test of personal involvement—the politician has more cause to worry. My own position at the United Nations was more worrying when I was a Minister of the Labour Government than when I had earlier been at the U.N. as a career service Ambassador. Whereas, while I was a civil servant, no one could fault me if I did not resign in a matter of policy, no matter how important, where I had nothing to do with either its presentation or its execution, a politician must feel an obligation on all major policy questions even when he is not, himself, directly involved. Two cabinet members have instructed me on this point. Iain Macleod once disclosed that he had twice contemplated resignation but had held back because in neither issue had he had direct departmental responsibility; R. A. Butler, too, expressed contempt for "open gestures of defiance." But I do not wholly agree: the fact remains that a member of the Cabinet cannot escape from responsibility for all the principal decisions of his Government. So to that extent, in spite of Disraeli's counsel—"never resign,"—a politician must be more ready than a civil servant to resign on an issue of policy.

But membership of the Government or Cabinet has another and contrary influence. Whereas Cabinet responsibilities may be used to justify resignation in the event of serious disagreement, it may also powerfully argue for drawing back from doing so in the interests of party loyalty. Prime Minister Balfour maintained that Cabinet Ministers are expected to preserve "an unbroken phalanx in the face of public opinion." Yet party loyalty may not always be a main motive. Randolph Churchill once said of Lord Curzon that "engagements to his colleagues were almost always vulnerable to an appeal to his patriotism, particularly when this was accompanied by the promise of high office."

But that is not the only dilemma—the conflicting influences of personal opinion and party loyalty—that the politician must face. The other dilemma involves what he can or should say when his resignation is announced. The fourth rule for civil servants also must be modified in reference to politicians. Some explanation, some justification, some defence is traditionally expected from a resigning Minister as he speaks on his return to Parliament's back benches. How much can he say? What can he disclose?

A resigning Minister is normally allowed and expected to reveal in public the reasons prompting his action, even if this involves disclosure of disagreement in the Cabinet. But beyond that, Cabinet secrets are expected to remain secret. Prime Minister Clement Attlee complained that Aneurin Bevan, in his speech resigning from Attlee's cabinet, disclosed something of what had taken place in the Cabinet, and his complaint emphasized both the importance of the rule and the rareness of its breach. More recently, memoirs of Prime Ministers and other Cabinet Ministers have knocked a few holes in the wall of Cabinet secrecy. But the basic rule is not disputed; and though it may be occasionally broken, it is quite clear that the British system of government—in spite of suggestions that we move to a more presidential system, with the Cabinet diminishing in power and importance in relation to the Prime Minister—requires free and frank discussion in the Cabinet. The whole system would be changed or even destroyed if the rule of Cabinet secrecy were abandoned.

So what are the restraints that a political resigner must contemplate? Many British political leaders have progressed to power through resignation. Lloyd George, Churchill, Eden, Bevan, Wilson all threatened to resign or actually did so, with no intention of leaving public life. On the contrary, they indicated and emphasized issues of major policy disagreement, and at the same time put up the stakes of political ambition. But the risk was there, even to powerful politicians such as those. It is greater for those of lesser rank. On the Suez issue two junior Ministers resigned, Edward Boyle and Anthony Nutting. Boyle subsequently reached the Cabinet. Nutting was never again appointed to a political office. The resigner can never be sure that he will survive. It was Churchill who said that "most men sink into insignificance when they quit office"; and former Foreign Secretary Samuel

Hoare "knew only too well," as he once said, "how quickly the river of politics flowed and how difficult it was for anyone who had left it to catch again the tide."[1] At any event, if anyone resorts to the extreme step of resignation, only in the rarest of cases can he get away with it a second time.

Two facts remain to be noted.

First. The threat of resignation is part of the common currency of political life. It should not be used too often (Asquith had a "drawer full" of Morley resignations, and Morley became known as an "inveterate resigner") but, if wisely used, the threat gives the individual Minister the opportunity and the right to exert pressure on his Government in a matter on which he feels deeply. It is a weapon to be sparingly used but never abandoned. As R. K. Alderman and J. A. Cross conclude in their study of the subject, "resignation is the metaphorical 'ultimate deterrent' of ministerial infighting and, like the nuclear deterrent, its real effectiveness may be said to lie in its potentiality rather than its use."[2]

Second. While the risks are great, I can vouch for the fact that the satisfaction can be overwhelming. The long anxiety, the persistent representations, the self-questioning, the arguments for compromise or delay are over. A burden is lifted. Concern about poverty and obscurity is for the moment forgotten. What a wonderful thing to be free, to dissociate oneself from contemptible policies and timid colleagues, to chart a new course of one's own. How good to walk out into the fresh air.

Resignation can be a poison-causing political suicide, but I am glad to say that it can also be a tonic—refreshing, satisfying, stimulating, exciting.

It is fine to be a martyr and fun to be a gambler. Best not to be afraid to be a bit of both.

---

1. R. K. Alderman and J. A. Cross, *The Tactics of Resignation: A Study in British Cabinet Government* (London: Routledge and Kegan Paul, 1967), pp. 48–49.
2. *Ibid.,* p. 57.

23

Resigning from Government and Going Public:
The Costs and Benefits of Speaking Up
and the Unwritten Vow of Silence

JAMES C. THOMSON, JR.

In early June 1970, after the Cambodian invasion, I communicated to three highly placed friends at the White House and State Department my hope that they might at long last consider resigning and "speaking out," individually or collectively, in order to help create a brake against further escalation in our involvement. My plea fell, I knew, on somewhat fertile soil: all three were opposed to the Cambodia move. Two replied that I had raised an important question; the third—the most disaffected—soon moved with apparent relief to a government agency that had nothing to do with the War.

Eight months later, in February 1971, after the Laos "incursion," I tried out the idea more publicly. In the course of a Harvard "teach-in" speech I suggested the creation of a "National Committee for the Regeneration of Conscience in Government." Such a group should be composed, I thought, of anti-war former officials, diplomats, and military men, and also, if possible, the college-age children of present officials. Its purpose should be to encourage individual and even collective resignations on grounds of conscience, resignations to be followed by speaking tours to take their anti-war dissent to the public. My proposal for this "Resigners Anonymous" elicited a handful of encouraging letters from local former bureaucrats, plus interested inquiries from one psychoanalyst and two clergymen. And from former Ambassador John Kenneth Galbraith came an important caveat. It would take artful wording, he said, to explain why those of us who were former officials were asking current officials to do what we had been un-

---

Mr. Thomson is Curator of the Nieman Foundation for Journalism and Lecturer on History at Harvard University. A former State Department and White House specialist in American-East Asian relations, he is the author of books and articles on the subject.

willing to do ourselves over the Bay of Pigs, the Dominican intervention, and the earlier Vietnam escalations.

Galbraith's point was hardly new to me, but it remains crucial. Why *hadn't* any of us resigned and gone public at once? Why hasn't anyone done so since on issues of foreign policy? Why, in the course of the longest and most unpopular war in American history, did no one exit and speak out right away? And why, over a longer time span, is it hard to find anyone at a Cabinet or sub-Cabinet or Assistant Secretary level who has left the U.S. Government on an issue of foreign affairs *and said so at the time?*[1]

One frequent use of secrecy in the making of foreign policy is to conceal internal disagreement. Yet one recourse of the dissenting official—in a democracy at least—should be to get out and take his case to that allegedly ultimate court, the voting public. So, noisy resignations over issues—as opposed to genteel departures on other grounds—should be one antidote to secrecy, one means of preserving openness. And the tacit *threat* of such a recourse for dissenters should be a constraint on the Chief Executives and an added strength to the dissenter's voice.

But that is not the way things work.

It might be argued that, in the case of Vietnam, some did resign and eventually speak out. The key word here is "eventually"—one to which we will return, for it shows that constraints continue to operate after departure. As for some of the high-level resigners who were doubters on Vietnam (we know of their doubts through either their later public statements or the Pentagon Papers): Far East Assistant Secretary Roger Hilsman was told to find other employment fast, which he did (early 1964); Michael Forrestal of the White House staff silently slipped back to the practice of law in New York (1965–66); so did Under Secretary of State George W. Ball (1966); John W. Gardner departed as Secretary of Health, Education, and Welfare (HEW) vigorously denying any disagreement over Vietnam (early 1968); Robert S. McNamara was removed as Secretary of Defense and allowed himself to be placed, mute, in the World Bank (early 1968); Chester L. Cooper of the White House staff quietly moved to the Institute for Defense Analyses (1968); Townsend Hoopes quietly resigned as Under Secretary of the Air Force (mid-1968). Others such as Clark Clifford, Averell Harriman, Chester Bowles, Cyrus Vance, and even Daniel Ellsberg, stayed on as full-time employees or periodic consultants to the Government until Richard Nixon's inauguration in January 1969.

There are certainly more names that could be cited. But the point becomes obvious: *When you leave, you go quietly; and at the very least, you*

---

1. Interior Secretary Walter Hickel is a special case. He parted company with President Nixon over other issues as well as Vietnam. But his parting was politely staged, and he did not "speak out."

stay quiet for a while. The question is, again, *Why?* And the answer is not simple.

How people act on leaving government service depends in part on why they left. And here one deals with a spectrum of possibilities. There is, first of all, exit through an overt, public firing. So, in a classic case, Truman got rid of Commerce Secretary Henry Wallace. That is a searing experience, but also potentially a liberating one in that it creates the immediate possibility of vocal opposition.

A more likely variant, however, is a concealed firing through apparently friendly resignation. Here the official—who may or may not have been a "dissenter," as opposed to merely incompetent, in the eyes of his superiors— is asked to leave (i.e., fired) but given a period in which to find alternative employment—and perhaps even assistance in finding it—prior to the cordial exchange of letters of resignation and appreciation. Such solicitude not only eases the blow to the resigner's ego; it also creates, for a while at least, a sense of obligation toward those who threw him out so gently.

More common, probably, is the muddled departure: the product not of firing but of frustration and fatigue. Mixed into the usually multiple reasons for this kind of resignation may be the following factors: simple exhaustion from long bureaucratic hours, a sense that one is losing more battles than one is winning, a sense that one has lost the ear of the powerful (perhaps never had it) and won't be advanced to a better spot, guilt about neglect of one's wife and children, concern about one's alternative career, and perhaps the financial limitations of government salaries. Included among such factors may be increasingly persistent and ineffective dissent on one or more issues; but this often gets blurred by the mix of other ingredients.

A further cause of resignation may be quite simply the apparent availability of much greener pastures elsewhere. This can relate to the previous point and become an inducement to exit in the midst of frustration and fatigue; or it can suddenly confront an otherwise content official in the form of that legendary unrejectable job offer—a great foundation or university or corporation presidency. Such men obviously leave with a minimal desire to "speak out," since they have little to speak out about.

There are, of course, a few rare birds who follow the angry-fed-up-blow-your-top route. General Patrick Hurley resigned (and blew his top) as Ambassador to China in late 1945; and under President Franklin Roosevelt Secretary Harold Ickes went through the motions repeatedly without being permitted to resign. Such impulsiveness is usually caught before it explodes in public: if the official cannot be dissuaded, a graceful departure is arranged (creating a sense of obligation); and if he does resign, the multiple pressures of bureaucratic life that have led up to the departure usually blur in his own mind, as well as others, the clarity of his stand on the specific triggering issue. He becomes in the eyes of others, perhaps in his own as well, a tired sorehead who couldn't play team ball.

The resignation spectrum includes, finally, the foul-up, or the ouster within (conventionally, the "kicking upstairs"—though it may often be sideways or even down). Here recurrent dissent alerts one's superiors to one's disaffection and hence potential disloyalty in time for the superiors to propose a new job, usually a respectable but non-sensitive ambassadorship, or perhaps the directorship of an international agency. At this point the would-be resigner is doubly trapped: on the one hand, it is hard to cut one's ties entirely, and perhaps some good might be done in the new job; and on the other hand, resignation *now* would look like personal pique over a job reassignment (ergo, selfish), not resignation on grounds of conscience.

ON NOT SPEAKING OUT

So much for some of the reasons people seem to resign or, in some cases, not quite resign. For those who do finally make the break, out of varying personal and political situations, what are the factors that prevent, inhibit, or at least delay their "speaking out?"

Here one deals once again with a number of variables, and their influence on any one individual will not be precisely their influence on another. The list that follows is only suggestive, by no means all-inclusive; nor is it possible to suggest any clear order of priority among the factors cited.

A sense of duty or loyalty to the Presidency

To those who have weathered the past decade, this thought will seem a bit archaic. Yet there does linger, in some exiting officials, a feeling that the Chief Executive is, for the time being, the only one we have (unlike in Parliamentary government, where ultimate national loyalty is not to the Prime Minister); a feeling, too, that one was in His Service, at his invitation, and owes him a debt of trust. It is simply ungrateful to bite the hand that gave you power and responsibility; and an attack on his policies is an attack on him—ergo, betrayal.

The fear of immediate retribution

The post-World War II U.S. Presidency is the world's most powerful institution of government. A former official is one lonely person—unless, of course, he has strong political roots of his own (as a previously elected official), or an influential constituency of colleagues in, say, business or banking or law, or can attach himself as a new recruit to an Opposition movement on the outside.

Even with such possible bases of support, he faces on exit the fact that the Executive Branch has instant and continued access to the media, has massive sources of support among its partisans throughout the country, and can make use, if necessary, of the FBI and the Justice Department to harrass an opponent. Lest this sound overdrawn, it should be noted that when Chester Bowles resisted his firing as Under Secretary of State in November 1961 and temporarily rejected an alternative job offer, preferring to "get out and speak out," President Kennedy's White House staff intermediary warned him, "We will destroy you." A fear of retribution in an electronic age—the unknown, what they may have on you, what they might do to you if only through denunciation and ridicule—is certainly an inhibiting factor.

The fear of barred return

Most men who have worked in high positions in government would like, however disaffected, some day to return—at least for a while, if the circumstances are right. Most departing officials are therefore careful not to do things that might bar such a return—that might burn their bridges once and for all. To be asked back you must behave like a team player. You may well have dissented openly, even passionately, within the councils of government; and your colleagues may really know why you resigned, if it was really over dissent. But you owe it to the Club—and to your continued membership in the Club, though temporarily on leave—to abide by the unwritten rule: *Dissent inside (and within limits) is fine; dissent outside, and in public, is bad form.*

Furthermore, an internal dissenter who becomes an external dissenter inevitably suggests the existence of previous internal debates and thereby breaks another Club rule, that proscribing revelation of the Club's internal squabbles to non-members. One might think that a two-party system would modify these rules—i.e., that an exiting internal critic would find welcome and refuge in the Opposition party. Such is the nature of foreign policy issues, however, cutting as they do across both parties; such is the nature of one's political allegiance (a dissenter doesn't necessarily want to join the other party); and such is the nature of the Club itself, providing foreign affairs officials to Administrations of *both* parties—that the barring of one's return means a barring of one's return *regardless* of party in power. The Club's grapevine crosses party lines; and once one is known as a rule-breaker under one Administration, the *fear,* at least, is that one will be barred from all future Administrations.

Anxiety over "security" regulations

This may seem a fairly trivial factor, hardly worth citing. Yet a man who has worked for an extended period within the special constraints of a system of *security* classifications as well as within the attendant *political* constraints—but without the harsh but clear guidelines of an Official Secrets Act—is very much at sea once he leaves government service. He has developed habits of discretion and prudence in his dealings with outsiders, even though he may have indulged from time to time in the tradition of selective leakage to friends in the press. Once on the outside, he is a bit unsure of the ground rules—of what to say to whom, where, and when. However much he may have dissented within, he is automatically careful, still weighing his words lest he let slip information or ideas that might somehow be "classified." The syndrome undoubtedly lasts longer in some than it does in others. But it operates as a strong constraint against "speaking out" at once.

The fear of intermediate ostracism

This is a variant of the earlier point about fear of barred return. It has not to do with government but with those adjuncts of government, the friendly watering places of other departed officials—such as, e.g., New York's Council on Foreign Relations, Washington's Brookings Institution, and periodic conferences hosted by foundations with an international interest.

Despite the jarring effect of Vietnam, intercourse between Government and the institutions of the external foreign affairs Establishment has continued. Former insiders often look forward to continued relations with present and former policy-makers—and a continued sense of involvement—through participation in such aspects of the extended Club. To speak out soon and bluntly, to be noisy or shrill, to break the internal Club's rules—all this, one fears, may ostracize one from even the status of friendly auditor. Since the other friendly auditors are men who will probably staff, or recommend the staff for, future Administrations, this fear reinforces the fear of barred return.

Anxiety about community

This is admittedly a subtle and highly speculative matter: the resigner's need for a sense of community once he has left the community of government officials and their associates. Once again, extended government service can isolate a man from previous communities: his former constituents, if earlier he had been an elected official; his students and faculty colleagues, if he was a teacher; his former business or professional associates. Relocating yourself takes time—especially psychic time. If you have resigned over an issue of policy, you may find that your recent community (government) is not immediately replaced by your previous community (particularly if it doesn't share your dissent); and to find a new community to encourage you and strengthen your voice takes time. Hence time passes; and one waits to "speak out."

Loyalty to the "good guys" still inside

Here we deal with another subtle matter. Most dissenters eventually find fellow dissenters. Most stay on for a while—sometimes forever—"conspiring" with their co-dissenters to make a few good things happen, keep a few bad things from happening. Once a man leaves, he knows that he has left behind a network of fellow believers who are still fighting the good fight. What is his responsibility to them? If he becomes an external nuisance to the Administration, he may well harm their cause, if only because they have usually been identified with him and his views by the higher-ups. Sometimes his external assaults can help them. But it is a hard matter to judge—and for a while he may opt to keep quiet and merely wish them well.

Desire for continued access, to influence even the "bad guys"

No one ever quite gives up on trying to influence his President, Secretary of State, or other inside superiors. Despite a formal parting of the ways, there lingers the hope that one can still get across one's message—perhaps even do it better—from the outside. Private letters or memoranda to one's former bosses; periodic visits; private collective efforts with other colleagues from the outside. The key here is access. Would it not be foolish to destroy the possibility of access by (prematurely) speaking out?

THE DE-COMPRESSION PERIOD

What all the foregoing add up to, singly or in concert, is a fairly formidable barrier to the unburdening of oneself at the moment of resignation from the Government. One must go first through a de-compression period; and for some it takes longer than for others.

My own experience, in this regard, is illustrative mainly of my own experience. But since I have been instructed by the Editors to be "personal," here is a capsulized account of my progression as a resigner.

To begin with, I wasn't fired nor did I actually resign. By which I mean that though I told my National Security Council chief, Mr. W. W. Rostow, that I would leave in the autumn (of 1966) to accept a teaching appointment at Harvard, I couldn't decide to whom I should send a letter of resignation, and therefore never sent one. As a 34-year-old East Asianist who had spent six years in the U.S. Government, I was still on the payroll of the Department of State, though assigned for two years to the NSC staff at the White House. I thought briefly of writing a Thank-you-and-Good-bye letter to Secretary Rusk; but since I had long viewed him as The Archenemy of wise East Asian policy, I decided to avoid any eleventh-hour hypocrisy. As for resigning to President Johnson, that seemed presumptuous, even perilous. ("Who the hell is *he* and why is he quitting?") A friend did get him to inscribe a photograph to me—misspelled, but with Best Wishes. And except for collecting accumulated vacation and sick-leave pay, plus arranging at the last minute to have the National Archives cart off my six years of chaotic files for the Kennedy Library, that was that. On September 15, 1966, I walked out of the Executive Office Building a free man.

I must now explain a thing or two. My "resignation" belongs, in retrospect, to the category of the muddled departure—i.e., it derived from several concurrent factors. Thus (in no particular order), I had come to Washington for two years and had stayed nearly seven; the policy frustrations and defeats had long since outnumbered the victories; I had recently lost my stimulating and demanding employer with the departure of McGeorge Bundy for the Ford Foundation; I was fatigued, and my family long since fed up, with endless bureaucratic days and evenings; Harvard had made an offer, and it was nearing time to choose between a base in the Academy or a long-term government career; AND my own central hopes for Sino-American *détente* seemed hopelessly obstructed by the Vietnam folly of the Johnson Administration.

Since "speaking out" is the subject at hand, I should say something about my Vietnam views as they evolved by September 1966. As one whose real interest since childhood was China, I had largely ignored and disdained Indochina during the Kennedy years, hoping that the problem might simply go away. During 1964 I found myself counting on a neutralist coup d'état in Saigon that would politely invite us out of Vietnam. And once the decision was taken in 1965 to escalate American involvement, I worked with others to bring about an end to the bombing, and negotiate a settlement.

Throughout this period it was my view that the alleged illegality and immorality of the Vietnam War was not the issue; but that the issue was instead the war's semi-suicidal stupidity in terms of American national interests. For a while I had hoped that this view, for which I found quiet support in many parts of the Government, might soon prevail. But by the time of my departure I had despaired of persuading Messrs. Johnson, Rusk, and Mc-

Namara to turn back from their chosen course. I felt, by then, totally alienated from the policy, yet helpless as to how to change it.

THE EXIT SYNDROME, PHASE I: THE SNIPER

Tucked in my briefcase as I left the Executive Office Building, in September 1966, was a piece of parody I had written on Cape Cod during a brief holiday earlier that summer. Entitled "Minutes of a White House Meeting, Summer 1967," it was a spleen-venting effort to satirize Mr. Rostow, our Vietnam policy, and a few of my NSC colleagues. Officials, it seems, find diverse ways to relieve tensions and frustrations. Mr. McNamara is said to have read Homer; one of my colleagues constructed entire miniature three-ring circuses in his basement; I tended to write parodies, all through my Washington years—and this was one of my best. On return to the job in August, I had shown it privately to some White House friends, and it had evoked much glee.

That parody was to become my first vehicle for "speaking out"; but it took seven months for the voice to be heard. The point is instructive. One refuge of the inside dissenter is the covert expression of disapproval— through private writings or a sharing with confederates of outrage, witticisms, ridicule, or despair. Once outside, my first instinct was to do more of the same—to pass the piece around to anti-war bureaucrats and academic colleagues. And inevitably two things happened: first, I was told that it must certainly be published; and second, it fell (thanks to Xerox) into a wider public domain and was referred to, without attribution, in the press.

By March 1967, when the piece was in press at the *Atlantic Monthly,* I found myself both excited and apprehensive. I had spent the previous autumn "de-compressing," which meant mainly sleeping late, finding out what Harvard students were like, and preparing a new lecture course. In my conversations with students I had been increasingly frank about my views on the War; but I had prudently stayed out of print. Meanwhile, in October, I had been asked to do an Asian-policy speech text for the President in Hawaii, which made me feel that I had not been forgotten or barred, despite my dovish inclinations.

Now, however, the parody was about to appear, with altered names— Herman Melville Breslau instead of Walt Whitman Rostow, for instance— but with my own real byline. (Professor Galbraith, an enthusiast for the piece, had offered me his *nom-de-plume,* "Marc Epernay," and I was deeply touched—until my canny wife pointed out that then Galbraith would get the credit for the article.) The fears of the unknown and of possible retribution were gathering.

One Saturday night I came home late, to discover that the White House switchboard (Mr. Rostow calling) had reached my wife close to midnight; he would call back. He didn't; but I wondered what was up, and tried to practice telling him that the whole thing was a joke, didn't he see? On Monday came the follow-up: a call from one of my Harvard bosses, who had been phoned by a Harvard professor who was still a member of the Rostow staff. My caller said that he didn't think I should take the message too hard, but that the Rostow man had warned that great damage would be done if my parody were printed, that I sure as hell would never get back into Government under any Administration, and that if Jim Thomson were declaring war on this Administration, they were ready for him. I responded weakly that I thought they had learned their lesson about non-essential, brushfire wars, and then asked what my caller thought this all signified. I was told that it meant trouble but that maybe things would blow over in a few years.

When the parody finally appeared in the May 1967 *Atlantic,* there were no audible thunderbolts from Washington—though I did later learn that the President had finally had his chance to say, "Who the hell is *he?"*

THE EXIT SYNDROME, PHASE II:
THE EPISTOLARY BREAKTHROUGH

I had, then, gone public—but only rather snipingly, using the tool of mockery. Yet confidence and indignation were gathering—thanks largely to the influence of some extraordinary Harvard undergraduates who were teaching me by their example to speak out on the war. (I was finding "community.") Their example was twofold: not merely the clarity and reasonableness with which they argued against Washington's policies, but the fact that *they* represented our cannon fodder, those numbers on Washington's charts.

Early in May I had talked with a high Yale administrator at a dinner in New Haven. He agreed that the War was a terrible thing, but then added that of course no "constructive alternatives" were now being offered in place of Washington's policies, nor had critics ever proposed such alternatives. These comments increasingly enraged me as I sped home on the train late that night, writing my final lecture in a course on American-East Asian relations for delivery the next morning.

The result of the challenge from that Yale official was several pages of lecture notes in which I argued that "constructive alternatives" had in fact been available and offered at each stage of our Vietnam involvement from at least 1961 onward; that such alternatives had been repeatedly rejected on the grounds that the price of accepting them would be higher than the price of deeper and wider intervention; but that in retrospect the price of further intervention had been infinitely higher.

Late that month, as the war turned sharply upward, I finally pulled myself together and transcribed these thoughts in the form of a letter to *The New York Times,* a letter in which I identified myself as a former State and NSC aide and argued that I knew from within that "constructive alternatives" to escalation had in fact been available but regularly rejected since 1961 when I entered government service. My closing paragraphs read:

> The Vietnam conflict is a needless war—one that could and should have been avoided. Its resolution today certainly lies with men in Hanoi and elsewhere as well as men in Washington. But the men in Washington bear the paramount obligation.
>
> For the greatest power on earth has the power denied to others: the power to take unilateral steps, and to keep taking them; the power to be as ingenious and relentless in the pursuit of peace as we are in the infliction of pain; the power to lose face; the power to admit error; and the power to act with magnanimity.

I had originally closed with the words, "and the power to lose wars," but was emphatically urged to delete them by another recent returnee from Washington.

The letter to the *Times* seemed to me, at the time, a large and perilous step: a move from ridicule to deadly serious stuff. I blew hot and cold, hoping at moments that the *Times* wouldn't use it or that no one would read it, at other moments that I would achieve at least minor fame through immediate public denunciation, or perhaps (a Walter Mitty daydream) that the President would be so moved and persuaded that he would stop the war at once. None of these things actually happened. The *Times* did run the letter prominently in its issue of Sunday, June 4, 1967; and it simultaneously ran a substantial editorial commenting favorably on what I had written.

That morning I felt exhilarated and scared. The phone soon rang, a long-distance call; and for an instant fear prevailed. It turned out to be a man in Harrisburg, Pennsylvania, who had just read the letter and had to tell me right away how grateful he was. Other calls that day were from friends, saying *Well done.* During the next week or so a score of letters arrived, many of them from former government officials, some known to me, some not. They were uniformly congratulatory. Meanwhile, from those inside there was silence. I began to breathe more easily.

Later that summer I slipped back into the State Department for the first time since my departure, at the invitation of a friend. There I encountered an assistant to one of my earlier State employers, and he told me that the former chief was furious that my letter had "cast aspersions on his honor."

I replied that it had cast aspersions only on his judgment. And there the matter rested until many months had passed and much had changed in me. In mid-March 1968 I received one further reaction to the *Times* letter—and perhaps to the parody as well—when McGeorge Bundy of the Ford Foundation preceded his Godkin Lectures at Harvard by a debate on the War, with Professor Stanley Hoffmann of the Harvard University Department of Government.

Bundy opened his remarks by setting some special ground rules: he would not talk about the past, period. He added, in rather vivid explanation, that those who had been entrusted with responsibility by a President had been handed a pistol along with that trust; and that those who later spoke out about their period of service not merely broke the trust but turned that pistol on the man who had trusted them and shot him in the head. As Bundy said this, my wife elbowed me and said, "He's talking about you." "No, no," I whispered, "he's talking about Arthur Schlesinger." As a small footnote to the domino-effect in guilt, I should report that I ran into Schlesinger the next day and told him the story. No, no, said Schlesinger—he was talking about Ken Galbraith and Dick Goodwin. (Later evidence indicated that my wife, as usual, was right.)

THE EXIT SYNDROME, PHASE III:
GOING (ALMOST) ALL THE WAY

By the time Bundy had delivered his grim injunction, my guilt, exhilaration, rage, and sense of impending doom had all reached a new height. Even as he spoke, the *Atlantic Monthly,* my wondrously supportive conduit, was already going to press with something that moved a good way beyond parody and letters-to-the-editor. It was a longer piece of reflection, intuition, illustrative anecdotes, and analysis, and entitled "How Could Vietnam Happen?" (The editor had added a premature subtitle: "An Autopsy.") That piece would appear in the April 1968 issue, out on the newsstands at the end of March.

This Vietnam essay was a product of serendipitous intervention. In August 1967 the psychoanalyst Robert Jay Lifton, a Cape Cod neighbor, had asked me to make the annual "outsider's" presentation to his Wellfleet seminar on psychohistory, a gathering of psychiatrists and historians who converse intensively about personality and history under the benevolent wing of Erik H. Erikson. Would I please think out loud, he asked, about how men and events had intersected to produce the Vietnam War? I agreed uneasily, free-associated for several days in the Truro sunshine, made extensive notes, and then held forth one evening. Things went quite well, and I felt stretched. You should really do an article, I was told; but I shrank from the thought. The *Times* letter had already strained me. Why take further risks?

And so things stood until the first weekend of December 1967, when I attended a very private conference sponsored by the Carnegie Endowment for International Peace and held in Bermuda. There, from all sectors of the foreign policy Establishment, were assembled sundry great men to ponder the War for two and one-half days and prepare a confidential message to the President urging de-escalation. That conference of decent and able but still cautious people, trying shrewdly to "work from within," took me right back to government days. (Of course none of us, our chairman had intoned, are for "withdrawal"—that then-anathema word.) I suddenly realized the qualities of pomposity and constraint I had hated—and how far I had come, for better or worse. I found at least two who shared my itchiness at Bermuda. Daniel Ellsberg and Frances FitzGerald, author of the acclaimed *The Fire in the Lake*. We became briefly a sort of token-Bolshevik cluster, and those two first-hand observers of the Vietnam scene reinforced my convictions and sense of community.

Bermuda sent me into a rage. The great men of the center, gathered in council, had come up with an obsequious, ameliorative (and private) petition to the White House.[2] Meanwhile, the best of my students faced the intolerable alternatives decreed by that White House: service in an immoral war (as I now agreed), or jail, or exile to Canada. On return to Cambridge I quickly and belatedly transformed my Cape notes into an article, tried to peddle it to *Life* (they said No), to *Look* (they said Yes, then weeks later reneged), and finally to Old Faithful, the *Atlantic,* which had wanted it in the first place but had seemed to me a journal whose readers were already persuaded.

Time wasted on *Life* and *Look* meant that my piece didn't run till the April issue. On the eve of its publication, President Johnson announced his abdication—not, I fear, a matter of cause and effect. And with its publication I felt I had finally come clean, had finally "spoken out." The response, again, was heartening; this time dozens of appreciative letters, from men inside Government, former officials, and a great many others. Most astonishing was a handwritten note from a Cabinet member, on official stationery, who agreed with what I had said but asked why I had not had the guts to add that Rusk and Rostow must go. But most saddening was one from a former boss I had much admired. I wonder, he wrote, in his most searing sentence, what standards of personal decency can have caused a man to do what you have done.

---

2. The Bermuda document was duly, and confidentially, presented at the White House, where our delegates were received by two junior assistants to Mr. Rostow.

There is no lesson to the foregoing account except that it took one foreign-affairs resigner, one whose departure was conventionally muddled but who dissented on a central issue, approximately eighteen months (including press time) to break through the multiple constraints that inhibit "speaking out" once one resigns from the U.S. Government. The circumstances were special —both mine and those of the issue—as they are in every case. But on the basis of this experience I have developed considerable compassion for those who don't speak out right away.

24

Dissemblement, Secrecy, and Executive Privilege in the Foreign Relations of Three Democracies: A Comparative Analysis

THOMAS M. FRANCK AND EDWARD WEISBAND

INTRODUCTION

Nearly three hundred years ago John Locke observed a degree of contradiction between democratic control of government and the exigencies of foreign relations. He concluded that the control exercised by the Legislature and by law over the nation's relations with other states, which he misnamed the "federative function," would perforce be less than that over domestic aspects of governance. External relations, he stated, are "much less capable to be directed by antecedent, standing positive laws" than domestic affairs, but must instead "necessarily be left to the prudence and wisdom of those whose hands it is in to be managed . . . by the best of their skill for the advantage of the commonwealth."[1] Moreover, to place this foreign relations discretion in any hands but those of the Executive would invite conflict and contradiction "which would be apt some time or other to cause disorder and ruin."[2]

Dr. Lemuel Hopkins, leader of the Hartford Wits, in his sardonic poem attacking populism and the confederal constitution, said much the same thing in the eighteenth century.

> But know, ye favor'd race, one potent head
> Must rule your States, and strike your foes with dread,
> The finance regulate, the trade control,
> Live through the empire, and accord the whole.[3]

---

1. John Locke, *Treatise of Civil Government* (New York: Appleton Century Co., 1937), pp. 98–99.
2. *Ibid.*, p. 99.
3. Lemuel Hopkins, *The Anarchiad*, published in the *New Haven Gazette* between October 26, 1786, and September 13, 1787, reprinted in part, including the quoted excerpt, in Vernon L. Parrington, *The Colonial Mind, 1620–1800*, I (New York: Harcourt Brace and Co., 1927), 372.

Some weight has even been given, indirectly, to this view of the institutional necessities for the efficient conduct of foreign relations by the Supreme Court of the United States. In the oft-cited United States v. Curtiss-Wright Export Corp. et al., the Court sustained a broad delegation by the Congress to the President of discretionary power to prohibit sale of arms and ammunition to parties in the Chaco war between Bolivia and Paraguay. Justice Sutherland, for the Court, spoke of the "exclusive power of the President as the sole organ of the federal government in the field of international relations" and noted that legislation having to be implemented on the basis of "negotiation and inquiry within the international field must often accord to the President a degree of discretion and freedom from statutory restriction which would not be admissible were domestic affairs alone involved."[4] Notable about *Curtiss-Wright* from the Constitutional point of view, however, is that this case and the very few similar cases[5] never question the right of the Congress to legislate in the foreign relations field but only test whether, in legislating, the Congress can delegate its own broad discretionary powers to the Executive. To this question, the Court has given a qualified affirmative response. But what the Congress has given must be the Congress's to withhold, to retrieve, to exercise without any delegation to Presidential discretion.

Whatever Justice Sutherland's dicta may have presumed, the Constitution of the United States is not John Locke's word made law, and quite specifically not in the matter of exclusive Executive authority over foreign affairs. Alexander Hamilton in *Federalist* No. 69 explicitly set out to quiet the fears of Americans that the Constitution did, in fact, propose to give the Executive such a monopoly. "The President," he wrote, "will have only the occasional command of such part of the militia of the nation as by legislative provision may be called into the actual service of the Union."[6] The President's power as supreme commander "would amount to nothing more than the supreme command and direction of the military and naval forces, as first general and admiral of the Confederacy," but it would explicitly not extend to the power of *"declaring* of war and to the *raising* and *regulating* of fleets and armies—all which, by the Constitution under consideration, would appertain to the legislature."[7] The President is also "to be authorized to receive ambassadors and other public ministers." But this, added Hamilton, "though it has been a rich theme of declamation, is more a matter of dignity than of authority."[8] Hamilton emphasized also the balancing power

---

4. 299 U.S. 304, 319–22 (1936).
5. See United States v. Chemical Foundation, 272 U.S. 1 (1926).
6. *The Federalist Papers,* ed. Edward Mead Earle (New York, Modern Library, 1938), No. 69, "The Real Character of the Executive" (pp. 445-53), p. 448. Italics added.
7. *Ibid.*
8. *Ibid.*

of the Senate to concur in the appointment of ambassadors, as did John Jay.[9] Jay added that the Senatorial role would ensure that "the affairs of trade and navigation should be regulated by a system cautiously formed and steadily pursued."[10]

Addressing himself squarely to the question of secrecy, Jay conceded that in the negotiation of treaties the Executive Branch might sometimes need "perfect secrecy" to achieve "immediate dispatch."[11] There would also be occasions "where the most useful intelligence may be obtained, if the persons possessing it can be relieved from apprehensions of discovery." There might be secret informants who would "rely on the secrecy of the President, but who would not confide in that of the Senate, and still less in that of a large popular assembly."[12] As Jay prophesied, however, "Those matters which in negotiations usually require the most secrecy and the most dispatch" would be "those preparatory and auxiliary measures which are not otherwise important in a national view." He added that the Senate's "talents, information, integrity and deliberate investigations" would always balance the Executive prerogatives of "secrecy and dispatch."[13]

It is not only in the United States but in every other democracy as well that the people have constantly sought reassurance that their Executive's need for "secrecy and dispatch" in foreign affairs would be balanced and checked by a vigorous, informed Legislature and public. In the words of the recent report of the Franks Committee in Britain,

> From the earliest times governments of all types have been anxious to pre-
> serve secrecy for matters affecting the safety or tactical advantage of the
> State. It is, however, the concern of democratic governments to see that
> information is widely diffused, for this enables citizens to play a part in con-
> trolling their common affairs. There is an inevitable tension between the
> democratic requirements of openness, and the continuing need to keep some
> matters secret.[14]

This checking and balancing has two functions: (1) to ensure that Executive discretion stays within the boundaries of the foreign affairs prerogative and does not replace legislation as the way to regulate the internal affairs of the nation; and (2) to ensure that the public is adequately, if not in every instance immediately, informed so that their Executive could still be held to

---

9. *The Federalist,* No. 64, *ibid.,* pp. 390–96.
10. *Ibid.,* p. 392.
11. *Ibid.*
12. *Ibid.,* pp. 392–93.
13. *Ibid.,* p. 393.
14. Great Britain, Home Office, Departmental Committee on Section 2 of the Official Secrets Act 1911, vol. 1, Cmnd, 5104 (London, H.M.S.O. 1972), p. 9; commonly referred to as the Franks Report.

account, even in foreign affairs. In the words of John Stuart Mill, "if the public, the mainspring of the whole checking machinery, are too ignorant, too passive, or too careless and inattentive to their part," democracy fails. "Without publicity," Mill asks, "how could they either check or encourage what they were not permitted to see?"[15]

Neither the written Constitution of the United States, nor the half-written Constitution of Canada, least of all the unwritten Constitution of Great Britain, has succeeded in establishing the balance decreed by democratic theory between the imperatives of Executive discretion and secrecy in matters of foreign affairs including defense, on the one hand, and on the other, the public's need and right to participate, knowledgeably, in the democratic process—either directly or through their elected representatives. There is no abstract basis upon which to reconcile the demands of the government for "secrecy and dispatch" with those of the demos for access to information.

When the Executive—the President, a Cabinet Minister, a senior bureaucrat—refuses information, the Government usually argues the case for security and speed and for preserving the integrity of an internal bureaucratic advisory process. But when legislatures, the press, and an aroused public demand information, they are really calling for the right to participate either in making, or in reversing, a decision. The Executive champions functional utility. The demos argues for the supremacy of democratic process. Without concern for utility, the society is doomed from without or disintegrates from within. Without concern for process, the society is scarcely worth preserving —at least for those who hold liberal democratic values. All democracies concerned for survival, therefore, must strive to maintain a functional balance between these competing demands.

Such a balance, however, cannot be captured in philosophic abstraction or even in Constitutional formulas. If there is a balance, it is likely to be an imperfect, shifting, dynamic, tension-filled equilibrium compounded by numerous small accommodations between the key actors in a society's foreign policy process. There can never be a final solution.

PRINCIPAL DOMESTIC ACTORS AND INTERACTIONS: A MODEL FOR ANALYSIS

Before examining the praxis by which three democracies, of varying international personalities and degrees of power, attempt to approximate such a balance, it is useful to define the *actors* in the balancing process. And since the subject of this study is *secrecy*, rather than the Constitutional balance of

---

15. John Stuart Mill, *Considerations on Representative Government* (London: Longmans, Green and Co., 1872), p. 13.

power in general, it is necessary to define the *role of secrecy* in the interactions between these actors.

The principal domestic actors in the field of foreign affairs[16] in Canada, the United States, and Britain are:

1. the Executive (consisting of the political head of Government, the Cabinet, sub-Cabinet, senior bureaucrats, and other special advisers and assistants);
2. the Legislature (including its committees and staffs, if any);
3. the press;
4. special and public interest groups (such as business associations, trade unions, public affairs organizations, consumer groups).

The states with which interactions occur, perceived as single entities or in terms of their multiple domestic actors, constitute additional actors in the field of foreign affairs. They, too, may play a part in our internal political interactions, directly or indirectly.

In our three countries there are general guidelines devised to harmonize the roles of the principal domestic actors. It is broadly agreed that the public and the special interest groups may play an important role through elections and may to a limited extent testify and lobby on issues before the Executive and Legislature. The Legislature in each country may ask the Government questions, examine policies in open debate, in committee, and in party caucus, and threaten to withhold funds or defeat legislation desired by the Executive. The press enjoys broad, but not unlimited, freedom to investigate and criticize Executive actions.

Despite these guidelines, tensions predominate and conflicts arise. It is to a considerable extent inherent in the role of each actor that this should be so. These tensions and conflicts frequently center on Executive secrecy. The press, Legislature, and interest groups want to share the Executive's virtual monopoly of secrets in the foreign affairs field. Thus the interaction would at first appear as a simple struggle for access to secret information between one actor and all the rest. This may be portrayed (as in Figure 1) as a tug-of-war over information that the Executive tries to keep in the realm of secrecy and the other actors try to pull into the public domain.

This is not, however, a universally valid representation of the struggle and conflict between the four principal actors. There are such situations, in which the Executive is confronted by a concurrent challenge to its secrecy from all three of the other actors (as in Figure 1), but these are rare. More usually, the interactions take the form of coalitions and alliances between

---

16. Throughout this essay, "foreign affairs" is used to denote the areas of (1) national defense, (2) diplomatic relations, (3) international trade, and (4) international monetary relations.

Figure 1

THE SUPERFICIAL "TUG-OF-WAR" MODEL

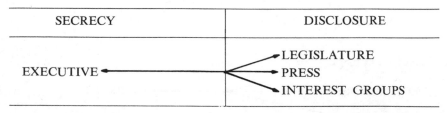

SECRECY	DISCLOSURE

the Executive and one or more of the other actors. These groupings may be based on selective sharing of secrets or simply on perceptions of mutual self-interest. Thus, both *The New York Times* and *The Times* of London have been told secrets by the Executive in order to secure the cooperation of those journals, and on the understanding that the information would not be revealed either to the legislature or to the public. Similarly, influential non-Cabinet members of the Legislature are sometimes co-opted by the Executive's selective revelations to them, always on the understanding that the secrets would be kept from their Parliamentary colleagues and the press.

Thomas L. Hughes, former director of the U.S. State Department's Bureau of Intelligence and Research, proposes in this book, that such co-option of key legislators be broadened and institutionalized.[17] The process is one of unstable coalitions and shifting alliances. In a war or a severe national crisis, as depicted in Figure 2, all the actors may rally patriotically

Figure 2

THE "INTERNATIONAL CRISIS ENCOUNTER" MODEL

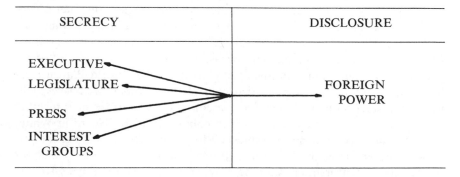

SECRECY	DISCLOSURE

behind Executive secrecy even without being co-opted. It is at such times that the Legislature, the press, and the public involved have sometimes

17. See Chapter 2, "The Power to Speak and the Power to Listen."

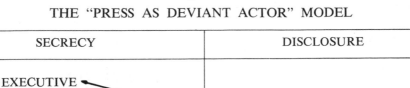

Figure 3

THE "PRESS AS DEVIANT ACTOR" MODEL

agreed—rightly or wrongly—to the enactment of broad Executive powers to classify, censor, and suppress as well as punish the leaking of information. Such Official Secrets and Espionage Statutes and classification regulations often survive long beyond the particular crisis and the patriotic coalition that made them possible.

A variation of this is the situation set out in Figure 3—also usually in wartime or in a severe international crisis—in which a newspaper or wire service breaks censorship or reveals information about troop movements or a key date, under circumstances deplored by the other actors. Here again, the Executive establishes a coalition built upon a common national team-interest and fear of defeat: a coalition favoring secrecy even at the cost of the public's right to know and participation in decision-making. In such cases there is a deviation that may lead to a serious conflict, one that is generally played out among the actors themselves but could conceivably become also a key issue in a national election or the subject of a criminal prosecution or civil litigation. This occasional umpiring role of electorates and courts is diagrammed in Figure 3. During the first World War in England it was, oddly, the Deputy Chairman of the *Military Mail* newspaper whose indiscretion landed him before a court. He was prosecuted together with his informant for the contents of a column entitled "Heard in Whitehall, by Mars." Both men were sentenced to two months' imprisonment.[18]

Such prosecutions are, however, extremely rare—as were press violations of security or censorship in wartime.[19] When violations do occur, offenders

---

18. (London) *Times,* April 3, 1916, p. 3, and May 4, 1916, p. 5. Franks Report, *supra,* list of prosecution, Appendix II, p. 116.
19. For an account of U.S. wartime censorship see James Russell Wiggins, *Freedom or Secrecy* (rev. ed.; New York: Oxford University Press, 1964), pp. 96–100.

are most frequently scorned rather than supported by the rest of the press. Conversely, however, when prosecutions or suits to prevent publication for violation of security are attempted in peacetime, or in wars legitimated neither by law nor by political popularity, the press generally rallies around the violator, as in the recent case of the Pentagon Papers published in *The New York Times*,[20] and when the British adviser's report on the Nigerian Civil War was published without authorization in the (London) *Sunday Telegraph*.[21]

There are also situations in which the Legislature has used its powers to attempt to force the Executive to reveal information that can be used to damage or persecute individuals (see Figure 4). Congressional committees

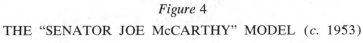

Figure 4

THE "SENATOR JOE McCARTHY" MODEL (*c.* 1953)

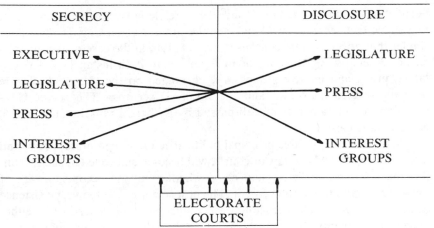

SECRECY	DISCLOSURE
EXECUTIVE	LEGISLATURE
LEGISLATURE	PRESS
PRESS	
INTEREST GROUPS	INTEREST GROUPS

ELECTORATE
COURTS

investigating disloyalty and subversion have sometimes succeeded in driving at least some of the press and some interest groups to rally on the side of Executive secrecy against abuses of Congressional scrutiny. In this encounter both courts and voters played an important role, not as parties directly involved in the action but as arbiters of the conflict. It should also be noted that the press and the Legislature, while directly involved, are not solidly ranged on one side but are divided in their support of the adversaries.

Diplomacy introduces the foreign government as actor. During diplomatic

---

20. United States v. New York Times Company, 403 U.S. 713 (1971).
21. For an account of this case see Jonathan Aitken, *Officially Secret* London: Weidenfeld and Nicolson, 1971).

Figure 5

THE "SECRET NEGOTIATION/AGREEMENT" MODEL

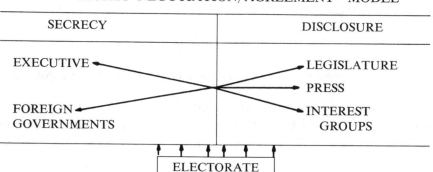

negotiations both the national and the foreign governments taking part may agree that secrecy would enhance the process of seeking agreement. A similar intergovernmental consensus may operate in the case of secret treaties and Executive agreements, as in Figure 5. In both instances the Legislature, press, and interest groups may be ranged on the side of disclosure in opposition to their own and the foreign Executive. The secret U.S.-Canadian oil quota agreement, discussed by Richard Frank in Chapter 16, is a dramatic case in point.

Whether or not the three principal political actors (Legislature, press, and interest groups) or the voters or courts, will become embroiled in such a conflict must depend, at first instance, on whether anyone becomes aware of the secret negotiation or agreement. The best secret is one the very existence of which is a secret. The occasion for a conflict will thus depend upon either diligent investigation by one or several of the other actors or upon a leak from within the Executive. Such a leak may range a disaffected part of the Executive on the side of the Legislature, press, and interest groups, as seen in Figure 6. In such incidents the courts are involved if prosecutions are brought against public servants for failing their vows of obedience and (verbal) chastity. Another kind of leak, however, involves no such sanctions. The Executive itself may selectively reveal hitherto secret information in order to mobilize public opinion for a new initiative or to secure funding of a pet defense project.

As noted, the Executive may seek to co-opt one, or several principal actors by means of selective disclosure in return for support for a policy and a promise not to disclose to others. An actor, however, may also actively solicit disclosure to himself and be equally exercised to prevent disclosure to others—that is, he may solicit co-option while hoping thereby

Figure 6

THE "ELLSBERG" MODEL (*c.* 1971)

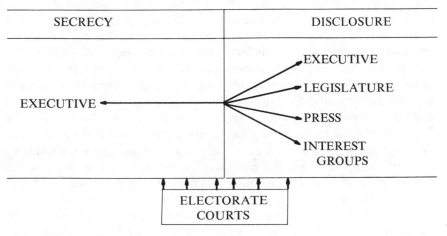

to co-opt. For example, in preparation for and conduct of trade negotiations, a special interest group representing export industries may find itself in conflict with the Executive in trying to discover what the State and Commerce Departments are thinking and planning. If the export group does gain access, it will be in conflict with the import industry's representatives and consumer groups both also trying to gain access in order to influence planning in the opposite direction. In the United States, this issue is currently hotly contested as between industry representatives who are allowed to populate Executive advisory boards on trade policy, and consumer representatives who are excluded.[22] In preparation of the U.S. policy for the 1973–74 Law of the Seas Conference, rival fishing interests—those fishing close to home and those fishing off foreign coasts—have vied with each other for the Government's ear.

Basic to these encounters is possession of a secret by the Executive and the countervailing efforts by one or several principal actors to have that secret disclosed, either to them alone or to the public. To that extent secrecy is the common element of interactions. To put it another way, secrets are power. It would seem to follow that the Executive's score in the larger power-balancing contest with the principal actors of the demos could

22. See Internal Memorandum of Secretary of Commerce Peterson, "Exemption of the Management-Labor Textile Advisory Committee from the Public Participation and Record Keeping Requirements of Executive Order 11671," August 31, 1972 (mimeo). See also, New England Governors Conference et al. v. Morton et al., Civil No. 13–59 (D. Me., filed April 27, 1972), which alleges failure by the Executive to engage in public consultation with interest groups before making oil import quota regulations.

be measured by how well it keeps its secrets. Conversely, the success of each other actor in the power balance would depend on how many secrets were pried out of the Executive. This is, however, a simplistic analysis. In reality secrets are kept by the Executive as defense against a *designated opponent* and are merely denied to other actors to ensure that the secret does not filter to the opponent. If an actor other than the opponent achieves disclosure, it is still only the opponent that benefits, and not the actor who achieved disclosure. To complicate analysis further, secrets are sometimes kept by the Executive even when none of the other domestic actors is a designated opponent. In such instances disclosure may impose a cost on the Executive without bestowing a gain on any of these other three actors. The only gain may, instead, accrue to a foreign actor. Or the real winner may be a disputing faction within the Executive. Secrets may also be kept by the Executive out of inertia or lassitude. Their revelation constitutes no power loss to the Executive and probably no power gain to any other actor.

There are other ways in which a direct power-secrecy correlation may be inoperative. A secret kept has a power value for the Executive quite different from its value to another actor when disclosed. The press, for example, does not gain power over foreign policy to the same extent that it denies prerogatives to the Executive by disclosure. And the advantage gained, by way of Constitutional precedent, when the Legislature forces a reluctant Executive to disgorge a secret, may be out of all proportion to the importance of the secret's substance.

A TAXONOMY OF FOREIGN AFFAIRS SECRETS

A taxonomy of secrets is a beginning toward understanding the role secrets play in the continuing power struggle among Executive, Legislature, press, and interest groups. Our taxonomy (1) sorts secrets into categories according to their content; (2) examines which actor or actors might stand to gain by disclosure (the secret's real "opponent"); and, (3) indicates what the Executive gains by denying the secret to the "opponent."

THE PRAXIS OF SECRECY AND DISCLOSURE
IN THREE DEMOCRACIES

Secrecy in Executive-Legislative Relations

In all three countries it is the Executive that possesses the secrets in the area of foreign relations, leaving the Legislature to try to find them out as best it can. This is not to say that the Legislature may not sometimes create secrets on its own. The Continental Congress of the United States resolved

TAXONOMY OF PRINCIPAL FOREIGN AFFAIRS SECRETS

CATEGORY OF SECRET	OPPONENT	REASON FOR DENIAL OF SECRET TO OPPONENT
Defense plans: strategy, operations, deployment	Hostile or potentially hostile foreign powers	To preserve tactical capacity to surprise enemy and reduce vulnerability to surprise by enemy
	Legislature, press, public	Prevent exposure of mistakes, debacles; preclude public participation in choice of plans
Weapons research and development	Other states	Surprise, options, flexibility; ability to market obsolescent weapons
	Legislature, press, public	Prevent intervention in key decisions; prevent investigation of policy, cost-over-runs, etc; prevent criticism for failure
	Interest groups	Reduce pressure, intervention
Diplomatic negotiations	Nations outside the negotiations	Prevent interference from those excluded, to facilitate "ganging up" by surprising those excluded
	Press; Legislature, public, interest groups of the negotiating states	Prevent interference by interest groups; prevent grandstanding by participants; encourage flexibility by making it easier to change positions without loss of face; prevent criticism for failures
Treaties, agreements	Nations against whom treaties directed	To preserve capacity to surprise; to avoid alarming prematurely, threatening those against whom treaty directed
	Own Legislature, press, interest groups, public	To avoid opposition, efforts to amend or prevent treaty or execution of treaty commitment; prevent criticism for failures
Information about other nations' defense plans, secret diplomatic negotiations, secret treaties and agreements	The nation whose secret it is	To preserve the predictability of opponent while retaining own option to surprise
	Own press and public	To preserve options without pressure from public to overreact

TAXONOMY OF PRINCIPAL FOREIGN AFFAIRS SECRETS

CATEGORY OF SECRET	OPPONENT	REASON FOR DENIAL OF SECRET TO OPPONENT
Executive process: Cabinet minutes, intradepartmental memoranda, expert advisory briefs, reports from diplomats	All other states	To prevent outside states from mistaking advice for policy and mis-reacting; to withhold "dirty linen" that affords other states propaganda advantage
	The Legislature	To preserve openness, integrity, of internal processes of Executive Branch by immunizing advisors, officials from Legislative review of their advice; prevent participation
	Special interest groups	To prevent pressure and deny participation
	The press and public	To prevent pressure, deny participation; prevent criticism for failures
Monetary negotiation	Currency speculators	Surprise; prevent intervention; retain flexibility
Executive preparations for tariff negotiations or new regulations	Special or public interest groups	To limit participation and opposition
Tariff or import agreements	States excluded from preferential treatment	To prevent hostility, retaliation, undercutting
	Legislature and special interest groups	To prevent participation and opposition
Intelligence reports from own agents	Most other states	Prevent identification of agents; retain surprise, options
	Legislature	Prevent participation in policy-making, opposition, and criticism for failure
	Press, public	Prevent participation in policy-making, opposition, and criticism for failure
Intelligence reports from allies	Most other states	Retain integrity of secret intelligence relation with ally; retain surprise, options
	Legislature, press, public	Prevent participation in policy-making, opposition

That every member of this Congress considers himself under the ties of virtue, honour, and love of his country, not to divulge, directly or indirectly, any matter or thing agitated or debated in Congress, before the same shall have been determined, without leave of Congress; nor any matter or thing determined in Congress, which a majority of the Congress shall order to be kept secret. And that if any member shall violate this agreement, he shall be expelled [from] this Congress, and deemed an enemy to the liberties of America, and liable to be treated as such.[23]

The Continental Congress, in 1775, established a committee "for the sole purpose of corresponding with our friends in Great Britain, Ireland and other parts of the world," and this actually became known as the Secret Committee, reflecting its preferred and accepted method of operating.[24] More recently, Congressional committees have sometimes met in secret, and so, on occasion, have British wartime Parliaments.[25] Even so, this secrecy is frequently no more than a symptom of co-option, the Executive whispering into the Legislature's ear.

To say that the Executive possesses most of the country's secrets could lead to the impression that a tight little island of government hoards information and defends it against all outsiders. When observed from within, the Executive is less than a unitary entity, and components keep secrets from each other. In Britain, for example, according to one writer, "The Prime Minister is the only member of the Cabinet who is informed of everything," since "the Cabinet office places at his disposal information on every single Cabinet activity, while ordinary members have detailed knowledge only of those matters dealt with in the various [Cabinet] committees of which they were members or of their own departments."[26] Particularly in defense and foreign policy, Prime Ministers at least from Disraeli forward, have operated primarily on their own, sometimes utilizing a small inner Cabinet committee, sometimes excluding most of the Cabinet while including some extra-Parliamentary members in a Committee on Imperial Defence, or a war Cabinet. More frequently Prime Ministers exclude the whole Cabinet while relying on their own secretariat and technical or bureaucratic advisers.[27] The Foreign Office in Britain, quite as much as the U.S. State Department,

23. Resolution of Secrecy Adopted by the Continental Congress, November 9, 1775, as in United States, 69th Congress, *Documents Illustrative of the Formation of the Union of the American States,* ed. Charles C. Tansill (Washington, D.C.: U.S., G.P.O. 1927), p. 18.
24. Samuel Flagg Bemis, *A Diplomatic History of the United States* (5th ed.; New York: Holt, Rinehart and Winston, 1965), p. 22.
25. The power, in the case of Parliament, appears to be inherent rather than statutory.
26. Humphrey Berkeley, *The Power of the Prime Minister* (New York: Chilmark Press, 1968), p. 51.
27. *Ibid.,* pp. 50–59.

has frequently been on the outside, looking in on foreign policy decisions made mainly by others. When Aneurin Bevan became Foreign Secretary in 1945, he was told by a departmental subordinate, "We have not been the Foreign Office for years. We have been merely a post office for Number Ten Downing Street."[28] Chamberlain had earlier carried on secret foreign relations with Mussolini without informing his Foreign Minister, Anthony Eden[29]; and Eden, in his turn, came to formulate his crisis policies toward Egypt in 1956 without consulting his full Cabinet until a few hours before the British-French ultimatum was dispatched to Nasser.[30] British negotiations with the Common Market were played close to the vest of Prime Minister Macmillan, with only a very few of the Cabinet's being informed or consulted.[31]

It is not only the legislators, therefore, from whom foreign policy secrets are kept. Adlai Stevenson's experience, as representative to the U.N. Security Council in arguing the American case during the Bay of Pigs incident, having been denied the facts by his own Government, is merely one dramatic instance of deliberate secrecy within the U.S. Executive Branch. There are many others.[32] Perhaps the most remarkable aspect of intra-Executive secrecy in Britain is the unwritten but iron-clad rule that a newly incoming Cabinet will not be shown the secret papers and records of its predecessor —that these will merely be summarized as the need arises, by the senior bureaucrats. In this way, as keeper of the secrets, the Civil Service obviously amasses considerable power. In the United States, the members of an outgoing Administration keep the secret files from their successors by shipping them home, or, under embargo, to repository libraries. But Mr. Nixon has sought to deny access to Presidential papers and tapes not only to the Legislative Branch in the Watergate case, but also to Special Prosecutor Archibald Cox, who operated within the President's own Executive Branch.

It is, however, the secrecy employed by the Executive to fend off inquiries from the Legislature that produces one of democracy's major headaches. In Canada, Britain, and the United States the Executive tends to deny secrets to the Legislature under three heads, the applications of which are set out in our taxonomy. Although these reasons differ in detail, they are broadly similar:

---

28. *Ibid.*, p. 56.
29. *Ibid.*, p. 58.
30. *Ibid.*, p. 59.
31. *Ibid.*
32. E.g., Lincoln White, speaking for the State Department, categorically denied the U-2 surveillance overflight without knowing what the CIA, the Russians, and soon the whole world knew about the matter. Roger Hilsman, *To Move A Nation* (Garden City: Doubleday and Co., 1967), pp. 83ff.

1. reasons of national security;
2. reasons of internal management;
3. reasons of Constitutional practice.

It is frequently pointed out by the Executive that secrecy is not directed *against* the Legislature or the public, but is rather designed to achieve security objectives that are to everyone's benefit. An insistence on disclosure, it is argued, would benefit no one except the "enemy." This contention is not invariably fanciful or paranoid. Thus, as Richard E. Neustadt has explained, Senate hearings on President Truman's Korean War policies after the dismissal of General Douglas MacArthur for insubordination placed the Executive in the position of having to expose its "innermost thoughts about the further conduct of hostilities."[33] In defending the Executive against the pro-MacArthur line taken by some Senators, its officials made a strong case against any further attempt to conquer North Korea, thereby also placing the "enemy" on notice, even before negotiations had begun, that U.S. policymakers had unilaterally renounced what might otherwise have been an important bargaining chip. Neustadt attributes the two-year stalemate in Korean truce negotiations in part to these revelations.[34]

The public Presidential agreement to cease bombing Cambodia after August 1973, unless specifically authorized by Congress to continue—whatever its merits in securing a domestic compromise on appropriations stalemate in Congress—certainly weakened the already weak U.S. hand in Cambodia. In Britain, the resignation in 1915 of Attorney General Sir Edward Carson in disagreement over British war plans relating to Serbia and, particularly, Gallipoli, led to an open discussion of these plans in Parliament.[35] This must have been more illuminating to the Germans and Ottomans than to the M.P.'s. The Suez crisis of 1956, on the contrary, came and went with Parliament left almost entirely in the dark, for fear of giving aid and comfort to the enemy. It is still in the dark about the truth of that affair. The crucial British issue as to whether it would abandon its historic military role "east of Suez" was briefly mooted to Parliament in 1966 on the occasion on the resignation of Christopher Mayhew, Minister of Defense. But thereafter the argument continued in secret inside the Cabinet until January 1968, when the final decision was announced, full-blown and unalterable, to Parliament.[36] Questioning of Cabinet members by backbenchers in Parliament generally stops short of anything that could aid an enemy. Neither in Britain nor in Canada is there a disposition to press Ministers for

---

33. Richard E. Neustadt, *Presidential Power: The Policies of Leadership* (New York: John Wiley and Sons, 1960), p. 30.
34. *Ibid.,* pp. 30–31.
35. 75 House of Commons Debates 535, November 2, 1915.
36. Patrick Gordon Walker, *The Cabinet* (London: Fontana/Collins, 1972), pp. 122–31.

answers once they have pleaded "national security," the Fifth Amendment of Cabinet officers.

Governments also tend to refuse information to the Legislative Branch on the ground that it concerns privileged communications either from friendly foreign Governments or from advisers within the Executive establishment. In either case, it is argued, the revelations would have a "chilling effect," embarrassing the source of the communication and discouraging frankness in future. The Canadian and British Governments both registered some dismay at the disclosure, via the Pentagon Papers, of communications made by them in confidence to Washington, and both privately expressed the resolve to be more guarded in future exchanges with the United States. But there is little evidence that this has actually happened. Conversely, in examining their own secrecy policies, Canadians have frankly admitted the necessity of remaining in step with British and American security rules since so much Canadian intelligence originates with those two nations,[37] and premature Canadian disclosure could embarrass its two larger allies and its allies' informants.

Similarly, in both Canada and Britain there operates an unwritten (but enforced) compact which requires the bureaucracy to remain wholly loyal and wholly silent and the Executive to act as a buffer separating and protecting the civil servant from investigation or criticism by the Legislature.[38] The silence imposed on a civil servant in exchange for this protection is re-enforced, in Britain and Canada, by sections 2 and 4 of their respective Official Secrets Acts.[39] The protection takes the form of Executive refusal to discuss with the Legislature the content or quality of the advice received from the bureaucracy. In the United States, then Attorney General Kleindienst stated in April 1973, that

> Congress likewise has recognized the validity of claims of executive privilege for internal advice to the President. The privilege has been invoked to promote frank advice within the executive branch and preserve confidentiality regarding conversations with the President.[40]

Constitutional doctrine is also invoked by these Governments to justify keeping Executive secrets from the Legislature. In Britain and Canada it is the doctrine of Cabinet "collective security" that serves. Broadly, as Patrick

---

37. Report of the Royal Commission on Security (Abridged; Ottawa: Queen's Printer 1969), p. 81.
38. Franks Report, *supra,* Note 14.
39. For Britain: 1 & 2 Geo. V, c. 28; for Canada: Official Secrets Act, 1939. (See Chapter 21.)
40. Statement of Richard G. Kleindienst, Attorney General, on S. 858 and S.J. Res. 72, Executive Privilege, Before the Separation of Powers Subcommittee of the Committee on the Judiciary and the Intergovernmental Relations Subcommittee of the Committee on Governmental Operations, U.S. Senate, April 10, 1973 (1973).

Gordon Walker has it, this "unwritten convention of the Constitution" holds that "every member of the government [Cabinet and Sub-Cabinet] must accept and if necessary defend cabinet decisions even if he opposes and dislikes them."[41] A common front such as this is deemed essential to the Parliamentary system—the common front being necessary not only to keep the Opposition at bay but to hold the Government's Parliamentary supporters in line and, in foreign policy matters to deny "aid and comfort" to foreign opponents. Crucial, therefore, is the deliberate "concealment of difference"[42] within the Cabinet. A Minister who disagrees with the views of his colleagues may resign and may even attack from the backbenches of the Commons or the Lords, but he may not, while remaining in Government, reveal anything of the frank and often bitter discussions and divisions occurring within the Government which are papered over by virtue of collective responsibility.

In the United States it is the Constitutional doctrine of the separation of powers which is often invoked to withhold Executive secrets from the Legislature. Unlike in the British or Canadian systems, the U.S. Executive's survival does not depend on retaining control of the voting majority in the Legislative Branch, and so secrecy cannot be invoked on grounds of partisan necessity. Instead, the Executive asserts that a Legislative incursion into the written communications, memoranda, intelligence, or other secrets of the Executive would represent an attempt by one coequal but separate branch of the Government to establish primacy over the other. This defensiveness is not a Watergate innovation. Thus, when a committee of the House of Representatives, in 1796, demanded to see copies of the instructions and other documents used in negotiating the Jay treaty with Great Britain,[43] President Washington held that "a just regard to the Constitution and to the duty of my office, under all the circumstances of this case, forbids a compliance with your request."[44]

William Howard Taft was equally confident of the Constitutional right to refuse.

The President [he wrote after his term of office] is required by the Constitution from time to time to give to Congress information on the state of the Union, and to recommend for its consideration such measures as he shall judge necessary and expedient, but this does not enable Congress or either

---

41. See Chapter 3.
42. *Ibid.*
43. For an interesting discussion of this episode see Raoul Berger, "Executive Privilege v. Congressional Inquiry," (1965) 12 *U.C.L.A. Law Rev.* 1044 at 85–93.
44. James D. Richardson, *Messages and Papers of the Presidents* (Washington, D.C.: U.S., G.P.O., 1897), p. 188. Cited in Joseph W. Bishop, "The Executive's Right of Privacy: An Unresolved Constitutional Question," 66 *Yale Law Journal* (1957), 500.

House of Congress to elicit from him confidential information which he has acquired for the purpose of enabling him to discharge his constitutional duties, if he does not deem this disclosure of such information prudent or in the public interest.[45]

This view, expressed sometimes more and sometimes less vociferously, appears to inhere in the office of Chief Executive.[46] President Eisenhower informed the Congress that "throughout our history the President has withheld information whenever he found that what was sought was confidential or its disclosure would be incompatible with the public interest or jeopardize the safety of the Nation." In particular, the President regarded it "essential to efficient and effective administration that employees of the Executive branch be in a position to be completely candid" and they "are not to testify to any such conversations or communications or to produce any such document or reproductions" before the McCarthy subcommittee. "I direct this action," the President emphasized, "so as to maintain the proper separation of powers."[47]

The three reasons commonly advanced by Governments to deny secrets to legislators are, however, much abused. Consider the reason of "national security." Legislative inquiry relating not to present but to past events cannot seriously be justified on this unfirm ground. Yet long-past events remain shrouded in secrecy in all three countries. Genuine concern for the integrity of confidences from other Governments is another reason. Yet this valid concern could be met, in most instances, simply by exorcising source identifications from secret information before it is disclosed.

Then there is the matter of protecting bureaucratic confidences. Undoubtedly, especially in periodic populist waves of witch-hunting, the Executive may be justified in protecting the anonymity of its internal advisory system by refusing to disclose controversial advice given it by members of the bureaucracy. Such protection may sometimes be necessary to ensure fearless, unpopular advice from within the Executive Branch, if the apparent purpose of seeking disclosure is to destroy the bureaucrat's radical independence. In most cases this, too, can be achieved by exorcising the name of the adviser. But it is doubtful whether there is so much unpopular, fear-

---

45. William Howard Taft, *Our Chief Magistrate and His Powers* (New York: Columbia University Press, 1916), p. 129.
46. See Irving Younger, "Congressional Investigations and Executive Secrecy: A Study in the Separation of Powers," 20 *U. of Pittsburgh Law Rev.* (1959) 755; Raoul Berger, "The Presidential Monopoly of Foreign Relations," 71 *Michigan Law Rev.* 1 (1972).
47. For a fuller presentation of the legal arguments used to support President Eisenhower's point of view see William P. Rogers, "Constitutional Law: The Papers of the Executive Branch," 44 *American Bar Association Journal* 941 (1958); the quotation is found therein.

less or dissident advice in need of protection. The Pentagon Papers indicate that the bureaucracy did not, in fact, challenge the political leaders with radical alternatives.

In Britain and Canada, too, there is a pervasive opinion among Members of Parliament that Executive secrecy is less intended to protect the bureaucrats from legislators' witch hunts than to preserve the civil servants' virtually exclusive access to the Ministerial ear. This opinion is coupled with another: that the bureaucrats' advice, protected from challenge by secrecy, tends to be conformist rather than innovative.[48] Thus secrecy may protect bureaucratic power more than bureaucratic independence. The two are not the same.

In Canada, of late, there is concern that the desire to protect the confidentiality of bureaucrats' advice is being extended, with much less legitimacy, to advice from outside consultants employed to advise Government. It has been the tradition of the British and Canadian systems that the usual form of outside advice—the Royal Commission Reports—be published promptly and in full, thereby allowing Parliament and public as well as the Government time to think and comment before the recommendations of the Commission were implemented, modified, or rejected. Since the early 1960's, however, the Canadian Government has begun to use task forces of outside experts as "informal administrative aids," and, as one writer states, unlike royal commissions, these "are not required by statute or convention to publish their reports or to make accessible, within a specified time, the research studies on which their recommendations are based."[49] The inclination in the Government, henceforth, appears to be to publish the data but not the recommendations of reports which are comparable to work that

---

48. For a British Parliamentary view to this effect, see Chapter 8, "Secrecy and the Right of Parliament to Know and Participate in Foreign Affairs." A similar Canadian Parliamentary view is expressed in Chapter 9, "The Role of Parliament in the Review and Planning of Canadian National Defence and External Affairs." Essentially the same view is expressed in an American context in Francis E. Rourke, *Bureaucracy and Foreign Policy* (Baltimore: The Johns Hopkins University Press for the Washington Center of Foreign Policy Research, 1972), esp. pp. 62–80.

49. Seymour Wilson, "The Role of Royal Commissions and Task Forces," in Bruce Doern and Peter Aucoin, eds., *The Structure of Policy Making in Canada* (Toronto: Macmillan, 1971), p. 124. In a recent statement the Canadian Government (March 15, 1973) sets out the general principle that "government papers, documents, and consultant reports should be produced" on motion to "enable Members of Parliament to secure factual information about the operations of government to carry out their parliamentary duties and to make public as much factual information as possible consistent with effective administration, the protection of the security of the state, rights to privacy and other such matters. . . ." House of Commons Debates, March 15, 1973, 2288. However, the recommendations of a consultant study need not be made public unless the nature of the projects has been designated, at its inception, "comparable to the kind of investigation of public policy for which the alternative would be a Royal Commission . . ." (*ibid.*).

might be done within the public service. This is either an advance or a defeat for openness, depending on whether one compares it to past practice regarding task force reports or to established Royal Commission practice.

As for the Constitutional arguments, it is evident that these, even if correct as stated, are being applied much more generously by the Executive to deny information to the Legislatures than is absolutely necessary either to preserve the separation of powers in the United States or to maintain collective Cabinet responsibility in Britain and Canada. In all three countries the overriding purpose of secrecy in foreign affairs is not to frustrate external enemies, nor to protect the integrity of the bureaucracy, nor even to safeguard Constitutional abstractions. The principal purpose of secrecy is to retain power—especially freedom of initiation—unfettered in the hands of the Executive. To share secrets is to share competence both to make decisions and to criticize them. In all three democracies secrecy is both symptom and, in part, a cause of Executive predominance in foreign affairs.

The Legislatures in the United States, Canada, and Britain are not, however, without some means for asserting at least a secondary foreign relations role, and efforts are underway in each to strengthen that role and to redress what is believed to be a balance tilted much too far in the direction of secrecy and unchecked Executive power. This does not, of course, ensure a wiser foreign policy. What Legislative participation tends to ensure is a broader base of consent for whatever policy is eventually decided. Lying to most members of the Congress and to the public about whether the United States was bombing North Vietnam or flying sorties over Cambodia between March 1969 and May 1970, and the cover-up of My Lai, have gained the U.S. foreign policy-makers no respite from foreign "enemies" since the North Vietnamese and Cambodians presumably knew that they were being bombed and the Vietnamese knew of My Lai. The real "opponents" from whom these secrets were being kept were the American people. But it is surely apparent now that in a democracy such secrets have a way of being found out, and that, when they are, the entire Executive Branch and all its works tend to lose public legitimacy. This ingredient of legitimation is important in democracies, not least to the Executive, which in its absence may find itself trying unsuccessfully to mobilize the country to a policy for which the people and their Parliament are unwilling to lend the necessary moral, financial, and physical support.

Moreover, legislative participation tends also to be a check on one-man decision-making, which, while sometimes brilliant, is prone to self-compounding error, ego justification, and even obsession. In Britain and Canada, the Prime Minister is usually surrounded by a Cabinet of men and women with sufficient political clout of their own to prevent this from happening, even without more Parliamentary participation. In the United

States, the Cabinet is far more subservient to the White House, and the White House is the instrument of one man. In practice, the President generally seeks and takes advice in foreign affairs. But neither his Constitutional relation to his Cabinet nor the balance of political power inside the Executive makes this inevitable. For this reason alone, Congressional participation can be of major importance to a healthy foreign policy.

Before examining the tool available for the assertion of such a role, it should first be noted, however, that in the United States, secrecy has perhaps become too central in the struggle to stake out a legislative role in the foreign affairs field. The British and Canadian Parliamentary Opposition parties seem somewhat less inhibited by lack of access to secret information in their criticism of Government policy. Of the United States, Richard Barnet has correctly asked:

> Should the fact that the citizen and his representatives in Congress share only a fraction of the information about the outside world that is available to the national security bureaucracy seriously inhibit them from making independent critical judgments about policy?[50]

During the Vietnam crisis, the Government constantly intimidated opponents with the warning that they did not know the whole story and should therefore suspend arguments based on nothing more than common sense. The Pentagon Papers have shown, however, that the secret intelligence reports hidden from the Congress, usually did no more than confirm the common-sense view and information readily available in *The New York Times* and *Le Monde*. The Congress need scarcely have hesitated to criticize the Executive security managers out of deference to what they knew but were not sharing. When the United States launched its invasion of Cambodia in 1970, lack of Congressional censure was not really primarily due to lack of information about the 3,630 secret sorties flown by U.S. planes in the previous months under cover of falsified records. Information can be a sacred cow, made too important. Indeed, lack of information can be an excuse for abdication. The Congress's failure to oppose the war earlier and more effectively is probably less due to a really debilitating lack of secret information than to the sharing by the Congress of the wrong-headed political assumptions of the Executive.

In all three countries the Legislatures possess certain powers to compel disclosure, but these are so Draconian as to be, in political practice, unusable. In the United States there is the power of Presidential impeachment. Only a little less drastic is the capacity of the British and Canadian Parlia-

---

50. Richard J. Barnet, *Roots of War* (New York: Atheneum, 1972), p. 285.

ments, in a vote over a matter of substance, to defeat a Government "on the floor." Normally, party discipline and the perceived self-interest of Members of Parliament in "voting at their party's call" would almost always prevent such an occurrence. Only a little less sledgehammer-like is the power of the Congress to fail to vote foreign and defense appropriations and the Canadian and British Parliaments' right to fail to vote supply. In practice, both involve a rare act of rash courage on the part of legislators, a firm belief that the Government, embarked on a disastrous course, must be stopped at all costs. In June 1973 the U.S. Congress did display such last-resort courage in using its fiscal powers to compel an end to bombing in Cambodia.

There are at the disposal of the Canadian and British Parliaments more finely calibrated weapons, but their effectiveness is quite limited in the face of determined Executive non-disclosure. The classic instrument for "finding out" is the question period at the beginning of the day's sitting. Members cannot, however, use this opportunity for free-flowing cross-examination. A Minister may postpone an answer by requiring "notice" and the questioner is allowed only one supplementary question beyond that put down on the order paper. Some "orchestration" of interrogation is possible if Members combine the thrust of their individual questions. It is all too easy, however, for the Government to parry, evade, or resort to witticisms, so that the specter of "national security" does not usually have to be raised. The inevitable consequence is that Members of Parliament in both Britain and Canada tend to regard Question Time more as an opportunity to draw attention or embarrass than to find out; more as an occasion to put their own opinions in the guise of a question than to solicit meaningful facts and opinions from the Cabinet. (For a full discussion, see Chapters 3, 8, and 9.)

Sometimes, however, intensive and punishing barrages of questions without adequate answers may raise doubts in the public mind which force the Governments in both countries to establish Commissions of Inquiry to investigate the matter. These commissions, as Professor Cohen points out in Chapter 21, may be—but are not necessarily—useful in getting facts before the public. In 1958 a British investigation tribunal, compelled by pressure in Parliament, looked into suspicious deaths at the Hola Mau Mau camp in Kenya and made public hitherto unknown facts about the treatment of prisoners; and this undoubtedly affected policy toward that colony.[51] Similarly, Canadian commissions have investigated circumstances surrounding the defeat and capture of Canadian troops at Hong Kong in 1942 and an earlier alleged scandal in arms and munitions.[52]

As part of their questioning procedure, both British and Canadian Par-

---

51. 605 Parliamentary Debates, House of Commons 563–564 (1958–59).
52. Report on the Canadian Expeditionary Force to the Crown Colony of Hong Kong (Ottawa: H.M.S.O., 1942); Royal Commission on the Bren Machine Gun Contract (1939).

liaments have a right to "call for the production of papers by means of a motion for Return." According to Erskine May, the power was "frequently exercised until about the middle of the nineteenth century." Although "rarely resorted to in modern circumstances," "[the] power has a continuing importance since it may be delegated to committees, thus enabling them to send for papers and records."[53] In Canada the procedure has recently been given new life by a Government statement outlining its purpose and scope.[54] The statement, however, exempts from the new requirement papers "dealing with international relations, the release of which might be detrimental to the future conduct of Canada's foreign relations (the release of papers received from other countries to be subject to the consent of the originating country)."[55]

Another recent and potentially promising development in the House of Commons both in Canada and in England is the appointment or strengthening of select committees composed of smaller groups of Members in proportion to their party's strength in the House. In 1968 Canada created a Standing Committee on External Affairs and National Defence consisting of thirty members and with the power to delegate to subcommittees. As described by Gordon Fairweather, in Chapter 9, the Committee may subpoena persons (including officials) as well as documents and records, and, at least in theory, arrest and bring to the bar of the House for trial and punishment anyone who refuses to answer the Committee's summons or behaves in contempt. Its terms of reference, however, are periodically determined by vote of the House—and there, presumably, the Cabinet commands majority support. Moreover, the Committee's members are chosen by the party whips, and this gives the Government control over the selection of the majority of members. Nevertheless, the innovation is important. In the Committee, Ministers and bureaucrats can be required to explain policies and may be cross-examined much more thoroughly than on the floor of the House during question period. In the words of the Conservative Party's Parliamentary spokesman on legal affairs, some committees are making a beginning toward equipping themselves with expert staffs, although these are still far from comparable in resources to the foreign affairs and defense committee staffs of the U.S. Congress.[56]

The British Commons drew up its first select committees in 1967, with powers of scrutiny and interrogation comparable to the Canadian. As with the Canadian committees, too, the British lack an autonomous power base and the developed staff and research backup of their American counter-

---

53. *Erskine May's Parliamentary Practice*, p. 250.
54. House of Commons Debates, March 15, 1973, vol. 832, cols. 2288ff.
55. *Ibid.*
56. Fairweather, Chapter 9.

parts. Significantly, however, the British Governments have never agreed to Parliament's setting up a Committee on External Affairs and Defence. Recently the Expenditure Committee was authorized to establish a Defence and External Affairs subcommittee, but its terms of reference are narrowly confined "to consider how, if at all, the policies implied in the figures of expenditure and in the estimates may be carried out more economically."[57] Of course Parliament itself grew from an acorn of Royal fiat not much broader than this; thus it remains to be seen whether the subcommittee will enlarge its own practice. (The Subcommittee is discussed by Robert Maclennan in Chapter 8.)

Britain has a device for disclosure not yet found in its Canadian counterpart, let alone in the U.S. Congress: the Parliamentary Commissioner for Administration, a post created in 1967 by Parliament.[58] This Commissioner is paid the salary of a High Court judge, may be removed only by vote of both Houses of Parliament, and appoints his own staff. His function is to investigate claims by individuals or corporate bodies to have sustained injustice in consequence of maladministration by the Government or its servants performing administrative functions.[59] He has subpoena, oath, and contempt powers, as well as access to all relevant documents except Cabinet papers and minutes.

The Commissioner's reports are made to the party alleging a wrong, to the Government, to the Member of Parliament who referred the case to him, and, if further remedial action is needed, to the House of Commons. Public disclosure of documents or information in such reports may nevertheless be vetoed by a Minister if it is deemed "prejudicial to the safety of the State or otherwise contrary to the public interest."[60] The Commissioner is barred by the statute from considering certain matters,[61] particularly those arising in the area of external relations.[62] Already, however, that limitation has been rather narrowly interpreted. The Commissioner has investigated a complaint alleging maladministration by the Foreign Office in denying to a group of former prisoners held at Sachsenhausen a share of the compensation fund made available by the West German Government for distribution to British concentration camp victims.[63] This appears to be a valu-

---

57. Maclennan, Chapter 8.
58. Parliamentary Commissioner Act, 1967, 15 & 16 Eliz. 2, c. 13.
59. Stanley A. de Smith, *Judicial Review of Administrative Action* (2nd ed.; London: Stevens and Sons Ltd., 1968), p. 40.
60. Parliamentary Commissioner Act, 1967, s.11(3).
61. *Ibid.,* ss. 4, 5; Schedules 2, 3.
62. *Ibid.,* Sched. 3.
63. House of Commons Paper 54 (1967–68); 758 House of Commons Debates (5th series), cols. 107–170 (February 5, 1968); Geoffrey K. Fry (1970) Public Law 336–358. See Professor de Smith's discussion in Chapter 18.

able precedent for interpreting "external relations" very narrowly. (A further discussion may be found in Chapter 8 by Professor de Smith.)

Since in neither Britain nor Canada does treaty-making Constitutionally require the participation of the Legislature, there are in theory greater opportunities for secret treaty commitments than would be the case in the United States. Under the so-called Ponsonby Rule, however, the tradition in Britain has been, since 1924, to lay all treaties before the Houses of Parliament at least twenty-one days before they are ratified by the Executive. In Canada the practice since 1926 has been to ask the approval of Parliament by resolution before the Executive ratifies treaties binding Canada to important military, economic, political, or fiscal obligations.[64] Since in Britain and Canada treaties do not automatically become part of the "law of the land" as in America, Parliamentary participation is in any event essential to the domestic effectuation of treaty commitments. On the other hand, while the U.S. Constitution requires the consent of two-thirds of the Senate prior to treaty ratification, many international commitments are made by Executive agreement free of this limitation. Only in 1972 did the House and Senate pass and the President sign a law requiring notice of Executive agreements to Congress within sixty days of their being concluded.[65]

The British and Canadian Parliaments have one other way to lift the veil of Executive secrecy: the resignation statements of Ministers. Resignation of Cabinet and sub-Cabinet officials over differences of policy occurs with much greater frequency than in the United States. Further, unlike the practice in Washington, the system in both London and Ottawa accommodates and to some extent encourages a public statement of these differences, and in the course of such a statement considerable hitherto secret information may be aired. While this information is rarely of the defense or security kind, much of it is valuable to the open political process. The practice of disclosure upon resignation has been referred to by Aneurin Bevan, himself a master practitioner, as "one of the immemorial courtesies" of Parliament.[66] The House even provides a time-honored place—the second bench below the gangway—from which the statement is made, and it is invariably received with much interest by Parliament and the media. In this way the public and its representatives sometimes catch a glimpse of the red flag of danger hoisted by a former Minister over a hitherto little-observed Government policy.

In the United States, too, the Congress has attempted in various ways to

---

64. Resolution of June 21, 1926. House of Commons Debates, 1926, vol. 5, col. 4758. See also A. E. Gottlieb, *Canadian Treaty Making* (Toronto: Butterworth, 1968), pp. 15–16.
65. Pub. L. No. 92–403, 92d Cong., S. 596, August 22, 1972.
66. Aneurin Bevan, 487 House of Commons Debates 34, 23 April 1951.

limit the Executive's commitment to secrecy. The separation and the equality of the Executive and Legislative branches colors the whole process of information flow. Unlike Canada and Britain, the United States does not have what would amount to a Parliamentary Opposition: rather, the Congress *is* the natural opposition to Government, required by the dynamics of institutional rivalry to play this role. While the British or Canadian Governments may be willing to share a few secrets with their own parties' loyal caucus, the U.S. President cannot really count on the same overriding loyalty on the part of his party in the Congress. The British and Canadian Cabinets exercise the discipline of nearly absolute power over their party in Parliament; the President has no such power over his party's Members of Congress. Thus a Canadian M.P., even if told a disagreeable secret, is really in no position to use the instruments of Parliament to do anything about it. The same is certainly not true of Members of the Congress. The President must always expect shared information to make for shared power. A U.S. Congressman, more readily than a British or Canadian Member of Parliament, can translate information into critical inquiry and into re-direction of policy. It is, therefore, predictable that the Congress at times struggles harder than British or Canadian M.P.'s to obtain information, and that the U.S. Executive may also resist harder. In the United States the battle is fought at a higher level of intensity because the stakes are greater and the institutional set-up is more conducive to conflict. This is illustrated by the 1969–70 Cambodian raids, covered up, denied, and lied about by the Executive in its relations with the Congress and even the Senate Armed Services Committee, but disclosed privately to a few trusted Congressional hawks for purposes of co-option. The falsification or denial of data and records in the Executive's struggle with the Congress had by 1974 reached a concussive climax. It, too, however, has a long history.

The Continental Congress, which established the Confederal Constitution, created a Department of Foreign Affairs in 1782 with a proviso that "any member of Congress shall have access" to the "books, records and other papers" of the department, except that no copies were to be taken "of matters of a secret nature without the special leave of Congress."[67] By 1789, however, confederal union had given way to federal union, and under the new Constitutional arrangement the Congress enacted a statute establishing an Executive Department of Foreign Affairs. Section 4 of the Act of 1789 entrusted to the Secretary "custody and charge of all records, books and papers" of his office without re-enacting the provisions for Congressional access.[68] This omission is somewhat accentuated by Congressional enactment, a few months later, of another law, this one creating the Executive

---

67. 7 Journals of Congress 219.
68. 1 Stat. 29 (1789).

Department of the Treasury. This law provides that the Secretary shall "make report, and give information to either branch of the legislature" concerning all matters delegated to him by the Congress or "which shall appertain to his office."[69]

It has been suggested, even by the Executive Branch, that no issue need be made over the inclusion of this provision in the law setting up the Treasury Department and its omission from the law setting up the Department for Foreign Affairs.[70] Nevertheless, in Louis Henkin's words, "In foreign affairs, in particular, Congress has itself recognized limitations, for while it has long demanded reports of all executive departments, it has requested them of the State Department only, 'if not incompatible with the public interest.' "[71]

It does not follow, however, that there is a Constitutional basis for this Congressional reticence. Rather, since the Congress and the Executive are assigned complementary powers over foreign affairs, it is generally assumed that there must be mutual accommodation. This process of accommodation is, by its nature, legally ambiguous. The first instance involved a Congressional investigation of a military expedition by General St. Clair. The Congressional committee called for the production of all Executive papers regarding the campaign. President Washington did deliver the papers but, according to his Secretary of State, Thomas Jefferson, who kept a private record of the Cabinet meeting, the President could "exercise a discretion" as to whether to do so or not, depending on whether "disclosure . . . would injure the public."[72]

Seen from the Congressional perspective, what matters is that the papers were delivered. From the Executive perspective, re-enforced by the subsequent controversy over the Jay Treaty papers, which were not delivered to the House of Representatives, what mattered was that the discretion was seen to reside in the Executive.[73] In essence, the accommodations prove conclusively neither that there is a Constitutional right on the part of the Congress to obtain information nor, on the contrary, an Executive right to withhold it. Accommodation, rather, has been evidence of mutual good

---

69. 1 Stat. 65–66 (1789).
70. 6 Ops. Att'y. Gen. 326, 333 (1856). The statute setting up the Department of State is: 1 Stat. 68 (1789). The statute setting up the Department of War is: 1 Stat. 49 (1789).
71. Louis Henkin, *Foreign Affairs and the Constitution* (Mineola, N.Y.: The Foundation Press, 1972), p. 112. See also J. G. Cannon's *Procedure in the House of Representatives,* H. Doc. 610, 87th Cong., 2d sess., p. 219.
72. Jefferson, *Writings,* ed. Paul L. Ford, I (New York: G. P. Putnam's Sons, 1892), p. 189; R. Berger, *supra,* Note 43, 1044 at 79.
73. Non-delivery can, however, be explained in this instance on the ground that the papers were being requested by the wrong House of Congress. Delivery was made to the Senate, which shares the treaty power; Berger, *supra,* p. 1086.

sense and a desire to make coordinate but separate powers work. It is this spirit of accommodation which appears to have broken down under the pressures of the Vietnam War and the Watergate scandal.

To compel disclosure of the name of an informer still employed in intelligence work, or the negotiating instructions of a diplomat still engaged in negotiating, or the precise strategic deployment of nuclear weapons, is as alien to the Congress's as to the Executive's sense of national security. But the Congress has never conceded that it is a sieve incapable of keeping a secret. A Committee of the House of Representatives during the controversy in 1843 with President Tyler over the alleged frauds of Indian Agents, specifically declared that Members of Congress are "as competent to guard the interests of the State, and have as high motives for doing so, as the Executive can have."[74] But the point has never been pushed to an absurdity. Very few disputes have arisen or are likely to arise over Executive secrecy in bona-fide defense and security matters.

Regarding this hard-core information, the Congress, by its voluntary reticence, has said in effect to the Executive branch: *We shall allow you to act as the judge of what may have to remain an executive secret in the field of foreign affairs, so long as we are convinced that you are keeping from us only those matters the withholding of which any reasonable Member would recognize to be absolutely essential to the national interest.* In 1930, for example, the Senate, as part of its advise-and-consent function, called on the Executive to show all papers relating to negotiation of the London Treaty for naval armaments limitation and reduction. The President resisted having to produce *all,* on the ground that some documents contained very frank comments on foreign officials. Although a majority of Senators in the debate confirmed the Constitutional right of the Senate to require production of all documents, the body nevertheless voted in favor of an amendment subjecting the demand to the usual "if not incompatible with the public interest" proviso.[75]

Unfortunately, the United States appears to have entered a period when the mutual confidence underlying this voluntary abstention is eroding. The responses recently elicited by Senator Sam Ervin's Judiciary Committee in questioning of the Department of Defense concerning Army surveillance of U.S. civilians and data-bank programs, as well as the Defense and the State departments' refusal of information to the (Congressional) General Accounting Office, taken together with Congressional reaction to these re-

---

74. A. C. Hind's *Precedents of the House of Representatives,* vol. 3 (Washington, D.C.: U.S., G.P.O., 1907–1908), p. 185.
75. 73 *Congressional Record* 86 (1930); Mary Louise Ramsey, Library of Congress, Congressional Research Service, American Law Division, "Executive Privilege," Memorandum of June 7, 1971, 43 at 43–45.

fusals, suggest that the erosion has gone rather far.[76] In these circumstances, the Congress has come to suspect that the Executive's application of the concept of "national interest" has become equated with the "Executive interest." The final warning signal was the White House's secret attempt in 1972–73 to suborn the CIA to perform in the domestic arena "dirty tricks" reserved by law and previous practice for use against foreign enemies. Inevitably, challenges have been laid down contesting the prerogative of the Executive to determine unilaterally what does and what does not come within the exempted categories. Such a challenge to the process of determination is the product not of any simple dispute about a particular item of information, but the result of a general dissatisfaction with the way the Executive has been exercising the right itself to make the preliminary determination: a right which the Constitution does not accord it, and which practice has assigned to the Executive only on the sufferance of the Congress.

When the impasse occurs, the Constitution, which is an instrument for all seasons, leaves the Congress and the Executive each to their own devices. The President may lock up the documents in his own office. Congress, in pursuit of its legislative powers, may subpoena and even attempt to lock up recalcitrant Executive officials.[77] War between the Executive and Legislative branches is, however, likely to yield the democratic system as its principal casualty. A better solution would be for each branch to admit that a lack of mutual confidence does not, for the time being, permit the Legislature to defer wholly to Executive judgment on what may or may not be revealed to them. The search could then begin—preferably a joint search—for a new process to ensure both Congressional access to necessary information and the safeguarding of essential secrets. While such a process can take many forms, one principle all forms must include: *It cannot be wholly within the power of either branch to make a determination binding on the other.* Operationally, this might suggest either a process of joint determination or one of third-party decision-making. Either of these approaches would probably have to be augmented with guidelines for resolving disputed cases.

A number of proposals have been made to establish such new machinery. Some deal only with the Congressional right to know, whereas other proposed legislation would be applicable equally to Members of Congress and

---

76. U.S., Senate Subcommittee on Separation of Powers of the Committee on the Judiciary, *Hearings,* "Executive Privilege: The Withholding of Information by the Executive," 92d Cong., 1st sess., 1971, pp. 5–6; see also, "Summary Listing of Significant Access to Records Problems in Recent Years," pp. 310–14.
77. McGrain v. Daugherty, 273 U.S. 135 (1927). Statement of Raoul Berger Before the Senate Subcommittee on Intergovernmental Relations and on Separation of Powers, April 12, 1973, mimeo. See also: *Congressional Power of Investigation,* Study Prepared at the Request of Senator William Langer, Chairman of the Committee on the Judiciary, by the Legislative Reference Service of the Library of Congress, U.S. Senate, 83d Cong., 2d sess. (Washington, D.C.: U.S., G.P.O., 1954), pp. 23ff.

to the public in general. The proposals dealing specifically with the Congress assume that the Legislative Branch has a right of—and need for—access to information distinguishable from that of the ordinary citizen, and thus this need must be met with speedier and more mandatory procedures.

One set of proposals, perhaps the simplest, refers the umpiring function to the courts. There are two separate but related routes to the court. One is via proposed statutory amendments like Congressman Moorhead's H.R. 15172 of 1972 and H.R. 4960 and 5425 of 1973. Each of these seeks to amend section 552 of Title 5 of the U.S. Code, broadening the range of judicial review in specific cases where information is refused, and thus making the courts the arbiters of whether a non-disclosure is a legitimate exercise of the limited Executive discretion set out in the statute.

The other approach, which has been described by Senator Mathias in Chapter 5, may be implicit in proposals by Senators Ervin and Fulbright.[78] This might be analogized to a "class action" by the Congress to determine the larger Constitutional issue the branches of government have so far managed to evade—i.e., does the Congress have the right to compel, by token arrest if necessary, the production of information in the Executive Branch's possession if the legislators deem it essential to the discharge of the legislative function? The first, judicial, approach avoids direct Constitutional confrontation, the second invites it. "In contemplating whether or not, or how, to take this issue to the courts," Senator Mathias has written, "the Congress must face some very difficult questions. There is, to begin with, the question of whether or not the issue is genuinely 'justiciable' or whether or not the Congress has legal 'standing.' "[79] Raoul Berger has emphatically answered this question in the affirmative during testimony before a Congressional Joint Committee.[80] When, on July 23, 1973, the Senate Committee investigating Watergate voted unanimously to subpoena White House Presidential tapes that Mr. Nixon had withheld in the name of executive privilege and the separation of powers, the Congress seemed embarked on a Constitutional voyage of discovery to have these questions answered definitively.

It should also be noted that the Ervin and Fulbright proposals, taken together, would require deliberate concurrent determinations by both the Legislative and Executive branches before a confrontation can occur. On the Executive side, under the Fulbright bill, a refusal to disclose based on the separation of powers or an assertion of "privilege" would require the participation of the Attorney General and the President. Full reasons would have to be given for invoking privilege. The Ervin resolution provides that

---

78. Senator Ervin's initiative is S.J. Res. 72, 93d Cong., 1st sess., March 8, 1973. Senator Fulbright's draft bill is S. 858, 93d Cong., 1st sess., February 15, 1973.
79. Mathias, *ibid.*, p. 26.
80. Berger, *Statement*, April 12, 1973, *ibid.*

ultimately it is the full Legislative chamber that "shall take such action as it deems proper with respect to the disposition" of an unresolved disagreement with the Executive on the matter of access.[81] This seems a more satisfactory procedure than a hasty *ad hoc* rush to the courts, for both sides would have time to reconsider and negotiate before squaring off in irrevocable confrontation.

The judicial approach has behind it the tradition obtaining in the United States—far more than in Britain or Canada—of using the courts as the umpires of intragovernmental contests. The principal disadvantage, aside from its procedural problems and delays, is that judges are neither necessarily expert at, nor eager to acquire expertise in, the intricacies of Government security management. This problem is faced in the Horton-Moorhead Bill, H.R. 4960, and the courts are provided with the option to seek the help of a special intragovernmental agency: the Freedom of Information Commission (see *below*).

Another third-party way of dealing with the problem is to appoint an administrative or arbitral tribunal specializing in security information cases. Britain and, especially, New Zealand, have set up their Parliamentary Commissioners as prototypes for filtering certain kinds of secrets. It is too early to assess their success. The Congress has been considering a proposal along these lines by Congressmen Horton and Moorhead. An earlier, somewhat comparable idea was advanced by Senator Edmund S. Muskie.[82] The Horton-Moorhead proposal, like that of Senator Muskie, pertains to disclosure equally to Members of Congress, the press, and the citizen. The Horton-Moorhead bill provides for a Freedom of Information Commission empowered to downgrade or declassify all government information. It would be composed of seven members, two appointed by the Speaker of the House of Representatives, two by the President Pro Tempore of the Senate (not more than one from the same party), and three by the President (not more than two from the same party).[83] The Muskie proposal would have created a Disclosure Board consisting of seven members appointed by the President, by and with the advice and consent of the Senate.

The Horton-Moorhead approach is somewhat weighted in favor of the Legislative Branch, although less so than in its earlier (1972) version in which there was a 6-to-3 ratio favoring the Congress. Its enactment might still depend on sufficient Congressional support to override a Presidential veto. For its part, the proposed mixed Executive-Legislative tribunal to review secrecy classification would undoubtedly help the cause of access. Its procedures would necessarily be much simpler and speedier (there is a

---

81. S.J. Res. 72, *ibid.*, s. 2.
82. S. 2965, 92d Cong., 1st sess., December 7, 1971.
83. H.R. 4960, 93d Cong., 1st sess., February 28, 1973.

thirty-day limit on making a determination) than those of the courts. Another useful innovation is the provision for an award of costs to the petitioner who proves that information has been wrongfully withheld.

If an administrative tribunal or court is to make difficult decisions, it must have a narrow, workable set of guidelines. If secrets pertaining to foreign relations are to be reviewed, there must be standards by which a review may be conducted. "Foreign relations" is often treated as a homogenous category, all components of which are presumed to be equally in need of the umbrella of secrecy. William Rogers, as Attorney General in the Eisenhower Administration, listed the categories of information that ought to be kept secret. One of these is "information which would adversely affect our national security." Another is "the field of foreign affairs" where there are "compelling reasons for non-disclosure."[84] In Rogers' view "foreign affairs" is a discrete category, separate from the "national security" category. In this view, everything pertaining to or affecting matters beyond the boundaries of the United States is potentially entitled to secrecy at the sole discretion of the Executive. Obviously, a third-party or joint review process could not function within such an overly broad exclusionary rule.

How well a tribunal is able to operate in reviewing classification must depend on the extent to which the traditionally hush-hush field of "foreign affairs" is divided between narrow security categories that may need protection and broad non-security categories—such as foreign trade and commerce, or environmental protection—that do not. Section 552(b) (1) of the Administrative Procedure Act's Freedom of Information sections exempts from disclosure all matters that are "specifically required by Executive Order to be kept secret in the interest of the national defense or foreign policy." This standard is extremely wide. The Muskie proposal (S. 2965) permits secrecy only for "information the declassification of which would clearly and directly threaten the national defense of the United States." Even this may be too broad. If a third-party process is to be used, then it should determine not only: "Is this a secret the revelation of which would do serious harm to the national defense?" but *also* "Is this a secret the continued suppression of which would do serious harm to the democratic or legislative process?" It should hear evidence on both points and weigh the balance. This could probably be done by an expert tribunal but almost certainly not by an ordinary court.

The Freedom of Information Commission, as contemplated by the legislation proposed by Congressman Moorhead in 1972 (H.R. 15172), did have a different sort of useful discretion. If this Commission believed that

---

84. William P. Rogers, "Constitutional Law: The Papers of the Executive Branch," in *Executive Privilege Hearings,* Committee on the Judiciary, *ibid.,* p. 551 at 552. Reprinted from 44 American Bar Association Journal 941 (1958).

certain information should be revealed to the Congress, or to some Members of the Congress, but not to the press and the public, it might balance the need of the Congress, of a Committee or of a Member of Congress against the extent to which disclosure "would be contrary to the public interest or would seriously endanger the national defense of the United States." In deciding to make information available, the Commission could "assure that access to the information be limited to, Members of Congress whose responsibilities require access to such information, . . ." and order that the "discussions with respect to such information shall take place in executive session of a committee of Congress and closed session of either the Senate or the House of Representatives."

The Muskie proposal also provides a separate procedure by which the Congress or component committees or designated Members thereof might be given a right to information, sometimes in secret, without the right's being necessarily and invariably extended to the press or general public.

Another group of proposals has been designed to achieve greater access without recourse to adversary or third-party process. One of the notably far-reaching—that of Thomas L. Hughes—proposes a Permanent Joint Committee on Intelligence Estimates composed of approximately fourteen Members of Congress, serving rotating terms, including the Speaker of the House of Representatives and the majority and minority leadership of both Houses, members of key committees having to do with foreign affairs, armed services, atomic energy, and appropriations, and also of other members. This Congressional group would receive *all* national intelligence estimates.[85]

The advantage of this proposal is that it requires no judicial or quasi-judicial enforcement and that it provides across-the-board disclosure of *all* information, thereby skirting the vexed question of appropriate standards for disclosure. There are risks: security risks for the Executive and risks of co-option for the Congress. But the intelligence community would probably welcome an opportunity to have the ear of key members of the Congress, if only because their views would then also have to be considered more seriously by the Executive Branch decision-makers.

A variation on this approach is the secrecy ledger. This proposal would require all classifiers in all departments to send weekly lists of current documents they have classified to a central registry office in the White House, together with a broadly accurate but discreet indication of their content. A consolidated register would be prepared and forwarded to all Congressmen, and they could then request, as a matter of right, access to a particular document. In a less radical version of this proposal, a request for access would take a vote by the Congress or by the responsible committee. Once made,

---

85. See Chapter 2, "The Power to Speak and the Power to Listen."

the request would have to be honored. There might be very narrow exceptions to cover negotiating instructions, names of informers or foreign informants, and purely in-house memoranda. Or the register might be made
available only to a committee of key members of the Congress, and these
alone would have the right to see any entry.

What most of these proposals incorporate is a set of three principles that
are probably essential to any reform of the U.S. information management
system as it pertains to foreign affairs:

> 1. That the Congress, in the field of foreign relations, has a particularly co-
> gent right to know, which is as real as that of the Executive;
> 2. That this right can be satisfied by the Executive either by a willingness to
> tell a select, representative group of Congressmen *anything* or by a willing-
> ness to tell *every* member of the Congress *almost anything;*[86]
> 3. That the alternative is for the Congress to set up a competing information-
> gathering network—but this would amount to admission of the failure of that
> co-operation between the two branches which must underlie any effective
> exercise of their coordinate foreign relation powers.

Foreign Affairs Secrecy and the Citizen

The citizen is politically affected by secrecy in the same way as a Member
of Parliament or of the Congress: that is, his political choice will be less informed and democracy will be undermined to the extent that his vote is
based on incomplete information or misinformation. But whereas the citizen will ordinarily be asked to pass judgment on the Executive conduct of
the nation's business only every four or five years, members of the Legislature must do so frequently. Again, although citizens are seldom likely to exercise their vote primarily on matters of foreign affairs, legislators do vote
on specific foreign affairs items, appropriations, and authorizations. The
legislator and the citizen thus differ as to the specificity and timeliness of the
information they need.

Paradoxically, the citizen's role in Britain, Canada, and the United States
is frequently emphasized by the Executive Branch. In British and Canadian
constitutional practice, the tight control exercised by the Cabinet over the
Parliamentary members of the party is rationalized on the ground that it is
the people, not individual M.P.'s, who elect and must ultimately pass judgment on the conduct of the Cabinet. Similarly, the relative abstinence of
courts from judicial review of Executive acts in Britain, Canada, and the

---

86. One step in the direction of a general requirement of production is Pub. L. No.
92-403, 92d Cong., sess. 596, August 22, 1972, which is an Act requiring that international agreements other than treaties (i.e. Executive agreements) entered into by
the United States, be transmitted to the Congress within sixty days after their execution.

United States is justified on the ground that the proper place to redress political grievances is in a general election.[87]

If the courts—and in Britain and Canada even the legislators—are to be kept on a short leash, then national elections assume a proportionately greater role in the democratic control of government. Lack of adequate information by the voters subverts that role as effectively as if there were no elections.

In the United States the Executive has withheld information from the Congress on the ground that as a separate, independent, and coequal branch of government it is responsible not to the Congress but to the voters. This implies a particularly direct accountability to those voters, not least to supply the data necessary to an informed election. The Executive quotes with approval Marshall's dictum in *Marbury* v. *Madison* that "By the Constitution of the United States, the President is invested with certain important political powers, in the exercise of which he is to use his own discretion, and is accountable only to his country in his political character, and to his conscience."[88] In Britain the Executive is accountable to Parliament (at least in theory), as well as to the people. To the extent that Executive accountability, in the United States, is squarely to the people alone, there would seem to be a special Constitutional requirement of openness. This has of course been recognized in the First Amendment to the Constitution, for which there is no British or Canadian parallel.

In democratic systems there are various ways in which the public can obtain information about the Government's activities. The Government's own voluntary disclosures is only one of these. Another is by means of invoking laws that compel disclosure. A third is by way of disaffected government officials who are willing to speak up or to leak information.

Laws compelling the Government to disclose information to citizens are confined primarily to a few democracies: Sweden and the United States in particular. Both the disclosure requirement embedded in the Swedish Constitution,[89] and the more recent (1966) American Freedom of Information Act specifically exempt defense and foreign relations from the requirement of disclosure. As noted, the first exemption in the FOIA relates to matters "specifically required by Executive Order to be kept secret in the interests of the national defense or foreign policy."[90] The general classification sys-

---

87. Diggs v. Schultz, U.S. Ct. of App. D.C., No. 72-1642, October 31, 1972, in which the Court held that the executive decision to violate the Rhodesian chrome embargo, although violative of international and U.S. treaty law, "present[s] issues of political policy which courts do not inquire into" (p. 6).
88. 1 Cranch.   (5 U.S.) 137, 164 (1803).
89. For a discussion of this provision of the Swedish Constitution see *Franks Report*, vol. 1, p. 33.
90. Title 5, section 552(b) (1), U.S. Code (1970).

tem set out in Executive Order 10501 as amended by Executive Order 11652 has been used to meet this requirement for a specific finding that an item ought to be kept secret. The Supreme Court, in the *Mink* case, has held that Executive self-determination to be unreviewable, apparently even for error or *mala fides*.[91] For the FOIA to have any effect on the citizen's right to know, the law would have to be amended to require judicial review (possibly *in camera*) and to narrow the category of what may be kept secret. The current category is arbitrary because there is nothing about foreign affairs as such which makes *all* information about it inherently sensitive. Within the defense and foreign relations field there are many kinds of information that are currently exempt from disclosure (see our taxonomy above). Very few of these sub-categories really need such blanket protection.[92] As in the case of the legislative right to know, so in the case of the public's quest for information, there should be an impartial administrative weighing of the consequences of disclosure and of non-disclosure. Only bureaucratic policy memoranda, negotiating instructions, and strategic defense information need categorical exemption.

Older provisions of the Administrative Procedure Act (APA)[93] suffer from disabilities similar to those of FOIA. The Act requires that an agency in the process of rule-making must give public notice, describe the proposed rule, give interested parties an opportunity to be heard, render a decision supported by the record, and state the basis and purpose of the decision. But these procedural safeguards do not apply "to the extent that there is involved a military or foreign affairs function of the United States."[94] Again, there is no convincing reason of security—as distinct from reason of politics—why this exemption could not be far narrower: confined, for example, as in the Muskie proposal discussed above, to "rule makings in respect of which the application of these procedures would clearly and seriously threaten the national defense."

As it stands, the FOIA and other APA provisions are virtually non-applicable to the whole vast foreign policy sector. And in Britain as well as Canada there is no right-to-know legislation at all. The upshot is that in all three countries, the public, with the help of the press, have had to rely wholly on what they were told officially, or else have devised their own self-help to get the information essential to an independent judgment of the Government's performance.

---

91. Mink *et al.* v. Environmental Protection Agency *et al.,* 93 S.Ct. 827 (1973).
92. The Moorhead proposal to revise FOIA, H.R. 15172, *ibid.,* also applies a "national defense interest of the United States of the highest importance" test for review of the executive classification by its proposed Commission. See Chapter 6.
93. 5 U.S.C. 551 *et seq.* (1970).
94. *Ibid.,* S.553(a) (1), S. 544(a) (4).

Whether such self-help is available to the public depends in part on socio-political and cultural realities: the degree to which the press, for example, diligently and independently ferrets out information, free of a governmental "buddy system" of extra-legal rewards and punishments. To a large extent, however, self-help, in the United States, Canada, and Britain, depends upon the willingness of some inside the Government to purvey information to the press and public without authorization. There are wide differences between Canada and Britain, on the one hand, and the United States on the other, in the way this "self-help" occurs and in the extent to which it is inhibited either by law or by professional sanction.

It has already been noted that the unwritten rules of the British and Canadian Parliamentary government do little to inhibit—indeed, they institutionalize—the Ministerial resignation statement. These statements frequently go into considerable informational detail by way of revealing the resigner's reasons for opposing a current government policy. Despite the broad sweep of the British and Canadian Official Secrets Acts, no Minister in either country, in this century, has been prosecuted for his revelations. The practice of making candid public statements is widespread: approximately half the British Ministers who resign make such disclosure statements. But public disclosure under these circumstances, provided there are no direct quotes from Cabinet documents, carries neither criminal penalties nor career-costs. A study by the present authors of all British resignations from Government between 1900 and 1970 reveals that those like Eden, Salisbury, and Wilson, who resign with calculated indiscretion, generally do at least as well, in terms of subsequent political career, as those of their colleagues who keep silent—in fact a bit better, on the average.

It is at least worth speculating how different the political temper of the Congress, press, and public in the United States might be, today, if a McGeorge Bundy, a Robert McNamara, or a John Gardner had "gone public" after leaving Government. Would it have been necessary for an Ellsberg then to have taken the Pentagon Papers to *The New York Times?* In the United States, however, there are hardly any instances of such public resignations. Despite the absence of an Official Secrets Act, the career costs of calculated indiscretions of the kind commonplace among British leaders, are horrendous in America. The few Americans to have tried it—William Jennings Bryan, Lindley Garrison, Webster Davis, Mabel Willebrandt—were never seen in Government again. Career costs are probably a more effective tool even than criminal law for silencing dissent.

Leaking, too, is a tradition in Britain, and while not exactly delighting the Prime Minister, it has a certain institutional respectability. Patrick Gordon Walker, himself a former Foreign Minister, makes a revealing distinction in Chapter 3 of this book between ordinary leaks of Cabinet secrets and the disclosure of true "state" secrets "such as the details of a budget, a decision to devalue, military and security matters."[95] Ordinary leaks are not only tolerable but, he believes, even necessary to the healthy operation of the system. Many of the most important permissible leaks of recent years have been in the field of foreign affairs, such as those in connection with the supply of arms to South Africa[96] and with Kenya's expulsion of Asians.[97]

Beyond such patterns and traditions of political behavior lies the law. As we have seen, in Britain and Canada there are Official Secrets Acts, and these are currently under review in both countries. In the United States there are the Espionage Statutes and these, too, are currently the subject of proposed amendments. But, while the British proposals, contained in the September 1972 report of the Franks Commission, bend in the direction of narrowing the use of the criminal law to discourage self-help, the U.S. trend appears to be in the opposite direction.

As the Official Secrets Act[98] of Britain now stands, its reach is broader than anything in the United States—indeed, than anything permissible under the U.S. Constitution. Section 1 of the Act has to do with spying, not with the communication or publication of official information for other purposes. There must be a showing of a subjective "purpose prejudicial to the safety or interests of the State" and it must further be established that the information "is calculated to be or might be or is intended to be useful to an enemy." Thus there are two tests: (1) prejudicial purpose, and (2) usefulness to the enemy.[99] In at least one instance, however, this provision has been used to convict persons who were not within the ordinary meaning of "spies." The leaders of the 1961 nuclear disarmament marchers who intended to occupy a military airfield to disable it temporarily were found to have conspired to invite persons to commit a violation of this section.[100]

Section 2 of the Act reaches a quite different category of acts and purposes. This provision makes it an offense for any Government official to disclose any official information (i.e., obtained in the course of his employment), whether secret or not, except to authorized persons. It is also an offense for anyone unlawfully given such information, even a journalist, to publish it or communicate it to anyone else. It is, further, an offense for any person having been entrusted with information in confidence, or as a government contractor, or employee of such, to disclose it under any but authorized circumstances. The possibilities for prosecution under this provi-

---

95. Gordon Walker, *The Cabinet*, p. 27; see also Chapter 3.
96. *Ibid.*, pp. 29–30.
97. *Ibid.*, p. 30.
98. Official Secrets Act 1911, 1 & 2 Geo. 5, c. 28.
99. Franks Report, *ibid.*, p. 111.
100. Chandler v. Director of Public Prosecutions (1964), A.C. 763.

sion are virtually unlimited. The fact that the provision has been used sparingly in Britain and very rarely in Canada does not preclude speculation about its "chilling effect."[101]

There have been very few prosecutions of newspapers or journalists in Britain, one exception being a military newspaper in World War I and the second a prosecution arising out of the Nigerian civil war. The Nigerian case was not only lost by the Government but even led the judge to ask whether the Official Secrets Act "had reached retirement age and should be pensioned off."[102] This, in turn, produced the Franks Committee and its report, with its recommendations for narrowing the law. But if there have been few British prosecutions of newspapermen it may be in part because of the Act's chilling effect and the D Notice system by which journals "voluntarily" muzzle themselves at the Government's suggestion when an item seems security-sensitive. Canada has no D Notice system, and no prosecutions have been taken against Canadian media, at least within the past few decades.

Moreover, there have been no prosecutions at all of the large number of British Prime Ministers, Ministers, and Members of Parliament who have taken to publishing "instant" memoirs. These recollections appear to be considerably more indiscreet than those of their American or Canadian counterparts and help to undermine the protective custody in which OSA places official information.

Disclosures by British and Canadian Ministers and ex-Ministers and their most senior Government advisers, it is generally accepted, are "self-authorized"[103] and thus invariably they escape the prohibition. In twenty-nine British prosecutions under OSA section 2, fully twenty-five of the defendants were present or former lower-echelon civil servants, contractors, or military personnel. Of those prosecuted, incidentally, nineteen were only fined, received suspended sentences, or had their charges dropped.[104] Among the rare instances of more severe penalties are cases of policemen who gave information to criminals.

It could therefore be argued that the British Act, in practice, is not so bad

---

101. This "chilling effect" in Britain is compounded by the "voluntary" D Notice system, which is not subject to criminal penalties for violation but nevertheless carries the implication that violators face charges under the Official Secrets Act. Canada has no comparable chiller.

102. The judge in an unreported opinion said, "The 1911 Act achieves its sixtieth birthday on 22 August this year. This case, if it does nothing more, may well alert those who govern us at least to consider, if they have the time, whether or not Section 2 of this Act has reached retirement age and should be pensioned off. . . ." See our Chapter 19, "Secrecy and the Citizen's Right to Know: A British Civil Libertarian Perspective."

103. Franks Report, *ibid.*, p. 14.

104. *Ibid.*, pp. 116–18.

as it looks. Indeed, the fact that the Act looks so bad may have had a reverse "chilling effect"—on prosecution. But, as discussed in earlier chapters, the Franks Committee has recommended fairly extensive surgery, proposing the repeal of section 2 and its replacement with an Official Information Act that would apply only to certain specified material, such as "classified information relating to defence or internal security, or to foreign relations"— but *only* where "the unauthorized disclosure . . . would cause serious injury to the interests of the nation."[105] This new standard, somewhat resembling several proposals currently before the U.S. Congress for narrowing the foreign affairs category, is an undoubtedly libertarian advance. The Franks Committee, however, proposes to leave the crucial determination of what revelation "would cause serious injury" in the discretion of the Government. No document found by the Government's pre-prosecution review to be improperly classified, and no information that is unclassified, or classified at a lower level than Secret could be the basis of any prosecution.[106] These proposals are not universally welcomed in Britain. They have led to vociferous criticism from British civil-libertarians who call for the total repeal of section 2, leaving only espionage subject to criminal penalties.[107] The exchange in this book between Professor de Smith and Professor Street adumbrates this argument.

In any event Britain can never be a model for the United States in respect of information flow between Parliament and Government, or Government and people. In the American system vast, almost total power over foreign relations has come to be centralized in one man: the President. To be sure, the President has his advisers and assistants on the White House staff and in the Cabinet, but these exercise no political clout of their own and they do not represent the public. The political power of decision-making in the Executive Branch, particularly in matters of foreign policy, tends to be, ultimately, a one-man process. This is not so in Britain or Canada, where the Cabinet members have independent power bases and can and do block Prime Ministerial decisions, even in the field of foreign affairs. Under the British system, foreign policy cannot be made by one man; Cabinet power may be diminishing, but it is still incomparably greater than in the United States.

Since American foreign policy can be made by one man, the role of the Congress and of the press as critic becomes much more important. Vigorous criticism by those outside the Executive depends, to an extent, on their access to key information. So far, the U.S. information laws have tended to reflect this difference, particularly by abstaining from making criminal the

---

105. *Ibid.*, p. 101.
106. *Ibid.*, pp. 103–104.
107. Street, *ibid.*

mere disclosure of official information. The law on this subject is to be found primarily, but not wholly, in the Espionage Statutes—but these laws are in what Professor Benno Schmidt in Chapter 11 has rightly called "a mess."

The principal thrust of the Espionage Statutes, as in section 1 of the British and Canadian OSA, is to prevent the deliberate transmission of valuable information to an enemy. The basic ingredients of the offense are, thus, *culpable intent* and *harmful effect,* and they are set out in most, but not all, the offenses.[108] Offenses lacking these appear to be the result of legislative inadvertence that should either be repaired by judicial construction or be held unconstitutionally vague and restrictive of speech.[109]

In addition to the Espionage Statutes, the United States also has in its armory Title 50 of the U.S. Code, section 783 of which—applying only to Government employees—makes it an offense to communicate any classified information to an agent or representative of a foreign Government or an officer or member of any Communist organization. The giver of the information must know that it is classified and that he is giving it to someone within the prohibited categories, but that is all the motive that need be proven. Culpable intent need not be shown, and the classification is not reviewable by the court.

In the new Criminal Code proposed by the Nixon Administration in 1973 there are much more extensive prohibitions to be enforced by criminal sanction,[110] apparently introduced, like the White House "plumbers," because of a deep concern that the leaks and unauthorized disclosures of the past few years are, in the words of Canadian diplomat Bruce Rankin, "only the tip of the Ellsberg." The further linking of classification with criminal sanctions against leaking by bureaucrats or other "authorized" persons is quite clearly a step towards greater suppression of all classified information.[111] The "authorized person" could then be punished for communicating to any "unauthorized person"—not just to a foreign government. This is obviously intended to catch much leakage that is in no way tainted with spying or harm to the nation or help to an enemy. The new U.S. proposals seek to stem the flow of unauthorized information by eliminating the need for the prosecution to show that a disclosure caused or could cause injury to the United States or benefit to an enemy. All "national defense" information becomes a ward of the criminal law, whether classified high, low, not at all, or incorrectly. Under the new proposals, a person is "guilty of an offense if

---

108. Title 18, ss. 794(a) and (b).
109. Title 18, ss. 793(d) and (e). See Chapter 11, "The American Espionage Statutes and Publications of Defense Information."
110. S. 1400, 93d Cong., 1st sess., 1973, ss. 1122-1126.
111. S. 1400, ibid., s. 1124.

he knowingly communicates information relating to the national defense to a person not authorized to receive it."[112] The definition of "information relating to the national defense," could include any information "relating to . . . the conduct of foreign relations affecting the national defense" whether the information were classified or not, harmful to the United States, or only embarrassing to the credibility of some of its political leaders.

Whatever the Congress does about reforming the uses of executive privilege and the FOIA, unauthorized information will remain democracy's principal antidote to unlimited, highly concentrated power, particularly when it prevails in foreign affairs. In recent years unfettered Executive discretion has occurred increasingly in all democracies; and yet, in part because of the U.S. Constitutional system and in part because of the exigencies of world leadership, it is perceived as a particularly acute problem in the United States. If proposals such as those in S. 1400 are eventually passed by the Congress, and the *Franks* proposals are adopted in Britain, the American restrictions on unauthorized disclosure will have the dubious distinction of having become more severe than England's Official Secrets Act. Such a development might well set the stage for further Vietnam-type disasters of arrogance: something the United States and, indeed, the Western Alliance could scarcely survive.

---

112. *Ibid.,* s. 1122.